In the Beginning, Man . . .

In the Beginning, Man . . .

Man and Myth
(An African Viewpoint)

David Carney

VANTAGE PRESS
New York / Los Angeles / Chicago

FIRST EDITION

Copyright © 1988 by David Carney

Published by Vantage Press, Inc.
516 West 34th Street, New York, New York 10001

Manufactured in the United States of America
ISBN: 0-533-07720-6
Library of Congress Catalog Card No.: 87-91760

To the three women in my life without whom this book would not have been written: Esther (mother), Helen (wife), and Ellen (wife).

Contents

Foreword

With the appearance of man on planet Earth began the odyssey of existence in search of meaning, of man in search of God and God in search of man. Which is another way of saying that man invented it all—the game of the meaning of existence and of the concept of God.

Humanity (including the founders of religio-theological systems) speaks in metaphors, parables, and myth when attempting to interpret the cosmos, reality, or being. Interpretation is all we can manage, for there is no explanation and the only answers we get to our questions are the ones we give ourselves; the only goals we attain in our questing are the ones we set for ourselves. As the psychiatrist, Sheldon Kopp, puts it, "there are no hidden meanings" (or interpretations) to be unlocked from within things and events.[1] The meanings are transparent for all to see, coming from an external source—ourselves. If they are "hidden" at all, it is within *ourselves* that they are hidden, and they must be unlocked from within *us*, being our own interpretations and nothing more.

Interpretations, however, do not exist in a vacuum but in a framework, a context—the framework or context that we create and use. Every framework, whether analogy, paradigm, or synthetic model, has implied or built-in answers to the questions put to it: answers that are meaningful in terms of the framework, but only if the questions posed are relevant to that framework. It is in this manner that, by adopting an existing framework or creating our own, we provide the answers to questions relevant to that framework. Hence, there are no hidden answers to be derived by revelation from outside the frame of reference as interpreted by us. Our answers are as good, or as bad, as the interpretive framework that we use to resolve our questions and our problems.

This thesis granted, religion, like theology, philosophy, or art, is merely a special kind of interpretation of cosmos, reality, or being. Philosophy, defined as the love of wisdom, is really no more than the search, through thought, for meaning within a context of interrelationships, interdependence, and unity of all things within the cosmos. Religion is the search for meaning or interpretation through feeling, conducted within

xiii

the context of interrelationships, interdependence, and unity within the cosmos. Theology is essentially thought plus feeling employed in the formulation of a doctrine of divine origin of the cosmos; that is, a doctrine of the creation of the cosmos by a god or gods and the accompanying feeling of dependence[2] of the cosmos on its divine creator(s). The framework utilized in this interpretation is that of a master craftsman—the Greek demiurge—who fabricates things that are, therefore, dependent on him for their coming into being in a certain form and continuing in that form.

There are many variants of the feeling-oriented framework of religious interpretation. Some variants emphasize the dominance of one species, mankind, in the total pattern of interrelationships and interdependence: all other species are regarded as relating to each other and the cosmos in general through man (anthropocentrism). Other variants, using as their model man in relation to his activities, creations, and moods, project this model on to the cosmos, which is then regarded as the creation of a being similar to man in its activities and moods (anthropomorphism, or the human paradigm). Here, religion passes over into theology. All these variants share a common characteristic: they are man-oriented or man-focused (anthropotropic), hence species-specific.

While the human paradigm is, understandably, the cosmic interpretive framework most ready-to-hand and widely used by man, the weakness of an anthropocentric or anthropotropic view of the cosmos and cosmic interrelationships is that it makes mankind and its planet the central preoccupation of the cosmos—without any supporting evidence—and eventually, within mankind, focuses on certain groups that regard themselves as most favored above the rest. There are many adverse consequences of this view. One of these consequences is suppression of one human group by another on the ground of the latter's assumed superiority, backed by brute force. Another consequence is the disregard by man of the nonhuman species, their right to a place in the cosmos, and their share of cosmic resources. From this has belatedly arisen, in our time, various movements concerned with the environment and its preservation for the benefit of all forms of life, including the endangered species. The pernicious result of the suppression of one group by another is ethnic discrimination and racism—the "most favored race," "chosen people," or "manifest destiny" complex. Undoubtedly of nonreligious origin, it survives as a feature of occidental culture uniquely connected with and perpetuated by the Semitic religions. Thus, racial oppression and intolerance and disregard of the claims of nonhuman species to a place in the cosmos are the price mankind continues to pay for using an inappropriate methodological framework for interpreting the cosmos.

The anthropomorphic view of the cosmos, which regards it as an artifact made by a god or superior being very much like man, has the effect of endowing this presumed being with human qualities—a being made in the image of man: it has feelings of pleasure, displeasure and wrath, concern and love and pity, as well as a providential attitude toward its creatures, but especially toward mankind. From viewing the cosmos within this human paradigm it is but a short step to mankind behaving as if it was the raison d'être of the cosmos, to thinking that man created the cosmos—almost. Something close to this thought occasionally comes through in the writings of Bishop Berkeley and Jean-Paul Sartre. If, therefore, there is such a thing as "original sin" by, and in, man, it would be this erroneous pride in a humanlike originator of the cosmos: a methodological error arising from the imposition of a human paradigm, as an interpretive framework, upon the cosmos.[3]

The combination of anthropomorphism and anthropocentrism in the human paradigm as a cosmic interpretive model leads not only to a god invented by man and endowed with human qualities—theology as anthropology, as demonstrated by Ludwig Feuerbach[4]—but also (and worse) to a "god in search of man," another central feature and doctrine of the Semitic religions. In short, we wind up with a god that would not exist but for man, that owes its very existence to man both as its conceiver and as its raison d'être. Man conceives a god for the sole purpose of seeking after man and creating the rest of the cosmos for man's benefit. Nothing could be more absurd—more absurd than attributing the creation of the cosmos directly to man.

Because of this dependence of the creator-god's existence and power on man's creative imagination and man's recognition, the ancient Jews' relationship to their god was a rather peculiar one: it could be dealt with as man's equal—praised, blamed, talked back to, and so on. It was in much the same vein that the ancient Romans treated their gods—in terms of law: the relationship between gods and man was a strictly legal and contractual one, the same as between citizens of the Roman state: "I will do thus and so [e.g., build a temple] in return for a favor or benefit received [e.g., victory in battle]"—a purely contractual arrangement for value given and received on both sides. This element of ancient Roman theology has passed over into institutional Roman Catholicism.

It should have become crystal clear that any species-specific interpretive framework applied to the cosmos contains the fatal weakness of extolling one species (or subspecies) above the rest of the cosmos, with all its attendant consequences, and that, in this respect, what is sauce for the goose is also sauce for the gander, as the British poet Rupert Brooke (1887–1915) expressed it so eloquently in his humorous poem titled "Heaven." In this poem he showed how the concept of heaven was relative to the environment, and the concept of god to the form, of the species that develops these concepts. Thus the god of fish is ichthyform and fishes' heaven a watery medium. Undoubtedly, the god of nonhuman animals based on land would be theriomorphic and their heaven one wide-ranging forest or savannah.

Mankind, in short, has no monopoly on a species-specific or species-oriented interpretation of the cosmos. A fish-specific, worm-specific, or monkey-specific interpretation would serve just as well as a man-specific interpretation. Indeed, the ancient Egyptians as well as the ancient Greeks did conceive and espouse theriomorphic gods—deficient, undoubtedly, but with probably less inimical consequences and a better feel for man's nonhuman neighbors and their common environment. While any species-specific paradigm has its weaknesses, it can at the same time have beneficial results if it could be generalized to other species-specific paradigms, thus serving as a basis for a more comprehensive and satisfactory interpretive model on the biological plane.

In later Judaism, however, the species-specific gave way to a non-species concept of god as spirit. This was a probable result of the influence of Zoroastrianism, the ancient religion of Persia. The spirit-god concept is inherited also by Christianity and Islam. "God is a Spirit and they that worship him must worship him in spirit and in truth," Jesus is reported to have said (Saint John 4:24), while reverting at other times to the human paradigm of a Father-God: "He that hath seen me hath seen the Father" (Saint John 14:9)[5]—a probable indication of Gnostic influence on early Christianity. In a similar manner Islam, inheritor of the ancient Jewish and Christian religious and scriptural traditions, makes reference to God as Spirit: "Verify, this Quran is a revelation from the Lord of the worlds. The Faithful Spirit has descended with it on thy heart, that thou mayest be a Warner, in plain Arabic tongue" (Sura No. 26, Al-Shu'ara, verses 193–194[6]).

Anthropocentrism naturally leads to geocentrism or, at least, reinforces geocentrism acquired on other grounds. It seems, however, that geocentric systems, such as those of the Babylonians and Ptolemy, were parallel to, or the consequent product of, anthropocentrism. Geocentrism in religion—which persists in spite of the Copernican revolution—not only makes planet Earth *the* (instead of *a*) center of the cosmos but, in combination with anthropocentrism, also makes the welfare of Earth and its human inhabitants *the* central feature of the cosmos. A certain geo-centrism in religion and theology is inescapable, man being basically earth-bound, even though he can rise in thought and body to the stars. However, it gives an unwarranted importance to Earth out of all proportion to its magnitude, compared to other astrophysical bodies, and in complete ignorance of the nature of other astrophysical systems. Such an unnecessarily restricted planetary orientation impoverishes religion and does an injustice to the cosmos itself.

This book is about the human activity of interpretation of the cosmos and man's environment, of existence itself. It shows how man has tended, all too naturally, to interpret the cosmos in terms of himself, producing—inter alia—an anthropomorphic theology no different in substance from anthropology (Feuerbach) and the secular ideologies of humanism (Feuerbach, Marx, Teilhard de Chardin, Julian Huxley, and others) and existentialism (Sartre). Even the religious and theological variants of existentialist ideology (e.g., Jesus, Kierkegaard, and Heidegger) are anthropocentric, because of the anthropocentric taint of their theological base. All these anthropocentric ideological products have exerted a strong attraction on human life and thought but suffer, nonetheless, from the obvious defects of a man-centered view of the cosmos. More important, the book shows that interpretation is a flexible, open-ended activity; that, consequently, no one interpretation can claim favor or adequacy as *the* interpretation of any given phenomenon or event. For all interpretations are relative in regard to both framework and purpose and therefore defective, because limited by this dual constraint.

The book ends with a plea for open-mindedness in examining all possible interpretations for whatever contribution they could make to science and the realm of values, and for a continuing search for new interpretations in order that man may escape the dead hand of the past and its dogmas, while continually enriching the meaning of his life. Thus every interpretation must be welcome for the nugget of wisdom, aesthetics, or whatever it contributes to life. For there is no doubt that, notwithstanding their pernicious effects, mankind has benefited in one way or another from the interpretive metaphors of human existence that have been contributed, for example, by various religions: by ancient Greek religion and mythology, the notion of human existence as a pilgrimage through life and beyond; by Zoroastrianism and Gnosticism, the notion of human existence as light at first trapped by, but eventually liberated from, darkness by a savior or Saoshyant; by Judaism, the notion of human existence as a journey into exile, estrangement, and lostness, redeemed by a return engineered by a gracious God in search of man, a leader in search of a followership (a notion inherited by Christianity and Islam); Christianity, as by African religion, the notion of human existence as family-centered in the trinity of father, mother, and child, the offspring constituting the locus of parental union (or at-one-ment) as well as the means of parental continuity; and so on.

xvii

It is the author's hope that through this book he has contributed as well as shared with others his contribution to the continuing quest of the human spirit for new paradigms and new interpretations of the all-pervading phenomenon of existence.

Tribute is hereby paid to the women in my life and their role in bringing this book to birth: to my mother, whose labor of love in my upbringing left indelible and beneficial imprints on my character, notwithstanding my early break with institutional Christianity; to my first wife, whose death triggered the writing of this book; and to my second wife, who encouraged and served as its principal reader and critic. To these three, a formidable trinity, this book is dedicated.

SEPTEMBER 1985   DAVID CARNEY

NOTES

1. Sheldon B. Kopp, *If You Meet the Buddha on the Road, Kill Him!* (Palo Alto, California: Science and Behavior Books, Inc., 1972), p. 165.
2. Outside of sacred texts such as the Torah, the Bible, and the Koran, numerous theses have been written on the subject of human dependence on the gods, a dependence that reveals itself in what has been described as the sense of the numinous or "the idea of the holy"—to use Rudolf Otto's striking phrase.
3. On this view, the original sin of pride is not a willful sin (sin of the will) as presented in the biblical book of Genesis and espoused by Saint Augustine, an early Church Father, among others, nor a sexual one such as was propounded by Origen, another early Church Father—although willfulness and sex are essential aspects of creative activity within the human paradigm.
4. Ludwig Feuerbach, *The Essence of Christianity* (New York: Harper Torchbooks, Harper & Row, 1957).
5. All biblical quotations throughout this book are from the King James or Authorized Version.
6. From the English translation of the Koran by Sir Muhammad Zafrulla Khan, c. 1981.

Autobiographical Preface

On the last day of her life I sat a long time by her bed thinking she was unconscious, when without opening her eyes she said in a steady hollow voice, "David, promise me never to make a bargain with God." A few minutes later she died.

—David Eccles,
Half-way to Faith

In this book I have attempted a wide-ranging examination of subjects in the related fields of metaphysics, theology, philosophy, religion, and ethics—fields that may properly be described as human aspects of existence. The book has its remote origins in my youthful experiences but was catalyzed in my maturity by a personal experience of catastrophe—the death of my first wife—the shock of which "made my world stand still," as the Yaqui Mexican Indians would say. But not for long. Instead of resuming its rotation and revolution in the usual direction, it reversed course, rotating and revolving the other way, which is another way of saying that I went back, and backward in time, to reexamine the bases of whatever views and beliefs I held, especially in the theological, religious, and ethical fields. In short, I had a rude awakening to an existence that had been largely taken for granted. But what I awoke to has been not, as I hoped, a discovery but, as I had never imagined, an unending quest full of adventure.[1]

I had been raised by a mother of strong character and devout theological faith and religious practice, in the Anglican confession, my father—through a politically related misfortune—having separated from my mother the year I was born. He eventually abandoned her to the combined roles of mother and father to her children—a role she acquitted most adequately, but only because of the fortunate circumstance of her having had a very good elementary and secondary education and subsequent training as an elementary school teacher. This family circumstance, naturally, was to affect my life significantly. Not only did I receive the greater part of my primary education at home from my mother, rather

xix

than at school, but my attitude and views regarding the female sex were formed from this experience. This latter facet of my personality is all the more evident when I compare my own life and career with those of my contemporaries presumed more fortunate in having been raised by both parents. I must confess that I have come to hold rather strong views on the subject of women—views that are not usually held by the human male in any society and particularly in African society. Since my childhood, I have held it as an article of faith (one of my very few articles of faith) that all girls should have access to an education and a profession or vocation, equally with boys, to enable them earn their livelihood and raise their children should marriage prove unworkable for one reason or another. This may not necessarily be due to the couple's fault: death or other catastrophe removing one partner (in this case, the father) is, in my view, a stronger argument in this respect than incompatibility or unfaithfulness in marriage. From a biological point of view, it is a woman's natural privilege to bear and raise children, male and female, with or without the conventional arrangements of marriage, just as it is a man's natural privilege (or misfortune, to the macho-oriented male) to be born of a woman. Placed beside this unshakable biological fact, all arguments, unless based on biopsychological factors, that would deny women equal access to educational, professional, and vocational opportunities prove superficial and weak and militate against the family and society in the long run.

Another indelible mark of my family circumstance is that I have grown up with a profound respect for women,[2] as compared to men, and for African women, in particular. (I do not say *womanhood*, of which I have no experience, as compared to *manhood*, of which I have some experience; both, naturally, are deserving of respect as given, but different, facts of life.) Correspondingly, I have developed a suspicion and a view about the dispensability—even the disposability—of the male sex in general and an unverified—and unverifiable—hypothesis about the biological superiority of the female to the male. Concerning this last, I am prepared to settle for a minimum: complementarity of the sexes, which is all that is biologically defined. Beyond this minimum, one is constantly reminded—by what transpires in the insect world of bees, termites, and praying mantises—of the precarious role of the male.[3]

To return to my upbringing, like all, or most, children I was the victim of conventional theological and religious brainwashing—of the Anglican Protestant variety, in my case—in the jesuitically crucial period before the age of seven. As soon, however, as I could begin to think for myself in these matters—a period that, fortuitously, coincided with my exposure, at the age of fourteen, to a brief course in "comparative"

xx

religion[4] at an Anglican grammar school (the C. M. S. Grammar School, later renamed the Sierra Leone Grammar School)—weak points and criticisms began to emerge on various aspects of the mythology of Christianity as contained in the New Testament and its foundation in the Old. By the age of seventeen I had quit the Church, but for other reasons, chiefly the uninspiring, rationalizing, question-begging, and question-discouraging sermons divorced from the realities of life, regularly delivered on Sundays by a mostly semiliterate clergy innocent of Greek and Latin. (There were brilliant exceptions, of course, in the university trained clergy from the local university college, but only on occasions that were few and far between.) These regular occasions of holy boredom were also occasions of priestly rhetoric featuring stock argumenta ad hominem, bookishness, and mnemonic skill in the retention of scriptural verse and the mythical history of the Children of Israel. The contemporary colonial history and daily burdens of the Children of Africa and, in particular, the Children of Sierra Leone went ignored, for the obvious reason that this was a subject implicitly and actively forbidden by the local and the metropolitan British colonial government and by the local and the metropolitan Anglican Church headed, respectively, by the English bishop and the English Archbishop of Canterbury. Holy Church in unholy cahoots with unholy State. It was all, to say the least, a holy exercise in irrelevance and futility.

It had its moments of comic relief, however. Sunday was the day of the split personality: its unrealistic atmosphere contrasted oddly with the grim atmosphere of the workaday world; its best apparel provided a welcome relief from the drabness of Monday-to-Saturday wear, as well as an occasion for furtive glances and envious comparisons among the women and overt peacockiness among the men. Children, who mostly went barefoot during the week, on Sundays strutted about in ill-fitting, pinching shoes and clothes too small or too big (to grow up in). Adults also suffered the punishment of ill-fitting shoes. It is remarkable how, until today, it sinks in rather slowly that imported shoes made to accommodate European feet will not do for African feet. No matter.

I quit the Church[5] but not religion. The damage had already been done, however, even unto this day: the indoctrination, I mean, and the chants and hymns set to beautiful music. I embarked on a conscious process of disindoctrination, of theological and religious detoxification. Difficult and not completely successful: a difficulty compounded by my parallel attempt to reconstruct my theological and religious orientation on a poison-free basis, making use of logical inquiry, scientific information, and whatever native philosophical talent I could muster from my own inner resources.

Not until the death of my first wife did I become aware of how much of the early indoctrination had remained with me and deeply underpinned my daily life, activities, and interpersonal relationships. I must confess that, until then, I believed very strongly, without the slightest evidence, in a personal God and in the automatic efficacy of prayer. Hitherto, somehow, all my prayers—wishes—seem to have been answered. I, somehow, had not given much thought and attention to the fact that while I had prayed I had also worked hard to bring about what I prayed for—that "God [if and in what form this being exists] helps those who help themselves," not those who merely pray. Similarly, I had not noticed that the illness of my first wife and her operation for breast cancer presented me with a situation in which I could only pray but do nothing to bring about what I prayed for: her survival and recovery. In retrospect, this naïveté seems strange and incredible. But it is a true measure of what passes today for simple, conventional Christian faith, regardless of confessional affiliation. Much of it is pure wishfulness where it concerns one's relation to one's self and pure superstition where it concerns one's relation to the actions of others. My relation to my wife's illness was what might be termed "pure superstition": I sought to influence, by prayer, what I could not control by action. She died (in 1976) of the complications from her illness, operation, and postoperational treatment. And I was shattered. Naturally, I was mad at the god who had "answered" all my prayers hitherto, but not this one that was so much more important to me than all the previous ones—this prayer for the life of a loved one. That god was eventually revealed to me as myself. I was the one who had answered my own self-related prayers by doing something about their objects. I was the one who had done, and could do, nothing about such other-related prayers as this one concerning my wife's health.

Until this insight broke upon me, I had asked myself, like the rest of humanity since time immemorial, the inane question, *Why this to me?* Realizing how stupid was the question, I gave myself three responses. First, I told myself, *Why not you, stupid? If it had to happen to someone, why not to you? What makes you so special or different from others?* Second, like C. S. Lewis,[6] I tried to rationalize away my pain. I composed an essay, beautiful and self-comforting, which I distributed to some of my friends (including one who was to become my second wife) in the hope—what conceit!—that it might offer them something of value. This phase, also, passed and I got on to the third response—the real business at hand. I tried to find out where and how I had been "had" by my Christian pastors and mentors, all of them descendants of "converted" Sierra Leoneans. For, in my childhood, the Anglican and Methodist Churches had long since matured to the point where Sierra Leoneans no longer received the "good news" direct from white, foreign missionaries but direct from their replacements—"the native clergy," as they were patronizingly called by the white missionaries. In this respect the Roman Catholic Church and various assorted schisms imported mostly from the U.S.A. (Baptists, Adventists, Pentecostals, et cetera) were the exception or, perhaps, the rule. Whatever. All the Christian churches were alike, however, in having white bishops, elders, or chairmen to keep them in line with the pure imported doctrine and the policies of the local colonial government, with the solitary exception of the African Methodist Episcopal Zion Church—a hybrid schism imported from the U.S.A., where it was established by emancipated blacks (Negroes).

This book is, in large measure, the result of my third response—a wide-ranging, no-holds-barred inquiry into things metaphysical, theological, philosophical, religious, and ethical, both ancient and modern, including ancient Roman religion, ancient Greek philosophy and religion, and contemporary religions—African and other. But especially the antecedents of the conscious occidental as well as the unconscious African theological, religious, and philosophical influences that had shaped my early life. For one whose active profession of economics and economic and social development and planning left (or ought to have left) him very little time for any other full-time pursuit, this book represents a heavy investment of private financial resources and private time outside of my everyday occupation, over a period of nine years. In the process of my inquiry I have become aware of how much more interesting and useful this "hobby" of mine is, compared to my professional pursuits. These pale in significance because of the normally narrow and inadequate training program for economists and planners offered at universities around the world: a program lacking in breadth, empirical tests and verification of theories or their implications, and practical apprenticeship, and unsuitable in every way to equip economists and planners for handling and resolving problems in their general field. For all the statistics and mathematics being applied in the field of economics and planning—which merely serve to fragmentate rather than integrate the subject matter—contemporary economic and planning theories differ little from contemporary religious and theological offerings: 90 percent opinion and rationalization, 10 percent paradigmatic and empirical relevance, on the most generous estimate.

I need hardly state that, my method of investigation being unstructured as well as wide-ranging, I found a multitude of interesting facts and things to say, but no particular plan or context in which to say them. Thus I accumulated an interesting jumble of related and unrelated bits of information, which I proceeded to ruminate upon, collate, and examine

xxiii

in various ways. I tried various arrangements. Gradually, after about five years of reading, writing, and reflection, the facts began to seek each other by affinity in an autonomous and self-evolving gestalt. A plan began to take shape, paradigms emerged, and a methodology of sorts was indicated. The result: this book.

Along the way, something new was attempted—the application to scientific study (or any other type of inquiry, for that matter) of a methodology that I have termed *helical thinking*. It is creative, dialectic, and dynamic thinking. It is a method of investigation in which problems are transformed by increasingly widening the framework within which they are assessed and interpreted. This is the process that scientific investigation in any field actually follows *over time*, a process adequately documented in Thomas S. Kuhn's *The Structure of Scientific Revolutions*.[7] Thus the process itself is not new. What is new is that, instead of leaving it to laissez-faire-ism and the attendant hazards of time, it is consciously organized as a regular method of inquiry, a way of devising hypotheses, with a view to accelerating the pace and increasing the yield of scientific interpretation. The ultimate intention is to ensure that, by the application of this method, scientific breakthroughs are made to occur at shorter intervals instead of the multicentennial intervals that separated the breakthroughs of, say, Copernicus and Newton or those of Newton and Einstein. It is Hegel's dialectical idealism (which he thought was revealed in the dynamic process of history through thesis, antithesis, and synthesis) consciously organized and raised to the level of scientific methodology: the helical method.

Although I have made but limited use of the methodology in this book because of the nature and constraints of the subjects treated—these being mostly topics and problems of cosmic dimension, leaving little scope for framework adjustment between the human and the cosmic paradigms—the results have been sufficiently encouraging and useful as to generate the expectation that similar fruitful results await the application of the methodology in other fields.

One problem that confronted me in the writing of this book was what to do about the conventional use of male patterns and figures of speech in the English language—a deeply entrenched consequence of male domination of our conventional world. As is generally known, however, the brute fact of domination is not necessarily in conformity with empirical truths in other respects. For example, the general use, in English speech, of masculine pronouns to represent female as well as asexual objects and concepts ignores, but does not eliminate, the fact that these nonmale entities exist. Quite often, it is the result of a perverse determination to not recognize these nonmale entities or their presence, just as the white racist determines not to "see" the black man whom he passes on the street in spite of the latter's high visibility (save to the black-color blind) or the white or black "liberal" determines not to "notice" the skin color of his cross-racial friend (save, again, to the truly black-color or white-color blind).

The sickness of modern language is male sexism—more appropriately, verbal sex discrimination. This is literally true because the language consciously or unconsciously disguises, and thereby prevents, important facts from becoming known, as well as unsuspectingly biases our judgment and conclusions in many and strange ways.

The solution, of course, is to use sex-neutral language, substituting the neuter for all objects, sexed and unsexed. This does not always succeed, and one eventually capitulates to convention. Thus, although a conscious effort has been made, wherever possible, to escape the adverse consequences of sexism in speech, it is necessary to state, at the outset, that wherever, faute de mieux, or in order to preserve elegance of expression or avoid complicated sentence structure and stilted language,[8] male sexist language is used in this book, it is intended to include the female sex. Similarly, the neuter will be used, even at the cost of seeming awkwardness, when it is important to stress that sex is an irrelevant consideration or that one could not presume to know the sex of the object or entity under discussion or whether the entity is, in fact, sexed. It goes without saying that the sexes will be distinguished where a distinction is necessary for the discussion.

Let me make clear what has been achieved in this intellectual odyssey. In the first place, the human paradigm has been dethroned as an interpretive model for the cosmos, but not decapitated. It is certainly not useful as an interpretive model for man—that would be tautological, yielding zero empirical content—but it may be useful for other organisms. (In the evolutionary scheme of things no superiority of man over other organisms may be assumed.) What, then, remains of the human paradigm, as of any other species-specific paradigm, is its *microcosmic* interpretive potential as well as its indicative nature. It does not interpret vis-à-vis the cosmos; it only indicates. And what it indicates is its component aspect *within* the cosmic paradigm. Whatever is true of the human (as of any other) paradigm is also true of the cosmos, but what is true of the cosmos or the cosmic paradigm is not necessarily true of every component paradigm. For the cosmos is more than any of its components and more than the mere aggregate of them. It is an integrate of components and component paradigms. An integrate is an aggregate of entities *in organic relationship.* Hence the cosmos and its paradigm is an aggregate of components and component paradigms in an organic relationship that transforms every component and paradigm to fit into, and yield, the flow-change organism and organic paradigm of the cosmos.

Thus, by its very inclusive nature, the cosmos is wise, loving, benevolent, understanding, et cetera, insofar as any of its components possesses any of these qualities. By the same token, the cosmos may be said to be jealous, destructive, evil, et cetera, insofar as any of its components possesses any of these qualities. However, one should be careful to note that these so-called qualities are no more than human evaluative interpretations of nonvalue characteristics that are part of the basic nature of the cosmos.[9] Whatever the characteristics (or qualities) possessed by any of its components, the cosmos possesses more than all those in an integral, organic way. This is a generalized and proper interpretation of the classic Stoic argument in support of the living, intelligent nature of the cosmos, in particular of planet Earth, based on the living and intelligent nature of one of its components, man.[10] If, as the Stoics argued, the cosmos was divine, then man and every other component unit of the cosmos constitute integral parts of divinity, endowed with divine nature. So that the divine cosmos does, itself and to itself, whatever every one of its components does. It is in this sense that can be interpreted the dictum of Aristotle, subsequently espoused by Spinoza, that God does not love man but only itself. By extension (again allowing for the interpretation of cosmic characteristics in terms of human values and sentiments) it may be said that the cosmic divinity loves and hates, laughs and cries, et cetera, doing all this itself and to itself: merely the human way of saying that the cosmos is alive and autonomous or, if one prefers, a living and autonomous *system*.

In the second place, this book contains a special implicit message from one African to other Africans who wish to preserve or rediscover their authenticity. The authentic African is the African in indigenous, traditional society, blessed with indigenous traditional values and customs. A return to authenticity is a return to one's roots, one's essence, one's past: but not to an outside-space-time Platonian or utopian past, or to a future outside-space-time Platonian ideal, mystical existence; rather to the actual within-space-time past, within the context of the unified community of ancestors, living dead and current survivors. A return to authenticity implies reconciliation to one's self, acceptance of one's self—identification of one's self with one's self and not with the self of another, beyond the seas or beyond the mythical skies: the end of self-alienation, of seeking after strange gods, customs, and ideas (ideologies); a reaffirmation of one's traditional customs and human values.

This book was intended originaly to be an autobiographical account of an experience of personal tragedy and its aftermath. It turned into an intellectual odyssey resulting from that tragedy—an odyssey that bears little or no trace of its triggering circumstances. Whence it became necessary to write this autobiographical preface in order to set the book in its proper context and forestall possible misunderstanding of its nature and intent. Notwithstanding the form and content it has assumed, it never set out to be a piece of academic research into the topics treated. The uneven style and format bear eloquent testimony to this fact, if testimony were required. Whatever research was done was not for the sake of the topics themselves, but in order to clarify my own interpretations of them—especially in order that, in showing how my interpretation of them differs from that of others, I may report correctly how others have interpreted them. Criticism of interpretation given by others has been only incidental to my own interpretation and was never a primary purpose of the research.

My interest has been primarily in my own interpretation of the subjects discussed and not in that of others, except insofar as their interpretation helps clarify mine by agreement or difference. Where I have pointed out inconsistencies in the interpretation given by others, these came to light partly as a result of my own different approach and partly as a result of my attempt to understand what the others meant. I did not set out to criticize but to understand. Criticism was, therefore, only an incidental part of the process of understanding. It could be that I may have occasionally misunderstood those criticized. I would be grateful, therefore, to be set right. The varying length of treatment of various topics reflects my free-wheeling thought and reaction, not the relative importance of the topics. Notwithstanding its style, format, and content, the result remains an intellectual autobiography, not a piece of academic research.

Finally, the results, findings, and interpretations presented in this work, like every human effort, remain provisional until new information and other—perhaps better—interpretations come along. Yet, as with any interpretation, I trust that they will disclose something valuable, some useful insight. In the meantime, readers are invited to read and enjoy, or disagree with, the contents and conclusions and, I hope send me their reactions through the publishers.

NOTES

1. This is the kind of unending quest for provisionally satisfactory answers to conventional questions, especially existential questions, that religio-theological dogma is designed to save by providing "sure and unchanging" answers. (See Book Two, Section B, chapter 8.)

2. My present (second) wife proposes a more general, and female, point of view supported by an African mother and mutual friend: namely, that mothers, as bearers and nurturers of the species, never cease to regard and treat their adult offspring as no more than grown-up *children*—their sons as strangers to domestic responsibility (there are exceptions, of course) and, I may add, their daughters as potentially responsible mothers. Thus (without mothers necessarily intending this result) love and veneration of mothers are fostered in the males, along with irresponsible behavior toward all other females in general (with exceptions, of course), while the females grow up as potential competitors to their mothers, mothers-in-law, and all females, in general, for the love and mothering of their fathers and husbands and all males, in general. Sons respect, daughters suspect, their mothers. And fathers have no *naturally* defined role save that of procreation. The stage is thus set for Freud's Oedipus and Electra complexes. I subscribe to all this with the exception—not unique—that in my case I was broken in by my mother and an aunt to a good deal of domestic responsibility and household chores.
3. Other than its complementary and procreative role, no other biological role seems to be clearly defined for the male save, perhaps, that of worker, which the human male everywhere—and irresponsibly—shunts, or seeks to shunt, off on the human female. Since he cannot claim an exclusive right to work, which is also a natural to the female as bearer and nourisher of the species, the human male has a hard time defining and justifying his worker role vis-à-vis the human female. His natural reaction toward the female seems, therefore, to be one of anger backed by attempts to put a corner on certain "privileged" occupations and by a domineering macho attitude—all sure signs of feelings of insecurity—aided by his acquired attitude of irresponsibility toward females.
4. Based on a book titled *Jesus Christ and the World's Religions*, whose author and publisher I no longer remember. The year of instruction was 1939, and the purpose of the text was to establish the superiority of—what else?—Christianity to all other religio-theological systems.
5. My pious mother continued to pay my church dues until she passed away in 1982. Now may come to pass what she most feared and sought to ensure against by paying the dues on my behalf: an unchurched funeral when I die.
6. See C. S. Lewis, *The Problem of Pain* (London: Collins, Fontana Books, 1976).
7. Thomas F. Kuhn, *The Structure of Scientific Revolutions*, 2d ed. (Chicago: University of Chicago Press, 1970). See especially chapters IX and X.
8. Such as using *he/she/it, he/she, his/hers/its, his/hers*, et cetera, all the time, and thereby increasing the printing costs of this book.
9. This should normally be obvious but for the fact that man is trapped in the human paradigm, interpreting everything in human language, terms, and sentiments.
10. See Cicero, *The Nature of the Gods* (London: Penguin Classics, 1972).

Introduction

In the beginning—that is to say, once upon a time—man looked at the environment around, above, and below him: the other animals, birds, insects, plants and trees, hills and valleys, rivers and streams; the sun, moon, stars and other planets; the seas and oceans and the fish and plants contained in their depths; and what lay underneath the soil. He wondered how it all came to be, and, especially, how man came to be and to occupy planet Earth. Man marveled at all the wonderful things around him, the dangers and the opportunities they presented. And, since he did not understand how it all came about, he decided to try to find out—if he could . . .

In trying to interpret—that is, understand—the cosmos, man, naturally, asks himself questions and attempts to provide answers to them. In order to pose his questions meaningfully, man needs a myth,[1] that is, a model or framework of perception, a window on the cosmos through which he could look out on it. The very idea of a framework or window implies a select view. For good or ill, this framework tends to be that of man himself—the only framework readily available and the one with which he is most acquainted. This framework he projects onto the cosmos, regarding it through the aperture thus provided both with his physical eyes and with his imagination (mind's eye). This select view is seen against the background of his past experiences, his inclinations, likes, and dislikes.

The framework provided by the human paradigm automatically decides for man both what he sees and the type of questions he asks of the cosmos, as well as the kind of answers he gives himself. Two basic questions, among others, keep recurring and will recur till the end of man:

(a) How did it all come about—man and his cosmic environment?
(b) How best can man relate to his fellowman and to the rest of his cosmic environment in order to survive?

The first question concerns *origins*, the second *interrelationships*. The investigations concerning origins fall under the heading *Theology*; those concerning interrelationships between man, on the one hand, and the rest of his cosmic environment, on the other, fall under the heading *Religion*. The two, theology and religion, may (but do not necessarily have to) be linked together. Essentially, they are two separate types of investigations of special interest to man, but concern all things. The relationship of man to his fellowman is also a part of religion, a special part that falls under the heading *Ethics*, as will appear in due course.

The fundamental problem inherent in any human interpretation of the cosmos is that of the part (man) trying to comprehend (understand) the whole (the cosmos) of which he is a part. The problem is further compounded—even confounded—when the interpreter, man (the part) is also the framework of interpretation (interpretor) as well as an integral part of what is being interpreted (interpretand). Thus

interpreter = interpretor = (part of) interpretand

The problem would not be so serious if the interpreter (man) or the interpretor (the human paradigm) were a microcosm or hologram of the interpretand (the cosmos). But this is not the case.

Just as a framework literally *contains* the entire photograph framed within it, so is there a tendency—and a danger—for the cosmos-interpreter (man) to regard the interpretor or framework of interpretation (the human paradigm) as containing (that is, enclosing) the entire cosmos, including man himself. From this it is but a short step to thinking (unconsciously) that man *is*, indeed, the entire cosmos or creator of the cosmos.[2] This is the occupational hazard that the cosmos-interpreter courts when using the human paradigm. Unlike the professional speech interpreter who is responsible for the interpretation that he gives but not for the speech interpreted (interpretand), the cosmos-interpreter using the human paradigm is tempted to consider himself responsible for *both* the interpretation and the interpretand (the cosmos).

Thus man runs the risk of confounding himself as framework of interpretation, with his interpretation and the cosmos itself. His interpretation is, consequently, vitiated by his involvement, as paradigm, in the interpretation. For even if the interpretor were such as to allow him to give an interpretation that reflected accurately the nature of the interpretand, both interpretor and interpretand would still be different entities. It is not immediately obvious why the confusion should arise, but a simple example should help clarify.

Let us assume that man wished to interpret the behavior of a primate, such as the ape, and used the human paradigm for his interpretation.

Then it appears that the ape behaves in most, if not all, respects like man, so that, approximately, we have a situation where

$$\text{interpreter} = \text{interpretor} = \text{interpretand}$$

or

$$\text{man} = \text{human paradigm} = \text{ape}$$

Here, the confusion of man with ape would be pardonable because of the close physical and behavioral similarities between all three elements in the continuous equation. But it so happens that, in fact, man does *not* make this confusion, in spite of the understandable similarities. Indeed, the greater the similarities, the more pains man takes to emphasize the differences. The average human being, curiously, does not wish to be considered an ape or even related to the ape. Why, then, does it happen that in a case where no greater difference could be discerned between interpreter and interpretand (or between interpretor and interpretand) than that between man (or human model) and cosmos, man so easily confounds himself with the cosmos to the point of regarding himself as its creator and superior?

One answer to this question might be to say that the confusion is an "original sin"—that is, fundamental error—due to human pride. This is the theologian's answer and reflects a subtle aspect of human psychology: a simultaneous fear of, and urge to dominate, what at first seems hugely different and, therefore, difficult to understand. Indeed, it would appear that the greater the difference (as between man and cosmos), the greater the fear and the urge to dominate; the less the difference (as between man and ape), the less the fear and the urge to dominate.

Theological pride thus consists in the substitution of the interpretive model (man) for the interpretand (cosmos). This sin (error) has two auxiliary consequences. The first is *metaphysical*: the thought that the being (or coming-to-be) of the cosmos is a product of the human mind and is otherwise unreal or "nonexistent" in the absence or nonfunctioning of mind. Hence mind (*m* upper or lower case) becomes the originator, the source of all existent entities,[3] with the exception—curiously enough—of man himself. This first consequence may also be called the *existential* consequence and serves an important function: *it takes away the fear of a thing if one created it.*

The second consequence is constitutive: the projection of human characteristics or qualities onto the cosmos. This serves another purpose: *investing the cosmos with human characteristics gives man the feeling that it may, thereby, be responsive to human initiatives and thus is made tamable. But in being thus rendered human and tamable the cosmos, like the ordinary human being, comes (or is thought) to have a beginning and an end. This second consequence may therefore be called, alternatively, the essential* consequence.

One may, therefore, conclude that the "original sin" of pride contains, as its inescapable ingredient, a human paradigmatic model of cosmic existence and essence. The cosmos is conceived in anthropomorphic terms as a humanlike construct. But it is clear to any observant person that the cosmos does not conform to this model, which thus becomes suspect.

Words, pictures, symbols, frameworks, models: whatever the interpretive tool, the aim and goal is the same—interpretation in terms of the characteristics of the tool. All interpretations are like so many worlds, all interesting and each relating to its paradigm. None is absolute or superior to another; all are satisfying in different ways because each answers to a different purpose, a different need. The crucial issue is always whether the model adopted is appropriate to, has a good fit with, what is being interpreted. In this respect it may be stated that the cosmos is an organic whole of all its components, held together by the principle of compensatory flow and change (flow-change), and any appropriate paradigm of the cosmos must reflect this principle. Similarly, all the paradigms of the components of the cosmos must, together, reflect this same principle of flow-change; and each paradigm must subscribe to, and be consistent with, this principle. Flow-change means continuity plus change.

Interpretations, however, are not always intended to reflect the nature of things according to experience. They may be intended to serve other purposes, such as to support a certain point of view, provide personal, psychological, or aesthetic comfort, et cetera. From the foregoing discussion we may, therefore, distinguish the following elements in the interpretive process:

(a) the interpreter (man);
(b) the object to be interpreted (interpretand);
(c) the interpretive framework, paradigm, model, equation, et cetera (interpretor);
(d) the interpretation or meaning given to the interpretand (value, significance);
(e) the purpose (telos) of the interpretation as stated or discerned, e.g.:
   (i) to establish correspondence or conformity to experience (i.e., scientific truth or provisional knowledge);
   (ii) to support a viewpoint, to provide personal, psychological, aesthetic comfort, satisfaction, pleasure, et cetera (opinion, feeling, therapy, et cetera);

(f) the relationship (i.e. consistency or inconsistency) of the interpretation to the cosmic principle of organic unity and compensatory flow-change.

In the final analysis, whatever meaning the cosmos, or any other term or concept, has for man is (or has been) given to it by man on the basis of an explicit or implicit model or framework. And in the case of the cosmos man's interpretation of it automatically determines, in turn, his conception and interpretation of his role and relationship to the cosmos and his fellowman. It is, of course, another matter whether or not the meaning-content of the interpretation has any empirical basis or confirmation. But a definition or meaning is no less one for lack of empirical content.

This introductory chapter anticipates much of the discussion that will follow and further elucidate many of the topics already introduced. In the meantime, we may summarize, in the form of questions and answers, the situation in which man finds himself in his attempt to interpret the cosmos by means of a human paradigm, as follows:

(a) How well does the paradigm fit, empirically? Poorly.
(b) What does man see in the cosmos through the paradigm? Form, order out of chaos (in this sense, confusion), uniformities, harmony, disharmony, et cetera.
(c) In the framework of the human paradigm, what kinds of questions does man pose concerning the cosmos? Origin, end, Creator (God), et cetera (theology, anthropomorphism).
(d) How does man view his relationship to the cosmos and its presumed Creator? Superiority to the cosmos, but child to parent vis-à-vis the Creator in a situation of dependence, obedience, love, fear, reward, punishment, et cetera, in a strange and hostile cosmic environment.
(e) How does man see his relationship to his fellowman? One of several children in a family, common parentage, brotherhood, common destiny, but not without sibling rivalry, conflict, self-interest, self-preservation, et cetera.
(f) What is the interpretational hazard connected with the human paradigm? Man makes (conceives) the Creator of the cosmos in his own image, thus throwing open the thought that man, through his mind, creates the cosmos.

There are, in general, no explanations to the questions man poses to himself concerning the cosmos—only interpretations or possible ways of accounting for some or all of a given set of facts or phenomena. The interpretation via the human paradigm is only one of many possible interpretations. But of all the possible interpretations, that which best fits the phenomena or the facts ("best possible fit") may be regarded as the most suitable hypothesis and, when empirically confirmed, as scientific truth or provisional knowledge until better interpretations are invented or suggested from a review of the facts.

NOTES

1. For the use of the word *myth* in this book, see the next chapter (chapter 1 of Book One).
2. The interpretational hazard associated with the human paradigm as an interpretive tool, namely, that man comes to think of himself as the creator of the cosmos, is very well illustrated in Christianity, where man, in the form of Jesus called the Christ, is believed to be the Creator-God of the cosmos. It is also apparent in Sartrean existentialist thought, as in Nietzsche's thinking, especially in his *Thus Spake Zarathustra.*
3. This is part of the doctrine of idealism.

In the Beginning, Man . . .

BOOK ONE
MYTH

Chapter 1

Definition of Myth

This chapter deals, briefly, with the uses of the word *myth* in this book. The *Collins Concise English Dictionary* (1978) gives the following definitions of the word, which itself derives from the original Greek *mythos*, meaning "word" or "legend":

1. a traditional story of unknown authorship, serving usually to explain some phenomenon of nature, the origin of man, or the customs, religious rites, etc. of a people: cf. LEGEND
2. such stories collectively; mythology
3. any fictitious story
4. any imaginary person or thing.

Without departing from the general sense of myth as defined above and accepted conventionally, the term will be used in this book in the wide sense of an "interpretation" or "hypothesis."

Thus *any* interpretation merits the name of myth. Accordingly, we may distinguish three principal types of myth:

(a) Scientific myth: A myth that is empirical, i.e., sense-verifiable, hence held as scientific truth or provisional knowledge. All established scientific hypotheses (laws) would fall into this category.
(b) Superstitious or dogmatic myth: A myth that has been exploded or contradicted by the test of sense experience but continues to be held or believed in. All superstitions (such as that an eclipse of the moon is caused by a demon attempting to gobble it up) and dogmas (such as the Roman Catholic and Orthodox Eastern church dogma of transubstantiation) fall into this category.
(c) Symbolic or metaphysical myth: A myth that is placed so far back, or so far forward, in time as to be unverifiable within the lifetime of the human species or that is couched in language that does not permit empirical testing. Such myths are usually retained for their symbolic, metaphorical, or aesthetic value. They point to some value,

3

moral or ideal beyond themselves that is desirable as a guide to conduct or as an aesthetic value for contemplation. The myth of heaven and hell (serving the end of behavior control) and the myth of the golden age (symbolizing the "enchanted distance fallacy" or natural human tendency to romanticize and idealize the past the further removed it is from any possibility of empirical confirmation of the events romanticized) fall into this category, which may also be denoted as "pure myth" or "mythology" in its strict sense.[1]

Any activity is myth making that seeks an interpretation of any given fact or phenomenon, whether in the field of metaphysics, philosophy, physical, or biological science or any other field of human endeavor. Preference for the use of the term *myth* in this book in place of, or as equivalent to, *hypothesis* or *interpretation* is based on the need to emphasize the fact that all interpretations of fact, phenomenon, or event do not exist objectively "out there" or independently of the human mind but proceed from man. As such, they are artificial in the sense of being artifacts, inventions, or creations of the human mind. It is very necessary and useful to underline this basic but not so very obvious fact, which is therefore liable to be often forgotten. The preference is also due to the desire to avoid the use of the term *explanation* since, in the first place, there are no explanations in the sense of a guaranteed, final, or fixed accounting for the presence of any fact, phenomenon or event; and, secondly, there is a popular tendency to associate the term, "explanation" with "unique" reasons or meanings, which is best avoided by using terms indicating the tentativeness or provisionality of meanings. This fact is best conveyed by terms such as "myth," "hypothesis" and "interpretation," which are relatively free of any of the undesirable connotations associated with the terms, "explanation" or "law."

NOTE

1. It is this third category of myth—pure or symbolic myth—that is the subject of the conclusion of Joseph Campbell's *Occidental Mythology* (New York: Viking Press, 1970). There he distinguishes four functions of mythology: (1) to elicit a sense of awe before the mystery of being; (2) to provide a cosmology appropriate to the sense of awe; (3) to support the current social order with a view to integrating the individual into the group; and (4) to initiate the individual into the realities of his own psyche for his own spiritual enrichment and realization.

Chapter 2

Myth: Matrix of All Knowledge

Myth is conventionally regarded as the embodiment of the traditional wisdom of any people. The definition given in the *Collins Concise Dictionary of the English Language* (1978 edition) quoted in the preceding chapter reveals the polyvalent nature of myth as an interpretive tool.

Basically, myth, philosophy, dogma, and scientific theory are the same: preestablished or ad hoc interpretations or hypotheses, differing only in the conditions governing their use as interpretive tools. The basic paradigm is the myth, possessing considerable potential. Taken in all its possible shades of interpretation (or meaning) and types of interrelationships, the myth transforms itself into *philosophy* (patterns of interrelationships, the knowledge of which constitutes what is traditionally called wisdom). Interpreted as a sensing and emotional appropriation regulating relationships between persons, on the one hand, and the rest of the cosmos, on the other, myth becomes *religion*—or *ethics*, if confined to interpersonal relationships or other kinds of mutual relationships. Assigned a unique interpretation without benefit of empirical confirmation and applicable under all circumstances, myth becomes *dogma* (fixed and certain truth). Assigned a unique interpretation confirmed empirically, for the time being, myth becomes *scientific theory* or provisional knowledge—that is, knowledge on trial, because subject to change in the light of better empirical data.

Because of its interpretive role in philosophy and its regulative function in regard to human conduct, myth is capable of being applied as a tool of psychoanalysis and psychotherapy. Also, because of its wide potential of meanings it furnishes models for interpretation and elucidation of certain kinds of literature, e.g., religious literature. In this domain it provides parables as well as hermeneutic principles often classified as literal, symbolic or analogical, tropic or moral, and eschatological. The same myth can furnish illustrations and interpretations in various fields.

5

Take, for example, the beautiful Greek myth of Cupid and Psyche,[1] which exhibits the following features in the fields specified:

(a) Psychoanalysis: sibling rivalry (Psyche and her sisters); mother-in-law and daughter-in-law rivalry and conflict (Venus versus Psyche).
(b) Religion and Ethics: trust or lack of it in interpersonal relations (Psyche and her sisters).
(c) Theology: dealings between god (Cupid) and mortal (Psyche) based on a nonreciprocal divine demand for blind human trust and confidence and suppression of human curiosity on pain of danger or death—curiosity always winning over danger and death; atonement by the son (Cupid) of a god (Zeus) for divine injustice (of Venus to Psyche); immortalization of a mortal female (Psyche) favored with immaculate conception (nonhuman, i.e. divine, fatherhood) of an offspring (daughter, Voluptas); immortality as a gift of the gods, as well as their greatest gift, to man.

Myth gives free rein to imagination, regardless of the plausibility or implausibility of the interpretations with which it is invested. Homer's stories of the gods, for example, have been traditionally criticized by Greek philosophers, including Plato, as both improbable and immoral—a criticism entirely beside the point of the Homeric myth. There is a strong presumption that Homer's intention was not merely to ridicule the gods but also had a more serious aspect to it that was lost on his critics: the "at-one-ment" or union between gods and mortals. If gods were like mortals, then mortals were like gods and the barrier separating the two sides was lifted. It is possible that, by his cavalier treatment of the gods, Homer was hinting at the divinity of, or in, man *regardless of man's condition*. Man was not alienated from the gods, and the gods were not—to use a modern-day theological phrase of Semitic origin—in a "wholly other" relationship to man. Homer thus appears to have been an early but unrecognized apostle of atonement of god and man. It all depends on the interpretation of myth, which has no limits.

Plato and others like him—Cicero[2] was one—were very strongly antimyth although spawning a few themselves,[3] precisely because of the myth's unlimited possibilities of interpretation and elucidation and especially because of its tremendous utility in politics.[4] Plato had only one overriding interest in myth: its dogmatic use for state propaganda purposes aimed at buttressing the conservative values and privileges of the aristocratic class to which he, himself, belonged. For this reason he advocated, in his "ideal" republic, a state monopoly on myth and myth-making activity. It was not through piety and respect for the gods that he criticized Homer's cavalier treatment of them, but because he wished to buttress popular belief in them as constituting a supernatural, superhuman authority for the sociopolitical system (aristocracy) that he wished to see established in Athens and other Greek city-states of his day. Plato's position was understandable: so long as others were free to create their own myth and interpret it in any way they liked, Plato's monopoly and dogmatic use of myth would be endangered. Hence his bitter attacks on poets and playwrights. Plato's attitude toward myth was therefore neither honest nor disinterested.

As interpretations—not explanations—of fact, some myths (or models) are more useful than others. As myths or models they may be already existing or newly constructed ad hoc frameworks superimposed on the reality or phenomena to be interpreted (the interpretand), without necessarily having any vital or other relationship to the interpretand, unless by sheer coincidence. For a myth or model negotiates or interprets reality on terms other than those of the reality itself, no matter how ingenious its interpretation may seem. It interprets reality in terms of its own framework. Therefore, care is needed in the handling of myth. It tends to dangerous confusion and error when its proper limitations (as defined by its framework) are exceeded or overlooked, and it becomes mistaken for reality or for explanation (rather than interpretation) of that reality or, worse, is believed, or intended to be believed, as fact.[5]

Myths may take their origin in fact—for example, they may be based on some historical event—or they may simply be invented ad hoc and used as interpretive devices or frameworks. The parable, so beloved of Jesus of Nazareth, falls into this latter category. For practical purposes it does not really matter how they arise. For the relevance of a myth does not consist in whether it is based on fact or contrived, but in whether it accounts in a plausible and/or desirable manner for the phenomenon to be interpreted. Thus the relevant question for a myth, as for a statistical equation, is: How good is the fit as an interpretation of something else?

MYTH IN RELATION TO TRUTH

According to the preceding test, the myth of Eden and the Fall of Man has been regarded by Christians as a sufficiently good interpretation of the human condition, to the extent that an entire theology of redemption has been erected upon it. To the modern Christian theologian it would be the nadir of unsophistication to even pose the question of the historical validity, or truth, of the myth. For it does not even originate with Christians or Jews! One of the significant aspects of myth in the modern world has been its contribution to our understanding of the term *truth* in its historical dimension. A modern-day philosopher, like Karl Popper, would define truth as correspondence with fact, making verification a crucial element in the definition.[6] What myth has taught us, on the contrary, is that verification or not, the fact to which truth corresponds, with the passage of time is not the historical fact but *our understanding* of the historical fact: the historical fact, *as we understand it*. Over time, therefore, authenticity yields place to *understanding*, to interpretation, of events.

It is for this reason that the modern Christian, for example, will have to come to terms with the central figure in his religion in the same way as he has come to terms with the myth of the Fall—if, indeed, he has not already done so: not by a naive quest to establish the authentic historical Jesus, but by a Schweitzerian quest—a mythical interpretation or reinterpretation—aimed at establishing the relevance of Christianity to modern life.[7] According to this aim, the crucial test is not whether Jesus existed as a historically authentic personality or was merely a fabrication of the early Christian sect (he seems to have been a bit of both), for this is of little relevance to the twentieth and future centuries; but how good is our understanding of the historical-cum-mythical Jesus as a fit, as an interpretation, of human life and destiny *as Christians desire it to be*. On the answer to this question will depend the future of Christianity, as of every founder-religion for that matter, in the centuries to come. Thus myth provides the same touchstone for dealing with the past in relation to the future as it applies for dealing with the past in relation to the present, and it applies equally to historical religious figures, such as Jesus, as to purely fictitious figures and events, such as Adam and Eve and the Fall. And the touchstone is that of interpretive relevance.[8]

MYTH AND INTERPRETATION OF TIME

Students of ethnology and African religion[9] maintain that African traditional society has no, or a very limited, concept of future time but strong concepts of time present (Sasa) and time past (Zamani). In African society, they affirm, the past is all myth or model, and the future does not exist except as a result of what use is made of past and present time.

The basic fund of time—according to the African view—is potential time, primarily vacant, nonactivity, chronological time, of which there is an inexhaustible amount available to man. Active time is activity time, for it is activity that makes time *pass*; so that, without activity, time does not pass. Past time is that slice of potential time already occupied by

8

activities of the ancestors, tribe, and family, the results of which are available in the form of stored harvests, huts, farming and hunting implements, cooking utensils, et cetera. Thus, socially accumulated capital is evidence of past time. Present time is that slice of potential time taken up with current activities, the fruits of which will become available subsequently in more stored harvests, huts, farming and hunting implements and cooking utensils, et cetera. More of the same in the future as was inherited from the past. Whence the future is the past repeated all over again—the "eternal return," in the apt description of Nietzsche adopted by Mircea Eliade.[10]

It is not, therefore, that there is no future time, or concept of future time, in traditional African society, but that the future is so much like the past, in terms of the product of activity—being a derivative of both past and present activities—as to be indistinguishable from it. Thus the phrase *eternal return* does more than express the cyclical nature of natural, environmental occurrences; it expresses, also, the *identity* of past and future (active) time. This implies, of course, that the clue to breaking the identity of past and future lies in the present, that is, in a pattern of current activities entirely different from that of the traditional past; which, in turn, means giving up the concept of the past as a source of emulation, of exemplary models.

Thus, basic to all African concept of time is activity, not chronology, and the clue to interpretation is the pattern of activity, reinforced by emulation. Activity time has proved a very useful concept in both traditional African society and modern occidental society. A change in the African concept and interpretation of time can only result from a surrender of the traditional habit of emulation of the past, and an acceptance of new patterns of activity dictated by technological change. Cyclicity will no more be an element in the substantive definition of future time but a mere feature of natural environmental events, of chronological time.

MYTH AND THE REINTERPRETATION AND TRANSVALUATION OF EVENTS

As already made clear, myth is interpretation with the aid of a preexisting or an ad hoc model or pattern. There is a widespread notion that associates myth with oral traditions, and another that regards myth as an inflexible and fossilized interpretation preserved by an unerring tribal memory and transmitted orally. Either notion is only partially true. Greek mythology, the most common example in the Occident, assumed written form quite early, through the efforts of the early poets, such as

Hesiod and Homer. The earliest type of written historical accounts (historiography) took the form of myth or preset patterns or molds into which accounts were uniformly cast. Such was the type of history written by Herodotus. The same procedure of using a fixed mold or pattern was also adopted in recording certain Greek myths such as in the *Iliad*.

It is not necessary to go so far back in time to demonstrate the existence of written myth or that the form assumed by myth, oral or written, is not an essential element, but that this consists universally in the application of a set interpretive framework to phenomena and events. The interpretive activity of the Pope, speaking ex cathedra, and of the Party Theoretician of the Communist Party of the Soviet Union, both applying preset models, is present and continuing evidence that myth is alive and well and in written form. What seems to escape attention frequently is that the interpretive pattern itself undergoes modification or change in the very act of interpretation. The *structure* of the myth may continue unchanged while the *meaning* given to it changes more often than is realized. This is, indeed, the problem at the heart of accusations of revisionism hurled by Communists at one another: the text remains unchanged while the meaning given to it changes.

Occasionally, if rarely, the pattern-text itself may change: the myth is rewritten and history as well, in order to support a differing point of view from that prevailing in the past. Again, the Soviet Union is a good example of a country that rewrites myth and history. So are post-Hitler Germany and Japan. Such attempts seldom pass unnoticed or unchallenged and may force other countries to make special mention of them in their own myth and history, insofar as the changes affect their own roles.

Whether regarded in its oral or its written form, myth, for all its preset ready-to-handness, is flexible and reinterpretable. And, essentially and truly, "the past is myth," interpretively malleable, in a very fundamental sense. For there is no *one* (or unique) way of interpreting or writing a myth or, for that matter, history—*rewriting* of history aside.

The past is myth. But it is also the *source* of myth in its dual aspect of: (a) *interpretive* model, employed to make sense of (give meaning to) natural phenomena and events of daily life; and (b) ideal or *exemplary* model selected from the past for emulation and reproduction, thus re-creating or commemorating events in the past of a tribe or people. This second aspect of myth, its hortative aspect, is what converts history into a reproduction of events in the past. Hence the basic feature of repetition in history. The question is not whether history necessarily repeats itself (seasonal cycles excluded) but whether history is supposed or expected to repeat itself. In traditional societies, the answer is, Yes.

10

With the preceding paragraph we arrive at the dialectical conflict at the heart of myth, its *interpretive role* providing, through reinterpretation, an element of flexibility that balances the rigidity of its *exemplary role*. *Myth* is thus a synonym for *dialectic*, the conflict of rigidity and flexibility (or change). While there are several interpretations possible for any given myth, interpretations that are polar or opposed naturally attract some measure of attention. It is this feature of myth, its perverse flexibility, that constitutes a danger, in the view of those who, like Plato, wish only their own preferred interpretation to prevail. The transvaluation of myth, that is, the giving of a meaning opposite to the traditional interpretation of a myth, is therefore of special interest.[11] An example of transvaluation applied to the myth of Adam and Eve and the Fall is provided in the appendix to this chapter.

MYTH AND PSYCHOTHERAPY

The versatility of myth is demonstrated in its utility as a problem-solving, psychotherapeutic tool in which the element of interpretation plays a very significant role. Its chief value, in this connection, consists in its dramatization of conflict and other kinds of psychological problems; or, as the psychotherapist would say, in its projection of a problem from the patient on to an objective plane on which the patient could study it and devise his own solutions. Here also, since the myth sets up the interpretive framework, the patient finds his solutions within that framework—be it the deliberately ambiguous pronouncement of an oracle or an ambiguous prophecy like that of the myth of Oedipus. Consequently, the solutions to his problems chosen by the patient will be as good as the relevance or fit of the myth's framework to the patient's perceived problems. For this reason psychotherapists, like their religious counseling counterparts, need to exercise great care in the use of myths as problem resolution tools.

This note of caution is even more necessary in intercultural transpositions of myth, since every myth encounters limitations when an attempt is made to apply it outside its cultural milieu. This handicap can, of course, be overcome by acculturation of the foreign myth, thereby providing it with a new lease of life as well as an expanded framework for problem resolution. Indeed, the dual need for mythological acculturation and framework adaptation may hold some promise for the future of psychotherapy as a problem resolution technique, as was hinted by Aldous Huxley in his novel *Island*.[12] There it was implied that the Oedipus myth, when transferred to some Southeast Asian island community, could munity, could have some relevance if it was adapted by dropping its traditional ending—if, that is to say, Oedipus did not have to marry his mother or, if he did and the mistake was discovered, Jocasta did not have to commit suicide and Oedipus did not have to blind himself, as these acts would appear pretty silly in a Southeast Asian culture. Such adaptation would accommodate the myth within the culture and mores of that society.

MYTH AND BELIEF

Belief is like myth and closely related to it, as will appear subsequently.[13] It arises as a conscious or unconscious protest against, a renunciation of, an existing experience or fact and seeks to provide an alternative which may or may not be actualizable in experience. Like myth, the relationship of belief to any previous or current experience is always an open question. The belief-content, that is to say, is always open to question as to whether or not it relates to a preexisting model or to actual experience.

The essential difference between myth and belief is that myth accepts and seeks to interpret an existing experience or reality, while belief rejects or repudiates it and proposes a substitute that may or may not materialize. Thus, in regard to attitude vis-à-vis a given reality, belief is at the opposite pole to myth, dialectically related with respect to their treatment—acceptance and rejection—of a given experience. This dialectical relationship endures up to the point where the belief-content (the proposed alternative to the given reality) becomes actualized. Once this happens, the dialectical relationship disappears; myth remains myth and belief becomes fact or experience to be, in turn, interpreted (myth) or repudiated (belief). Thus the actualization of belief constitutes a dynamic, generative element in myth-making activity as in belief-making activity, and vice versa.

MYTH: A SUMMARY

The myth is a model or paradigm, derived or not from previous experience, employed to interpret, comprehend, or give coherence to a fact or set of facts of experience with which it may have no rational relationship. Thus the three elements of the myth are:

(a) an existing or ad hoc model;
(b) a fact or experience to be interpreted or understood;

12

(c) the relationship (if any) of the model to any previous experience or to the experience to be interpreted.

Any interpretation of experience or reality is basically mythical because it involves the use of a model or paradigm (which may or may not be based on experience) to interpret a given experience without reference to fit. Only subsequently, if at all, is the question addressed of the goodness or accuracy of the fit of the model to the experience. Normally, an attempt is made to interpret new or previously unknown facts in terms of a previously known model.

When, subsequently, the question of goodness of fit of the myth is addressed, five options present themselves:

(a) Test the myth by the facts, repeatedly, for conformity to the facts, and if validated—myth always conforming to fact—the myth becomes a scientific law, knowledge on trial, or provisional truth.
(b) Retain an exploded or fact-rejected myth as a superstition.
(c) Conform the facts to the myth (i.e., rationalization) and so establish the myth as dogma, definition, or certainty.
(d) Retain a factually untestable myth as pure myth for its aesthetic, philosophic, or therapeutic value based on the elasticity of its interpretation.
(e) Reformulate an exploded myth to establish a new myth subject to all the five choices listed here.

From the preceding choices it becomes clear why myth is the basis of all knowledge, all philosophy, all art, all science, all dogma, and all superstition.

APPENDIX

1. A MYTH TRANSVALUED: EDEN, ADAM AND EVE, AND THE FALL

The Creation story of the Book of Genesis was advanced not as a theory with empirical content, but as a myth that, however, lends itself to more than one interpretation. The interpretation given here is a transvaluation, or contradiction, of the ostensible meaning of the biblical version. The following are the elements of the interpretation:

(a) The creature, man, is a plaything made at the whim of the Creator

13

and always at his mercy. (This is not a flattering picture of the Creator.)

(b) Ignorance has a premium, while knowledge is at a discount. Ignorance is rewarded with eternal life, but knowledge, born of curiosity and experience, with punishment: hard labor as the cost of daily subsistence, painful child bearing, and, eventually, death. (This interpretation could easily result in leaving knowledge entirely in the hands of the priestly class—the class that spun the myth—as it was in the Middle Ages.)

(c) Presentation of alternatives (fruit of the tree of life and of the tree of the knowledge of good and evil) by God implies the grant of choice and free will to man. Free will implies the freedom to choose and to order one's priorities as one wills, including an order of priority different from that of God. An order of priority conforming to that desired by God makes of man a conforming robot, not an agent possessed of free will. For free will involves the *voluntary* assumption of consequences, including negative consequences, of one's choice for the sake of achieving goals that one values. Thus the Genesis story represents a contest between power (God) and free will (man).

(d) Man prefers—and chooses—the risk of knowledge with certain death to the riskless tranquillity of eternal life in obedient ignorance (or ignorant obedience). He opts for free will in the face of power. Therefore, in exercising his free will Adam committed no sin (offence), unless it is a sin to accept the choice of alternatives offered, in the first place. (Moral: Cooperating with power may be at the expense of one's free will, and there is no reason why one's choice must necessarily conform to that desired at the seat of power.)

(e) Lack of curiosity regarding the fruit of the tree of the knowledge of good and evil would have put Adam outside the "game" of God by removing the means of negative cooperation with the "game," the object of which was to test Adam's willingness to cooperate or not in God's design—discouragement of knowledge: in short, to test man's free will to the full, to bring out his order of preference as between knowledge and eternal life. Adam was the Hebrew Prometheus, negatively interpreted (transvalued).

(f) In exercising his curiosity and his preference man kept himself within the "game," putting himself completely within the power of God. The result: a demonstration of God's power and an exercise of man's free will—an opposition of two assertive modes. (Moral: Conflict is the price of liberty of action.)

(g) Considering the Creator's responsibility for the creature (man) and

14

the fact that, by presenting a choice, the Creator accorded man free
will:

(i) Attaching a penalty to one choice represents an attempt by the
Creator to influence the creature's choice. A choice under duress
would not have been a free choice. Adam rejected such a choice
to his enduring honor.

(ii) The penalty for rejecting the Creator's preference negated the
free will already accorded to man and was therefore unfair, an
"Indian" gift (with apologies to the red man).

(iii) If, therefore, there was any subsequent need for reconciliation
between God and man, it was on the part of God not of man.
Christians affirm that Jesus was the mediator of such reconciliation, sent by God to man. If so, Jesus' mission on earth was
misunderstood and misinterpreted by his followers. Rather than
pay the price of man's sin (there was none), he paid the price
of God's original sin of injustice to man, thus reconciling Creator
to creature. (The embarrassing question will always remain under
the Genesis or this transvalued interpretation of the myth: If a
reconciliation was, indeed, effected by Jesus, why, then, does
man continue to die? Man seems to have lost both ways—losing
eternal life without gaining much knowledge: even fools die.)

It is clear from this reinterpretation of the Genesis myth that the
pertinent mission of Jesus to man was not salvation (soteriology) but
reconciliation (atonement). For this, it was only enough that the Word
(Logos) become flesh. For since God did not wish man to become like
himself ("like gods"), knowing good and evil, it was only necessary,
for the purpose of reconciliation, that God become man, experiencing
suffering and death, the very curse he laid on man.

It hardly needs pointing out that in this transvaluation of the Genesis
myth man emerges with a better showing, his dignity and honor intact,
both of which he forfeits in the Genesis interpretation. The conclusion
is clear: if man was given free will by his Creator, then his treatment by
the same Creator in the Genesis myth was manifestly unjust.

2. MYTH IN RELIGIOUS PSYCHOTHERAPY: JUDAIC AND CHRISTIAN MYTHS OF REPENTANCE, JUSTIFICATION, AND REMISSION OF SINS

Both the Judaic and the Christian theological myths postulate an

15

anthropomorphic, male Creator-God of the cosmos, including man. In Judaism he is "wholly other," a being entirely removed from the cosmos that he created—transcendent in the highest degree. But he has a special relationship of partiality for man, and particularly for the original twelve tribes composing the Jewish people and their descendants, as against the rest of mankind and the rest of his creation. In Christianity, he is "wholly other" but not to the same degree as in Judaism, since he deigned to become incarnate in the man, Jesus. Nonetheless, he is separate from his creation, yet having a special relationship of partiality for mankind in general, as against the rest of his creation. Furthermore, according to the Christian myth, his incarnation in Jesus made possible a rapprochement between mankind and himself.

For all this partiality enjoyed by the Jews or mankind, man is regarded in both myths as by nature evil (Adam's original sin); that is, tending to produce suffering and misfortune in the world (if not in the cosmos at large), to the detriment of the human race and the rest of God's creation. This evil tendency disturbs the "favored-creature" relationship with God, perpetuating sin, that is, estrangement or psychological alienation of Jew and all mankind from God. The special relationship is thus perpetually in danger—all through man's fault, because of his inherently evil nature.

The concepts of evil (that which causes suffering and misfortune) and sin (psychological alienation) constitute the core of the Judeo-Christian myth of the man-God relationship, fulfilling the central role of disequilibrators or destabilizers in that relationship. But this disequilibrium is soon remedied by the special provision made available in both myths. For easy comparison, the provision is outlined in summary form in both cases, in order to bring out the similarities and differences.

A. Judaism

(a) (Jewish) Man's responsibility for evil and sin on every occasion of perturbation of the man-God relationship is remedied by
(b) Renunciation, which implies
   (i) Acknowledgment of personal responsibility for evil and sin;
   (ii) Rejection of the disequilibrium caused in the man-God relationship;
   (iii) Resolve to avoid future actions of evil and sin, hence, of disequilibrium;
   (iv) Rectification of the relationship with God (i.e. justification or making right) by *animal* sacrifice (unblemished scapegoat),

16

which could remove the personal responsibility for the particular evil or sin from oneself onto the sacrificial animal, depending on the acceptability of the sacrifice to God.

(c) Remission of sin follows through the grace of God if the sacrifice is acceptable to him; that is, if conditions i, ii, and iii preceding are genuinely fulfilled and the ritual involved in condition iv correctly executed.

(d) Token of Remission of Sin: Material blessings and prosperity for the individual Jew and, in the end, the millennium-on-earth for the Jewish people.

(e) Repeatability of the Renunciation procedure in full for every subsequent case of sin or evil.

B. Christianity

(a) Man's responsibility for evil and sin on every occasion of perturbation of the man-God relationship is remedied by

(b) Renunciation, which implies
  (i) Acknowledgement of personal responsibility for evil and sin;
  (ii) Rejection of the disequilibrium caused in the man-God relationship;
  (iii) Resolve to avoid future actions of evil and sin, hence, of disequilibrium;
  (iv) Rectification of the relationship with God (i.e., justification) by *human* sacrifice (Jesus the unblemished, sinless scapegoat), which could remove the personal responsibility for the particular evil or sin from oneself onto Jesus, who is an acceptable sacrifice to God.

(c) Remission of sin follows through the grace of God, if the sacrifice is acceptable to God (which it is, in the case of Jesus his Son, who is also God himself incarnate) provided conditions i, ii, and iii preceding are genuinely fulfilled.

(d) Atonement: In addition to being reconciled to God man is *made one with God* through the self-sacrifice of Jesus who being man, puts himself (the spotless ''sacrificial lamb'') in man's place and, being God, raises man to the level of God.[14]

(e) Token of Remission of Sin: None—hence, as Paul put it, every man will have to work out his salvation, incessantly, with fear and trembling.[15] Material blessings and prosperity are not guaranteed to the repentant sinner; on the contrary, persecution is promised (and expected) to those who accept and follow Jesus' Gospel.[16] There is, however, the consolation of the Kingdom of God on earth (the Church) and, in the end, the Resurrection and Last Judgment followed by Paradise for the Just.

(f) Nonrepeatability of the Renunciation procedure in full for subsequent evil or sin, since the sacrifice of Jesus was once and for always in the same manner as the renunciation of sin through (adult) baptism is once for all. Therefore, all evil and sin should be avoided after baptism. However, this being humanly impossible, each subsequent evil or sin could be atoned for by genuine fulfilment of the renunciation conditions i, ii, and iii and by faith in the atonement of Jesus accompanied by appropriate works ("fruits worthy of repentance").[17]

It should be noted that the goal of the renunciation procedure in Judaism is strictly the restoration of the disturbed equilibrium in the relationship between God and man. Nothing more, such as the promise of atonement (at-one-ment = union) with God in the Christian myth—an impossibility in the Judaic myth since the Jewish God (Yahweh) is absolutely transcendent, "wholly other." Thus, the main difference between the Judaic and Christian myths of renunciation and remission of sin is the Christian doctrine of atonement resulting from the transvaluation of the Judaic scapegoat into Jesus, the man-God. The doubling of the role of scapegoat (transvalued from the celebration of Passover in connection with the liberation from Egyptian slavery to the celebration of the Resurrection or liberation from mortality) and mediator by Jesus, as affirmed in the Christian myth, involved his atonement in two senses: (a) the reconciling of good and evil and (b) the reconciling of man and God. But Christians also believe that he thereby abrogated the natural law of justice (cause-effect or karma) in favor of man above every other living creature in the cosmos.[18]

It is also interesting to compare the two myths with their Dionysian equivalent. The central idea in all three religions is the sacrificial feast:

(a) The Dionysian feast in which the god Bacchus (or a surrogate animal) is sacrificed, and the animal's flesh eaten raw and its blood drunk warm. This represented, symbolically, partaking of the flesh and blood of the god, to which was added the drinking of wine, the god being the original cultivator of the vine.

(b) The Jewish Passover in which the unblemished lamb is sacrificed and eaten roasted and its blood smeared on the doorposts.[19]

(c) the Christian Eucharist (a transvaluation of the Jewish Passover feast) in which the bread and wine are symbolically (or transubstantially, according to the Church of Rome) eaten and drunk as the flesh and blood of Jesus, the human sacrifice.[20]

The affinity between the Dionysian and Christian feasts need hardly be remarked upon. Both share the belief in man's immortality by reason of their basic faith in a dying and resurrecting god/God[21]—a belief (in resurrection) also shared only by the Pharisaic sect among the Jews.

NOTES

1. The version of the myth used here is taken from Walter Pater, *Marius the Epicurean* (New York: A. L. Burt Company, Publishers, n.d.) pp. 54–81.
2. Cf. Cicero, *On the Nature of the Gods* (Penguin).
3. Cf. Plato's myth of the ideal republic.
4. The modern-day equivalent to the use of myth in politics is the puppet theater, which, in the absence of strict censorship, could easily doom contemporary dictatorships, where, incidentally, they have achieved great popularity. Jokes and cartoons also play a similar role.
5. E.g., Plato's myth of the various metals of which the different social classes are made, as recounted in his *Republic*.
6. Karl R. Popper, *The Open Society and its Enemies*, vol. 1 (London and Henley: Routledge & Kegan Paul, 1962) p. 274; *Objective Knowledge* (London: Oxford University Press, 1981) pp. 44–46, 127–28.
7. See Albert Schweitzer, *The Quest of the Historical Jesuss* (London: A & C Black, 1954).
8. The criterion of interpretive relevance constitutes an automatic built-in obsolescence factor for all original historical models.
9. Cf. John Mbiti, *African Religions and Philosophy* (Heinemann, 1969).
10. Friedrich Nietzsche, *Thus Spake Zarathustra*, and Mircea Eliade, *Myths, Dreams and Mysteries* (Collins Fontana Library, 1977).
11. The term *transvaluation* is often associated with Friedrich Nietzsche, who made a specialty of espousing interpretations and views opposite to those conventionally held, as in his writings titled, *Twilight of the Idols, Beyond Good and Evil, Thus Spake Zarathustra*, et cetera. This tactic seems to have brought him quick public notice that apparently counted, for him, as the equivalent of the fame enjoyed by the conventions and idols whom he admired and attacked.
12. Aldous Huxley, *Island* (New York: Harper & Row, 1972), p. 251.
13. See Book Two, Section B, chapter 8.
14. This is why it was necessary for the Councils of Nicea and Chalcedon to affirm the two natures of Jesus, as otherwise atonement with the divine nature of God could not follow from the ritual self-sacrifice of the human nature of Jesus.
15. Philippians 2:12.
16. Saint Mark 10:28–30.
17. Saint Luke 3:8; also James 2:14–26. James preached faith with works, Paul justification by faith without the deeds of the law (Romans 3:28). There would seem to be no incompatibility here, as Paul was referring not to works of faith outside the law, but to the ritual works and sacrifices of Jewish law.
18. This aspect of the myth is anthropocentrism gone wild.
19. Exodus 12.
20. Matthew 26:26–30; Saint Mark 14:22–26; Saint Luke 22:14–20.
21. Cf. Edith Hamilton, *Mythology* (Mentor Book, 1942), pp. 47–62. There is little doubt that the rites of Dionysus as dying and resurrecting god (Bacchanalia) and of

Demeter (Eleusinian rites) in honor of her daughter Persephone, the dying and resurrecting goddess, served, like the Christian Eucharist and belief in the resurrecting Jesus, to allay men's fear of death in their time. No other interpretation would fit Cicero's comment on the Eleusinian rites in the century before Jesus: "Nothing is higher than these mysteries. They have sweetened our characters and softened our customs; they have made us pass from the condition of savages to true humanity. They have not only shown us the way to live joyfully, but they have taught us how to die with a better hope" (op. cit., p. 48). Or Plutarch's comment on the Dionysian rites to his wife, on the occasion of the death of their daughter around A.D. 80: "About that which you have heard, dear heart, that the soul once departed from the body vanishes and feels nothing, I know that you give no belief to such assertions because of those sacred and faithful promises given in the mysteries of Bacchus which we who are of that religious brotherhood know. We hold it firmly for an undoubted truth that our soul is incorruptible and immortal. We are to think (of the dead) that they pass into a better place and a happier condition. Let us behave ourselves accordingly, outwardly ordering our lives, while within all should be purer, wiser, incorruptible" (idem, p. 62).

Chapter 3

Origin of Philosophy in Myth

Philosophy, in the Greek tradition, originated in myth—the fable or *mu-thos*—usually a pseudo-historical account encapsulating the wisdom born of the experience of a people or community. The magical character of myth derives from the fact that the account is often a kind of "open sesame" or fiat, whereby things come into being in a contingent manner, that is to say, without any logically compelling reason for their coming to be; they could as well not be. To the extent that it is concerned with the *being* or *existence* of things in a general sense, myth is, in part, metaphysical. To the extent that it also deals with the *origin* of things, myth is also protological—often theological—concerned with the abrupt and sudden origin of things, their *coming to be*. But, however the being of things originates, myth is generally concerned with the interrelationships between and among things, events, entities—hence with the knowledge or wisdom of *how things function in context*: in short, philosophy. Thus philosophy usually contains both metaphysical and theological elements intimately bound up with it—these elements constituting the contingent or magical features of the embodying myth—but which are not really necessary to an interpretation or understanding of the relationships among entities (i.e., the philosophy) once such entities are assumed to have originated and, therefore, to exist.

The magical and contingent nature of myth reflects the corresponding nature of things in their coming into existence and of existence itself. As a pseudo-historical account it is intended to serve both as a multidimensional model or paradigm of interpretation of things[1] and as a summary account of the lessons of experience of the folk group in question. However, this does not imply any necessary logical, or even empirical, connection between the myth-model and the experiences for which it serves as a peg; the experiences may be real enough but may not constitute any confirmation of the model. For this reason, and because the theological and metaphysical elements of myth are not essential to the interpretation of interrelationships among things, it is important for the philosopher to be able to distinguish and separate myth from experience and indicate where myth is empirically valid as well as what relational insights could be derived from it.[2]

The early Greek philosophers, as indicated above, were mostly myth-makers. Since myth employs a lot of symbolism, they were also symbol manipulators.[3] Plato and Aristotle were eminent practitioners of the art, inventing myths and symbols as well as ingeniously manipulating them. Not all of these early philosophers were mythologists of this type, inventing pure myth. The Ionian philosophers were less inclined to pure myth and more given to empirical observations, although handicapped in regard to experimental devices. It must be recognized, however, that pure myth is merely an elaborate way of formulating hypotheses, its principal feature being an excess of imagination and fantasy and a minimum of empirical foundation and, therefore, of credibility.

The main concern of the Greek philosophers was to find out what kind of substance or material things were made of and how they functioned. In this connection they could not help basing their interpretation on the human model. Eventually, they had to turn their attention to investigating the nature of man himself.[4] Because they had to rely on concepts, thought, and contemplation (reflection) as their main tools of investigation, and particularly on reason or logic for drawing out the implications of their interpretive framework, they mistook these tools for the essence of philosophy, which they thought to be a love of, or indulgence in, thought and contemplation. As a result they missed what was, in fact, the very substance of philosophy, namely, "thought and contemplation of *what*?" The answer: general interrelationships among entities, whether these entities are physical (phenomena) or mental (forms, ideas, concepts). *General*, as distinct from *specific*, interrelationships distinguish philosophy from its constituent or derivative disciplines, such as religion, ethics, psychology, et cetera, as well as the innumerable breed of subconstituents denominated by "philosophy of," followed by almost any substantive intellectual category selected at will.

Not only the Greek philosophers but their successors up to the present day have missed this relational, and most fruitful, approach to the nature of philosophy; their successors, by reason of the pull exerted by tradition and by the universal tendency of most men to venerate their predecessors as well as their ancestors. This has led to a continuation of the early tradition of myth making, mysticism, and symbol manipulation and a lot else besides that, unfortunately, continues to pass for philosophy. Indeed, as has been truly said, all Western philosophy consists of footnotes to Plato.[5]

NOTES

1. I.e. interpretation of their various aspects, theological, metaphysical, philosophical, et cetera.
2. The emphasis in this book as regards philosophy is on interrelationships—the relational aspects of things—and how philosophy differs from theology, religion, ethics, and other kindred pursuits.
3. Mathematical, especially geometrical, symbols.
4. See R. G. Collingwood, *The Idea of Nature* (London: Oxford University Press 1945), Part I, Chapter I.
5. A remark by A. N. Whitehead mentioned by Karl R. Popper: see K. R. Popper, *Objective Knowledge* (London: Oxford University Press, 1981), p. 122.

BOOK TWO
THEIR MYTH

SECTION A
PHILOSOPHY AND METAPHYSICS

PART I
GREEK ACADEMIC PHILOSOPHY; OR, PLATO'S MYTH

Chapter 1

Definitions and Summary of Basic Tenets of the Academy*

Plato and his Academy propounded the doctrines that are set forth below.

1. PLATO'S THEORY OF FORM AND MATTER

There are two basic, preexisting elements of being, both coeval and perpetual:

(a) *The Idea or Form of a Thing:* There is only *one* specific idea or form per object or species of object,[1] and it is fixed, nonpliable, and perpetual. Not only each form, but the total number of forms is fixed, unchanging, and perpetual.

The collection of determinate, unchanging, and perpetual forms is called God—a kind of Super-Idea or Super-Form containing all forms within itself. (The terms *Idea-Group, Form-Group, Group-of-All-Ideas*, and *Group-of-All-Forms* are each interchangeable with the term *God*.)

(b) *Matter:* This is the substance or receptacle in which objects appear. It is also perpetual and indestructible, but divisible and pliable, and means the same as *space*.

---

*As used in this book in connection with the Academy, the term *academic* relates to the philosophy and thought of Socrates, Plato, and Aristotle, because Plato recorded the thought of Socrates (who left nothing in writing) and Aristotle that of Plato. Strict usage should confine it to Plato and those who were successively in charge of his Academy in its five different phases of orientation: Plato, Speusippus, Xenocrates, and Polemo; Arcesilas; Carneades, and Clitomachus; Philo of Larissa; and Antiochus of Ascalon. (See the Introduction in Cicero, *The Nature of the Gods* [Penguin Classics]). Though an alumnus, Aristotle was never in charge of the Academy but founded his own school, the Peripatetic School of philosophers, whose tradition was carried on after Aristotle's death by Theophrastus and Strato. A more precise heading for this chapter would be "Greek Classical Philosophy: The Socratic-Academic-Peripatetic Myth." The exposition owes much to Betrand Russell, *History of Western Philosophy* (Unwin Paperbacks, 1979), Book One, Part 2.

Other than its being indestructible, divisible, and pliant in character, nothing is said about the *volume* of matter, because no one in the Academy knew anything definite about it. This ignorance has caused much trouble before and since Plato's time. (*Parmenides* thought that there was a single, finite, fixed, and indivisible volume of matter, within which there could be no motion—notwithstanding all appearances to the contrary. He called it The One. *Heraclitus* thought that, finite or infinite, matter was mobile, while the Greek Atomist philosophers thought it was also finitely divisible, subject to an irreducible and indivisible smallest unit called the atom. *Kant* could not make up his mind whether it was finite or infinite; he thought it could as well be the one as the other (hence his famous antinomies) and, since he could not say which, decided it was neither—all appearances to the contrary—but only a subjective phenomenon, a built-in feature of the way man sees and perceives objects. Thus Kant side-stepped rather than resolved the problem. *Einstein* and some modern physicists decided that matter or space is of finite volume.) The question of the volume of matter has significance, at least for spaceship Earth, in regard to the transformation of matter, of which biological reproduction and mass-energy transformation are important aspects.

Thus, the *difference* between form and matter is in regard to plasticity and divisibility: form is nonplastic (fixed) and indivisible, matter plastic and divisible. Both are *similar* in being preexisting, coeval, and indestructible elements of being.

2. ARISTOTLE'S THEORY OF FORM AND MATTER

(a) *Form—Universals versus Particulars*: Aristotle criticized Plato's theory of ideas (forms) by saying that what is signified by proper names of persons or things (like *John, moon, bed*) is a particular or unique *substance* (a "this"), whereas what is signified by an adjective or class-name (like *hard, round*, et cetera) is a universal quality shared in by many things—a *sort* of thing, not the actual thing (a "such").

Plato's "idea," Aristotle says, was a substance peculiar to a particular thing and not to anything else (like the idea of a bed); it was not, as Plato intended it to be, a universal or class characteristic in which all particular things of a given class shared. For a universal is a common quality belonging to more than one thing, not peculiar to any one of them. Aristotle called this impersonal or universal quality a Form. Thus, according to Aristotle, a *particular* thing can exist by itself, whereas a *universal* could not, but only in particular things. In short, universals are derived from particulars, forms from particular objects—not the other way round.

31

(b) *Form and Matter:* Form is that in virtue of which matter is some definite thing; that is, that in virtue of which a thing has individuality or identity. (As will appear later in this chapter, soul plus plasticity—or recalcitrance—of matter gives an object identity or individuality.)

The form of a thing is its essence and primary substance. (This contradicts Aristotle's own theory of form as relating to universals ["suchness"] and not to particulars ["thisness" or substance]. He thus contradicts his own criticism of Plato on this point.)

Form is actuality; matter, in its "unformed" state, is a potentiality that can take on any form. Change is evolution in the sense that after a change there is more form (substance) in a thing than before the change. That which has more form is considered to be more actual. God is pure form, pure actuality, and therefore there can be no change in God.[2]

3. SUPER-IDEA OR SUPER-FORM AS PROPULSIVE (PLATO) OR ATTRACTIVE (ARISTOTLE)

The fixed Group-of-All-Forms called God was regarded differently by Plato than by his pupil, Aristotle. Whether due to the mystic influence of Pythagoreanism or not, both viewed this fixed collection of forms as a force—or, as endowed with force, and simultaneously possessing anthropomorphic guise (it has a mind and loves itself). But, for Plato, it was an *active, propulsive* force that moved matter about in order that it may assume, approximately, the shape of the forms or ideas contained in God's mind. It was thus a *creative* force. But it also did a strange thing: it created (that is, molded) out of matter the first object, endowed it with the same creative force as itself, then set it up as a surrogate for itself to continue the work of creating other things. This surrogate-God was called the Demiurge or Artificer-God and, once in place, God, the Group-of-All-Forms, retired from the work of creation. (This is a pretty myth and pure, and can survive as such,[3] provided one does not start asking questions such as, What was the form of the demiurge—a representative sample of God? How could it propel matter *outward*, instead of drawing it *inward*, toward the forms whose semblance it wished to incorporate in matter?, et cetera.)

Aristotle saw things differently. The Group-of-All-Forms was a *passive, attractive* (and anthropomorphic) force, somewhat like gravitational force, which pulled matter toward it in order that it may assume, approximately, the shape of the various forms or ideas. (Aristotle was a more logical thinker than Plato in this respect, detecting that attraction, not propulsion, was the only way in which matter could be in-formed, i.e. assume the shape of forms or ideas.) But, again, a strange thing happens with Aristotle's God. This passive, anthropomorphic force is blind—to everything except itelf. It neither sees, nor is aware of the presence of, matter. It sees and loves only itself, and can only think about itself and the other forms conceived and contained within its mind. (Since the Group-of-All-Forms is blind it may be assumed that each individual form is also blind and possessed of the same attractive force as the group taken together.[4])

4. PHYSICAL AND MORAL FORMS

There are two kinds of forms:

(a) *Physical forms* (i.e., forms of physical entities): These are incorporable, imperfectly, in matter and beyond the control of the physical entity (which is under the influence of the appetites or vegetativeness of soul, as will shortly appear).

(b) *Moral forms* (or forms of behavior): These are the standards or norms of human conduct and action, conforming to the rule of virtue or the golden mean. Unlike the forms of physical objects, which are only imperfectly, because approximately, incorporated, moral forms are perfectly apprehended by the intellect and perfectly incorporated in man and could, in principle, be perfectly reflected in human conduct. They are pure forms, without any attachment of matter—like God himself—hence are the only type of forms that man shares with God and the means whereby man shares in the divine nature. Mathematical forms (concepts or ideas) are like moral forms—pure forms perfectly comprehended by the human intellect and without any matter attached. For example, points have no magnitude, lines and surfaces no thickness, in the geometry of Plato's day. This similarity of mathematical to moral forms explains why mathematics was so closely linked to the ethical and theological aspects of Greek religion and mysticism (Pythagoreanism and Orphism) and constituted an indispensable qualification for admission to Plato's Academy. For mathematical forms were pure and perfect forms suitable for regulating human conduct in the same way in which they regulated the movements of the planets and provided the constitutive bases of the elements, fire, air, and water.[5]

5. THE SENSIBLE AND SUPRASENSIBLE WORLDS, RESPECTIVELY, OF MATTER AND IDEA

Academic philosophy postulated two separate domains inhabited, respectively, by the basic elements of being, idea and matter. Phenomena, consisting of physical objects, belong in the world of sense—the "sensible" world where objects are subject to change, composition, and decomposition. But the world of forms or ideas was a different world beyond the reach of the senses, being the special habitation also of God, the Form of forms, the Group-of-All-Forms. This world, like the forms, can only be intuited by man, not sensed. Philosophers, in particular, are best placed to intuit and comprehend (understand) the ideas or forms, since they are given wholly to a life of thought and contemplation.

The ability of philosophers to intuit the forms does not come naturally but through their training (in schools such as the Academy), which acquaints them with, among other subjects, the metaphysical aspects of mathematics. Having qualified in mathematics before embarking upon a course in philosophy and metaphysics, they are able to appreciate the nature of moral forms in their similarity to mathematical concepts and how they differ from physical forms. All forms, however, are alike in being completely divorced of matter and are alternatively known as noumena (singular, *noumenon*).

The perfect comprehension (understanding) of intelligible forms by man, the perfect incorporation of moral and mathematical forms in man as guides to conduct, and the imperfect material comprehension (incorporation) of physical forms in objects raise difficulties for the theory of forms, the separate existence of form and matter, and the separation of the sensible and suprasensible worlds. These will be discussed in the next chapter.

6. ETERNITY

The quality of unchangingness, of fixity, of form is called *eternity*,[6] meaning, outside time. The relationship between plastic matter and rigid form—both indestructible—is called *time*, which was defined by Plato as *the moving image of eternity*.[7] This simply means that *matter is plastic and sequential, rather than instantaneous, with regard to the incorporation of form* or idea, which, however, is *fixed and rigid with regard to matter*.

Phenomena (i.e., the appearances of forms in material guise) result

34

from the process of *incorporation* of the *semblance* of forms in divisible, plastic matter. This process is called entelechy and takes place over time. Thus entelechy and time are parallel events but different aspects of the relationship between fixed form and plastic matter. Alternatively, time may be regarded as a dimension of entelechy.

(It may be noted that while entelechy involves time, the converse is not true, as when, for instance, two phenomena (say, the sun and the earth) move relatively to each other; thus, chronological time without entelechy. A comprehensive statement of the relationship between form, matter, phenomena, time, and entelechy would be: form and matter find their synthesis in phenomena through the process of entelechy over time, and their desynthesis in entropy and disintegration.)

7. RECALCITRANCE OF MATTER

Phenomena (objects or things) incorporate form but only imperfectly. They incorporate only a semblance (a "poor copy of a copy") of the corresponding pure or perfect forms. This is due to the fact that matter, being plastic and continually changing, lacks, therefore, the ability to "stay put" for any length of time and thus reproduce the perfection of rigid form. This quality, the resistance of matter to perfect molding, is referred to as the *recalcitrance* of matter.

(It may be argued, however, in objection to Plato, that if it is the recalcitrance, or resistance, of matter to perfect "forming" that prevents the reproduction of facsimiles of pure forms, then the form that is incorporated in matter is not an "imperfect copy" or semblance but the pure form itself whose perfect outlines are hidden, or *appear* to be distorted, by the plasticity and instability of matter. Thus, there is no reason why pure form cannot be incorporated in matter and yet *appear* distorted, just as a straight stick immersed in water *appears* bent, even though the immersed section remains straight. This would imply that the perfect form that lies hidden in the distorting medium of matter could be derived by, and as, an idealization of the *apparent* forms of several objects of the same class rather than that (as Plato argued) the apparent form is derived from the pure form as a "poor copy of a copy" of it. On this showing, there is really no need for the distinction (and separation) between pure form and its semblance made in Plato's doctrine of forms. For it is not the pure form that is distorted in matter, but matter itself that is distorted.)[8]

8. SOUL (ARISTOTLE)

Soul is a metaphysical concept denoting a Form-giving cause or device and is employed to account for entelechy, the response of matter in its incorporation of forms, as well as for the biological differentiation of things into animals and plants. (Minerals and the planets constituted two other groups, the planets being some sort of gods of lesser category than Plato's demiurge—which involves the presumption that the planets are representative samples of God, the Group-of-All-Forms or Form of forms.) This device is an integral part of the constitution of matter and consisted of two elements: (a) a rational element called mind or intellect, which is of the same nature as idea or form; (b) an irrational element, or propensity to emulate form or idea, which may be called *soul proper* and consists of "appetites" (literally, tendencies to *actively* seek or emulate) in the case of animals and "vegetativeness" (literally, tendencies to passively emulate without apparent motion or bodily exertion) in the case of plants.[9]

Mind is higher than *soul proper* because it is pure intellect and therefore divine, being one of the qualities found in, or possessed by, God. Also, mind, like idea, is indestructible and separates from matter at the death or dissolution of the animal or plant, while the matter including the *soul proper* of the animal or plant disintegrates.

The primary role of soul, in particular *soul proper*, in regard to its differentiation of matter into plant or animal, is to give the plant or animal not only a form or shape but also a unitive organic structure; that is to say, a structure that integrates different but complementary constitutive, physical elements. It is implied, but not stated, that *soul proper* also plays a role in the disintegration or dissolution of organisms.[10]

9. IMMORTALITY OF THE SOUL

According to Aristotle, the intellectual or rational part of the soul—i.e., the mind—has no identity, demarcation, or individuality and therefore unites man (and plants) without distinction, rather than separates them as does the irrational part (appetites and vegetativeness). This rational part is the immortal element in man, as it is in God. (It is not stated, but implied, that the mind of plants is also immortal.) In so far as men are rational they partake in God's immortality. But this is not a *personal* immortality (as Socrates and Plato believed) but an impersonal kind, like that of the Hindus and Buddhists—a Nirvana.[11]

36

Mind is that part of soul that understands mathematics and philosophy. Its objects are timeless like itself. The soul proper (the irrational part) is that part of soul that moves the body and perceives sensible objects: it is characterized by self-nutrition (which is also the only psychic power possessed by plants), sensation, feeling, and motivity. But mind has the higher function of thinking—a function unrelated to the body or the senses, hence undecomposable, while the rest of soul is decomposable and disintegrates with the body.[12]

10. TRANSMIGRATION OF SOULS (OR METEMPSYCHOSIS)

In sections 10, 49, and 50 of the *Timaeus* Plato formulated his myth of transmigration of the human soul, which is, indeed, a theory of human devolution—in line with his doctrinal prejudice that all change is toward corruption and degeneration.

Cowardly and immoral men degenerate into women at rebirth; empty-headed, harmless men who only trust to their senses become birds; men lacking in philosophy degenerate into land animals, and the most unintelligent and ignorant men degenerate into fish, shellfish, and every other marine animal. (How seriously Plato took his theory is questionable: one can almost see him enunciating it, tongue in cheek. It might have gone well with nonphilosophers, the simple-minded men who regarded the arcane reaches of Plato's mathematical philosophy with reverence, and whom he despised.)

Thus, women and all nonhuman animals derive directly—and degenerately—from the human male (shades of Genesis!). There is no process of devolution of one nonhuman animal from another nor, inversely, evolution from lower, nonhuman animal toward the human male.

11. VIRTUE

Virtue is defined in academic philosophy as action that reproduces a form, and moral forms are that category of forms to which action relates. Virtue thus becomes a relationship of conformity of action to moral form. The form being assumed to be good, the action that reproduces it is likewise assumed to be good.

Man has control over moral forms insofar as he has control over his actions that are directed toward reproducing those forms in his behavior. But over physical forms man has no control since not only are the pure

37

versions of those forms beyond the grasp of matter, but the versions (poor semblances) within grasp are automatically realized (incorporated) through the autonomous action of soul.

Conceptually, there are two kinds of virtue corresponding to the two parts of the soul: *intellectual* and *moral*. Intellectual virtue relates to the mind and results from *teaching* good behavior. Moral virtue relates to the appetites or passions and results from good habits or actions. It was the business of the legislator to make the citizens good by teaching them, and forming in them, good habits.

Virtue was held by the Greek philosophers to be a golden mean between two extremes of action, each of which was a vice; e.g., courage is a mean between cowardice and rashness, proper pride a mean between vanity and humility, wit a mean between buffoonery and boorishness, modesty a mean between bashfulness and shamelessness, and so on. Hence, virtue came to be regarded as a matter of "avoidance of extremes," of "moderation," of "prudence in the pursuit of pleasure," each of which leads to individual salvation.[13]

12. THE THREE KINDS OF SUBSTANCES (ARISTOTLE)

There are three kinds of substances:

(a) Sensible and perishable (decomposable): plants and animals.
(b) Sensible and imperishable (nondecomposable): the heavenly bodies, which were believed to undergo no change but only motion (thus agreeing with Plato, who believed that change was the start of inevitable degradation).
(c) Nonsensible and imperishable: God, ideas, the rational soul in man.

13. THEOLOGY (ARISTOTLE)

Aristotle gives *First Cause* as the argument for the existence of God—a force or being that originates motion without being moved and must, therefore, be eternal (unchanging) and imperishable, substance and actuality: the object of *desire* (irrational soul) and of *thought* (rational soul). All other things cause motion by being in motion.

All living things are aware of God and are moved to action by admiration and love of God (Greek *eros* = aspiring love). Thus God is the final cause of all activity.

Change consists in giving form to matter. Only God consists of pure form without any matter and therefore, alone, does not change. All sensible (i.e., material) things tend to evolve toward God (pure form) but not completely: a substratum of matter always remains in sensible things (which is why they are sensible objects), as they would not otherwise retain their individuality.[14] Individuality is bound up with the appetites, the irrational part of soul—the part that makes it possible to distinguish one man from another, one plant from another. The rational part of man's soul—mind, reason, intelligence—unites men without distinction or individuality, being their common possession, and, as part of God's reason and immortality, is *shared* with God. (It is clear that mind does not *unite* man to God, who is pure form, since matter adheres to man.)

God, being pure form and perfection untainted with matter, is complete and, lacking nothing, seeks nothing outside of himself. Lacking matter, God has no appetites (desires) and, unlike objects with appetites (plants, animals) is not moved by admiration and love of anything but himself. Consequently, God does not love man or any other object, is even unaware of their existence—unaware of any other but himself.[15]

(It is therefore a concession—but an inconsistency—on the part of Aristotle when he defines the relationship of God to man by the term *agape* (condescending love) or the love of a superior for an inferior that is all right and good in its proper place and function: an inconsistency, because God is not supposed to be aware of the existence of man. Perhaps, however, the relationship—if one exists—is better expressed by the Greek word for "justice" (*dikaiosyne*), meaning duty or proper behavior toward other people—especially one's superior, keeping within one's proper station in life, performing the socioeconomic tasks assigned to one according to the social division of labor within one's community. Thus, the relationship of God to man would consist in the satisfaction felt by the superior (God) at having ordered things in such a manner that each object fulfills its proper function in the scheme of things; and of man to God in the satisfaction felt by an inferior (man) at having performed his duty toward his superior (God).)[16]

14. THE "TWO WORLDS"
AND THE DESTINY OF THE SOUL

As stated in section 5 of this chapter, the two worlds of matter and idea, phenomena and noumena, the sensible and the suprasensible, formalize the dichotomy between the two basic elements of being. However, the two worlds run parallel, the phenomenal world, like the forms incorporated in matter, being a poor copy of the noumenal world inhabited by the pure forms and God. Thus, the noumenal world is merely more of the same things found in the phenomenal world, shorn of matter and at a higher pitch of intensity and purity.

Being as well as its mode (biosis) is therefore a synthesis—albeit imperfect—of its two basic elements, a synthesis in which soul plays a crucial role. This role is a duality involving a split within the soul itself. Torn between the two worlds, the soul is never at rest until the divorce of matter and form at death, when soul rejoins Super-Soul, that is, mind rejoins Super-Mind.[17]

This myth, which clearly bears some relationship to the ancient religion of Persia, constitutes the basic model for Christian and Islamic eschatology that has remained unchanged until the present day.

NOTES

1. It may be noted that shape or graphic form is the visual representation of philosophic idea or form. For an exposition of Plato's theory of forms, see G. C. Field, *The Philosophy of Plato* (Oxford, London, New York: Oxford University Press, 1969).
2. It may be noted that although *eternal* and *immortal* tend to have the same meaning—"lasting forever"—it is convenient to use them in two different senses: *eternal* to mean "unchanging" in *form* or shape, fixed; and *immortal* to mean "indestructible, imperishable, continuing forever even though decomposable, changing in form or shape."

   These meanings are in keeping with the discussion in the philosophical system of Plato and Aristotle. Thus form is eternal and immortal, matter noneternal (because changeable in form) and immortal.
3. It continues today in the doctrine of deism, which holds that God created the world and then retired (or withdrew) from it, leaving it to run according to fixed laws.
4. Leibniz's monads, the basic element of matter in his system, bear a striking resemblance to the Aristotelian form or idea in being blind but coordinated—by God (Aristotle's Form of forms) according to a preordained harmony. The monads are both coordinated and synchronous in their blindness, while reflecting each other. Leibniz's myth is clearly a rehash of, if not a gloss upon, Aristotle's.
5. In the *Timaeus* (sections 22–24) Plato constitutes the elements fire, air, and water from geometrical solids—pyramid, octahedron, and icosahedron, respectively, composed of scalene triangles—and earth from the cube, composed of isosceles triangles. The first three elements are, thus, inter-transformable; i.e. can be decomposed and recomposed into one another. This is an excellent example of non-empirical connection between interpretor (myth of geometrical solids) and interpretand (the elements) in spite of their common feature of possessing transformable components.
6. See note 2 earlier.
7. Plato, *Timaeus* (New York: Penguin Classics), section 7.
8. More will be said on this in the next chapter.
9. The "propensity to emulate" an animal or vegetable form (soul proper) taken together with the mind or intellectual part of soul stirs up thought of the modern DNA, the special protein that contains all the information relevant to the nature and structure of a biological organism, and is self-activating and self-implementing. Since Aristotle's philosophic forms are an attracting force, and if unlike elements (form and

matter) attract each other, it is not clear why a mental element similar to idea is necessary in matter in order to enable it emulate ideas—unless on the unlikely theory that like elements attract one another, so that a formlike element is necessary in matter for it to be attracted by an external form. This incorporation of a mental element in matter, however, somewhat invalidates the distinction between the dual elements of being—form and matter—as well as the distinction between sensible and suprasensible worlds and leads to an inseparable tandem of idea-matter, much like Einstein's mass-energy, both occurring in the sensible world.

10. In both processes—integration and disintegration of matter—soul proper would seem to be similar to, or another name for, the metabolic process in organisms.

11. Plato, like Socrates, believed in a *personal* immortality—hence in an individual rational soul. Otherwise it would not be possible for the rational soul (an element without identity or particularity) to transmigrate among species of animals. In a later age Schopenhauer believed, like Aristotle, in an indivisible, nonindividual soul common to man, animals, and other objects. But he called it *will*.

12. It is necessary, here, to distinguish between immortality (imperishability) and decomposability. Mind, like idea, is immortal and undecomposable. Matter, however, is *both* decomposable *and* immortal. Thus immortality may include or exclude decomposability. The two terms are different but not contradictory. Matter decomposes but does not disappear, and nothing, including mind or idea, disappears. All is immortal.

13. This is the ideological origin of the occidental wisdom that favors the "middle-of-the-road," the avoiding of extremes, especially in politics.

14. Furthermore, so long as any sensible object contains any element of matter the form toward which it evolves is always a *semblance*, not the pure form itself.

15. Aristotle's monotheism is monotheism proper, strict and all-comprehending. There is no other God beside. This contrasts with traditional, classical Greek super-theism, a hierarchy of gods topped by a super or most powerful god, Zeus, in a pantheon. So-called Hebrew monotheism is not strict monotheism in the Aristotelian sense but preemptive or monopoly theism. Jahweh knows, is aware, that there are other gods but simply *refuses to recognize them*, being jealous of what he regards as his prerogatives, especially his relation to his special people, Israel. The subsequent stage in Israel's theological development at which Jahweh is regarded as the God of the cosmos and all mankind is not a development toward monotheism, contrary to the general opinion. For Jahweh is still not the *only* God, like Aristotle's, but universal *only if* adopted by other people and *on the condition* that they become either ethnic or spiritual Jews—just as Zeus, as Jupiter, became the God of the Romans by simple adoption, involving the adoption also of Greek culture and civilization.

   The God of Aristotle is the same God adopted by the Marcionites, a second-century Gnostic Christian sect and, much later, by the philosophers, Spinoza and Leibniz: monotheism in its strict meaning, except that Spinoza's God was also pantheist, being both matter and pure thought.

16. A most appropriate expression of the relationship may be found in the famous eighteenth-century hymn by Mrs. C. F. Alexander beginning, "All things bright and beautiful," and containing the following verse:

> The rich man in his castle,
> The poor man at his gate,
> He made them high and lowly,
> And ordered their estate.

For all the difference in their conception of God, Plato and Aristotle were at one in that their God was a gentleman's God, a God of the leisured class who did no work and did not involve himself in the affairs of the cosmos—a view espoused by Epicurus (fourth–third century BCE). (Epicurus believed in the gods but not in religion, because of its encouragement of fear of the gods.) When he fashioned anything at all (Plato) he did so by proxy (the demiurge, whose fashioning was the only work he ever did), since a member of the leisured class performed no work. The demiurge was thus the slave of Plato's God. Aristotle did even better—his God was more of a gentleman's God who made absolutely no concession to labor. He did not even bother to fashion a slave, but simply attracted matter to "in-form" itself, thus regulating the affairs of the cosmos by remote control. Thus, the concept of a God by proxy or of an unmoved mover of things is the origin of the concept of deism—the gentleman's concept of God.

17. As we shall see in the critical review that follows in the next chapter, its metaphysics or theology (for Aristotle, the two terms were interchangeable)—that is, its theory of being—is the Achilles' heel of the academic philosophy. The reproduction theory of matter in the sensible world could only make sense if there was some mechanism in matter that could "see" or "intuit" the forms to be copied in matter. Physics not being advanced enough in his time to the point where gravity could be recognized as an impersonal force in its own right, Aristotle devised "soul" as the active principle (or mechanism) containing an intelligent element, mind, that established rough correspondence between form and matter. A brilliant piece of ingenuity, to be sure, but one that erased at the same time the distinction between the intelligible and the sensible worlds, since matter—one of the exclusive, coeval, and preexistent components of being—had thereby become intelligent. Thus we end up, effectively, with one world and one mode of being consisting of the inseparable form-matter element.

Closely bound up with the Achilles' heel of the two worlds is the doctrine of time (which holds sway in the phenomenal world of change) and of eternity, change-lessness or outside-time (which holds sway in the intelligible or suprasensible world). This doctrine, like the "two worlds" doctrine, is correspondingly tainted.

The doctrine of the liberation of mind from matter and its union with Super-Mind or God, so that matter and soul become restored to their original separate worlds, shows suspicious traces of Indo-Persian religion and its evolution into Gnosticism. The latter emphasized knowledge (a major topic of academic philosophy) and the liberation of light from darkness so as to restore the original separation of the two (academic metaphysics is heavy on the liberation of mind-soul, as distinct from soul-soul, from matter). Separation of soul from life forms in the wheel of life and its union with Super-Soul (Brahman) in Nirvana is a dominant theme in Hinduism-Buddhism. The importation of Indo-Persian religious influences into Greek metaphysics and philosophy was regarded by Bertrand Russell as a sinister event attributable to Pythagoras. (See Bertrand Russell, op. cit., Book One, Part 1, Ch. III.)

Chapter 2

Critical Appraisal of Greek Academic Philosophy

1. TWO VIEWS OF PURE FORM—
ITS SEPARATION FROM MATTER

The metaphysical building blocks and basic concepts of Academic philosophy—idea and matter—prove, on closer examination, to be flawed. But, first, a brief recapitulation of the basic doctrine regarding the concepts.

Idea, like matter, is immortal but, unlike matter, is nonplastic, unchanging, and outside of time. However, its realization in matter takes time, matter itself being in time. Matter being subject to motion, ideas become dynamic through matter. The ideas realized in matter, however, are not the pure ideas themselves but approximations.

(Time, as Hegel was to show, subsequently, is history and history the time dimension of philosophy. History is the time element in the manifestation of God [Absolute Idea, to Hegel] in matter and human events [phenomena]. Thus, phenomena derive their dynamism from the dynamic nature of idea-in-matter.)

Ideas lie outside the reach of the senses but are directly apprehensible by the mind. In moving and realizing itself in matter over time the idea-semblance leaves a "mark," casts a "shadow," on matter. It is thus simultaneously *visible* (reflected in matter), *invisible* (intelligible to the mind), and *dynamic* in time. Time itself is an invisible, dynamic "image" of the idea-semblance in the process of its incorporation in matter and, like the idea, is beyond the reach of the senses but not of the mind.

So much for the bare bones of the basic doctrine. Since idea, pure and simple, was held by Plato to be outside time and the phenomenal world of matter, it was logically necessary, for incorporation purposes, that only a poor semblance (not the pure idea itself) be incorporated in matter, which exists in time. The trouble with this neat trick is that pure idea could just as easily be derived as an idealization of perceived idea-semblances in objects of the same class. And by thus reversing the process (and there seems to be no valid argument against it) it would require more than sophistry to show that an idealized concept derived from the phenomenal world exists in a totally different world. On the other side, it can easily be argued that since matter is the unstable medium, in process of continual change—hence, deceptive—there is no logical contradiction in assuming that it is, indeed, *pure* form or idea that is incorporated in matter, its purity being disguised and revealed only approximately through the unstable and distorting medium of matter, much like the distortion of a straight rod that appears bent when partially immersed in water.

What seriously invalidates the metaphysical separation of idea and matter, however, is the organic incorporation, by Aristotle, of rational mind (an element assumed to be outside time and the phenomenal world) in soul and of soul in matter as its integrative, entelechian constituent. This ingenious device invalidates, at one stroke, Plato's and (without apparently being aware of it) Aristotle's separation of idea and matter and the two worlds of sense and supra-sense. The resultant is *one* compound metaphysical building block, idea-matter, instead of two and *one* metaphysical world instead of two.

(In view of this radical, if long undetected, modification of academic philosophy by Aristotle, the continued opposition of idealism and materialism in the subsequent history of occidental philosophy implied a false dichotomy and an unwitting anachronism. It is interesting, in this respect, to note that African peoples, for example, make no sharp distinction between "material" and "spiritual" (ideal) or in terms of two worlds; the two concepts shade into one another through the mediating link of the human being, and both inhabit the same phenomenal world of sense. The result is an unusual and interesting brand of metaphysics.)

There is no empirical or other evidence for a two-world metaphysics. Plato's error was one of inattention and bias: either he failed to notice or he tried to conceal the fact that concepts, ideas, forms were the brain-children of man, that definitions, including those of mathematics, and dogmas are human inventions and do not exist on an independent footing outside the mind of man in some different, supra-sensible world.[1] The concepts of man cannot but inhabit the same sensible world inhabited by man. All that Plato did was postulate a definition or concept ("the idea" that he also called "the thing itself"), endow it with the unchanging perfection of a mathematical concept, then use it as a reference model for comparing actual instances or phenomena. These, quite naturally, fell short of such unchanging perfection. It should be added, in this connection, that Plato committed the error of confusing mathematics with phi-

44

losophy, holding to the view that one could not philosophize without an adequate knowledge of mathematics. (The motto at the entrance to his Academy warned all mathematical illiterates to keep their distance.)

Plato's obsession with mathematics and mysticism (which recalls a similar tendency on the part of some contemporary economists) was a Pythagorean heritage that reinforced, and was reinforced by, his aristocratic tendency toward conservatism. Like any Athenian aristocrat of his day, he was all too aware of the unsettling nature and consequences of change in the social as in the phenomenal world. The reverses suffered by the aristocratic class at the hands of Athenian democracy totally biased him against any kind of change, in nature as well as in society. He longed for stability, even—unrealistically—static and immutable conditions, in order to preserve his aristocratic privileges.

He regarded a static order as the real, the true nature of things, and change as unreal, untrue, and degenerative, whether in nature or in human affairs. If things did not change, they would reflect their true nature, their "pure forms." Plato's rule of life was very simple: "if things change, they get worse." Thus believing that things can only change for the worse, Plato regarded perfection in terms of a static mathematical concept, never achieved no matter how close one comes to it—like an asymptote. Such then are the physical and moral forms—unattainable levels of perfection: the physical forms, because of the supposed recalcitrance of matter; the moral forms, because of the apparent conflict between the two elements of soul (one perfection-oriented, the other appetite-oriented) resulting in the compromise of virtue, or the "golden mean." [2] (The affinity to, and reinforcement of, the Christian doctrine of human nature provided by the Platonian-Aristotelian doctrine of forms is quite evident.)

2. TWO-WORLD METAPHYSICS CORRECTED: ONE EXISTENTIAL WORLD, TWO ASPECTS

With the introduction of soul into Greek metaphysics Aristotle abolished the two-worlds doctrine of Plato, leaving what turns out to be merely two aspects of the same metaphysical world. The "worlds" translate into "aspects" as given in the interpretation below. The interpretation is given in the framework of Plato's myth.

(a) *The sensible (phenomenal) "world"*: This is our actual or present world *as it is*, with form (idea) and matter present. The form is the "pure" Platonian form, with plastic matter moving over and incorporating it. This dynamic world is "sensible" because the senses are being continually stimulated in the various ways appropriate to them by the movement of changing matter: sight by light waves or particles, hearing by sound waves, smell by olfactory waves, taste by the effect of chemical reaction on the taste buds of the tongue, touch and feeling by pressure and temperature variation. It is thus, by the movement of matter, that the senses are able to detect change, growth, and disintegration in physical objects.

(b) *The supra-sensible (noumenal)"world"*: This is our actual world as it would be if the senses lacked the different stimuli appropriate to them from the motion of matter—a sensation-free world. It is a "conceptual" world in the true meaning of the term: an imagined world, a world intelligible or apprehensible directly by the mind (reason)[2] instead of indirectly by, or through, the senses. It is the world with direct perception of forms or ideas instead of their indirect perception through matter. The "supra-sensible" world is, therefore, *not* some "heaven above the bright blue skies" but our actual world (supposedly) devoid of all stimulation of the senses—a state approximated by people who spend time experimentally in subterranean caves, devoid of external stimulus and all notion of the passage of time. (Incidentally, Plato did use the cave example to illustrate his conception of the phenomenal world as opposed to the supra-sensible world, in his example the actual world of sunlight outside the cave.[3] Although Plato uses the cave illustration in the opposite manner to that given in this book, what is significant is that in both cases what is being illustrated belongs entirely within the same phenomenal world that we all know.)

3. UNITY OF THE EXISTENTIAL WORLD

We may borrow some concepts from modern physics (with modifications) and parapsychology to elucidate the basics of Greek academic philosophy, shorn of its mystical elements. The concepts of mass and energy serve very well provided the following correspondences with academic philosophical and terminology are established:

$$\text{Energy} = \text{form, idea}[4]; \ \text{Mass} = \text{matter};$$
$$\text{Matter} = \text{form} + \text{matter} = \text{Energy} + \text{Mass}$$

The senses are the capacity of the sense organs to apprehend (respond to) form (Energy) (i.e., all of the senses); or to matter (Mass) (i.e., touch and feel); or to Matter (form + matter = Energy + Mass) (i.e., all of the senses). Sense perception is then sense-induced mental perception.

Intuition, then, is direct (sense-free) mental perception caused by

46

certain types of form or energy that bypass (or are not apprehensible by) the senses, such as are involved, for example, in extrasensory perception and other so-called Ψ-phenomena. The domain of intuition and Ψ-phenomena approximates the noumenal world—the world of ideas, "things themselves" without mass, pure energy as the attractive as well as the motive force of material entities. This would be roughly equivalent to "soul" (anima)—the energy or "thing itself" of every material entity.

In the light of the preceding clarification, experience would appear to consist of mental perceptions obtained directly by intuition and indirectly through sensation, with sensation acting as control on intuition, sense-experience cross-checking and verifying intuitive experience.

It seems clear, then, that our actual world is an organic whole consisting of pure form (energy) and varying combinations or syntheses of form (energy) and matter (mass): a world composed of sensation and extra-sensation (intuition).

The mysticism is thus taken out of the concept of the supra-sensible form inhabiting a supra-sensible world, the supra-sensible and the sensible being merely two dimensions (intuition and sensation) of the one and same physical world.

Granted this correction and elucidation of the two-world metaphysics of academic philosophy, one may conclude that Socrates could not have gone to another world after his death, as he fondly believed would be the case when he so calmly and contentedly drained the proffered cup of hemlock. Indeed, Aristotle's doctrine of the impersonal, if immortal, nature of the mental part of soul confirms this conclusion. He should, on this showing, be somewhere within our physical, noumenal-phenomenal world—as, indeed, African philosophy and religion hold to be the case with the dead. There is little doubt that some degree of this Socratic illusion about the nature of the after-death underlies some suicides and suicide pacts: the hope and expectation of another and happier existence in a kind of supra-sensible world.

Nothing said so far, however, constitutes any kind of valid argument against the possible existence of another world of the mystic type believed in by Pythagoras, Socrates, Plato and his school, and the Stoics. All that is implied is that if such a world, indeed, there be, little warrant for it can be found on the basis of a critical examination and strict construction of the concepts of Greek academic philosophy.

4. CHANGE, TIME, AND ETERNITY

All material entities (energy and mass) are composable and decomposable, hence, subject to change. Thus, change is the mode of being of material entities. And change implies and contains time. Hence, different times and rates of change of time (for example, as between planetary revolutions) constitute different modes of being. But change, as a continuing process, is also the only mode of being that does not change. Thus the paradox of change as a dual existential mode—at once in time and outside time (eternal).

Time, as a mode of being, is thus a dimension of change, hence of eternity. With time in—and a dimension of—eternity, any *opposition* of time to eternity would be nothing but sophistical.

5. SEPARATION OF MIND-SOUL FROM MATTER AT DEATH

It has been shown that Aristotle's endowment of matter with mind-containing soul invalidates the distinction and separation between the world of mind or intellect and the world of matter. Yet it is still the common theme of various metaphysical doctrines to assume an original separation of these two elements of being that then subsequently, somehow, get marginally mixed up in one another. At that point, salvation—in the sense of the restoration of the original separation of the two elements—comes into the picture, with the separation of the confused marginal portions and their reunion (or fusion) with their respective original sources. This salvific myth continues in occidental religion as well as in the oriental religions from which it derives: in Hinduism it is atman or individual soul (or breath) that has to be separated from the human body and reunited with Brahma, the world soul (or breath) and ground of all being; in Zoroastrianism and its Gnostic derivations it is the separation of light from darkness and its reunion with the Father of Light (Ahura Mazda or Ohrmazd); the Zoroastrian doctrine of bodily resurrection finds an echo in Pharisaic Judaism, and in Christianity where the Apostle to the Gentiles, Paul, reinterpreted resurrection of the carnal body into resurrection of a spiritual body—an obvious attempt to bring in the oriental notions of light and breath.[5]

There is hardly any question that classical Greek metaphysics derived its doctrine of the liberation of mind-soul from body at death from Indo-Persian religious sources. The date of Zoroaster has been variously given at anywhere from 1000 B.C.E. (*Cambridge Ancient History*, vol. IV, p.

48

207) to approximately 618–541 B.C.E. (Trevor Ling).[6] One may assume that the Persian prophet lived and preached no later than early sixth century B.C.E., which would make him a predecessor of Pythagoras, the man most credited with the introduction of religious mysticism into Greek metaphysics and philosophy.

Where the oriental mind was still bogged down in concrete symbolism and metaphors, the Greek mind, no longer so constrained, was able to move from metaphor to metamorphosis, process or transformation.[7] Thus, at the early stage of Greek mythology the metaphor of the revelation of truth as by a shining light was represented anthropomorphically by the god, Apollo. And while this metaphorical stage of the association of light with truth, darkness with error, still held sway in the Indo-Persian religion the Greek mind had moved on to a contemplation of the process by which truth became metamorphosed into knowledge by the activity of mind. Thus light and truth became metamorphosed into mind and knowledge in Greek philosophy so that, in the tradition of Pythagoras and Socrates, Plato and his Academy could speak of the separation of mind (or mind-soul) from matter and its reunion with super-Mind or God, while Zoroastrianism continued to talk of the separation of light from darkness and its reunion with the Father of Light. In this manner was Indo-Persian theology accommodated, by acculturation, to Greek theology and metaphysics.

The source of the myth of the liberation of mind-soul from appetites and matter in Aristotle's metaphysics being thus explicated, it becomes clear why this element, being foreign, did not ride well with the traditional Greek myth of Olympus for the gods and Hades for the Human dead (itself a two-world doctrine of a different kind); nor with the one-world consequences of Aristotle's witting or unwitting compromise of the endowment of matter with mind-soul.[8] This compromise effectively put idea, God,[9] and matter in the same sensible world.

NOTES

1. Professor Karl Popper's objective world of knowledge (World Three) is similar to Plato's "form"—independently existing. But, unlike Plato's static forms, Popper's objective world is subject to growth. Like Plato, he does no more than postulate the existence of such a world, his arguments establishing its independence remaining totally unconvincing. (See K. R. Popper, *Objective Knowledge*, Rev. Ed. [London, New York: Oxford University Press, 1981].)
2. The ancient Greeks set an inordinate store by reason, interpreted as the pure activity of mind, involving direct perception without the intermediary of the stimuli provided by the senses. This they thought possible only in mathematics, neglecting, as it were,

the basic process involved—intuition—which is not confined to mathematics. In any case, they thought so highly of the sensation-free type of mental activity that they considered it the "real" or true world. Conversely, they considered the sense-induced type of mental activity or other activity the "unreal," the untrue world. This was unfortunate, as it led to a lot of muddled thinking in philosophy, which has persisted until today. The excessive emphasis put on reason was also misguided in that reason was regarded as a heuristic, rather than a purely explicative methodological, tool. Without underestimating the contribution of the ancient Greeks to philosophy, it may fairly be said that many of the difficulties confronted by philosophy in that early period arose from the lack of clarity regarding (a) the nature of perception (mental apprehension) of phenomena and events; (b) the means of perception—direct (intuitive) and indirect (sense-induced); (c) the nature of reason or mental activity; and (d) the nature of experience—intuitive and sensible, with the sensible serving as the control on the intuitive.

3. Plato, *The Republic* (London, New York: Penguin Classics), Part VII, section 7.
4. This could also be interpreted to mean that energy is the basis or stimulant of ideas.
5. I Corinthians 15:42–55.
6. Trevor Ling, *A History of Religion East and West*, p. 75.
7. See George Santayana, *The Life of Reason*, vol. 3: *Reason in Religion* (Dover Publications, 1982), pp. 87–90, for that author's insightful analysis of the Greek mentality in relation to the doctrine of the Eucharist.
8. This is in line with the hylozoic doctrine of matter propounded by the Stoic philosophers.
9. Through the incorporation in matter of the various ideas or forms that constitute God.

PART II
LEGACY OF GREECE AND THE NEAR EAST TO THE OCCIDENT: PHILOSOPHY AND METAPHYSICS (SELECTIVELY ILLUSTRATED)

Chapter 3

Philosophy

INTRODUCTION

The ancient Greek philosophers established a body of thought that has survived various vicissitudes, especially the ravages of time and destruction wrought by human political and religious-theological conflicts. By a fortuitous chain of transmission through Arab learning and culture and the Roman Catholic Church, which served as the conservator of learning throughout the Middle Ages, the philosophical legacy of the Greeks was bequeathed to Western Europe, in particular, and eventually to the world in general.

Western Europe has appropriated Greek lore with prideful claim, its leading thinkers having assimilated, rearranged, and laid consanguinary accretions upon the basic structure of Greek thought. These accretions have fallen wholly within the Greek intellectual tradition, so much so that modern occidental philosophy is little more than extension, commentary, and gloss on the original.

The circumstances in which Western Europe rediscovered Greek learning—through Latin translations of Arabic translations from the Greek—gave the product an aura of accidental discovery of a great treasure. Consequently, the treasure was accepted, for the most part uncritically, and acclaimed in an atmosphere of near reverence normally reserved for Holy Writ. No doubt the part played by the Church in the transmission of the treasure was largely responsible for the association of reverence with Greek philosophical writings. Thus Greek philosophy was accepted with all its strengths and weaknesses, and its conceptual confusions, contradictions, and errors were perpetuated across the centuries during and after the Middle Ages as before.

It is only in the present century, especially since the Second World War, that the errors and biases—personal and social—of some of the Greek philosophers are beginning to be revealed, notably through critical studies like those of Karl Popper.[1]

In this chapter, a selection of major occidental philosophers who have worked and made contributions within the Greek philosophical tradition is presented and their thought critically examined, as briefly and concisely as possible, allowance being made for the personal predilections of the author in their selection and treatment.

1. RENÉ DESCARTES (1596–1650)

René Descartes is best known for his famous dictum "Cogito ergo sum"[2] (in French, his mother tongue, "Je pense, donc je suis"), which, literally translated, is: "I think, therefore I am." This dictum is generally known as the cogito.

It is a matter of dispute whether Descartes intended to infer existence, i.e., *empirical* existence, from thought. If he did, it would be in the tradition of Greek academic philosophy, especially Greek metaphysics, in which thought or reason was an existential ingredient. In that case the statement expressed in the cogito is a non sequitur and should rather read the other way round: "I am, therefore I think." Martin Heidegger reminds us,[3] and Hans Küng does likewise,[4] that, as Descartes himself emphasized,[5] the *ergo* (or *donc*) in the cogito was used incidentally, rather than inferentially, to imply the conclusion of a syllogistic argument. Both Heidegger and Küng go on to explain what, in effect, amounts to a matter of emphasis, namely: *I* think, therefore *I* am. This shifts the emphasis from *think* and *am*, in what would otherwise be the normal interpretation, to the subject of thought and existence, namely, *I*. In which case the cogito is no more than a compressed syllogism that, expanded, becomes:

> Any thinking being exists.
> I am a thinking being.
> *Therefore*, I exist.

This expanded form of the cogito links thinking and existence concomitantly rather than (con)sequentially. It is an acceptable version stating, correctly, that thought is given with existence. It is also free from Kant's fatal objection to which Anselm's ontological proof of God's existence succumbed: namely, that existence is not a predicate. Yet, however one looks at the cogito or interprets it—whether as meaning the opposite of what it says, or as a compressed syllogism in which thought and existence are correlated as concomitants, so that Descartes is seen as merely correlating his thought and his existence in order to claim membership in the class of thinking existents—the *ergo* (*donc* or *therefore*) definitely had an inferential function, as becomes clear from what follows.

In the light of the exhaustive discussion by Descartes himself, in which he is concerned to make the point that, as a thinking or doubting being—thinking or doubting his own existence or that of any other person or thing—his existence is assured as the condition of his thinking and doubting activity, the cogito may be regarded as an elliptical statement that can be fully expressed as follows:

"I think that I am, therefore I am"

or, from the doubting aspect,

"I doubt that I am, therefore I am."[6]

This expansion on the cogito serves to reveal its weakness: the implied assumption that the object of thought or doubt automatically exists empirically, an error not easy to detect since the object of Descartes's cogito is himself. Once the object becomes other than Descartes himself, however, the erroneous nature of the assumption reveals itself. For mere thought or doubt about (the concept of) a thing—e.g., a unicorn—does not automatically imply an empirical counterpart of the thing. It is the same old Achilles' heel of Greek academic philosophy: automatic ascription of an empirical counterpart to a nominal object of thought, rather than to the thought or concept alone. This was the same error involved in Anselm's ontological proof of God, which Descartes accepted.[7]

The concept of a thing commits us to the existence of only the concept itself, not of the thing conceived—as Kant was to point out more than a century after Descartes wrote and published his *Discourse*. Similarly, there is no necessary empirical validity to the consistent conclusion from the major premise of a syllogism unless the major premise is itself empirically valid.[8] Empirical existence cannot be assumed unless it has first been tested and confirmed or else brought about by appropriate action. Thus, before the Wright brothers (Orville and Wilbur) of Dayton, Ohio, came along there was no empirical counterpart to the concept of an airplane as a ship that flies. The Wright brothers made the concept come true to life—brought it into empirical existence.

In this connection, an interesting distinction may be noted between Gallic and Anglo-Saxon habits of thought. The French, apparently profiting from the weakness of Descartes's cogito, wisely make a distinction between *theory* and *practice*, recognizing that there is no automatic empirical counterpart to a concept. The British tend to make no such distinction, arguing that "sound in theory is sound in practice."[9] The implied assumption here is either that there is an automatic empirical counterpart to a concept or that such a counterpart can be brought about (like the Wright brothers' airplane). Obviously, the first alternative alone is not true, and the second is not necessarily true since there is no guarantee of a successful transition from blueprint to empirical reality. It would, therefore, seem that the Gallic manner of thinking does not make sufficient allowance for the possibility of making ideas come true by appropriate action where they do not already have an empirical counterpart; whereas the Anglo-Saxon habit of thought overlooks the fact that it is sound practice that makes theory sound, not vice versa. To the Gallic mind, events, regardless of theory, realize themselves more or less in the manner of a law of nature only where the conditions are right. To the Anglo-Saxon mind, where the theory is right events can be brought about according to the theory.[10]

Another defect in Cartesian philosophy, as in its Greek antecedent—and one that appears as the other side of the defect already discussed—is the myth of the preeminence of reason. Like the ancient Greek philosophers he wrongly regarded certainty as the hallmark of knowledge, and reason as the heuristic tool of knowledge rather than what it really is: an analytical tool for explicating the implications of any hypothesis. There is no path from reason to empirical reality. In short, the cogito is a glaring error in philosophy. Neither Descartes nor anyone else can establish the fact of his own empirical existence (or anyone else's) by reason alone, much less arrive at certainty through reason. The entire exercise of the cogito was doubly misconceived by Descartes.[11] Firstly, as already pointed out, reason does not discover knowledge, as Descartes sought to do. But, given knowledge—a matter of empirical fact (using *empirical* in its widest meaning of sense and intuitional experience)—reason can *show* all the consistent implications of that piece of knowledge. Secondly, there is no certainty or certain knowledge, in fact and in philosophy.[12] For knowledge or scientific truth, born of experience, is never certain, only provisional at best, being subject to change.

2. IMMANUEL KANT (1724–1804)

The discussion of Kant's thought, based on his *Critique of Pure Reason*, published in 1781, will concentrate on four major elements of the myth that he built up into a philosophical system. They are his concepts of (1.) space and time, (2.) thing-in-itself, (3.) mind or will, and (4.) morality or duty.

55

1. SPACE AND TIME

The modern view of nature posits a rule of "minimum space, minimum time" required as a condition for things to come into being—in Plato's terminology, for the semblances of pure forms to be incorporated in matter—and so be recognized as the particular things that they are. This view implies that space and time are objective entities. Kant, however, regarded space and time as subjective preconditions of perception, that is, necessary for man's recognition of objects.

Once recognized, Kant maintains, a thing will always be recognized *as such* in the future because of the *unchanging* category of perception (Kant's equivalent of Plato's [semblance of] ideal form), which is imposed on it at its very first recognition. That is to say, a particular thing will always *conform* to the category (or form) previously imposed upon it by our reason. Recognition of the thing is then simply the repeated imposition of the identical category each time it is encountered. (This is pure Plato: preexisting or a priori forms [or, as Kant prefers, categories] are imposed on [sensations derived from] matter in order to give them identity.)

The implication of Kant's doctrine is that either things do not change over time (in spite of the recalcitrance of matter to perfect molding, of which Plato assures us) or, if they do, they only change proportionally in all their dimensions and parts. This would include the human observer, among "all other things." But on this latter condition we should never know whether the cosmos is becoming bigger or smaller (as astrophysicists of opposite persuasions maintain), since change within the cosmos would be proportional, affecting everything the same way.

The doctrine that space and time, or space-time, is built into our perception as a precondition of our recognition and knowledge of things is what Kant means by denoting space and time as transcendental or intuitive categories; that is, they are subjective and beyond experience, but not beyond knowledge.

Knowledge, for Kant, is thus not merely reminiscence of what is already known a priori (as Socrates taught—a reminiscence called into being in the present by the dialogic or dialectic [question-and-answer] method of discussion, in a manner similar to a midwife delivering a baby that is already there, in its mother's womb); it is also reminiscence in a space-time dimension, a dimension already built into our perception, thus given with our existence, and by which we organize and identify our experiences. It should be noted that Kant's gloss on Plato makes space (matter) and time subjective, where Plato makes matter objective, within the empirical world. In this respect, Kant differed also from his predecessor, the philosopher-mathematician, Gottfried Wilhelm Leibniz

(1646–1716), who maintained the opposite view, namely, that space and time are objective relations among things.[13] By making space and time subjective Kant adopted the position that it is impossible to know the world objectively, since our experience of it is derived indirectly through our senses and perceptions.

One stage removed from perceptions are concepts, being derived from perceptions; they are therefore beyond the reach of space-time and experience, as well as of the analytical operating rules of the mind—logic and mathematics. They are, that is, transcendent—nothing could be known about them. This applies to metaphysical concepts such as God, immortality, and freedom.

The scope of knowledge, according to Kant, is thus limited to such things as can be *organized* by the mind's subjective, space-time framework of perception and on which the mind can *operate* according to its own rules of logic and mathematics. There are, accordingly, two kinds of knowledge:

(a) *Analytical* or certain knowledge, a priori and tautological (implicit) and always true, derived purely from the mind's own operations and rules; and

(b) *Synthetic* or empirical knowledge derived from experience via the senses, organized and interpreted by the mind's space-time framework and conforming to the general principles of logic and mathematics (hence predictable); such knowledge goes beyond the merely tautological in adding something new, so that it is not certain knowledge or always true because it is about things that are not known a priori but only indirectly through the senses, hence subject to error. Outside of these two kinds of knowledge nothing can be known. The operations of the mind on concepts fall into this category. For concepts, being derived from perceptions, lie beyond the realm of the knowable, that is, beyond certainty and beyond empirical knowledge.

Kant was troubled by the concepts of space and time because he could not determine by reason or by experience whether they were finite or infinite. Reason seemed to admit of either possibility as he demonstrated by his antinomies (whose theses and antitheses became the source for Hegel's method of dialectic idealism). He therefore concluded, in the light of his criteria for knowledge that space and time were neither in the domain of analytical or certain knowledge nor in that of synthetic or empirical knowledge. This left only one domain, the metaphysical, which dealt only with concepts outside the domain of reason. Hence he concluded that both space and time were metaphysical concepts (like God, immortality, and freedom), purely subjective and given with our existence. But whereas he found a practical role for these concepts—the ordering and interpretation of perceptions derived from the empirical world—he stopped short of prescribing a similar role for other metaphysical concepts like God, immortality, and freedom. He, at least, left it to be inferred that these also were given with our existence without actually saying so. Thus these transcendent concepts (as he designated them) were beyond knowledge and experience and given with our existence.

Kant's space-time concept has a dual interest for us. First, it constitutes the link between the metaphysical and the empirical world and helps us situate Kant's thought within the Greek academic philosophical tradition. Metaphysical concepts correspond to Plato's pure forms or ideas—beyond knowledge and experience, in a transcendent, suprasensible world. The space-time metaphysical concept and mechanism enables us identify empirical objects through the categories of the mind imposed on them and to which they conform. These categories correspond to the Platonian semblances of forms or ideas. Second, Kant's space-time concept provides a good illustration of problem supersession by paradigm change—a change from regarding a problem (space and time) within an objective, empirical framework (Plato, Leibniz) to regarding it within a subjective framework (Kant). As a case study in Thomas Kuhn's "structure of scientific revolution by paradigm change"[14] it demonstrates the opposite of Kuhn's thesis that scientific progress proceeds by paradigm change, that such change occurs because it solves many more problems than before. Kant showed that paradigm change could lead equally to scientific regress along with problem elimination. His conclusion that space-time was subjective, beyond the reach of empirical knowledge, was a step backward in philosophic and scientific thought.

2. THING-IN-ITSELF

Working within the Platonian tradition, Kant reexamined the concept of "form" or "idea," that is, the essence of a thing—Plato's "thing-itself" that, in his philosophic myth, lies outside the corresponding sensible thing as well as outside the domain of all sensible things and in some suprasensible world. For Plato, it is that idea or shape that, lying outside and beyond it, the object in question seeks to reproduce by imitation, albeit poorly or imperfectly. Kant took the Platonian "idea" and modified its original meaning of suprasensible and unknowable idea to *semblance* of idea located in the sensible world *within* individual objects

58

instead of outside them, transmitting sense data and causing sensation but unknowable. He renamed this modified concept "thing-in-itself."

Thus, whether he was aware of it or not, Kant effectively reversed the meaning of Plato's *thing-itself*, bringing it down from a supra- to an intrasensible world, and from outside to within the object in question. The confusion created by maintaining practically the same terminological equivalent ("thing-in-itself") as Plato's "thing-itself" while changing its sense was not lessened by his comparing it indirectly to the human will.[15] For an instructive comparison and clarification, Popper's foray into the same field may be mentioned.[16]

Popper took the middle ground between Plato, on the one hand, and Kant, on the other, interpreting the Platonian concept of pure form to mean a property lying *outside* of a thing but *within* our sensible world. All attributes of things are thus assigned an objective existence of their own, independent of the human mind and thought although originating therein, and termed *objective knowledge*, meaning the world of language, mathematical and scientific theories, arguments, problem situations, et cetera, contained in libraries. These elements, although owing their existence to man in the first place, eventually become independent of man, according to Popper, and by their use scientific knowledge increases.[17]

We may illustrate the three interpretations given to the Platonian idea, including Plato's own interpretation, by the following table:

Form, Idea, or Property of an Object

		Location of Concept			
Philosopher	Terminology	Inside Object	Outside Object	Sensible world	Suprasensible world
Plato	Pure Form (Thing-itself)		X		X
Kant	Thing-in-itself	X		X	
Popper	Objective Knowledge		X	X	

3. MIND OR WILL

Just as he rebaptized Plato's semblance of pure forms of physical entities as "thing-in-itself," so Kant rebaptized virtue, the semblance of moral forms (the pure forms of human behavior or action) as "mind," which reveals itself as "will." [18] Like the "thing-in-itself" of any physical object, "mind" or "will" is not a datum given a priori to man, but unlike a thing's "thing-in-itself," which cannot be known but only thought, the human mind *can* be known or revealed in action as will. Will is thus the revelation of mind when it achieves its own reality and consciousness, and turns out to be the same as an object's thing-in-itself in action.

Here, again, we see how Kant takes an academic philosophical concept ("mind"), which originally implied a transcendent or suprasensible entity, and brings it down into the sensible world, retaining its name while changing its sense to that of its semblance ("virtue").

4. MORALITY OR DUTY

As space and time conditioned man's perception in Kant's system, so morality or duty governed man's action or behavior. And it is toward morality and moral ends that man's reason may rightly be used. Morality is the law that commands specific actions as a duty binding on all mankind regardless of their consequences or effects, much the same as a law of nature is binding. He calls it a "categorical imperative."

Kant makes a distinction between morality or "categorical imperative"—a command of reason compelling to the will without conditions—and "hypothetical imperative" or conditional command, conditioned by its effects. The categorical imperative commands one to "act as if the maxim of your action were to become through your will a general natural law," regardless of its consequences. The hypothetical imperative, by contrast, enjoins one to act only in ways that ensure favorable or prevent unfavorable consequences to oneself.

For all its high-sounding tone, Kant's morality, duty, or categorical imperative is flawed—in two ways. First, the desire to have the maxim of one's action become a general law binding on all mankind does not carry any guarantee that everyone else would accept the same maxim in the same light. The "rule" of moral action, as presented by Kant, is solipsistic not objective in regard to other persons, regardless of an individual's will that it become so (objective). It is, as Bertrand Russell says of conventional morality, "fundamentally an attempt, however disguised, to give legislative force to our own wishes." [19] It amounts to no more than "dependent benevolence" masquerading as "independent benevolence," i.e., independent of one's own wishes. [20] Second, there is no objectively necessary action prescribed for human society by a nonhuman agency. All such "absolute obligations" are legislated by man, hence open to question by those who disagree. They are not considered absolute by others, or independently of their effects. It is the old argument by Thrasymachus, in Plato's *Republic*, about moral laws being imposed by the dominant class on the rest of society. Herein lies the weakness of Kant's categorical imperative. It is no more than the ancient Greek philosophers' (Plato's and Aristotle's) aristocratic concept of duty or obligation of the inferior to the superior class, laid upon it by the guardians of society. It is not reciprocal but based on the master-servant relationship within a slave, or any class-structured, society; hence it is immoral.

Following in the new trail made by Kant, Arthur Schopenhauer sought, unsuccessfully, to give precision to Kant's concept of the "thing-in-itself" or "will"—a solipsistic concept like Hegel's "Spirit" (in practice, German nationalism apotheosized)—as meaning, specifically, the "will to live and to procreate." In thus giving a little more concreteness to "will" Schopenhauer unintentionally spawned a whole new brood of "will" philosophers including himself, Nietzsche ("will to power"), and Adler ("will to excel") as well as existentialist theologians and philosophers (Kierkegaard, Jaspers, Sartre) who placed undue emphasis on the individual, willing self as paramount; biologists who emphasized the survival instinct (Darwin) or blind *elan vital* or life force (Bergson) as the motor that drives the evolutionary process; and psychoanalysts, starting with Freud, who boiled down all psychic drives to the procreative instinct or libido.

In the realm of will, any interpretation would seem to do—anything goes. One finds oneself in the paradoxical situation of being in the sensible world with a nonobjective, nonempirical concept that is supposed to motivate empirical objects but can only be interpreted solipsistically to cover a wide range of nonrational forces and drives.

Thus far has Kant's mythical concept of "thing-in-itself" led. Lacking in precision and rational content and flexible enough in interpretation to cover a multitude of instinctual and unconscious drives, it has sparked an antirationalist revolt that has not yet run its course in the twentieth century.

The imprecision brought into philosophy by Kant's legacy of the "thing-in-itself" and its antirationalist tendency, coupled with his solipsistic and transcendent concepts of "God," "freedom," and "immortality," led eventually in recent times to the effort initiated by the Logical Positivists to reverse the trend by their legitimate insistence on the need for clear definitions and empirically testable propositions. As a result, much emphasis was placed on linguistics, which, unfortunately, tended to become substituted for, and confused with, philosophy. Nevertheless, the Logical Positivists performed a very useful service and necessary prerequisite to the effective pursuit not only of philosophy but also of any other branch of study. They stressed clear thought, definition, and expression as a prerequisite to fruitful inquiry in every field, but especially in philosophy.

3. GEORG WILHELM FRIEDRICH HEGEL (1770–1831)

The major elements in Hegel's philosophic myth are best presented in summary form, as follows:

1. ABSOLUTE IDEA, SPIRIT, OR REASON

The Platonian-Aristotelian concept of God as the Form of all forms or Idea of all ideas, thinking out and contemplating the constituent forms or ideas in his eternal mind is rebaptized by Hegel as Absolute Idea, Spirit, or Reason. It is this Absolute Idea (or collectivity of ideas) that is worked out—poorly copied, according to Plato and Aristotle—in matter over time.

2. CONCEPT OF HISTORY

According to Plato, ideas or concepts are traced and filled out imperfectly in matter (owing to the recalcitrance factor in matter) not all at once, but consecutively over time. Hegel sees this process as constituting the essential definition of history. History, therefore, becomes the working out or realization of the collectivity of ideas (Absolute Idea) in matter over time. Thus Hegel gave explicit formulation to an idea that was already implicit in Plato's philosophical system.

3. CONCEPT OF ALIENATION

Absolute Idea, Spirit, or Reason in being worked out in matter over time is said, by Hegel, to alienate itself (from itself) in history: alienation, because ideas and matter do not mix; the one (ideas) being eternal (outside time), the other (matter) being ephemeral (changeable) in conforming to ideas because operating in time, hence in history. Thus, eternal Absolute Idea is, as it were, encapsulated or trapped in matter that, in working out the pattern of ideas over time, generates history.[21]

62

4. CONCEPT OF THE "CUNNING OF REASON"

Hegel terms the alienation of Absolute Idea in history the *cunning of Reason*. The basis of this concept lies in the Aristotelian definition of soul as consisting partly of a rational element, mind, which is part of the mind of God (Hegel's Absolute Idea) and partly of an irrational element—appetites or soul proper (emotions or passions) in animals, vegetativeness in plants; and as constituting the unitive organic and organizing force that molds matter into plants or animals, as the case may be. The "cunning of Reason," therefore, consists in the rational element of soul (which is of the same nature as Reason) influencing or using the irrational element (vegetativeness or animal, including human, passions) to realize, through matter, its own ideal goals in history.

5. DIALECTICAL IDEALISM

Absolute Idea is a dynamic entity that moves in a dialectic (or dialogic) process whereby any given idea (thesis) generates its opposite (antithesis) and both then associate to form a new and broader idea (synthesis) in which elements of both opposing ideas are represented—like the Yin and Yang of Taoist philosophy. It is by this dynamic process that ideas progress (literally, move forward) in history. This process is what is termed *Dialectical Idealism* (the dialogue of opposing ideas). It contrasts with the similar process supposed to take place in the realm of matter, propounded by Karl Marx and dubbed *Dialectical Materialism* and modeled on the pattern of Hegel's *Dialectical Idealism*.

6. INCARNATION OF ABSOLUTE SPIRIT IN THE CONTEMPORARY DOMINANT NATION IN WORLD HISTORY

According to Hegel, the dominant nation at any time in world history incarnates Absolute Idea or Spirit and is the standard-bearer of its ideal designs. He held the Germany of his day to be the dominant nation and current representative of Absolute Idea or Spirit.

7. GLORIFICATION OF INTERNATIONAL CONFLICT AND WAR

The principle of synthetic resolution of dialectical conflict or differences propounded by Hegel was held by him to apply in the internal affairs of nations, as in the realm of ideas, but not (inexplicably) in international affairs. Each nation is *a* manifestation of Absolute Idea, but only the leading or dominant nation is *the* standard-bearer and representative of Absolute Idea or Spirit. This exclusion of the dialectic method from international affairs led Hegel to espouse national sovereignty as an absolute value and to glorify international conflict and wars as the logical means of selecting the victor and dominant nation to represent Spirit.

8. RISE AND FALL OF NATIONS

Hegel's doctrine of representation of Spirit by the dominant nation on the stage of World History implies a theory of the rise and fall of nations.

Appraisal of Hegel's Myth

Hegel made significant contributions to philosophy or, more appropriately, philosophic myth. These are mainly:

(a) his concept and doctrine of dialectical idealism;
(b) his derivation of history from philosophy;
(c) his dubious if noteworthy thesis of the dominant nation on the international scene as the spearhead and standard-bearer of Absolute Idea or Spirit as manifested in world history.

These ideas are evaluated in what follows.

(a) An important contribution by Hegel consisted in his advancing a new dynamic for philosophy. In Plato's philosophic system dynamism is provided by the creative and propulsive activity of God and the demiurge, in Aristotle's by the gravitational or attractive force of God as unmoved mover of the cosmos. Hegel shifted the dynamic role from God to the ideas *explicitly*[22] and changed its nature from one of propulsion or of attraction to the all-inclusive one of *dialectics*—the self-generation of ideas by movement, conflict, and synthesis in the mind of God or Absolute Idea. Thereby he combined Plato's and Aristotle's concepts of God or Collective Idea. It is this dialectic movement of ideas that generates history. Thus Hegel achieved the overt and complete dynamization of the metaphysical basis of Greek academic philosophy, demonstrating for the first time (what Plato

64

cryptically expressed) that time was history and history the moving image of Absolute Idea as it sought to realize itself through matter and events, that is, phenomena.

(b) In explicitly dynamizing the ideas Hegel became the first philosopher in the Greek philosophic tradition inherited by the Occident to explicitly derive history from philosophy—just as Parmenides was the first Greek philosopher to derive metaphysics from thought expressed in language, reasoning from language to the outside world.[23] This derivation of history from philosophy by Hegel may have misled the historian R. G. Collingwood, into thinking that philosophy *was* history. As T. M. Knox, the editor of *The Idea of History* (published posthumously from Collingwood's notes) puts it, perhaps a bit unkindly, "he seems to have been inclined to draw the conclusion that philosophy was simply identical with whatever he happened to be studying most intensively at the time," namely history, in this case.[24] Actually, the fact is otherwise: instead of philosophy being absorbed in history, as Collingwood would have it, it is history that is absorbed in, because derived from and therefore a part of, philosophy—as Hegel makes clear.

(c) Hegel advanced the thesis that at any stage in world history the dominant nation is the spearhead and standard-bearer of Spirit in its movement in and through world history. This thesis is interesting but empirically invalid in that there have been single as well as several dominant nations at various periods in world history. Even at those times when there have been great empires in the Occident there have also been dominant nations and empires elsewhere.

And in nonimperial periods in the Occident and elsewhere there have been several dominant nations—for example:[25] in the fifteenth and sixteenth centuries England, Portugal, Spain, and France and in the eighteenth and nineteenth centuries England, France, and Germany, to take only the Occident. In the twentieth century, the list includes England, France, Germany, the U.S.A. until 1914; England, France, Germany, the U.S.A., the USSR, and Japan until 1939; England, France, China, the U.S.A., and the USSR until the 1950s; and the U.S.A. and the USSR in the second half of the twentieth century. Thus even in Hegel's own day his thesis about *the* dominant nation was at odds with the facts, thereby invalidating as well his thesis on international conflict and war in relation to the emergence of *the* dominant nation.

(d) It is generally agreed that Hegel's system is flawed by his espousal of national sovereignty as an absolute value in international affairs and consequently his glorification of international conflicts and wars.

65

The tragedy here is that Hegel (as well as others) got taken in by his own myth, that a nonempirical myth glorifying sovereignty and war should have been taken as unquestioned fact, whereas it was based on a piece of pure myth about Absolute Idea or Spirit and a dubious hypothesis erected upon it, namely, that Absolute Idea can only be represented at any time in world history by a single dominant nation.

Like Marx after him, Hegel was a tolerant dialectician in philosophy and the world of ideas generally, but an intolerant eliminator in the world of affairs. His excessive German nationalism blinded him to the contrary evidence of history in the formulation of his single-dominant-nation thesis.

(e) *Hegel's Legacy in International Affairs: Chauvinism and Racism*: If the Germans or other European peoples were to continue to accept the myth of the incarnation of Spirit at any historical time (Zeitgeist) in a single dominant nation, chosen by the natural selection of conflict, wars of elimination and victory to be the current standard-bearer of Spirit—à l'Hegelisme—there should always tend to be wars of elimination in Europe, and nationalism would tend to be identified with, or assimilated to, theology and religion, as was the case in Germany before each of the two World Wars.[26]

When any group puts itself at the center of humanity, as its standard-bearer and archetype—as did the ancient Jews and the Germans after Hegel—it is only a short step to one man putting himself, or being put, at the center of that group (and humanity) as the *human* archetype, as the Christians did with Jesus and Hitler with Aryan man. The ultimate is reached when the group or individual is self-identified, not as *an* but as *the* incarnation of God (Hegel's Germany and Jesus of the Christians).[27] Hegel applied the ancient oriental custom and formality of the deification of individuals (adopted by the ancient Greek and Romans) to the German nation as the Elect of God, thus setting the Germans, implicitly, in competition with Jews (the only group that had previously so self-selected itself). Hitler literally took the story on from there (as Nietzsche's superman) discerning a competition between Jews and Aryans for the place of the Elect of God, requiring the displacement of the contemporary Jews by a war of elimination—à l'Hegel.

So much havoc can pure myth inflict on mankind, since not only Jews but also all non-Germans outside the charmed circle of the Axis Powers had to feel the weight of German "superiority."

66

4. ARTHUR SCHOPENHAUER (1788–1860)

If one wished to give a summary of Arthur Schopenhauer's philosophical myth it may be put this way: The appearance of persons and things is *my* idea of them; their inner nature is inaccessible to me but is identical to mine and is the same as my will. Appearances divide, will unites, persons and things. One detects in this summary a combination of Plato's theory of phenomena as appearances and appearances as poor semblances of pure forms or ideas and Aristotle's rephrasing of the same theory in the concept of irrational soul (appetites or vegetativeness) that gives identity to, and therefore divides, persons and things; together with Aristotle's theory of rational soul (or mind) that is impersonal, without identity, and therefore unites all persons and things. Thus, Schopenhauer's is basically a reformulation of Greek academic philosophy, directly linked to a similar reformulation by Kant. This summary of his thought will now be elaborated in first personal presentation, since Schopenhauer's myth is essentially solipsistic.

Phenomena or things are the specific ideas, or semblances of ideas, incorporated in things as I perceive them. And the way I (or anyone else) perceives each person or thing is through my (their) senses. The result of this perception—the appearances of persons and things—is thus only an idea, *my* idea of that person, thing, the world. But my idea is not the same as the true nature or essence of whatever I perceive. That essence—Plato's semblance or poor copy of the pure form of the object of perception or Kant's equivalent, the "thing-in-itself"—is inaccessible to me, just as an artist's original vision or conception is inaccessible to me or anyone else when I study his painting or sculpture.[28]

My own essence or thing-in-itself I take to be my will, which is accessible to me alone. Therefore, Schopenhauer concludes by analogy, the thing-in-itself of every person or thing is their will, and this, he further assumes, must be of the same nature as my will. And my will is, primarily, my *will to live and procreate*, basically my *sex drive*, my desire to perpetuate myself. Thus the *will to live*, not Hegel's Absolute Idea or Spirit, is the essence and motivating force of the phenomenal world and its constituents. In Aristotelian terms, the choice facing Hegel and Schopenhauer for the motivating force and essence of persons and things lies between the two elements of soul: rational or mental soul (reason), which is Hegel's choice, and irrational soul or psychic drives, which is Schopenhauer's choice.

Given that rational soul was idea and irrational soul was attached

67

to matter, it is the familiar but false conflict between idealism and materialism in another guise; the same false dichotomy that later separated Marx from Hegel. Both sides to this conflict seem to have overlooked that, for Aristotle, soul was a unitive integrating factor with merely two aspects that collaborated inseparably so long as the organism persisted.

The will to live (as manifested in the sex drive) is a blind, unknowing, goalless, incessant impulse—a vitality that is common to organic as well as inorganic Nature, leading to self-realization and individuation through procreation, hence to mutual opposition, conflict, and suffering in the phenomenal world. Liberation or salvation from this suffering can come only through a denial and abandonment of the will to live, all desire, all selfness—asceticism—and, finally, death. For, without the will to live there is no self, no idea, no world. (This conclusion—liberation from will to live through self-denial and death—is generally credited to Schopenhauer's readings in Buddhism. It is well to note, however, that it is the same conclusion indicated in Aristotle's metaphysics: one is rid of irrational soul [Schopenhauer's will to live] only at death.)

One further conclusion that was clear to Schopenhauer was that since will led, through procreation and competition, to suffering it was not moral—it carried no duty or categorical imperative to procreate. Thus, there was no happiness in the world, and all that man can do is, not bring about happiness but reduce unhappiness in the world by denying his will, his instinct to procreate. This tenet has obvious kinship with the similar Gnostic doctrine of the Marcionite variety,[29] with which Schopenhauer may or may not have been acquainted.

Such was the philosophy[30] that Schopenhauer strove to perpetuate, competitively but ineffectually, against Hegel's dialectic idealism and philosophy of history at the University of Berlin.[31]

It is interesting to note that Schopenhauer's concept of will (to live and procreate) provided the basis for Sigmund Freud's concept of *sex drive* (libido) in his psychological writings and Adler's *will-to-excel* (competitively); Nietzsche's *will-to-power*; and Henri Bergson's *elan vital* or blind, unknowing, nonteleological, evolutionary force. This elevation of will or blind instinct to a position of primacy over idea or reason (replacing Hegel's "cunning of reason" with Schopenhauer's "cunning of will or instinct") had the adverse effect of devaluing reason and extolling passion, started a trend to antiintellectualism in Europe and led, via Nietzsche, to Hitler.[32] This antiintellectualism has two aspects: a revolt against abstract intellectual inquiry, connoted by the term *idealism*, which is held to have little effect on human action and is supposed to be the special activity of the traditional philosopher: and increasing attention to the influence of nonrational, unconscious attitudes and feelings on human action.

It is also ironical that Schopenhauer's myth of will should lead to the same results and through the same channels (Nietzsche and Hitler) as Hegel's myth of Spirit and dominant nation, absolute national sovereignty, and international wars, and for the same reasons: both myths are two aspects of the same Aristotelian concept of soul, and both play on human instincts and passions that are more readily aroused to action than abstract intellectual activity. Schopenhauer, like Hegel, was a symbol manipulator, executing a purely mythological operation with terms like *idea* and *will*, without any presumption of empirical content or confirmation. He made the transition from a purely solipsistic position to what he believed was a universal empirical position solely on the basis of analogy, rather than experience. This was an illegitimate use of analogy since only *correspondence*, not *empirical identity* can result from the analogy:

my idea of self and world: my will $=$ your idea of self and world: your will

It is not possible to pass on from this position of correspondence to the identity proclaimed by Schopenhauer:

$$\text{my will} \equiv \text{your will}$$

Unlike Kant, Schopenhauer had no theory of morality, categorical imperative, or duty that, in theory, would have made all wills identical by action in ways considered objective and binding on all. And if he had had one, it is unlikely that it would have been different from the traditional conception of morality that, as we saw in the case of his mentor, Kant, related to relationships between individuals and classes that were not reciprocal but acropetal (one way, from the lower to the upper unit), hence essentially immoral.

5. KARL HEINRICH MARX (1818–83)

Karl Marx is universally regarded as an economist who, within the tradition of the British classical economists, especially David Ricardo, developed a labor theory of value and a theory of institutional economic change. The latter was based on Marx's reading of economic history, interpreted in the light of his inversion of Hegel's dialectic model of philosophy. But for all his activism in the working-class movement of his time and his classic study on capital and capitalism and other similar writings, Marx was more philosopher than economist. His doctoral dissertation presented and accepted at the University of Jena was on the topic of the difference between the natural philosophy of Democritus and Epicurus with regard to the atom. Democritus espoused a vertical fall of atoms, indicating thereby the impact of necessity on the cosmos. Epicurus, on the other hand, espoused a sloping fall of atoms diverging from the vertical, thereby indicating a departure from necessity due to the individuality, indeterminism, or free will of man. Marx had inclined to the side of Democritus: inevitability, as against individuality and free will. In fact and in practice, he made some allowance for human action in bringing about the inevitable. Man's individuality and free will are denied, leaving him no choice but to aid the inevitable. This view is best expressed in Marx's famous dictum that philosophers had in the past been content to *interpret* the world while their duty was to *change* it.

Marx's espousal of the working-class movement was, for him, primarily an opportunity to put into practice this dictum. He interpreted the process of institutional economic change as an inexorable progression from feudalism to capitalism (the stage at which Europe had arrived in his lifetime) to socialism,[33] in Hegelian dialectical fashion, and called upon the working classes to throw their weight on the side of the inevitable next stage of the historical evolution of capitalism, namely socialism, and so hasten its advent. In short: free will in the service of determinism, Epicurus in the service of Democritus.

Marx will, therefore, be treated here as a philosopher or a philosopher-turned-economist, economics being merely an area for the application of his view of the philosopher's role, just as politics and government provided a similar opportunity for Plato's application of his philosophy. In this respect, Marx was in the great tradition of Greek academic philosophy while, at the same time, following in the classical economic tradition established by Adam Smith, founder of British economics. He complemented Smith's theory of laissez faire capitalism with his own theory of institutional economic change, with the corresponding difference that Smith was a nonactivist laissez faire economist while Marx was an activist economist. In this role Marx provided a historico-philosophical underpinning for the tradition of state economic intervention that preceded Smith's time and which, today, is carried on by all countries of the world in more or less degree.[34] Indeed, from a technical point of view, Marx was a better philosopher than economist. As an economist he may be faulted for ignoring organization or entrepreneurship as a special kind of labor and, therefore, a factor of production. As a philosopher he was the first to effectively link the Greek philosophers' two worlds in a derivative manner (the ideal from the material world), although he committed the error of assigning primacy to one of them (the material world). Thus he committed the reverse error of all occidental philosophers up to his day, who assigned primacy to the ideal over the material world.[35]

MARX'S DOCTRINE

Marx's doctrine is simplicity itself. Taking off from Democritus and his material (atomic) basis of the cosmos—as opposed to Plato's threefold basis (God, ideas, matter)—and Hegel's dialectical method of thesis-antithesis-synthesis, Marx held matter to be the sole basis of existence and that the material arrangements for production and those controlling them in any society dominate the climate of thought and ideas, including ideas about religion. Somatopsychism, in short, as opposed to the psychosomatism of Hegel. The dominant economic group in society develops ideas arising from, and consonant with, its economic position or class in society. That is to say, ideas are a derivative of matter and material arrangements for production.

Ownership of the means of production of a given society pits owners against nonowners who have only their labor to sell to the owners of the productive resources. Thus a dialectic clash or conflict of interests of the "haves" and the "have nots;" hence, dialectic materialism. The owners of productive property exploit the labor of the workers, paying them subsistence wages and expropriating the surplus (between their output and their wages) for formation and accumulation of more capital (produced means of production). From this expropriation arises the alienation of workers (literally) from the surplus product of their labor. (This parallels the other kind of alienation that Ludwig Feuerbach had highlighted in his *The Essence of Christianity*: man's alienation of his good qualities and projection of them onto an objectified concept, called *God*). The corrective to the exploitation of the workers through the expropriation and conversion of their surplus into capital is for them to recover their surplus, thus ending their alienation from it. (Feuerbach gave similar advice in respect of man's alienated godlike qualities).

The method proposed by Marx for recovery of their surplus by the workers differs from the solution to the Hegelian dialectic by synthesis or assimilation of contraries. The solution to the Marxian dialectic is not joint ownership of capital (as would normally be expected) or assimilation of capitalists and the working classes in society for mutual advantage, but a forcible expropriation of capital, a war to the death by the displacement and annihilation of capitalists by the working classes, followed by the establishment of a working-class dictatorship represented by the state. The state, henceforth, would own and control all the means of production on behalf of the workers. Such was the socialist "dialectical" solution advocated by Marx.[36]

Before undertaking a critical examination and assessment of Marx's philosophy and practice, it is necessary to take a look at some of the decisive factors that influenced his thinking.

DECISIVE FACTORS IN MARX'S THOUGHT

Some of the main influences on Marx's thought were the following:

(a) *Anti-Jewish Attitude*: Although himself a Jew, Marx was noted for his anti-Jewish strictures and his tenet that money is the Jew's god. His own wasteful use of his family's money may or may not have been a consequence of his disrespect for money. He overtly renounced Judaism in his personal life, which was hardly surprising since his parents were neither practising nor believing Jews.

(b) *Disrespect for Conventional Religion and Theology*: Marx had a strong disrespect for religion, especially the Christian religion with its theology that cheapened itself by the forced conversion of Jews (including Marx's father and himself, brothers, and sisters) to Christianity as a condition for their access to opportunities for professional and social advancement.

(c) *Ludwig Feuerbach's View of Theology as Anthropology*: The thesis propounded by the German materialist philosopher Ludwig Andreas Feuerbach (1804–72) that God was a creation of human thought, by the alienation of all that was best in the human race and its projection onto an objectified concept called *God*,[37] had a profound influence on Marx's thinking. He interpreted the thesis to mean that God was a projection, in the realm of ideas, by a species of matter called man, in his effort to safeguard the property rights and production arrangements of the dominant economic class in society. In short, theology was the idealist product of the material arrangements of a capitalist society. This was a less flattering view than Feuerbach's which placed accent on the outward projection of the *best qualities* of the inner self of the human race. Marx changed Feuerbach's concept from an anthropological to a crassly economic concept, with implications in the domain of property law. (From a pragmatic point of view, Marx was undoubtedly right, considering the use made of Christian religion and theology in his day to select (by exclusion and inclusion) those who would be permitted access to economic and social opportunities.)

72

(d) *Hegel's Philosophy of Dialectical Idealism*: Once he was won over by Feuerbach's view of theology Marx reacted in contradiction to Hegel's philosophy of dialectical idealism. Hegel's primacy of ideas over matter was replaced by Marx's primacy of matter over ideas, the dialectical process being retained. Thus Hegel's dialectical idealism was replaced by Marx's dialectical materialism. This was but the application of the dialectical process in the materialistic field.

EVALUATION OF MARX'S PHILOSOPHY

1. Marxism as Religion

Marxism, like Christianity, is a religion, being concerned inter alia with interrelationships among human beings and between human beings and the rest of their environment. However, Marxism erected itself into a bitter foe of Christianity, with which it has common roots in the Jewish sectarian tradition of the Essenes. Insofar as they are both apocalyptic millenary religions Marxism and Christianity share a common characteristic, differing only in their time perspective of the advent of their predicted apocalypse and accompanying millennium. For Marxism, it is apocalypse and millennium *now*, rather than, as for Christianity, *later* (at the end of the world and humanity). Insofar as both seek to create a "new man" under their regime—respectively under communism and in Jesus Christ—through adherence to the party (Marxism) and rebirth through baptism (Christianity), they differ merely in the specific mechanism (or lack of it) for bringing about the new man: Christianity using the church seeks to bring about the "new man in Christ" through internalization of the ethical control mechanism that should automatically regulate the relationships among men in society: the love of God and of one's neighbor as oneself; Marxism has no equivalent or substitute for this internal control mechanism, once the external control of the state (supposedly) withers away under communism (stateless socialism), no mechanism, that is to say, for fostering the internalization of its own ethic ("from each according to his ability, to each according to his need"). Consequently, in the absence of an internal control mechanism under Marxism, the state is unlikely to wither away and the millennium, if not the apocalypse, to arrive. For Christianity, through the institutional paraphernalia of church and priesthood, seeks, on a regular (weekly, if not daily) basis, to indoctrinate its disciples with its ethic from birth till death—admittedly, with mixed results. Marxism's party and party theoretician perform no such role, neither weekly nor over the lifetime of its card-carriers. Although itself a religion, by attacking religion, especially Christianity and its church, with which it has common roots, Marxism cut itself from adopting a serviceable internalization mechanism and the steady and continuing nourishment that it provides, and came adrift. It continues to drift to this day.

Thus the quarrel between Marxism and Christianity, properly understood, is an internal, family quarrel,[38] in which an accommodation can only be reached by Marxism returning to its roots: by recognizing itself for what it is: a religion, and by recognizing as well as accepting the necessity for the internalization of its own ethic as the only possible guarantee of the emergence of the "new man under communism" and the advent of the millennium. Until this lesson is learnt by Marxism and actively practiced by both Christianity and Marxism, it will not be possible to put their respective claims, if ever, to the test.

Strictly speaking, God or theology does not enter into the Marxist-Christian quarrel, since the point of engagement between the two movements is religion—ideal human interrelationships in society to be achieved in the here and now—not theology. For theology is about *origins* of things, an issue with which Marx was not concerned. Rather was he concerned with the *current and future state of things in human society*, which is a religious concern. Thus, Marxism-Communism is technically a-theistic or a-theological, that is, not concerned with theology; which is not the same thing as being atheistic in the conventional sense of antitheological—although it was that as well, in bias if not in content.

Nor can it strictly be said that Marxism is antireligious, for it is itself a religion, as has been demonstrated. It is, however, anti-Christianity in rejecting the Christian position (or what Marx regarded as the Christian position) of apocalypse and millennium later, instead of now. This, however, was only one (and probably not the most important) of the positions adopted and promoted by Jesus. There is nothing in the ethical system of Jesus that could be contrary to that of Marx (if one overlooks Marx's unethical sanctioning of violence and liquidation of the capitalist class); for Jesus preached justice among men in the here and now, with appropriate rewards for the just, which, however, could only be *guaranteed* for and in the hereafter, if not in the now.

It is necessary to remark, at this point, that although for the convenience of economic and social advancement Marx, like the rest of his family, was compelled by the laws of the State of Prussia to convert to Christianity, such conversion, understandably, was only superficial. There is no evidence that, as a Christian by duress, he was taught, or grasped, much about the reported teachings of Jesus.

74

Whatever the case, he was too busy attacking institutional Christianity to make a distinction between the teachings of the Church and those of its founder (as reported in the Gospels). This is probably part of the reason why he seems to have missed the crucial point about Christianity as it related to his own movement, namely, that as reportedly presented by Jesus, Christianity was a program for the *individual*, unlike Marxism which was a program for *society*. In his thus failing to recognize the *complementarity* of the two religious programs Marx's fire against Christianity was largely misdirected.

2. Marx's Apparent Antireligious and Antitheological Bias[39]

Marx's open disrespect for, and bias against, the Christian religion, as institutionally preached and practiced, arose from personal and family as from institutional reasons and is often taken as evidence that Marxism is antireligion essentially. It should be borne in mind, however, that Marx did not prepare a full-scale attack on religion—for two reasons: first, because he concluded that Feuerbach had presented all the necessary criticisms on the subject in his *The Essence of Christianity*; second, because in Marx's philosophical system religion belonged in the realm of ideas, which was a derivative or secondary realm based, and erected as a defensive superstructure, upon the material arrangements for production. Consequently, religion did not rate as a principal adversary of socialism: that place of honor belonged to the private capitalists who owned and controlled the means of production in society—resources that properly belonged to the entire working class and the state as their representative. And, in Marx's view, once the means of production were taken over by the state, religion as a derivative product would disappear.[40] For along with the annulment of the alienation of the material surplus would go the annulment of the alienation of man's best qualities from himself and their projection on an objectified concept named *God*. There would be no more God as a separate entity (theism), but man would become his own God, a man-God (anthropology),[41] as he takes back unto himself his hitherto projected best qualities.

In keeping with his dual approach to philosophy—interpretation and statement of the inevitable backed up by action to assist the advent of the inevitable—Marx was not content to wait for the inevitable disappearance of religion with the advent of socialism, but was eager to give it an assist. This explains his frequent contradictory statements on the subject. Thus, on the one hand, he opposed all efforts by sympathizers and followers of socialism aimed at a frontal attack on theology and religion. In his *The Holy Family* he criticized the theologian and critic of religion, Bruno Bauer, for attacking religion as an independent entity, autonomous in its

75

own right, whereas it was but a derivative of the system of production. A rearrangement of the system, and religion (theology) would die a natural death. Similarly, he criticized Feuerbach in his *German Ideology* for giving too important a place to the struggle against religion. On the other hand, Marx regarded antireligious (antitheological) criticism as an important tool in achieving the social revolution that he preached. In his view, it was necessary to free the workers from religious affiliation, since this prevented them from thinking about the revolution.[42]

In his "Introduction to the Critique of Hegel's Philosophy of Law," which appears in a collection of his "youthful writings," Marx writes as follows:

> Criticism has stripped the imaginary flowers from the chains [of bondage], not so that man may bear his chains without fantasy and without hope, but in order that he may throw off his chains and gather the living flowers. Criticism of religion destroys man's illusions in order that he may think, act, construct his reality as a human being without illusions, a human being who has attained to the age of reason; in order that he may revolve around himself, his real sun.

Again, in his *On Religion* Marx advocates that each man ought to satisfy his religious needs in the same manner as his physical needs without intervention by the state police, yet he denies that this liberty of conscience implies tolerance of all kinds of religion by the party of the workers, which should, instead, work to free the worker's conscience from the horrors of religion. This would seem to imply some kind of endorsement for some form of state religion to be freely propounded, while denying similar freedom to all privately organized religious systems—provided, of course, that the state is vested with ownership and management of all the means of production.

This ambivalent attitude on the part of Marx is reflected in the Constitution of the USSR, which simultaneously provides for freedom of religious and of antireligious propaganda. It casts doubt on the inevitability of the demise of religion (theology) under a socialist system and seems to say: "If religion fails to disappear under socialism, the Party should hasten its demise." In any case, what Marx's doctrine and prescription to "assist the inevitable" indicates is that no system is necessarily inevitable.

The subsequent history of religion and theology in the USSR has proven Marx wrong, since religion and theology still survive in its socialist economy as much as in private enterprise capitalist economies. Furthermore, religious and theological ideas flourish especially in agrarian societies, including those where the basic means of production, land, is socialized—for example, in Africa. These examples show, if anything, that theology—in the context of Marx's philosophical scheme—is a permanent by-product of *any* and *all* material arrangements for production in *any* and *all* societies. It, therefore, survives regardless of the system of production in vogue in any given society. But while this does not necessarily contradict Marx's doctrine that ideas (including religious and theological ideas) are derivative products of matter or material things, it does show that religion and theology are not the unique by-products (if at all the products) of private enterprise capitalism. Consequently, this showing must prove fatal to Marx's attempt to link his materialist (appropriated surplus) alienation doctrine to Feuerbach's human self-alienation doctrine of theology. There is no logical connection between economics and anthropological theology in this regard. Accordingly, Marxism has no really valid basis for an attack on religion and theology, as such, as distinct from the institutional misuse of Christian doctrine.

If—to go one step further—like Marx, one denies the Platonian metaphysical transition from suprasensible ideas to sensible idea-incorporating matter (the foundation of Hegel's idealism and his doctrine of the "cunning of Reason") and, instead, asserts the validity of the contrary transition from sensible matter to sense-based ideas, including the idea of God as a separate category of ideas, one is led to conclude that matter is the original God or, at least, to assert the *inseparability* of matter and God. One thus arrives at what may properly be termed "a [Marxian] philosopher's God" in a sense that lays claim to empirical validity such as Blaise Pascal could never claim for the Aristotelian philosopher's God, nor for his "God of Abraham, Isaac and Jacob." Marx, of course, made just such an assertion in his article on "The Jewish Question" (*Zur Judenfrange*) in 1843:

> Money is the devouring god of Israel before which no other god can exist! Money humiliates all the gods of man transforming them into saleable goods.

Or again:

> Money is god manifest . . . the divine power of money is implicit in its essence . . . it is the alienated power of mankind.
> *Youthful Writings* (Ecrits de jeunesse)

Thus, a strict construction of Marxist doctrine leads not to "materialistic atheism" or "godless materialism" (as the Roman Catholic Church would have it) but—ironically—to "materialistic theism" or "godful materialism." This, in turn, leads—again ironically—to another contradiction in Marx's doctrine of man being the God of man: if money is man's god, then man cannot at the same time be man's god after reclaiming his expropriated surplus nor, even, after reclaiming his good qualities from that onto which they have been projected and apotheosized.

Marx's rantings on religion and theology (other than his justified criticisms of institutional Christianity) make good polemics while being flawed with inconsistencies. For all that he tried to appropriate Feuerbach's man-god, around whom man would revolve after reclaiming his divinity and his expropriated surplus, it turns out that man discovers his true god to be the same expropriated surplus in the guise of money!

3. Marxism as So-called Exact Science or "Scientific Socialism"

Marx's insistence on the dominant role of materialism (the economic basis of life or its infrastructure) and the secondary or derivative role of ideas—politics, law, philosophy, religion, art, et cetera (the superstructure)—raises serious question for Marxism itself as a philosophy and, therefore, as a part of the superstructure of the private enterprise capitalist mode of production. This follows from the simple fact that Marxism emerged under the private enterprise capitalist system rather than under the socialist (state enterprise) capitalist system with which it is concerned and which was as yet nonexistent. This meant that, in principle and according to Marx's theory of the derivative nature of ideology with respect to economic systems, a theory of socialism could not precede the existence of a socialist economy. *Ergo* Marxist socialist theory is, ipso facto, invalid as a theory of socialism, being really a dialectical complement of the private enterprise capitalist system. Beyond this, one does not need to go in dismissing Marx and his theory. And the clear implication of it all is that with the passage of the private enterprise capitalist mode of production would disappear both the theory of private enterprise capitalism *and* the theory of state enterprise capitalism (or socialism). Equally clear is that there is no way of knowing or predicting what type of economic system would succeed the private enterprise capitalist system, other than a mixed, private-state enterprise system.

The trouble with Marx is that he committed a worse fault than he accused the philosophers of—interpreting the world instead of changing it. In his case, he did not even have a world to interpret—the world he wished to have. He ought, first, to have changed the world (to socialism) before derivatively interpreting it. Instead, he did worse than the philosophers: interpret a nonexistent world before it existed—before bringing it about. He thereby demonstrated that dialectic idealism was, contrary to his own thesis, independent of dialectical materialism.

This much was clear to Engels, Marx's collaborator, from the very beginning and subsequently to others among the faithful, including Stalin and Georg Klaus. It was clear that language, linguistics, mathematics, the natural sciences, formal logic were all idea systems independent of any particular system of production and, therefore, were not—so it was argued—in the same derivative category as politics, law, philosophy, and theology.[43] They constituted, it was argued, neutral factors or idea systems belonging neither to the base (system of production) nor to the super-structure (derived ideas).[44] Thus Georg Klaus argues:

> All pre-Marxist theories of society are in the nature of the superstruc-ture of their respective eras and disappear with them. They cannot operate on different bases.
>
> As an "exact science" historical materialism is born under the cap-italist regime but does not belong to the superstructure of capitalism.[45]

Klaus's arguments are interesting for the following reaons:

(a) They attempt to establish the claim of any branch of study to scientific status on the neutrality of its idea system, that is, its generality and its independence of the material basis of production prevailing in a given society. It is on this basis that Marxism is said to be a science, an "exact" one.
(b) They deny scientific status to any system of ideas that can be shown to be dependent on, and derived from, a given system of production with whose passing the system of ideas also passes.
(c) They imply, furthermore, that the essential criterion of "scientificity" is neither substantive *content*, nor *method* of study, nor yet *relativity* to any system of production, but the *absoluteness*, the pureness of its ideas (shades of Plato!).
(d) In stating that Marxism though born under private enterprise capi-talism does not belong to it, they imply: (i) that Marxism is pure idealism—like Hegelianism—in the tradition of Plato rather than Democritus, in short, that if Marxism has any effect at all on the material world it is due to the primacy of ideas (idealism) not, as Marx believed, to the primacy of matter (materialism); (ii) that the ideological superstructure of private enterprise capitalism provokes Marxism as its dialectical antithesis, in which case we are back with Hegel's dialectical idealism, and Marxism is seen as confirmation, not contradiction, of Hegelianism as Marx supposed.

However one examines Klaus's arguments, Marxism has succeeded in standing Marx, not Hegel, on his head and become a resounding confirmation of Hegel, explaining the world like all traditional philosophers who, if they change the world, do so by the force of their ideas, not by violence, and revolutionary programs and activities. Moreover, Klaus's criterion of science as being neither systematic organization of ideas, nor method of study, nor empirical validity but absoluteness and certainty of ideas is the diametrical opposite of the modern criteria applied to science. Rather is it the criterion for obscurantism, definition, and dogma: always true under all conditions, because independent of conditions.[46] Marx would have resisted to the death any interpretation of his ideas by his followers that converted him into a Hegelian. Nevertheless, that is clearly what the attempt by his supporters to invest his doctrine with the aura of an exact science has brought about. If, indeed, Marxism is scientific, this has yet to be demonstrated according to accepted modern criteria.

4. Fatal Weakness and Indeterminacy of Marxism

Contrary to Georg Klaus's arguments, Marxism *is* a product of, and belongs within, the private enterprise capitalist system insofar as it is the antithesis of private enterprise capitalistic ideas. It fits within the framework, and is a powerful application of Hegel's dialectical idealism. Consequently, the appropriate solution of the Marxian dialectic is not displacement and elimination of the private capitalists but a synthetic solution that finds room within the economic system for private capitalists and "have not" workers to co-exist and cooperate.

This, in fact, is what has happened in the world of private enterprise capitalism. A synthetic combination of private enterprise and state capitalism has replaced the largely private enterprise economies that formerly existed in Europe in Marx's day. And even in the USSR elements of private enterprise capitalism coexist with the dominant state capitalist sector, even though they survive, formally unacknowledged, underground. Hegel, not Marx, has won the battle of the dialectics, proving that synthesis, not conflict, compromise, not elimination, is the appropriate, dialectical solution.

Even if, for the sake of argument, one were to assume that full-blown socialism or communism existed already in place of private enterprise capitalism, Marxian dialectical materialism would lead one to expect the emergence of an antithetical economic system and corresponding ideology. What this would be is indeterminate; it could be private enterprise capitalism, large and/or small cooperative enterprises, et cetera, or a mixture of all of these eventually, as each thesis provokes its antithesis. A pluralistic mixed economy could thus emerge from a dialectic

80

mixed economy. The essential point to note, however, is that, theoretically, Marx's dialectical materialism leads to an indeterminate successor system, not to socialism as the culminating point of the economic evolution of human society.

Marx and Engels must, undoubtedly, have speculated on the further development of their theory of socialism. They also must have reflected on the possible scenario of socialism leading on dialectically to another economic system—possibly back to capitalism (at least partially)—via a split in the working class, but rejected this possibility; not because it would have undermined Marx's theory (it would not) but because it would have taken the fight out of their crusade for a working-class revolution against the private capitalists. For what would have been the use of fighting for socialism (which was inevitable, anyway) if private enterprise capitalism (for capitalism of some sort there must always be under some form of control) would again, inevitably, be restored at some future time or, if socialism would lead inevitably to another form of capitalism—say, a mixed economy of state and private enterprise capitalism, as already exists in many countries of the world today? It is legitimate to speculate that it was in order to forestall such a possibility that Marx decided on the eliminatory instead of the synthetic solution to the dialectical problem. He reasoned (wrongly) that if existing private capitalists were eliminated instead of coopted into a socialist economy, new private-capitalist–minded individuals would not arrive in the future. In this way he vainly sought to thwart the working out of the dialectic in the future.

5. Residual Element of Marxism

Given Marx's doctrine of dialectical materialism and its modus operandi, the following conclusions set forth in the doctrine do not strictly follow from it and have been shown to be empirically invalid:

(a) Religion and theology are uniquely the ideological superstructure of private enterprise capitalism.
(b) Socialism-Communism is the final stage in the historical evolution of the human economic system.
(c) The state will wither away under socialism, leading to the emergence of communism and the new man under communism (in spite of the lack of a mechanism for the internalization, by the individual, of the socialist ethic).

The bedrock element of Marxism that has survived unscathed—so far—is the general thesis of the primacy of matter over idea, of materialism over idealism, or, at least, the inseparability of matter and idea, of materialism and idealism. Hegel's doctrine of ideological primacy is invalid for the simple reason that ideas do not exist independently of man—a material agent of thought and ideas. Even though they may be recorded in books and other documents ideas do not autonomously activate themselves, but must be retaken into the mind of material man and put into effect in a material way. Marx's doctrine of idealism as a derivative of materialism is only plausible since empirically untestable in a manner that would demonstrate conclusively that matter and idea are in sequential rather than concomitant relationship.

6. Marx and Hegel

It is often claimed by Marxists that Marx founded a science of history. This, of course, is not the case, as there is no such thing as a science of history. All Marx did was borrow and apply Hegel's dialectical method to the study and interpretation of historical events connected with the disposition (ownership) and use of the capital instruments of production. In short, thanks to Hegel, who saw history as a dynamic movement generated by the dialectic clash of ideas, Marx applied this dynamic method to the study of history.[47] His was an interesting achievement, since history is essentially all movement, dynamics.

Protagonists, respectively, of form (idea) and of matter, Hegel and Marx dynamized these concepts. Hegel dynamized the perfect, eternal, and suprasensible idea of Plato by inventing the locomotive device of synthetic dialectics, hitching it to Absolute Idea (or Spirit), dubbing the contraption *dialectical idealism* and installing it as the motor of historical development in the sensible, phenomenal world. Under the disguise of a critique of Hegel, Karl Marx borrowed Hegel's invention (without payment of royalty), hitched it to sensible matter (system of economic production), renamed it *dialectical materialism* (or *class struggle*), and installed it as the motor of economic development in the sensible phenomenal world. In addition, Marx hitched Hegel's Absolute Idea to his contraption, thereby claiming to regulate the workings of Hegel's machine by his own (that is, idealism as a derivative of materialism). Marx committed a flagrant act of intellectual poaching while denigrating the Master to cover up his act. Hegel had put the Germany of his day in the driver's seat of his contraption, Marx the England of his day in the driver's seat of his, and both contraptions immediately developed engine trouble. (Hegel's machine developed trouble because of his unjustified chauvinism and glorification of international conflict and war; Marx's machine, because of his unwarranted attack on religion and theology, as distinct from the institutional misuse of the Christian religion.)

82

What struck the imagination of the world, after Marx had "rectified" the work of Hegel, was the damage done by Marx's engine, as much as the engine itself. The world suddenly woke up to the fact that there was no more a suprasensible world of God (Absolute Idea) and the eternal ideas, separate and independent from matter and the sensible world of the here and now. The suprasensible had been collapsed into the sensible world.

The "enormity" of what Marx had done can be appreciated if one takes the Hegelian position as a point of departure. Hegel had maintained the Platonian duality of suprasensible and sensible worlds, the latter deriving from the former—especially from God, the Super or Absolute Idea in the former world. So far, all had gone well with theology, religion, and philosophy. The origin of the organized sensible world was an *eternal given* located in "the other" world, hence exogenous. Even when installed in the sensible world in and through the process of history this origin became immanent *in* the sensible world but still not *of* it: separate, although within it. When Marx, however, latched Hegel's suprasensible world onto his contraption he literally made it an appendage as well as a part of the sensible world. Henceforth, the origin of the sensible world was no longer exogenous but endogenous, and the sensible world became an autonomous, no longer a heteronomous, entity as well as the *only* metaphysical given.

Marx, however, did not bother to explain what he had done to theology; he took it for granted that Feuerbach, on whose work he had relied, had said it all in his *Essence of Christianity*. But here Marx was wrong. For Feuerbach had only maintained that "theology is anthropology," that God was man (humanism or humanistic theism).[48] This had been shocking, but not devastating, since man still remained superior to the rest of Nature (as Genesis had declared) and could still take pride in his continued good fortune.[49] Moreover, the idea was not so strange, after all: Jesus (as the author of the Fourth Gospel and Paul in his epistles had declared) was God in the form of man. These two biblical personalities, strictly speaking, were the original sponsors of the theology-is-anthropology thesis long before Feuerbach. But this was quite a different proposition from what Marx was now advocating. He not only had accepted Feuerbach's thesis; he had also gone beyond it to imply that God is matter ("theology is materialism") when he asserted that "money is god manifest . . . the alienated power of mankind" (p. 77 above). If theology was anthropology, man, by implication, was also mere matter. Marx thus transformed Platonian-Hegelian *idealistic theism* ("God is Absolute Idea") into Democritian *materialistic theism* or *pantheism* (often misrepresented as *atheism* or *atheistic materialism* or *godless Communism*—in unfairness to Marx).

Friedrich Nietzsche seems to have been the first writer of any importance to take stock of the consequences of the revolution in theology and philosophy that Marx had brought about by the application of the Hegelian dialectic—a method Nietzsche was also to apply in his own thinking and writing, eliminating, in true Marxian fashion, every conventional position by the substitution of its dialectical opposite, rather than searching for a synthetic solution.[50] Nietzsche took note of the fact that, with Marx, theology had been absorbed in the philosophy of dialectical materialism, as a part of the phenomenal world and was no longer a feature (the most important feature) of the transcendent world of ideas. He summed it all up in his famous dictum, "God is dead" ("Gott ist tot")[51] in his *Thus Spake Zarathustra* and was promptly branded a madman, like his Zarathustra, and an atheist, like Feuerbach and Marx.

What is really important in all this for the history of human thought is the power of myth—especially pure myth—over the human mind and the effect of the manipulation of mythological symbols on human affairs and historical developments.

Here we confront the case of a Greek cosmological myth, elaborated in Plato's *Timaeus* and riddled with little-noticed contradictions, being accepted, without empirical proof or testing for confirmation, as truth and hallowed for millennia as such by the Semitic religions adopted by the Occident and further elaborated upon. Then comes along an effective symbol manipulator like Hegel who modifies the Greek myth ("Idea has primacy over matter," "History is the incorporation of Absolute Idea in matter over time," "the dominant State is the incarnation and standard-bearer of Absolute Idea at any given stage of world history"), followed by another and equally effective symbol manipulator, Marx, whose further modification ("God is matter [money]," "Idea is a by-product of matter") effectively changed the myth and revolutionized the world picture that went with it, but still dealing in the realm of pure myth. The mythologies of these two myth makers are each the equivalent of a Copernican revolution in their effects, but without the empirical confirmation that went with it. There is no empirical confirmation of Hegel's myth of the primacy of idea over matter; nor for much of Marx's doctrine of dialectical materialism, especially of his thesis that private enterprise capitalism is the stage before socialism as the final stage, that state capitalism is followed by stateless capitalism (or communism) accompanied by the emergence of the new man under communism. Moreover, on the basic issue of the primacy of matter over idea, in Marx's doctrine, there is also no empirical confirmation, plausible as it may seem.

Modern physics, after Einstein, has confirmed the equivalence of mass and energy, via a transformation factor, both being regarded as

84

matter, and nuclear physics has, to some extent, confirmed the doctrine of the ancient Greek atomist philosophers. It may very well be that ideas and concepts are manifestations of energy, hence forms of matter. If this is empirically confirmed—as it may well be—Marx would have won the argument concerning the dominance of matter, but not its primacy over ideas. Instead, matter and ideas, like mass and energy, would be equivalent, and theology would be materialism.

Be all this as it may, the important lesson to be learnt from this historic example of the evolution of a myth through symbol manipulation is that philosophy encounters pitfalls and confusions by the failure of its practitioners to distinguish clearly between its mythology (that is, the models and interrelationships from which it presumes to derive both nonempirical and empirical consequences), on the one hand, and the empirical testing and confirmation of the content and consequences of its mythology, on the other. The latter constitutes the valuable and useful part of philosophy and is what distinguishes it from, say, mathematics and other definitions and dogmas that are pure inventions of the mind—symbols and symbol manipulation exercises—without any necessary empirical consequences.[52]

6. FRIEDRICH NIETZSCHE (1844–1900)

Nietzsche is a classic study in Adlerian striving for excellence—to equal or surpass rivals (or those he considered rivals)—with the resulting neurotic problems, including self-alienation from man, woman, God, religion, and Bible and setting up his own equivalents in a fantasy world.

Nietzsche's God—Superman—was the dialectic (antithesis) of the Christian God: a god of the rich, the aristocratic, elect few, the strong, the wicked and hating, the uncompassionate, et cetera. Nietzsche was the antithesis of existing systems and values, the theoretical Alistair Crowley, the left-hand pathman, et cetera—all because of his jealousy and grudging respect and admiration of the founders of existing systems and his desire to rival and outdo them, in the manner of Schopenhauer striving to surpass Hegel. Like some envious people, he tried to obtain quick and easy fame (or notoriety) by contradicting the behavior and doctrines of supposed rivals. Yet all he said was not necessarily nonsense or worthless; he merely expounded opposing viewpoints for what they might be worth.

Just as Sigmund Freud based his psychoanalytical system on Schopenhauer's *will* (to survive by procreation) or sex instinct, so Alfred Adler based his psychoanalytical system on Nietzsche's *will to power*, or competitive instinct, toward success and perfection. The one (sex instinct) was a universal instinct, the other (striving for excellence) an individual instinct, an instinct of the few. (Hence Freud's was group-oriented, Adler's individual-oriented psychoanalysis. Morever, Freud's *individual* unconscious was socialized into the *collective* unconscious in Jungian psychoanalysis.)

Again, just as the ex-clergyman, Thomas Robert Malthus, formulated his theory of population on the basis of competition for limited life-sustaining resources, thus transferring industrial competition to the population-resource field, so Darwin applied the Malthusian theory to the wider field of biology. In turn, Nietzsche adopted Darwinism—survival of the fittest, not the weakest, as in Christianity—to the general principle of life: survival of the strong, the elect, the uncompassionate, not the weak, the many, the compassionate; selection and breeding of the fittest and elimination of the weak (euthanasia.)

Darwin, however, may have had a much earlier model than Malthus: Plato, the Greek philosopher, whose *devolutionary* theory, as expounded in the *Timaeus*, is the exact antithesis of Darwin's evolutionary theory. Darwin merely stood Plato on his head and thus may have been the first "transvaluer" in the Nietzschean sense and, in this respect also, a spiritual precursor and mentor of Nietzsche. In this connection, however, one must not overlook Marx, another transvaluer—of Hegel, same as Schopenhauer. Schopenhauer stood Hegel on his head by extolling the Greek irrational element of soul—appetite, renamed will by Schopenhauer—at the expense of the rational element, that is, mind, reason or idea, which Hegel extolled. Similarly, Marx extolled matter (dialectical materialism) over form or idea, which was Hegel's preference (dialectical idealism). Thus the dialectic opposites, Plato-Darwin, Plato and Hegel-Schopenhauer and Marx, were the true spiritual precursors of Nietzsche, furnishing appropriate models in the domain of transvaluation of values.

Jean-Paul Sartre's concept of "being and nothingness" is a witting or unwitting takeoff on Nietzsche's "superman," that is, the self-overcoming or self-surpassing man. The "self" that superman overcomes is the self of "being and nothingness"—the self that can be typed or stereotyped (the self of being) and that, when surpassed, is reduced to "nothingness"; it is the *static self* of convention. The self that surpasses, the overcoming self, is what Sartre refers to as the "self of existence," the self that stands out of its (static) self (*ex-sistere* in Latin = to stand out) and takes stock of the possibilities open to it: the *dynamic self* that is always on the move, always achieving, and therefore cannot be typed or stereotyped. For it is never long enough in any one role to be captured, pigeonholed, and given a label, a nature, or an essence.

Nietzsche's *Beyond Good and Evil* (1886) was based on his assumption that there are higher criteria that override the conventional antithetical values and that these conventional values must serve whether good or evil, true or false: e.g. the higher criterion of survival; even mendacity is justified (according to Nietzsche) if it promotes self-preservation. This viewpoint is reminiscent of, and is of the same kind as, Plato's argument for deliberate deception by governments in the higher interest (i.e., survival) of the state. At this level, Nietzsche seems to have already surpassed the issue of transvaluation (i.e., inversion) of values (such as the Schopenhauerian inversion of the Hegelian reason-over-matter to will(matter)-over-reason). In fact, however, he has not done so. Instead of a higher value (synthesis) superseding the dialectical components he merely returns to the process of transvaluation in another guise: he first *transvalues* conventional values by espousing opposing values, then *subsumes* the conventional values in their opposites. In practice, subsumption is impossible, amounting to *elimination* of the conventional values and the substitution of their opposites.

This issue is of more than formal interest. For Nietzsche, "beyond good and evil" means "beyond true and false," and vice versa, so that, for him, the epistemological problem (truth and falsehood) is the reverse side of the ethical-moral problem (good and evil). What is important here to note is that this position leads straight to dogma. In applying the Cartesian touchstone of doubt to dialectical values Nietzsche is not thereby led to Cartesian self-certitude but to dogmatic doubt (cynicism) and to dogma. For beyond true and false lies reason, which serves both truth and falsehood, as well as dogma, which, like reason, is neither true nor false because beyond sensible and nonsensible (intuitive)—but especially sensible—empirical confirmation or disproof. The test of sense-experience serves as the ultimate check on nonsensible or intuitive experience. Thus, in espousing a position beyond true and false Nietzsche is, in fact, making an appeal to reason that is also an appeal to intuition and to dogma. Reason, definition, and dogma are the only *absolute* values that lie beyond the clash and reach of dialectics. All else is *relative*, good as well as evil, truth as well as falsehood: *relative* (to experience) hence *provisional* and, therefore, subject to change. There is no absolute value, no certitude except value judgment (on which logic, i.e., reason, goes to work explicatively), reason itself, definition, and dogma. Since, however, logic or reason accommodates all absolutes, it is the absolute of absolutes.

It could be concluded, therefore, that in *Beyond Good and Evil* Nietzsche was not interested in the validity of experience but in the ancient Greek mystic of reason and other nonheuristic dogmas.

Nietzsche furnishes in himself a classic case of the trinity of Admiration-Envy-Hatred (the basis of Adlerian psychoanalysis). He begins by admiring his heroes or role models; then, desiring to become like them, envies them; then, unable to become like them and feeling inferior, hates them. In the end, he contradicts them, as the quickest and cheapest way to become (he believes) as famous as they. This may be termed the dialectical route to fame or notoriety. His is a very complex—and complexé—case of the secret admirer: in regard to his idols (and supposed opponents) a poseur who, as it happens, also calls attention to opposing points of view for what they may be worth; in regard to himself, a sincere man.

A nay-sayer to the negative (negation of negation) thereby becoming a yes-sayer to the positive: this is how Nietzsche portrays himself. He is the transvaluer of all existing (and impliedly negative) values into their positive, dialectical opposites. However, he does not altogether denounce what he regards as negative or evil—he feels it has a role to play in life as much as its opposite value: the Greeks, he asserts, were first savage before becoming civilized, overcoming their barbarism. Whence barbarism, he holds, is an inevitable prelude to civilization. Nietzsche's self-appointed role was therefore to accentuate the opposite, not to synthesize dialectical values in Hegelian fashion. For he sees in life merely a continuing alternation, not a synthesis, of dialectical values.

NIETZSCHE AND NIHILISM

The concept of nihilism contains the following elements:

(a) Goallessness, like evolution: everything lacks meaning, value.
(b) Contrary to, and destructive of, life.
(c) Reduction of morality to nothing:
     (i) by judgment
     (ii) by action

For Nietzsche, there must be added a fourth element:

(d) Reconstruction of new values—the transvalues: hence the "eternal return" or recurrence—continual destruction and reconstruction in the realm of values, more or less Heraclitus's continual destruction of the cosmos by conflagration and the resurrection of a new order, phoenixlike, from the ashes.

Thus nihilism is a point of view that holds that everything lacks meaning and therefore value, both intrinsic and extrinsic: intrinsic because meaningless, extrinsic because lacking purpose or goal. In short, there is nothing to existence. Hence, so-called traditional or conventional values and beliefs are without objective foundation or empirical truth (the Thrasymachian doctrine). Consequently, all systems of social organization and morality deserve to be destroyed—reduced to nothing.

In strict logic, nihilism should not be followed by any construction or reconstruction but should, in the political arena, result and remain in anarchy: complete destruction of government. However, this was not the case so far as Nietzsche is concerned. For him, nihilism represents a transition from "No" to "Yes," from devaluation to revaluation (transvaluation) of all existing values. In short, in the thought of Nietzsche, *nihilism is the destruction of conventional values and the setting up in their place of their dialectical opposites* (the same procedure that Marx adopted via-à-vis Hegelian idealism). Although what Nietzsche dubs the "eternal return" is the never-ending cycle of destruction-reconstruction, what returns is never the same as what is destroyed, but its opposite. This means *an endless alternation of dialectical values, rather than a recurrence of the same values.* Thus the small, weak, and decadent man so much detested by Nietzsche to the point of disgust will return alternatingly with his superman. This is in keeping with *Nietzsche's yea-saying to all aspects of life, provided dialectical aspects do not co-exist but alternate.* For Nietzsche is not a Hegelian synthesizer but a Marxian eliminator of what exists and its substitution by its opposite.

NIHILISM AND HISTORY

The evolutionary theory of history (R. G. Collingwood, *The Idea of History*) holds that there is no goal of history—only a movement from an unknown past to an unknown future.

Hegel held that history has a goal *within* it, according to which human passions (intuition, feelings) serve the cunning ends of human reason and, *a fortiori*, of Absolute Idea or Spirit; while Reinhold Niebuhr held to the opposite view, that history has a goal *outside* it in Jesus Christ, its beginning (first coming) and its end (second coming or parousia) as proclaimed by the Christian religion and the Church. (Nietzsche's view, be it noted, is a variation on the "savior doctrine" of the old religion of Persia preached by Zoroaster.)

Both Hegel and Niebuhr reject the evolutionary theory of history, which clearly reflects the doctrine of nihilism, espoused by Nietzsche.

GOD AND SUPERMAN

Feuerbach was enamored of man and wanted him to reclaim his divinity from the phantom God of Christianity. Nietzsche went further: once man reclaimed his divinity, the phantom God was no more, and in his place Nietzsche would install man in the guise of superman—the self-surpassing, self-overcoming man, the man become God. The phantom God was dead for good. ("Gott ist tot.")

The principal characteristic of Nietzschean superman is that he is above (super) all morality, all conventional dialectical values of good and evil, true and false, because he makes his own values to serve his own interests, not those of others. On the contrary, he makes others serve his own interests, not their own. He is none other than Machiavelli's prince under another name.

NIETZSCHE AN ATHEIST?

Nietzsche was neither anti-Christ nor anti-God, but anti– a certain conception of Jesus and of God—that developed by institutional Christianity as represented by the Church. Nietzsche admired heroes—those who had achieved and become famous and recognized by all men. These were the role models he sought to emulate.

So far was Nietzsche from being an atheist and, on the contrary, so much did he want to be like Christ, like God, like every one of his heroes, that his excessive admiration turned to envy, then hatred (the Nietzschean syndrome)—and eventual madness[53]—because of his self-acknowledged weakness and inability to become like, and achieve the fame, respect and admiration accorded, his role models. He, consequently, sought the quickest and cheapest route to fame or notoriety: the dialectical route of contradiction of the positions represented by his role models, the inversion (transvaluation) of the values that they espoused. In this manner, he sought, by contradiction, to free himself of the hold his models had on him. Once free, however, he became lost and had to find his bearings back to some order—by rebuilding something the opposite of what he destroyed, not the thing that he envied and destroyed, as indicated by his doctrine of eternal recurrence. Unlike his later, apparent disciple, Sartre, Nietzsche never found his way back to conventional values.

It may thus be concluded that Nietzsche was not a genuine atheist, in the conventional sense, but a fake atheist, a poseur—an atheist by default, by the accident of not being able to be like his admired heroes: God, Christ, Schopenhauer, Wagner, et cetera. Nietzsche was possessed of a great desire for fame at the same time that he was possessed of a great sense of inferiority.

INFLUENCE OF FEUERBACH, SCHOPENHAUER, AND MARX ON NIETZSCHE

Like Feuerbach, Schopenhauer, and Marx, Nietzsche was an iconoclast, a destroyer of sacred and conventional idols, more in the spirit of rivalry that marked Schopenhauer vis-à-vis Hegel than in the spirit of inquiry that distinguished Marx.

Again, like Schopenhauer and Marx, who attempted to discover completely different systems from Hegel's—with Schopenhauer substituting *idea* for *matter* (*world*) and *will* for *idea* as the true equivalent for Kant's *thing-in-itself*; and Marx substituting *matter* for *idea*—Nietzsche destroyed any given position in favor of its opposite. Combining the spirit of rivalry with the dialectic technique, he neither invented something new nor moved on to a development of his thought.

The concept of "eternal return" was a primordial concept dating back to Heraclitus. Nietzsche only gave it a new meaning as the alternation of dialectic positions. His "superman," while interesting, turns out not to be a superior kind of human being. Supposedly above the dialectics of moral values, superman merely makes his own values by opting for those values condemned by society: selfishness, naked power, et cetera. He neither rises above nor synthesizes values. Rather is he partial to the unconventional.

Nietzsche's "will to power" is a variation on Schopenhauer's "will" (to live and procreate), power being what Nietzsche, physically and mentally sick, needed most to compensate for his inferiority complex, his deteriorating health that would eventually lead to an early death. He regarded sexuality as an expression of the "will to power," to dominate, and as being secondary to power, in the same way that Marx regarded "idealism" as secondary to "materialism."

The "God is dead" idea is not original, going back to Feuerbach.

Nietzsche merely reversed the order of things. Instead of man regaining his divinity, God becoming man, as was Feuerbach's intention, man becomes God (anthropology becomes theology) in the form of Superman in the Nietzschean inversion of Feuerbach.

Nietzsche's claim to fame rests not on his ideas but on the fact that he tilted at conventional values by calling attention to their opposites.

SARTRE AND NIETZSCHEAN SUPERMAN

Jean-Paul Sartre's concept of "being and nothingness" is a conscious or unconscious takeoff on Nietzsche's superman, the self-overcoming or self-surpassing man. The self that superman overcomes is the self of being and nothingness, the self that can be pigeonholed and typed, that has nature or essence (''being'') and that when surpassed is reduced to nothingness.

So long as one exists, one has no being, only existence or becoming. Only at death does one have being, nature, or essence. At death existence degenerates into being.

There is, however, one respect in which Sartrean existential man differs from Nietzschean superman, at any rate in Sartre's later period. In his early period, before he converted to Marxism, Sartre's existential man is identical with Nietzschean superman: he makes his own values, serves (and makes others serve) his own interests. Others are objects to be used by existential man for his own benefit. In his later period, after converting to Marxism and discovering humanism—the value of the individual-in-society, of man as species rather than an atomic unit—Sartre seemed to have returned to some conventional values, and to cease regarding others as objects, a situation that superman inhabits permanently. Thus once he rediscovered society through Marxism, Sartre rediscovered morality within society.

DESTRUCTIVE FALLOUT FROM NIETZSCHE'S IDEAS

Nietzsche's ideas may properly be described as ''half-baked'' or incomplete, and his work fell short of the goals that he apparently set himself. His very first published work, *The Birth of Tragedy Out of the Spirit of Music* (1871), in which he sought to combine Arthur Schopenhauer's metaphysic of will with Richard Wagner's theory of art (as a blend of poetry, music, and drama), sets out the pattern of what he sought to achieve in life but never did, a work that was never equaled by anything he subsequently wrote. The basic ideas of *The Birth of Tragedy* are three and simple:

(a) In the beginning: Apollo and Dionysus are in conflict in Greek antiquity (order or idea versus destructive and creative power).
(b) Later: Apollo crushed Dionysus during the (Socratic) period of science and the Englightenment in Europe, when reason triumphed over blind destructive power.
(c) Then and finally: Dionysus (as creative power) triumphed over Apollo (reason) in the romantic period of Schopenhauer's philosophy and Wagner's music. The defeat of reason is just, in Nietzsche's view, because behind all reason, all logic, stand the irrational value judgments, appetites, and biases, the self-interest of the scholar—even the will to deceive.[54]

In his subsequent works Nietzsche was never able to use the creative force of Dionysus to produce something new. He remained trapped in the destructive stage of his Dionysian potential. It may be that his short life was responsible for this apparent arrest in his development.

It is clear, in any case, that admirers of Nietzsche (like the Nazis) failed to recognize both the relativity and the flaws in his ideas. For example, he approved of all primordial instincts or basic values—the so-called Aryan values: elitism, the master-race concept, et cetera; not as being good or evil, per se, but as being basically *necessary* in order to be subsequently brought under control, that is, sublimated or spiritualized, so as to yield culture—any kind of culture.[55] The primary instinct, for Nietzsche, is *violence*, not sex, and he saw the "sweetness and light" of Greek culture as being the result of the sublimation of the combative instinct of the ancient Greeks. The "sublime" arises, thus, from sublimating what originally existed in nonsublime form. These so-called primordial values were, therefore, not ideals or ends in themselves, but raw material for the fabrication of culture. Nietzsche's admirers conveniently ignored this fundamental aspect and *sine qua non* of his "master race" doctrine.

Furthermore, Nietzsche, in contrast to Kant, makes clear that morality—i.e., all values, whether Aryan or other—is *never absolute* or valid for all societies and all times, but relative and valid only for the particular society in which, and for those within it by whom, it is espoused.

Gobineau, Hitler, and others who were attracted by Nietzsche's Aryan master-race concept and sought to apply it to other groups not only missed or ignored all the fine points and qualifications of his doctrine, but changed what Nietzsche regarded as a sociological into a "biological" and "scientific" concept, transforming into an absolute what Nietzsche propounded as a relative concept with a pragmatic goal: its transcendence or sublimation in cultural creativity. However, those who sought to apply the master-race concept to others have logic, if not science and biology, on their side. A master race cannot be master except in relation to all other races—Nietzsche's qualifications notwithstanding. A master race cannot be a concept relative only to a single society.

Even with all the qualifications necessary for the proper interpretation and understanding of Nietzsche's so-called Aryan values and concept of morality, his doctrine of sublimation of primordial values is of questionable validity. What, after all, Nietzsche is saying is that there was a time when the ancient Greeks lacked culture, as did the Germans of his day. This kind of statement is nonsense to all but those who—like Plato and Nietzsche, among others—make arbitrary judgments and distinctions between those they choose to call barbarians and those they choose to call civilized. So far was Nietzsche himself from understanding the implications of his own Dionysian model that he either ignored the *simultaneous* presence of the destructive frenzy and the creative elements—religious and viticultural aspects—in Dionysus or else he arbitrarily assumed—as he, in fact, did—that violence or raw power and culture are sequential and mutually exclusive forces. Which, of course, is nonsense, since violence is not excluded from any kind of culture.

In regard to morality Nietzsche was a humbug. He wrote a lot about morality—which is nothing if not ethics or mutuality—but apparently misunderstood everything about it. Exposing cant, as he did, is one thing, and here he did a good job on the church as an institution—he merely followed in Marx's footsteps. But reversing ("transvaluing," as he termed it) established doctrine is not the solution to cant. Rather is it a replacement of one form of cant by another. Morality implies reciprocity, mutuality of action, of benefits. On no principle of morality could the Nietzschean concept of superman, the man above all law, all morality, be justified in any society. There cannot be a *class* of supermen, only one individual: the god or tyrant of the society. Even Plato's "guardians" of society were within the law. In effect, Nietzsche's superman is but another version of Machiavelli's Prince—the unscrupulous, amoral, unethical individual whose every action is its own justification: whose selfish ends are the sole criterion of a morality that relates to him alone (a contradiction in terms).

Only a Nietzsche or a Machiavelli would write books advocating and extolling the tyranny of the individual. And only a man without conscience, both individual and social, would enunciate a superman doctrine.

NOTES

1. See Karl R. Popper, *The Open Society and Its Enemies*, vols. I & II (London: Routledge & Kegan Paul, 1945). Also, Bertrand Russell, *History of Western Philosophy* (George Allen & Unwin, 1946), passim.
2. René Descartes, *Discourse on Method* (London: Penguin Classics, 1975).
3. Martin Heidegger, *Basic Writings* (London: Routledge & Kegan Paul, 1948), p. 279. Heidegger goes on to point out that, in fact, the inverse is meant: "I am, therefore I think" ("sum, ergo cogito"), *sum* being the ground of *cogito*, existence the ground of thinking.
4. Hans Küng, *Does God Exist?* (New York: Vintage Books, 1981), pp. 13–14.
5. Descartes states in Discourse 4: "I see very clearly that in order to think one must exist" (London, New York: Penguin Classics, 1975), p. 54.
6. As will be seen, from a different perspective, in Book Three, chapter 5, *thought* and

doubt were the two necessary and sufficient conditions for human existence, according to the ancient Greek academic philosophers. Hence, anyone who thought and doubted must automaticaly be regarded as an empirical existent: thought, because it implies *idea* (or *form*) and doubt because it implies unreliability of the human senses in regard to *matter* (or material objects). These conditions, however, are both inadequate and nonsensical as confirmation of the empirical existence of an object which is also the thinking subject. Thus, Descartes's proof of his own existence is seen to be nonsensical.

7. Anselm (1033–1109 C.E.), the eleventh-century Archbishop of Canterbury, argued that God, being the most perfect being conceivable, must necessarily exist really or he would not be the most perfect being; hence, God exists. This, of course, is nothing but circular reasoning since Anselm regards real (i.e., empirical) existence as one of the elements in his definition of perfection. Not only can one not demonstrate by argument what is assumed in the argument, but, as Kant pointed out, empirical existence is not an attribute of perfection or anything else. Anselm's error is traceable to the automatic ascription of empirical existence to any object of thought.

8. E.g., the syllogism: The sun is in my cigarette lighter, My cigarette lighter is in my pocket, Therefore, the sun is in my pocket. The conclusion is consistent but empirically invalid because the major premise is empirically invalid.

9. This is a question-begging phrase since sound in practice is the test of a sound theory, not the other way round.

10. An interesting example of this is Karl Marx's theory of ''dialectical materialism'' as the ''inexorable law of economic evolution,'' involving the replacement of capitalism by socialism. In spite of the presumed automatic effect of his ''law,'' Marx did not leave things to chance to work themselves out, but sought, simultaneously, to implement his ''sound law'' by organizing the workers and inciting them to take the necessary revolutionary action that would ensure that socialism *did*, in fact, come to pass, replacing capitalism: a judicious combination of theory and practice, or idealism and pragmatism. Marx lived long enough to recognize that there is no automatic guarantee of a successful transition from blueprint to empirical reality. His successors have yet to grasp the lesson of experience: that it is the empirical reality that tests the theory, not the other way round.

11. See especially, Descartes, op. cit, Discourse No. 4.

12. Only definition and dogma are certain, but they do not count as knowledge.

13. Leibniz's view is correct in that the world is apprehensible through the senses, and even nuclear particles are inferred to exist objectively through the traces they leave on an emulsion. Kant is right, however, in that sensation mediates between man and an external object.

14. See Thomas S. Kuhn, *The Structure of Scientific Revolutions* 2d ed. (Chicago: University of Chicago Press, 1970), chapters IX and X. The subject of paradigm change will be discussed in more detail in Book Three, chapter 4.

15. As we shall see in another section of this chapter, Arthur Schopenhauer adopted Kant's interpretation of ''thing-in-itself'' as ''will,'' making it the subject of a lengthy dissertation in his famous book, *The World as Will and Idea* (1818).

16. Karl Popper, *Objective Knowledge*, rev. ed. (London, New York: Oxford University Press, 1981), pp. 194–97, 261–65, and passim.

17. For further examination and criticism of Popper's view see Book Three, chapter 4, section 8 (b).

18. The relationship between the two kinds of ''thing-in-itself'' of the human being—physical and moral—is not clearly stated by Kant. But it is left to be inferred that they are one and the same thing—mind, which becomes known only in action as will.

19. Bertrand Russell, *A Free Man's Worship* (London: Unwin Paperbacks, 1976), p. 105.
20. See R. B. Perry, *Realms of Value* (Cambridge: Harvard University Press, 1954), pp. 82, 94.
21. The concept of alienation of Absolute Idea has intellectual affinity with the Gnostic concept of alienation of soul or light in the darkness of the world made by Ialdabaoth, the God of Justice. The Gnostic concept seems also to have inspired Heidegger's concept of *Dasein* or "thrownness into the world." Neither Hegel nor Heidegger, however, has any equivalent of the Gnostic (individual or personal) Savior in his system. This was left for other minds (notably, Nietzsche and Hitler) to supply.
22. The dynamic nature of the ideas was only implicit in Plato's system, as could be inferred from his definition of *time* as the "moving image of eternity," eternity consisting of the eternal forms or ideas that, by Plato's definition, are outside time.
23. See Bertrand Russell, *History of Western Philosophy* (London: Unwin Paperbacks, 1979), p. 67.
24. Editor's preface to R. G. Collingwood, *The Idea of History* (London, New York: Oxford University Press, 1980), p. xv.
25. The list of dominant nations is not intended to be exhaustive but only indicative.
26. In this connection it is interesting to note that in the Germany of before both World Wars the melodic pattern of patriotic songs was indistinguishable from that of church hymns. The classic example is the German national anthem, which is both patriotic song and melody of a religious hymn.
27. Most would agree that any individual or nation is *an* incarnation of Absolute Idea, Spirit, or God. It is a different matter altogether whether or not a given individual or nation is *the* incarnation of such entity.
28. See Book Three, chapter 7, on Religion where the relationship between religion and art is discussed.
29. See Book Two, section B, chapter 14.
30. Expounded in Schopenhauer's *The World as Will and Idea* (1818).
31. The author is indebted to the following sources for Schopenhauer's thought: the Penguin edition of Schopenhauer's writings and Bertrand Russell, op. cit., Book Three, Part 2, Ch. xxiv.
32. See Crane Brinton, *The Shaping of the Modern Mind* (Mentor Books, 1953) chapter 7. This is a useful historical survey of ideas and intellectual movements by a noted historian.
33. Marx was not the originator of socialism or communism (stateless socialism). This ideology dates back, in the Jewish tradition, to the Essenes and the early Christians (Acts 2:44–45; 4:31–37), who modeled their communal life on the practice of the Essenes. What was truly Marxian was the method he advocated for the establishment of socialism: *force*, namely, a working-class dictatorship and elimination of the rich and all opponents of the dictatorship, in place of *voluntary choice*, the method used by the Essenes and the early Christians. Marx himself was, throughout his adult life, a dialectical phenomenon conforming to his own doctrine: owners(hip) of capital (Engels, his friend and benefactor, and the capitalists) balanced by nonowners(hip) of capital (Marx and the working classes). And whereas his doctrine did not produce a Hegelian synthetic, but an Aristotelian eliminatory solution, his dialectical relationship to Engels produced a true Hegelian synthesis in their collaboration and writings.
34. Marx was not the first to espouse a doctrine of state intervention in the economy. The Mercantilists preceded him in this, and even Adam Smith propounded a doctrine of limited state intervention in the domain of defence, justice, education, and public

works (*Wealth of Nations*, Book V, chapter 1). Both Smith and Marx were philosophers-turned-economists, although with different approaches to policy. Twentieth-century economists, lacking the broad liberal and philosophical background of the earlier British and Continental economists tend to go the other way, ending their careers as philosophers.

35. As indicated earlier (Book Two, section A, Part I, chapter 2), occidental philosophers overlooked the effective compression of the two philosophical worlds into one by Aristotle's concept of soul.

36. Karl Marx, *Capital*.

37. L. Feuerbach, *The Essence of Christianity* (1841), transl. into English by George Eliot (1853) (New York: Harper Torchbooks, 1957).

38. The religious nature of Marxism-Communism and its close ties to Christianity—for all of Marx's vituperation against that religion—is strikingly brought out by the oft-recorded fact that if, for one reason or another, a Marxist-Communist breaks with the Party he will not give up the millennial dream, but is only likely to exchange apocalypse and millennium now for apocalypse and millennium later. In short, a disillusioned Marxist-Communist is apt to convert to Roman Catholic Christianity, which, additionally, is structured on similar authoritarian lines as the Party.

39. Much of what follows on the evaluation of Marx's philosophy has benefited from a reading of Helmut Gollwitzer, *Athéisme marxiste et foi chrétienne* (translated from the German by Bernard Delez [Casterman, 1965]), from which the quotations are culled and translated into English by the present author.

40. In the light of Marx's own theory, this expectation was naive. For if his theory is correct, that the God-concept was developed by capitalists to provide a safeguard for property rights, then even a one-class state would still have need of a theology both to justify its exclusive ownership of the means of production and to protect its rights against opponents since, in the nature of the dialectic process, opposition is bound to arise even to a one-class society.

41. This notion of man as God was worked up in Nietzsche's *Thus Spake Zarathustra* into the entity known as Superman (self-overcoming man, a Dionysian) and was reflected in Martin Buber's super-Jew and Hitler's Aryan man. Ironically, Marx's endorsement of Feuerbach's man-God (or God-man) thesis was an unintended affirmation of the central doctrine of Christianity (the very butt of Marx's attack!) just as Martin Buber's super-Jew is a secular reflection of Jesus.

42. This opinion is shared by a leading Ceylonese (Sri Lankan) Christian, Daniel T. Niles, who wrote in *Die Botschaft für die Welt* (Munich, 1960), p. 38 ff: "The Gospel lends importance to the struggle for life while assigning it second place . . . To bread is given the role of assisting and assuring authentic living and the struggle for bread is freed from the bitterness which it would otherwise engender. It is correct that religion is the opium of the masses; because true religion puts to sleep the desire for revenge" (Helmut Gollwitzer, op. cit., p. 31).

43. It has been argued above that philosophy and theology are also independent of any particular system of organization of production. The same can be said for politics and law, which exist under every economic system.

44. This argument is equally fatal to Marxism as dialectical *materialism* since it is, in fact, admitting that it is dialectical *idealism*, independent of matter. But the argument is less extreme than its presentation warrants: all that can properly be said is that Marxism (dialectical materialism) is independent of a particular system of production, not of matter as such. But if it is, then it collapses as a theory, for there is then no basis for linking socialism with private enterprise capitalism, attacking that form of capitalism, or ever knowing how, when, or if socialism can ever come about.

45. Georg Klaus, *Jesuiten, Gott, Materie. Des Jesuitenpaters Wetter Revolte wider Vernunft und Wissenschaft* (Berlin, 1958), pp. 126, 127.
46. It may be noted that—*pace* Plato—philosophical ideas are neither absolute nor certain but, like scientific ideas, provisional and subject to doubt and change.
47. Arnold J. Toynbee was later to apply this same dialectic method, which he redesignated "challenge and response" to his monumental *A Study of History*.
48. This view was subsequently revived in the biological sphere by Julian Huxley (*Religion without Revelation*) in another brand of humanism ("theology is human evolutionary biology"). Père Pierre Teilhard de Chardin (*Le Phénomène Humain*), combining palaeontology and biology with philosophy and Christology, concluded from this hybridization that "theology is noetics"—more or less—the evolution of mind or soul.
49. Darwin had not yet come along to dethrone man from his biblical pedestal in the Book of Genesis.
50. With the apparent exception of his *Beyond Good and Evil* in which he outlined a "code of morality" for his superman (the new Machiavelli). Being beyond conventional notions and standards of good and evil, this being devises his own morality that could use good and evil methods indifferently to achieve his objectives.
51. He should have added: "Long live God, matter!" Instead he intoned: "Long live superman!" He adopted the humanism of Feuerbach rather than the materialism of Marx.
52. Where a society's myth enshrines empirical wisdom it is also scientific.
53. It is possible, as some maintain, that Nietzsche's madness was brought on by syphilis, which affects the brain in its later stages. This author is convinced, however, that even in the absence of syphilis Nietzsche would have become mad, in any case, because of his great envy and hatred of the great.
54. Hegel's Aristotelian theory that behind all passions stands the cunning of reason as their directing force is here inverted (transvalued) by Nietzsche.
55. This is a strange and noninformative argument, saying in effect whatever is, is necessary.

Chapter 4

Metaphysics: Nature and Destiny of Man

1. THE PERSIAN BEQUEST

Occidental metaphysics is a product of many sources, but major credit must go to Zoroastrianism, the religion of ancient Persia. The doctrines of spiritual forces of Light (Good) and Darkness (Evil), the Last Days of conflict between the supporters of these two forces (eschatology), and the emergence of a Savior of Mankind (Saoshyant) who would raise the dead and restore them to the Light or consign them to the Darkness after Judgment: these are basic Persian ingredients in the blend of contemporary occidental metaphysics with strong theological undertones.

From the doctrine of spiritual forces of Light and Darkness sprouted the concept of the soul of man in affinity with the World Soul, God or the Good: the Atman and Brahma of Indian mythology, the human and divine soul of Socratic and subsequent Greek metaphysics and philosophy, and the similar doctrine of the Semitic religions of Judaism, Christianity, and Islam.

The doctrine of last things—of global conflict and the coming of a Savior who would raise the dead—started a similar tradition in Pharisaic Judaism, as well as a tradition of avatars, specifically the reincarnated saviors of mankind: Krishna, Buddha, and Jesus, among others.

The doctrine of man as a being composed of a duality of matter and spirit (or soul), of elements of both Good and Evil, is a basic plank in occidental metaphysical and philosophic thought, deriving from the ancient religion of Persia, and is a fundamental tenet of Hinduism, Buddhism, and the Semitic religions. Similarly, the doctrine of the destiny of the human being—to reunite with, or stand in the presence of, the Great Light or Spirit—finds sympathetic echoes in Hinduism, Buddhism, and the Semitic religions.

2. CHRISTIAN THEOLOGY

The renowned American Protestant theologian, Reinhold Niebuhr, is chosen as a representative of the Christian theological doctrine of the nature and destiny of man. No attempt is made here to expound all of Niebuhr's ideas or to present the entire gamut of his thinking. Only a summary—very brief—of his main ideas is attempted in a way that highlights his views on the nature and destiny of man.[1]

In order to appreciate Niebuhr's thought it is necessary to know his concept and understanding of history. Basing his view on strictly biblical (New Testament) literature, he defines history as the temporal interlude between the first and the expected second coming of Jesus. He thus ignores all that went on before the birth of Jesus as unimportant except in leading up to his birth. The present, therefore, consists in history as he defines it, the future in the posthistorical (or nonhistorical) sequel. The transition from history (present) to the future is through the cataclysms of the Last Day and the Judgment that follows it. In this final Judgment consists the fulfillment of history—an event outside history itself. (This is the typical view of those who—like Plato—do not trust the world of change, for one reason or another, and prefer to put the *raison d'être* of the world—which is conveniently identified as the authority of their pet desires—outside of the world itself.)

The present (history) is, accordingly, finite and mutable—subject to the change that will intervene at the Last Day. Therefore, no finalities or goals could be found *within* history or historical time. All finalities lie beyond and outside history. Within history (the Christian's vale of tears) one only encounters the dialectic of good and evil, rise and downfall.

Man is, by nature, a finite and mutable animal living within a finite and mutable history. His finiteness and mutability constitute the limits of his freedom—his freedom to create. For these limits provoke tension[2] within man, leading to creativity and corresponding possibilities in the spiritual arena. Two choices are open to man: either to accept the responsibility of his creative freedom or to shirk, by seeking to escape, his responsibility.

Where he ignores his finiteness and mutability man falls into the sin of pride. He so falls when he seeks finality or finite goals within history—e.g., the goal of perfection (shades of Plato!). On the other hand, where he seeks to abdicate his responsibility and escape from his creative tension, he descends into materialism, sensuality, or lust. Either way, the consequences are destructive for man. Like a daimon, man is creative where he acknowledges his responsibility, destructive where he chooses ignorance and lust (shades of Nietzsche's Dionysian man!).

100

Man's search for finality within history—such as the perfectionism of progressive movements—is evidence of his sin and pride and is doomed because he ignores the final Judgment that goes with fulfillment. For man, like history itself, stands under the Judgment of God at the end of history. His destiny is Apocalypse, the new Heaven and the new Earth, and Judgment, with Paradise and Hell as appropriate rewards.

Such is Niebuhr's conception and doctrine of the nature and destiny of man. His definition of history is strictly New Testament, as is his doctrine of the fulfilment of history (which is faithful to the Heraclitian myth of the eternal cosmic return following periodic cosmic conflagrations). Like Plato, Niebuhr denigrates the world of sense and finds no final or satisfactory answers in it, such as, for example, the concept of society as the guarantor of human values. And, like Plato, he finds only degeneration, collapse, and decay.

Niebuhr condemns the idea of progress, an idea oriented to the future though not to future existence but to the future conceived within history (present existence) and for this very reason regarded as reprehensible. Niebuhr is therefore opposed, in principle, to all who seek and hope for goals within history (Marxists, for example) or who do not posit an existence or goals outside history. Existentialists are right, according to Niebuhr, to see no meaning or goal in history and historical existence, but wrong in seeing no goal for present historical existence. Similarly, Niebuhr would agree with Darwin and Bergson in seeing evolution as purposeless within history, but disagree with them for seeing no goal or purpose for historical existence itself or, for that matter, evolution.

No attempt will be made here to examine Niebuhr's basic assumptions, as these stand or fall by his definition of history. Suffice it, therefore, to say that his definition is a nonempirical one, hence, purely mythical. Having said this, it is appropriate to observe that, like Plato, Niebuhr is the ideal utopian, his utopia (future existence) occurring beyond and outside of historical (present) existence. By contrast, utopians of the classical type, starting with the prototypical Sir Thomas More, have always located their utopias in the present historical existence, even if they did not specify a particular geographical location. Niebuhr's utopia is Plato's ideal type shared in common with the Semitic religions and ushered in by some kind of catastrophe (death in the case of Plato, Apocalypse in Niebuhr's case). However, proceeding by structure rather than by terminology alone, it could be argued that the true prototypical utopia is the ideal one of Plato and the Semitic religions (including Niebuhr's) while those of More, Marx, et alii, are departures from the prototype in regard to existential rather than geographical location.

It is consequently true to say that Niebuhr is an existential dialectician contrasting, like Plato, the finiteness and mutability characteristic of present historical existence with the infiniteness and eternal changelessness of future nonhistorical existence. What is most striking about Niebuhr's approach to the nature and destiny of man, however, is the pontifical manner in which he denies others the right to their own dreams and myths—good dreams at that—and the dogmatism with which he presents his own dream as the *only* viable one. As Perry rightly points out:

> Nor is there any duty which forbids man to accept his good dreams as true, provided they do not conflict with his waking knowledge.[3]

The impossibility of empirical testing does not confer an aura of truth on Niebuhr's dream, even if this-world utopian dreams frequently encounter stupendous obstacles to their fulfillment.

3. EVOLUTIONISM: DARWINIAN AND NON-DARWINIAN THEORIES

A. Darwin's Theory of Species Survival by Genetic Mutation and Environmental Adaptation

Darwin's basic doctrine[4] presented in his *Origin of Species* is that species survival is a resultant of two different but concomitant factors:

(a) genetic mutation;
(b) environmental compatibility (or adaptability) (termed "natural selection" by Darwin) of mutants in a changing environment.

Those species that have a greater environmental adaptability survive better than others by having a higher reproduction rate. Not all mutants possess environmental compatibility, even in the artificial breeding of animals and plants.[5]

The crucial issue is thus whether environmental adaptability can be transmitted along with genetic mutation. Says Darwin, those mutants that inherit or possess a higher degree of environmental adaptability will outproduce other mutants and eventually displace them.

One thing is clear: adaptability to environment is not entirely an inherited characteristic but can also be culturally (i.e., socially) transmitted or acquired where not genetically transmissible. These cultural adaptive traits have to be taught and learned by each new generation.

This is the case with the human species. Hence, a restatement of Darwin will read:

Species survival is a resultant of two different concomitant factors—

(a) genetic mutation;
(b) environmental adaptability of mutants to a changing environment, a factor that can be (i) inherited and/or (ii) acquired.

In short, species survival is a matter of gradual and continuing ecological adaptation of random genetic mutations.

Now, of the two motive forces of survival—genetic mutation and natural selection—genetic mutation is a matter of chance, hence unpredictable in its occurrence and results; natural selection is an empirically valid hypothesis, hence predictable, once the adaptability potential is known. Thus there are two elements in survival: chance and law. Since chance, however, is an outcome of law (the product of a fortuitous conjunction of laws, hence unpredictable), species survival is basically a matter of natural law.[6]

Darwin goes on to show that species survival is marked by:

(a) lack of aim or goal (nondirectedness);
(b) lack of any progress orientation;
(c) materialism (i.e., material basis of existence and all its characteristics).

A complete statement of Darwin's theory would therefore run as follows:

Species survival is a matter of gradual and continuing ecological adaptation of random genetic mutations[7] resulting in an undirected, unstructured, and dynamic materialism with regard to any given species.

Darwin's theory is no more than that. It is nonempirical in form and only analogical in its paradigms: Malthus's competitive theory of population[8] and the practice of animal cross-breeding. Its nonempirical nature is underlined by the fact that the time span required for the mutation-ecological adaptation process to work out far exceeds the time span of human and national life and so precludes observed repeatability of the phenomenon; and by the fact that the nonavailability of lost phyla makes the theory only probable. It is, at best, a very good theory and currently the best available that interprets coherently all the known facts.

The traditional presentation of Darwin's theory, following Darwin himself, is open to the logical objection that chance genetic mutations, per se, have nothing to do with species *survival.*The theory merely destroys the creationist doctrine of fixed species propounded in the Book of Genesis. Environmental adaptation is what has to do with species survival. The logically acceptable formulation of Darwin's theory would therefore be the following:

(a) There are no fixed biological species because of chance genetic mutations among species, independently or as a result of environmental changes (genetic mutations).
(b) Those mutations that are best adapted to the environment (which itself is not fixed but always changing) have the best chance of survival, reproducing their kind in greater numbers than others less well adapted and crowding out the latter. By contrast, those mutations that are not adapted to the environment die out (natural selection).

Combining these two statements yields the following:

Species *change* according to chance *genetic mutations* and *survive* according to *natural selection.*

The only point that Creationists and Darwinians have in common is this: at any given time and epoch the species that survive are the best adapted to their environment and their functions.

Cosmic Mutation (Accidents and Shifts) and the Contingency of Life Forms

Since all life is contingent, including that of the planets, any planet that explodes leaves a vacuum that is filled by simultaneous and mutual adjustments among the remaining planets in its solar system. When such a shift occurs there would be a concomitant change in planetary eras that would translate to a geological era for our planet, Earth, putting an end to some species of life and altering the previously existing relationships among the surviving species. Such a situation could have occurred in the past, providing a plausible interpretation of the geological evidence of a flood or an ice age in a bygone era, the disappearance of dinosaurs, and the emergence of the human species to a favorable position on the biological map, owing to a new and more congenial environment. Similar catastrophes may yet recur or others of less than cosmic proportions—such as an uncontrolled use of nuclear weapons—that on a negative hypothesis may endanger the life of various biological species and even extinguish human life in a moment, as was apparently the case with the dodo.

If the foregoing thesis is valid, it implies that human life is contingent over time. It also implies that there is no reason to assume that contemporary man is the final stage in the evolution of the human species. This

104

is in keeping with Darwin's theory of evolution, except that to genetic must be added cosmic (including planetary) mutations as another source of mutation of biological species. The hypothesis of cosmic mutation further implies that neither man nor any other species is a *preferred* life form (manifestation) in the cosmic scheme, less still *the* superior or highest species. Survival would be merely proof of varying degrees of environmental fitness, not of "goodness," "betterness," or "bestness" in any moral or intrinsic sense.

Thus hanging, like the sword of Damocles, over the illusion (derived from procreation) that the human (or any other) species will continue endlessly is the stark fact of the contingency of any manifestation of life. One cosmic catastrophe or terrestrial calamity, and new environmental conditions and a new geological age would result, which could be favorable or hostile to man and/or other biological species.

Geo-Darwinism

From the geological perspective, therefore, the "fittest species" are those that survive through the geological ages: man, the dog, the rat, the ant, the roach, et cetera. In any geological era, man is a product of two forces: his *inherent* and his *acquired* characteristics (i.e., "nature" and "nurture") combined in inverse proportions. Cultural innovations (acquired characteristics for environmental adaptation) play a greater role than genetic mutation (inherited characteristics) in the geobiological evolution of man and inversely in that of most nonhuman animal species. (Exceptions would be, for example, the bee and the termite, which parallel the case of man). Therefore, what most distinguishes man from most other animals is culture rather than heredity, cultural selection rather than genetic heritage. Man's culture and his tools condition his survival, to the extent that he can control the destructive potential of his tools.

The cultural factor in man's adaptation to his environment is so important as to merit being separated out into a special category in the determinants of man's biological evolution. These determinants become three instead of two: genetic mutation, natural selection, and cultural innovation (in response to environmental challenges). Thus, depending on his cultural innovations, man may at one geological age be an earth-bound animal that survives by the bow and arrow, the flint and the hoe. In another geological age or with other cultural implements man becomes an animal that sails the seas, crossing from one part of his planet to another, flies through the air, and journeys to other celestial bodies.

Without his more recent cultural innovations man would remain, like most other animals, completely earthbound and depend for his survival merely on purely biological adaptation to his environment.

Darwinism: The Unpredictable in the Cosmos

Manifestations of being (existence) proceed according to two fundamental principles: (a) law and (b) chance or contingence. Chance (contingence) is a consequence of law in the sense that the conjuncture of the various laws or uniformities of nature is a random affair, occurring in no particular order; whence the consequences of such conjuncture are always unpredictable. Cosmic manifestations therefore conform to the two concomitant principles of predictability and unpredictability, and existence becomes a joint affair of these same principles.

Darwinism emphasizes the contingent aspect of existence, the chance element in survival. We know that life forms will always survive, but which ones cannot be predicted in advance. Darwinism is the contingency aspect of every law in the natural domain, of every scientific hypothesis or provisional truth. It is the element of chance by which any given natural law may be modified or annulled by the impact of other natural laws. It is this possibility that confers a provisional character on every scientific law.

This interpretation of Darwinism makes it possible to understand the nature of Quantum Theory as a discontinuity (or annulment of continuity) brought about by a random conjuncture of other natural events. The same is true of what is called Catastrophe Theory. Thus Evolution Theory, Quantum Theory, and Catastrophe Theory are different names for the same thing manifesting itself in different ways: chance. In the theological field the corresponding term is *free will* (unpredictability), which is contrasted with *predestination* (predictability).

It is evident, therefore, that "unpredictability" is as much a "scientific" principle as "predictability," both being associated with different kinds of impact by factors that are essentially predictable. A God that does not play at dice (Einstein's God) is as much a scientific God as one who does (Planck's God). The manifestation of phenomena is as much a matter of chance as of law.

Science and Darwin's Theory

In his *Language, Logic and God*, Frederick Ferré stated three of the principal characteristics of scientific method as follows:[9]

(a) *Specificity*: It must be of limited generality, i.e., it must explain some events but not others and certainly not *all* events, as otherwise it loses meaning.

(b) *Uniformity, hence predictability*: It must enable the user to project or expect recurrence of the given phenomenon under the same given conditions, so that the future resembles the past.[10]

(c) *Extensibility*: It must have application beyond its immediate data to other data of a similar nature; i.e., it must have general application as an interpretation of events of the particular kind of which it treats.

A fourth characteristic, not mentioned but implied in Ferré's discussion, is:

(d) *Empirical Verification*: It should admit of independent empirical verification of the relevant data by third parties.

Ferré shows how on the basis of these characteristics no scientific method exists capable of establishing God as a scientific concept or entity. By these same tests Darwin's theory cannot be scientifically established. Far from being empirical and predictable, it highlights the *unpredictable* in biological evolution. It imports the element of chance into, and thereby upsets, the principle of predictability ("the future will resemble the past"). It should be noted that chance is not an intervention from without into the phenomenal world—an external intervention or theological miracle, so to speak—but an internal ("endogenous") interruption of normal expectations resulting from the conjunctural operation of uniformities. This principle of "chance within uniformity" or "scientific" (as opposed to theological) chance is as scientific as anything could be within the phenomenal world. To this extent, Darwin's theory, though by its very nature nonempirical, may be said to be scientific.

This same argument necessarily applies to concepts and theories of development in economics, development being the same in conception as Darwin's evolution, namely, an unpredictable course of events. The nondevelopment (chiefly noninnovation) aspects of economics—such as production and pricing theory and demand and consumption theory—are fairly predictable. But both development (chiefly technological) and nondevelopment aspects fall within the scientific domain.

Darwin's theory is not a theory of progress, although it has been misrepresented as such and thereby made to seem to suffer from an internal contradiction. Thus Julian Huxley should be faulted for asserting man to be the goal and pinnacle of the evolutionary process—a declaration made in presenting his argument for a scientific religion—religion without revelation—the religion of evolutionary humanism: man as the goal, the means, and the spearhead of the evolutionary process.[11] Evolution being a theory of the unpredictable, there is no way of predicting its outcome in advance. Darwin shows man's destiny to be unpredictable.

B. NON-DARWINIAN EVOLUTIONISM: TEILHARD DE CHARDIN[12]

In his famous work titled *The Phenomenon of Man*[13] Père Pierre Teilhard de Chardin, Jesuit priest and renowned palaeontologist, sought to reconcile what he evidently thought to be Darwinism (actually Darwinism misconstrued or reinterpreted in a non-Darwinian fashion) with the "creationist" doctrine of fixed species recorded in the Book of Genesis. His effort pleased neither Darwinians nor the Roman Catholic Church and merely earned him, for all his pains, a proscription (indexing) of his works and interdiction to teach his (or any other) doctrine.

Teilhard theorized that all terrestrial life evolves from matter with minimal spiritual content (inorganic) through forms with increasing spiritual content (organic) including plants and animals, the entire gamut culminating in man, the most evolved animal and the form with highest spiritual content. Man, however—according to Teilhard—will continue to evolve to the next higher stage and form: all spirit or mind, no matter; a community of souls that he termed the *noosphere*. This entire evolutionary process is held together by Jesus Christ, who descended into matter, as Alpha, and raised the entire material creation through increasing accretions of spirit unto himself, as Omega, in the noosphere—a beautiful myth and clever compromise, reminiscent of elements of Simonian, Valentinian, and Manichaean Gnostic doctrines.[14]

This compromise only led to ostracism by Darwinians and Creationists alike, by Science and the Church. It offended the spirit of Darwinism, which is neither goal- or progress-oriented and is materialistic in the best Marxian sense of matter having primacy over mind or spirit. Teilhard's theory is goal-oriented (to the noosphere) as well as progress-oriented and creationist, man being the apex of cosmic manifestations as well as lord of the Earth. Moreover, spirit evolves completely from matter. Marxians would disown Teilhard's speculation on the ground that there cannot be pure mind (or spirit) without matter or a material base. The concept of the noosphere is formulated in nonempirical terms—a further strike against him as a scientist. To the Roman Catholic Church Teilhard was not creationist enough inasmuch as man is not a fixed or final type, being the product of the evolution of matter as well as a transitional stage toward the disappearance of man himself. This objection did not seem to have been affected in any way by the fact that the noosphere concept is, at least, in line with orthodox Christian doctrine of a post-resurrection community of souls, felicitously described by Teilhard as a "union of differentiates."

Father Teilhard's work is significant as much for its eclectic character as for its misinterpretation (or misunderstanding) of Darwin. If, however, one assumes that Teilhard was, undoubtedly, fully acquainted with the essence of Darwin's theory and its unstructured, goalless, and purposeless character, then Teilhard's work appears not as a misinterpretation of Darwin nor a mere attempt to reconcile Darwin or Marx with Creationist doctrine, but as an original contribution and *reinterpretation* of Darwin designed to give a smattering of scientific background to the creationist story of Genesis. Teilhard, however, made no such claim to reinterpreting Darwin.

4. HUMANISM

Theology, in general, maintains that man exists for the glory of God. It does not follow, however, that without man to proclaim God's glory, God would not exist. Only anthropocentric conceit could lead to this viewpoint. Worse still, only ethnocentric or elitist conceit would go one step further to hold to the view of "God in search of man," man being interpreted as a favored, chosen tribe. Humanism, by contrast, subscribes to the view that man exists for the advancement and glory of man.[15]

These two presumed goals of human existence—glorification of God and of man—are, formally, quite separate and distinct, unless a deliberate connection is made between them. Such a connection was made by the German philosopher Ludwig Feuerbach, who argued that theology is anthropology—hence humanism—since the concept and person of God was an alienated, objectified projection (or hypostatization) of the best qualities of the human species, so that, in effect, God is only mankind's "good face" hypostatized.

Humanism, or the doctrine that man, human values, and human welfare constitute the highest goal of man, has a long and ancient history. Its resurgence in modern times has been generally associated with Feuerbach. But its roots go far back in history, to Plato at least. There is, however, an important distinction between ancient Greek and modern humanism. Plato's was a two-world humanism. The highest manifestation of man in this sensible, phenomenal world was the philosopher-king: his humanity was gilded by a tinge of the divine mind, but all of the divine mind remained virtually inaccessible in a separate, suprasensible world.

This two-world setting remains the background of Adam Smith's humanism in which the highest manifestation of man in the phenomenal world is "economic man"—the individual completely free to own property and pursue his own ends unhampered by the state, under the guidance of an "invisible hand" that harmonizes the actions and activities of all individuals.

With Ludwig Feuerbach, the ancient two-worlds tradition ends. Modern humanism becomes a one-world humanism, the sensible and the suprasensible being combined in one sensible phenomenal world. For the suprasensible world of God is shown to be no more than a projection of the ideas of man, a denizen of the sensible world. Marx, Nietzsche, and other modern proponents of humanism have operated within this one-world framework. The group includes Julian Huxley and a later convert to humanism, through Marxism, Jean-Paul Sartre. Although Sartre falls within the group, other existentialist philosophers are excluded, such as Kierkegaard and Heidegger. These philosophers are not humanists but proponents of individualism in a theological setting. They trump up the individual, not as an end in himself, but as an important and sacred value, a value made sacred in reference to a superior power, God, disguised as Being by Heidegger, dwelling in a suprasensible world.

In this section, the development of humanism is presented in its dual aspect, social and teleological. Social humanism will be traced through Plato (*The Republic*), Adam Smith (*Wealth of Nations*)[16] Ludwig Feuerbach (*The Essence of Christianity*), and Karl Marx (*Capital*). These writers and philosophers see humanism as a contemporary social goal. Teleological humanism is represented by Teilhard de Chardin and Julian Huxley, who regarded humanism not as a contemporary goal of society, but as a very distant goal in time or outside time in Teilhard's case, which is also eschatological. The humanism of these two representatives is more destiny (long-term) than social objective (short-term) or a guide to everyday living.

SOCIAL HUMANISM (SHORT-TERM OBJECTIVE)

A. Plato

Plato may be regarded as a prominent exponent if not the father of humanism in ancient times, for Plato's doctrine of the philosopher-king, the man who was both royal (by birth and status) and divine (by possession of an element of the divine mind, or reason) was a sort of hypostatization of man, the highest development that man was capable of achieving in this phenomenal world. Unlike Feuerbach's humanism, which was a democratic concept capable of being realized by *all* men, Plato's was an elitist concept possible of achievement only by a few, the aristocrats by birth, the guardians and leaders of society. Even more elitist was Nietzsche's "humanism," its product, the superman, being that rare individual, a Napoleon, that fortunate one-in-several-million survivor and goal of Nature's prodigal reproductivity.

Plato, and Nietzsche in a later age, correctly saw that in the natural state of things, the highest state of human development was not a democratic, but an elitist, autocratic one. It was based on an uneven distribution of property, including property in human beings. This was possible only in a slave society, where not only property but also its fruits were unevenly owned and distributed. In short, inequality of property and income was the basis of Plato's, as of Nietzsche's, humanism. It was on this basis of inequality—unacceptable, from the modern democratic point of view—that the ancient Greek educational system (inherited by the Occident and romanticized, perhaps ignorantly, as the "humanities,""the liberal arts") was erected. It was an elitist education for the few, not for the many. It was on this same basis that the concept of "morality" or "duty" (also inherited by the Occident) was erected by the ancient Greek philosophers: the concept of social obligation by the inferior toward the superior (the foundation of the caste system) and the complementary noblesse oblige, the condescending patronage by the superior toward the inferior.

It was, similarly, on this basis that the Greek concept of love (properly, affection) was differentiated: *eros*, or aspiring affection of the inferior toward the superior, and *agape*, or condescending affection of the superior toward the inferior.

B. Adam Smith

Ignoring the lessons of history so clearly evident in the time of Plato and his school of philosophy, Adam Smith, Scotsman, professor of moral philosophy, and economist, sought successfully, like Plato, to establish humanism on an economic basis; but, unlike Plato, erroneously, expected the outcome to be democratic. For he aimed to demonstrate that a system of private ownership of the means of production, coupled with laissez faire, i.e. an environment in which each man sought his own self-interest or economic gain, was productive of the most good for each individual and, mystically, for society as a whole. This was a doctrine of individual (and, only incidentally, collective) humanism—a doctrine that the highest development of man, individually and collectively, depended on absolute freedom for the individual to pursue his own self-interest. The collective aspect of the doctrine was based not on demonstration, but on indulgence in a bit of mysticism in the form of the dogma of the "invisible hand" that automatically harmonized private and public self-interest.[17]

That Adam Smith's doctrine sold extremely well is all the more surprising since history, both before and since Plato, had shown the doctrine to be patently false as concerns both the good of every member of society and the public good. It became the economic doctrine of the new republic of the United States of America, which was born the same year in which Smith's *Wealth of Nations* was published (1776). The more successful achievements of U.S. society in the economic sphere, as compared to those of ancient Greece, may have been due to several modifying factors, among them: (a) the abolition of slavery, (b) replacement of the aristocracy of birth by the aristocracy of achievement, and consequently (c) the emergence of the guardians and leaders of society from various strata of society rather than from an elite or aristocratic group. These factors were the very opposite of what had obtained in Greek society. Nevertheless, the fact remains that the unequal ownership of property with the accompanying unequal distribution of its fruits has prevented, in modern America as it did in ancient Greece and eighteenth-century England, the emergence of a democratic humanism—a humanism for all, effectively accessible to every individual. Economic laissez-faire is the death knell of democratic humanism, for complete and unregulated individual freedom in economic matters does not promote the fullest development or unfolding of each and every member of society but only of a segment—those who survive the competition either by the fortuitous circumstance of property ownership or by the possession of more than average energy, intelligence, or fraud.

C. Ludwig Feuerbach

One tradition regards Feuerbach as the father of modern humanism—the doctrine that human welfare is man's highest good since, according to Feuerbach, the highest good, or God, was no more than man's best qualities voluntarily alienated from himself and projected into an objectified concept, God. God was a hypostatization of man's best qualities. The worst qualities, only, remained with man as his property after the projection. All that was necessary for man to become his complete self once more was to reclaim his divinity, thereby becoming his own God, highest good and sun around which he would revolve.[18]

112

Feuerbach was, therefore, strictly speaking, the first philosopher to abrogate the occidental philosophical tradition, inherited from Greece, of a divorce between the sensible and the so-called suprasensible world—a tradition that continues, nevertheless, to dominate occidental philosophy to this day. So strong is the power of old ideas, hallowed by centuries of tradition, even when they are patently erroneous. The two-worlds concept simply refuses to die.

The doctrine that theology is anthropology has several facets to it, not all of which were fully explored by Feuerbach. Some of them are, briefly, the following:

(a) The alienation, objectification, and hypostatization of mankind's best qualities left man with the worst qualities of his species, implying that the Devil was also the hypostatization of those residual worst qualities of the human species.

(b) By reclaiming his best qualities, his own godhood, man was reuniting his best with his worst qualities, his constructive with his destructive forces, his Apollo with his Dionysus. This consequence was clearly seen by Nietzsche and fully developed by him into his doctrine of superman—the man beyond good and evil, God and the Devil. It was similarly developed by Freud in the psychological arena and exploited by him in the practice of psychoanalysis.

(c) Not only was theology anthropology, according to Feuerbach's doctrine, but so also was demonology, according to the full implications of that doctrine. And when Freud came along psychology became, technically, an aspect of anthropology and psychiatry its applied or practical side. For Freud, therefore, theology was psychology, a part of anthropology.

It should be pointed out that an outstanding weakness of Feuerbach's doctrine was the absence of any discussion of the economic conditions necessary for the democratic achievement of this philosophic humanism. In this respect, that is, in terms of scope, his doctrine was both defective and inferior to that of Plato, which set out the economic, social, and political structure necessary for the realization of his elitist concept of humanism.

D. Karl Marx

Grasping fully the economic facts and lessons of ancient and modern history, Karl Marx recognized that private ownership of the means of production resulted in an elitist humanism from which, consequently, the major part of society was excluded. Private ownership in property, he sought to demonstrate, resulted in an alienation of a part of the material product of society (the part devoted to capital formation) from its rightful owners, the workers. This product alienation constituted the material basis for that other alienation expounded by Feuerbach—the ideological alienation and hypostatization of mankind's best qualities into God. It was therefore not enough, argued Marx, for man to reclaim his divine qualities in order to become his own God. It was also necessary, he emphasized, for man to reclaim the alienated product of his labor in the form of capital or private property and socialize it, in the first place, in order for his divinity to be completely and automatically restored. For it was this alienation of a part of his material product that generated the emergence and alienation of his ideological property in the concept of God. Only the material "haves" could become fully human (that is, divine as well), not the material "have nots." For humanism to become completely democratized—that is, completely *individualized*—according to Marx, property should become completely *collectivized*.

What a doctrine! Partly unusual, partly beguiling! The unusual part: Divinity requires a material basis, and particularly that part consisting of productive capital. Automatically, whoever controls productive capital (whether private entrepreneurs or the state) controls theology. The beguiling part: For humanism to become completely democratic, i.e., *individualized*, property and productive capital should become completely *collectivized*. In short, individualization of capital deprives some part of the population of that capital, while collectivization of capital democratizes (individualizes) it. The latter argument is beguiling because collectivization of capital does not imply more than a collectivization of its benefits, without any automatic commitment to individualize those benefits. A separate and additional commitment is required for that and is provided by the socialist ethic "from each according to his ability; to each according to his need." However, this ethic was to be enforced through state intervention at first, which intervention was to disappear eventually, leaving in its place an automatic system of production according to ability and distribution and consumption according to need. Leaving aside, for the moment, the imprecision of the terms *ability* and *need*, there was no automatic mechanism installed to ensure the automatic operation of the socialist ethic after the state "withers away." In the absence of such a mechanism or the internalization of the socialist ethic by each individual, Marx's economic and democratic humanism symbolized by the "new man under Communism," ethical and responsible, could hardly arrive.

It is instructive to end these observations on Marx's humanism by noting that both Adam Smith and Karl Marx were in the same tradition, which regarded humanism as basically inconsistent with state intervention. Both subscribed to the tenet that that government is best that governs least. Marx took this to the logical conclusion that no government is the test of humanism at its best—which is synonymous with communism.

TELEOLOGICAL HUMANISM (LONG-TERM DESTINY)

The discussion in section 3 of this chapter shows that Darwin's evolutionary speculation leaves the beginning and the end of man uncertain. This "biological uncertainty principle" of evolutionary theory was unsatisfactory to some and regarded as a challenge—to be taken up by, notably, the Jesuit priest Teilhard de Chardin in several of his writings on the subject of human destiny, but chiefly in his *The Phenomenon of Man*; and by the biologist Julian Huxley in his *Religion Without Revelation*. Both writers base themselves on Darwin's evolutionary theory but misuse it in a way that leaves the goallessness and uncertainty out of it. By giving it a *direction* and a *goal* they offended against the central feature of the theory. The result is an anthropocentric, mankind-enhancing interpretation of evolution, little different in spirit from that of the Book of Genesis.

E. Pierre Teilhard de Chardin

As indicated earlier, Teilhard's theory postulates an evolutionary development of matter and spirit in inverse proportion with man, as the cap of the structure, possessing most spirit and least matter. This is a nonempirical postulate. But man will continue to evolve in the direction of increasing differentiation of his nervous system and increasing development of his mind to its next higher form and destiny of all spirit (or mind), no matter. This stage that emerges at the death of the human individual signals the institution of a community of souls, termed the *noosphere* (the sphere of the intellect, soul, or mind), located above the biosphere. One soul is different from another, like the individuals from whom they derive, so that the noosphere is a union of differentiates. This entire process of *directed evolution* is taken in charge by Jesus Christ, who unites it organically with himself, descending as Alpha into the heart of matter and raising the entire material creation through successive stages marked by increasing accretions of spirit finally unto himself, as Omega, in the noosphere.

Teilhard's right to create his own myth of the "after-life" in competition to that of the Roman Catholic Church was challenged, especially as it introduced a strong element of imprecision into an otherwise clear and precise domain—the Christian Paradise—whatever else its merit might be. Without any substitutes his myth eliminated the furniture of the after-life: gold-paved streets, robes of white, golden crowns, everlasting songs in praise of the Creator, et cetera. Besides being less attractive than the ruling myth, it was apt to dishearten the faithful as a portrait of man's long-term destiny.

F. Julian Huxley

Julian Huxley propounded a theory of human destiny that he termed *Evolutionary Humanism* and can be summarized as follows. It postulates that man's destiny is to spearhead, as agent and leader, the evolutionary process on planet Earth. For this function, religion of some kind is necessary in order to cope with the problems of human destiny, but not a revealed religion, not a religion with a god, for "Gods are no longer spearheads of history"[19]; only man is spearhead of both history and evolution, so that evolution theory becomes no more than anthropobiology.

What Huxley did was to reinterpret the Christian Trinity, substituting matter and mind for the first and third persons of the Trinity, respectively[20]; he then substitutes man for the second person and makes him the spearhead of evolution on Earth.[21] This is merely another version of Teilhard de Chardin's Christocentric model of the evolutionary process, in which Jesus Christ is the spearhead of evolution.

Huxley assigns to science the task of creating the new religion for humanity, a religion without revelation. But how this religion should take form is unclear and unpredictable. What is clear to Huxley is that this new religion, like man, is to become "an organ of destiny,"[22]—man's evolutionary destiny. Three passages convey the gist of Huxley's theory (italics supplied):

Biology, I repeat, has thus revealed man's place in nature. He is the *highest form of life* produced by the evolutionary process on this planet, the latest dominant type, and the only organism capable of further major advance or *progress*. Whether he knows it or not, he is now the main agency for the further evolution of the earth and its inhabitants. In other words, his *destiny* is to realise new possibilities for the whole terrestrial sector of the cosmic process, to be the instrument of further evolutionary *progress* on this planet.[23]

116

And again:

> From this point of view, the religion indicated by our new view of our position in the cosmos must clearly be one centred on the idea of fulfilment. Man's most sacred duty, and at the same time his most glorious opportunity, is to promote the maximum fulfilment of the evolutionary process on this earth; and this includes the fullest realisation of his own inherent possibilities.[24]

Finally:

> Evolutionary humanism has the further implication that man is at one and the same time the only agent for realising life's further progress, and also the main obstacle in the path of its realisation. The hostile outer world was his first obvious adversary; but the only opponent ultimately worthy of his steel is himself. Man has learnt in large measure to understand, control and utilise the forces of his own nature.[25]

The italicized words in the first quotation—*highest form of life, progress*, and (manifest) *destiny*—show to what extent Huxley, like Teilhard, departs from the substance and spirit of Darwin's evolution theory, a theory that specifically excludes the concepts contained in those words. There is no higher or lower, superior or inferior species, no progress or regress, no manifest or known destiny of any species in a theory that emphasizes the ideas of contingence, undirectedness, goallessness, and uncertainty. Huxley's excessive anthropocentrism is neither consistent with evolution theory nor warranted by the available evidence.

5. EXISTENTIALISM: MYTH OF HUMAN EXISTENCE

A. EXISTENTIALISM DEFINED

The theme of existentialism—the nature of human existence—is both ancient and modern: as ancient as Plato, and Zoroaster earlier on, and as modern as Kierkegaard, Heidegger, and their successors, occurring also in various currents of thought in between. The emphasis is on the existence of the *individual* self and on its true happiness as consisting in a transcendent sphere or power beyond itself and its sensible world. Or, alternatively, in some modern versions, the true happiness of the self is conceived as consisting in its self-transcendence through sublimation or

117

supersession of a specified aspect of the self in or by its opposite (or another) aspect.

Thus, for Søren Kierkegaard, as for Martin Heidegger, both of whom are regarded as the modern precursors of existentialism, the human self's highest good or salvation consists in being "grabbed" by a higher power that reveals itself to man by its own grace in a free and willing act of self-disclosure. This power is variously denoted as God, as manifested in Jesus Christ, who in turn manifests himself to man (Kierkegaard) or as Being (Heidegger). The road that prepares the human self for the possibility of this event is sublimation of inauthentic existence (i.e., being in *and* of the contemporary world) in authentic existence (being in, but *not* of, the contemporary world). Similarly, Friedrich Nietzsche's superman, or self-overcoming man, who says "yes" to life sublimates negative, life-denying tendencies in positive, life-affirming tendencies and moves beyond the conventional norms of good and evil to a "higher" personal standard or law, in which the welfare of the self is all that counts. A similar thought of self-transcendence is implied in Paul Tillich's "courage to be" or "self-affirmation of being," which takes one's "nonbeing" into one's "being" or "courage."[26]

Existentialism is an intellectual movement[27] that usually emerges in societies in the process of disintegration, where the traditional and familiar moral and social values have collapsed and life seems insecure and absurd—as in Europe after the First and Second World Wars or, much earlier in antiquity, in the society of Plato's time. The prevailing attitude in such an environment usually is: "the codes which have broken down were imposed by a dominant group on the rest of society in order to serve their own class and selfish interests. Therefore, now that they have broken down, it is everyman for himself."[28]

The weakness in this existentialist position, however, is that no man lives unto himself—"No man is an island"—but has to depend on others, on society, if each must live a full and satisfactory life. Every individual is a product of the union of two individuals of opposite sex, a liaison that constitutes the basic unit of society. It is not surprising, therefore, that sensitive existentialists, such as Jean-Paul Sartre, were obliged to review their solipsistic position. Sartre, in later life, turned to Marxism in order to remedy this defect in his philosophy by embracing society once more.

Conscious that man cannot survive—or even be born—without society, great social reformers have always rejected the solipsistic existentialist position and sought to reconstruct society along new lines on the basis of interpersonal relationships. Plato, for example, accepted the basic criticism regarding the origins of moral codes—that they are imposed by, and serve the interests of, the dominant group—but sought to establish

118

principles on the basis of which the interests of the dominant group could be transformed into those of the entire society. This he did by eliminating any personal economic stake by the dominant group, the guardians, in the reconstructed social and economic order by substituting, instead, a singleminded devotion by each guardian to the pursuit of philosophy, and by rationalizing in the name of the principle of justice or division of labor (i.e., complementarity of the socioeconomic functions of various social groups) the respective roles of the guardians, the military class, and the farming and business class. (The slaves who did the rest of the work—the "dirty work"—of the society did not count as citizens and barely as persons.)

At the level of society as a whole, Marx, on the other hand, sought the same objective as Plato—socializing the interest of the dominant group—by eliminating the previous dominant group (the capitalists) and replacing it with a new dominant group, the one-class proletariat; this new group would be temporarily represented by the state until such time as the latter would wither away with the advent of the new citizen, the new man under communism, who guides his behavior by the new socially oriented code. In this way, all of society becomes *the* dominant class. Marx seems to have aimed further than Plato: beyond socializing the moral values, he aimed at socializing man himself. Plato did not have to concern himself with the latter, since this theory of moral values postulated a direct and automatic access by each individual to the concept of *the* good (or God).[29] Marx, however, was not so trusting, believing that material interests were so corrupting that the entire economic system, and thus the whole man, had to be socialized with the communist ethic ("from each according to his ability; to each according to his need") in order to guard against that source of corruption. It is therefore surprising, at first, that Marx did not assign to the state or any other institution the role of socializing the individual in preparation for the eventual withering away of the state. This failure in praxis is a grave weakness in Marx's system. There is an obvious explanation for this omission. In attacking the Christian religion, the religion of Western Europe, and a significant part of the population of the USSR—justifiable from an institutional point of view—Marx, unfortunately, overlooked the salutary role of the Church as an instrument for the socialization of man through the inculcation or internalization of Christian moral values. Every effective religion exhibits two aspects: (a) the social, comprising the web of external interrelationships that cement the society together and to the rest of the cosmos, and (b) the personal, comprising the process of socialization of the individual through his internalization of the ethic regulating the web of interrelationships within society—a process familiarly known as "indoctrination" of the individual. In failing to provide for the moral indoctrination of the individual, Marxism fails to complete its character and its religious mission.[30]

The attitude of "Every man for himself, the devil take the hindmost" or "Look out for number one (oneself)" that is implied in both theological and secular existentialism is counterbalanced by the arguments of existentialists like Camus and Sartre to the effect that the individual finds himself saddled with an existence and a corresponding responsibility that he did not seek and does not want.[31] What, then, is he to do if he does not wish to take the way out through suicide? Accept his fate, naturally. There is no other alternative. This, indeed, is the answer given by Camus and Sartre. The individual should recognize and willingly accept his fate. Thus existentialism comes to be associated in the popular mind with defeatism, pessimism, and fatalism—with the Hobson's choice of accepting life as it is, with all its absurdities. The secular existentialist ends on an upbeat note, however: by willingly accepting his fate the individual thereby transcends it; he rises above his fate by scorning it. He may even find happiness in accepting his fate and, like the (Christian) theological existentialist, exult, "O death, where is thy sting? O grave, where is thy victory?"[32]

Three variants of existentialism may, therefore, be distinguished: Christian (or ethical), theological and secular. Christian existentialism emphasizes interpersonal relationships as the essence and goal of human existence—"thy brother's keeper." Theological existentialism finds the goal of human existence in a solipsistic relationship to a superior (and superhuman) power that willingly discloses itself to, and grabs, man; while secular existentialism finds the goal in self-interest and self-reliance alone, in facing and accepting human existence as a goalless and insoluble situation. These three variants may now be examined, each in its turn.

B. CHRISTIAN EXISTENTIALISM

The ethical teachings of Jesus lay emphasis on physical and spiritual alienation of man from fellowman, and its adverse consequences, as the central fact of human existence; and on the consequent need to overcome this alienation by each individual assuming *personal* responsibility for the state of his spiritual condition as well as of his relationship with his fellowman. The same standard of what is best for oneself—the basis of one's self-love—is to be applied in one's dealings with one's fellowman, friend and foe alike. The privileged position of belonging to a special nation or a special tribe of the elect of God—Israel—is not an adequate

120

basis for personal existence. It needs to be complemented by personal responsibility for the welfare of one's nation or one's tribe, starting with its individual member, and by extending this responsibility to cover individuals outside of one's nation or tribe. In short, one's welfare is conditioned on the welfare of others—of one's neighbor. One must transcend the love of self to the love of the other.

Such is the basis of Christian existentialism, of the existence of Christian man: personal responsibility, on an individual and reciprocal basis, as the sufficient and satisfactory condition for individual existence, as well as for any acceptable relationship with any higher or superhuman power. No doubt, it is claiming too much to describe this position as Christian, for it is neither unique nor Christian, being as old as Judaism and older. Nevertheless, it may justifiably be labeled Christian in that it was revived and given a new emphasis by Jesus at a time when it was apt to be overlooked and buried under the weight of claims to special and exclusive privileges, such as those of Roman citizenship, and membership of various groups—Roman, Greek, Jew, et cetera. More will be said subsequently on the subject of Christian existentialism (Book Two, Section B, chapter 11). But enough has been said here to convey its flavor.

C. THEOLOGICAL EXISTENTIALISM

The distinguishing feature of theological existentialism, as noted already, is the personal relationship of the individual existent to a superior power that willingly discloses itself to man and grabs all of his attention and himself. In this respect, the existentialism of both Kierkegaard and Heidegger is of the same variety—theological—although Heidegger is commonly regarded as a proponent of secular, nay, atheistic existentialism. This conventional view seems mistaken, however, and is probably due to the fact that Heidegger talks not of God, as did Kierkegaard, but of Being. In fact, however, all of Heidegger's discussion of Being is nothing but pure theology, tinged with a Gnostic flavor about man as a stranger in an alien world and disguised as philosophy. Consequently, Kierkegaard and Heidegger will be discussed together under the heading of theological existentialism[33]—even though they differ in their views of the relationship of the self to the world and, therefore, of what constitutes authentic and inauthentic existence.

For the purpose of exposition it is convenient to discuss theological existentialism with reference to the following major topics: (a) Existence, (b) Care, (c) Authentic and Inauthentic Existence, (d) Means to the attainment of authentic existence, (e) Death, and (f) Role of "the Other" in one's existence.

(a) Human existence is generally conceived by theological existentialists as a being-in-the-world—being-there (*Dasein*), facticity. However, the nature of this being-in-the-world differs in conception as between Kierkegaard and Heidegger. For the former, it is a being-*alone*-in-the-world; for the latter it is a being-*with-others*-in-the-world. "And thereby hangs a tale." In either case, being-in-the-world is a being unto, or toward, death. Existence, in short, is death-oriented—to the existent's own death. And in facing one's own death one is alone and lonely, for no other can die one's death except oneself.

(b) Care, or anxiety, is central to one's death-orientation and manifests itself in a temporal spectrum that covers the *past*, over which one has no control; the *present*, the domain of action (*falling*); and the *future*, the domain of choice (*possibility*). The ultimate in care is death itself, being the one potential event that satisfies all three temporal dimensions of care: *potential* facticity, falling, and ultimate possibility ending all other possibilities.

(c) The tale that develops from being-in-the-world differs as between Kierkegaard and Heidegger according to their differing conceptions of the role played by others ("they") in the individual's existence. For Kierkegaard, for whom existence is being-*alone*-in-the-world, the other is an obstacle; hence, complete withdrawal from the other, the world, is the essence of *authentic* existence. This is not true for Heidegger, for whom the other is necessary to one's existence, defined as being-*with-others*-in-the-world. Thus, the other is consistent with authentic existence for Heidegger. It follows that, for Kierkegaard, being involved with others, the impersonal collectivity of the "they" and its affairs, is the hallmark of *inauthentic* existence. Withdrawal from the world (as Kierkegaard did in canceling his marriage intentions in order to devote himself to God) would not rate as authentic existence for Heidegger. However, his definition of *inauthentic* existence is different, being cast in terms of less than total involvement in all three temporal dimensions of care simultaneously. Thus, to be preoccupied with only one of these dimensions, especially the present, would be *inauthentic* (i.e., disunited or time-fragmented self) existence; while, living in all three dimensions simultaneously, with thought of one's own death as the cement that binds all three, would constitute *authentic* existence (or unified self).

Whence, for Heidegger, conscience becomes defined as the silent call of the authentic (integrated) to the inauthentic (fragmented) self to choose responsibly in the face of the master possibility of death. Correspondingly, self-acceptance implies voluntary choice among possibilities that are still open in the light of the master possibility of death; nonacceptance of self, the opposite. The failure to heed the call of conscience, i.e., to choose responsibly and willingly in the face of the possibility of death, is guilt. And the self that continues to choose responsibly, consciously, and willingly in face of the possibility of death overcomes guilt through the grace of Being and, thus overcoming transcience (i.e., the succession of nows or falling), achieves immortality.[34]

(d) The means to the attainment of authentic existence is the same for both Kierkegaard and Heidegger: the grace or voluntary self-disclosure to man by a superior power, called different names by both. God in the person of Jesus Christ (Kierkegaard) or Being (Heidegger) reveals himself to man and grabs him. Thus the attainment of authentic existence is not within the power of man but of a superior power outside and beyond him.

(e) Death plays a central role in the different variants of existentialism in two respects: (i) existence is death-oriented (a being-toward-death) and (ii) no one can take another's death upon himself, die another's death. In these two respects combined resides a unique feature of all existentialist thought: the loneliness of self-existence, culminating in the fact that man dies alone, even while being-with-others-in-the-world.

Theological existentialism, however—and unlike secular existentialism—assigns a positive role to death, based on its centrality: that of serving as an integrative link among all the temporal facets of care and personality, since it participates in all these aspects as a certain, if fortuitous, event in human life. Death binds together the time-integrated self, even though its central role may be ignored or overlooked by the time-fragmented self.

(f) It has been shown that "the other"—the world—plays a part in the definition of *inauthentic* existence for Kierkegaard, while for Heidegger it is an essential part of the definition of *existence* itself. Kierkegaard sees "the other" as being in competition for the grace of authentic self, as well as for scarce life-sustaining resources. The other is thus an obstacle to the attainment of authentic self, especially since what scarce resources are used by the other are not available to oneself. To Heidegger, there is no self, no existence, without the other.[35] Hence "the other" is accepted in the definition of "self." And selfhood, in temporal terms, is, for Heidegger, the identifiable segment of existence between (or bounded by) birth and death that integrates, and is integrated by, the three dimensions of time—past, present, and future.

D. SECULAR EXISTENTIALISM

The leading representatives of secular existentialism are Jean-Paul Sartre and Albert Camus, the former being by far the better known for his prolific writings and social activism, besides being older than, and out-living, the latter. Accordingly, Sartre's existentialist thought will be examined here as the best representative of the secular genre.

Jean-Paul Sartre's thought is structured on, and will be discussed with reference to, the three following elements:

(a) *dynamic time*, involving any two consecutive moments of time:
    (i) preceding moment, t_{n-1}, or nothingness; and
    (ii) succeeding moment, t_n, or the instantaneous now of existence;
(b) *static time*, fixed perpetually at, and from, the moment of death; $t_{\bar{n}}$;
(c) *interrelationships* between and among persons.

Dynamic time is the moving link between the *now* (t_n) and the preceding (superseded) moment or nothingness (t_{n-1}). That is to say, one exists, dynamically, from moment to moment, continuously re-creating oneself. Sartre associates this dynamic situation with the phenomenon of choice. Thus, at any moment one could change one's life, futurewise, since every moment presents one with an opportunity to choose and, in choosing, to reorient one's life. Anyone in this situation does not have or "possess" a nature or essence, and every change or reorientation cancels the previous orientation, reducing it to "nothingness."

Existence is self-affirmation, that is, affirmation of oneself as an absolute entity. As such, it is an affirmation of one's potentialities and one's ability to freely orient one's life—according to one's interpretation of one's situation and the resulting choice of action or inaction—from what it is to what it will become, but is not yet. It is the self that one is to become by orienting one's life toward a future different from one's present, on the basis of an interpretation of one's present situation, subsequently confirmed by one's corresponding choice of action or inaction.[36]

This self-affirmation is absolute, solipsistic: exclusive of every other entity, human and nonhuman, except oneself. No other entity exists or counts, since one can only know of one's own existence. Every other entity merely possesses formal and fixed qualities, attributes, or essence, having meaning only with reference to oneself.

Néant or nothingness is the cancellation of a previous orientation of one's life by a new one. It is the annulment of the self that one *was* by the self that one is *now*, or of the self that one is now by the self that one is to become. In a dynamic situation one is continuously annulling

124

(*anéantissement*) and re-creating oneself (that is, existing), moving continually from "nothingness" to "existence."[37]

Choice is the engine of this continuing dynamic. "Man is condemned to be free," says Sartre. That is to say that as an existential entity in the world man is condemned to be "free to choose," regardless of the nature of the situation in which he happens to be; and, in choosing, man reveals the sense, interpretation, or meaning that he gives to the situation. Thus one interprets the situation in which one finds oneself in the world and, according to this interpretation (or orientation) that one gives to the situation, one makes one's choice of action or inaction in response thereto. Thus also, once one interprets a situation, giving it a meaning, one's choice is determined and, therewith, one's liberty of action is constrained, narrowed down to one or, at best, a few alternatives. One is not, therefore, as free an agent in regard to one's choice as Sartre (or Kierkegaard, for that matter) would think; for, in fact, one is never faced with the multiplicity of choices that Sartre implies and believes possible. By one's interpretation or sense of the situation, which precedes one's action or response, one limits one's freedom of choice in order to act. Hence Sartre may appropriately be paraphrased as follows: Man is condemned to interpret his situation in order to choose, by action or inaction, an appropriate response. Man's *freedom* consists of, and is exercised, in his *interpretation* of his situation, his *interpretation* limits his *choice*, and his *choice* involves the exercise of his *reponsibility* to act or not to act. At the point of choice one's freedom is limited to acting, or not acting, responsibly.

To summarize. With every moment of choice one determines one's future just as one's present situation results, inevitably, from one's past choices. One is what one has been (Hegel) and will be what one chooses *now* to make of oneself (Sartre). Thus the law of cause and effect (karma, of Hinduism and Buddhism) holds irrevocably throughout. "You are nothing but your life," says Sartre; i.e., you are only what you have been and what you will make yourself become.

In the continual movement of annulling and re-creating oneself from nothingness to existence there is no resting place, no goal. The essential of existence is in the continual reorientation, the doing, the activity of one's life. There is no fixed or final goal of achievement, because one is perpetually achieving by annulling one's life of yesterday, of the last hour, the last minute. In principle, this is a more exciting venture than the dull Sisyphean task to which Sartre compared it: forever rolling a stone uphill only to have it roll down again, once the crest is attained, and to start the chore all over again. Existence, certainly, is not that dull. In the exciting task of existence there is no crest, no set, beaten path to tread uphill or down. Existence, like evolution, is open-ended, always leading not, indeed, to nowhere but to some place we know not where—until death its final, resting place (according to Sartre). Because of this perpetual excitement it is enough to just keep going on on the endless journey, go on existing, not caring where the road may lead; for it will lead where it will, with enough excitement on the way, according to the choices one makes.

Static time, the period from death (t_n) on, defines the state of *being* when, in spite of the passage of chronological time, there is no movement and the nature, essence, or character of a person is fixed, once and for always: one finally *possesses* a character, becomes a statistic, history, at death.

Being (*être*) is the possession of an attribute or essence. One's opportunity to choose and thereby orient one's future life ends with one's death. With death, one's life becomes a thing entirely of the past, an unalterable,[38] noncontinuable record of past events to be presented to, and objectively discussed by, others. One's life has become destiny, i.e., known, fixed and unalterable. With death, also, the *existence* of man becomes—is transformed into—man's *essence*, for he now possesses, for the first and only time, a fixed nature which he did not have before. Being is, thus, a static state ensuing at death[39] and existence (continual remaking of oneself) precedes essence (one's fixed qualities at death).

Two interesting aspects of Sartre's concept of being are its implication of the finality of death for the human being and its association with the concept of atheism. Both aspects are contestable: the finality of death from the viewpoint of physics, and atheism from the viewpoint of definition.

Sartre's theory of *interrelationships* between and among persons is modeled on those associated with the human paradigm: *personalization* (I/Thou), *personification* (I/He, I/She), and *objectification* (I/It). Thus the actual relationship between any two persons will conform to one or other of these patterns. It is on this basis that Sartre's lifelong companion, Simone de Beauvoir, described the role of the female sex in society as defined less by biology and more by social conditioning;[40] that is, a relationship and a role dictated by choice, education, and culture, the cultural aspect including the objectification of the female by the male sex. She did not imply, nor intend in any way, any denial of the biological fact of sexual differentiation of male and female, as Claude Tresmontant would have it believed.[41]

Notwithstanding the attention given to interpersonal relationships, Sartre's existential system is basically nuclear, solipsistic, and ruggedly individualistic, without the saving grace of a Smithian "invisible hand"

126

to reconcile, automatically, the welter of conflicting individual interests: a veritable Hobbesian world in which the life of man is "nasty, brutish and short."[42]

The doctrine that the human self alone exists and other persons or things exist only through, by courtesy of, or with reference to the self—solipsism—rules out humanism, strictly defined as the primacy of the human species and its well-being as the instrument and end of all biological evolution.[43] The individual, not the species, counts. Thus Sartre's existentialism, like Kierkegaard's, is a glorification of the self and egotism, contrary to Buddhist and Christian teachings.

This characteristic of Sartre's intellectual system derives from its historical background of the breakdown of European society during the First and Second World Wars. The effect was to throw individuals back on themselves and their individual resources. The climate of suspicion and mistrust in countries that, like France, capitulated to the German invasion of the Second World War easily led to an objectification of persons and interpersonal relations. What Sartre did not recognize until much later in his life was that the breakdown of society accompanied by traumatic consequences was always a temporary condition, and that man could not long survive except in society. Whatever of the social fabric was destroyed must eventually, be reconstructed.

The absence of social relationships in the original Sartrean system laid open to question its claim to being a philosophic system. The defect was eventually corrected in his subsequent intellectual development, when he recognized the need for the existence of society as a condition of the existence of the individual and espoused Marxism, thus supplying a humanistic context for his system. It finally acquired a philosophic context in the sense that paired or discrete interpersonal relationships were replaced by a web of interpersonal relationships.

Thus, at the end, Sartre incorporated a fourth element into his system: Marxist humanism, in which the ideals and welfare of man-in-society constitute the ultimate raison d'être of human interrelationships. But, strictly speaking, Sartre's solipsistic existentialism did not evolve into humanism—it became merely *associated* with it through his later espousal of Marxism. Contrary to what he believed and wrote,[44] his brand of existentialism is *not* humanism. Imported into his system like a deus ex machina, dialectical materialism played the same complementary and conciliating role in Sartre's solipsistic existentialism that the "invisible hand" played in Adam Smith's laissez-faire economy.

With its humanistic trappings Sartre's system is rigidly anthropocentric without being humanistic—hence of restricted scope—rather than embracing the general field and scope of philosophy. It relates more to ethics and morality (a branch of philosophy) on the human plane than to interrelationships of all kinds in general (the proper subject of philosophy). Without its humanistic trappings, solipsistic existentialism is egocentrism, inevitably—a trait that revealed itself in Sartre's desire for immortal literary fame. As always, it is but a short step from anthropocentrism to egocentrism.

E. EXISTENTIALISM: IDEOLOGY OF A SOCIETY IN TRANSITION

Secular existentialists view existence as a trap from which there is no exit. Man, they argue like the Gnostics of old, finds himself in a world in which he did not ask to be placed and from which he could not escape but is doomed to die in. Man may therefore despair of his situation or boldly accept and live with it. These are the two adaptation alternatives possible.

Existentially speaking, the adaptation of despair does not follow rationally from the finitude of conscious human existence, since this is a datum beyond human control. To despair on account of one's not liking the world, and therefore to reject it and ensconce oneself in a cocoon of solipsism, is not a rational solution. To despair on account of the multitudinous choices theoretically possible is to refuse to interpret one's existential situation, for interpretation narrows possibilities and facilitates choice. Equally irrational is the way out of the existential dilemma by suicide, for since death is an inseparable part of the human lot, one does not escape death through death by suicide.[45]

Rationality in the face of existence is to accept the world as a datum, dislike it as one may, and to interpret it.[46] Once one accepts the world, existential solipsism disappears; and once one interprets it, alternative possibilities become limited in number and choice becomes possible.

Acceptance and interpretation of the world and one's existential situation imply hope—optimism in the possibility of choice and orientation of one's life. One is seen to be "in and of" the world, not "in but not of" it. To be in and of the world is the only way to actualize one's possibilities. The vaunted self of Kierkegaard is inadequate, un–self-sufficient if one must ex-sist (or stand out to face one's possibilities) in the Sartrean sense. Thus one must take the risk of Kierkegaard's "inauthentic" existence if one is to contribute to the construction of a just society—a "Christian" society, for Christian existentialists.

When "things fall apart" one tends to reject, and withdraw oneself from, the crumbling edifice of society or world into a solipsistic shell.

This action, though instinctive, does not release one from one's nexus to the world. Sooner or later, one will have to start recognizing and reaccepting the world, to rebuild it, to pass from "authentic" to "inauthentic" Kierkegaardian existence.

Existentialism is thus the ideology of a society in transition from disorder to reorder. It is the temporary ideology of withdrawal, of solipsism and despair of a self forced back upon itself and its own resources in a disintegrating society, a self searching for the road to resocialization; the road to a self that needs its fellowman and society at large in order to actualize its existential possibilities. It is, in short, the ideology of a society *en panne* searching for the means of its *dépannage*.

F. SUMMARY AND CRITICISM OF EXISTENTIALIST THOUGHT

Summary

Terrestrial existence, according to Socrates, Plato, and Aristotle, is a dynamic journey from what one is (in a previous, suprasensible world) to become what one is (in the same previous, suprasensible world, to which one returns after death).[47] That is to say, motion without change of origin and destination, both being the same. Time (or temporality) is not the essence, but a superficial and illusive index of an underlying unchangingness. Selfhood and existence are interchangeable terms and open-ended, unbounded by life and death: *a dynamic within a static.*

According to the existentialist view, terrestrial existence is a dynamic journey of a blank, fortuitous self through the three dimensions (past, present, and future) of time and care to become, through continual choice among one's possibilities, the action-filled self whose nature is determined—and, therefore, arrested—only at death. The "before" and "after" death do not exist. Selfhood or human existence is bound by birth and death. The self is a statistic, a stereotype, only at birth and at death. In between, one never *is* anything in particular, because one is in the perpetually changing process of "becoming"—again, as with the ancient Greek philosophers, *a dynamic within a static.*

Existentialists view existence, therefore, as *an unending becoming in the now*, a standing out before one's possibilities (*ex-sistere*). Accordingly, selfhood is seen as:

(a) an unending becoming in the *now* (the telescopic point of past and future, of facticity and possibility);

(b) a continuing and dynamic choice of possibilities conferring a dynamic content on the existence of the self, and

(c) that portion of existence sealed off between birth and death.

And *death* is that event, that master possibility to end all possibilities, that gives the final, fixed, and forever static content to the self.

Thus death becomes the *goal* of existence, which, accordingly, is viewed as a *being-toward-death*. Existence, for all its dynamism, is *death-centered* in two ways: (a) death is the goal of existence and (b) death is the central integrative factor of the self and its various temporal modes of existence. These temporal modes of existence are past, present, and future, constituting what Heidegger calls "care," and are linked to, and distinguished by, their corresponding characteristics:

Facticity: all the givens or data with which the self is confronted;
Falling: preoccupation with affairs of the present (or past or future) alone, the hallmark of the "fragmented" self (in contrast with the "unified" self, which considers all three time dimensions, always in the light of the master possibility of death); and
Possibility: all the choices remaining open, not yet preempted by previous or past activity.

As the ultimate possibility to end all possibilities—the ultimate, certain, and fortuitous (because liable to happen at any time) possibility—death, and particularly the thought of death, wraps up and integrates all modes of care and existence, giving the latter meaning at the same time as it terminates the existent as a being-in-the-world. Death, as a fortuitous and certain event, is neither *future* (as it can happen in the instant present) nor *contingent* (as it is certain to occur). It is this *fortuity-cum-certainty* of death that marks it as unique among all possibilities, all other possibilities being both *future-oriented* and *contingent*.

Given all the foregoing, the authentic self or existent is that which lives at once in all three dimensions of care or temporality—facticity (past), falling (present), and possibility (future)—using the death-thought as an integrating principle of life. The inauthentic self or existent is that which lives in only one of the three modes or dimensions, but especially in the present or falling mode. Accordingly, the inauthentic existent gets involved with the world and forgets about dying—is "in and of" the world. The authentic existent, thinking always of death, does not become involved with the world—is "in but not of" the world (Kierkegaard). In consequence, other existents (the "they") who get involved with the world could impede one's attempt at authentic existence if they succeed in getting one involved, like themselves, in the world (Kierkegaard). Authentic existence, moreover, is impossible without the aid of Super-Existence (Kierkegaardian "God" or Heideggerian "Being"), who grabs man and reveals itself to him in a freely granted act of grace.

Criticisms

(i) The Existential Interpretation of the Ontological Dictum That "Existence Precedes Essence." Existentialist thought—at least the brand promoted by Heidegger and Sartre—is essentially about individual human character formation by means of individual choice among *given* alternative possibilities involving human action (or inaction). Existence is defined in this character-forming sense as freedom and ability to constitute one's character (i.e., make and remake oneself) by free choice among alternative possibilities that are continually confronting everyone. But character forming being a continuing and dynamic process is never completed until the day of one's death. Then, and only then, does one have or possess a *complete* character or *essence.* It is in this sense that existence (continual remaking of oneself) precedes essence (the final, sum total of one's character)—according to the Heidegger-Sartre brand of existentialism.

It is a case of multiple confusion and error for Sartre to insist that one does not possess a character or essence until one's death. Firstly, he failed to recognize the "stickiness" and cumulative nature of character-formation—that the past cannot be simply erased by the present in the realm of character-formation. What one has been persists to a large extent in influencing what one now is and will be in the future. One merely adds to, not subtracts from, one's essence as one's life and time proceed. Thus Sartre failed to distinguish between one's *interim* character, which one has at any given moment, and one's complete or *final* character at death.

And even this is not "final," as we have learnt regarding the theory and practice of personality cult in authoritarian societies.[48]

Secondly, Sartre and other existentialists of his persuasion concentrate on character formation to the total exclusion of physical existence. Hence, they are able to ignore, artificially, the social context of man, present in the act of human reproduction. In thus failing to distinguish between *character existence* (which is all they care about) and *physical existence* (which they blandly ignore) they overlook two important facts:

(a) that there are other physical existents than man;
(b) that while an individual forms his character by choice among given,

131

or presented, possibilities (for which he is not responsible) his character is not entirely the sum total of his own choices and actions. Another and very important part of his character is formed by the choices of others—his parents, teachers, and other people who raise him since infancy and influence him as role models and in other ways, his peers—as well as by his environment, generally: all of which stamp his character indelibly without his necessarily being aware of it or exercising any *conscious choice* (or lack of choice) in their favor. Thus this brand of existentialist thought not only ignores the physical existence of other human and nonhuman existents but also, as a result, their input into one's character formation. This is a very serious lack.

Thirdly, and in consequence of the preceding defect, existentialist thought ignores the dependence of its interpretation of existence ("existentialist existence" or character formation) on physical existence. It is in this latter, and original, sense that "existence (physical existence) precedes essence (character formation)." This is the traditional meaning of the famous dictum in the ontological controversy initiated by Anselm, the eleventh-century Archbishop of Canterbury, and concluded, after a fashion, by Kant, the eighteenth-century German philosopher. However, existentialists of the persuasion under discussion ignore this traditional interpretation of the dictum, in favor of theirs in which existence (= continuing, dynamic choice among possibilities and corresponding continuing character formation) precedes essence (= complete and final state of character at death). This latter meaning, while interesting, is less fundamental than the former and overestimates the permanence of character at death, given revisionist tendencies of historians and authoritarian governments as these affect the type of character associated with the historical figures that they present to succeeding generations.

(ii) The Central Role of Death in Existentialist Thought. In existentialist thought death is seen as the ultimate possibility—the possibility that ends all possibilities. This view is not valid, existentially speaking, since death is *not* the end of existence—not even the end of *human* existence, but of human *biological* existence. Therefore, it is necessary to qualify death in its character as a possibility. Death is transformation but not the transformation to end all transformations, for transformations continue after the death of the human body. Death is much more than possibility. Even so, too much emphasis is placed on death and its role in human existence when it is described as death-integrated, death-centered, death-oriented, and death-terminated.

Existence, in its proper sense of becoming, is an open-ended and

132

continuing process without beginning or end and marked by continuous transformation. Life and death are inseparable components of this transformation. Death is only one of various possible organizing principles of *human* existence; others may be power, religion, peace or conflict avoidance, et cetera. Being open-ended, existence cannot be death-centered, nor can there be any *ultimate concern* of existence (such as death or other) as theologians are fond of orating, except existence itself—continuing transformation or change.

Regarding human existence as a being-toward-death, existentialists hold that it behooves every human being to be (i.e., make himself/herself) available or *free for death*. Death marks the *finite temporality* or *finitude* of man. In this respect, Heidegger criticizes Hegel for regarding man as being caught up in the infinite, unending process of history. This is hardly a valid criticism, given the distinction between the individual human existent and the human species. While the individual is made finite by the certainty of death, it is otherwise with the species in that individual reproduction in a more than one to one correspondence cancels out the effect of individual finitude-through-death, making the species as a whole less finite. The finitude of the species is governed less by the death of its individual members than by biological and cosmological catastrophes that threaten the entire species. Here Darwin, not Kierkegaard or Heidegger, holds the key to the riddle of the species' existence. Thus in order to properly appreciate the role of death in human existence it is necessary to distinguish between *micro-existentialism* and *macro-existentialism* and, correspondingly, between the *certain finitude* of the conscious, individual human existent and the *contingent finitude* of the human species.

What gives meaning to human life is not necessarily one's own death—not even for those (like the Christians) who, while directing their current terrestrial life in the shadow of death-thoughts, believe in a heavenly and a hellish afterlife. There are various possible meaning-conferring criteria. If, for example, the criterion is one that piles up for a blissful life in heaven due to good works on planet Earth, then thoughts of death are futile. If the criterion is power on Earth, then terrorizing people with death-dealing atomic weapons as a means to power confers meaning on the life of the tyrant, provided there is no competition in the terror department. If, however, the organizing criterion is "no criterion" and life is regarded as having no particular meaning or significance, except continuing change or evolution—as Sartre and Camus maintain—then anything goes: no action is futile—even in the face of death; any and every action is worthwhile, even if meaningless.

Whatever one's criterion for a meaningful, conscious existence, one does not need death-thoughts to make it fruitful. On the contrary, a death-oriented thought-life may generate psychological morbidity and paralyze responsible, meaningful, and decisive action. One may be better off *forgetting* about one's death in such a case. Likewise, a falling or in-authentic existence in which one is preoccupied with the present, being "in and of" the world, is precisely what is called for if, according to Sartre, existence is a continuing decision and choice among possibilities that yet remain open—a continuing reduction of one's past to "nothing-ness" as one chooses a new orientation. One must always live in the present in order to make such choices. Indeed, one is more "free for death" when one does not think about it. For death, being fortuitous though certain, there is no way one can "prepare oneself" for it.

The real issue about death is not with thinking or not thinking about it, as Heidegger maintained, but with the nature of one's myth concerning one's state of existence after death (beyond the obvious fact of physical disintegration), and the extent to which one can contribute during one's lifetime to enhancing the afterlife. For Christians who believe in a grand Judgment as introduction to the afterlife, frequent death-thoughts may serve as a salutary reminder summoning to good behavior during their lifetimes. Others who conceive of the afterlife differently and those who have internalized good behavior may not need frequent death-thoughts in order to direct their daily lives. And there is nothing to deplore in that, contrary to Heidegger's point of view. Epicurus, after all, may have had the last word on the subject of death: it is neither of consequence nor of concern to us, for it is not present when we exist consciously, and when it is present we do not consciously exist. Conscious existence and death never coexist in the same existent.

(iii) Secular Existentialism and Atheism. Jean-Paul Sartre created a minor scandal when he equated secular existentialism with atheism. Nothing in Sartre's writing, however, lends support to his claim that secular exis-tentialism is, indeed, atheism—as the internal evidence will show. As to his own self-proclaimed atheism, Sartre appeared to be no more than a poseur who delighted in shocking others who professed a belief in God.

Sartre's interpretation of atheism was ambiguous from the outset, as he used the term in two senses: first, to mean antitheism or disbelief in God; second, to mean a-theism or neutrality regarding a belief in God. In his work titled *Existentialism*[49] the following passages occur, equating secular existentialism with antitheism:

> Atheistic existentialism, which I represent, is more coherent. It states that if God does not exist, there is at least one being in whom existence precedes essence, a being who exists before he can be defined by any concept, and that this being is man. . . . Thus, there is no human nature, since there is no God to conceive it. [p. 15.]

134

When we speak of forlornness, a term Heidegger was fond of, we mean only that God does not exist and that we have to face all the consequences of this. [p. 21.]

The existentialist . . . thinks it very distressing that God does not exist because all possibility of finding values in a heaven of ideas disappears along with him. [p. 22.]

Dostoievsky said, "If God didn't exist, everything would be possible." That is the very starting point of existentialism. Indeed, everything is permissible if God does not exist, and as a result man is forlorn, because neither within him nor without does he find anything to cling to. He can't start making excuses for himself. [p. 22.]

In other words, there is no determinism, man is free, man is freedom. On the other hand, if God does not exist, we find no values or commands to turn to which legitimize our conduct. [p. 23.]

On the other side, we find the following passage, which makes the concept of God not invalid but only *irrelevant* to the concerns of existentialism, that is, a-theism:

Existentialism is nothing else than an attempt to draw all the consequences of a coherent atheistic position. . . . Existentialism isn't so atheistic that it wears itself out showing that God doesn't exist. Rather, it declares that even if God did exist, that would change nothing. There you've got our point of view. Not that we believe that God exists, but we think that the problem of His existence is not the issue. (p. 51)

This last passage shows that Sartre is not an atheist in the sense of antitheist, but an atheist in the sense of one who is neutral in the matter of whether or not there is a God. What is more, Sartre is not even an agnostic. But most interesting of all are the following passages from a translation of his famous work *Being and Nothingness* (L'Etre et le néant),[50] which not only indicate that his antitheism was probably no more than a pose but also that his existentialism defines man in terms of God. Dealing with human responsibility, he writes:

Yet this responsibility is of a very particular type. Someone will say, "I did not ask to be born." This is a naive way of throwing greater emphasis on our facticity. I am responsible for everything, in fact, except for my very responsibility, for I am not the foundation of my being.

And again:

It is precisely thus that the for-itself apprehends itself in anguish; that is, as a being which is neither the foundation of its own being nor of the Other's being nor of the in-itselfs which form the world . . .

135

These two passages do not sound like an espousal of antitheism. Writing of man in relation to God, Sartre penned the following revealing passage:

> The best way to conceive of the fundamental project of human reality is to say that man is the being whose project is to be God. Whatever may be the myths and rites of the religion considered, God is first "sensible to the heart" of man as the one who identifies and defines him in his ultimate and fundamental project. If man possesses a pre-ontological comprehension of the being of God, it is not the great wonders of nature nor the power of society which have conferred it upon him. God, value and supreme end of transcendence, represents the permanent limit in terms of which man means to reach toward being God. Or if you prefer, man fundamentally is the desire to be God.[51]

It seems clear that, far from being antitheist, secular existentialism consists essentially in this, that man, not God, provides the ultimate answer and solution to the problem of man's facticity as a being-in-the-world; namely, to reconcile himself to the world, get involved in it through actions resulting from his continual exercise of choice among his possibilities, thereby continually reconstituting his own character in a meaningful way.

6. THE DESTINY OF MAN: A SUMMARY

The various cosmologies (or theologies of the cosmos) speculate upon not only the origin and destiny—beginning and end—of the cosmos but specifically also upon the origin and destiny of man. In regard to man there are more speculations than pronouncements based upon evidence or experience.

Ancient Greek philosophical and metaphysical thought propounded the myth of the two worlds—sensible and suprasensible—based on the mystical tradition of Pythagoras and his predecessors. This duality was reflected in the nature of man, part body *(physis)*, part soul. The latter consisted of intellect *(nous)* and appetite *(nisus)*, with appetite linked to the body and intellect merely associated with it. The destiny of man is the dissolution of body-cum-appetite from the intellectual part of soul that regains the suprasensible world in which it originated. This main doctrine is supplemented by a devolutionary theory of metempsychosis or transmigration of souls, traced only in outline by Plato in his dialogue, *Timaeus*. According to this theory, in their next incarnation in the sensible world, cowardly men will become women; light-minded men, unlearned in mathematics, will become birds; those men who have no knowledge of philosophy will become land animals—including the belly-crawling serpent—while the most stupid will become fishes.

The Hindu-Buddhist conception of human destiny has common elements with the ancient Greek myth on the subject. Existence is conceived as consisting in two phases or worlds: a sensible world in which operates the "wheel of life," the continuing cycle of birth and death, and a suprasensible world, "nirvana," or state of perpetual bliss. The sensible world is the theater for the enactment of metempsychosis, or devolutionary process, on lines similar to those sketched by Plato in the *Timaeus*. There are successive reincarnations (births, deaths, and rebirths) until the time when one lets go of the wheel and enters, after a final death, the state of nirvana.

With the cessation of the cycle of births and deaths the individual soul or life force (Atman) unites undifferentiatedly with the universal life force (Brahma). The destiny of man is thus the merging of the individual with the cosmic life force in a "union of undifferentiates."

For all the comfort they may bring to their adherents, the Semitic theologies, like any theology regarding the destiny of man, are no more than what they contain—pure speculations or myths, crude analogies patterned on man's earthbound existence. As analogies, however, they can be ranked and compared in order of attractiveness. The messianic speculations of Judaism about apocalypse followed by final judgment and a millennium of peace and social justice somewhere are, on the one hand, too general, lacking specifics, and, on the other, too tied to the destiny and eventual comeuppance of the Israelite tribes to be of universal interest, especially to non-Jews.

The Christian speculations, based on the Jewish model of apocalypse—last judgment—millennium, contain few improvements in the line of specifics and succeed only in presenting a general picture of monotony and boredom: the Christian Elect among the resurrected (corresponding to the Elect among the twelve tribes of Israel) are presented as inhabiting a land flowing with milk and honey—a postresurrection land of Canaan—located on the metaphorical thither side of a metaphorical river Jordan, its capital (the metaphorical New Jerusalem) paved with gold. There is to be found the throne of God around which stand the Elect, dressed in robes of spotless white and wearing golden crowns, incessantly singing day and night, praising God and saying, "Worthy is the Lamb that was slain to receive power, and riches, and wisdom, and strength, and honour, and glory, and blessing."[52]

Islam, with all the advantages of the late starter, was able to study and compare the anthropotheological fables of its predecessors and come up with a picture a little less general, gayer and fun-filled—consequently,

137

more attractive. The Elect dwell in the mansions of Paradise, amid well-watered gardens and oases overflowing with milk, honey, and dates. The male of the species disport themselves in these elysian surroundings, each accompanied by numerous houris (beautiful, chaste, female companions).[53] With such a delightful prospect, small wonder if Islam should exert a greater pulling power on converts (predominantly male, of course) than its two predecessors. Promising to deliver such an attractive *au-déla* (beyond death) Islam, naturally, walks off with the competition and the honors.

In both Christianity and Islam the non-Elect—or the Damned—receive the same treatment: the lake filled with fire and brimstone, called Hell, where the unlucky ones burn forever without being consumed, in unending torment.

In contrast to the foregoing speculations, Darwin's theory of evolution of species through genetic mutation and natural selection (environmental adaptation) assigns man no destiny. The same goes for any other species. The prospect offered to man is the *contingent* survival of the species, for evolution leads always to something new but unknown: it may be survival or its opposite, disappearance.

Basing themselves on Darwin's theory, Teilhard de Chardin and Julian Huxley attempt in different ways to work in the substance of Christian theology as well as Christology. Either way, man becomes the spearhead and goal of all evolutionary processes, as Jesus Christ or simply as man. The destiny of man is man transformed.

Of all destiny theories Darwin's seems the most plausible. Yet even its most enthusiastic supporters admit that the evidence for applying it to man is very slim, for the following reasons[54]:

(a) the phyla or branches from or through which man could have evolved are lost in the mists of antiquity and palaeontology;
(b) the evidence of human existence goes only as far back as the neolithic age, say, some three to five hundred thousand years back;
(c) man has not changed genetically, anatomically, or physiologically throughout the known period of his existence since the neolithic age;
(d) human environmental adaptation and survival has been due rather to cultural than to genetic adaptation to environmental changes; and cultural, unlike genetic, adaptation is not inherited but taught anew in each generation;
(e) human culture has hardly changed regarding the general artifacts and arrangements of domestic and social life.

The upshot of all this is that neither Genesis nor Darwin says anything about the destiny of man, and the available evidence does not give any ground to expect, under either theory, that the human being of the future is likely to be any different, by and large, from the human being of the past or the present. But there can be no guarantee.

NOTES

1. The presentation given here is based on Niebuhr's Gifford Lectures, collected in the volume titled *The Nature and Destiny of Man* (New York: Charles Scribner's Sons, 1953).
2. In the "Books of The Times" column of *The New York Times* of Thursday, January 2, 1986, p. C16, Walter Goodman, reviewing Richard Wightman Fox's biography of Reinhold Niebuhr, quotes a British Niebuhrian who wrote: "The true believer / In Reinhold Niebuhr / Is apt to mention / The fact of tension."
3. R. B. Perry, *Realms of Value* (Harvard University Press, 1954), p. 491.
4. Misnamed Evolution Theory, though he himself called it a theory of "modified descent" of species.
5. For example, Ndama cattle are better adapted than zebu to a tsetse environment, but zebu cattle give more meat. Crossing the two is supposed to result in a tsetse-resistant (ndama strain) meat-producing (zebu strain) new species of cattle. Whether the new breed surives is a chancy affair, as this will depend on its ability to resist tsetse; but this cannot be taken for granted since there is no guarantee that the tsetse resistance of the ndama will be passed on. To take another example from botany: the green revolution aims, by genetic cross-breeding, to produce higher yield seeds. Whether these seeds are better adapted to a given environment than the local seed varieties is a chancy question. If they are not, they may succumb to local plant pests and diseases.
6. There is some relationship between chance and chaos, the latter being a state of confusion that proceeds according to some order. (See "Science" section of *Newsweek*, 18 July 1983, p. 45: "Finding the Order in Chaos.")
7. It should be noted that Darwin compared genetic mutation in nature (unplanned) to genetic mutation by animal breeding, except that this form of animal (or even human) husbandry can be artificial (planned) or natural (unplanned).
8. T. R. Malthus, *An Essay on the Principle of Population* (1798).
9. F. Ferré, *Language, Logic and God* (Westport, Conn.: Greenwood Press, 1961), pp. 23–24.
10. Kant, in his *Critique of Pure Reason*, posited that objects conform to our knowledge, thus reversing the normal order of things in scientific inquiry and making phenomena and scientific laws a subjective affair, beyond all possibility of empirical verification.
11. Julian Huxley, *Religion Without Revelation* (New York: Mentor Books, 1957).
12. Julian Huxley's speculations about religion and human evolution fall in the same category but are treated, for convenience, in the following section on humanism.
13. Teilhard de Chardin, *The Phenomenon of Man* (Collins, Fountain Books, 1977).
14. See Book Two, Section B, chapter 14.
15. The socioeconomic viewpoint is similar, namely, that man exists for, and is simultaneously the instrument of, the advancement and welfare of man.
16. Strictly speaking, Adam Smith's humanism is more individual than social—he is a strong advocate of that "rugged individualism" associated with theoretical private enterprise capitalism—social goals and benefits being merely incidental and a spinoff from individual objectives. His humanism is here treated as "social" in the sense

that it is regarded as a desirable goal for society and achievable in the short term.

17. This bit of mysticism begged the question and thereby prevented the rational use of foresight, of preventive action against foreseeable adverse consequences, and of a proper assessment of the environmental and social consequences of unbridled individual initiatives. Hence the human suffering and social ills of the Industrial Revolution in Britain.

18. Presented thus, humanism is egocentrism—much worse than geocentrism, anthropocentrism, and ethnocentrism. It may have some redeeming feature if interpreted as anthropocentrism as, indeed, Feuerbach intended it to be. Even so, however, it is just as flawed as geocentrism was, compared to heliocentrism, or, paradoxically, just as valid. For the essence of the Copernican revolution is that any point in the cosmos could be regarded as its center. This paradox, which really does not dethrone geocentrism, anthropocentrism, or ethnocentrism but renders them equally valid with any other x-centric doctrine, contains a difficulty that has seldom, if at all, been addressed: the geometry and general mathematics of an n-centered system—a very difficult topic as well as a very difficult picture of the cosmos to comprehend.

19. Op. cit., p. 59.

20. The transposition of God into Huxleian "matter" and Holy Spirit into Huxleian "mind" results in an inverse variation of matter and mind when inserted into Teilhard's evolutionary model.

21. Op. cit., chapter 2, pp. 37–48.

22. Op. cit., p. 208.

23. Op. cit., p. 193.

24. Op. cit., p. 194.

25. Op. cit., p. 196–97.

26. Karl Marx—less strictly an existentialist in the sense that he was concerned with groups or "classes" rather than individuals, but still in the tradition of the existentialist solution of self-transcendence transferred to the level of the class, where it becomes the suppression of one class by another—may be regarded as a *group-oriented* rather than an individual-oriented existentialist. Viewing the social system rather than the individual (hence as a "group-oriented" existentialist rather than as an "individual-oriented" existentialist or existentialist proper), Marx dwelt on the internal contradictions of the private enterprise capitalist system and the desirability of suppressing or eliminating one contradiction (the "haves") by its opposite (the "have-nots"). Henceforth, society would no longer be composed of two classes but of one—the working class. In this event, according to Marx, lies humanity's highest good.

27. There is some question as to the appropriateness of the term *philosophy*, as applied to existentialism. Christian existentialism, as defined later in this section, may be called a philosophy since it involves interpersonal relationships. Theological and secular existentialism reject interrelationships for solipsism, even in a context of interrelationships. These pseudo-philosophies as well as the philosophical brand of existentialism may together be best described as an "intellectual movement."

28. The argument of Thrasymachus in Plato's *Republic*.

29. Plato thus set the tradition later adopted by the Christian theologians, including theological existentialists, who argue solipsistically that morally the individual relates directly to God, not to the world.

30. The religious nature of Marxism has been discussed already in chapter 3 of Book Two, Section A, Part II, preceding.

31. Dramatized in Sartre's play, *No Exit*.

32. I Corinthians 15:55.

33. The discussion is based on various writings by Kierkegaard but, notably, *Fear and Trembling, The Sickness unto Death* (Princeton, N.J.: Princeton University, 1941, 1954); and on Martin Heidegger, *Existence and Being* (Henry Regnery Company, 1949) and *Basic Writings* (Routledge & Kegan Paul, 1978).

34. Heidegger conceives of immortality in an unusual manner, as being within time but transcending transcience, i.e., the succession of "presents" or "nows." This same concept, for Sartre, becomes continuous choice among one's possibilities and re-making oneself—Sartre's very definition of existence as standing outside and in front of one's possibilities in order to choose.

35. This is very much like the Buddhist doctrine that self-knowledge (knowing who one is) involves, and cannot be achieved without, knowing the other and thereby recognizing the unity underlying the appearances of differences among persons, and the nothingness underlying all appearances of concreteness. In Hindu philosophy this sameness and nothingness are symbolized by the deity, Shiva, the creator of appearances (maya, illusions) and the destroyer of concreteness (reduction to nothingness).

36. The correspondence of this interpretation of existence to the Darwinian meaning of evolution is rather striking, revealing existentialism to be the interpretation or application of evolution theory at the level of the individual member of a species—at least so far as secular existentialism is concerned.

37. Sartre shows a bit of naiveté, or error, in maintaining that past choices and their effects are eliminated, nullified, by present choices—wiped clean without any trace or contribution to one's interim character and one's final character at death.

38. In this respect, also Sartre may be judged a bit naive or unacquainted with the theory and practice of the mutable past under secular authoritarian regimes that "impersonify," "depersonify," and "repersonify"—and even create fictitious persons, according to their will. George Orwell's *Nineteen Eighty-Four* (New York: Penguin Books, 1954) immortalizes this theory and practice.

39. The Sartrean concepts of "nothingness," "existence," and "being" contrast with the African philosophic concept of existence as a thorough and continuing state of dynamism, beginning but without ending. Sartre also overlooks the fact—noted in Book One, chapter 1, and subsequently in Book Three, chapter 10—of the malleability of history and so-called fixed statistics, both through reinterpretation (Book One, chapter 1) and through subsequent alteration of records (Book Three, chapter 10). To this extent Sartre's existential theory is empirically defective.

40. Simone de Beauvoir, *The Second Sex* (Bantam Books, 1961).

41. Claude Tresmontant, *Sciences de l'Univers et problèmes metaphysiques* (Paris: Editions du Seuil, 1976), p. 9.

42. Thomas Hobbes, *Leviathan* (New York: E. P. Dutton, 1950), part I, chapter XIII, p. 104.

43. See section 4, E and F, of this chapter.

44. J.-P. Sartre, *Existentialisme est un humanisme*.

45. This argument is on a slightly different plane from, but of the same type as, that of those who choose suicide in order to avoid or terminate pain and suffering in their human existence. Their assumption is that consciousness, along with its psychological pain and pleasure, does not survive the physical dissolution of the human organism. This is a moot point. But the possibility that consciousness does outlive the mortal body should not be entirely ruled out merely on the ground that what we do not know now won't hurt us later when, and if, we come to know it. For nothing is impossible in our open-ended cosmos. The conclusive answer, of course, is that if consciousness does survive mortality, then suicide becomes a matter of choice—of

substitution at the margin—among the modes of pain, not a matter of avoidance of pain: we merely make a marginal substitution of after-death psychological pain for a temporary combination of physical and psychological pain before death. In this case, there is nothing in the argument or in the world to forbid anyone to make the choice of suicide, except ignorance on the question of the survivability of consciousness and its states after death. In the circumstances, it will ever remain a moot point whether a willing suicide would carry through with the act if he or she had prior knowledge of the "fact" of postdeath consciousness. Since, however, no one possesses valid information on this point, none is competent to lay down the law on suicide or to forbid another from taking that course. And even if such valid information existed, no one could claim competence to decide for another who consciously chose suicide. In this matter the decision of the suicide is supreme—as it is in every case of suicide. Naturally, of course, the same argument holds in our present state of ignorance, for there is no valid reason to prefer submitting to dissuasion by others in the face of ignorance to bravery in the face of ignorance.

Notwithstanding the foregoing argument, it remains true and should always be borne in mind that death, however it comes to us, does not enable us to opt out of existence; for existence is unoptable—in spite of death.

46. This point further clarifies the difference in the respective stance of existentialists as a group (Christian, theological, and secular) and Karl Marx. Existentialists are concerned only with themselves, whether or not they accept the other, the rest of the world outside of themselves; and change, if any, is brought about in themselves not in the world. Karl Marx, no existentialist, was concerned with the world outside of himself, not with himself, did not accept the world as it was and, therefore, was concerned to change it *in addition* to interpreting it. Essentially, therefore, the difference is between changing oneself (existentialists) and changing the world (Marx). Yet, essentially also, the end result could be the same, since by changing oneself—provided everyone else does the same—one changes the world. And herein lies the real difference—in terms of *effectiveness* of the change: the world is more quickly and effectively changed if everyone aims to change themselves. This is the truth that escaped Karl Marx—that in spite of his antagonism to Christianity, the Christian message of changing-the-world-through-changing-oneself is a potentially more effective weapon of change than the Marxian weapon of direct frontal attack on the other, the world.

47. Provided one does not earn a lower-than-human-male status by Platonian devolution through living a less-than-fully-human-male existence. (See Plato, *Timaeus*, section 49).

48. See note 32.

49. English translation of the original French, presented in *Existentialism and Human Emotions* (New York: Wisdom Library, 1957).

50. Idem, pp. 57, 59, 63, respectively.

51. This passage is reminiscent of Friedrich Nietzsche's similar ambition to become Superman, God. (See F. Nietzsche, *Thus Spake Zarathustra*.)

52. Revelation 5:12.

53. The Koran (New York: Penguin Classics), trans. N. J. Dawood: 4:58, 13:36, 32:18, 39:21, 47:16, 55:47–79, 56:2–41.

54. See V. Gordon Childe, *Man Makes Himself* (London: C. A. Watts & Co., 1956).

PART III
AFRICAN METAPHYSICS

Chapter 5

Metaphysical Structure of African Society

For the African, tribe or society is a system of relationships and inter-relationships founded upon something fundamental: the relationship of man to land. And land is a space fragment, a portion of the cosmos consisting of a given mass (or condensed energy). It is a basic meta-physical unit and, as in economics, must be invested with a wider inter-pretation to include not only soil and mineral resources but also climate: in short, the biosphere or ecology of man. Thus erected on the land is the first tier of relationships—the ecological relationship of man to land.

Following upon and closely bound up with the ecological relationship are the social relationships. These include family and other kinship ties, religion as well as ethics. Religion comprises the relationships pivoted on man and ethics the mutual, personalized interrelationships prevailing, normally, among the human members of society. The social relationships together constitute the web that holds the members of the tribe or society together.

On the social relationships are based, in turn, another system of relationships linking tribe or society to the extraterrestrial elements of the cosmos. These relationships are mostly theological, manifesting them-selves in prayer, incantations, sacrifice, and offerings to the tribal gods and to the one great God or Spirit, but also to the tribe's founders, heroes, and ancestral spirits who share the biosphere with their survivors.

The African thus erects a vertically structured network of relation-ships and interrelationships founded on the basic man-land structure. This network we may term the existential web, the constituent elements of which (man, other animals, climate, and other natural resources) are always in a permanent state of flux. The entire system rises literally, from the ground up and beyond to the outer limits of the cosmos. Land is thus the basis, physical and metaphysical, of African society.

This vertical existential web accounts for two important features of African life: first, the fundamental importance of land to the African, economically and metaphysically; second, the structure and nonproselytic character of the African religio-theological system.

144

Anthropologists have made various studies confirming the extremely important role that land plays in the African social scheme, as the bond between past, present, and future in the life of the community and among the ancestors, the current sociobiological community, and the unborn generations to come. Its economic role is, of course, paramount: the source of the community's sustenance as well for man as for the domesticated and wild flora and fauna—its food (grain and meat and fruits), fiber, and water.

The social, religious, and theological role[1] of land is only slightly less than its economic role and is equally well documented by anthropologists. It is where the sites of the sacred shrines and fetishes are to be found, attesting to the numinous: the spirits in water, tree, forest, grove, and mountain—the local divinities. In some societies, it is also where the umbilical cord of each member of each family in the tribal community lies buried at the root of its appointed tree. It is the last resting place of the ancestors, containing their graves marked by mounds, circles of stone, and broken utensils (calabashes and earthenware) that testify that their owner is no more in the sociobiological—though continuing in the sociometaphysical—community.

Most important from the sociometaphysical point of view is the fact that the tribal land is the only geographical space—and no other—where the religious myth and rites of family and tribe can be practiced: the birth, pubertal, marital, and funeral rites; the offerings and sacrifices, symbols of continuing contact, sharing, and communion with the dead ancestors, very much alive in the minds and memories of their survivors. Even in spiritual form, these ancestors are permanently in the land of the living, tribal community. This is why, when they are forced by natural or other calamities to move from a tribal area, the members of a tribe feel obliged to take with them from the old to the new tribal land all their fetishes, shrines, and other ritual property as well as the remains of their ancestors.

The land, as family and tribal property, is therefore rich in connotations. There is so much that links the society to its tribal lands that should shifting cultivation make some land apparently vacant, it would be a grave error to assume or think, as did the Boer trekkers in South Africa in the latter part of the last and early part of the present century, that there were no owners of such land. Land that still contains the bones of the ancestors is not vacant land, appearances to the contrary, but very much "owned" and "possessed." In tribal Africa, there are no vacant, unowned lands. Even anthropologists miss the most important and crucial aspect of land in African society—its metaphysical aspect. The entire concept and structure of being, in the dynamic sense of existence, is erected vertically upon the tribal land, as we have seen. Consequently, to take away an African's land, his tribal patrimony, is literally to deprive

145

him (her) of his (her) very existence, to rob existence of all meaning.

In keeping with the vertical dimension of African metaphysics—from land (including buried ancestors) through family and tribe to the Great Beyond—African religion and religious practices are also vertically structured. Religion is, on the one hand, a direct relationship between an individual and, on the other, his dead relatives, ancestors, and other spirits, his shrines, family and tribe and, beyond, the sun, moon and stars. Similarly, theology is a direct relationship between an individual and the "lesser gods" (actually, spirits) as well as the Supreme God conceived in Cartesian terms as wholly other and preserver of the cosmos. Nothing horizontal in all this: all is vertical. The land containing the ancestral remains and the shrines is literally below the individual; at his level come the family, within a hierarchically structured tribe; above him the ancestral spirits, and higher still the sun, moon and stars; and, far and away beyond all, the Supreme God.

There is, therefore, no room for proselytism in African religion and theology. These are very personal matters, confined within the family and the tribe. No family converts another, no tribe another tribe. In sum, religion and theology have no horizontal dimension in the life of the tribal African, that is, outside of his family and tribe. Each individual relates directly and personally to the spirits of the local shrines, to departed relatives and spirits, to his family and tribe, working out his own "salvation" with joy, or with "fear and trembling," as the occasion may demand. A man's religion and theology have no meaning outside of his family and tribe or for another tribe. It is thus no accident or miracle that religious or theological wars are never fought in indigenous Africa. Such conflicts, typical of the Semitic religions, when they do occur have always involved adherents to these foreign religions—chiefly, Christianity and Islam. These two, like their Judaic archetype, are by nature and tradition intolerant and proselytic.

Given the vertical structure of African metaphysics, African philosophy is inevitably concerned with the general relationships within this metaphysical system; African religion is concerned with the individual African as the focus and radial point of these relationships, and African ethics basically with that part of the religious network subject to reciprocity and mutuality. These relationships are depicted in the two diagrams that follow.

NOTE

1. A good reference is John Mbiti, *African Religions and Philosophy* (Heinemann, 1969). The French edition is titled *Religions et philosophie africaines* (Yaounde, Cameroun: Edition CLE, 1972).

AFRICAN SOCIO-COSMOLOGY

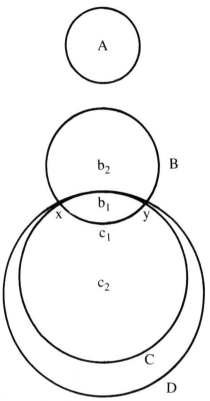

Legend

Circle A = Deity

Circle B = Past community of ancestors = Intercessors with Deity for
the living

composed of: b_1 = the living dead, i.e., the personalized
spirits of the dead within living memory

b_2 = the depersonalized spirits of the
unknown dead

Circle C = Present or contemporary community

composed of: b_1 = the living dead

Arc xc_1y = witch doctors, on the fringe of intercessors with Deity for the living
(Circle B)

c_2 = rest of the contemporary community

Circle D = Biosphere of animals (including contemporary human community),
plants and other vegetation, nonbiological entities, and their
environment

(Note: The relative sizes of the circles are not significant.)

147

AFRICAN COSMOLOGY

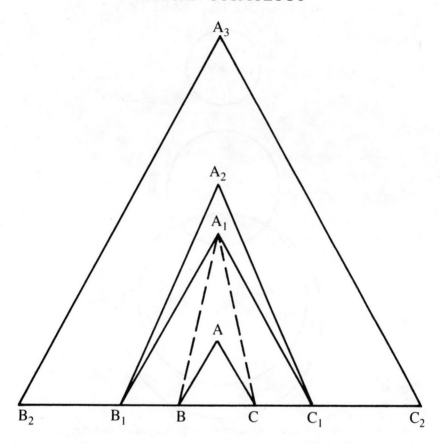

Legend

$$
\begin{aligned}
ABC &= \text{Contemporary human community (physio-mental}\\
&\quad\;\text{personalities) including the living dead (mental}\\
&\quad\;\text{personalities)}\\
A_1BACA_1 &= \text{Depersonalized spirits}\\
A_1BB_1A_1CC_1 &= \text{Minerals, vegetation, other animals (nonhuman)}\\
&\quad\;(= A_1BB_1 + A_1CC_1)\\
A_1B_1A_2C_1A_1 &= \text{Environment of } A_1B_1C_1\\
A_2B_1C_1 &= \text{Biosphere}\\
A_2B_1B_2A_3C_2C_1A_2 &= \text{Rest of Cosmos}\\
A_3B_2C_2 &= \text{Cosmos}
\end{aligned}
$$

(Note: The relative sizes of the triangles are not significant.)

Chapter 6

African Existentialism: The African View of the Nature and Destiny of Man

This chapter presents the essence of the African view concerning the nature and destiny of man. It is a view that differs greatly from the occidental view inherited from the ancient Greeks.

Two basic elements constitute the structure of a human being:

(a) the body (soma): the palpable physical element of man;
(b) the mind-spirit: the intellect, emotions, and psychic energy of man.

These two elements combine to form the vibrant psycho-soma known as the human being. This psycho-somatic unity generates an aura of its own consisting of the total integrate of impressions emanating from it and received by other human beings and known as its *personality*. The personality is thus a kind of superstructure erected on the psycho-soma.

Personality is attached to *persons* in two ways: first, to the physical person to whom it belongs and who carries it about inseparably while psychosomatically alive; second, to those who know the person to whom it belongs in the form of mental impressions of that person's personality. Thus there is a multidimensional relationship between the personality and its owner, and between it and those who know the owner.

The human being passes through three phases. The first phase consists of the psycho-soma, body-mind-spirit personality. The second phase sets in with the disintegration (through death) of the soma, releasing from its union with the soma the mind-spirit. This leaves us with the mind-spirit personality, which survives only in the minds and emotions of those who knew the deceased. This is the phase of "personal survival" (*survie personnelle*) of the deceased, which is supposed to be capable of taking on visible form on occasion, appearing as a disembodied entity recognizable as the deceased. This is the deceased's apparition or ghost. Meanwhile, the number of survivors who knew the deceased personally, including offspring, other relatives and friends, acquaintances, colleagues, and strangers, continues to diminish as these die off, one after another, with the passage of time.

The main characteristic of the second phase is that its duration is equivalent to that of the concurrent life of all the survivors who knew the deceased. Normally, therefore, the greater the number of survivors and the more spaced out their age distribution, the longer the duration of the deceased's second phase. For even apparitions of the deceased have a point only if, and so long as, they can be recognized as such by those who knew the deceased. Thus apparitions derive their importance from the survival of impressions of the personality of the deceased in the minds of those survivors who knew the deceased.

It is generally regarded as a good thing for the second phase of the deceased to have as long a duration as possible. To this the deceased can have contributed personally by having as many offspring as possible. This ensures not only his biological continuity but also the existence of a second phase and its duration for as long as possible. Herein lies the metaphysical basis for the African's predilection for as large a family as possible, consisting of as many children, grandchildren, great-grandchildren, et cetera, as can be. It is thus that, in determining family size, metaphysical take precedence over economic and other considerations—for *both* parents, be it noted. Consequently, despite the risk to the mother's health and life and the economic hardships that often result from too large a family, both parents have a metaphysical investment and interest in the outcome.[1]

It is easy to understand, therefore, why childlessness is regarded in Africa as a curse, for this means not only that one will have a shorter duration of personal survival than may otherwise be the case; but also that the deceased will have no near and dear one to perform the last rites of closing one's eyes in death and similar related last duties normally performed by the eldest surviving male child (for the father) or daughter (for the mother).

The mind-spirit personality is assumed to have great influence, for good as for evil, on its surviving relations, especially in regard to such matters as honoring the last wishes of the deceased and in executing traditional rites in honor of the dead, both at the time of death and periodically thereafter in remembrance of the dead. One courts blessings and avoids misfortunes by carrying out all the observances prescribed by tradition.

The third phase of human existence is ushered in with the death of the last survivor who knew the deceased[2] and the consequent disintegration or disappearance of the last human impressions of the personality

150

of the deceased. With this event, the mind-spirit personality is divested of its mind *and* its personality, surviving only as *spirit—depersonalized spirit*—so far as the community is concerned; that is to say, unremembered (because personally unknown to any physically living member of the community), an *amorphous spirit*, an entity without any recognizable form or personality. In this third phase the amorphous spirit is assumed capable of unlimited mischief and of being manipulated, for evil purposes, by those with special powers enabling them to do so, namely, sorcerers and sorceresses.

In the metaphysical system of indigenous Africa the destiny of the human being is thus seen to be a devolution from a personalized to a depersonalized entity capable, in the hands of competent manipulators, of unlimited mischief to the community. The entire process can be aptly described by the phrase, "the birth, development and abrupt loss of personality."

Man both enters and exits psycho-physical existence, as man, through man.

NOTES

1. This is the reason why it is difficult for family planning and economic considerations to prevail over the large-family tradition and the Roman Catholic large-family dogma in Africa. This difficulty seems likely to persist until a rational and feasible alternative solution can be found capable of satisfying the metaphysical desideratum.
2. It is important to recognize that the last survivor on whom the duration of the deceased's second phase of existence depends need not be a child or other relative. This point is both crucial and important in opening the way to that rational alternative solution (see the preceding footnote) that should satisfy both the metaphysical requirements of the last rites and the second phase of existence, as well as the objectives of family planning. These requirements and objectives could be met if: (a) the priest–medicine man performs the ceremonies of the last rites for every deceased member of his community, and (b) there are more community activities or functions to provide maximum social exposure for each individual in order to increase his/her circle of acquaintances. These two measures should reduce the metaphysical need to have many children, allowing economic and family planning considerations to determine family size. However, the success of the proposals—especially the first—would depend on their acceptance by the community.

Chapter 7

Evaluation of African Metaphysics

The African view of human existence and its development in three phases is scientific in a formal and technical sense: in the formal sense a well thought out and systematic view, in the technical sense an empirically verifiable thesis.[1] The implication of the thesis is clear: there is no human existence outside of human society, since man as an individual exists only *because* of society. All three phases of human existence depend on, and occur because of, human society. The first phase defines the status of all living persons in society; the second phase, that of personalized spirit or the "living dead," defines the status of recently dead relatives (ancestors), friends, and well-known persons; the third phase, that of depersonalized spirit, defines the status of long-dead ancestors, heroes, and founders of society no longer remembered personally. Thus human society, like its collective memory, regresses dimensionally into the hazy past.

The third phase of existence, the depersonalized phase of amorphous spirit, is assigned an ethical interpretive role for the occurrence of evil in human society. The thesis is that spirits are evil-tending elements that could be harnessed by evilly disposed persons (sorcerers, sorceresses, and magicians) to cause harm to other persons. This interpretation is not scientific in the sense of being open to empirical testing, either directly or in regard to its implications. Moreover, the presence of evil in human society is not inconsistent with other alternative interpretations such as, for example, the existence of a principle of evil, the devil, or whatever. For these reasons, while it is permissible to say that the destiny of man is depersonalization, one cannot go further to say that the destiny of man is *evil*. Until it can be tested empirically (if ever) the thesis of the depersonalized spirit as the source of evil in human society is no more than pure myth. Even so, it has its uses[2]—one of which is integrative, rather than empirical. For it serves to integrate evil into the existential system—even while disapproving it in human society—in a manner that exculpates God (defined in African theology as Creator and Sustainer of

152

the Cosmos) and implicates every human being as its ultimate cause and some human beings as its immediate cause and agency. Thus God takes all the credit for all the good, man for all the evil in human society. Feuerbach would have agreed.

Man is thus beginning and end of man in human society, taking complete responsibility for what happens in society. Save for the presumed human manipulators of evil spirits, there is no direct individual self-responsibility for evil or misfortune; no "mea culpa," no devil theory of responsibility, either, but *other* human responsibility—recently dead ancestors, displeased and particularly active in dreams, and the spirits of long-dead ancestors manipulated by some individuals regarded as marginal to society. The scapegoat for evil in African society belongs in the past, the past of the dead, with an assist by some living malefactors. It is always "the other, not me."

From a comparative viewpoint the ethical implications of the third phase—the anthropogenesis of evil—are quite interesting. The Semitic religions as well as Buddhism place the blame for evil in human society squarely on man—as does African religion also.

But there is this important difference. These other religions declare that "man is by nature evil," while African religion says "man is born unto evil and destined to become evil." The contrast is between evil as *human nature* and evil as *human destiny*. In the Semitic and Buddhist religions, "the devil of evil is *in* me." In African religion, "the devil of evil is *outside* me, manipulated by *other* persons to my disadvantage."

There is, for the indigenous African, only *one* existence and three phases of that existence for man, all found in the historical and contemporary society, an existence that is perpetual even after biological death, so long as human society endures. The biologically living and dead belong together in the same historical milieu, constituting one great family and tribe of man across time and sharing in all activities: eating, drinking, rejoicing, and sorrowing and in all events that concern the family and the tribe.

African religion, inseparable from the metaphysical interpretation of the cosmos, is built from the ground up, from that part of Earth that constitutes the tribal lands upward and outward. Accordingly, the religion of a tribe cannot be exported to another tribe and its homeland, for it has no meaning outside of each particular tribe. Thus it can never be a bone of contention provoking war nor a cause of proselytism.

Anchoring religion in the tribal lands, however, invests land and every other aspect of tribal life with an aura of sacredness, since the religion of the tribe cannot be practiced outside of its tribal lands. This explains the fierce resentment and opposition in Africa to deprivation of land, banishment or exile from tribal lands under colonialists and racist regimes, for such measures touch the very being of the persons against whom they are directed, their relation and orientation to the cosmos. They are more than punishment, constituting ontological extinction.

The structure of African religion proclaims the unity of existence: land, climate, seasons, animals, plants, trees, minerals, tribe, clan, ancestor, family, birth, initiation rites, marriage, health, sickness, death, work, leisure, song, dance, sacrifice, offerings, prayers, celestial bodies, spirits, et cetera—each and all of these have their place in the close-knit interpretive framework imposed on the cosmos to hold it together and give it meaning. African religion is a web of interrelationships and interdependencies of rights and duties among men and women in family, clan, society, between ancestors and their living survivors, all finely regulated by custom. The influence of custom and the rites and observances marking the principal events from cradle to grave is very powerful, and the individual has his place and functions defined by society. The individual self and personality have meaning only in society, as they are defined and regulated by society. It is a collective, not an individual, personality so long as the slightest thread of connection binds the individual to society. The psycho-soma of the individual is formed in terms of the progression of rites and functions prescribed by society; the period of personal survival after death is equally determined by society in terms of the severance of the last connecting thread of remembrance by the death of the last surviving associate.

Marx's doctrine of social determinism of the individual and his character finds resounding confirmation in African society and religion, for the African personality is nothing if not a collective or tribal personality. But there is no confirmation of the implied Marxian theory of the primacy of matter over mind or idea, of the material arrangements for production as determining the religious ideas of the individual and tribe; and this for the simple reason that the African makes no distinction between the material, on the one hand, and the spiritual or ideological, on the other. There is also no African theory or philosophy of recompense to man in an afterlife for the deprivations suffered or imposed by others in the present life, because all existence is one and indivisible. There is no need for a Marxian type doctrine of apocalypse plus millennium *now* rather than later, because traditional African society does not have a landless proletariat, and the millennium or golden age has already existed in the past and continues by emulation into the present and the future. Nor is there any existential dialectic of internal contradictions awaiting to be eliminated, *à la* Marx, or synthesized *après* Hegel; for society is always a synthesis and always in synthesis, because it contains the past and the present in human destiny, and the future is, in theory, a reproduction of the golden past.

154

And what society, reluctantly, synthesizes—the depersonalized spirit of man—is a potential antisocial destructive force against which it is always on guard, protecting itself by appropriate sanctions against those who would lend themselves to antisocial action by manipulation of malevolent depersonalized spirits and other destructive forces of nature. How effective this protection is it is difficult to say since, so far as is known, there is no empirical confirmation of the existence and role of depersonalized spirits.

African theology—the doctrine of origins—postulates a Creator-God of the cosmos, but so far removed from humanity and the rest of its creation, so extremely ''wholly other'' as to be definitely unapproachable. One, therefore, does not concern himself with One so unapproachable as God (in other words, with the question of origins), as a rule, although one could offer prayers directly or through intermediaries—chiefly, the ancestors, professional mediums, and priests–medicine men. But the aim of such prayers is not reconciliation or unification with God—which is impossible—but communion and request for help and favors. Thus while there are intermediaries for prayer there is no mediator in the sense of a personal savior between man and God; there is no need for such mediation since there is neither hope nor possibility of atonement with God—hence no theological mysticism.

The cosmos, according to African theological doctrine, does not perish but is eternal and immortal. And in a world that does not perish, where the human being merely sheds his mortal wrappings and continues to survive indefinitely in other forms, the question of *resurrection* does not arise, since man never disappears from the community or the cosmic scene.

Nor does the question of *existential doubt, anxiety, or anguish*, for the destiny of man is clearly defined: transformation, ending in depersonalization, not destruction. One is always around, no matter what happens, and therefore has no fear of death or disappearance into nonexistence (which is impossible). There is always—and only—existence or becoming in some form or condition. A tribal African cannot, therefore, be an occidental existentialist (religious or secular, Kierkegaardian or Sartrean), for there is no end to man's existence.

Nor does the possibility of metempsychosis or transmigration of souls arise, for where there is no resurrection there is no transmigration of souls. There may be *partial* reincarnation, that is, reincarnation of parts of deceased persons through reproduction of the living by the living so that a descendant bears certain features of a deceased forebear, but no complete reappearance on the biological scene of a deceased person. There is no fear of a worse state to follow after death, nor hope of a better.

There is the equivalent of a pristine-innocence-and-subsequent-fall theory of man in African theology, but no equivalent doctrine of *original sin* or *essential evil* of human nature. Since all evil comes from without and could be parried by prescribed offerings, sacrifices, rites, and ceremonies, there is no after-burden of personal guilt, only relief. Human nature is by definition good, although evil powers could be manipulated by evil persons. But these malefactors attract communal sanctions of the most severe kind, if discovered.

Sickness and misfortune count among the external evils afflicting man; and death, for all its lack of terrors, is seldom regarded as occurring naturally. More often it is regarded as the work of malefactors who have to be flushed out, exposed. This follows from the belief in the manipulation of malevolent forces by evil persons.

Metaphysician par excellence, the African is not concerned with *how* things happen but with *why* they do. How they do happen belongs in the realm of the physical. This, in the final analysis, does not much matter, for various countervailing reasons connected with personal survival, the nature of time and the relation of past to present. For example, sickness and death may cut down one's biological life, but this can be compensated for by having more children, friends and relatives to prolong one's personal survival after death. Or, again, because the golden age lies always enshrined in the myth of the community's past, wherein are extolled its exemplary models (heroes) death does not deprive a community of any great future potential. Greatness having already occurred in the past, the future can only reproduce, not excel, the past. For all these reasons the why of things is more important than their how, especially in view of the ever-present unknown, invisible, and evil-tending forces. If one could divine the why of events, one could then adopt the necessary diversionary or protective measures. For this, knowing how things happen is of little help.

NOTES

1. The third phase is readily sense-verifiable as regards depersonalization rather than as regards "spirit." It should also be borne in mind that in the African conception "spirit" is a physical entity.
2. For the uses of pure myth, see Book One, chapter 1.

156

Section B
Theology and Religion

Chapter 8

Cult of Dionysus: Archetype of Christianity and Paradigm of Faith*

The main features of Christianity are so strikingly similar to those of the cult of Dionysus (or Bacchus, the god of wine) that its legends and rites seem to have been modeled, to a large extent, on those of Dionysus, apparently in order to win over the Greek[1] and Hellenized populations who constituted its most important target group. The members of this target group were adherents of various Greek mystery cults, chiefly those of Demeter (the Eleusinian Mysteries); Dionysus (also at Eleusis, where Demeter's cult was installed); Pallas-Athena at the Parthenon in Athens; Orpheus (Orphism) and its offshoot Pythagoreanism; Apollo, the god of Truth whose temple was at his birthplace, Delos, and his Oracle at Delphi; and Apollo's sister, Diana (Artemis).[2] Christianity thus furnishes a case study of the classic tools of religious conversion at work: transvaluation by the Christian missionary of rival religious systems, and acculturation of the new religion by both converts and missionary.

The cult of Dionysus suited the human condition and Christianity perfectly. Dionysus, according to Greek mythology, was the son of Zeus and the Theban princess Semele, a mortal subsequently assimilated to divinity, and was the only god whose parents were not both divine.[3] This parallels the case of Jesus (as presented in the Gospels), whose father was reputedly the Jewish God, Jahweh (the Jewish equivalent of Zeus), and his mother, Mary, a mortal subsequently assimilated to divinity (according to Roman Catholic tradition). Like Dionysus, Jesus was also

---

*The main references for this chapter are: Edith Hamilton, *Mythology* (Mentor Books, 1942), pp. 54–62; the Synoptic Gospels; and Acts of the Apostles. This chapter was already written before the author came to read John Hick (ed.), *The Myth of God Incarnate* (SCM Press, 1977), especially chapters 5 and 8. While there is general agreement with the views in that book, the approach adopted here differs significantly in regarding the Dionysian rites as the appropriate archetype of the Christian religion and in taking a more general view of myth as the matrix of all knowledge.

reputedly both mortal and divine (a simple case of two natures, which was further reinforced in the case of Dionysus by the dual nature of wine—benefactor and destroyer). The relation Zeus-Semele-Dionysus was thus the paradigm for the relation Jahweh-Mary-Jesus, for Jesus' Dionysiac birth and the deification of himself and his mother, Mary.

In being both mortal and divine Dionysus was also Christianity's paradigm case of the atonement of God and man, the latter's hope being to become like God. Every mortal woman in the Hellenistic culture hoped to be favored by Zeus and that her son would be the son of Zeus or, failing that, the object of deification rites.

Greek mythology records that Dionysus introduced the culture of the vine, as well as his own cult, to men. Jesus is reported to have introduced, if not his own cult, a memorial rite, the so-called Last Supper[4]: the breaking of bread and drinking of wine—an ancient Greek rite linked to the worship of the Earth divinities, Demeter and Dionysus.

Dionysus exerted pressure on men—by miracles and by punishment—in order to get them to adopt his worship. Jesus, similarly, collected a lot of following by his miracles and threat of damnation to the unbelievers—a practice continued by his disciples after his death, and in his name, by which the movement appeared to spread like wildfire.

Most significant parallel of all is that both Dionysus and Jesus were dying and resurrecting gods and both descended into Hades. The Last Supper, or what became the sacrament of the Eucharist, reflects the essence of the Dionysiac orgy: the sharing in the sacrificial feast of the torn god and mystic union with the god by passionate, sympathetic contemplation of his suffering (passion), death, and resurrection (new birth). In Christianity, Jesus holds the central place in the Eucharist that Dionysus holds in his orgy, the bread and wine representing symbolically Jesus' pierced and crucified body and his flowing blood.

Gentile Christianity with its institutions was thus pure Greek in its religious inspiration and Hellenistic in its culture. In this respect it falls within the tradition of the miracle and mystery cults that competed quite vigorously with it.[5]

A summary of the main parallel facts and events in the mythical cult of Dionysus and the historical cult of Christianity follows in tabular form.

Dionysian and Christian Cultic Rites and Features

Rites and Features	Dionysian	Christian
1. Father-of-the-god (immortal)	Zeus (chief god of Pantheon)	Jahweh (triune deity)
2. Mother-of-the-god (mortal)	Semele	Mary

160

3. Trinity of Father-Mother-Child	Zeus-Semele-Dionysus	Jahweh-Mary-Jesus
4. Assumption of god's mother (into godhood)	Semele	Mary
5. Miracle-working god	Dionysus	Jesus
6. Staunch cultic support by women	Maenads	Influential women converts
7. Institutor of cultic worship or memorial	Dionysus	Jesus
8. Sacrament or common meal (transubstantiated into the god)	Sacramental orgy	Eucharist or Communion
9. Ecstatic revelation of the god during sacrament	Dionysus	Jesus
10. Mystic union with the god during sacrament by passionate, sympathetic contemplation of his passion, death and resurrection	Dionysus	Jesus
11. Mystery, truth or dogma	Transmigration of souls	Resurrection of the body
12. Dying and resurrecting god	Dionysus	Jesus
13. Descent into Hades or Hell	Dionysus	Jesus
14. Missionary activity by god and his followers	Dionysus	Jesus

The mystery, metaphysics, and theology of these two cults, the one with its dogma of Zeus and Olympus, the other with its dogma of Jahweh and Heaven, reflect the two-worlds doctrine of the Greek Academic philosophers and its accompanying mysticism.

In its historical aspect as a religion originating within Judaism, Christianity appears as a cross between Jahwist monotheism and oriental deification of mortals. From Judaism's viewpoint, therefore, it takes on the appearance of a degenerate movement within Judaism, being:

(a) Judaism's "society for the propagation of Jahwism to the gentiles," but using the gentile tool of deification of mortals to elevate the man, Jesus, to the status of the Jewish Jahweh[6];

(b) a humanization of Jahweh the Spirit, hence a reversal to primitive Jewish anthropomorphism[7] and debasement of Jewish theological coinage;

(c) a competitor with other forms of gentile religion and theology on their own terms and a form of idolatry, specifically, Christolatry (Christians, however, preferred to regard their religion as monotheism or monolatry).

FACT VERSUS FAITH

The tabulation of correspondences between the Dionysiac and Christian cults serves to establish the basic nature and essence of faith or belief, as distinct from (empirical) fact. It is simply this—that fact is *not* necessary to faith, only to truth. The "pagan" cults (like the Dionysiac and Eleusinian rites) had faith in propositions that were not factual but relating to pure myth: e.g., the principal figures, Dionysus and Demeter, were fictional characters around whom cultic faiths were built. There was nothing originally empirical or historical about these characters—they were simply made up: figments of the imagination that were, nevertheless, given *unconditional acceptance* and *complete emotional commitment*, the two basic ingredients of belief or faith.

Faith, accordingly, may be defined as unconditional acceptance of, and complete emotional commitment to, a given proposition, in spite of contrary evidence or fact. It is roughly equivalent to what Paul Tillich calls "courage."[8] Fact, by contrast, is indispensable to truth, truth being that which is empirical—verified by sense experience—and, like sense experience, subject to change.

Truth is therefore always on trial, always provisional until modified by further experience. Truth may, therefore, be defined as that which is accepted on the evidence of sense experience, on a provisional basis, being subject to change with changing experience.

All this does not imply that Jesus was not a historical but a fictional character, a figment of the imagination, like Dionysus or Demeter. Nor does it imply that fact may not be mixed up with belief in various ways. All that is implied is that belief, in Jesus for example, does not require that he be a historical, an empirical event, a fact. And this goes for all types of belief, both ancient and modern, for it is the nature of belief that it does not require a foundation in fact. In short, the historical existence of a man called Jesus is neither required nor relevant for the validation of belief in Christianity, just as belief in the Eleusinian rites and the Dionysian cult did not depend on the truth (i.e., empirical existence) of Demeter and Dionysus. The *truth* of Christianity, however, depends on the *actualization* or experience of the manner of living that it advocates.

ANATOMY OF FAITH

Why is fact unnecessary to faith? The answer is simple and found in the raison d'être of faith: facts are sometimes awkward and unacceptable to man. So it becomes necessary to change them, if possible, and substitute or create new ones. Thus faith—rather, the content of faith—becomes the new fact that it is desired to substitute for the old or existing fact. The content of faith becomes the experience desired *ex ante* but yet to be actualized. Paul had a correct conception of the matter when he wrote: (the content of) "Faith is the substance of things hoped for"—the desired fact or experience to be brought about—"the evidence of things not seen"[9]—the *ex ante* experience yet unseen but to be actualized and made *ex post*. It is precisely because the existing fact is unacceptable but there is no guarantee that the desired alternative fact or situation (the content of Faith) is feasible that fact is not necessary to faith.[10]

Faith always involves a protest (implied or expressed) against the existing order of things, against reality—a renunciation of existing fact. Hence it is *always oriented away from the present* order of things and is forward-looking, *future-oriented*. Once the content of faith or belief is entertained, one has already oriented oneself to the desired state of things, made oneself right with it. This "making right with," this orientation toward the content of faith, Paul calls "justification"—"justification by faith."[11]

Orientation to the content of faith—justification—is not enough, however. To stop at orientation would mean that the content of one's faith, the substance of one's hope, would die and be of no effect. One must go beyond that and try to actualize by appropriate action ("works") the content of one's faith. As the Apostle James counseled: "Even so faith, if it hath not works, is dead, being alone[12];" "But wilt thou know, O vain man, that faith without works is dead?"[13]

If one's efforts (works) succeed in bringing about the new fact, experience, or content of one's faith, one then becomes liberated from the old, existing, and undesirable fact into the domain of the new. One is "saved." The success of one's efforts to actualize the content of one's faith is, to a large extent, a matter of chance depending on the conjuncture of external events that may help or hinder those efforts. Some who dislike the idea of chance and prefer to talk in terms of God would say, with Paul, that one's success would depend on the "grace of God": "For by grace are ye saved through faith; and that not of yourselves: it is the gift of God." "Not of works, lest any man should boast."[14] Chance or God is just another name for that conjuncture of events, that intervention in one's efforts from the outside that may aid or prevent the actualization of faith. The terminology may differ, but the meaning is the same whether one thinks in terms of God or Chance as the determining factor in the saving liberty of an actualized faith.

Nietzsche argued in his *Thus Spake Zarathustra* that dissatisfaction with the world could lead to rejection of it and its experiences by those so dissatisfied. These, he says, are the nay-sayers who despise the earth, the flesh, and its joys and sorrows. Nietzsche's perspicacious analysis thus delineates and establishes the ground of faith. Thus all the great rejectors or nay-sayers from Buddha (to go no earlier) down to the present, including Pythagoras, Socrates, Plato and his Academy, the Hebrew prophets, Jesus (following in the footsteps of his predecessor John the Baptist), Muhammad, Marx, Gandhi, and Martin Luther King—to be selective—have been essentially purveyors of faith. Faith is what has sustained their dissatisfaction with the world, their religion, philosophy, and metaphysics.[15]

Plato's suprasensible world was the faith content of his alternative to the sensible world with which he was dissatisfied from a social point of view, because of the wars that had devasted Athens of his day and destroyed its aristocratic privileges. His suprasensible world delineated in the *Republic* and *The Laws* was pure myth.

The faith content of Buddha's doctrine was Nirvana—like Plato's, a pure myth about which little could be done by the believer. The faith content of Jesus' belief was the kingdom of God on earth, in preference to the real world of his day; of Muhammad's a male-dominated paradise in life and after, complete with lovely maidens; of Marx's the socialist economy; of Gandhi's an economy of cottage industries in an India freed from British colonialism; and of Martin Luther King's an America of various ethnic groups living in harmony founded on the principle of freedom and equality under law. All these beliefs, with the exception of Buddha's and Plato's, had empirical content that their proponents sought to, and did, actualize—even if only partially.

One can, therefore, say that an element of faith underlies activity in various fields or disciplines, including the direction of scientific research. As the Apostle Paul observes: "We walk by faith; not by sight."[16] We also *work* by faith.

What does all this mean in practical terms? Firstly, that where there is faith there is *renunciation, protest against existing fact or experience.* The object of renunciation may be the colonial yoke of Rome on a proud people, such as the Jews, or living on harmonious terms of equality with the black majority in South Africa whom the white minority, especially the Afrikaner, would like to eliminate, if this were possible or convenient. Secondly, renunciation or protest provides faith with its content, namely, the *proposed alternative to the unwelcome fact or experience* by which believers are oriented. The content of faith may be the Messiah who should come to liberate the Jews[17]; or the policy of *apartheid* by which the white minority of South Africa seeks to oppress and control the black majority and impose an unequal and inferior status on them forever, if possible. Thirdly, the content of faith leads to action—*creative action toward establishing the proposed alternative.* The action is necessarily creative, since it involves bringing somethng new into existence, even in destroying the old situation. It is no less creative for being unpleasant as for being pleasant: liberation by a Messiah would be pleasant to the Jews, unpleasant to the Romans; *apartheid* is pleasant to the Afrikaner, unpleasant to the black population—and, indeed, even to some minority of the Afrikaner population. Fourthly, successful faith-induced action liberates from the yoke and unpleasantness of existing fact (Roman colonialism or the "threat" of equality and dominance by the black population) through *establishment of the proposed alternative.* Fifthly, success in establishing the alternative will depend on the conjuncture of events variously called *Chance* or *the grace of God.*

Faith, like everything else—hypothesis, knowledge, or provisional truth, as well as error—is subject to the analysis of reason, to understanding. But faith that is empirically verified becomes knowledge.

Hypothesis that is empirically verified by fact also becomes knowledge. But fact that is conformed to hypothesis is sheer rationalization, such as theodicy or the attempt to "justify the ways of God to man"—in the elegant language of John Milton's *Paradise Lost.*

FAITH VERSUS EXPECTATION

The anatomy of faith just concluded differs from the popular understanding of the term, namely, a belief in God or in the traditional doctrines of a religion. This understanding is consistent with the analysis but is too restricted, being limited to a specific type of faith-content, rather than to the entire range of the concept embraced in its five aspects.

In popular parlance, also, faith is often regarded as equivalent to expectation, but this is essentially a different concept from that of faith. The principal differences in the content of the two concepts are the following:

(a) The content of faith does not depend necessarily on previous experience, although it is a reaction to previous experience; the content of expectation does. One expects something to happen on the basis of previous relevant experience.
(b) Faith involves action on the part of the believer to actualize its content; expectation does not—on the contrary, it involves no action to bring it about. One only waits for the expected event to happen, while taking consequential measures premised on the fulfillment of the expectation.
(c) The actualization of the content of faith depends both on one's action (works) and on chance or God's grace (external factor); the actualization or fulfillment of an expectation depends solely on chance or God's grace.
(d) One does not normally insure for or against the actualization of the content of faith by appropriate action; but one can, in the case of an expectation, by hedging, since one is not actively involved in bringing about the outcome (success or failure) as in the case of faith. In the case of faith, one is committed to one outcome only—success; with an expectation one seeks to profit from its fulfilment or nonfulfilment.

These differences between faith and expectation can be strikingly illustrated between two Christian dogmas: the Kingdom of God on earth and the Last Day (of Judgment). The former pertains to faith, since one is required to take appropriate action for its actualization. The latter belongs in the realm of expectation since one can do nothing to bring it about except wait—if one can live that long.

CONVERSION OR THE IMPLEMENTATION OF FAITH

The five-stage process involved in the operation of faith—its implementation—is also denoted by the term *conversion* in the sense of changing the present situation of oneself or of others. It elucidates the blueprint for all missionary activity before and since Paul, the founder of Gentile Christianity. It also describes the attempt of white South Africa to sell and implement its program of *apartheid* on the black (as well as Indian and "mixed race") population. The mechanism of conversion in regard to religious or theological doctrines is discussed in detail in a subsequent chapter.[18]

INTERNALIZATION AND EXTERNALIZATION OF FAITH

A faith or belief system remains internalized within the individual—"the kingdom of God is within you," to use Jesus' colorful expression of the matter—until externalized in action leading to its actualization. But externalization or actualization of faith is the same as its implementation, or what has been alternatively called conversion in the preceding section.

Externalization of faith is intimately connected with religious systems because the latter are often based on belief or faith (protest plus alternative to be actualized—whether, in fact, actualizable or not). Hence one may appropriately talk of "religious beliefs," that is, beliefs on which religious systems are based. Since beliefs are primarily internalized and secondarily externalized systems, successful externalization assumes and depends upon successful prior internalization. Thus Marxism is a religious (person-focused relationship) system based on belief in an alternative system (socialism) to that of private enterprise capitalism; an alternative system that has only been partially actualized because of the same obstacle encountered by early Christian communism: inadequate prior internalization of the socialist ethical belief to the degree required for successful and consistent external conduct.[19] And where a belief falls short of actualization, it may continue to be conveniently entertained provided it does not occasionally lead to behavior that conflicts with normal experience.

SCIENCE AND FAITH

Science is experience-based knowledge fully explicated by reason and, therefore, becomes truth. Truth is provisional knowledge or *knowledge on trial* because based on changeable experience. Belief or faith, as such, is not based on experience, although arising out of protest against a given experience. It is therefore not knowledge; it is not truth. But once actualized, made empirical, a belief becomes *new knowledge* that did not exist before. It is then no different in nature from science or scientific knowledge.

The dividing line between science and faith is therefore, like knowledge itself, a provisional matter: always on trial. Once faith is actualized this putative line disappears forever. Those—theologians, mostly—who, in the tradition of Descartes, Pascal, Kant, and others (a tradition inherited from Pythagoras, Socrates, Plato, and Aristotle), make a sharp and arbitrary distinction between science and faith (or science and religion) in the mistaken hope that this compartmentalization will preserve faith and religion from attack by scientists, do themselves a disservice: they either ignore or overlook the possibility that faith *can* become fact, hence science, through successful implementation. And while living the pattern of life preached by Jesus (as interpreted by Christianity) does not necessarily imply the historical existence of Jesus—just as a practicing Dionysian or nuclear physicist does not necessarily imply the historical existence of Dionysus or the existence of quarks—it does demonstrate that the Christian pattern of life (where successfully implemented) has become a fact of experience, like nuclear fission and fusion. Belief specialists, certainly, do underrate themselves vis-à-vis the scientists—not as theologians, but as practitioners of their beliefs. Scientists and believers are united in this: the object and goal of their hypotheses and beliefs is *practice*, validation in experience.

APPENDIX

THE MYTHICAL CONTENT OF THE BELIEF IN LIFE AFTER DEATH—REINCARNATION AND RESURRECTION

Reincarnation and resurrection doctrines may be termed "mythical beliefs" because they fall in the category of pure myth as well as in the category of belief. As pure myth they have no empirical content, possessing only aesthetic appeal and reflecting a desire for rectification of the "injustices and imbalances" of this life in another. As beliefs they are unidimensional, possessing only the possibility of internalization and none of externalization (actualization), although having empirical value as psychotherapeutic aids.

Reincarnation is a Hindu-Buddhist myth that makes its appearance in Plato's *Timaeus* as a human devolutionary theory. In this respect it merits interest for two reasons: (a) as illustrating the retributive aspect of the law of karma (cause-effect) in a metaphysical dimension, i.e., an interexistential phenomenon spanning several existences; (b) as a possible source of reference for Darwin's (reverse) evolutionary theory. (Darwin was certainly acquainted with Plato's writings.) But the essential feature of reincarnation (Hindu-Buddhist or Plato style) is that it promises no biological *improvement* on the human form. Buddhas keep on reincarnating as human beings until they let go of the wheel of life and enter the blissful, undifferentiated spiritual state of Nirvana.

Resurrection doctrine, by contrast, promises only a once-for-all reincarnation of man in an improved spiritual body (Pauline version) that then becomes subject to either the blissful state of paradisial happiness or the retributive punishment of hell. No time is wasted on devolutionary retributive experiments.[20] On the other hand, it beats Darwin's evolutionary theory in pretending to know the next stage of human evolution—spiritual body (whatever this may mean)—while Darwin contends that evolution being a contingent, chancy affair can, by this very fact, have no prescribed goal knowable in advance.

All doctrines of transmigration of individual souls are internally inconsistent. The inconsistency lies in the tenet that the individual soul (mind) or breath (Atman) being a part of the universal or world soul (mind) or breath (Brahma) joins the latter at the death of a human being. This implies—as Aristotle pointed out—that the individual soul lacks a personality or individuality. Therefore, it cannot become reincarnated as a previous identifiable personal or individual mind in *another* biological organism, however many or few its successive cycles of birth and death before it ends all reincarnation. Indeed, it cannot be reincarnated even once. Thus, in principle, reincarnation is impossible.[21]

The Judeo-Christian-Islamic doctrine of resurrection of the body or one-time reincarnation in the *same* or similar biological organism as was possessed before death—a doctrine of Zoroastrian origin that has survived in Hindu-Buddhist religion as a repeatable privilege only for the Buddha himself—is a drastic modification of the original doctrine, a modification that confers on it an entirely different character. Bits of the original Light entrapped in Darkness come to assume individual personalities corresponding to identifiable biological organisms of the human species. At death, these bits of light (individual souls) hover around, go into purgatory or some equivalent region or state, where they are kept on "hold" until the final day—the Day of Resurrection—when they reunite with their recomposed original (or spiritualized) bodies. Once resurrected, soul-cum-body enters the presence of God, to be judged and rewarded or punished, as the case may be. The fortunate ones constitute (or are constituted into) Teilhard's "union of differentiates" (as distinct from the Hindu-Buddhist "union of undifferentiates") for an eternal "sing-in" (Christian version) or a hyped-up Hollywood version of a perpetual "love-in" of the beautiful people (Islamic version).

Unlike in the doctrine of metempsychosis, there is no internal inconsistency in the resurrection doctrine. Both beliefs are widely held, since time immemorial, among mankind and, like all beliefs, are open to reason—in principle—but not necessarily to experience. If they became open to experience as well, they could cease to be mere beliefs and graduate to the status of empirical fact. The only obstacle to this, of course, is that both doctrines make it crystal clear that, given the average span of human life, there is neither world nor time enough to put them to the test—a most unfair play.

As belief systems, reincarnation and resurrection satisfy the basic criterion of protest[22] against apparent reality: the apparent disappearance of the human body without trace at death. This is, for occidental man as much as for oriental man, an unacceptable experience; hence the protest leads to a belief content—reincarnation or resurrection—which, however, is nonempirical, for all practical purposes.

The mythical content of the belief in life after death survives and is likely to continue to survive for the following reasons:

(a) as pure myth it has aesthetic and therapeutic value as man's futile response to his existential protest;
(b) it does not seem to lead to any real-life action that seriously conflicts with normal everyday experience.

NOTES

1. Ref. Acts 17:4 and 12: "And some of them believed, and consorted with Paul and Silas; and of the devout Greeks a great multitude, and of the chief women not a few." "Therefore many of them believed; also of honorable women which were Greeks, and of men, not a few."
2. Whose cult, we are told, flourished at Ephesus during the evangelization of the Gentile world by Paul and Barnabas (Acts 19:23–28).
3. Exception made of the Heroes, such as: Epaphus (son of Io and Zeus), Minos and Rhadamanthus (sons of Europa and Zeus), Perseus (son of Danaë and Zeus), and Hercules (son of Alcmena and Zeus).
4. See Saint Matthew 26:26–30, Saint Mark 14:22–26, Saint Luke 22:7–20. This ritual is paralleled in Vedic ritual by the drinking of the soma juice, known in Zoroastrian ritual as the drinking of the haoma juice. (See Trevor Ling, *A History of Religion East and West* [London: Macmillan Press, 1984], p. 82.)
5. There was competition also from the metaphysical and philosophical systems of the Epicureans and Stoics (Acts 17:18), Neoplatonists, as well as from the counter-Hellenistic religion of Gnosticism (direct descendant of Zoroastrianism), not to talk of various types of sorcery and common magic (Acts 8:9–13).
6. Deifying and raising Jesus to the status of the Jewish Jahweh meant constituting Jesus into a gentile Jahweh. The Jewish Jahweh is a jealous god, intolerant of other gods, and is a spirit besides. He could not be represented by images, graven or other (being an unbodied spirit). The Christian Jahweh is also a jealous god, like his Jewish homologue, intolerant of other gods, but only a mortal deified in gentile fashion and represented by a human image. In this respect, Islam may be regarded as a movement of purification recalling Christianity to its Jewish roots in imageless, spiritual divinity.
7. This is true notwithstanding that, in the rabbinical interpretation of the Torah that has developed through the centuries (i.e., the Talmud) emphasis is now put on the analogical rather than the literal meaning of the Old Testament. Thus the modern

rabbi will probably argue that the writers of the Pentateuch knew that God was not a human being but that they had to employ human analogies in order to convey the divine message to the profane.

8. Paul Tillich, *The Courage To Be* (Fontana Library, reprint of March 1977), pp. 89, 152, 167–68. In his definition of "courage" Tillich lays stress on "self-affirmation" and "acceptance" "in spite of" everything to the contrary. In this sense, the definition of faith is the same for dogma.

9. Hebrews 11:1.

10. This lack of any necessary *ex post* link between faith and fact may be the reason for intolerance and persecution in the Semitic religions, as there is no empirical landmark to which reference could be made. And if the content of one's faith cannot be implemented, but is held onto emotionally, nonetheless, then one is living in a dreamworld, cut off from the empirical world every time one reenacts that faith. This is why convents and monasteries are colonies or strongholds of the neurotic. It is also why Paul's definition of faith is also a perfect definition of the neurotic condition.

11. Romans 5:1: "Therefore being justified by faith, we have peace with God through our Lord Jesus Christ." Galatians 3:11: "The just shall live by faith." II Corinthians 5:7: "For we walk by faith; not by sight."

12. James 2:17.

13. James 2:20. Herein seems to lie the difference between *faith* and *expectation*. In faith, one does something toward the actualization of the desired objective. In expectation, one does nothing to bring about the anticipated event, but merely takes precautionary or other action against its occurrence. In neither case is there any guarantee that the event desired or anticipated will occur.

14. Ephesians 2:8, 9.

15. It may be noted that rejection is only one of various possible reactions to the world. The reverse, acceptance, manifests itself in different ways. The Ionian philosophers accepted the world with curiosity and set about examining and analyzing it. The end result was positive, like the actualized faith of successful rejectors. Epicurus and his school accepted, for beneficial use, the pains and pleasures, sorrows and joys, of the world. The Stoics accepted the world with indifference, without emotional involvement. This reaction of resignation and indifference was, perhaps, the only one with a negative end result or, at least, without a positive result.

16. II Corinthians 5:7.

17. Jesus so regarded himself, preaching and expounding a doctrine of renunciation (repentance) and faith in the gospel of "the kingdom of God" (the desired alternative to the current situation), even though this was a different kingdom from what the Jews expected (Saint Mark 1:14–15).

18. Book Two, Section B, chapter 13.

19. The couple, Ananias and Sapphira, were not completely won over from the system of private to that of community ownership of property. Failing to internalize the system, they brought disaster upon their own heads and probably an end to the experiment (Acts 2:44–45; 5:1–11).

20. This, however, entails the loss of the protean dynamism of the Hindu doctrine, for which is substituted the static alternative of reanimation: a single kiss of life in place of a continuing dynamic process of countless kisses of life—a saving of the same life in place of adventure in a variety of (albeit devolutionary) life-styles.

21. It is necessary to qualify the content of this paragraph to the extent that Hindu-Buddhist doctrine does provide for an intermediate "hold" stage for the soul between the death of the human being and the final merger with Brahma. In this intermediate

stage—equivalent of the Christian purgatory—the soul remains until, and between, reincarnation(s) prior to the letting go of the wheel of life and the merger with Brahma in Nirvana. This arrangement merely postpones, but does not remove, the inconsistency: if Atman does not join Brahma immediately at death various adventures are open to it, in principle, but the question remains whether Atman has a personality, an individuality, or not. If it has not (the condition for an undifferentiated union with Brahma), how is it possible to know which soul is being reincarnated in which form? Or, if it has, how does it come about that it disappears in the union with Brahma? Thus the provision of a holding stage between death(s) and Nirvana merely complicates, by postponing, the internal inconsistency.

22. Unlike most other peoples, Africans find no need to protest at the phenomenon of death because in their metaphysical system human existence does not become extinct and biological existence is only one of the three phases of human existence. It is quite possible that prior to the Babylonian exile of 586 B.C.E. Jews adhered to a metaphysical system similar to the African system, which may explain the absence of a belief in resurrection before the exile. In that exilic period they came under the influence of the Persian religion in which resurrection and a savior were essential elements and which led to the postexilic emergence of the sect of the Pharisees (Hebrew equivalent of Parsis or Parsees, a Zoroastrian sect, that held to a belief in resurrection.

Chapter 9

Proto-Christianity: Sectarian Jewish Political Revolt and Religious Colonialism

Christianity (a term that throughout this chapter refers to original Christianity) represents a third stage in the evolution of Judaism, the religion of the Jews. This religion, a tribal religion, underwent three stages of development, as follows:

First, the stage of a *tribal religion* associated with Jahweh, the tribal god of the Jews, who loves and saves only Jews—especially the elect among the twelve Jewish tribes.
Second, the stage of *proselytization*, in which the tribal religion and its god are made accessible to non-Jews on the condition that they become Jews by conversion, that is, by spiritual and physical adherence, through conversion of mind and body, to the Jewish tribes.
Third, the stage of *evangelization* or *religious colonization*, in which access to the tribal religion and its god is made available to non-Jews on the condition that they adhere spiritually only (not physically as well) by mental conversion, to the Jewish tribes.

This third stage is Christianity, the society for the propagation of the Jewish tribal religion (SPJR). Christianity is often regarded and presented, mistakenly, to and by its adherents, as a different religion from Judaism and as a detribalized, universal religion. The fact, however, is that it is neither—not even in the twentieth century after its establishment—as the enumeration of the three stages in the development of Judaism indicates and as will be further made clear in what follows.

Especially under Roman domination Judaism assumed very strong political overtones, becoming the focus of Jewish resistance to Roman power. This naturally came to be the case in view of the Roman custom, inherited from the Greeks and other tribes on the eastern outposts of the empire, of deification of outstanding citizens, especially the Roman emperors. Claiming allegiance to their tribal god, Jahweh, as their highest and indivisible allegiance that could not, therefore, extend to any mortal albeit deified, the Jews resisted all attempts to compel them to pay symbolic obeisance to the statue of the emperor, even though all Roman citizens did so. Their resistance was all the more fierce inasmuch as tribal religion, like tribal loyalty, is very exclusive by nature.

Like other Jewish leaders of political resistance to the Romans, Jesus used the Jewish religion as a powerful emotional weapon. But his brand of power tactics[1] was new on the scene. He reinterpreted the Jewish Scriptures in a manner bound to lead to direct conflict with both the Jewish religious authorities and the Roman political authorities. He made allegiance to Jahweh and spiritual renewal the condition of political renewal, putting himself in the direct line of prophecy as "he who is to come" to free the Jews from political bondage and restore the ancient Kingdom of Israel. Except that his kingdom was, first of all, a spiritual kingdom. It is not clear precisely how Jesus hoped, by this very Nietzschean transvaluation of values, to accomplish his purpose of overthrowing the Roman power, but this much is evident: he was probably the first to combat Rome with nonviolent noncooperation, or passive resistance, as a moral weapon to achieve political ends with both Jewish and Roman authorities. Apparently, also, he had determined that if his tactics failed to secure the liberty of the Jewish people (Stage One), he would then take the struggle to the furthest bounds of the Roman empire, hoping that by his preaching a loyalty higher than to the Roman emperor and other tribal gods the empire would collapse in chaos (Stage Two). In the end, his Jewish spiritual kingdom won over the Roman political kingdom under the Emperor Constantine in 313 C.E.—long after his own death—but the Roman empire of his day did not collapse and the Jews did not gain their freedom. On the contrary, they were subsequently dispersed to the ends of the earth.

The consequences of the Jesus movement were far-reaching, nonetheless. When the movement apparently collapsed with the crucifixion of Jesus by the Roman authorities, thanks to the clever and successful machinations of the Jewish authorities, Stage Two of the movement's strategy (taking the struggle outside Judaea to the furthest bounds of the Roman empire) was put into operation by the disciples of Jesus in a two-pronged campaign.

The first prong, directed by Peter and James—the Apostles to the Hebrews—took the movement to the Jewish colonies in the empire. This was the easier campaign: Jewish religious traditions and customs, including the crucial rite of circumcision—the hallmark of Jewishness for Jews—were strictly observed; only a little bit of brainwashing through

174

superior rabbinical interpretive skills was necessary to show that Jesus was "he that should come," the Messiah foretold in the Scriptures. He had come in the person of Jesus, the Super-Jew and visible representation of Jahweh, as well as the very last of the prophets.[2]

The aim of the movement among the Jews was to vulgarize the traditional Jewish rebellious spirit expressed in their fierce tribal allegiance to their god, Jahweh: an allegiance exceeding all loyalties, including that to the Roman emperor (especially as deified) and all other civil authorities. The renaissance of this rebellious spirit in allegiance to Jahweh would lead to Rome's overthrow. It was an allegiance not only, or simply, to Jahweh but also to Jesus the Messiah who was to come to free the Jewish people from their political yoke but whom the Romans had put to death—a very powerful appeal against Roman injustice and to Jewish national pride.

The second prong of the campaign, directed by Paul[3] and Barnabas—the Apostles to the Gentiles—took the movement to non-Jews throughout the empire. The most significant group of non-Jews were the Greeks and Greek-speaking (Hellenized) populations (which, ironically, included considerable numbers of Jewish descendants of the Babylonian diaspora no longer acquainted with the Hebrew tongue) as well as the Roman population itself. To the Gentiles the good news (evangelion) was spread:

> The Jewish god, Jahweh, no longer loves exclusively the Jewish tribes, including those who become Jews through proselytism. He now loves all of mankind, including Gentiles—but at a price for Gentiles: the price of faith—faith in Jesus as the son of Jahweh and Savior of Gentiles as well as Jews, Jesus the Anointed One who atones (makes one) with Jahweh all the peoples of the earth.[4]

Thus the love of Jahweh for the Gentiles, as preached by Paul, Barnabas, and other Jewish disciples of Jesus, is not free but available at a price. This is the catch that reconverts an apparent detribalization of the Jewish god and religion into a retribalization of the same. Gentiles no longer have to become Jews by both spiritual and physical conversion (the latter symbolized by circumcision). All they need do to become Jews is undergo spiritual conversion (symbolized by baptism) without circumcision—in the first place. This guarantees their becoming spiritual Jews. But instead of circumcision a new condition was added as a means of access to the love of Jahweh: belief in Jesus as Jahweh's son and Savior of mankind—Jew and Gentile alike. This condition of restricted access was, supposedly, imposed by Jesus himself, with a bit of spiritual black-

175

mail attached. "No man cometh unto the Father but by me," Jesus is reported to have preached,[5] and he is reported to have gone further to threaten, "He that believeth and is baptized shall be saved; but he that believeth not shall be damned."[6]

This is, perhaps, the most objectionable feature of Christianity, that it offers, with one hand, the promise of love and salvation by Jahweh while taking from the prospective convert, with the other hand, his dignity and freedom, as a rational human being, to examine and voluntarily appraise the "free" gift that is offered. The only way out of this indictment is to cast doubt on the authenticity of the Synoptic Gospels in this respect—which is plausible, considering that the earliest of them (disputably, Mark or Matthew) was written long (maybe seventy years or more) after the death of Jesus. The authenticity of received Christian literature is also very much in doubt, considering the bitter quarrels that raged among the various early Christian sects, their controversies marked by mutual recriminations, book burnings, tampering with and forging of one another's literature, et cetera.[7] However, authentic or not, this is the message that reached the Gentile world and continues to reach it today.

Once the Gentiles became spiritual Jews (by the circumcision of the "foreskin of their hearts" instead of their penises)[8] *and* Christians by their belief in Jesus as Savior, they could join the authentic tribal Jews everywhere in the revolt against Rome and the overthrow of its empire as a means of freeing the Jews from the Roman yoke. This, in turn, was but a step toward the establishment of a Jewish political kingdom and with it (as was hoped) the ushering in of the Jewish millennium.

There was, thus, a double aim to Gentile conversion:

(a) to make spiritual Jews and Christians of the Gentiles, then
(b) to mobilize the Gentiles in the struggle to overthrow the Roman empire and free the Jewish people.

In short, the Christin sectarian design was for Jews to achieve their freedom by involving the rest of humanity in their cause, thereby making it the cause of all humanity within the Roman empire—a very clever strategy, indeed.

Christianity is, therefore, the equivalent, in the religious field, of colonialism (or imperialism) in the economico-political field. It is, baldly put, sectarian Jewish religio-theological imperialism that, in modern times, is exerted through already religio-theologically colonized Europeans and Americans serving as surrogates for the Jewish tribes. It is ironic, all the same, that one type of imperialism, the economico-politico-religious imperialism of Rome, was being countered by another but simpler type, religio-theological imperialism, by Christian Jews under the very noses of the Romans, and that the pawns in this Jewish-Roman contest were as much the Jewish people as the rest of the world. Thus the interesting spectacle of the twentieth century and, probably, of the twenty-first as well, of most of the world—both so-called developed and so-called underdeveloped, perpetuating as surrogates the ancient sectarian Jewish-Roman religious imperial contest, now become transformed, for the most part, into a purely intertribal contest between the Jewish and Arab branches of the Semitic tribes, with most of Christendom virtually on the Jewish side.

A further irony, it may be noted, is that the genuine (i.e., tribal) spirit of Judaism, as expressed in the traditional saying of Jews—"to each his own"—disavows any kind of religio-theological imperialism, such as the efforts by the sectarian Jews, Paul and Barnabas, and their modern-day successors, and rightly so. It is understandable, therefore, apart from any other motives, that traditional Judaism should have resisted—with all the means at its disposal—the Jesus movement and its evangelical message as a deviation from the tribal nonimperialist spirit of Judaism.[9]

This brief critical survey of the historical origin and development of Christianity does not, and is not intended to, detract from its merits as a religious and ethical system. Divested of its theology and its political and imperialistic aspects, Christianity compares most favorably with other ethical and religious systems of the world.

NOTES

1. See Jay Haley, *The Power Tactics of Jesus Christ* (New York: Avon Discus Books, 1969).
2. Saint Luke 7:19; Acts 21:15–32; Galatians 2; James 1:1. However, the Messianic "proofs" in the Gospels were hollow non sequiturs.
3. Just as it took a Super-Jew, Jesus, to acclimatize, by reinterpretation, traditional Jewish doctrines to the necessities of his Jewish liberation movement, so it took another Super-Jew and reinterpreter, Paul, to accommodate Jewish doctrine to the understanding and philosophy of the Gentile world, in order to win its support for the Jesus movement.
4. Acts 9:11–16, 13:1–46, 15:1–32; Galatians 2. Also Ludwig Feuerbach, *The Essence of Christianity* (New York: Harper Torchbooks, 1957), chapter 26, especially pp. 263–66.
5. Saint John 14:6; Galatians 2:16—justification by faith: the pillar of Martin Luther's Protestant Reformation.
6. See Saint Mark 16:16.
7. Walter Bauer, *Orthodoxy and Heresy in Earliest Christianity* (Philadelphia: Fortress Press, 1971), chapters 7 and 8.
8. Deuteronomy 10:16.

9. The tribal ethic of Judaism, like that of indigenous African religion, is averse to running after strange gods and, like African religion, averse to imposing its own god on others. Yet Africans (and other non-Jewish peoples) have been less successful in resisting the onslaughts of foreign religions, particularly Christianity and Islam which, being offshoots of Judaism, also espouse the Jewish aversion to strange gods. But this message seems to have been lost on all non-Semitic peoples who have fallen victims to Christianity and Islam, and given up their own gods. The reason, of course, is Semitic intolerance and the characteristically imperialist nature of these deviants from Judaism which have sought to impose themselves on others by fire and the sword. Judaism itself, however, was not entirely free from intolerance and imperialism in its early stages, as recorded in the Pentateuch, as it was by this means that the tribes established themselves in Palestine. Once their land-grabbing phase was over and they had established themselves in the fertile areas of Palestine, they returned to the true spirit of their tribal religion.

Chapter 10

Jesus the God:
The Ancient Custom of Deification

It was a custom among the nations of the ancient world, in Europe and the Orient, Near and Far—with, perhaps, the sole exception of the Jews in their postpolytheistic stage—to deify outstanding individuals: heroes, successful warriors, persons endowed with unusual gifts or talents such as strength, powers of healing, et cetera.

The Greeks had their twelve major divinities, but they also regarded outstanding individuals as being of "divine descent," chiefly heroes and heroines believed to be the sons and daughters of gods and men. Divinity, with the Greeks, was therefore either an original quality (as with the gods and goddesses of the pantheon) or acquired by putative descent (as with heroes and heroines). In exceptional cases it was also acquired, by the grace of the original divinities of the pantheon, by assimilation or elevation to that status. But these exceptions were made only for the mortal mothers of the sons and daughters of gods. Such was the case with Semele, mother of the god Dionysus, and with Psyche, wife of Cupid and mother of their daughter, Voluptas.[1]

The Romans adopted the Greek pantheon and borrowed the custom of other nations of elevating distinguished mortals to the rank of god.[2] This concerned, chiefly, the outstanding generals who acquired territory or empire, hence the Emperors, in particular the Caesars of both the Julian and the Claudian families.

Subsequent to their polytheistic stage, the Jews declined to acknowledge any other gods but their own Jahweh, whom they elevated from tribal to universal status, at a time when other nations still had their pantheons under the dominion of a supreme deity. Least of all were the Jews inclined to deify human beings.[3] Thus, what set the Jews apart from the other tribes and nations was not their later monotheism (other nations also acknowledged a single supreme deity above all other deities) but their later abandonment of the worldwide custom of the time of deifying outstanding human beings.[4]

179

The author of Saint Matthew's Gospel links the birth of Jesus to an oriental mythical tradition, common at the time of the Roman Empire,[5] that a great man from the East would become monarch of the whole world. This was supposed to refer to Emperor Vespasian but was, naturally, interpreted by the Jews to refer to themselves and their Messianic tradition. The Messiah ("messenger," "sent one," "anointed one") would come to liberate the Jews from their yoke—at the time the Roman yoke—and, for Jews, this meant only one thing: a Jewish King who would rule the world, with Jerusalem and Judaea supplanting Rome and Italy as the hub of that world, a purely political affair. It could never have meant a deified human liberator. The source of this tradition, however, seems to have been the Zoroastrian doctrine of a world Savior or Saoshyant who would appear at the end of time and the world to judge and rule over mankind.

In presenting himself as the Messiah, Jesus adopted an unusual, but essentially Jewish, tactic for the overthrow of Rome: a moral and spiritual movement of revolt[6] in which allegiance to the Jewish God overrode all other allegiances,[7] including the political allegiance of Jews to the Roman Emperor. In the Roman state, political allegiance involved formal obeisance to the Emperor or his representative—his statue, an act that was construed by Jews in a religio-theological sense. This construction was not wrong, since the act of obeisance to the Emperor's statue was also part of the ritual of the Roman state and imperial religion. However, Romans did not regard the act as anything more than a formality that did not elevate the Emperor to the status of their most high god, Jupiter. Indeed, it was no more than the equivalent of the modern-day oath of allegiance to a monarch or the state (represented by its flag) taken at a church or other religious service. But Jews did not make this distinction.

Thus Jesus aimed to start—if not lead—a moral and spiritual revolt in Judaea, by which he and his followers hoped to supplant the Roman governor and his Jewish lackeys in synagogue (High Priest) and state (the Rome-appointed Jewish King). If the Judaean revolt did not come off or result in the downfall of Roman power there, then his supporters—but principally his disciples—would fan out throughout the Roman Empire, preaching moral and spiritual revolt[8] in the name of the higher allegiance to Jahweh. In this respect, his doctrine was a direct attack on the Roman state and imperial religion. Furthermore, he not only proclaimed himself the only authentic prophet of Israel[9] but, anticipating the failure of his movement in Judaea, also provided sustained interest and support for his movement by promising to reappear a second time to rule the world (exception, apparently, made of his reported postresurrection appearances).[10] This, in effect, was a promise that his movement could not be defeated by failure or his own anticipated death, but was bound to succeed in the end.

With few exceptions—notably the disciple John and the Apostle Paul—the Jewish disciples of the Jesus movement did not regard or interpret their leader as a god or as God.

But once the movement took hold outside of Judaea it was inevitable that, to non-Jews, any individual powerful enough to claim an allegiance higher than that to the Roman Emperor would have to be of divine origin or else favored by the gods. Indeed, he was presented as both by John and Paul. Furthermore, deification was inevitable in the face of apparently sworn accounts of Jesus' death, resurrection, and ascension to heaven (Olympus to Greek audiences).

Paul, the shrewd evangelist, who regarded himself as specially chosen to take the movement to the pagan (Gentile) world[11] was very knowledgeable in the ways of that world. He apparently recognized that the best and quickest way to get the movement going was to deify Jesus,[12] thus profiting from a well-established pagan custom. Knowing the customs and habits of the various ethnic communities, he knew how to communicate effectively with each group in putting Jesus across. His strategy was to tailor his message to the prejudices and sentiments of each community. This was the basis of his famous statement to the Corinthians espousing expediency as his modus operandi.[13] By the same token he knew how to exploit sectarian prejudices in order to get himself out of tight spots.[14]

John, another Apostle to the Gentiles, also encouraged the deification of Jesus among Hellenistic populations.[15]

Peter, Apostle to the Jews, was under no compulsion to deify Jesus, as the tenor of I and II Peter shows—the Jews refusing to deify a mortal—notwithstanding that the Gospel by Matthew records Peter as having confessed Jesus as the Son of God.[16] Mark, on the other hand, records Peter as having only referred to Jesus as the Christ or Anointed One.[17] In any case, it is clear that Peter could not have presented Jesus as God or the Son of God to Jewish audiences. On the contrary, among Jews Peter was a very strict observer of Jewish law and ritual, unlike his more relaxed practices among the Gentiles, for which deception Paul took him strongly to task.[18]

From all the foregoing it appears that Christianity could not have spread rapidly as a movement throughout the Roman Empire had it not "degenerated" into "paganism" by the practice of deification of Jesus. Thus we witness the ironic spectacle of a movement born within Judaism and rooted in its theological and religious beliefs adopting "pagan" practices foreign to Judaism in order to win converts to its subtle message of revolt against the Roman Empire.

181

NOTES

1. This recalls the parallel case of Mary, the mother of Jesus by divine (immaculate) conception to whom the custom was applied by Christians of a later day, being assimilated to divinity by her assumption into heaven.
2. There seems to have been a difference, nevertheless, between the Greeks and the Romans in the practice of conferring divinity on mortals: with the Greeks the initiative came from the pantheon (Psyche, Semele); with the Romans, from men, subject to the approval of the gods as determined by augury.
3. It is possible, however, that the originators of the twelve tribes of Israel were mythical heroes, equivalents of the twelve deities of the Greek and Roman pantheon. The parallel is inescapable. Furthermore references may be found in the Old Testament to ''sons of God'' or ''son of God'' (Genesis 6:1–4; Psalms 2:7), which indicate that the Jews at an earlier stage observed the oriental custom of deification of outstanding individuals and only subsequently abandoned it.
4. For this reason a Jew who became Christian and acknowledged Jesus as God or of divine status was a technical impossibility, a contradiction in terms. After Paul's reported healing of the cripple at Lystra, the Lycaonians are recorded as having said of him and Barnabas, ''The gods are come down to us in the likeness of men,'' and proceeded to deify them, respectively, as Mercury (Hermes) and Jupiter. The two were scandalized and restrained the priest of Jupiter from proceeding with the ceremony and sacrifices (Acts 14:8–18).
5. Flavius Josephus, *The Jewish War* (New York: Penguin Classics, 1980), p. 350.
6. The terms *moral* and *spiritual* are used in this context to indicate, respectively, what relates to the regulation of external behavior (moral) and what relates to the internal discipline of thought and feeling (spiritual), both being compatible and complementary. For other views about Jesus and his movement, see Hugh J. Schonfield, *The Passover Plot* (New York: Bantam Books, 1967) and Jay Haley, *The Power Tactics of Jesus Christ* (New York: Avon Books, 1969).
7. Aptly expressed by Paul in Acts 10:36: ''. . . Jesus Christ: (he is Lord of all)'' and in his epistle to the Ephesians (4:5–6):
   One Lord, one faith, one baptism
   One God and Father of all, who is above all, and through all, and in you all.
   Thus Jesus as ''Lord of all'' is equivalent, and as ''Son of God'' superior, to the Roman emperor.
8. The charge to his disciples, given *after* his resurrection, was in this sense an admission of failure to bring off the revolt in Judaea (Saint Matthew 28:19–20):
   Go ye therefore, and teach all nations, baptizing them in the name of the Father, and of the Son, and of the Holy Ghost:
   Teaching them to observe all things whatsoever I have commanded you: and, lo, I am with you alway even unto the end of the world. Amen.
9. It is difficult to conclude otherwise in the light of Saint John 10:7–10:
   Then said Jesus unto them again, Verily, verily, I say unto you, I am the door of the sheep.
   All that ever came before me are thieves and robbers: but the sheep did not hear them.
   I am the door: by me if any man enter in, he shall be saved, and shall go in and out, and find pasture.
   The thief cometh not, but for to steal, and to kill, and to destroy: I am come that they might have life, and that they might have it more abundantly.

These verses are reinforced by the even more remarkable one at Saint John 14:6: "Jesus saith unto him, I am the way, the truth, and the life: no man cometh unto the Father, but by me."

10. Three postresurrection appearances are reported in Saint Mark 16.

11. Galatians 2:7–8:
. . . the gospel of the uncircumcision was committed to me, as the gospel of the circumcision was unto Peter;

"(For he that wrought effectually in Peter to the apostleship of the circumcision, the same was mighty in me toward the Gentiles:)"

12. Philippians 2:5–6:
Let this mind be in you, which was also in Christ Jesus:

Who, being in the form of God, thought it not robbery to be equal with God.

13. I Corinthians 9:19–22:
For though I be free from all men, yet have I made myself servant unto all, that I might gain the more.

And unto the Jews I became as a Jew, that I might gain the Jews; to them that are under the law, as under the law, that I might gain them that are under the law;

To them that are without law, as without law, (being not without law to God, but under the law to Christ,) that I might gain them that are without law.

To the weak became I as weak, that I might gain the weak: I am made all things to all men, that I might by all means save some.

This was the first classic statement of the practice of expediency—the end justifying the means—as well as the first prescription for the conduct of anthropological field surveys. Paul was an excellent practitioner of Picasso's rule for conversion: "mixing what they know with what they don't know."

14. Thus when Paul was presented before the Sanhedrin in Jerusalem to defend himself against assorted charges, including pollution of the temple by bringing Greeks into it, he was quick to exploit the doctrinal difference between Pharisees and Sadducees regarding the possibility of resurrection (Acts 23:6–7):
But when Paul perceived that the one part were Sadducees, and the other Pharisees, he cried out in the council, Men and Brethren, I am a Pharisee, the son of a Pharisee: of the hope and resurrection of the dead I am called in question.

And when he had so said, there arose a dissension between the Pharisees and the Sadducees: and the multitude was divided.

15. Thus Saint John 1:14, 34:
And the Word was made flesh, and dwelt among us, (and we beheld his glory, the glory as of the only begotten of the Father,) full of grace and truth.

And I (John the Baptist) saw, and bare record that this is the Son of God.

Also, Saint John 10:36, where Jesus is reported to have referred to himself as "the Son of God": "Say ye of him, whom the Father hath sanctified and sent into the world, Thou blasphemest; because I said, I am the Son of God?"

The Lucan account of the birth of Jesus (Saint Luke 1:30–37) may be regarded as a posthumous attempt to rationalize the deification of Jesus by ascribing to him divine conception.

16. Saint Matthew 16:16: "And Simon Peter answered and said, Thou art the Christ, the Son of the living God."

183

17. Saint Mark 8:30: "And he saith unto them, But whom say ye that I am? And Peter answereth and saith unto him, Thou art the Christ."
18. Galatians 2:11, 12, 14:

> But when Peter was come to Antioch, I withstood him to the face, because he was to be blamed.
>
> For before that certain came from James, he did eat with the Gentiles: but when they were come, he withdrew and separated himself, fearing them that were of the circumcision.
>
> But when I saw that they walked not uprightly according to the truth of the gospel, I said unto Peter before them all, If thou, being a Jew, livest after the manner of Gentiles, and not as do the Jews, why compellest thou the Gentiles to live as do the Jews?

Chapter 11

The Jesus of the Gospels

The Synoptic Gospels are neither autobiographical nor biographical accounts of Jesus' teachings and activities, although they may read like a
mixture of both. Bearing in mind that they were written long after the
death of Jesus,[1] that the practice of faking documents was not uncommon
in the early history of the Christian Church;[2] and that the original band
of twelve disciples, which included four fishermen, was reportedly dull
at understanding that common staple of oriental discourse employed by
their Teacher, the parable and the metaphor, and was therefore unlikely
to have been good scholars and biographers; it is clear that the Gospels
are anything but eyewitness accounts of the person and activities of Jesus.
More likely, they are impressions of Jesus dictated, at best, by disciples
or acquaintances of Jesus and written by persons at several removes from
direct acquaintance with his person. The same conclusion regarding their
authorship applies even more to the New Testament epistles.

All these considerations must be borne in mind as we attempt to
derive an understanding of Jesus from the Gospels. They rule out not
only attempts to treat the Gospels as biographical materials but also, a
fortiori, any attempt to derive a self-understanding of Jesus from them.
All that is open to us is to evaluate the impressions of Jesus projected
through the Gospels, as we understand them, and, in our turn, interpret
the evidence and the projected impressions in the light of the accumulated
information at our disposal. What is most important in these circumstances, after all, is not so much the authenticity, or otherwise, of the Gospels
as what they mean to, and for, us in our contemporary situation. For the
great problem in regard to Jesus—and Christianity—is, and forever will
be, the hopeless task of separating fact from pure myth and fantasy, in
order to avoid throwing out the baby, Jesus (who, in manhood, transvalued Judaism's precepts and doctrine of love as well as pronounced
the Beatitudes) along with the bathwater of fiction and invented tradition.

The scanty biographical record of Jesus' life given in the Gospel of
Saint Luke records only four events: (a) his birth (2:11); (b) his circum-

cision and naming on the eighth day followed by his presentation in the temple (after sixty-six days) with the necessary offering of "a pair of turtle doves or two young pigeons" (2:21–24); (c) his presence in the temple at age twelve among the doctors of the law (Torah), "both hearing them and asking them questions" (2:42–47); (d) the start of his three-year mission at age thirty subsequent to his baptism by John the Baptist and his preparation in the desert (3:23). This leaves us with two huge gaps between his birth-cum-circumcision-cum-presentation and age twelve, and between ages twelve and thirty. The so-called *Aquarian Gospel of Jesus the Christ*[3] attempts to fill in the eighteen-year gap between the ages of twelve and thirty with a presumed account of Jesus' journey and sojourn in India at the feet of Buddhist monks, in Persia, Assyria, Greece, and Egypt.[4] No one has yet attempted to fill in the gap constituted by the first twelve years of his life.

Nevertheless, there is enough material in the Gospels and Pauline Epistles to enable us piece together a broad picture of Jesus as: (a) Reformer and spiritual successor to John the Baptist, engaged in a (b) Mission of Miracle, Mystery, and Authority on behalf of the Kingdom of God—a mission that, although involving his (c) Crucifixion, reported Resurrection and Ascension, and Prediction of his Second Coming, was designed to establish him as (d) Political and Spiritual Rebel and Ethnic Leader whose (e) Ordinary human, but unusual, life as a prophet and reformer has been grossly idealized by the Church. The material also enables us to evaluate (f) the claims regarding the Messiahship of Jesus and (g) Jesus as an Existentialist Teacher.

1. REFORMER AND SPIRITUAL SUCCESSOR TO JOHN THE BAPTIST

The image of Jesus as reformer and spiritual successor to John the Baptist comes through very strongly in the Synoptic Gospels. Such recent discoveries as the Dead Sea Scrolls,[5] the parchments in the cave at Qumran, and the Nag Hammadi fragments[6]—Coptic translations of Gnostic writings, merely confirm and enlarge upon the picture derived from the Gospels. John and Jesus were contemporaries and cousins with an age difference of six months in favor of John, if the Lucan account has any validity at all.[7] It is, therefore, stretching things a bit to describe Jesus as John's successor; but this is the way the Gospels present the picture, undoubtedly with the benefit of hindsight, since John was imprisoned and beheaded by Herod early in the mission of Jesus.

Both John and Jesus were, apparently, adherents to the sect of the

Essenes, a monastic sect that flourished in the Palestinian desert—a sure sign of the insecurity of the times—and observed a strict ascetic and communal life. Both were destined to be great, and John was to be a reformer with tremendous influence.[8] As they were cousins, it is remarkable how little they knew of each other.[9] Yet there seems to have been some common knowledge and understanding between them. This is the impression given by the Gospel accounts of John's baptismal activities and Jesus' baptism by John, which show that their work was related and that it was understood that the one should carry on and complete the work of the other.[10]

Their work of reform centered on the message of the Kingdom of God, the substance of which was fully contained in the teachings of Jesus as recorded in the Gospel of Saint Matthew,[11] and on the institution of adult baptism. This was symbolic of a reformed life based on repentance (conversion) on the basis of faith in the teachings about the Kingdom of God backed by appropriate works to implement the substance of those teachings. As will subsequently appear, the ultimate goal of this reform was political as well as spiritual. But the secret of Jesus' spiritual reform was a reinterpretation as well as transvaluation of Jewish scriptural teachings. His method of expounding the Torah by parables was designed to convey the spirit of the law to the common people whose intelligence had been insulted by the literalness of the law as expounded by the rabbis. He shifted emphasis from ritual observances back to the meaning and spirit behind the rites, which alone gave them significance. It was a work of spiritual purification that badly needed doing at the time. Jesus' teachings were therefore not original, but his interpretations were, and were delivered with authority.[12]

TRANSVALUATIONS OF JEWISH TEACHINGS BY JESUS

The Eight Beatitudes (Saint Matthew 5:3–10) are the least—the minimum canons or rules of behavior—to which a Christian is required to subscribe, assuming the Jewish Decalogue as a base. Their fulfillment satisfies "the righteousness of the scribes and Pharisees" (Saint Matthew 5:20). To become a Christian, to enter the Christian "kingdom of heaven," requires more than "the righteousness of the scribes and Pharisees," more than the minimum required by the normal rules of behavior enshrined in the Beatitudes. For that, one must add adherence to the transvalued (reinterpreted) teachings of Jesus concerning:

(a) Anger: Anger is murder (Saint Matthew 5:21–22).
(b) Lust: Lust is adultery (Saint Matthew 5:27–28).

(c) Divorce: Divorce or remarriage after divorce is adultery (Saint Matthew 5:31–32).

(d) Oath: Taking an oath is evil because it seeks to compel belief by annulling reason (Saint Matthew 5:33–37).[13]

(e) Vengeance (*Lex talionis*): Vengeance, resisting evil, is evil (Saint Matthew 5:38–42).

(f) Reciprocity: Reciprocity is the crassest form of self-interest. Nonreciprocal, zero self-aggrandizing action for the benefit of others in the face of evil, loss, or disadvantage is the real test of (Christian) love (Saint Matthew 5:43–48).

(g) Public almsgiving: Public charity (almsgiving) is hypocrisy because, far from being nonreciprocal, it is reciprocated by public approval, which is its true objective (Saint Matthew 6:1–4).

(h) Public prayer: Public prayer is vanity and self-righteousness (Saint Matthew 6:5–15; Saint Luke 18:9–14).

(i) Public fasting: Public fasting is hypocrisy because its true objective is public approval, not repentance (Saint Matthew 6:16–18).

(j) Material possessions: Material possessions confer no real security or peace of mind; only right living according to moral principles does (Saint Matthew 6:19–21, 31–33).

(k) Fault finding: Fault-finding self-righteousness is hypocrisy, for there is none that is good but God (Saint Matthew 7:1–5, 19:16–17; Saint Luke 18:18–19).

(l) Precept: Precept is easy but not enough—performance is its real test (Saint Matthew 7:15–20).

(m) Miracles: Miracles are easy but not enough, because they seek to compel belief; conviction by simple action and right attitude is more effective (Saint Matthew 7:21–27).

The paradox of the teachings of Jesus lies in the fact that, for all their lofty moral tone, the Beatitudes and the transvalued teachings are all self-serving, tinged with self-interest in one way or another.

Given the wide range of the teachings of Jesus, it would be invidious to attempt to select and categorize some as more important than others. Nevertheless, Paul seems to have done just that in his Epistle to the Hebrews,[14] where he lists the following doctrines[15]: (a) Repentance; (b) Faith toward God; (c) Baptism(s); (d) Laying on of hands (a rite Jesus performed on children[16]); (e) Resurrection of the dead (in which the Samaritans, like the Sadducees, did not believe[17]) (f) Eternal (last) judgment.

It is significant that Paul did not include in the list the Eucharist or sacrament of the Last Supper, with its Dionysian overtones of devouring the flesh and drinking the blood of the god[18] and, therefore, presumably

188

abhorrent to the Samaritans; nor the doctrine of the Trinity (Father, Son and Holy Ghost or Comforter), which would have offended the Samaritan Gnostic Binity[19] or Dualism of the True One, or Pristine God, and the Glory (Jahweh). No significance, however, should be accorded to Paul's list, since it was selected for a specific target group—Samaritans—and (in keeping with his proselytizing principle of expedience, of being all things to all men in order to win some souls for Jesus) would probably vary according to the target group of the moment.

2. JESUS' MISSION OF MIRACLE, MYSTERY, AND AUTHORITY

Jesus' "forty days in the wilderness," that is, his period of sojourn in the desert and preparation for his mission, has been presented in the Gospel accounts as an ordeal during which he was subjected to temptation or enticement to do wrong by Satan the Arch-Devil. A critical examination of the temptation accounts, in the context of other accounts of Jesus' subsequent mission, leads to the view that the desert sojourn was, for Jesus, a period of reflection on all the available options that could guide his mission. No doubt, the physical conditions of life in the Palestinian desert—living on locusts and wild honey with camel skin as the material for raiments, if the case of John the Baptist may be regarded as typical[20]—were severe. But such ascetic conditions were, equally undoubtedly, conducive to sober reflection and firming up of one's resolve after mature consideration of the often conflicting options that test one's will. Indeed, it was a period of intense preparation in building up stamina and physical hardihood to confront the trials involved in dealing with crowds on a continuing basis and with the gamut of reactions ranging from enthusiastic support to deadly opposition. Modern army survival courses would probably rate a poor substitute.

The temptation accounts were therefore either slanted to conform, presumably, to some standard or conventional pattern of reporting on the preparatory stage of the lives of great social reformers of the age; or else reflect the lack of sophistication, that is, the dull-wittedness of the majority of Jesus' disciples.[21] The second alternative, however, is not easily distinguishable from the first, since both may present an aspect of simplicity and lack of sophistication. Furthermore, given the legitimate doubts about the authorship of the Gospels and the ability of any of the twelve disciples to write them, they may very well represent a concerted (hence synoptic) group effort to create a body of basic Christian literature or Scripture and a record of the life of Jesus for use by Christians, similar to the Torah, the sacred literature of the Jews.

That the need for such literature would arise is only to be expected, since the Torah could not be used by non-Jewish converts to Christianity during its first century. This would explain why the Gospels were composed long after the death of Christ and at a time when the original disciples were either dead or too old to compose such literature themselves.

Fyodor Dostoyevsky in *The Grand Inquisitor*[22] presents an excellent account of the three pillars of Jesus' mission—miracle, mystery, and authority. Indeed, these are the leading themes of the temptation accounts as well as of Jesus' mission. In the temptation stories each theme is balanced against an alternative:

(a) the *miracle* of conversion of stones into physical bread, as against the bread of spiritual sustenance provided by the word of God, that is, the message of the *mystery* of the Kingdom of God, as the drawing power for building up a following (converts);
(b) worship of the Devil as against the worship of God, that is to say, temporal power and *authority* (the kingdoms of the world) as against spiritual power and authority (the Kingdom of God);
(c) physical demonstration of faith in the saving power of God to interpose a safety net of angels in Jesus' fall from a pinnacle of the temple, as against quiet undemonstrative faith and confidence in God; that is to say, again, the striking evidence of miracle as against direct appeal to the will, the hearts and minds of people (i.e., faith) as the motive force of conversion.[23]

Thus the temptation accounts appear to be less a record of the Devil's attempt to seduce Jesus and divert him from his mission—as the simplistic conventional reading would seem to indicate—than a statement of the alternatives considered by Jesus as open to him in the pursuit of his mission as successor to John the Baptist. These alternatives are cast in the form of a conflict between Good and Evil, thereby reflecting the various influences and movements—Gnosticism, Zoroastrianism, et cetera—prevalent at that time. The accounts also indicate Jesus' internal conflict regarding the choice of a political or a spiritual route toward the liberation of the Jewish people.

There is hardly any doubt that miracle (common magic at the least), mystery (in the form of occult or esoteric doctrines, which in Jesus' case were adapted to presentation in the form of parables for the exoteric group of his followers), and authority (based on claims to divinity—divine descent and divine powers) constituted the common coinage of social reform movements in Jesus' day, as well as before and, occasionally, since.

190

The decisions or resolutions with which Jesus emerged from his sojourn and preparation in the desert are of much interest. First, he saw himself as successor to John the Baptist (indeed, he is so presented in the Gospels) and decided to continue, with his disciples, John's mission and message of repentance and the kingdom of heaven (God) both before [24] and, especially, after the latter's imprisonment and execution. Accordingly:

(a) he preached the same Gospel as John, commanding his disciples to do likewise, namely: (i) the baptism of repentance (renunciation and conversion) for the remission of sins; (ii) the kingdom of heaven (God)[25]; (iii) appropriate works of faith in the Kingdom of God ("fruits worthy of repentance");
(b) he baptized, as also did his disciples[26];
(c) he commissioned and dispatched his disciples and Apostles, two by two, on their mission on the standard instructions of the Essene sect used by John himself[27];
(d) he taught his disciples to pray, as John did his.[28]

Indeed, so similar were the doctrines and practices of Jesus and his disciples to those of John and his disciples—all based on those of the Essene sect—that, with the addition of the miracles of healing, feeding, and the resurrection of the dead, Herod the Tetrach, who had beheaded John, was deceived into believing that Jesus was John resurrected and performing great miracles.[29] Eventually, Herod sought to kill Jesus also.[30]

Far from repudiating any of the alternatives open to him (as the temptation accounts would have it), Jesus decided to adopt *all* of them in the prosecution of his mission: miracle (people love it), mystery (people worship it), and authority (people gladly submit to it, in order—as Dostoyevsky puts it—to escape the burden of freedom and decision making). Jesus performed (or is supposed to have performed) miracles of feeding and healing and resurrection of the dead, preached the mysteries of the Kingdom of God in parables, and became the source of authority, both temporal and spiritual, of the church established through the missionary activities of his followers. For himself he claimed divine authority as the Son of God[31]—blasphemy to the Jews, who had fallen out of a tradition they themselves had once espoused, as passages in the Torah and the Psalms bear witness[32]; and the worshipping crowds accorded him kingly status, hailing him as the King of Israel.[33] This honor, bestowed by the crowd on his triumphal entry into Jerusalem at the feast of Passover, constituted a basis for the charge on which Jesus was finally ordered crucified by Pilate, the Roman Governor of Judaea.[34]

191

The miracles helped spread Jesus' movement like wildfire and encouraged his worship by the crowds of both sick and healthy people. It is true that he did not attempt to fall from a pinnacle of the temple. (At least, there is no record of such an attempt.) Apparently, this was a standard act (jumping or attempting to fly from eminences) as demonstration of divinity or the possession of divine powers, from time immemorial. The ancient Greek philosopher-prophet Empedocles (circa 440 B.C.E.) was reported to have attempted to establish his claim to divinity by jumping into the crater of Mount Etna—presumably under the influence of some drug. Contrary to his own expectations, he did not survive the roasting. Simon, the Samaritan Gnostic (the Magus of Acts 8:9–24), is reported to have unsuccessfully tried to establish his divinity by attempting to fly or ascend to heaven. He was killed in the fall.[35] However, when the worshippers in the synagogue at Nazareth, annoyed at Jesus' sayings, sought to throw him from the brow of the hill on which the city was built, Jesus is reported to have miraculously passed through their midst and gone on his way.[36]

By his miracles Jesus surpassed John the Baptist, who while in prison sent two of his disciples to inquire of Jesus whether he was the hoped-for Messiah of Israel.[37] By the same means he attracted a considerable following. The miracles, combined with his unusual but popular approach to Jewish Scripture and traditions, threatened the position of the Jewish religious hierarchy.

One final point about Jesus' mission: He regarded his work as principally concerning the Jews (children),[38] not the Gentiles (dogs), salvation, in his view, being the privilege of Jews. He was not, at first, concerned to "save" all mankind—naturally, because the Messiahship concerned the political liberation of Jews. How it came about that Jesus involved the Gentiles in the political liberation of the Jews and, toward the end of his mission, charged his disciples to preach the Gospel to the Gentiles and involve them in the struggle has already been discussed in a previous chapter.[39]

3. THE CRUCIFIXION, RESURRECTION AND ASCENSION, AND SECOND COMING OF JESUS

While the crucifixion of Jesus is scarcely in doubt,[40] his resurrection is very doubtful. First, the Synoptic Gospels record that he was seen *after* he was risen and also seen *ascending*, but nowhere is it recorded that anyone actually *saw* him *rise*. This constitutes as good an argument for the docetic belief of those who held that he was divine (a god or God)

192

as for the opposite belief of those who held that he was only a mortal.

Second, Luke's account gives strong support for the complete humanity of Jesus, who appeared to his disciples after his supposed resurrection and not only insisted that he was flesh and bone and no spirit (Saint Luke 24:39–40)—*pace* Paul's doctrine of spiritual resurrected bodies (I Corinthians 15:42–44)—but confirmed it by eating fish and honeycomb (Saint Luke 24:41–43).[41] This is strong presumptive evidence only of *resuscitation*, not of resurrection.[42]

Third, the preceding point makes pure myth of Paul's doctrine of resurrection of a spiritual from a mortal body, supposedly based on the experience of Jesus, whom Paul, in any case, apparently neither knew nor met (I Corinthians 15:3–8).

All the evidence (or lack of it) on the subject of Jesus' resurrection has been widely available since the books of the New Testament were canonized toward the latter part of the second century of the Christian Era. That no firm evidence exists of Jesus' resurrection merely confirms that belief, essentially, has little or nothing to do with evidence or empirical fact. It also attests to the fact that the Church, as an institution, has successfully promoted a belief-system based on message (*kerygma*) about a supposed empirical event (the resurrection of Jesus) for which it has no evidence, oral or written, of eyewitnesses.

While there is no eyewitness account anywhere in the New Testament of the actual event of Jesus' resurrection, there is apparent evidence of his ascension and second coming in the Gospel of Saint John. There, at chapter 20, it is recorded that on the first day of the week, immediately after his resurrection, Jesus appeared to Mary Magdalene and forbade her to touch him as he had not yet ascended to his Father in heaven (verse 17). The same evening, Jesus appeared to his frightened disciples where they were closeted for fear of the Jews and breathed on them the gift of the Holy Ghost (verses 19–23). This implies that he had ascended into heaven *and* come again the *second time*, bringing with him—rather than his Father or himself sending—the gift of the Holy Ghost, the Comforter. This is a legitimate interpretation in the light of what is recorded at chapter 14, verses 1–3, 16–20, 25–28, and at chapter 16, verses 7, 13, 16, and 22. And confirmation is given by Jesus' invitation, at chapter 20, verses 24–28, to Thomas Didymus to verify by touch that it was indeed he, Jesus, that had appeared in flesh and bone with all the stigmata of his crucifixion showing. Prior to his ascension he did not want to be touched.

We here limit ourselves to the documentary evidence and its interpretation, without inquiring into such difficult and insoluble questions as how it was possible for Jesus to carry about with him for over a week the apparently serious and unhealed wounds inflicted upon him on the

193

cross and at the same time appear well and healthy, flesh and bones, able to eat without problems. Absolutely incredible for one who averred himself to be no spirit but fully flesh and bone.

Also ignored is the apparently thorny issue of the nature of Jesus. If, as he averred in Saint Luke, at the passage referred to above, he was no spirit but flesh and bone after his resurrection (resuscitation), then the Chalcedonian two-natures doctrine is also open to question. Basing ourselves on the evidence of Luke alone, we can reasonably say that if Jesus had a second and divine nature there is no way of knowing it. What is clear from the Synoptic Gospels about the nature of Jesus is this: they do not constitute, nor seem intended to be, accounts of what Jesus actually was but are, rather, accounts of how the different writers (or their narrators) regarded him and interpreted his nature, whatever that may have been. This would not be surprising, given the time lag between Jesus' death and the dates of composition of the accounts; so that, looking back over the events, the writers (or narrators) benefited both from hindsight and from the romantic enchantment of distance in time. They were certainly not writing from diary notes compiled over the years that Jesus lived.

Thus Luke saw Jesus purely as a human being—as may be expected of one reputed as a physician. John, steeped in Hellenistic philosophy and culture, saw Jesus in metaphysical terms as preexistent form, reason, soul, logos, mind—all being elements shared with God—and incorporated in matter in the guise of a human phenomenon; hence, for John, Jesus would be both human and divine. Against the background of Socratic and Platonic metaphysical ideas, this was not saying much—at least, not more than a Platonic philosopher would say in describing the nature of any other human being. But John mixed his Platonic with Persian Gnostic ideas, so that one gets the impression that he was more concerned with showing off his composite learning than addressing himself to the subject in hand: Jesus. No doubt, each Gospel writer was a missionary type and wrote with a specific audience and readership in mind. And certainly, some parts of the Gospels (for example, the last chapter of Mark) read as though they were derived from prior sources; while other parts (for example, the last verse of John) sound much like an attempt at generalization by a man working with scanty materials but wishing to give his reader the opposite impression.

The Synoptic Gospels were, therefore, interpretations of Jesus' role and significance vis-à-vis the movement that grew out of his teachings and activities. The Pauline letters represented another type of interpretation by one who neither knew nor experienced the historical Jesus. In this, his tremendous labor of love, Paul clearly showed that faith is not necessarily allied to experience. He, especially, set the precedent for other interpretations by people several generations removed from the historical scene. This led to a proliferation of interpretations and nuances of interpretations, the most widespread and competitive being those based on Gnosticism, a movement that long preceded Christianity.

Understandably, there was a widely felt need and demand for restoring some order and discipline in the plethora of interpretations, to set basic ground rules for interpretation and narrow limits for divergencies of interpretation. This is what the controversy over orthodoxy and heresy within the early Church was all about: setting rigid limits, spelled out in dogmas that served as guidelines to hermeneutic activity. But for the involvement of the hermeneutic struggle with power, influence, position, and money, which stir up blood, passions, and burnings at the stake, its true nature would easily appear as a case study in the evolution of myth, in the broad sense of interpretation, over time. In the event, as so often happens, there is neither orthodoxy nor heresy, only successful and unsuccessful interpretations, accepted and rejected points of view, without any necessary implications of truth or falsehood on the part of winners or losers. For, with the passage of time, the issue of truth or falsehood becomes irrelevant to the hermeneutic enterprise, while its purpose and utility become increasingly the most important consideration.

4. JESUS THE SPIRITUAL AND POLITICAL REBEL AND ETHNIC LEADER

The rebellious spiritual and political activities of Jesus have been summarily examined in a previous chapter[43] and will not be repeated here. An interesting psychological study on the subject has been made by Jay Haley and is rewarding reading.[44] Moreover, the preceding chapter has presented the background of the subsequent deification of Jesus,[45] and another elucidated the form and structure of the religious cult that was established after his death.[46] All these sources provide a sufficient context for placing and interpreting the Gospel references to Jesus' career as a spiritual and political rebel and ethnic leader against the Jewish and Roman religious and political establishments of his day.

Jesus' reported claim to sonship of God[47] constituted the highlight of his spiritual mission and served to buttress the further claim made by himself or, on his behalf, by others to be "a prophet sent from God." His reported identification with his "Father,"[48] which provoked in the Jews a desire to stone him for blasphemy, could be interpreted, rather, as an identification of his mission with the will of God than as an identification of himself with God. But it may also reflect the adhesion of the author of Saint John's Gospel to an element of Gnostic doctrine, according to which the Father sent his Son to save mankind trapped in the domain (*heimarmene*) of the Jewish Just God, Ialdabaoth. This Son was the Light Jesus (Luminous Jesus).[49]

The highlight of Jesus' political career, based on his purported claim to Messiahship, was his triumphal entry into Jerusalem at Passover, when he was hailed by the worshipping crowds as king.[50] His acceptance of this kingly adulation by the crowds was seen as a provocation by the Jewish religious and political hierarchy as well as by the Roman power. It is significant, therefore, that the inscription on his cross—"King of the Jews"—was the one charge (sedition) that could legally be brought against him.[51]

It is important to bear in mind that, to the extent that he regarded himself as Messiah and Savior, Jesus was, throughout his life and in keeping with his Jewish background and tradition, a strictly ethnic (that is, Jewish) not a world Messiah and Savior. His entire life was spent in teaching, preaching to, and healing mostly Jews. He did not minister to Gentiles.[52] The mission to the Gentiles was sanctioned by him only *after* his death and presumed resurrection, being undertaken by some of his disciples who fled Jerusalem after his crucifixion, but chiefly by Paul, the former persecutor of the Jesus movement. The New Testament is very clear on this point; nor did Paul, the premier Apostle to the Gentiles, have any misconception on the matter. The following passages are eloquent:

(a) Jesus declares his ethnic mission in clear terms to the Syro-Phoenician woman of Canaan, terms that gave a rather unflattering picture of himself:

And, behold, a woman of Canaan came out of the same coasts, and cried unto him, saying, Have mercy on me, O Lord, thou son of David; my daughter is grievously vexed with a devil.

But he answered her not a word. And his disciples came and besought him, saying, Send her away; for she crieth after us.

But he answered and said, I am not sent but unto the lost sheep of the house of Israel.

Then came she and worshipped him, saying, Lord, Help me.

But he answered and said, It is not meet to take the children's bread, and cast it to dogs.

—Saint Matthew 15:22–26

(b) Jesus gave strict instructions to his disciples while he was alive, that they should confine their mission to Jews and avoid Gentiles and Samaritans:

These twelve Jesus sent forth, and commanded them, saying, Go not

196

into the way of the Gentiles, and into any city of the Samaritans enter ye not:

But go rather to the lost sheep of the house of Israel.

—Saint Matthew 10:5–6

(c) Jesus commissioned his disciples to take his movement to the Gentiles, but only after his reported resurrection:

Go ye therefore, and teach all nations, baptizing them in the name of the Father, and of the Son, and of the Holy Ghost:

Teaching them to observe all things whatsoever I have commanded you: and, lo, I am with you alway even unto the end of the world.

—Saint Matthew 28:19–20

(d) Paul made it clear that Jesus confined his mission to the circumcision (the Jews) while he himself was the minister of Jesus to the Gentiles:

Now I say that Jesus Christ was a minister of the circumcision for the truth of God, to confirm the promises made unto the fathers.

—Romans 15:8

Nevertheless brethren, I have written the more boldly unto you in some sort, as putting you in mind, because of the grace that is given to me of God,

That I should be the minister of Jesus Christ to the Gentiles, ministering the gospel of God that the offering up of the Gentiles might be acceptable, being sanctified by the Holy Ghost.

—Romans, 15:15–16

And that the Gentiles might glorify God for his mercy; as it is written, For this cause I will confess to thee among the Gentiles, and sing unto thy name.

—Romans 15:9

5. AN UNUSUAL PROPHET WHOSE HUMAN LIFE WAS GROSSLY IDEALIZED BY THE CHURCH IN ITS CONFLICT AND COMPETITION WITH GNOSTICISM

There is little doubt that the life and activities of Jesus have been grossly idealized by a Church that began to document the accounts of Jesus some half a century or more after his death. With the aim of not merely holding together the group of Christians by providing them with "approved" Scriptures but also of increasing its membership, the compilers of the accounts that have survived the selection and weeding out process over time succumbed to the enchanted distance fallacy. Only such an occupational hazard could account for a tradition that has turned a blind eye or glossed over obvious evidences of inconsistencies and nonideal behavior of the hero of the Christian confession, most of whose

197

life remained a closed book to his followers. This idealization was also inevitable in the context of the teachings of the Gnostic religion against which Christianity had to strive, and whose ideal theological system Christianity had to borrow in order to make itself at least as attractive as Gnosticism.

By his denunciations and threats of doom (Saint Matthew 23; Luke 11:29–54) and by his reinterpretations and transvaluations of the traditions and teachings of the elders, Jesus put himself in direct line with the prophets from Jeremiah to John the Baptist.[53] Naturally, in reinterpreting and transvaluing the teachings of Judaism he was within the rabbinical tradition but, by refusing to quote rabbinical precedents, he taught entirely on his own authority—"Ye have heard . . . but I say unto you" (Saint Matthew 5)—and not as the scribes who relied on citations of chapter and verse for every word or interpretation: ". . . they were astonished at his doctrine: for he taught them as one that had authority, and not as the scribes"(Saint Mark 1:22).

Jesus advised his followers to do what the scribes and the Pharisees taught them but not practice what they did. The same advice, ironically, holds for Jesus himself, who seldom practiced what he preached, as Haley amply points out[54]: he not only judged and denounced his opponents while counseling others to refrain from judgment[55]; he preached peace to others[56] while he himself came, as he put it, to cause division by the sword and create strife within families.[57] He treated his anxious parents and brethren in cavalier fashion,[58] and on occasion was impolite to his host.[59] He preached forgiveness and love of one's enemies but never forgave his enemies; on the contrary, he denounced them, as we have seen.

Incidentally, Jesus' unforgivingness raises a serious obstacle for Christian faith in regard to the so-called Last Day, the Day of Judgment at the end of the world. Normally, one would not consider it sound judicial principle to have the same person as prosecutor, judge, and jury in his own cause. But this is exactly what Christians preach and believe about Jesus, who, they hold, was wronged by the world—as witness the Apostles' Creed[60]—even though he is supposed to have died *voluntarily* for the sins of the world.[61] It is an even more serious matter when the prosecutor-judge-jury, Jesus, was himself a man who never forgave his enemies. His cry for forgiveness on the cross was addressed to God as a general prayer—not a direct offer of forgiveness from himself to anyone.[62] The impartiality of his judgment at the Last Day would therefore be open to question.

Considering what the Church has made of the life of Jesus, it is obvious that only those with a specific aim in view other than an objective examination of the evidence would idealize the events and behavior examined in the two preceding paragraphs, not to mention their misuse of the privilege of hindsight. Similarly, it may be said that the messiahship of Jesus was anything but doubtful, the claim of his followers notwithstanding. Firstly, he was clearly *not* the messiah expected in Jewish tradition—even if it is permissible for any one to transvalue and reinterpret the content of messiahship in the light of the totally different events that transpired in the life of Jesus. Secondly, the so-called "proofs" of the messiahship of Jesus given in the Gospels are non sequiturs.

They may be in line with accepted corroborative evidence according to the practice of that era. But they certainly cannot survive rational scrutiny. A more detailed examination of the claims of messiahship follows.

6. THE MESSIAHSHIP OF JESUS

The New Testament contains many affirmations that Jesus was the expected Messiah of the Jews, as well as attestations by Jesus himself to that effect.[63] Some of the affirmations are based on so-called proofs of Jesus' messiahship, others on alleged miracles of healing and other events. However, none of them adds up to firm, incontestable evidence. First of all, Jesus did not conform to the traditional Jewish concept of Messiah—the ideal Priest-Prophet-King of the Davidic line who should come to liberate Israel from its current foreign yoke (whether Babylonian, Greek, or Roman) and reestablish a royal and priestly kingdom of Israel.[64] Even as late as the Zionist Congress held in Basle in 1897 when the founding of a state of Israel was proposed, there were Jews who objected to its establishment before the Messiah had come, thus implying that no Jewish leader up to that time had a profile corresponding to that of the still-expected Messiah.[65]

Anyone, of course, is at liberty to reinterpret the messiah-concept to suit a particular individual, as the Christians did in the case of Jesus, transvaluing the concept from that of a liberating and conquering king to that of a suffering servant.[66] But the traditional concept of the messiah expected then and now by Jews remains that of the conquering warrior-king.

The affirmation of the messiahship of Jesus by two or more witnesses (as required for corroboration by the Torah) does not necessarily establish it as fact—indeed, it does not so long as Jesus did not fit the traditional Jewish concept. It would certainly be going too far to suggest that the Jews could not recognize their Messiah, when he did come, in the person of Jesus. Only Jews are competent to judge of this matter. And their judgment is that Jesus was only a prophet and did not conform to their messianic expectations. Against this judgment neither the testimony of a few Christianized Jews, nor that of the Gentile world, nor yet that of the whole of Christendom could prevail.

Given the questionable opinion that the Jews, unlike the ancient Greeks, were not a people inclined to philosophy,[67] the so-called biblical proofs of Jesus'messiahship—however much they may be in line with the rhetorical and literary practice of the time—are nothing but non sequiturs structured on the following three-step paradigm:

(a) Quote a prophecy or myth. (There was a prophecy, A.)
(b) Affirm a fact about Jesus. (There was a fact or event, B, with all the earmarks of A.)
(c) Claim the fact (B) as confirming the prophecy or myth (A). (Therefore, B happened in order to fulfill A.)

All the New Testament "proofs" of Jesus' messiahship are of this kind, as the following examples show.

(a) *Saint Matthew 1:18–24:*
 (i) It was prophesied that a virgin should conceive and bring forth a child, Immanuel (Isaiah 7:14).
 (ii) Mary, wife of Joseph, conceived a child, Jesus (before they came together).[68]
 (iii) Therefore, Jesus was the prophesied Immanuel, or Jesus was born in order to fulfill the prophecy.
(b) *Saint Matthew 2:1–6:*
 (i) It was prophesied that out of Bethlehem would come the Governor of Israel.
 (ii) Jesus was born in Bethlehem of Judaea.
 (iii) Therefore, Jesus was the prophesied Governor of Israel, or, Jesus was born in order to fulfill the prophecy and become Governor of Israel.

The problem with these "proofs" is that they do not demonstrate conclusively, if at all, that the prophecies referred to Jesus and not to any other male child, known or unknown, born to a virgin (young woman) in Bethlehem, in the past or in the probable future. In other words, how does one know that the conclusion (iii) about Jesus is valid? That Jesus (ii) was a unique fulfillment of the prophecy (i)? That there was a unique one-to-one correspondence between (iii) and (i)? The stock answer:

(a) Take it on trust, and if you do you will be rewarded with a life in paradise, if you do not, then with damnation in hell—after death.

200

(*Argumentum ad hominem*, consisting of bribery and threat—plain duress.)

(b) If you still do not accept it on trust, under promise or penalty, then look at the reported signs, wonders, miracles, and gifts of the Holy Ghost credited to Jesus (Saint John 14:6–11; Hebrews 2:4). (Special pleading.)

All three types of statements—conclusion (iii), (a), and (b) are non sequiturs—irrelevant as incontrovertible proof or evidence of a connection between prophecy (A) and event (B).

Similarly, it was "proved" that John the Baptist was the forerunner of Jesus prophesied by Isaiah:

(c) *Saint Matthew 3:1–3:*
   (i) Isaiah prophesied that a forerunner of the Messiah would emerge from the desert (Isaiah, 40:3–5).
   (ii) John the Baptist emerged from the desert preaching the baptism of repentance for the remission of sins (Saint Luke 3:2–6).
   (iii) Therefore, John the Baptist was the forerunner prophesied by Isaiah, or John the Baptist came along in order to fulfill Isaiah's prophecy.

John, however, was not the only desert prophet who preceded Jesus with the message of repentance and baptism.

Whatever may be the truth, or lack of it, regarding the Jews' alleged lack of inclination toward philosophy, one thing is certain: those among them who advanced the foregoing type of "proofs" as well as those among them to whom they were presented were fully aware of their inherent weakness. Hence a sign—an "incontrovertible" sign—was often demanded and/or given, whence the common saying that "the Jews require a sign."[69] Thus miracles and signs had to replace the textual "proofs," since these, lacking the rigor required by reason, were no proofs at all. This may be one reason that the Synoptic accounts of the ministry of Jesus are miracle-studded. It is, however, another matter whether miracles are necessarily proofs of anything at all, including the messiahship of Jesus. Reason cannot arbitrate in such matters, since more than reason and experience are involved—namely, belief or faith. Hence in the absence of miracles an appeal was frequently made to belief—sometimes *in addition* to the miracles, notably by Jesus himself.[70] When faith tended to be weak—even in the presence of miracles—it had to be buttressed by positive and negative sanctions: spiritual rewards for those who believed and damnation for those who did not, after death.

In any case, no conclusive proof could be given of Jesus' messiahship. The message had to be put across, in the absence of convincing argument, by the bludgeon method of (alleged) miracle and sign (or magic) or by the carrot-and-stick method of after-death promise-and-threat, reward-and-damnation. Especially for those who were being pros-elytized centuries after Jesus' death, it was a psychological tactic designed to *compel belief*, rather than a method conducive to conviction by reason.

In the final analysis, the validity or invalidity of the messiahship of Jesus is of little consequence in the context of faith. For, as we have seen,[71] the content of faith, as a reaction stemming from rejection of an existing reality, is not necessarily based on empirical fact or evidence; it could be independent of experience, even though accessible to reason. Therefore, nothing prevents those who want to believe that Jesus was the expected Messiah of Israel from so doing. They merely elect to bring into being—if at all possible—a new experience, a new reality, based on such a belief. There is no guarantee, of course, that the new reality to which they look forward will actualize. Nevertheless, in default, the belief must not clash with other experiences or empirical facts if it is to continue to be held comfortably and without neurotic effects on the be-liever.

From a purely religious standpoint, the impression of Jesus that the Gospels project is that of a prophet in the Danielic tradition and a Messiah-Saviour of the Gnostic type, namely the Messenger of Light sent by the Father to retrieve and "gather in" the scattered bits of light (each spark of life or pneuma) entrapped in the darkness of the world ruled by the "Prince of this world" (Saint John 14:30). The appellation, Son of Man, was appropriated for themselves by certain of the Jewish prophets, notably Daniel and Ezekiel.[72] The same designation is reportedly used by Jesus in reference to himself, in all four Gospels, implying succession in the tradition of Daniel and Ezekiel. Thus the authors of the Gospels have, at least, a common aim: to present Jesus as a prophet. Indeed, he is widely regarded as such in Judaism (where the prophetic literature was regarded as closed with the Book of Malachi)[73] and in Islam, which regards Muhammad as the last in a long line of prophets of the three Semitic religions.

The scenario of the *parousia* or second coming of Jesus "with the clouds of heaven" as well as of the resurrection of the dead on that last day, which Jesus is reported in the four Gospels to have employed on occasion in the course of his teaching, comes straight out of the Book of Daniel,[74] but has a far older antecedent. It dates back to ideas of a Savior (or Saoshyant) and the resurrection of the dead in the religion of the Prophet of Persia, Zoroaster.[75] These ideas were borrowed by Judaism during the Babylonian exile. As preached by Jesus, they were, therefore, not original. Indeed, they had become the common stock of Gnosticism.

202

In this connection, the Johannine Gospel differs from the other three in projecting a Gnostic impression of Jesus, thereby suggesting that it may have been an adaptive composition by a Gnostic Christian that was later adopted by the Church, in order both to hold on to its Gnostic converts and to combat Gnostic doctrines in their original form. Be this as it may, Jesus is there portrayed as the Son (or Logos),[76] identifying himself with the Father (God), who has sent him as his chosen Messenger to preach salvation to those souls trapped in human bodies in the darkness of the world ruled by the ''Prince of this world''—otherwise known as Ialdabaoth, the ''Prince of Darkness'' (Ephesians 6:12)—and to unite them with his Father (the Father of Light).[77]

We may conclude, on the whole, that the life and teachings of Jesus, as portrayed in the Gospels, did not represent something extraordinary or unique in the religious tradition of Judaism—whatever his political intentions may have been. Even his crucifixion was not a unique or unusual form of punishment in his day. It was the ancient parallel to more sophisticated modern methods of torture. His reported declaration that he came to fulfill, not destroy, the Jewish religious law and the prophets[78] is an accurate and perfectly acceptable presentation of his religious mission, except that he gave the law interpretations that brought out the spirit behind its otherwise dead letter. It is in his interpretation, reinterpretation, and outright transvaluations of the traditional teachings of Judaism that his contribution as a Jewish religious teacher lies. Most outstanding of his teachings and interpretations are those concerning Love and the Kingdom of God, in terms that today may be described as existential. But Jesus' brand of existentialism may be described as Christian, as distinct from Kierkegaard's and Heidegger's theological, and Sartre's secular, existentialism. One might go so far as to say that Jesus' unique contribution to Jewish religion was his existentialist interpretation of Judaism's law and the prophets. He examined every issue from this angle: How does the individual relate to this problem? How does the individual, as a human being among other human beings, stand in regard to this issue? In this approach he was among the ancient forerunners of the existentialist tradition in religion[79]: he interpreted human existence in terms of love of oneself and this, in turn, as the key to the love of God and of other human beings. It was a new approach to the Jewish doctrine of love as commanded in the Torah,[80] by which the doctrine was reinterpreted to include enemies as well as friends among one's neighbors. The practice of this reinterpreted doctrine of love, Jesus taught, elevated the individual to the moral state that he termed *the Kingdom of God*. This Christian existentialist doctrine of the Kingdom of God eliminated all differences among human beings, such as the distinction between Greek and barbarian,

Roman citizen and slave, Jew and Gentile (Colossians 3:11). It was a revolutionary doctrine—imagine loving the enemies of Rome!—that, whether Jesus intended it or not, was bound to have short- as well as long-term political repercussions, subvert the established order, destroy the psycho-cultural foundations of empire and imperial domination, and transform the relationships between imperial citizens and imperial subjects.[81] Such a change would liberate both Jews and Gentiles from the Roman imperial yoke but without restoring the kingdom of Israel. Clearly, Jesus was not the expected Messiah of Jewish tradition but a revolutionary. He paid with his life for his novel existentialist doctrine.

It is therefore necessary to close this chapter, fittingly, with a brief examination of what has been called the Christian existentialist approach adopted by Jesus in his teaching, showing how it both differs from and completes other brands of existentialist doctrine.

7. CHRISTIAN EXISTENTIALISM[82] AND THE ROLE OF THE CONCEPT OF SIN IN HUMAN EXISTENCE

The Jesus of the Gospels, like the Apostle Paul, may be "made all things to all men"[83] in the process of winning adherents to Christianity, but his principal teaching, like that of John the Baptist, was concerned with *sin, repentance*, and the *Kingdom of God*, with *love* playing a crucial role in the entry to that kingdom. These four topics are essentially existentialist themes, that is to say, they concern human existence. Love, however, was central to the others.

Sin, in its original Judaic conception, means estrangement or alienation—regarded chiefly as alienation from God, but also from one's fellowman. From this point of view sin is an existentialist condition of man but one that, Jesus taught, could be overcome by man's act of love leading to atonement or reconciliation in unity with God and one's fellowman. Thus sin is an original human condition and atonement its cure.

Sin enters human existence in three ways. First, by self-estrangement pure and simple, that is, alienation from oneself. One "stands beside and apart from" oneself—a condition regarded as the common type of mental ill health, requiring reintegration with oneself. It was, somehow, never regarded in Judaism as a religious problem, although, in fact, it is one, in the strict sense of religion.[84] Rather was it regarded as an anormal condition, the self-integrated individual being regarded as the norm. Second, sin enters human existence by self-estrangement from God (conceived as "wholly other," completely "transcendent" vis-à-vis man).

If God be defined as Existence itself, or Being (better still, Becoming), then sin, as estrangement of man from God or Existence is man's conceptual doing; for it is man that, falsely, conceives of God as being "wholly other," estranged from man or vice versa—a view easily fostered by the anthropomorphic conception of God.[85] Third, sin as physical alienation of man from man is built into human existence by the mere physical separation of one human being from another, each inhabiting their own body. Of the three kinds of alienation this is the only one that truly can be called an original condition of man, of human existence. It implies a subjective or solipsistic (that is, vicarious or mediate) experience of the other person, not a direct or immediate one. Physical alienation of man from man is then easily reinforced by psychological or emotional alienation, whether mutual or nonreciprocal.

In regard to man's conceptual self-alienation from God/Existence this is easily remedied, for each human being has a direct and immediate awareness of, and link with, Existence in the sense of the Whole of which each human being is a part, an integral part. All that is necessary, therefore, is to reconceive man's relationship to God/Existence, so that each human being is immanent in God/Existence which, at the same time, transcends each and every human (or other) being. Thus immanence defines man's relationship to God/Existence, transcendence the relationship of God/Existence to man. The traditional immanence-transcendence, man-God relationship remains true but is only the same relationship viewed from its two ends. It may be expressed, accurately, by the term *pan-en-theism* or its equivalent, *pan-en-cosmism*: everything in God/Existence/Cosmos which, in turn, transcends every individual entity or thing.

As to the biopsychological phenomenon of interpersonal alienation, this may be overcome by interpersonal atonement, reconciliation, or love—according to the teaching of Jesus, love being the will to include, and the actual inclusion of, consideration of the welfare of "the other" (the neighbor, that is, friend as well as foe) in all considerations of one's own well-being. Thus we do our own atoning, our own reconciliation vis-à-vis "the other." No one can do that for us.

Basically, therefore, man overcomes sin or alienation by being existentially (and automatically) "at one" with God/Existence, being immanent therein, while it requires an act of will to be "at one" with "the other." The "new man," in Jesus' teaching, is the man who has found the "kingdom of God/Existence" within himself, who is "at one" with God/Existence and "at one" with his fellowman.

The teaching of Jesus regarding the Judaic concept of sin found an echo in Gnosticism, where "sin" is replaced by "ignorance." Here alienation of man from God and from man is due to ignorance. Thus the man who has overcome alienation is the one who has overcome ignorance by obtaining knowledge (*gnosis*) of man's proper relationship with God and with his fellowman.

This knowledge starts with "self-knowledge"—the motto of the Delphic Oracle, adopted by Socrates—leading to an identical union of "knower" and "known" (the "unknown" being God as well as man). This "union-through-knowledge" is the equivalent of Christian "love" or atonement, operating in its threefold aspects: love of God for man—love of man for man—love of man for God, by which the cycle is closed.

Repentance involves a *stock taking* of our daily ongoing activities and a *reorientation* (in some cases, an about-face-turn) of those activities. This exercise is symbolically represented in the Gospels as a once-for-all effort sealed by the rite of baptism. However, it is a daily, ongoing exercise. Each of us lives and relives his life each day, reorienting it as well as its program of activities. The orientation that Jesus preached was toward a specific goal: the Kingdom of God.

This Kingdom of God, which exists within every person,[86] is founded on love—love of God and "the other" which, in turn is based on love of self. Self-love exhibits its full scope in the three kinds of personal interrelationship: I-I, I-God, I-Other (Other being neighbour—stranger, friend, or foe).[87] These correspond to the three basic existential relationships found within the Kingdom of God: solipsistic, theological, and communal. They are the three dimensions of what may be called Christian existentialism. In sum, the solipsistic or self-regarding and self-preserving relationship, based on love of the self, is incomplete unless extended to include love of God and of the Other: self-love completes itself by submergence in love of transcendent Existence as well as of the neighbor or stranger, friend or foe. The gateway to the love of Existence and of others is the self, the first object of one's love. The communal dimension of existence consists of the sum total of one's neighborly (or I-Other) relationships, namely, the Church or externalized Kingdom of God on earth, for the promotion of which Jesus is reported to have conferred a special commission on Peter.[88] Through the communal dimension one approaches the theological dimension of human existence, namely, man's existential relationship to Existence itself.

Christian existentialism—as distinct from the solipsistic theological existentialism of Søren Kierkegaard, Karl Jaspers, Martin Heidegger, and others of their following, on the one hand, and the solipsistic secular existentialism of Jean-Paul Sartre, Albert Camus, et al., on the other—contains the missing complement of these others: the communal dimension. And the essence of the communal dimension is "being-*among*-others-in-the-world," a quite different matter from Heidegger's "being-*with*-others-in-the-world." In Christian existentialism, "being-*among*-others" is necessary to authentic existence and involves love, while Heidegger's "being-*with*-others" is no more than an incidental aspect of human existence, and does not enter into his definition of authentic existence, this having to do with the centrality of death in human life. Thus the communal dimension of Christian existentialism completes the other types of existentialism—theological and secular. Indeed, as pointed out already, the extreme solipsism of Kierkegaard is contrary to the thrust of Christian existentialism, which devalues it in favor of relationships to man and God.

In addition to providing the missing (communal) element in the other two types of existentialism, Christian existentialism differs radically from both in its attitude to death. For the Christian existentialist, unlike the theological and secular existentialists, death is not the end, but only an aspect of existence. There is more beyond death as indicated in the doctrine of resurrection—a principal tenet in Jesus' teaching borrowed from Zoroaster.[89]

The key word in Christian existentialism, we may conclude, is *love*, on which hang all the law and the prophets of Judaism.[90] The law and the prophets and the doctrine of love were basic to Judaism, except that the scope of love toward man was limited to friends, excluding one's enemies.[91] In extending the scope of love to include one's enemies Jesus included all of mankind in it.[92]

The schema of Jesus' teaching on love, as recorded in the Gospels, is as follows:

Kingdom of God within man: I — God (love of God) / I (self-love) / Other (love of Other)

In an innovation to his teaching, knowledge is assimilated to self-love and the love of God and man in the first of the Johannine epistles, an innovation that betrays the influence of Valentinian Gnosticism on the author. Thus a Gnostic flavor was added to the existentialist teaching of

Jesus, without detracting from its essence.[93] The modified schema becomes:

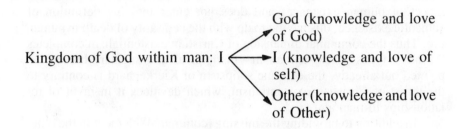

Kingdom of God within man: I

God (knowledge and love of God)

I (knowledge and love of self)

Other (knowledge and love of Other)

APPENDIX

1. A NOTE ON THE DOCTRINE OF ORIGINAL SIN AND ALIENATION OF MAN FROM GOD

The doctrine of Original Sin was formulated by Origenes[94] Adamantius (Origen, for short), a Gnostic Christian born in Alexandria around 186 C.E. (died around 256 C.E.) in a manner that emphasized (and condemned) sexual intercourse and lust as its chief characteristic, with resulting "alienation" of man from God. This doctrine, which was Gnostic rather than Christian, may be interpreted in at least four possible ways, all sex-related in one way or another and all involving "physical" alienation of the person or an organ or part of the body:

(a) The sin of desiring knowledge of good and evil—like gods—committed by Adam in the Garden of Eden, through his eating of the fruit of the tree of knowledge of good and evil in disobedience to God's command (Genesis 2). This disobedience led to physical alienation of Adam and Eve from their anthropomorphic God through their expulsion from the Garden of Eden, on pain of toilsome labor for Adam and sorrowful childbirth for Eve.

(b) The sin of self-castration committed by Origen, who thereby physically estranged or alienated an organ of his body from himself. This was the probable cause of the refusal to ordain him as a priest.[95] Thus rendering himself physically chaste and celibate, he was physically less than a whole man.

(c) The sin of sexual intercourse and procreation whereby Ialdabaoth, the Just God of the Jews, desired his creation, Adam and Eve, to multiply humanity in order to further imprison (physically alienate) and disperse in little bits the light from the Father of Light, Ohrmazd (Ahura Mazda). This light was already captured by the darkness of Ialdabaoth's world, the cosmos. Its dispersal and imprisonment in little bits within human bodies made more difficult the task of re-demption of the light, that is, its collection or gathering in by the Savior, Jesus. Procreation also involves the physical alienation of man from man by the giving birth to, expelling or alienating, off-spring, as well as the alienation by the mother of a part of herself.

This is the Gnostic doctrine on which Origen based his definition of "original" sin as sexual intercourse. In obedience to this doctrine he, as a devoted Gnostic, sought to defeat Ialdabaoth's evil purpose of procreation by rendering himself impotent through self-immola-tion.

(d) The Gnostic doctrine of the passion of the Sophia for the Father of All in wishing to know him and to procreate without her consort—which led to abortion of her passion in the hypostatized form of her "strengthless female fruit" and daughter, the Lower Sophia (or So-phia Prunikos). The sin in this case is the passion to know and procreate with the unknowable Father—a kind of Electra complex—and involved a dual physical alienation: of the Sophia's consort and of the aborted fruit of her passion, the Lower Sophia.

The prominence of the Gnostic themes of *gnosis* (knowledge), sex, and procreation in these interpretations is the genuine hallmark of the doctrine of "original sin." It indicates a probable Persian-Gnostic, if not a Babylonian, origin of the Genesis Creation Myth.

Further References

Bible.
Trevor Ling, *A History of Religion East and West* (London: Macmillan Press, 1984), pp. 172–174.
Hans Jonas, *The Gnostic Religion* (Boston: Beacon Press, 1963), chapter 8.
Walter Bauer, *Orthodoxy and Heresy in Earliest Christianity* (Philadel-phia: Fortress Press, 1971), pp. 48, 54–59, 106.

2. THE MYTH OF THE DEATH OF JESUS CHRIST FOR THE SINS OF MANKIND

Notwithstanding the modern existentialist wisdom that no one can die another's death, the myth of the death of Jesus for mankind remains robust after many centuries. It happens, of course, that in any human society innocent people are often made to suffer for wrongs committed by others against the society. Occasionally, also, an entire community may suffer the wrongs committed by a few. The myth of Jesus, an innocent man, being made to suffer the wrongs of others is, therefore, not a unique event in human history. What seems unique about this legend is the claim by partisans of Jesus that he voluntarily suffered for the wrongs and sins of all mankind committed before, during, and since his time on planet Earth. And here arises the difficulty.

One may define a wrong with reference to a given society. But different societies of mankind have different standards of wrong and right, so that it is impossible to define uniform standards of right and wrong for all mankind, at any one time, let alone for all mankind of the past, the present, and yet to come. How, then, could one individual, a Jesus Christ, be wronged in his person by mankind-of-all-time? And by what universal intertemporal standard of right and wrong?

Substantiation of the claim by Christians would require that the following conditions be met. First, it should be possible to identify at least one universal rule of conduct valid for all mankind. Second, this rule must be shown or known to be regularly violated, at the least, by *some people* in *all societies* at *all times* and by *all people* in *all societies* at *some times*. Third, there must be one person representing (or incarnating) this rule that is violated regularly by all men in all societies at all times, past, present, and future.

It readily can be shown that there is at least one rule of conduct that can claim universal validity for all men at all times: the Golden Rule of Reciprocity, which has been variously formulated by various great religious figures. Confucius expressed it simply as: "Do as you would be done by" or, in the literature of the New Testament; "Do unto others as you would they should do unto you."[96] In both Judaism and Christianity there is also a nonreciprocal formulation of this ancient rule of reciprocity: "Thou shalt love thy neighbor as thyself." This, however, is a more limited form of reciprocity in Judaism, since it is limited effectively only to friends and not extended to enemies. The rule of reciprocity ("Do unto others . . .") is, at least formally, unlimited since it could be argued that *others* includes everybody, friend as well as enemy. In extending love to enemies Jesus was, in this respect, not formulating a new rule. Buddhism, which antedates Christianity, goes even further to espouse the "abolition of distinctions" between man and man and between man and the rest of Nature. The Buddhist version is certainly the most far-reaching and comprehensive of the formulations, extending beyond the human species to which the rule of love seems limited in Confucianism, Judaism, and Christianity.

There is evidence that one or another version of the rule of reciprocity or mutuality is subscribed to, or is at least not in conflict with other ethical rules accepted, by other societies of man than those already indicated. Whether formulated as the principle of mutuality or reciprocity[97] (Confucianism, Judaism, Christianity) or as the principle of nondistinction (Buddhism), the common essence of the rule in behavioral terms may be expressed as follows: "Take only such action as benefits oneself and others at the same time." Expressed in this form, there can be very little doubt that this principle of action has been and will be violated by all men of all times, considering that its opposite—selfness, self-preservation, and concern for one's own interests and safety, sometimes exclusively—is the very basis of individuation and biological survival.

Granted all the foregoing, it may be said that Jesus was certainly not the *only* representative of the Golden Rule nor, metaphorically speaking, its sole incarnation.

Confucius and Buddha were equally impressive champions. Thus every time the rule is violated the persons of Confucius, Buddha, Jesus, et cetera, are violated in a metaphorical sense. The claim of the Christians is, therefore, true in a metaphorical sense, but is certainly not unique. The crucifixion of Jesus was a violation of the rule but so, in every sense, has been the murder of any innocent human being, any animal or plant; so, in general, is every antiecological act, and so, in the final analysis, is the very cosmic principle of mutual cannibalism for survival viewed in a human rather than cosmic context.[98] However, the claim becomes banal when account is taken of the violations of the mutuality principle by Jesus himself at various times in his life: he took pride in sowing antagonisms within families, setting parents against children (Saint Matthew 10:35); he cursed the fig tree and withered it (Saint Matthew 21:18–19); ultimately, he ate meat, cereal, fruits and vegetables, and fish in order to survive. Thus, from a human point of view, every other great religious leader has similarly violated the mutuality principle in fulfilling the general cosmic rule of survival.

The myth of the death of Jesus for the sins of the world may be interpreted in a sense opposite to that of his followers when placed in the context of the myth of the Garden of Eden and the Fall of Adam and

211

Eve. Here God, as creator of Adam and Eve, cannot escape responsibility for their actions.[99] It therefore seems unjust to punish them with banishment, death, toil, and sorrowful childbearing for eating the forbidden fruit of the tree of knowledge of good and evil. Furthermore, it may be assumed that Adam and Eve had eaten of the fruit of the tree of life, which had not been forbidden to them. Thus they were being punished, unwarrantedly, with death in being deprived of an existing benefit to which they were entitled (deathless life). (The implication that knowledge is more important than life, in the view of both God and Adam, is seldom mentioned in the exegetical treatment of the myth. This contrasts with the parallel case of Prometheus in Greek mythology, where his theft of fire from the gods for the benefit of man is treated approvingly.)

In the circumstances, it would seem only logical and fair that God, in the person of his son, Jesus, should suffer sorrow and death in order to make amends for his injustice to the first man and woman, thus calling it quits. On this interpretation Jesus did not atone for the sins of mankind but for the injustice of God.

Again, from the viewpoint of reciprocity enshrined in the Golden Rule the sacrifice of Jesus in dying for mankind would be ethically unacceptable if it benefited only mankind but not himself. This objection reaches to the very heart of the Christian doctrine of Grace—unmerited favor that puts man in debt to God for all time, without recompense. Grace takes away from man his responsibility for his own welfare and salvation, deprives him of the opportunity of working out his own salvation, whether or not with fear and trembling.[100] In thus being one-sided the relationship of grace is ethically unacceptable. Moreover, the self-sacrifice of Jesus, which Christians declare to be a free gift of love, turns out not to be so but is conditioned on belief,[101] the narrowest of all dispositions and one opposed to reason, morality, and love.[102]

Finally, the voluntariness of Jesus' self-sacrifice is called into question by the passage, recorded in the Gospels, where in his last hours he prayed that the cup of suffering should pass from him—if God (not Jesus) willed it.[103]

The discussion up to this point has revealed the complexity of a myth that, at first sight, would appear as one of the simplest and most straightforward of its kind. The analysis has revealed its rather unattractive features. Why such a complicated, unattractive, and unconvincing scenario, as presented in the Genesis myth of the Fall, when a more convincing one could easily have been concocted? To repair the consequences of the Fall and restore Paradise to man, either God could have formed a second Eve out of the second Adam—Jesus—conceived by Mary through God's instrumentality; or God could have been the instrument of another immaculate conception, a girl, a second Eve, who, with Jesus, could have procreated a new and redeemed race of mankind. Clearly, the opportunity for this second alternative was missed when the two cousins, Elizabeth and Mary, immaculately conceived two boys—John and Jesus—instead of a boy and a girl to redeem the fallen race of man. The Christian myth makers seem to have bungled their job—or else were more interested in promoting their hero, Jesus, than in restoring Paradise to man.

Notwithstanding the foregoing exegesis, the truth regarding the myth (or dogma) of Jesus' voluntary death for the sins and salvation of mankind is probably much simpler than would appear. It is no more than a composite myth (Greek Dionysus plus Persian-Gnostic Savior) devised specifically for proselytic purposes by the followers of Jesus. No more profound exegesis is required beyond this simple statement.

NOTES

1. The Gospels of Matthew and Mark vie for the title of earliest of the Christian writings, the date being generally fixed at around 70 C.E., the date of the destruction of the Jewish Temple at Jerusalem and the sacking of Jerusalem itself by the Romans. Internal evidence for this date is usually based on Jesus' reference to the destruction of the temple, if the reference is not regarded as a prophecy. However, the reference is found in three of the four Gospels, at: Saint Matthew 24:1–2; Saint Mark 13:1–2; Saint Luke 21:5–6. On this evidence alone it would seem that three, rather than two, of the Gospels are involved in determining the issue of priority.

2. The competition and mutual interaction between Gnosticism, a long-established product of Zoroastrianism, and Christianity, which came into a field already preempted by Gnosticism, was carried on by various methods: trading of charges and counter-charges of heresy, mutual excommunication and persecution, forging and counter-forging of supposed Scriptures, financial bribery and corruption, executions, destruction and burning of the books and other literature of the opposition, et cetera—not unlike the practices of the Spanish Inquisition. In the event, Christianity gained the upper hand by its successful conversion of the Emperor Constantine (baptized on his deathbed) and its alliance with the Roman imperial power, which enabled it the better to suppress its opponents. Even so, Christianity could not avoid bearing some of the marks of the struggle: it employed the time-honored method of competition of stealing some of the enemy's thunder and powder—in this case the adoption and adaptation (including transvaluation) of some of the enemy's tenets. Thus clear evidence of Gnostic ideas survives in the Gospel of Saint John: the Gospel of truth and light-in-darkness and of the Messenger-Son of the Father of Light sent down into the world to save the souls (sparks of light) imprisoned in the darkness of the world by the "prince of this world" (Saint John 3, 8, 10, 12, 14, 17).

The Apostle Paul, a past master at the game of thunder-and-powder stealing as well as the philosopher-apostle of expedience in order to win souls for Jesus was, in this respect, the ideal warrior—and original Jesuit. The epistles credited to him are redolent with the fragrance of Gnosticism. For accounts of the conflict

213

and methods used in the competition between Gnosticism and Christianity, see Walter Bauer (ed. by Robert Kraft and Gerhard Krodel) *Orthodoxy and Heresy in Earliest Christianity*, (Philadelphia: Fortress Press, 1971); Trevor Ling, *A History of Religion East and West* (London: Macmillan Press, 1984), pp. 169–172, 174, 176, 183; Hans Jonas, *The Gnostic Religion* (Beacon, 1963); Elaine Pagels, *The Gnostic Gospels* (New York: Vintage Books, 1981).

3. Levi, *The Aquarian Gospel of Jesus the Christ* (De Vorss and Co., 1979).

4. *The Aquarian Gospel* and other studies constitute a basis for the view that Christianity owes its doctrine and character to Buddhism. But another view could equally be argued, to the effect that, in reaching out to the Gentiles—including Hindus and Buddhists—Christianity had to become doctrinally flexible and eclectic, if there is any validity at all to the analysis of the process of conversion given subsequently at Book Two, chapter 13. Like Paul, Christianity became all things to all men in order to win souls for Jesus. See also Elaine Pagels, *The Gnostic Gospels* (New York: Vintage Books, 1981), introduction, pp. xx–xxv.

5. See A. Powell Davies, *The Meaning of the Dead Sea Scrolls* (Signet Key Books, 1956).

6. See Elaine Pagels, *The Gnostic Gospels* (New York: Vintage Books, 1981).

7. Saint Luke 1:36.

8. Saint Luke 1:15, 32, 16–17.

9. Saint John 1:29–34; Saint Luke 7:19–20.

10. Saint Matthew 3, Saint Mark 3, Saint John 1:19–34.

11. See especially Saint Matthew 5, 6, 7.

12. Saint Matthew 7:29: Unlike the scribes, Jesus did not quote any authority for his interpretation, except himself: "I say unto you . . ." This was a rather unscholarly approach, given established rabbinical tradition.

13. Cf. Saint Matthew 14:1–11 and Saint Mark 6:21–28 for another kind of evil resulting from swearing an oath: Herod's beheading of John the Baptist against his reason and his conscience.

14. Mostly Samaritan Jews with a Gnostic background who converted to Christianity. See John Hick (ed.), *The Myth of God Incarnate* (SCM Press, 1977), chapter 4, especially pp. 65–67.

15. Hebrews 6:1–2.

16. Matthew 19:13–15; Mark 10:15–16.

17. John Hick (ed.), *The Myth of God Incarnate* (Philadelphia: Westminster Press, 1977), p. 73.

18. Cf. Jesus' Dionysian reference to himself, which foreshadows the institution of the Eucharist: John 6:48–59.

19. Hick, op. cit., pp. 71, 73.

20. Matthew 3:4.

21. If the accounts of their vocational background and their inability to grasp and interpret Jesus' parables are to be believed. (Cf. Matthew 13:36, 15:15–20; Mark 4:13, 7:17–23, 8:14–18; Luke 10:9, 11.)

22. F. M. Dostoyevsky, *The Brothers Karamazov*, (New York: Penguin Classics, 1978), Vol. I, Part Two, Book Five, chapter 5.

23. Saint Matthew 4:1–11 and Saint Luke 4:1–13 give details of the temptation, while Saint Mark 1:9–13 merely records Jesus' baptism followed by his departure into the desert to be tempted.

24. Saint John 3:26. This seems to have raised a jurisdictional issue among John's disciples.

25. Saint Matthew 4:17; Saint Mark 1:14–15; Saint Luke 4:43.
26. Saint Luke 7:29; Saint John 3:22–23.
27. Saint Matthew 10:5–42; Saint Mark 6:7–13; Saint Luke 3:1–18, 9:1–6, 10:1–20.
28. Saint Matthew 6:9–15; Saint Luke 11:1–4.
29. Saint Matthew 14:1–2; Saint Mark 6:14–16; Saint Luke 9:7–9.
30. Saint Luke 13:31.
31. Saint John 5:25, 9:35–37, 10:36.
32. Genesis 6:2, 4; Psalm 2:7.
33. Saint Luke 19:28–40; Saint John 6:15, 12:12–15.
34. Saint Matthew 27:24–26, 37; Saint Mark 15:15, 26; Saint Luke 23:23, 24; Saint John 19:12–19.
35. Hans Jonas, *The Gnostic Religion* (Boston: Beacon Press, 1963), chapter 4.
36. Saint Luke 4:28–30.
37. Saint Luke 7:11–20. Jesus' answer was rather evasive (verses 22–23).
38. Saint Matthew 15:24; Saint Mark 7:27; Saint John 4:22.
39. Book Two, Part III, Section B, chapter 9 of this book.
40. Josephus, *The Jewish War* (London: Penguin Classics, 1980) pp. 396–400. Even those inclined to question this source would, at least, agree that Jesus lived and stirred violent reactions against himself and his mission.
41. There is presumptive evidence at Saint John 21:1–15 that Jesus ate with Simon Peter and six other disciples at his third appearance after his reported resurrection. But it is not definitely stated that Jesus himself ate anything. Only his disciples are clearly stated to have eaten at Jesus' invitation (verse 12).
42. Certain observations are in order at this point on the topics of transmigration of the soul and resurrection of the body. Transformation which, according to Plato in the *Timaeus*, is decomposition and recomposition—disintegration and reintegration, in other terms—into a *different* entity from what was broken down, is a Hindu-Buddhist concept. It constitutes the physical basis of metempsychosis or metensomatosis (literally, reembodiment of the soul in different bodily elements) which, broadly, means the passage of the soul of a human being or other animal at, or after, death into a new body of the same or different species (*Shorter Oxford English Dictionary*)—usually a different species.

Assuming the validity of soul as the animating and motivating element of an animal or plant—according to the Aristotelian definition of soul—it has been shown why transmigration of soul is theoretically impossible, given that its mental component is an impersonal element that unites all biological entities without distinction (see chapter 8 immediately preceding on Cult of Dionysus, et cetera).

Resurrection of the body—an Indo-Persian concept adopted by the Semitic religions of our day—is *not* transformation in the Platonian sense, since decomposition is succeeded by recomposition of the *same*, rather than a different, entity as that which originally decomposed.

If the mental part of soul is impersonal and its nonmental part decomposable like the body and recomposable into the same or different species, then all that it is permissible to say (again, within the context of academic Greek philosophy) is that soul *manifests* itself in different species, rather than migrates from one species to another. And this is certainly consistent with what can be observed in the world of Nature. The myth of metempsychosis is inconsistent with the rest of the metaphysical myth of Plato and Aristotle. For this reason, the Lucan account of Jesus' bodily appearance after his resurrection (24:39) would not have made much sense to a Greek or Hellenist philosopher (although it would have been acceptable to its Zoroastrian source) while Saint Paul's concept of transformation into a *spiritual*,

215

hence different, body would, in principle, be listened to but declined with politeness, since a *spiritual* body (nonmaterial) would not make much sense, either—unless it meant the pure form of the material body. Like metempsychosis, resurrection does not make sense on the basis of the Aristotelian conception of soul and for the same reason. However, unlike the Greek soul, the Christian soul is a personalized soul that will claim its human body on the Last Day and, therefore, cannot transmigrate.

43. Book Two, Section B, chapter 9.
44. Jay Haley, *The Power Tactics of Jesus Christ* (New York: Avon Discus Books, 1969).
45. Book Two, Section B, chapter 10.
46. Book Two, Section B, chapter 9.
47. Saint John 10:36.
48. Saint John 10:30: "I and my Father are one."
49. Cf. Hans Jonas, op. cit., chapter 9.
50. Saint Luke 19:28–40.
51. Saint Matthew 27:37; Saint Mark 15:26; Saint Luke 23:38; Saint John 19:19.
52. Notwithstanding that he is recorded as saying, at Saint John 10:16, "And other sheep I have, which are not of this fold: them also must I bring, and they shall hear my voice; and there shall be one fold, and one shepherd."
53. That Jesus did regard himself as a prophet is clear from his reported reply to those who advised him to flee Jerusalem and Herod: "For it cannot be that a prophet perish out of Jerusalem" (Saint Luke 13:31–33) or, again, from his statement to his audience at Nazareth who were inclined to belittle "Joseph's son": "No prophet is accepted in his own country" (Saint Luke 4:24).
54. Jay Haley, op. cit., pp. 53–55.
55. Saint Matthew 7:1–2; Saint Luke 11:43–48.
56. Saint Matthew 5:9.
57. Saint Matthew 10:34; Saint Luke 12:51–53, 14:26.
58. Saint Luke 2:41–49, 8:19–21.
59. Saint Luke 11:37–44.
60. "Suffered under Pontius Pilate, Was crucified . . . He ascended into Heaven, And sitteth on the right hand of God, the Father Almighty; From thence he shall come to judge the quick and the dead" (repeated in similar wording in the Creed of Saint Athanasius).
61. Saint John 10:17–18.
62. Saint Luke 23:34.
63. E.g., Saint John 4:25–26:
    The woman saith unto him, I know that Messias cometh, which is called Christ: when he is come, he will tell us all things.
    Jesus saith unto her, I that speak unto thee am he.
64. This concept of the Messiah is outlined at various places in the Old Testament, but principally at Isaiah 9:6–7 and 11:1–12. It was held also by Jesus' disciples, who are reported to have asked him *after* his resurrection, "Lord, wilt thou at this time restore again the kingdom to Israel?" (Acts 1:6.) John the Baptist must have held a similar expectation, as he apparently had doubts about Jesus' messiahship when he sent from prison to ask him, "Art thou he that should come? or look we for another?" (Saint Luke 7:20.)
65. Trevor Ling, *A History of Religion East and West* (London: Macmillan Press, 1984) pp. 362–63.
66. This is the Pauline concept of the Messiah as recorded at Philippians 2:5–11, which,

216

in turn, is based on the suffering servant of Isaiah 53. This transvaluation seemed necessary to Paul (who never knew Jesus), since it was obvious that Jesus was not the kingly Messiah of Jewish expectation.

67. George Santayana, *Reason in Religion*, vol. 3 of *The Life of Reason* (New York: Dover Publications, 1982), p. 14.

68. The Hebrew word for "virgin" (a young woman) was misinterpreted as "sexually innocent young woman" in the Christian literature, thus providing the basis for the myth (pure) of immaculate conception.

69. I Corinthians 1:22.

70. As in the case of the cured blind man *after* his cure (Saint John 9:35–38) or *before* the raising of Lazarus (Saint John 11:25–27).

71. Book Two, Section B, chapter 8.

72. Daniel 8:17; Ezekiel, passim.

73. Trevor Ling, op. cit., p. 123.

74. Daniel 7:13:
    "I saw in the night visions, and, behold, one like the Son of man came with the clouds of heaven."
    Daniel 12:2:
    "And many of them that sleep in the dust of the earth shall awake some to everlasting life, and some to shame and everlasting contempt." (Cf. Saint Mark 14:62.)

75. Trevor Ling, op. cit., pp. 75–82.

76. In the appropriate sense of *message*.

77. The Johannine Gospel constitutes a bridge between the other three-synoptic Gospels and the rest of New Testament literature. The latter portray not only a more diversified understanding of Jesus but also the heterogeneous nature of the early Church, For, whatever diverse factors and considerations determined their production, selection, and canonization, the books of the New Testament are a heterogeneous collection portraying the early Church as an equally heterogeneous and loose group of sects, doctrines, and brands of Christianity: those of the Gentile-Pauline-Gnostic doctrine of justification by faith and salvation by grace (Romans 3:28, 30; 5:1; Galatians 3:11; Ephesians 2:5, 8, 9; Hebrews 10:38, 11:1) as against those of the traditional Jewish doctrine of justification by faith made efficacious by works which entered Christianity through the Jerusalem branch of the Church (James 2:14, 17, 18, 20, 24, 26); Gentile as against Jewish Christianity (Galatians 2:7, 8; Philippians 3); various Gentile Christian sects known by the names of their founders (I Corinthians 3:3–11, 21–23; 4:6, 14–16) as well as manifesting Gnostic, prophetic, glossolalian, et cetera, tendencies (I Corinthians 1:10–16, 3:3–7, 11:18, 19, 12:4–12; 14)—to mention some examples.

78. Saint Matthew 5:17.

79. Others were Zoroaster and the Gnostics, Buddha, and Socrates—to name a few.

80. See Leviticus 19:18, 34; Deuteronomy 6:5, 10:19, 11:1.

81. Saint Augustine went to great lengths to deny the accusation that Christianity contributed to, or had anything to do with, the downfall of Rome (sacked by Alaric in 410), arguing that Christianity looked to the establishment of a heavenly City of God, while Rome was concerned with the earthly City. Augustine downplayed the effect of Christian doctrine and teachings on political life. From the granting of full equality and citizen rights to Christians in 313 by Constantine, followed by his deathbed conversion to Christianity in 337, to the sacking of Rome in 410 is just under a century. But it took only this relatively short period of time for Christianity to work out its socially insidious and subversive effects on the estab-

lished order, to "soften it up" for a fall. The process had begun long before, of course, since the first missionary activities of Paul to the Gentiles and was serious enough to warrant injunctions by Church leaders, especially Paul himself, against disobedience to established authority, and by slaves to their masters. (See Ephesians 6:5–9, Colossians 3:22, 23, 4:1; I Timothy 6:1, 2; I Peter 2:12–16, 18–25; Romans 3:1–8). There was certainly some truth in the accusations against the Christians. (See Saint Augustine, *City of God*, Part I, Book I, chapters 1–3 [Pelican Classics.])

82. See Book Two, Section A, Part II, chapter 4 above for a more extensive discussion of existentialist doctrines.
83. I Corinthians 9:22.
84. See Book Three, chapter 7, following.
85. The self-imposed concept of divine alienation leads to both mysticism and neurosis as its end products.
86. Saint Luke 17:20–21. This precept was alredy foreshadowed in Deuteronomy 30:11–14.
87. Saint Luke 10:29–37.
88. Saint Matthew 16:18–19.
89. Saint Matthew 22:32, Saint Mark 12:24–27, Saint Luke 7:22, 14:12–14; Saint John 11:25.
90. Saint Matthew 22:35–40.
91. Leviticus 19:18, 34; Deuteronomy 6:4, 5.
92. Saint Matthew 5:43–48.
93. I John 2:3–5, 4:6–8. This Gnostic influence, which also involved denigration of the world (I John 2:15) was a prominent element in Paul's teaching (borrowing or preempting the thunder of the opposition) and a marked feature of Kierkegaard's existentialism.
94. Whence, probably, the adjective *original* (*origenal*) in the term *original sin*.
95. See G. L. Prestige, *Fathers and Heretics*, (London: SPCK, 8th, 1977), p. 47.
96. Saint Matthew 7:12; Saint Luke 6:31.
97. This may be strictly referred to as *positive* mutuality, since its negative version exists in the *lex talionis* of Judaism: "an eye for an eye, a tooth for a tooth." In short, the comprehensive principle of mutuality says: "Love those who love you; hate those who hate you."
98. For further discussion, see Book Three, chapter 8.
99. See Book One, Appendix to chapter 2.
100. Paul's advice in Philippians 2:12.
101. Saint John 3:16.
102. Ludwig Feuerbach, *The Essence of Christianity*, trans. George Eliot (New York: Harper Torchbooks, 1957) pp. 264–265 and footnote.
103. Matthew 26:39; Mark 14:35; Luke 22:42; John 12:27.

Chapter 12

Christian Ethics: Evolution[1] of the Christian Concept and Doctrine of Love

Christians fondly claim that their religion is a (if not *the*) religion of love and that this characteristic sets it apart from all other religions. By this they do not, of course, intend to mean that love is not preached by other religions—this would be manifestly incorrect insofar as (to mention only two examples) Judaism (the mother of Christianity) and Islam (the reform movement of Christianity) are concerned. What they intend to say is twofold: firstly, that no other religion puts as much emphasis on love as Christianity does; secondly, that only within Christianity is love preached and (practiced) to its highest degree, that of sacrificial love.

This claim of Christianity will be examined in what follows. It will be shown that the Christian doctrine of love is not an original contribution but a composite of borrowings from other sources, reinterpreted—as need be—to suit the circumstances of Jesus' times. The various nuances of love are analyzed, in increasing order of benevolence, under four categories with their likely sources indicated:

1. *Direct Reciprocity among Friends and Peers* (Reciprocal Dependent Benevolence). Sources: Confucius' Golden Rule (positive aspect), Judaism's Law of Revenge (negative aspect).
2. *Indirect Reciprocity with other than Friends, Peers, and Kinsmen* (Indirect Reciprocal Dependent Benevolence). Sources: Divers cultures.
3. *Nonreciprocal Beneficial Relationships with one's "Neighbor"* (Independent Benevolence). Sources: Judaism, Greek philosophic theology (Aristotle).
4. *Perfect Nonreciprocity with all of Mankind* (Perfect Independent Benevolence). Sources: Dionysian rites, Buddhism.

The highest form of benevolence (Type 4), known in Christianity

219

as sacrificial love and regarded—by reason of the death of Jesus on the cross—as the most distinctive aspect of Christian love is also the most unclear in meaning in New Testament literature, as well as the most controversial in the early history of the Christian Church. Unless interpreted according to Buddhist doctrine or in the light of Gnostic myth, it makes very little sense in the Christian context. The historical test to which it was subjected in the life of the early Church—martyrdom—had the same effect as the death of Jesus: an increase in the number of adherents. Of course, Christian martyrs were seduced by the promise of the kingdom of heaven to the persecuted, which is contained in the Beatitudes. Although not subject to independent confirmation, this promise shows that sacrificial love is not without self-interest, hence not without reciprocity, since the killer bestows on the martyr the opportunity of achieving the reward. The increase in membership of the cult is hardly what one would associate with the concept of sacrificial love; but to the extent that it may be regarded as a beneficial result of the self-sacrifice of Jesus and subsequent Christian martyrs, it is no longer true that there was no self-interest or reciprocal benefit (direct or indirect) from inflicting and voluntarily undergoing suffering, killing and being killed for one's Christian beliefs and teachings. The self-sacrifice constitutes the reciprocal bond between tormentor and tormented, similar to that constituted by the act that binds the sadist and the masochist. Even in Buddhism, the Mahayana Buddhist who delays his entry into Nirvana in order that the rest of the world may enter with him must, certainly, derive untold satisfaction from the pleasure of their company.

In his interesting book titled *The Four Loves*, C. S. Lewis distinguishes among Affection, Friendship, Eros, and Charity.[2] A brief description of each shows their different characteristics.

Affection (Greek = *storge*): Parental-filial love. It is need-love and gift-love at the same time, or need-gift love—a love that *needs to give*, not a love that is needed. Hence it is love on the parent's side, whose proper goal is to work toward the elimination of its need to give, toward the independence of its object of affection, toward its own abdication. It is the humblest and most catholic of the four loves because it is the least discriminating. It can exist even for the most unlovable of persons.

Friendship (Greek = *philia*, from *philos*, dear, friend; Lat. *amicitia*): This is a love based on shared interests and is shareable with (i.e., extendable to) others if they have the same common interests. Hence it is the least jealous of the loves because involving open personalities.

Eros: Aspiring love (not sexual love, though this also—naked bodies—may be involved in the desire to be one with the object of aspiring love); striving or seeking to be like the beloved object. It is jealous love,

220

hence not shareable with any other but the loved one or object. It is direct and exclusive. (Aristotle regarded eros as the essence of the love of man for God—i.e., man's aspiring to be like God.)

Charity (Greek = *agape*, Latin = *caritas*): Gift-love or sharing love; gift-love on the part of the giver, need-love on the part of the receiver. (This meaning derives from the original meaning of *agape*, namely, the love of a superior for an inferior that is good and proper for, and in, its place. This original meaning is not discussed by Lewis. Aristotle regarded *agape* in this sense as the essence of the love of God for man—somewhat inconsistently, since God neither knows nor, therefore, loves man. For God, being by definition a perfect and complete being and, therefore, needing nothing outside of itself to aspire to, can only love itself. This contradiction, however, is easily reconciled by Aristotle's argument that man's sharing in the *nous*, i.e., the mind and self-knowledge of God, enables him to share in the life of God and thus to be brought within the circle of God's self-knowledge, *ergo*, within God's self-love.[3])

Lewis regards *agape*, gift-love, as the ultimate or highest of the loves and the essence of Christian love: the love that freely gives and is freely given, *without merit* on the part of the receiver. This is true only in a general sense. For gift-love can take several forms different in intent and spirit. There is the gift-love in which others' interests are taken into account in addition to one's own but made dependent on one's own interests. There is also the gift-love that is like the preceding but differs in that the interests of others are not dependent on, but independent of, one's own interests. (This is genuine agape or gift-love in its strict sense of sharing love.) Then comes gift-love in its highest sense, in which the gift takes the form of the ultimate sacrifice of all one's interests to the independent interests of others—in particular, the giving of oneself, one's life—and gift-love becomes transformed into *suffering* sacrificial love.[4] All gift-loves are, in a sense, sacrificial, in that they involve giving up a part of one's interests and substituting those of others. But not all sacrifices are genuine or uncompensated—as will appear in due course. Indeed, it is doubtful whether there is ever a case of genuine sacrifice in this sense, even where, as in the case of sacrificial love, the totality of one's interests is sacrificed. Subsequent discussion should illuminate this issue.

Lewis's understanding of agape (unmerited gift-love) is the standard Christian doctrine of love, the love that freely gives. The related doctrine of salvation by grace—i.e., salvation as a free gift on the part of God—is a doctrine shared with Marcionite Gnosticism and, like this branch of gnosis, preaches salvation as obtainable by man through faith alone in

Jesus Christ. However, it is specifically the ultimate gift of self-sacrifice by Jesus on the cross in order to win salvation for meritless mankind, that is, suffering sacrificial love, rather than agape in the sense of sharing love, which is held up in New Testament literature as the exemplary model for emulation by the followers of Jesus. This is also the raison d'être of the Eucharist as instituted by Jesus as a commemorative feast (Saint Matthew 26:26–28; Saint Mark 14:22–24; Saint Luke 22:14–20), although it tends to get mixed up with sharing love. This is because the Last Supper was an occasion of sharing love in commemoration of (the forthcoming) suffering, sacrificial love.

The evolution of the Christian concept and doctrine of love can be traced in the reported teachings of Jesus in the New Testament. It is necessary, however, to remind ourselves that, whether in the Aristotelian sense or in the Lewisian sense, the love of God for man (agape) and the love of man for God (eros) are nonreciprocal affairs, notwithstanding their opposing directions. They are both one-sided affairs that are parallel, neither coinciding nor intersecting. This is also the traditional Christian view and is a hangover from the suprasensible-sensible, transcendent-immanent orientation of Greek academic philosophy on which it is based—a dichotomy now known to be flawed and erroneous. Furthermore, as R. G. Collingwood points out, in the view of Aristotle "the love that makes the world go round is neither God's love for us nor our love for each other, but a universal love for God which is wholly unreciprocated."[5] (Again, this is consistent with the distinction, in Greek academic philosophy, between the parallel worlds of the sensible and the suprasensible and the doctrine of eros or seeking to reproduce the perfect forms of God—albeit imperfectly—that sets the world of matter in motion.)

The difference between the Aristotelian and the traditional Christian view of "the love that makes the world go round" is that the Christian view is a transforming gloss upon the Aristotelian view, namely, that the love of man for God (which makes the world go round) is achieved through man's love for his fellowman. And since loving one's fellowman involves loving one's enemy, this is unmerited and unrequited love—very much like the love of the Aristotelian God for man. Thus, insofar as one's enemy is concerned, one can only love God (whom one has not seen) by behaving—condescendingly—toward one's fellowman as God himself would behave toward man. God's presumed activity of love thereby becomes a role model, an exemplary model, for man in regard to his enemies. This kind of love is certainly not a genuine feeling; besides condescension it involves a certain intention of discomfiture or embarrassment of the enemy; in short, it aims to "heap coals of fire on his

222

head," according to Paul's advice to the Romans in this matter. The reported teachings of Jesus, however, go beyond this model to that of sacrificial love, which is not partial but *total* "gifting," the gift being one's self, one's all.[6]

The Christian doctrine of love is not a single nor a simple one. An eclectic mix scattered throughout the Gospels, it ranges from simple reciprocity—prudence or dependent benevolence, in the terminology of R. B. Perry[7]—and meanders through various nuances of nonreciprocity to end in the extinction of selfhood, a level of love higher than agape, as we shall see. In what follows, the various kinds of love are ranked from the lowest to the highest.[8]

1. DIRECT RECIPROCITY AMONG FRIENDS AND PEERS (RECIPROCAL DEPENDENT BENEVOLENCE)

Therefore all things whatsoever ye would that men should do to you, do ye even so to them: for this is the law and the prophets.
—Saint Matthew 7:12[9]

And as ye would that men should do to you, do ye also to them likewise.
—Saint Luke 6:31

This is the case described by Perry as "dependent benevolence" where the interest of A in the interest of B depends on the interest of A—and vice versa. It may also be called the Rule of Prudence. (A acts to avoid B's hostility or to secure some benefit in return.) It is also the same as Confucius's Golden Rule: "Do unto others as you would they should do unto you" or "Do as you would be done by." Reduced to simpler terms, it says: "Love those who love you; do good to those who do good to you; lend to those who lend to you."

Naturally, there is the negative equivalent of this positive reciprocal dependent benevolence covered under this same case of simple reciprocity and is applicable to enemies, but also to friends. It is the *lex talionis*, or law of tooth and claw, of vengeance. The classic statement of negative simple reciprocity is found at Exodus 21:23–25 in the case of a pregnant woman hurt by a man so that she aborts and other adverse consequences (mischief) follow:

And if any mischief follow, then thou shalt give life for life,
Eye for eye, tooth for tooth, hand for hand, foot for foot,
Burning for burning, wound for wound, stripe for stripe.

223

The law of revenge is, however, generalized in Leviticus:

> And if a man cause a blemish in his neighbour; as he hath done, so shall it be done to him;
> Breach for breach, eye for eye, tooth for tooth: as he hath caused a blemish in a man, so shall it be done to him again.
> —Leviticus 24:19–20

Obviously, simple reciprocity among friends and peers is not a high standard of love but a very ordinary one. As Jesus pointed out, even ordinary people and the hated publican (the Jewish tax collector hired by the Roman colonial administration in Judaea) observed it in their daily lives:

> For if ye love them which love you, what reward have ye? do not even the publicans the same?
> And if ye salute your brethren only, what do ye more than others? do not even the publicans so?
> —Matthew 5:46–47

> For if ye love them which love you, what thank have ye? for sinners also love those that love them.
> And if ye do good to them which do good to you, what thank have ye? for sinners also do even the same.
> And if ye lend to them of whom ye hope to receive, what thank have ye? for sinners also lend to sinners, to receive as much again.
> —Saint Luke 6:32–34

The Christian is called upon, and required, to do better by extending his dependent benevolence to those outside his circle of friends, peers, and kinsmen, even though the self-interest involved is indirect:

> For I say unto you, that except your righteousness shall exceed the righteousness of the scribes and Pharisees, ye shall in no case enter into the Kingdom of heaven.
> —Saint Matthew 5:20

2. INDIRECT RECIPROCAL RELATIONS WITH OTHER THAN FRIENDS, PEERS, AND KINSMEN (DIRECT NON-RECIPROCAL OR INDIRECT RECIPROCAL DEPENDENT BENEVOLENCE)

Better still it is to entertain nonreciprocal relationships with anybody, whomsoever, both within and outside one's circle of friends, peers, and kinsmen, but especially those who, obviously, cannot reciprocate nor threaten one's interests:

And it came to pass, as he went into the house of one of the chief Pharisees to eat bread on the sabbath day, that they watched him. . . .

Then said he also to him that bade him, When thou makest a dinner or a supper, call not thy friends, nor thy brethren, neither thy kinsmen, nor thy rich neighbours; lest they also bid thee again, and a recompense be made thee.

But when thou makest a feast, call the poor, the maimed, the lame, the blind:

And thou shalt be blessed; for they cannot recompense thee: for thou shalt be recompensed at the resurrection of the just.

—Saint Luke 14:1, 12–14

This is the opposite of Type 1 benevolence in being indirect rather than direct, nonreciprocal instead of reciprocal, both types being dependent. One's self-interest is involved in the form of an other-worldly (post-resurrection) reward for the Christian believer. This conditions the act of benevolence, which is thereby made dependent on one's self-interest.

Both types of benevolence, being dependent, are therefore the lowest kind of love: self-interest kind of sharing love with some expected parallel benefit, direct or indirect.

Type 2 benevolence descends even lower when done for public show: such as the public display of almsgiving (Saint Matthew 6:1–4), which, like public show of praying (Saint Matthew 6:5–6) and fasting (Saint Matthew 6:16–18), is done specifically in order to be ''seen of men'' and so secure their glory and esteem—which becomes the specific indirect benefit desired. In such cases the reward is direct and immediate, although the act is ostensibly done out of ''pure benevolence'' with no other end in view than an indirect reward ''at the resurrection of the just.'' Thus the act is hypocritical, being done under false pretences—the pretence in either case being to create the impression of unselfish motivation and interest when, in fact, selfish motivation and interest (the esteem of other men) is being directly sought and obtained in return, in addition to the gratitude of the recipient in the case of almsgiving: two immediate rewards plus one expected future reward for the price of one gift.

3. NONRECIPROCAL BENEFICIAL RELATIONSHIPS WITH ONE'S "NEIGHBOR" (INDEPENDENT BENEVOLENCE)

(1) First, among one's group and tribe: the neighbor within one's group or affiliation.

> Jesus said unto him, Thou shalt love the Lord thy God with all thy heart and with all thy soul, and with all thy mind.
> This is the first and great commandment.
> And the second is like unto it, Thou shall love thy neighbour as thyself.
> On these two commandments hang all the law and the prophets.
> —Saint Matthew 22:37–40

> And one of the scribes came, and . . . asked him, which is the first commandment of all?
> And Jesus answered him, The first of all the commandments is, Hear, O Israel; the Lord our God is one Lord:
> And thou shalt love the Lord thy God with all thy heart, and with all thy soul, and with all thy mind, and with all thy strength: this is the first commandment.
> And the second is like, namely this, Thou shalt love thy neighbour as thyself. There is none other commandment greater than these.
> —Saint Mark 12:28–31

> And, behold, a certain lawyer stood up, and tempted him, saying, Master, what shall I do to inherit eternal life?
> He said unto him, What is written in the law? how readest thou?
> And he answering said, Thou shalt love the Lord thy God with all thy heart, and with all thy soul, and with all thy strength, and with all thy mind; and thy neighbour as thyself.
> And he said unto him, Thou hast answered right: this do, and thou shalt live.
> —Saint Luke 10:25–28

This corresponds to Perry's case of independent benevolence in which the interest of A in the interest of neighbor B is independent of the interest of A. This case should be carefully distinguished from that of Type 2 benevolence (direct nonreciprocal beneficial relationship with one's neighbor). It is equivalent to one half of the Type 1 relationship without any expectation of the other and reciprocal half. An example will show the difference.

I bestow a pair of shoes on a neighbor who has none and is too poor to reciprocate. My gift may be made for any or a combination of various reasons. I may make the gift purely and simply to enable him keep his feet warm (Type 3—independent benevolence). Or the shoes may be out of style, too tight, or slightly damaged, or I may want to save myself the embarrassment of being seen in public conversing with a barefoot neighbor (Type 2—indirect reciprocal dependent benevolence: the reward of the just after resurrection, with or without the good opinion of the public towards me and the gratitude of the recipient); et cetera. How, then, can a third party tell whether my benevolence in this case is independent or dependent on my own interests? No way. Only the giver knows, knowing his own motivation. Jahweh's comment to Samuel in the matter of anointing one of Jesse's sons is apposite in this case also: ". . . man looketh on the outward appearance, but the Lord looketh on the heart" (I Samuel 16:7).

In this connection it should be noted—as indicated in the preceding chapter—that, in Jewish tradition, the command of Jahweh to the Jews to love him and their neighbors as themselves antedates the times and teachings of Jesus, who merely recites the injunction:

Hear, O Israel: the Lord our God is one Lord:
And thou shalt love the Lord thy God with all thine heart, and with all thy soul, and with all thy might.
—Deuteronomy 6:4, 5

Thou shalt not avenge, nor bear any grudge against the children of thy people, but thou shalt love thy neighbour as thyself: I am the Lord.
—Leviticus 19:18

(2) Then, among strangers unrelated to one by tribe or other affiliation: the case of the Good Samaritan and the Jew ("the stranger within thy gates"—Deuteronomy 5:14).

. . . And who is my neighbour?
And Jesus answering said, A certain man went down from Jerusalem to Jericho, and fell among thieves, which stripped him of his raiment, and wounded him, and departed, leaving him half dead.
. . . there came down a certain priest that way . . . saw him . . . passed by on the other side.
And likewise a Levite . . . came and looked on him, and passed by on the other side.
But a certain Samaritan . . . saw him . . . had compassion on him,
And went to him, and bound up his wounds, pouring in oil and wine, and set him on his own beast, and brought him to an inn, and took care of him.
—Saint Luke 10:29–34

Love of the stranger was enjoined by God to the Jews according to Old Testament Scripture, long before the birth of Jesus:

> Love ye therefore the stranger: for ye were strangers in the land of Egypt.
> — Deuteronomy 10:19

> Ye shall have one manner of law, as well for the stranger, as for one of your own country: for I am the Lord your God.
> —Leviticus 24:22

> But the stranger that dwelleth with you shall be unto you as one born among you, and thou shalt love him as thyself; for ye were strangers in the land of Egypt: I am the Lord your God.
> —Leviticus 19:34

By turning the Old Testament injunction around so that it is the stranger that loves the Jew, Jesus sought to show the possibility of universal application of the precept, knocking down the narrowness of ethnic preferences and teaching the Jew humility at the same time.

(3) Eventually, with all men in general, including one's enemies, that is, those who not only will not reciprocate even if they could but, worse, go further to wish one evil (malevolence),[10] harm one's self-interest and oneself.

> Ye have heard that it hath been said, Thou shalt love thy neighbour, and hate thine enemy.
> But I say unto you, Love your enemies, bless them that curse you, do good to them that hate you, and pray for them that despitefully use you and persecute you;
> That ye may be the children of your Father which is in heaven: for he maketh his sun to rise on the evil and on the good, and sendeth rain on the just and on the unjust.
> —Saint Matthew 5:43–45

> But love ye your enemies, and do good, and lend, hoping for nothing again; and your reward shall be great, and ye shall be the children of the Highest; for he is kind unto the unthankful and to the evil.
> —Saint Luke 6:35

In this case, the interest of A in the interest of B is positive and independent of the interest of A, while the interest of B (the enemy) in the interest of A is negative and dependent or independent of the interest of B. In this manner one (A) approaches divine love in the sense of agape or sharing love that is unmerited, unrequited, and independent of one's

228

(A's) interest. But one still retains a part of the totality of one's self-interest. There is, however, no direct compensation for the part of one's interest shared with others. The compensation is indirect—the status of "child of the Highest."[11] Such unmerited love on the part of the enemy is the ideal case of agape: sharing out of one's fullness, one's overflowing love, but leaving some love for oneself (self-love).

All three types of love or benevolence, both dependent and independent, direct and indirect, reciprocal and nonreciprocal—that is to say, any act that wills and seeks the welfare of another in addition to one's own, any act of altruism—therefore, *always* contain a certain amount, however small, of one's own self-interest that is not sacrificed in order to accommodate the interests of another.

The case of sacrificial love in which the amount of one's self-interest in the benevolent mix of self-interest and others' interests is zero is really a special case of the third kind of Type 3 benevolence and, as such, is equivalent to Type 2 benevolence. Yet it is generally regarded by Christians as the highest form of love, being the perfect case of nonreciprocity and, as such, is often mistaken for perfect independent benevolence—a case that does not exist within the Christian context. This will become apparent in what follows. Although the case will be treated as a fourth type of benevolence because of its special nature, it should be regarded, correctly, as only a special form of Type 2 benevolence.

4. PERFECT NONRECIPROCAL BENEFICIAL RELATIONSHIP WITH ANY AND ALL OF ONE'S FELLOWMEN (PERFECT INDEPENDENT BENEVOLENCE?)

This is the putative case of Jesus' sacrifice on the cross—the Christian's highest ideal of love. It is also, in the sense of elimination of selfhood, the ideal pursued by the Boddhisatva in Buddhism.

I am the good shepherd: the good shepherd giveth his life for the sheep.

—Saint John 10:11

Greater love hath no man than this, that a man lay down his life for his friends.

—Saint John 15:13

It is clear from the context of the discussion in John's Gospel that *friends* in the second quotation includes "enemies." This type of love

229

is, then, the perfect love—or is supposed to be—with zero self-interest and the interest of others constituting its totality. It is truly sacrificial love. Besides Jesus, Dionysus is also said to have bestowed this kind of love. So did the widow with her two mites,[12] although she did not need to give her life as well. It is higher than the divine love of agape, sharing love with a remainder for the sharer; hence the highest type of love.

Sacrificial love (zero selfhood) is the dialectical opposite of total selfishness (total selfhood). These two qualities are represented in Buddhism by the Boddhisatva and the Arhat, respectively; the one postponing personal salvation (letting go of the wheel of life in order to gain Nirvana) until the entire race of man is saved, the other concerned only with his personal salvation. In Buddhism, as in Christianity, therefore, the highest form of love or benevolence is self-sacrifice—suffering self-extinction (Christianity) or temporary foregoing of Nirvana (Buddhism)—for the sake of others. However, in both Buddhism and Christianity there *is* some self-interest involved in total self-sacrifice—in the form, at least, of self-satisfaction at saving others through one's sacrifice. Hence perfect independent benevolence exists only in theory, never in practice, while its opposite side, perfect nonreciprocity, could also be said not to exist insofar as the other provides the opportunity (hence reciprocity) for one's total self-sacrifice. Yet such self-sacrifice converts the giver immediately into a cause célèbre, a law of great good establishing itself. All this is made clear in the following sayings ascribed to Jesus on the subject of self-sacrifice:

> He that findeth his life shall lose it: and he that loseth his life for my sake shall find it.
>
> —Saint Matthew 10:39

> For whosoever will save his life shall lose it; but whosoever shall lose his life for my sake and the gospel's, the same shall save it.
>
> —Saint Mark 8:35

> For whosoever will save his life shall lose it; but whosoever will lose his life for my sake, the same shall save it.
>
> —Saint Luke 9:24

> He that loveth his life shall lose it; and he that hateth his life in this world shall keep it unto life eternal.
>
> —Saint John 12:25

In this teaching, *for my sake* or *for my sake and the gospel's* refers to the cause of Jesus, presumed to be the salvation of mankind. It is won by the complete extinction of oneself, lost by excessive love of one's life. The condition attached ("for my sake") constitutes a benefit for the sacrificer, thus qualifying the perfection of this type of benevolence. The teaching itself is an existential paradox hard to substantiate empirically—for the obvious reason that no one has any conscious experience of the benefits of self-sacrificial love in a nonpersonal existence; therefore, such benefits cannot be compared with those of total selfishness (or self-interestedness) in a personal existence. This precept is therefore no more than a Christian dogma about the benefit of self-sacrificial love.

There is another more likely but equally dogmatic—because purely mythical—interpretation of self-sacrificial love based upon the Persian-Manichaean Gnostic doctrine of salvation through rejection of the evil world created by the Chief Arkon (Ialdabaoth), as well as sex and pro-creation. This would give the precept the character of a Gnostic inter-polation that somehow found its way into all four Gospels or else imply—which may or may not be the case—that Jesus was familiar with pre-Christian Gnostic doctrines and incorporated this particular Gnostic precept into his teachings in eclectic fashion. The aim would be to convert Jewish (Samaritan) Gnostics to his movement on the basis of his claim to be the Messiah (Saoshyant) of Israel.

According to Gnostic myth (or precept) salvation consists in the gathering-in of the bits of light that descended from the realm of the Father of Light (Ahura Mazda, Ormuzd, or Ormazd) and lie imprisoned in the evil world created by Ialdabaoth; this latter also created Adam and Eve to procreate and thereby disperse further—and make even more difficult the collection of—the bits of light (pneuma or spirit) imprisoned in mankind. Therefore, the cause of salvation will be served by any action that prevents the further dispersal of the light in man—such as male castration (à l'Origen) and abstention from sexual intercourse, marriage, and procreation—thus defeating the evil purposes of Ialdabaoth.

Interpreting Jesus' saying against this Gnostic background, saving (that is, continuing) one's physical life by means of sex, marriage, and procreation will lead to the dispersal and loss of one's spiritual life (the light, spirit, or pneuma in man); by contrast, losing (that is, not contin-uing) one's physical life by these means will save one's spiritual life by preventing the light or spirit in man from being lost through procreative dispersal. This interpretation, though intelligible, lacks empirical veri-fication for its content; and in the context of what it is supposed to elucidate—suffering, sacrificial love on behalf of others (taking also into account cases of self-mutilation as practised by Origen and other Christian Gnostics)—it is somewhat irrelevant. For the light (spiritual life) that is saved is that of the chaste, not that of others—unless by the powerful influence of example.

A third interpretation of the paradox of sacrificial love, that of the Buddhist doctrine and practice of Boddhisatva (the Buddhist who postpones his own access to salvation, Nirvana, until the rest of mankind is saved) is probably the most conformable with the spirit of sacrificial love, although also without empirical substantiation. In which case one may regard the Christian doctrine as a syncretic borrowing from Buddhism for the purpose of enriching Christian teaching or converting Buddhists. Indeed, there is a tradition that Jesus sojourned in India during the middle period of his life for which no record exists.[13]

The Christian doctrine of love is thus a composite doctrine interpretable at its lowest level in terms of material and psychological rewards involved in a simple reciprocal relationship (dependent benevolence). Increasingly higher levels of love involve a nonreciprocal relationship with an ever-widening circle of mankind (including, ideally, nonhuman organisms) as well as a progressively decreasing content of self-interest and an increasing content of the independent interests of others in the mix of one's love (independent benevolence). Theoretically, in the ultimate, love becomes an extinction of self-interest—a zero content of self-interest and a total content of the interests of others or, if need be, literal self-extinction in the service of others (perfect independent benevolence). (This level of love, so far as we know, is beyond human experience, including that of Jesus.) "Christian love" thus runs the entire gamut from Confucian love (the Golden Rule) through Aristotelian agape or sharing love of ancient Greek religion (Eucharistic sharing) to Dionysian/Buddhist self-abnegation (suffering sacrificial love), that is to say, from simple reciprocity through nonreciprocal sharing with others of the excess or surfeit of one's abundance, to giving one's all.

It is a fact worthy of note that there arose in the early Church a bitter controversy over the significance and practice of martyrdom or suffering sacrificial love. In view of the nonempirical nature and various possible interpretations of the doctrine that lost life is found life, this is not surprising. The occasion of controversy was the persecution of Christians under various Roman Emperors for their disregard of, and opposition to, the Roman state religion based on deification of the Emperor. The occasion simultaneously provided a mundane (empirical) test of the meaning and implications of the doctrine of sacrificial love. The Nag Hammadi finds of Christian Gnostic literature in December 1945 in Upper Egypt have thrown considerable light on the nature and effects of the controversy.

Elaine Pagels[14] reports Tertullian's view that the Gnostic theological "heresy" known as docetism was first advanced in connection with the persecution of Christians by the Roman state, as a theological justification for the opposition of mostly Gnostic Christians to martyrdom (or "blood witness'') on behalf of the Christian faith. Positions were thus taken on the issue of the proper attitude to adopt towards Jesus' passion and death: positive, by the organized, apostolic Church (''orthodoxy''); negative, by the unorganized Gnostic opponents—Simonians, Valentinians, and Marcionites (admirers of the Apostle Paul[15])—all ''heretics'' to the organized Church. Those on the side of orthodoxy based their encouragement of martyrdom on Christ's own reported teachings in the Gospels, which urged upon his followers a duty to take up their cross and follow him, expecting to suffer persecution and death gladly, in the same manner as these would be meted to himself.[16] These warnings by Jesus were, of course, normal expectations, rather than prophecies, based upon the history of Rome-Jewish relations. Besides the practical consideration that persecution strengthened Christian faith and increased Church membership,[17] the orthodox also argued that martyrdom brought forgiveness of sins and salvation as promised by Jesus; and that it was the human and divine Jesus, both, that suffered on the cross in a dramatic gesture of suffering love. This last claim became the point of contention with the Gnostics, who argued that the divine Jesus merely *seemed* to die on the cross (hence, docetism) but did not, and could not; that it was only the human Jesus that actually died on the tree, the divine Jesus ascending straight to the realms of light whence (according to Marcion) he descended, in the first place, directly on the synagogue at Capernaum without being born. Thus there was no point in Christians going to their death in the mistaken belief, encouraged by orthodoxy, that the divine Jesus had suffered as well as the human Jesus on the cross. For only the human element would similarly suffer in every Christian believer who underwent martyrdom, the divine spirit within transcending both suffering and death.[18]

As a refutation of the orthodox position that the divine Jesus died on the cross, the argument of the Gnostics seemed to be correct and supported by internal evidence from the Old and the New Testament:

(a) The suffering servant of Isaiah 53 is a man (human being).
(b) The Jesus who died on the cross was a man who felt abandoned by God (Saint Matthew 27:46).
(c) The Jesus of Saint Luke who was resurrected (or resuscitated) declared himself a man and no spirit (Saint Luke 24:39).
(d) The Jesus of Paul's Epistle to the Philippians, the suffering servant, was not only a human being but also one who had ''emptied himself'' of his divinity (kenosis) in order to become man (Philippians 2:5–11).

Thus, by all accounts, the Jesus who died on the cross was only human, not a divine being. But the refutation by the Gnostics did not constitute a valid argument against martyrdom per se. For, granted that it was only the human Christ that suffered and died, nothing in the Gnostic position prevented any human follower of Christ from similarly suffering and dying, if he or she so wished. It will always be the human element that suffers and dies, not the divine, in any case. Docetism did not, therefore, weaken the argument for martyrdom.

The orthodox theology may have been faulty. Indeed, Irenaeus, Bishop of Lyons and a staunch opponent of the Gnostics, paid tribute to the attempt of the Gnostics to raise the level of theological understanding, but correctly argued that this did not warrant their attempt to undermine the solidarity of the Christian Church by discouraging martyrdom at a time when the very existence of the Church was at stake. Orthodoxy may have been wrong and Gnosticism right on the doctrinal issue, but both arguments were irrelevant to the issue of whether a man or woman wished to bear "blood witness" for the faith as Jesus did. This was the crucial issue, and orthodoxy made the correct decision for the Church in the circumstances—the only decision warranted on the basis of the history of the foundation of the Jesus movement and its Synoptic Gospels. The conflict was less a matter of doctrine than of attitude: a bold stand by the orthodox for freedom of conscience, regardless of the consequences, in opposition to a cautious stand by the Gnostics dictated by a desire to escape adverse personal consequences of persecution, at the risk of destroying the entire Christian movement.

APPENDIX

THE ROLE OF LOVE AND MERCY IN CHRISTIAN THEOLOGY

Love and Mercy (Compassion) constitute a tandem of great importance in Christian theology, their role being to annul the Law of Compensation, Retribution, Justice, or Cause and Effect—a basic law of being. Christian theological doctrine employs the two concepts in order to focus attention on the Christian metamorphosis of the Jewish God of Justice into a personal God of Love who, out of compassion and partiality for man, annuls the universal law of justice or compensation in favor of the individual human being by taking upon himself, in the person of Jesus, and in place of man, the full impact-effect of the universal law of Cause and Effect.

What, however, is this Justice that is annulled? In the Judeo-Christian-Islamic myth, it is the penalty for man's disobedience, in his pristine state in the Garden of Eden, to God's dietary prohibition against partaking

234

of the fruit of the tree of knowledge of good and evil. This penalty consisted not only in Adam being deprived (along with Eve) of the fruit of the tree of eternal life (which had not been forbidden to them) but also being cursed with hard labor in earning his livelihood. For Eve the penalty was sorrowful childbirth and enmity between her and her brood, on the one hand, and the serpent, on the other.[19]

Anyone familiar with the Genesis myth and conscious of God's voluntary responsibility for creating the human species (among his other works of creation) cannot but be struck by the harshness of the penalty inflicted on archetypal man and woman.[20] From this viewpoint, the myth of the suffering God—through his son Jesus—makes a great deal of sense; but not as Jesus atoning for man's sin, but for the harsh and unjust treatment of man by God. Atonement, indeed, there needs to be: not of man with God but of God with man. Jesus is thus seen as redeeming God in the eyes of man, rather than man in the eyes of God. It is, therefore, man, not God, that has to accept this sacrifice.

Within the context of the Genesis myth the preceding comment redresses the imbalance in the traditional interpretation of the Christian doctrine of Atonement through Sacrificial Love. The traditional interpretation is clearly one-sided: the fault is all on the side of man, the right all on the side of God, but only by overlooking the harsh and unwarranted punishment of man by God in the Garden.

Properly speaking, atonement is a two-sided affair: A is reconciled to B and B to A. This presumes shortcomings on both sides. However, it is difficult to see where man went wrong in the Genesis myth.[21] Thus the self-sacrifice of Jesus has to be acceptable to man, not to God.

The use of Love and Mercy to promote partiality and a privileged position for man within the cosmos, to the point of annulling a basic natural law in man's favor, betrays the heavily anthropocentric bias of Christianity—a bias that is not only outdated, and therefore in need of correction, but also prone to ridicule: cosmic laws being bent to accommodate an insignificant, conceited and vainglorious part of the cosmic order. This myth does not even have the merit of a fable, nor the aesthetic beauty or therapeutic value of pure myth, being conflict-creating within the cosmos as well as unjust and therefore in need of creative obsolescence.

NOTES

1. It is not intended to imply that such an evolution did actually occur, for that was most unlikely to have happened in view of the eclectic nature of Christian teachings and rites. It is merely a methodological assumption adopted for expositional purposes

235

only and for ease of comparative evaluation of the various Christian teachings on love.

2. C. S. Lewis, *The Four Loves* (Collins Fontana Books, 1976).
3. R. G. Collingwood, *The Idea of Nature* (London: New York: Oxford University Press, 1945) pp. 87–89.
4. It would be a mistake, however, to regard this highest gift-love, of which Jesus' · suffering on the cross is the Christian instance, as a unique possession of Christianity. It was also a feature of the Dionysian cult, where Bacchus (or Dionysus) was the suffering god par excellence, either as the torn god or the pruned vine.
5. Idem, p. 87.
6. ˆSuch a gift was Christ's self-sacrifice on the cross or the widow's gift of her two mites—all she had (Saint Mark 12:41–44; Saint Luke 21:1–4).
7. R. B. Perry, *Realms of Value* (Harvard University Press, 1954), p. 82.
8. Equivalence with Perry's terminology is established throughout, to the extent possible. See, in particular, R. B. Perry, idem, chapters III–VII, for his terminology, definitions, and examples.
9. All quotations from the Bible are from the Authorized or King James Version.
10. R. B. Perry, op. cit., p. 82, where malevolence is defined as "negative interest in the fulfilment of another's interest; or the desire to frustrate it . . . the malevolence of one person to a second person means that the first person is interested in the frustration of the totality of the interests, positive or negative, of the second person."
11. This status seriously compromises the independence of the benevolence, converting it to indirect dependent benevolence (Type 2).
12. See note 6.
13. See, for example, Levi H. Dowling, *The Aquarian Gospel of Jesus the Christ* (DeVorss & Co., 1979) chapters VI and VII. Also, Elizabeth Clare Prophet, *The Lost Years of Jesus* (Summit University Press, 1984). The theory that Christianity is an offshoot of Buddhism—which would be appropriate in relation to the cult of Dionysus whose institutional and cultic rites constitute a paradigm for Christianity—seems to be based on the emphasis in the Gospels on (a) love of neighbor as oneself or independent benevolence (Saint John's Gospel is the Gospel of love, par excellence); (b) self-sacrifice for the benefit of mankind as the ultimate in love; (c) equality of all men in the sight of God as preached in the various parables attributed to Jesus. These features are similar to the Buddhist doctrine of abolition of distinctions generally (though the doctrine is confined in Christianity to relations among human beings) and the role of the Boddhisatva. However, this is not the entire message of Christianity as recorded in the Gospels. There are other messages, such as (d) to refrain from passing judgement on others (moral judgment); human welfare as the primary objective of laws, social, religious, et cetera ("The sabbath was made for man, not man for the sabbath"—Saint Mark 2:27); and so on.

In order to appreciate the inevitable syncretic nature of the Christian message, including the teaching on love, it is important to recall the central objective of the movement—to convert all the world, at the time split among various existing religious systems and cults: the cults of Bacchus, Diana, Ra (the Egyptian sun-god), Judaism, Buddhism, Confucianism, the Roman state religion founded on deification of the Emperors, et cetera. It was therefore natural that the Gospels and Epistles (as distinct from the personal mission of Jesus himself) should be addressed to all these religions and their adherents and, consequently, contain borrowings and transvaluations from all of them, but subordinated to the dominant theme of Christianity: loyalty to a power higher than the deified Roman Emperor or any other deity—a power capable of raising men from the dead and making their afterlife welfare his special concern.

It is not, therefore, that Christianity had its origins in Buddhism—or any other religion for that matter, except Judaism—but that it borrowed doctrines from all of them. A good example is Gnosticism, with which it had a lively and mutual exchange of ideas. Christian Gnosticism was the work of "converted" Gnostics who assimilated (or back-referenced) the message and mission of Jesus as Messiah to that of the Zoroastrian Messiah or Saoshyant, which was the original source.

14. Elaine Pagels, *The Gnostic Gospels* (New York: Vintage Books, 1981), chapter IV, "The Passion of Christ and the Persecution of Christians."

15. Paul's attitude on the matter was in line with that of the Gnostics, holding that Jesus made one full and sufficient sacrifice for sin, a sacrifice that was therefore not repeatable by him or anyone else (Hebrews 9:25–28, 10:10–12, 26, 27).

16. From the Gospel of Saint Matthew alone:

> Blessed are ye, when men shall revile you, and persecute you, and shall say all manner of evil against you falsely, for my sake,
>
> Rejoice and be exceeding glad: for great is your reward in heaven: for so persecuted they the prophets which were before you.
>
> —Saint Matthew 5:11–12
>
> And fear not them which kill the body, but are not able to kill the soul: but rather fear him which is able to destroy both soul and body in hell.
>
> —Saint Matthew 10:28
>
> . . . If any man will come after me, let him deny himself, and take up his cross, and follow me.
>
> —Saint Matthew 16:24
>
> Then shall they deliver you up to be afflicted, and shall kill you: and ye shall be hated of all nations for my name's sake.
>
> But he that shall endure unto the end, the same shall be saved.
>
> —Saint Matthew 24:9, 13

17. Thus it was that many years after the death of Jesus came the empirical test and meaning of sacrificial love: increased faith and Church membership—one life lost through martyrdom, many lives found (saved, through faith) for the Church to the credit, and merit, of the martyr. This was neither Gnostic self-salvation, nor Buddhist delayed salvation of one man (Boddhisatva) until the salvation of all men is assured, but plain increase in followership—a not-so-inspiring interpretation of this highest ideal of sacrificial love. Even politicians know of less painful ways of increasing their followership—through prudence, expedience, charisma, and plain demagoguery. One thing seems clear: mere increase in Christian followership could not be the meaning of the high ideal of sacrificial love. Thus, even with subsequent experience, the paradox of sacrificial love remains.

18. Islam also subscribed to the docetic doctrine of the Christian Gnostics, but went further to deny that even the human Jesus died on the cross, holding in the Koran (Suras 3, 4, 5 respectively, titled "The Imrans," "Women," and "The Table") that he was removed from the cross after he had fainted, for Allah had promised him that he would die a natural death.

19. Genesis 3.

20. This was, undoubtedly, one of the telling points in the opposition of Gnostics to the Jewish God of Justice with whom they contrasted their own God of Goodness—Plato's and Aristotle's God in another guise.

21. See the Appendix to chapter 2 of Book One.

237

Chapter 13

The Nature and Mechanism of Religious Conversion

The obvious question now poses itself: If all that has been said about the structure of African metaphysics and religion is true, why was it so easy to convert Africans to Christianity and Islam? The answer depends on what is meant by *convert*. *Collins Concise English Dictionary* (1978) gives the following two relevant meanings: "(a) to cause to change from one belief, religion, etc. to another, (b) to exchange for something equal in value." Anyone familiar with the activities of missionaries in Africa, their "sales technique," and the response of Africans to their "sales pitch" is likely to attest that the interaction between missionary and "convert" can hardly be described in terms of the dictionary meaning of convert. Indeed, doubts may be expressed as to whether conversion in the dictionary meaning ever takes place—at least in Africa. It is there-fore necessary to take a close look at the mechanism of what is generally described as "religious conversion" in Africa, in order to determine whether or not, in terms of religious views and practices, the missionary does "cause the convert to change" and the "convert" does make an "exchange;" that is to say, whether or not the converter does *convert* and the convert is *converted*.

The missionary seeking to convert an African engages in a two-part process involving, first, the establishment of contact on the basis of a common ground of ideas, views, or beliefs shared with the African, followed by a transvaluation of those other ideas, views, or beliefs that he wishes the African to surrender or abandon. Thus, in establishing contact he would make reference to man's universal belief in a Supreme Deity, souls and spirits of saints and other departed persons, principalities and powers or forces of good and evil, et cetera, all of which find an echo in the African's religious system. This part can best be described by what Picasso called "mixing what they know with what they don't know." A full description is given in the relevant passage quoted from the book by Françoise Gilot and Carlton Lake, *My Life With Picasso*, in David Eccles' *Half-Way To Faith*:

> (Picasso speaking) "How do you go about teaching something new? By mixing what they know with what they don't know. Then when they see vaguely something in their fog, something they recognise, they think 'Ah, I know that'. And then it is just one more step to 'Ah, I know the whole thing'. And their minds thrust forward into the unknown."[1]

This passage mirrors faithfully the first impact of Christian and Islamic evangelism on the mind of the African.

The actual thrust at conversion comes with the discouragement of African ideas and practices regarded by the missionary as wrong, contradictory to the missionary's religion, or downright evil. This part of the process is known as "transvaluation," that is to say, the attachment of negative values to ideas and practices that have positive values in the African religion but are rejected by the missionary as contradictory to his. Thus "idols" and "fetishes," which represent spiritual forces with which the African is in communion (i.e., an intimate and deeply understanding relationship) with a view to sharing of the good things of life (offerings) or appeasement (sacrifices), are usually candidates for condemnation by the missionary. They are given a negative value (e.g., they are said to be "of the Devil") in the religion that the missionary is trying to sell, chiefly because they are the elements that, by reason of his bias, the missionary does not, cannot, or will not understand.

On the part of the African candidate for conversion a corresponding two-part process is enacted in response to the missionary's effort. The first part is identical to that of the missionary—the establishment of contact on the basis of common ideas that are found in both religions. This may be called the blending process by which the two religions become linked. It is the stage at which the missionary and the African truly interact, the stage where the missionary engages in "mixing what they know with what they don't know," and the African likewise. In a dual sense not intended by Picasso but truer than he realized, both the missionary and the African engage mutually in "mixing what they know with what they don't know" on either side; what they both know are the common elements or ideas in both religions. These the missionary mixes with what he does not know (the idols, fetishes, and other practices by the African), and the African with what he does not know (Virgin Birth, Jesus, Trinity, Transubstantiation, et cetera, or Muhammad, Fast, et cetera). Corresponding to the missionary's thrust at conversion —transvaluation—is the second part of the African's response: revaluation, that is, transformation by positive reinterpretation, of the new beliefs and elements in the foreign religion in terms that he understands and that accord with his religious system. For example, the Eucharist is assimilated to a "communal cook" similar to the "family cook" of which living survivors as well as recent and long-dead ancestors partake. Obviously, ideas that cannot be easily revalued in local terms and institutions would either be abandoned or cohabit uneasily with the rest like an undigested morsel.[2]

It appears, therefore, that the process of religious conversion in Africa is not a grafting of a foreign onto a local religious system. That would imply that the foreign religion was inserted unchanged into the local one, in the hope that the graft would "take." This would carry a high risk of failure. Nor is it an elimination or surrender of a local religious system by the substitution of a foreign, for substitution, by itself, does not eliminate. The local religion would in that case be merely displaced but continue to hang around and be available in case of need. Nor, finally, is religious conversion an elimination of a local religion *and* the substitution of a foreign one. Not only does this not happen, as we have seen, but, if it did, it would amount to grafting the foreign religion, unchanged, onto the rest of the local culture with a high risk of failure.

What happens, rather, in religious conversion is a process of acculturation or assimilation, after suitable modification, of the foreign by the local religion. This takes place through the process of blending of elements common to both religions in order to establish a link ("Ah, I know that"), a process requiring the collaboration and interaction of both sides to the transaction. This is followed, on the part of the missionary, by a transvaluation of the remaining elements in the local religion and, on the part of the candidate for conversion, by a revaluation through reinterpretation in local terms and imagery of the remaining elements in the foreign religion ("Ah, I know the whole thing") leading to elimination or uneasy cohabitation of indigestible residual elements. It is by this process that the foreign gets absorbed into the local religion.[3]

The implication of this entire process of religious "conversion" is clear. In the first place, the local religion is definitely *not* displaced nor is it eliminated by the foreign religion. Instead it absorbs or assimilates it after suitable modification and digestion. The local religion continues as before, suitably augmented and enriched by the foreign import. The supposed "convert," the African, is really the "converter" who transforms, by revaluation or reinterpretation, the foreign into the local religion. The supposed "converter," the missionary, by contrast, is the "convert" in the sense that his religion is converted or assimilated into the local one.

240

It is a measure of the success of the "conversion" process as described above that—and when—the "converted" African maintains both systems of religion in an easy combination. The African Imam or priest who performs the mosque or the Church rites on Friday or Sunday following up with those of the indigenous religion, or who combines with the mosque or Church rites the observances of the local fetish, is a good example of the successful convert.[4] This may certainly not be in accordance with the intention or desire of the missionary who prefers, and works for, the complete abandonment of the local religion. However, as we have seen, the intentions and what actually happens are inversely related. This may account for the widespread verdict of "failure" of missionary activity in various parts of the so-called Third World, and calls for a closer study and reevaluation of the results of missionary effort in the light of the analysis that has been given.

Cases of apparent failure of evangelization, from the missionary point of view, but of successful acculturation by the other side would include, in the case of Christianity, the fragmentation of various Christian denominations into various local sects with a large admixture of indigenous elements. One of the notable indigenous elements in African religion is the healing art (by laying of hands) practiced by Alice Lenshina and Roman Catholic Archbishop Emmanuel Milingo, both of Zambia. The latter was placed on interdiction in 1983 and removed from his archdiocese to Rome for "discipline" and "treatment," at the successful conclusion of which he was promoted to be in charge of immigrant workers in Rome.[5]

The spread of a rash of black Jesus and black Madonna-and-child in the black world of Africa, the Caribbean, and the Americas (including an interesting case of a black Jesus and disciples in the Roman Catholic Church at Soufrière on the Caribbean Island of St. Lucia) marks an advanced stage of failure and distortion of fact, from the missionary standpoint, but of successful "conversion" on the other side.[6] Similarly, in Islam, El Haj Marwa Maïtatsine, the "black Muhammad" who objected to an Arab religious leader for black Africans (but not to Islam as a non-African religion), represented a failure of institutional Islam but a successful acculturation from the other side. Maïtatsine was killed in religious riots connected with the spread of his Islam in Kano, Nigeria, in 1980. Since his death, regarded by his followers as religious martyrdom, the movement has been growing and causing more disturbances in northern Nigeria.

The approval by Vatican II, under pressure, of the celebration of the Mass in the vernacular instead of Latin was an apparent failure from the traditional institutional viewpoint, but a successful acculturation from the other side. There are still grumblings, dramatized by Archbishop Lefebvre's traditional seminary at Econe, Switzerland, subsequently abandoned or played down after successful pressure by John Paul II in his bid to call the errant Archbishop to ecclesiastical obedience. What is strange here is that there was opposition within the Church hierarchy to a measure that, undoubtedly, would have won the approval of that archevangelist, Paul, who went so far as to discourage the exercise of the gift of speaking in tongues (*glossolalia*) unless interpretation was provided simultaneously in the local language.[7]

Not surprisingly, the early Church did engage in quite a bit of acculturation of the teachings of Jesus to the practices of non-Jewish populations—a tradition that seems to have been largely abandoned by the modern-day apostles. Exceptions, of course, may be found in dire cirumstances, such as in wartime emergencies when, it is reported, the scarcity of grape wine during the Second World War obliged some churches in Africa to substitute palm wine in the celebration of the Eucharist. Paul, following the example of Jesus (himself a practised acculturator: "Ye have heard it said . . . but *I* say unto you"[8]) quoted the teachings of Jesus, then made modifications in appropriate cases: for example, in marital relations between believing partners ("I command, yet not I, but the Lord"[9]) and between a believing and an unbelieving partner ("But to the rest speak I, not the Lord[10]). In general, Paul, as also did Muhammad, respected local customs and advocated that they be observed—but in the Christian spirit—as being consistent with Christian doctrines: for example, respect and obedience to political authority; observance of social institutions and customs such as obedience of slaves to their masters, the inferior social status of women and children, obedience of children to their parents and of wives to their husbands, et cetera. (All of these were also endorsed by Muhammad, including wife-beating in disobedience cases.[11]) However, formal acculturation of the Christian religion was simultaneously subverted by Paul through the doctrine of brotherhood and equality of all men in the sight of God and in Jesus as the true spiritual relationship among Christians.

There are other side effects of missionary activity, moreover. One of the most interesting is that of the opportunist convert who formally adheres to the religion in order to gain some material benefit. This was a widespread phenomenon in Kikuyu-land in Kenya, where the Protestant missionaries provided education only for converts. This was an open invitation to false converts—people merely joining the Church in order to obtain an education, without in any way adopting the faith.

Some apparent damage was done to the local religious system when not only missionaries but also "converts" engaged in orgies of idol-smashing and fetish-burning, to the great delight and satisfaction of the missionaries. Many cases, from the side of the Africans, were "staged" for some ulterior benefit. And, in any case, there is no way in which it is possible to know whether or not—and what—anyone, especially in indigenous Africa, does believe or hold to specifically in religious or theological matters, given the local tradition of religious privacy, absence of discussion of religious matters outside the family and tribe, and non-proselytism.

It has been argued above (Book Two, Section B, chapter 9) that Christianity originated in religious colonialism and continues as such. The same goes for Islam, which has the same tradition of intolerance—perhaps even more of it. The point is not that people outside the Judeo-Christian-Islamic tradition also believe in a Supreme Deity but that, to those within the tradition, they believe in the *wrong* Supreme Deity and lack the means or the knowledge of approaching the *right* one. And since the Judeo-Christian-Islamic religions each claims a monopoly on the right God as proclaimed, respectively, by Moses, Jesus, and Muhammad it follows that the salvation each offers is not free but offered at a price—the price of belief buttressed by certain rites or, which is the same thing, the price of surrender of reason and experience. Whether the belief required is in Jahweh (the God of Abraham, Isaac and Jacob), or in Jesus as God or the Son of God, or in Allah (the God of Muhammad), in view of the nature and mechanism of the process of religious "conversion" as described in this chapter, it is arguable whether, and to what extent, the price demanded of supposed converts (at least in Africa) has been rendered or is being rendered. To the extent that the price of religious colonialism has not been truly paid in Africa, this may be the saving grace of the process of religious "conversion."[12]

NOTES

1. David Eccles, *Half-Way To Faith* (Fontana Books, 1968), p. 46.
2. What actually occurs in such cases is somewhat more complex. Where an imported and nonunderstood religious doctrine cohabits uneasily with other acculturated elements in an African's religious baggage, the way is easily opened to doubt when questions arise. And where such doubt is suppressed by the weight of external authority fanaticism tends to result. There is a parallel here with the traditional reaction of parents to the questions of children in indigenous African society. Because of lack of knowledge of what answers to give (similar to the lack of knowledge of the meaning of indigestible religious doctrines) parents generally display annoyance at being asked questions by their children and vigorously discourage them, reinforcing their interdiction with a moral in the same sense drawn from a fable. Consequently, the African child in traditional society tends to be accepting and uninquisitive.

3. The same mechanics and process of "conversion" are seen more openly at work in the political domain in contemporary postindependence Africa. Whatever the occidental political institutional model adopted, whether British parliamentary or French presidential, it was foisted by the political missionaries on the colonial population, and accepted by its leaders, as a condition of political independence. This was, again, a case of "mixing what they know with what they don't know." On the metropolitan side, "what they know" was the imposed political model; "what they don't know" was the indigenous political system—or, if they knew it, they did not want it. The opposite was the case on the side of the colonial population. They knew only the system of hereditary chieftaincy elected by ruling houses and guided by councillors and advisers selected to represent the population at large (not forgetting the court jester and the *griots* or paid chanters of praises or misdeeds). They did not "know," although they were acquainted with, the occidental political model. Thus, unlike in the religious situation, there were no common elements in the knowledge possessed by both sides.

Once independence was declared and the indigenous government installed, the process of acculturation or assimilation of the foreign political model began, buttressed by the concepts and traditions of a tribal system. "What they don't know" had to be reinterpreted and transformed into something locally recognizable by the local government and population. The periodically elected prime minister or president and his government had to be transformed into a traditional chieftaincy ("life president") and councillors ("one-party state"), the politically dominant tribe (that of the president or prime minister) having all the plums and suppressing all the other tribes—including the "white tribe" if (as in Kenya or Zimbabwe) there was a local, settled white population.

4. Similarly, in the medical field, the successful African medical convert is the practitioner who knows how to absorb occidental medical systems into the traditional medical and healing system, so that the limitations of the one are compensated by the other, and vice versa.

5. *Jeune Afrique* (Paris), nos. 1139, 1176, 1182, 1192, 1198. It is surprising that the practice of healing by laying of hands, which was a trademark of Jesus, the founder of Christianity, is being criticized and forbidden as "of the devil" two thousand years later, by the very institution he is said to have inaugurated. Pope John Paul II, like Dostoievski's Grand Inquisitor, would, undoubtedly, forbid Jesus to practice his art if he returned to Earth today—even though Jesus bestowed the art, as well as power over devils, on his disciples (Saint Luke 9:1)—for fear of competition with the modern-day Peter to whom all powers in heaven and earth had been surrendered as his (Jesus') vice-regent. The annual trip to the Lourdes is all right and, apparently, not evil or superstitious, if made and presided over by John Paul II, but no competition from any other (unauthorized) source within the Church. *That* would be superstition.

6. This process of indigenization of the Holy Family is not, of course, unique to Africa. On the contrary, along with the adoption of local motifs in Church decorations, it has been one of the earliest and most universal forms of religious acculturation in Christianity—in contrast to Islam, where the acculturation process has been much slower. For examples of indigenization of the Holy Family by the Indians of South America, see *Américas*, Vol. 25, no. 11–12, published by the Organization of American States. A more general study is contained in Frederick Buechner, *The Faces of Jesus* (New York: Simon and Schuster, 1975), excerpted in the *Smithsonian* magazine of November 1974.

7. I Corinthians 14:27–28.

8. See various examples in Saint Matthew 5.
9. I Corinthians 7:10.
10. I Corinthians 7:12.
11. The Koran, Sura 4:34 (New York: Penguin Books), trans. Dawood.
12. The criticism of theological missionary activity presented in this chapter does not overlook the considerable benefits of nontheological missionary work—e.g., the health, medical and educational services provided by theological missionaries—even though all cultural contacts involving different groups tend to be disastrous in some way or other where such contacts are imposed by one group on another, regardless of their concomitant or presumed benefits.

Chapter 14

From Zoroastrianism to Gnosticism: A Case Study in Religious Conversion and Acculturation

Zoroaster, the Prophet of Persia (circa 628–551 B.C.E.), also known as Zarathustra, established a theological system of dualized monotheism centered on one supreme, wise Lord of Light, Ahura Mazda (O[h]rmazd or O[h]rmuzd). There was, first, the dualism of Light and Darkness, since the assumption of a Lord of Light automatically implied the existence of Darkness: everything outside of Light is Darkness, thereby also implying a limit or dividing line between the two, as well as their co-existence rather than their alternation. A second dualism occurs within the godhead in order to account for the existence of spiritual goodness and spiritual evil, respectively represented by Ahura Mazda (with whom the Good automatically associates) and Ahriman, the opposing dialectic principle of Evil.

The material world is the creation of Ahura Mazda and is good. The later tradition whereby the material world is considered evil is the product of the Manichaean adaptation of Zoroastrianism known as Manichaeism or Manicaean Gnosticism (Greek *gnosis* = *secret knowledge)*. What Zoroastrianism and Gnosticism lacked was a synthesis of their dualism in which the two elements, light and dark or good and evil, were integrated rather than unmixed opposites (like oil and water), with light being implicitly regarded as the more potent of the two.

The theology of Zoroastrianism underwent various modifications over time in the different versions that came to constitute what is known as Gnosticism. These versions are the differentiated evolutionary by-products as Zoroastrianism adapted itself through the centuries, by the process of eclectic borrowing or syncretism, to Judaism, Greek religion, and Christianity as these religions became dominant and competitive. But it had previously contributed to Judaism and, through Judaism, to Christianity the ideas of spiritual dualism (Good and Evil), resurrection of the dead, and the coming of a savior (or Saoshyant) at the end of time to establish a kingdom of righteousness and to reward the good and punish the evildoers.

The adaptations of Zoroastrianism, involving both reinterpretations and transvaluations, were made within the guest religions from which the various elements were borrowed. In other words, they were made by Gnostic converts or associates to these religions who learnt enough about them to be able to adapt them to Zoroastrianism and then defect in order to establish the various modified forms of Zoroastrianism grouped under the label of Gnosticism. Consciously or unconsciously, these various adapters functioned as moles within the guest religions to which they were "converted" or with which they were associated.

The contributions of ancient Greek religion and Zoroastrianism to Judaism and the later adaptations of Zoroastrianism to the Greek, Judaic, and Christian religions are shown in schematic form below. It is difficult to summarize satisfactorily what may be regarded as the common tenets of the various Gnostic sects. However, an excellent summary of the three major issues that divided the Gnostics from the early Christians—especially those of Jerusalem and Rome—is provided by Trevor Ling:

> First, the Gnostics identified Jahweh, the God or Israel, with the inferior god, the creator of the evil, physical world, and for this reason Gnosticism was on the whole strongly anti-Jewish. Second, the Christian idea that the divine Saviour had actually suffered and died was rejected by the Gnostics: a divine being could not suffer, and most certainly could not suffer death. They therefore introduced the idea that the Jesus of Christian tradition had been not a real human being but only by outward appearance human. (From the Greek verb dokein ''to seem'' this doctrine became known as Docetism.) Another Gnostic idea was that the divine Saviour who had inhabited the body of Jesus had returned to heaven before the Passion so that it was only a 'seeming' death, an illusion to deceive the evil spirit-powers of this world. Third, since it was held by the Gnostics that it was by sexual reproduction that the divine spark imprisoned in man was transmitted to other bodily prisons, their attitude to married life such as Jews and Christians practised was one of hostility: some sought to prevent procreation by taking refuge in celibacy, while others debased the sexual relationship with the aid of some rather disagreeable contraceptive practices.[1]

Zoroastrianism: Contributions and Adaptations
(a) Contributions
Homer (ninth century B.C.E.) → Judaism: Greek-type Jahweh of fire, thunder, smoke, and wrath who dealt with

247

Moses; giants having affairs with the daughters of men.

Zoroaster (sixth century B.C.E.) → Judaism: Dark/Light, Good/Evil conflict; man's freedom of moral choice but preferably in favor of Light, Good, and Order against Darkness, Evil, and Chaos; Savior at the end of time and his establishment of a reign of righteousness after the defeat of the forces of Evil; resurrection of the body, Last Judgment, and reward or punishment.

Cyrus the Persian (sixth century B.C.E.) → Judaism: Return of Jews from Babylonian captivity and rebuilding of the Temple destroyed by Nebuchadnezzer.

Greek civilization and expansion: from sixth century B.C.E.

Alexander the Great and Expansion of Hellenistic civilization: from fourth century B.C.E.

(b) Adaptations

Roman Empire (first century B.C.E.) and Christianity (first century C.E. onward)

Light: Domain of Gnostic God—Greek Zeus, Father of Light; Glory of Jahweh—Samaritan Gnosticism: Simon Magus

Darkness: Domain of Jewish God, Jahweh, Creator of the World, Just and Jealous—transvaluation of Jahweh to Ialdabaoth, Arch-Archon: Valentinian Gnosticism.

Genesis of Dualism: Greek mythology—androgyny: Zeus/Athena: Valentinian Gnosticism.

Light/Dark Conflict: (a) Christos and Light-Jesus rescue Lower Sophia: Valentinian Gnosticism (Zoroastrianism from Christianity).

(b) Primal Man, Living Spirit, Messenger and Light-Jesus versus Ialdabaoth the Chief Archon and other Archons and the cosmos: Manichaean Gnosticism (Zoroastrianism from Judaism and Christianity).

Material Cosmos as Evil: Handiwork of Prince of Darkness: Manichaean Gnosticism (Zoroastrianism from Judaism).

Saoshyant or Savior: Light-Jesus, Jesus of Christianity: Marcionite Gnosticism (Zoroastrianism from Christianity).

It was inevitable that the ancient world dominance by Greece and, subsequently, Macedonia with their Hellenic and Hellenistic civilization, respectively—their theological, religious, and cultural ideas—should have left indelible marks on the theology and religions of the peoples within their dominion. This is particularly true in the case of Judaism,

248

Gnosticism, and, through its attempt to convert peoples of Hellenistic culture, Christianity. Greek theogony—Hesiod's mythology of the origin and descent of the gods—incorporated both heterosexual and androgynous patterns of reproduction, the former pattern involving liaisons between male immortals and female mortals. This pattern has come to be known in Christian tradition as immaculate conception or virgin birth and was exemplified by two famous cases: Dionysus, the male offspring of Zeus and the female mortal Semele, and Voluptas, the female offspring of Cupid and the female mortal Psyche.

The immaculate conception paradigm left its mark on the literature of Judaism in the apparently interpolated passage at Genesis 6:1–4, where it is recorded that the sons of God (otherwise known as Titans, in Greek mythology) had children (Nephilim or giants—same as the heroes of Greek mythology) with the daughters of men. It is also possible that Isaiah 7:14 falls within the pattern of immaculate conception, the essence of the "sign": for a virgin (young woman) conceiving a son, Immanuel, would not be a "sign," something extraordinary, if it was meant to refer to the normal maculate, conception.

Christianity, at any rate, preferred the immaculate conception interpretation of Isaiah 7:14, as is clearly indicated in the account of Jesus' conception in Saint Luke 1:26–38 and of his conception and birth in Saint Matthew 1:18–25.

Thus Judaism and Christianity bear the hallmarks of Greek theological myth. With Gnosticism, the pattern changes from heterosexual to androgynous reproduction or (as the Gnostics preferred to call it) emanation. The Gnostic God, or Father of All, is the equivalent of a male God (Zeus) who, impliedly possessing female genetic characteristics as well, gives birth to the equivalent of a female offspring (Athena) all by himself. The Gnostic Athena is variously called the Female Thought of God, Epinoia, Ennoia, Sophia, Grace, Silence, et cetera, in the same way that Athena was the brainchild or female thought of Zeus.

In order to better appreciate the subtleties and interrelationships involved, the theogenetic patterns of Greek mythology are set out and those of Gnosticism and Christianity related thereto, all within a general classification of types of reproduction, both asexual and sexual. (Definitions refer to *Webster's Collegiate Dictionary*, 7th ed.)

As a complex politico-religious phenomenon antedating Christianity, Gnosticism is a theo-religious system whose intellectual and religious antecedents hark back to the Delphic Oracle and whose political antecedents go back to the time of Alexander the Great. In its active period, during Alexander's time, the intellectual, religious, and political aspects were intimately fused so that it appeared as a religious cloak for anti-colonial revolt in the realm of ideas and culture as well as in direct opposition to Judaism. It created a counter-cultural movement on the literary, and eventually on the linguistic, front as well as transvalued long-established Jewish religious concepts. The linguistic innovation came during the early Christian era when Gnostic literature was produced in Syriac through the initiative of Valentinus, Mani, and Ephraem.

Reproduction Patterns and Theogony

A. Asexual Reproduction: Cellular division (fission)
B. Sexual Reproduction: Cellular fusion and separation

I *Parthenogenesis or Female Unisexual Reproduction* (F → F)

   Reproduction by development of an unfertilized gamete (as occurs in some plants and animals). E.g., female birds → female birds.

II *Heterosexual Reproduction* (M = F → M/F)

   (1) *Immaculate Conception*: Conception in which the offspring is preserved free from original sin by divine grace, especially held in Roman Catholic dogma to be the manner of conception by the Virgin Mary.

   (Note: Original sin = original *human* sin, i.e. by human heterosexual contact. Divine grace = gift of a god.)

   Hence, immaculate conception = *human female* conception and parturition without human male sexual contact, but by *divine male* sexual contact, supposed to be the manner of conception of Jesus.

   The concept derives from Greek mythology, which features two well-known cases:

   Zeus = Semele → Dionysus (m)

   Cupid = Psyche → Voluptas (f)

   Cf. Christian God = Mary → Jesus (m)

   The myth of Jesus' birth follows the Dionysian pattern and implies an adoption of Greek mythological concepts in Old Testament prophetic as well as New Testament literature.

   (2) *Maculate Conception*: Heterosexual reproduction *within the same species*.

   (i) Divine: e.g., offspring of Zeus and Hera

   (ii) Human: normal human reproduction through union of male and female

III *Androgynesis or Hermaphrogenesis* (M(F) → F or F(M) → M)

   Reproduction by an organism possessing both male and female characteristics, with offspring being sexually opposite to the apparent sex of parent.

   This concept also derives from Greek mythology, which features two well-known cases: Zeus → Pallas Athena (Minerva) (M(F) → F)

   Hera → Hephaistos (Vulcan) (F(M) → M)

   Cf. Gnostic God (Father of Light/Father of all) → Female Thought (Sophia) (M(F) → F)

250

The Simonian, Valentinian and Manichaean Gnostic myth of the Father of All (the Original One, Abyss) conceiving his Female Thought (Epinoia,Ennoia, Wisdom, Grace) derives from the Greek mythological paradigm of Zeus/Athena.

On the religious front, the main target was the religion of the Jews, whose God, Jahweh, as well as the world he was supposed to have created—according to the Genesis story—was transvalued from a power of light and goodness (which it also was as the creation of the Demiurge in Plato's *Timaeus*) to a power of darkness and evil. It is believed by some authorities that this transvaluation began within the Jewish religion itself, with the Samaritan branch of Judaism opposing the Jerusalem or Judaean branch. The Samaritan branch was based on the Pentateuch, the Judaean on the Pentateuch and the Prophets; so that it looked like a simple opposition of "the Law" to "the Law and the Prophets." Whatever its origins, it is clear that Gnosticism transvalued the Good God of Judaism into a Just God known for his vengeance and creation of an evil world, in opposition to the alien and Good God of Gnosticism, directly unknown and unknowable.

When Christianity later made its appearance as a protest movement within Judaism it was only natural that Gnosticism should find in it a useful ally against Judaism. Gnostic was adapted to Christian doctrine and vice versa, in joint opposition to Judaism and in various degrees of collaboration. Where the mutual adaptation was very close, as in Marcionite Gnosticism, a mutual antagonism subsequently developed in the competition for territory and adherents.

Following is a brief summary of the struggle of Christianity with Gnosticism, its main antagonist and ally, as well as with other divergent views within early Christianity. A correspondingly brief exposition is then given of the main variants of Gnosticism. Finally, the metaphysical aspect of Gnosticism is examined, bringing the chapter to a close.

GNOSTICISM VERSUS CHRISTIANITY

Gnosticism was the occasion that gave rise to the use of the word *heresy* in early ecclestiastical Christianity.[2] Simon Magus was regarded as the father of all heresy by the Fathers of the early Church[3] and Marcionite Gnosticism as the strongest challenge among the Gnostic sects to the Church because it was the closest, doctrinally, to Christianity.[4] In the first century C.E. the dominant branch of Christianity was, naturally, Jewish Christianity headquartered in Jerusalem, and it continued to be

251

so until the fall of Jerusalem in 70 C.E. Then leadership passed on to Gentile Christianity headquartered in Rome. Jewish Christianity had to contend, in the first place, with Pauline (Gentile) Christianity,[5] which preached a doctrine of salvation by faith alone (in Jesus) and the resurrection of a spiritual body, while Jewish Christianity emphasized faith with the works of the law (Torah)—circumcision, at least, and dietary rules. The conflict between Paul, on the one side, and Peter and James, on the other, led to the Jerusalem compromise that exempted Gentiles from circumcision but not from the dietary laws, a minimum observance of which was prescribed.[6] Paul's emphasis on faith in Jesus as the only road and requirement to salvation, whether expediently borrowed from the Gnostics or not, proved a valuable point of agreement and alliance between him and the Gnostics, especialy the Marcionites.

Simon Magus, the Gnostic, and his sect constituted the genesis of heresy within the Church. Having been baptized and admitted into the Church[7] Simon eventually had to separate himself (or be separated) from the Church. His Samarian brand of Gnosticism based on the Pentateuch was too strong a catalyst within the Church. He declared himself a god and was worshipped as such by his followers—"the power of God called Great"[8]—in competition with the god, Jesus, who seems to have been regarded as a previous incarnation of Simon himself.[9] His brand of Gnosticism was the apparent paradigm for the Valentinian system, which later elaborated the origin of the spiritual split within the Gnostic godhead.

With the fall of the temple in Jerusalem, Rome took over the leadership of the Church and a change occurred in the character of Christianity from Judaic to Gentile, even though Roman Christianity was originally established by Judaist apostles and sympathizers. Thus by the second century C.E., Roman Gentile Christianity entered in the struggle against Gnosticism as well as against Judaic Christianity. In regard to the latter the struggle was focused against Jewish legalism in religious matters. Two Gnostic sects, the Valentinians and the Marcionites, proved formidable competitors, the Marcionites more so. The Valentinian Gnostics (Syro-Egyptian type) set up a rather elaborate system that was easily distinguished from Christianity by its emphasis on the source of spiritual dualism within the godhead. The Marcionite type was similar in doctrine to Christianity and was therefore more easily confused with Christian doctrine and more difficult to combat. Both Paul and Marcion emphasized faith in Jesus as the means to salvation and the abrogation (Marcion) or suppression by fulfillment (Paul) of the Old Testament law and the prophets by the coming of Jesus. The Marcionites were, therefore, the Gnostic sect with which the word *heresy* was most frequently associated by the early Church Fathers.

252

In the third century C.E. and after, a new sect of Gnostics came on the scene to challenge Roman Christianity. This was the Persian type developed by Manes (or Mani) and laid stress on the drama of the conflict between Light and Darkness, borrowing elements from Buddhism, Zoroastrianism, and Christianity.

THE MAJOR GNOSTIC SECTS IN EARLY CHRISTIANITY

1. SIMONIAN AND VALENTINIAN GNOSTICISM

The Zoroastrian doctrine of spiritual dualism was a principal feature of both Simonian[10] and Valentinian Gnosticism, but was fine-tuned by Valentinus, who was born in Alexandria in the early part of the first century C.E. Both developed a doctrine of the genesis of dualism within the godhead of the one, wise Father of Light, using for this purpose a model similar to the Greek theogonic model of androgyny[11] associated with Zeus in connection with the birth of Athena. On this paradigm the Father of Light emanated his Female Thought (Sophia). In Simonianism the Female Thought descends into the regions of Darkness and produces angels and powers who imprison her. She is eventually rescued by Simon in her incarnation as Helena, a whore whom he had found in a bar—the lowest level of degradation to which she had sunk. Together they promise salvation to mankind through faith in themselves, the divine couple.

In Valentinianism, the Father and his Thought together produced Mind (Nous—male) and Truth (Aletheia—female); this pair, in turn, produced Word (Logos—male) and Life (Bioté—female), and these, in their turn, produced Man (Homos—male) and Church (Ecclesia—female). These eight Aeons constitute the original Ogdoad (octet). Word and Life produced ten additional Aeons and Man and Church twelve, making in all fifteen pairs or thirty Aeons constituting the Pleroma (or Fullness)—that is, the Fullness of the Divinity (divine characteristics) or the free and adequate self-expression of the fully explicated manifold of divine characteristics.

Evil in the world arose because the female Aeon of the fourteenth pair, Sophia, wished to know and procreate with the Father of Light instead of with her male consort. She conceived and aborted a formless emanation that was cast out of the Pleroma into outer Darkness, because it was the evil fruit of her evil passion, and prevented by the Limit (separating Light from Darkness, and the unbegotten Father from the begotten Aeons) from regaining the Pleroma. This emanation received external formation into the female fruit—Lower Sophia or Sophia Prunikos, Wisdom the Whore—of the first Sophia by Christos, the male consort of Holy Spirit, with whom he constituted the fifteenth pair of Aeons (produced by the Father of Light and his Female Thought). The Aeon, Jesus (or Light-Jesus), was produced as the male common fruit of the entire Pleroma and sent as consort to "inform" or en-light-en the outer Sophia with the knowledge (gnosis) about the unknowability of the Father, a task similarly performed for the first Sophia by the Limit and by Christos for the other Aeons.

The Lower Sophia also had passions that were separated from her by Jesus, these solidifying into matter from which things external are created—first, the demiurge Ialdabaoth, who, in turn, created the rest of the material world of things containing matter and soul. After receiving the light brought by the angels of Jesus, the Lower Sophia conceived pneumatic (spiritual) fruit in the image of herself and the Light-Jesus—fruit that was the source of the pneumatic element (spark or spirit) in the world, especially in mankind.

The Light-Jesus accompanied the Lower Sophia, now purified and enlightened, back to the Pleroma, which by reason of the enlightenment effected by the Limit and Christos was restored to its original harmony and separateness from the Darkness. Salvation thus consisted in restoring the original and separate integrity of the Pleroma in Light, unsullied by the Darkness. This is achieved by dispelling the ignorance of the Aeons through the imparting of knowledge (enlightenment) about the unknowability of the Father. This salvation was clearly the gift of the Pleroma, unmerited by man.

The foregoing is a very much abbreviated account of a much more complex system in which, eventually, man is shown the way of his own ascent to the Pleroma. It is significant to note that evil arose within the Pleroma by the desire of the Aeons to know the Father, that is, from their ignorance of the unknowability of the Father, an ignorance dispelled with their enlightenment. The implication here is that with knowledge evil disappears.

An interesting detail of Valentinianism is the docetic doctrine that maintains that the Light-Jesus and Christos descended upon the human Jesus at his baptism and left him before his passion so that death was deceived. Thus it was affirmed that the real Jesus, the fruit of the Pleroma, did not suffer and die on the cross. Similarly, Christian doctrine was reinterpreted by the Valentinians in regard to the passion of the human Jesus. The real passion, it was said, was not that of the human Jesus but of the Sophia for the Father (which disturbed the harmony of the Pleroma) and of her daughter, the Lower (outer) Sophia for Christos whom she wished to follow into the Pleroma after her external formation, but she was barred by the Limit from doing so.

2. MARCIONITE GNOSTICISM

The adaptation of Christianity to Gnosticism was most successfully made by Marcion and his sect. This version of Gnosticism cut the complications of Valentinus that resulted from his attempt to derive Zoroastrian dualism as well as the subsequent process of separation of Light from Darkness. Instead, it substituted God and Jesus for the dramatis personae, interpreting both in Gnostic terms. It eliminated the immaculate heterosexual descent of Jesus, holding to the androgynous reproduction model: thus Jesus came directly from heaven as the Mind (Nous) of the Father. Like Christianity, it offered salvation through faith in Jesus. And, like Christianity, its God was wholly alien but good, offering salvation to mankind without strings attached—other than faith in Jesus.

The Unknown God (or Hidden God) of the Areopagites to whom an inscription was erected on Mars Hill in Athens[12] was not a pagan god nor the Greek god Zeus whose main characteristics of Reason was *known* and whose behavior was predictable: terrible with his lightning bolts and thunder when angered, carousing and philandering when in his soft, sweet moods. Nor was he the Jewish God, Jahweh, creator of the world, who was *known* to be just, jealous of other gods, and petty, visiting the sins of the fathers on the children for several generations ("the fathers have eaten sour grapes and the children's teeth are set on edge"). No, he was a Gnostic God, utterly alien and *unknown* to the world, so transcendent as to be "wholly other," *unknowable except by revelation of his unknowability*.

Jesus had come to abrogate, not complete, the rule of the Jewish God along with his "law and prophets" and to purchase salvation for mankind by liberating man, with the purchase price of his blood, from the rule of the Just God. Man, the creature of the Just God, should help defeat his power by opposing his laws, negating marriage, which merely creates more slaves for the domain of the Jewish God, and by having as little to do as possible with the world created by him. This meant asceticism and celibacy, not for self-purification but for the defeat of the Just God. The Good God sent Jesus to bring this message to mankind, which is in a relationship of mutual alienation and ignorance with the Good God. The Good God offers salvation to mankind in order to defeat the Just God.

255

The gnosis or secret knowledge of Marcionism was, thus, the unknowability of God, the fundamental doctrine of all variants of Gnosticism. Neither love, nor knowledge, nor good works is required on the part of man for salvation or liberation from the power of the Just God; herein lies the mystery of salvation. And those who reject such salvation and continue to remain under the power of the world creator do so by their own choice.

Although Marcion had a tremendous respect for the apostle Paul as mentor, and both expounded a doctrine of salvation by grace, the differences of interpretation between them were very significant, as Jonas makes clear.[13] Grace was freely given: for Paul, in the face of human guilt and inadequacy; for Marcion, in the absence of human merit and in the face of mutual alienness of the giver and the receiver of grace. For Paul, God was both Just and Good; for Marcion, only Good. For Paul, the Just and Good God is necessarily involved in man's destiny; for Marcion, not so. Sin, for both Paul and Marcion, is alienation from God; but, for Paul it is an offence against God ("For all have sinned and come short of the glory of God."[14] But "Thanks be to God for his unspeakable gift."[15]); whereas, for Marcion, the question of offence against God does not arise since there is no history of any connection between God and man. Thus for Marcion there is no divine love or mercy for man or any of the creatures of Jahweh's world on the part of the Good God; no call to repentance, fear and trembling, and atonement on the part of man; no final judgment. Given these fundamental differences, it is no surprise that Marcionism was the bitterest Gnostic enemy of Roman Christianity. Both were most closely allied in doctrine but worlds apart in interpretation.

Finally, it may be noted that Marcion was the first to establish a canon of Scriptures for his followers: Luke (expurgated) and the ten Pauline letters or letters attributed to Paul (carefully amended and excised). The canon established by the Roman Church was in direct response to Marcion's canon and included, naturally, the Old Testament ("law and prophets"), Marcion's meager selection, and much else besides.

3. MANICHAEAN GNOSTICISM

Mani (or Manes), founder of the Gnostic sect that bears his name, was an innovator who aimed to construct a syncretic system out of Buddhism, Zoroastrianism, and Christianity, with a view to dramatizing the conflict between Light and Darkness, Good and Evil. Starting with the basic Zoroastrian dualism of Light and Darkness, he initiated the drama with the assault of the forces of Darkness on those of Light.

The Gnostic God, sole *Father of Light*, responded by calling forth the *Mother of Light*, who in turn called forth *Primal Man*, who called forth his *Five Sons of Light*. Primal Man and his Five Sons were sent by the Father to do battle against the powers of Darkness—the Arch-Devil and his Five Devils or Archons—and were defeated, the forces of Light being entrapped by the Darkness. The Father then called forth the *Friend of Lights*, who called forth the *Great Architect*, who in turn called forth the *Living Spirit*. Living Spirit was sent to the rescue but succeeded in retrieving only Primal Man, the Five Sons of Light remaining entrapped. A third creation of the Father, the *Messenger*, was sent to rescue them, but the Prince of Darkness countered by creating Adam and Eve to procreate and, with their brood, to continue to entrap and disperse the Light in innumerable bits, thus making it difficult to separate and retrieve the bits of Light from the Darkness.

It is at this stage that the Luminous Jesus (or Light-Jesus) is created to rescue Adam and Eve and their brood. He is also the suffering form of Primal Man, the "passible Jesus" who hangs from every tree and every day is born, suffers, and dies in his unending task of liberating the elements of Light until the end of the world.[16]

In the Manichaean system the material world is evil, being the substance of Darkness out of which, also, Adam and Eve were created with the express purpose of procreating and making the liberation of the Light more difficult. Thus Adam and Eve and their brood—the entire human race—are evil. Consequently, mankind is not alien to the world but belongs to it. The evil nature of matter and man calls for asceticism and the minimizing of contact with the substance of Darkness—the world and all that is in it.[17] This asceticism involves abstinence from eating ensouled and sentient things (things containing elements of Light) but preference for eating vegetables and other nonsentient things (all made of the substance of Darkness).[18] It also involves abstinence from the delights of love, marriage, and procreation—all instruments of entrapment of the Light.

Salvation in the Manichaean system, as in the other systems of Gnosticism, consists in the separation of the Light from the Darkness. The final separation is achieved in a great cosmic conflagration at the end of the world (the kind propounded by Heraclitus) followed by the emergence of a new Aeon in which the powers of the Light will reign. Also, the secret knowledge in Manichaeism, as in other Gnostic systems, is the unknowability of the Father.

Mani's very dramatic and syncretic system reveals two important

257

aspects, among others. First, its heavy debt to Zoroastrianism, Buddhism, and Christianity: its asceticism from Buddhism; its dualism and soteriology (the three "creations"—Primal Man, Living Spirit, and Messenger) as well as its cosmogony from Zoroastrianism; and its eschatology from both Zoroastrianism and Christianity. Second, its principal aim, which was to estalish a continuity in prophetology from the Buddha, through Zoroaster and Jesus, to Mani himself, the latest in the line of prophets to reveal the message of the Father of Light and his unknowability.

4. CONCLUSION ON THE VARIOUS TYPES OF GNOSTICISM

(i) Gnosticism Reopens and Leaves Unresolved the Problem of Good and Evil

The double dualism of Zoroastrianism consisted in spiritual and moral polarization: spiritual in regard to the dualism of Light and Darkness and moral in regard to the dualism of Good and Evil within a single godhead of Light. Light and Darkness are coeval, without any implication of Evil being attached to Darkness. Thus Zoroaster resolved the moral problem of good and evil by placing responsibility for both within the godhead. However, Zoroaster propounded a doctrine of moral choice by man in favor of Good, Light, and Order and against Evil, Darkness, and Chaos. This had the effect of aligning Evil with Darkness, making it (like Darkness) external to the Light and, therefore, no longer within the godhead. Thus Zoroaster's own theory of moral choice converted his moral monotheism into moral duotheism, alongside his spiritual duotheism.

Mani seized on this implicit result and made it explicit in a thorough and simplified doctrine of duotheism, both spiritual and moral, in which Darkness came to have the connotation of evil, and the world as well. (According to Zoroaster, the world was created out of Darkness by the Father of Light himself and was, therefore, good.) Moreover, by putting it outside the responsibility of the godhead, Mani left the problem of Evil unresolved. In the same manner Christianity also leaves the problem unresolved.

(ii) Gnostic Heresy as Dynamic Religious Acculturation

A perspective view of the heresiological controversy between Gnosticism and Christianity reveals two important aspects. The first concerns

258

the dynamics of so-called heresy. Stripped of all its acrimony, its devilry and unethical methods of competition, the heresiological controversy is no more than a symptom of, as well as fallout from, the process of religious acculturation that is always involved in so-called religious conversion. The mechanics of this process have been discussed in the preceding chapter and need not be repeated here beyond saying that what in the new religion (Christianity) was similar or related to features in the old (Gnosticism) was easily assimilated directly, by reinterpretation or by transvaluation, into Gnosticism; what was different, inconsistent, or incomprehensible was rejected or remained undigested.

The second aspect of the controversy concerns the end result of the acculturation process: who wins and who loses in the struggle. This is where the true nature of "heresy" as an institutional (as distinct from an acculturation) phenomenon emerges clearly. As Bauer convincingly argues in his excellent study,[19] "orthodoxy" is the brand of doctrine preached by the party—in the event, the church of Rome—which could back up its claim of direct apostolic succession from Peter or other of the Apostles with organization and means superior to those of its competitors; "heresy" is the brand of doctrine preached by those who lost in the contest, namely, those who either could not claim direct apostolic succession or could make such a claim or any other, but could not back it up with effective organization or means, or both, to carry the day. This was the case with the Gnostics, whose various sects were disunited, hence unable to present a common front to ecclesiastical Christianity.[20]

There is, therefore, in the final analysis, no inherently "right" (orthodox) doctrine as there is no inherently "wrong" (heterodox) doctrine or "heresy," only successful and unsuccessful challenges and interpretations of a given (or reference) doctrine. In the competition for the minds and hearts of men, the successful challenges and interpretations—the winners—become the "orthodox" doctrines, the unsuccessful ones—the losers—the "heretical" doctrines, regardless of the nature of the doctrines in the contest. Gnosticism was thus both an acculturation of Christianity (and vice versa) and an unsuccessful challenger in the bid to achieve supremacy.

(iii) Gnosticism as Existentialism

Gnosticism propounded a metaphysical doctrine that sought to account for the being of the cosmos and that of man. In the latter respect it anticipated and may have been one of the conscious or unconscious antecedents of Kierkegaard's and Heidegger's theological philosophy of existence. In his definition of human existence Heidegger makes frequent

259

use of the metaphor of light (in the forest clearing) which was fundamental to Gnosticism.

The existentialism of Mani emphasizes the literally "fallen" nature of Primal Man (not Adam and Eve, who are products of matter and part of the cosmos created by the Arch-Archon, Ialdabaoth, and are therefore not alien to the world). Primal Man is "fallen" from the upper realms of Light into the lower realms of Darkness, where he finds himself a "thrown" being (Heidegger's *Dasein*) in an alien world. Salvation (which is the goal of human existence in Gnosticism and of the theological existentialism of Kierkegaard and Heidegger) comes in Gnosticism when Primal Man, who is all Light, is rescued by Living Spirit proceeding downward from the Father of Light, and raised back upwards into the realms of Light, his original home. An "en-lighten-ment" of Adam and all mankind occurred subsequent to their creation by Ialdabaoth for his evil purposes. This is effected by the Light-Jesus sent for this purpose from the heavenly realms of Light and through whom salvation comes to man when the Light in mankind is restored to its original source.

For comparison, it may be noted that Heidegger's existentialism starts with the existence of man as a "being there" (*Dasein*) and proceeds with a description of the "thrown-ness" of man into a world in which he finds himself an alien and superior existent. (Here Heidegger assimilates mankind to the Gnostic Primal Man.) But Being (Existence) "gives itself" or "discloses itself" to man, while man's understanding (or knowledge) of Being is in the nature of a gift, grace, or favor by Being toward man, in order for man to find his true humanity, salvation, or joy in his existence.

NOTES

1. Trevor Ling, *A History of Religion East and West* (London: Macmillan Press Ltd., 1984) p. 171–72. These "rather disagreeable contraceptive practices" are detailed in Joseph Campbell, *The Masks of God*, vol. IV: *Creative Mythology* (New York: Viking Press, 1970), pp. 159–61.
2. Trevor Ling, op. cit., p. 170.
3. Hans Jonas, *The Gnostic Religion* (Boston: Beacon Press, 1963), p. 103.
4. Hans Jonas, op. cit., p. 137.
5. W. Bauer, *Orthodoxy and Heresy in Earliest Christianity* (Philadelphia: Fortress Press, 1979), p. 236.
6. Acts 15:12–31; Galatians 2:1–10.
7. Acts 8:9–24.
8. W. Bauer, op. cit., p. 232.
9. Hans Jonas, op. cit., p. 103.
10. It is assumed that the founder of this sect, Simon Magus, is the same referred to in Acts 8.

11. It is pertinent to note here that Socrates used this same model as metaphor in describing the function of the philosopher, namely, to serve as midwife to the (female) thoughts of (who else?) men. Socrates' mother was also a professional midwife.
12. Acts 17:22–23.
13. Hans Jonas, op. cit., pp. 143–44.
14. Romans 3:23.
15. II Corinthians 9:15.
16. This is strongly reminiscent of the ever-dying and resurrecting God of the Vine, Dionysus, who is also brought to mind by Jesus' reported comparison of himself to the vine: "I am the true vine, and my Father is the husbandman" (Saint John 15:1). This may have been intended as a transvaluation, with followers of the Dionysian rites in mind. And again: "I am the vine, ye are the branches" (Saint John 15:5). Equally interesting is the nature of the salvific process common to all types of Gnosticism: the liberation of the Light from the Darkness—the "in-gathering of the Light." This is a major hallmark that stamps Gnosticism as basically an oriental religion exhibiting the oriental mystic process of reunion of energy in the form of light with its source (the Father of Light). In Eastern mysticism the bits of light are undifferentiated, whereas in Western mysticism they are regarded as spirits endowed with individual, differentiated personalities; whence Eastern mysticism is a union of "undifferentiates," Western mysticism a union of "differentiates."
17. Thus Gnosticism is a spiritual progenitor of Kierkegaardian existentialism in that the latter favored complete withdrawal from the (evil) world. This compares with the withdrawal of the Hindu ascetic, which was based on the illusive nature of the material world.
18. There is affinity here with the similar vegetarianism of Pythagoreans and Brahmins.
19. Walter Bauer, op. cit., especially chapters 6–8.
20. Walter Bauer, op. cit., chapter 10.

Chapter 15

Philosophy, Politics, Religion, and Racism

Plato was the father of occidental philosophy, just as Jesus was the main inspiration of occidental religion. Plato espoused a myth of the earth-born—the myth of blood and soil—as the anthropological base for his philosophy and his ideal state. The earth-born consisted of men in whose blood God had put gold—they are the rulers formed in the golden age; followed another age and race of men in whose blood was silver—the auxiliaries or fighting class; last of all, the age and race of men in whose blood was iron and copper—the lower classes constituted of peasants, merchants, and other producing classes. Thus race was assimilated to social class and social class regarded as indicative of a difference in race. This was Greek philosophical myth, not empirically verifiable information, used to rationalize the existing social structure.

The men of the golden age were best qualified to be the guardians and rulers of Plato's ideal state: to this group belonged Plato's aristocratic class, which, supposedly, automatically qualified Plato for a leadership role in his or any other Greek city-state. The lower classes (hoi polloi) were only fit to perform all types of drudgery required for the maintenance of the state, for which some of them needed to be enslaved; but best suited of all to be slaves were the non-Greeks or barbarians. Thus slavery, especially of non-Greeks, became an integral part of Greek political racism, its *political rationalization* consisting of the argument that non-Greeks, being foreigners as well as barbarians, could not be citizens but only slaves on whom was incumbent all the drudgery of household and state. It followed that race-mixing (mixing of the classes) would upset the delicate equilibrium of the state and was therefore to be avoided. Plato speaking.[1]

Racism was further provided with a *philosophical rationalization* by Plato in the form of the strange but abominable argument that slavery of non-Greeks was justified since, without slaves to do all the drudgery, the philosopher-guardians of the state could not be free from toil and have the leisure to philosophize, that is, engage in a life of contemplation. To

262

this Plato added a *moral rationalization* of racism and slavery in the equally abominable argument that non-Greeks, being outside the pale of civilized (Greek) society—which is what the term *barbarian* connoted —merited whatever treatment was meted out to them as the price they had to pay for being in contact with civilization. Such was Plato's political, philosophical, and moral rationalization of state-sponsored racism, social discrimination, and slavery. In short, being a non-Greek implied a penalty in the form of racism, discrimination, and enslavement. Such is the political, philosophical, and moral heritage of the occident from the ancient Greeks regarding the norms that were supposed to govern contacts between one group or tribe and outsiders. The religious and theological heritage, as will shortly appear, was little better.

Jesus was supposedly largely responsible for much of what passes today for occidental theology and religion, a heritage of Semitic origin with important contributions from Plato's metaphysics and, especially, from Aristotle's theology. Racism is also endemic in the Semitic theologies and religions. It is a part of the heritage of Judaism and, by succession, of Christianity and Islam. Judaism postulates a Creator-God, maker of heaven and earth and all therein, but having a special relationship with the tribes of Israel against, and exclusive of, all other tribes who are saved or admitted into the Creator-God's presence through the intermediary of Jews—subsequently, through Christians and subsequently through Moslems, all of them originally Semitic tribes. Thus the theological and religious rationalization of racism inherited by the Occident.

This assumption of a special relationship between the Creator-God and Jews is reflected in the ethnography and anthropology of Judaism in the myth of Shem, Ham, and Japheth, the three sons of Noah,[2] from whom all mankind is supposed to descend after the Flood[3]: Shem was the progenitor of the Semitic (that is, Jewish and Arabic) peoples of whom Abram,[4] one of Shem's descendants, was the most famous of patriarchal figures claimed by Jews (as well as by the original Christians and Moslems). Ham was the father of the Hamitic peoples, chiefly, the African branch of mankind. Ham, who saw his father, Noah, drunk and naked, reported this incident to his other two brothers, who, walking backward so as not to see their father's nakedness, covered him up. For seeing his father's nakedness Ham was cursed by Noah—who, apparently, had a right to be drunk and naked but not to be seen in that state by his children—to be the servant of servants to his two brothers.[5] In other words, the African peoples were to be the servants, forever, of the Semitic (Jews, Christians, Arabs) and other branches of mankind.

The Semites, naturally, believed their own myth—some non-Semites believed it as well—and behaved, accordingly, as the "superior people of God," but especially the Jews who came to appropriate the term *Semitic* to themselves alone and to regard themselves as *the* chosen people of God.

Ham, representing the Berber, Nilotic, and other dark-skinned peoples of Africa destined, according to the Semitic myth, to be "hewers of wood and drawers of water" for the rest of mankind, thus provided the *anthropological rationalization* on which rested the superiority of Shem and Japheth, Semitic and other peoples of the earth. It is also on the basis of this mythical superiority that Jews make a distinction between themselves and the so-called Gentiles (Goi) or the rest of mankind. (Compare the Greek *hoi polloi*.)

Jesus accepted this Semitic anthropology in declaring to the Samaritan woman that "salvation is of the Jews,"[6] and to the Syrophenician woman (of Canaan) whose daughter was possessed: "Let the children (Jews) first be filled: for it is not meet to take the children's bread, and cast it unto the dogs (Gentiles)."[7] He also commanded his disciples to take their missionary activities first to the Jews ("the lost sheep of the house of Israel"), then to the Gentiles[8]—which not only indicates a racist attitude but also is in keeping with his own assessment of his mission, as expressed in connection with the Syrophenician woman's request to have a devil cast out of her daughter: "I am not sent but unto the lost sheep of the house of Israel."[9]

All European peoples who became converted to Judaism, Christianity, and Islam have swallowed whole this myth of Semitic superiority (since the Scriptures of Christianity and Islam accept and include the Judaic Scriptures as their base) and made it their ground of justification for enslaving and colonizing other peoples, but especially Africans—just as the Jews enslaved and colonized Palestine and the Arabs were to do centuries later in Europe and Africa.[10] The Afrikaners, with less imagination than the other Europeans, did no less than they, regarding and treating the indigenous South Africans as Kafirs (heathen) and inferior to the invading "white tribe." All is based, of course, on the Bible—as the Afrikaners were careful to point out.

There is little doubt that Jewish racism was the result of their violent reaction to their Egyptian slavery (if that myth is founded); for it is only natural for the persecuted to think that their socially inferior position created by their persecution is due to their possession of some special qualities envied by their persecutors,[11] and from this idea to go on to imagine that they are consequently superior to their jealous persecutors and to act accordingly whenever they have the opportunity to do so. This complex may be termed the *paranoid-megalomaniac* or *inferiority-superiority complex*. It is a dialectic of extreme reactions similar to those of a manic-depressive patient.

Thus in the Occident, Christian and Islamic theology and religion combined with Plato's pseudo-philosophic, pseudo-sociological, and pseudo-moralistic justification to provide a powerful foundation for racism, slavery, and colonialism. The Christian missionary operated within this powerful and ancient tradition, aptly reflected in Bishop R. Heber's hymn:

> 1. From Greenland's icy mountains,
>   From India's coral strand,
>   Where Afric's sunny fountains
>   Roll down their golden sand . . .
>   They call us to deliver,
>   Their land from error's chain.
>
> 2. . . . In vain with lavish kindness
>   The gifts of God are strown;
>   The heathen in his blindness
>   Bows down to wood and stone.
>
> 3. Can we, whose souls are lighted
>   With wisdom from on high,
>   Can we to men benighted
>   The lamp of life deny? . . .[12]

What superiority! What special divine relationship and favor to these missionaries whose "souls are lighted with wisdom from on high"!

Jan Christian Smuts, founder of modern racist South Africa and a Christian in name as well as confession, was a perfect product of occidental Judeo-Christian-Islamic Graeco-Roman civilization: he knew his Bible as well as his Plato very well, backward and forward, being also a first-class Classics scholar. Thus the world has witnessed the paradox of an ideal product of this occidental civilization as well as his successors being condemned by others of the same occidental matrix!

It is, therefore, no accident that the three major unsolved problems of occidental civilization to the present day are Race, Religion, and Rule (politics and government). What, however, constitutes the tragedy of this civilization is that very few recognize the sources of its inspiration as the sources of its problems and, possibly, of its eventual destruction if its three primary problems continue to resist correction.

It has been pointed out and is undoubtedly true that all the ration-

265

alizations of racism in its variant forms and aspects stem from basic insecurity and fear vis-à-vis the new and the strange when perceived as a threat to established positions and inherited or acquired advantages. There is, however, something unusual and unique about Semitic, in particular Jewish, racism (this being the acknowledged source of Semitic scriptural racism): it is the only racism on record that claims *divine* authorization for its unique combination of aggression and racism against others. The Afrikaner may rationalize his racism by a combined appeal to Scripture, his civilizing mission, and supposedly vacant lands. But only the Jew could make bold to claim divine sanction and authorization for dispossessing others of their patrimony on the ground of their presumed wickedness.[13] Following this brilliant precedent, the Christians of the Crusades and the Inquisition, as well as Islam, have also claimed divine authorization for destruction of all who resisted conversion—auto-da-fé or jihad.

The significance of racism for nonoccidental countries and peoples lies in the fact that in those countries where society is organized on tribal lines tribalism is easily perverted to constitute a form of racism in the same sense as Greek or Semitic racism (between different peoples and between different classes or castes of the same people). Tribalism becomes racism when it favors one tribe above another or others and seeks to aggrandize the favored tribe at the expense of other tribes or to oppress other tribes to the advantage of the favored tribe. But tribalism per se is not racism to the extent that it does not regard one tribe as superior to another or fabricate rationalizations for presumed superiority. This distinction, however, merely shows that there are different kinds and aspects of racism.

Occidental racism is obviously more pernicious than perverted tribalism or tribal racism in that it is buttressed by rationalizations founded on pseudo-arguments in the areas of philosophy, government, anthropology, theology, and religion—rationalizations and pseudo-arguments that have become hallowed by the passage of centuries. For this reason there are, naturally, very strong objections to any attempt or form of occidental missionary activity—religious and theological evangelism—in so-called Third World countries both because it transmits a pernicious and vicious form of racism and concomitant political and economic colonialism. There is little gain and all loss in adding to the indigenous and milder forms of racism more virulent forms of this human and social disease imported from the outside world.

NOTES

1. It is interesting to note that the Greeks who originated the concept of "race mixing" used it originally in a sociological, not necessarily a biological sense. Modern Caucasian racists have thus either misunderstood the ancient Greeks, or deliberately reinterpreted their meaning solely in a biological sense thus betraying their ignorance or disregard of Mendel's Law.
2. Genesis 5:32, 6:10.
3. Genesis 7:11–24, 8:9, 9:18–19, 10:32. A flood myth is found in the mythology of most peoples. The Greeks, for instance, had their Deucalion and Pyrrha, who survived the flood sent by Zeus and his brother Poseidon to drown the world. They raised a race of men from the stones of the earth—the autocthonous race of men (the stone men). Noah was to the generations after the flood what Adam was to the generations before the flood. Noah was thus a kind of second Adam, procreationwise, to whom as to Abram, God gave the command and promise: "be fruitful and multiply and replenish the earth" (Genesis 9:1, 7; 17:2, 6).
4. Later renamed Abraham ("father of many nations") by God (Genesis 17:5).
5. It did not seem to matter that, but for Ham's seeing what the problem was and alerting his brothers, these latter would not have been able to avoid seeing their father's nakedness. The curse of Ham is thus a strange type of justice, but the Old Testament is full of similar strange things.
6. Saint John 4:22.
7. Saint Mark 7:27; Saint Matthew 15:22, 26.
8. Saint Matthew 10:5, 6; Saint Luke 24:47.
9. Saint Matthew 15:24.
10. Even among the colonized, those converted to Christianity tended to regard themselves as superior to the non-Christians (Moslems included) as, for example, the Sierra Leone Creoles and the Americo-Liberians vis-à-vis the indigenous peoples of the countries where they settled. Similarly, the later Moslem converts regarded themselves as superior to all non-Moslems (Jews and Christians included). Most interesting of all, but hardly suprising, within contemporary Judaism in the state of Israel Jews of European provenance regard themselves as superior to, and discriminate against, Jews of African provenance, including, of course, the Falashas of Ethiopia.
11. This is obviously not a universal reaction as it seems to have been absent—so far—among enslaved Africans or liberated ones, vis-à-vis their persecutors.
12. *Hymns Ancient and Modern Revised* (William Clowes & Sons, Ltd.), no. 265. This hymn gives a clear indication that self-conceit, self-righteous prejudice, and power, rather than common sense or reason, constitute the basis of any evangelizing activity.
13. Genesis 12:1, 13:7, 14–18; 15:7, 18–21; 17:8. Contemporary orthodox rabbinical Israel is bent on reenacting the Genesis myth as history. It should be noted, however, that many contemporary Jews, in and outside Israel, are embarrassed by their own mythology of the Chosen People and its pernicious consequences and would like to have this part of their mythology expunged.

BOOK THREE
MY MYTH

Chapter 1

Clearing the Ground

Book Three sets forth my myth: that is, my interpretation of things in general as they present themselves under various aspects—mainly metaphysical, philosophical, theological, religious, and ethical. The received conventional wisdom in these areas is no more than a body of interpretations handed down from time immemorial, as augmented, reduced, modified, and reinterpreted from time to time. In these matters no interpretation, however, hallowed by time, is sacrosanct or eternally valid, each being provisional and subject to change in the light of changing evidence and experience. Only one piece of wisdom emerges as eternally valid, namely that "New occasions teach new duties" and "Time makes ancient good uncouth."[1]

In presenting my myth it is necessary to clarify and lay the conceptual groundwork by introducing my preferred definitions. These do not necessarily conform to accepted or traditional definitions, concepts, and usages, but merely present the manner in which I view the concepts and issues involved.

1. DEFINITIONS

(a) *Physical objects* are organizations, or functions, of mass-energy (as defined by physicists) which, in turn, are functions or ways of organizing matter (= nuclear and sub-nuclear particles).

(b) *Energy waves* are transformations of mass or extensions of the mass-energy structure of physical objects.

(c) *Sensations* or *impressions* are energy waves proceeding from, or transmitted by, physical objects to, and through, the sensing organs and mechanisms of the human body and received and organized by the human brain in a contextual web known as *mind.*

(d) *Intuitions* are energy waves transmitted by objects directly to the brain, by-passing the body's sensing organs and mechanisms.

271

(e) *Ideas* derive from sensations or impressions, or from intuitions, being functions of, or ways of organizing or processing, sensations, impressions, and intuitions stored in the mind.

(f) *Experience* consists of everything apprehended by the brain, through sensations and intuitions, as ideas, forms, or organizations of energy waves. Experience is thus the content of the mind, namely, sensations, impressions, intuitions, concepts, ideas, et cetera.

(g) A *function* or *interrelationship* is a state of composing (i.e., "entering into") or being composed (i.e., "being entered into") or of decomposing (i.e., "coming out of") or being decomposed (i.e., "being taken out of"). In short, it is a relationship of integration or its opposite, disintegration.

An idea or concept is thus a type of organization of a group of nuclear or subnuclear particles, or matter, into mass-energy or of mass-energy into objects or groups of objects (i.e., phenomena). This is the same as the old Platonian philosophical notion of form or idea. It differs from it, however, in showing the proper relationship of form to matter, namely, that form and matter are inseparable, form being an organizational aspect of matter, not something separate from, or imposed upon, matter. In other words, in the phenomenal, sense-empirical world there is no form without mass-energy and vice versa, since mass-energy is analyzable into nuclear and subnuclear particles, each of which consists of a certain organization of nucleus and other elements. Thus form and matter compose and decompose at the same time.

If objects (composed of mass-energy) disintegrate, we are left with no specific form or a new form of elemental matter (particles), just as stripping the layers of an onion leaves us with no onion-form but only the material components of the former onion, themselves organized in new forms.

Ideas, concepts, or forms, however, can exist as such *in the mind*, without any sensible corresponding matter, as mere patterns of organization. But they cannot exist *on their own*, independently of the human mind. At least, one could not become aware of them without the activity of mind. Once they are recorded in writing or in other ways, they become associated with matter (or mass-energy). Other than being in the mind of man or on some record, they disappear into "nothingness." Thus "nothingness" is a purely definitional, not an intuitive-empirical or a sense-empirical, concept in this context. It means merely the absence, disappearance, suppression or nonevidentiality, vis-à-vis the mind, of something that previously existed as concept or object. But when something (an object or concept) disappears, its place is not vacant but is occupied by matter in the form of pure energy, so that our "nothing"

272

is really energy—intuitive-empirical or sense-empirical pure energy. Thus an object or concept "disappears," vis-à-vis the mind, by being displaced by, or transformed into, another object or concept.

It follows that the basic metaphysical (or existential) elements are:

(a) sense-empirical matter (mass and energy) together with its associated idea, form, or concept, and
(b) intuitive-empirical, i.e. purely mental, or brain-intercepted, energy (ideas, forms, or concepts).

In order for intuitive-empirical concepts to become viable and useful, they need to be "objectified" in two ways:

(i) by common agreement or convention regarding their precise meaning (objective meaning) and, where possible,
(ii) by sense-empirical verification of the content (if any) of their objective meaning.

From the foregoing definitions it is clear that sensations, impressions, concepts, ideas, and chains of thought are not *superstructures* of the mind erected on objects (as Karl Marx suggested) but *extensions* or *integral parts* of the mass-energy structure of those objects. Consequently, the old controversy of idealism *versus* materialism, or of the primacy of the one over the other, is seen to be both artificial and false. In the first place, it does not translate into the language of mass-energy so far as objects are concerned, these being both mass and energy combined. In the second place and in consequence of the first, the correct situation is revealed as an inseparable mass-energy continuum.

While the mind-versus-matter or idealism-versus-materialism controversy is false, the doctrine of materialism is true in the sense that everything is matter, once it is understood that "matter" consists of mass and energy—or subnuclear elements, in the final analysis. Whence existence, by which is meant *phenomenal* existence, is all material being mass and energy in a variety of combinations.

2. NATURE AND PROCESS OF HUMAN PERCEPTION AND KNOWLEDGE OF THE PHENOMENAL WORLD

A. NATURE OF THE OUTSIDE WORLD (PHENOMENA AND EVENTS)

The outside world (the rest of the cosmos apart from oneself) consists of phenomena and events experienced mostly, but not entirely, through our senses. This experience consists in their relationships to us via our senses, and these relationships may be termed *reality* (*"thing-ness"*) *relationships* or simply *relationships*.

There are three types of reality relationships with phenomena and events:

(a) Presentation of their *external aspects*, at first hand, to our senses and, through our senses, to our brains and minds at second hand. This is the reality relationship we denote by the term *phenomenon* or *event*—both dealing with the externality of thing-ness (re-ality).

(b) Representation of (i.e., standing for) their *internal aspects* via their external aspects, which are their contact points with our senses. This internal aspect we denote by the term *noumenon* or *in-vent* and is a relationship that may or may not be reflected in the external aspects of things; but to the extent that it is, it is a relationship at *third hand* because it is negotiated to us, first to the external aspects of things (firsthand), through these to our senses (secondhand) and, finally, through our senses to our minds (thirdhand).

(c) Direct (firsthand) presentation of the knowledge of things to our minds without the mediation of our senses (*"sensation"*)—what is commonly referred to as *intuition*. The process by which intuitive knowledge is transmitted to our minds without (i.e., by bypassing) the mediation of our senses is, undoubtedly, physical, living as we do in a physical environment, although not enough is known about the nature of the process. (In this case, the internal aspects—noumena or in-vents—of things are negotiated second-hand by the mind.)

It must be pointed out that the above definitions and concepts are arrived at *analytically* and that this manner of proceeding does not imply that the processes involved operate sequentially. On the contrary, our experience indicates that the various steps or processes operate synchronically.

B. ROLE OF THE SENSES

Our senses lock us *in*—in both our external and internal dimensions—from the *outside* world (the cosmic web of things and events distinguishable from ourselves). Conversely, our senses lock the *outside* world—in its external and internal dimensions—*out* from us. Thus our experiences of the world are mediated, mostly through our senses (allowance being made for the part played by intuition) and our knowledge of the world is, correspondingly, mostly mediated, not direct. That is, we know *about* things; we do not directly *know* things, for the most part, so far as sensation is concerned, except for intuition. In short, most knowledge is *indirect* or sense-*mediated* knowledge; some knowledge, through intuition, is *direct, immediate*, or *nonmediated* knowledge.

The dual role of our senses is, therefore, clear: they *insulate* us from, as well as put us in *contact* with, the outside world, so that by their means we *know* (externally and indirectly) and *do not know* (internally and directly) our cosmic environment. Knowledge itself—the apprehension, cognition, and recognition of things and events—insofar as it is derived via the senses is thus a dialectical relationship with things and events: a *knowing* and *not knowing* them, linked together at the contact point with them—our senses. Awareness or paying attention plays a role, of course, in sense-mediated knowledge, for it is an essential ingredient in the transmission of such knowledge. It is well known that lack of attention may block the transmission of knowledge even while sensation is active. One may see or hear a person or thing, but lack of attention may prevent one from knowing what it is one hears or sees.

Our existence—i.e, our physical-being-in-the-world—is, therefore, mostly a *hyphenated* existence, because it is mediated or brought into relationship with the existence of other things and events mostly through our senses. Our senses are the *hyphens* or *mediators* of our existence, except when intuition takes over. This merely reflects the fact that each human being is, physically, a separate individual.

C. NATURE AND ROLE OF INTUITION

Intuition is the capacity to know things and events—relationships—directly, without the mediation of the senses. It is direct cognition by the mind, through a process still incompletely known but undoubtedly physical in nature—possibly, energy transmission of a special sort that has a direct impact on the mind. The process has to be physical in order to traverse our physical environment and reach to, as well as be received by, us in our capacity as physical receptors.

Allowing, then, for this role of intuition, one may say that our physical existence is sense-and-intuition-bound, hyphenated as well as direct, vis-à-vis our environment.

It thus becomes possible for us to derive physical pleasure and pain through our senses, as well as psychological pleasure and pain through our intuition—but also through *reminiscence* of the nature of physical and intuitive pleasure and pain.

D. KINDS OF PHENOMENA

Three kinds of phenomena may be distinguished:

(a) integrated units of differentiated constituents ("integrated differentiates") perceived through our senses and termed *organic* phenomena: mostly, biological entities;
(b) integrated units of undifferentiated constituents ("integrated undifferentiates") perceived through our senses and termed *inorganic* phenomena: e.g., minerals;
(c) phenomena, including knowledge and relationships, which we perceive directly and intuitively, bypassing the senses.

The entire cosmos is composed of sensible (organic and inorganic) and intuitive phenomena and relationships—viewed from the human standpoint—and is thus an integrated whole in itself, a biophysical entity.

E. DIMENSIONS OF PHENOMENA

As entities (*res*), phenomena are *re-al* to us, via the mediation of our senses, in regard to their outward or external dimension. They are also *re-al* in their internal dimension, that is, *in themselves*, but *not* to us because their internal dimension (what Plato called "the thing itself" or noumenon and Kant, at a different level, "the thing-in-itself") is not directly accessible to our senses, only inferable through their mediated external dimension after a series of tests. However, "things-in-themselves" may be directly known through intuition, although sense-empirical confirmation, where possible, is necessary to verify the result of intuition.

The external reality of phenomena (which is what the term *phenomenon* [appearance] implies), the aspect that is accessible to the senses, was much emphasized by Epicurus, the Greek philosopher (c. 342–270 B.C.E.), but downgraded earlier by the Academic philosophers, Plato (c. 427–347 B.C.E.) and Aristotle (384–322 B.C.E.) and their followers. These philosophers placed more emphasis on the *internal* reality of phenomena—their noumena—which was generally inaccessible to the senses, but could be intuited. Arguing from the perspective that the external reality (which was a dimension subject to change) did not directly reflect the internal reality (which was a dimension unknown to the senses but which they held to be static), they concluded that the external aspect of a thing

276

was not a true or reliable indication of the sensibly unknown internal aspect: it was, that is, untrue to its inner, static self and therefore deceptive, illusory (in the sense of deceptive, not of a mirage)—hence worthless. The real worth or essence of a thing was, for them, the unknown, inaccessible internal dimension, presumed to be unchanging. Epicurus, by contrast, argued—correctly—that the external dimension of things was, at least, true to itself and therefore had value as such. The weight of tradition, however, favored the earlier Academic philosophers, not the later Epicureans.

The Academic philosophers, whose view has dominated in the heritage of Greek philosophy bequeathed to the Occident, committed two errors. First, there was no a priori reason why the internal dimension of phenomena should remain static while the external dimension exhibited change. They thus failed to allow for the possibility (now known to be fact, as a result of modern atomic research) that in a physically changing world all dimensions change, however imperceptibly. Second, phenomena are no less real for being externally accessible than for being internally inaccessible to the senses. In thus devising a single theory about the sensibly inaccessible, namely, that it is static and unchanging, the Academic philosophers tended to encourage the growth of obscurantism as well as superstition in philosophy.

F. THE MECHANICS OF KNOWLEDGE

The state as well as the quality of knowledge (i.e., the apprehension, cognition, and recognition) of phenomena and events is a resultant of three factors:

(a) the degree of accuracy with which our senses present the external aspects of phenomena and events;
(b) the accuracy and extent to which the internal aspects of phenomena (noumena) and events are reflected in, and by, their external aspects;
(c) intuition of the phenomenon, verified by the senses where possible.

The first is a function of the efficiency of our senses, aided or not by sense-extending or sense-amplifying instruments, *in the light of pre-(vious)-conceptions impinging on the sense-presentation of phenomena.* Hence the necessity for independent verification by several other persons in order to minimize the influence and residue of preconceptions and other idiosyncratic factors on the sensible apprehension of phenomena.

The second is a function of whether or not there is a connection between the external and internal aspects and, if so, the extent or degree to which the external presentation reflects or represents this connection and the internal aspect.

The third depends on inadequately known factors.

Since there is no guarantee that there is a connection between the internal and external aspects of an object—although it is highly unlikely that there is no connection—we are obliged to make two alternative assumptions, that there is and that there is not such a connection, then work out, with the aid of reason, the implications of each assumption and by subsequent testing (i.e, referral to sense experience) determine which set of implications (and, therefore, which assumption) is valid.

Throughout the operations for determining the validity of our knowledge, reason is involved in the vital role of explicating the implications of every assumption or hypothesis.

Insofar as knowledge can be gained through intuition, bypassing our sensing organs, human beings are not as insulated from their physical environment as our senses would seem to indicate. Intuition provides direct access for our minds to the world outside us, although the nature of the process is not, as yet, precisely known.

Intuition and sensing therefore constitute our two major routes to knowledge, to cognition and recognition. But until the process of intuition is better known and empirically determinable, empirical confirmation by the senses provides the only dependable means of verification and control of intuitive experience. Such verification and control, naturally, can only be applied to the implications—i.e., the sensible implications—of the intuitive experience.

G. THE NATURE OF KNOWLEDGE

We have seen that our senses enable us to know *about* things but not to know them directly. Added to this limitation are others, two of which are most important for our purposes, both of them mutually reinforcing in their effects: namely, that the nature of our contact with the external aspects of things (external reality) is both *disintegrative* and *analytical* (discrete and step-by-step).

Biophysical Disintegration of the Cosmos

We experience the world as single or discrete organisms, entities, and appearances or as a limited and discrete group of such entities at any given time. It is impossible to take the whole world in at a given time. These discrete encounters are, of course, real experiences but, being isolated from their cosmic context, are not cosmically organic, although they may be in themselves complete individual organisms. Thus the thrust of our experience of the world, the cosmos, is to disintegrate not integrate it. Such is the result of our own individual limitations as infinitesimal units vis-à-vis the world, the cosmos.

Moreover, our curiosity leads us to dissect and analyze individual phenomena in order to see what they are made of and how they function (what makes them tick), and in so doing we destroy their organic or inorganic unity.

Both these factors—disintegration and dissection or analysis—are mutually reinforcing, and the consequence is serious because we never succeed in restoring the cosmic context, the cosmic unity, and the organic or inorganic unity of the phenomenon under study.

Finally, even in sensing phenomena as discrete entities, we fail to sense each entity completely. This is due to the fact that a phenomenon may not be accessible to all, but only to some, of our senses. Furthermore, in regard to those senses to which a phenomenon may be accessible, the partial impression of it obtained through those senses will vary according as the sensing is synchronous or consecutive for each of the senses involved.

Mental Disintegration of the Cosmos

While we physically disintegrate the cosmos and its individual phenomena through the process of sensing, in the attempt to apprehend or know something about the constituent elements, the mental process of cognition tends to have the same disintegrative effect. Mentally, we classify things *out* of the cosmic whole on a uniform, homogeneous basis, in order to arrive at generalities that we hope may yield uniform "laws of nature." Thus, mentally as well as biophysically, we tend to disintegrate the unity and integrity of things in order—so we believe—to know them better.

It thus seems that "to know" (cognize and recognize) is "to destroy," "to disintegrate" without ever being able to reintegrate things. At best, we merely "aggregate" what we "disintegrate." Phenomena are sensibly and mentally wrenched from their cosmic, organic unity at the biophysical as well as at the mental level. At the biophysical level, the organic or inorganic unity of individual entities may be preserved, but not their cosmic integrity. At the mental level, where we pass on to dissect and analyze, neither cosmic nor individual integrity is preserved in the process of "knowing" the phenomenon or entity under study. Our human knowledge is mostly of the analytical kind, emphasizing homogeneity, consistency on prescribed narrow bases of classification. What we generally most lack—and this is crucial for problem-solving exercises—is integrative knowledge, the kind that requires heterogeneity and tolerates inconsistency because released from narrow classifications, the kind that relates to the cosmos itself.

3. THE "AFTER-WORLD" AND THE "WORLD OF INTUITION" AS IDENTICAL WITH THE PHENOMENAL WORLD

The Semitic religions espouse a doctrine of "compensation" in another and future world, after death, for the vicissitudes of the present existence: good/evil here and now will be "compensated" by good/evil in the there and then of that "after-world." The corresponding Hindu doctrine is that of the law of karma (cause and effect), which, as with the Semitic doctrine, is played out between at least two, but certainly more, existences. Isaac Newton expounded the equivalent law for this present existence in his Third Law of Motion, where compensation takes place within the same existential world. Thus the existential worlds across which compensation takes place are linked consecutively in the Semitic and Hindu religious systems, rather than simultaneously and identically as in the Newtonian scheme. However, in the two religious systems the "compensatory" existences are formally similar, though not equal nor opposite: goodness in this existence, more goodness in the other; evil in this existence, more evil in the other. Plato's devolutionary existence followed this same pattern in the *Timaeus* (section 49). There is thus no basis, according to the Semitic and Hindu religions, for anticipating that the other existence will be substantially or essentially different from the current one. This, coupled with the evidence on which the Newtonian law is based, leads to the conclusion that man does not pass out of the present existence ever, but *always* is in it. In short, *there is no existence different from the present one*, and nonexistence is not given in human experience.

Since sense-mediated knowledge as well as direct, nonmediated knowledge (based on phenomena, intuition, parapsychological occurrences, et cetera) both occur in our experience in this same material or physical existential world, we may also conclude that intuition or any type of direct, nonmediated knowledge is physically transmitted and received and confined to this, our current, existence. This type of knowledge, moreover, must derive from manifestations or forms of mass and energy.

The nonsensible world of intuition is thus not different from or unconnected to our physical world but is merely another dimension of it. The ancient Greek Academic philosophers associated the occurrence of nonsensible phenomena (the so-called intelligible forms apprehended by intuition) with immobility or absence of motion, apparently believing that the senses were activated by matter-in-motion. Since, however, intuition seems to be direct apprehension, by brain and mind, of knowledge borne, as it were, on energy waves that bypass the senses, we encounter here a paradox in which energy waves of a certain kind—the kind that relates to intuition—move (like any form of matter) and yet do not move since, according to Greek Academic philosophy, the senses are not stimulated and therefore are not involved.

This paradox can be resolved on the assumption that, if intuition is, indeed, related to some special kind of energy wave, then the speed of this type of wave must greatly exceed the speed of light so as to be instantaneous and ubiquitous,[2] hence gives the impression of motion-lessness and surpasses the capacity of any of the senses to detect it. This assumption implies that our existential world is a world of thoroughgoing motion, in which various velocities or speeds appropriate to various types of energy exist. Taking the standard velocity to be that of light (radiant energy), then super-radiant–energy velocities would give the apparent effect of no-motion because of the impression of instantaneity and ubiquity created by such velocities. Subradiant-energy velocities may also give the apparent effect of no-motion, such as the effect of stationariness produced by a body traveling at the same speed as another, as in the case of geo-stationary satellites that move at the same speed and in the same orbit as the earth or the effect of stationariness of any object on earth by reason of the fact that it is carried around by the earth at earth speed. Either way—above or below radiant-energy velocities—the apparent world of no-motion (or imperceptible motion), which is produced by instantaneous ubiquity as by synchronous velocity, is not a different world from our material world of sense, but merely two different motion dimensions having an impact on our very same world.

The foregoing argument and conclusions all point to the same unique result: there is only ONE existential world—the physical or material world of sense and intuition—and only ONE existence lived in our cosmos. Whether it is possible for the *same* individual to repeat this *same* existence several times in this same cosmos is, of course, another matter, which does not directly concern us here, but one which opens up interesting speculations.

Other related conclusions which flow from the above are the following:

(a) The human being is a complex unit of mass-energy and is therefore thoroughly material and materialistic in outlook. (It should be remembered that *all* types of energy are here regarded as physical, as is inevitably the case within a material cosmos.)
(b) Transmigration of souls (regarded as energy packages of an as yet unspecified and unknown kind), if it does occur, occurs within this ONE existential world of sense and intuition and—on the available evidence of so-called parapsychological phenomena and accounts of prenatal and out-of-body (including postdeath) experiences, for what they may be worth—seems to be strictly intraspecies, *not* trans-species as Plato believed.

4. THE NATURE AND MEANING OF THINGS

The question that preoccupied the Greek Academic philosophers —What is the nature or essence of a thing?—may be interpreted in three ways:

(a) What is its physical *structure* or composition, i.e., *what* is it *made of*? (This aspect fascinated the early Greek philosophers from Thales on.)
(b) What is its *function*, aim, or purpose, i.e., what does it *do* or what is it supposed to do? (Teleology: an aspect that also interested the early Greek philosophers, whether historicists, like Plato with his notion of *justice* [the equivalent of the modern concept of division of labor] as the purpose and function of all things; or philosopher-theologians, like Aristotle, with his notion of *nisus* [or "striving to become like" the ideal form] as the end and function of all things—as much as it interests the modern philosopher or theologian.)
(c) What is its *behavior*, comportment, or manner of operation, i.e., *how* does it *do* it? (This is an aspect of great interest to physical and social scientists.)

Any question regarding the nature or essence of a thing may be termed an *essential* question, and one or other of its essential aspects may be more emphasized than the rest. The three different interpretations are but three different and inseparable aspects of the *same* essential question. It is therefore legitimate to address oneself to all three aspects at the same time. This inseparability of the three aspects is revealed in the fact that in the early development of Greek philosophy questions about "structure" became resolvable into questions about "function."[3] Granted the inseparability of the three aspects, the attempt by a modern philosopher, Karl Popper, to distinguish between "structure" questions and "behavior" questions, but to reject the "structure" questions, seems untenable.[4]

Another important consideration relating to essential questions is the obvious fact that the nature or essence of a thing resides *in* the thing, not outside it, pace Plato,[5] who sought to discover the essence of things—their nature, reality, or reason (the so-called Platonic forms or ideas)—*outside* of themselves; that is, outside of their sensible, phenomenal appearances in our sensible world and in some putative, prenatal, suprasensible world. Such an attempt seems clearly illegitimate because the forms and ideas are defined in a manner that puts them beyond the reach of empirical verification, so that everyone is entitled to their own notion of the Platonic form or idea. In short, Plato's forms fall into the category of pure myth. Popper's property of things fares little better, except for being situated in the sensible world.

Aside from essential questions there is another category of questions equally as important: meaning or interpretation questions of the type "What does this thing mean to me?" The meaning given to a thing is very important for assessing its role or significance vis-à-vis man, the interpreter and giver of meaning, but also vis-à-vis other things that are similarly given different meanings by man. Meanings given to things may also include arranging them in order of importance according to some criterion.

Essential questions are *objective* questions in the sense that the standard of reference is the thing itself. Meaning questions, on the contrary, are *subjective* questions in the sense that the standard of reference is man, not the thing or entity concerned. But both types of questions are not mutually exclusive. Indeed, wherever possible, it is advisable to pose both types of questions, since the mutual consistency of the answers to them (or the lack of consistency) is a good prima facie test of their empirical validity or scientific truth. The answer to the one could provide a check on the reasonableness or accuracy of the answer to the other. Scientific hypotheses may start as meaning hypotheses, but must end as essential hypotheses if they are to be tested for empirical validity.

This important feature of scientific hypotheses highlights the difference between such hypotheses, on the one hand, and dogma and definition, on the other. Dogma and definition deal solely with meaning, are therefore subjective, and remain in a private world. They fail to pass over to the objective world, where by fulfilling the sense-empirical test of validity they may become uniquely identifiable public property. Consequently, unless they are made objective *either* by common agreement (convention) on their specific meanings, or by verifiable sense experience, or both, they tend to vary in meaning according to different individuals and, therefore, to generate controversy while—and because—still remaining in a private world.[6] Scientific hypotheses, in contrast, pass over from the private world of variable subjectivity of meaning into the public world of double objectivity where their meanings are determined by convention and their content verified by sense experience.

It may, therefore, be argued that any meaning (or hypothesis) that has not been made doubly objective by *both* common agreement *and* sense experience (for example, dogma or definition) is both incomplete and, especially from its tendency to generate needless controversy, illegitimate and counter-productive.

SEPARATION OF NATURE AND MEANING IN GREEK PHILOSOPHY

The weakness of Greek Academic philosophy (as represented by the teachings of Plato and Aristotle as well as their precursor, Socrates) was not so much the distinction between the nature (structure) and the meaning of things, between essence and meaning (interpretation), between objective and subjective, as the failure to establish a bond of legitimacy between the two by the requirement of double objectivization of subjective meaning, namely, by (a) convention or common agreement about meanings (objective meaning) and (b) empirical verification of objective meaning in sense experience.[7]

By thus keeping meaning and essence separate and parallel, the Academic philosophers created the false idea and tradition of two separate and substantive worlds of meaning and of essence where, in fact, there is only *one* substantive world—the sense-empirical world—at least in so far as human beings are concerned. Unlike the Greek atomist philosophers and, much later, Karl Marx and his followers, the Greek Academic philosophers did not seem to have recognized the need to conform mind, thought, or meaning to their objective material base.

It is by the separation of meaning from essence that theologies are created, having appeal and reference to a supernatural and suprasensible world. The creation of sophistical worlds of meaning is an age-old and popular pastime as well as a rhetorical device that permits everyone to say what they wish without fear of contradiction. This is possible because, as we have seen, there is neither empirical evidence nor objective (conventional) standard of meaning regarding the existence of such worlds, to which reference could be made.[8]

Thus under the assumption—it is no more and no less than an assumption—of the existence of a suprasensible world, paradises and hellish infernos have been woven out of imaginative whole cloth with the sole objective of cajoling or browbeating and certainly brainwashing the unimaginative majority into submitting to, and executing, the wishes of the clever and imaginative minority.[9] So, for example, has it been with Greek Academic philosophy and occidental theology and theologians of whatever persuasion—starting from Socrates, who heard the voice of a god within him and preached the existence of a suprasensible, prenatal, and postmortem world of the soul, gods, dead heroes, and philosophers; passing through conservative and reactionary idealists like Plato, and on down to the modern representatives of all varieties of occidental theology.

The foregoing critical analysis of the nature and meaning of things is unlikely to put an end to the creation of suprasensible (outside space-time) worlds, nor is it necessarily intended to do so. For the creation of such worlds is, after all, a pleasant and creative pastime, much as the painter or the sculptor engages in fanciful creativity. Rather is it the intention to direct attention to the ground rules (if any) of the game, less for the benefit of the players than for that of the game's unsuspecting victims—its spectators.

New worlds are daily being created in and outside space-time. Worlds created outside of space-time (usually denoted by the term *utopia* or *pure myth*) present us with great difficulties. Since they are not phenomenal worlds, that is, have no direct contact with, and therefore no relevance to, intuitive or sense experience, they can be created in great profusion without hindrance.[10] There are no ground rules for their creation. The prototype of outside–space-time worlds is the mythical and mystical world of the early Greek philosophers, celebrated in the Dionysian and Eleusinian rites, the Orphic and Pythogarean rites—all of which were basically related, being different versions of the same world. The great exponents of this prototype were Socrates, Plato, and Aristotle, who regarded this outside–space-time world as the *true* world, that is, the true metaphysical world. This Greek prototype had much in common with the corresponding Judeo-Christian-Islamic model.

Although anyone is free to fabricate outside–space-time worlds without limit, no one is free to apply conclusions derived from them to our space-time sensible world unless certain restricting and empirical conditions are respected. For the great weakness (from an empirical point of view) of outside–space-time worlds and speculations connected with them is their great flexibility and elasticity, as a result of which they can be used to support various different positions and propositions, as well as their implications—no matter how diametrically opposed—for which no empirical basis exists. It is in this lack of empirical foundation, rather than the diversity and conflict of derivable positions, that the weakness of outside–space-time worlds consists.

While there are no ground rules governing the creation of outside–space-time worlds, the creation of space-time worlds, by contrast, is subject to one overriding rule: they and/or their implications must be amenable to confirmation in sense experience. In short, they must be empirical. The creation of new communities intended to survive in space-time must pass this empirical test to be of any practical or lasting value. By the same token, outside–space-time worlds and their implications have not only to be recast in empirical terms but also modified, through empirical testing, in order to have any relevance at all for the space-time world of our planet Earth.

NOTES

1. *Songs of Praise*, enlarged (New York: Oxford University Press, 1948), no. 309, verse 3.
2. Physicists maintain that there is no speed in the cosmos exceeding that of light. This does not, however, interdict anyone from making a different assumption in this open-ended cosmos where everything seems possible, including new discoveries about speeds of entities within it. Indeed, paradox or inconsistency is the very stuff of the cosmos.
3. R. G. Collingwood, *The Idea of Nature* (London, New York: Oxford University Press, 1945), p. 16.
4. Karl R. Popper, *Objective Knowledge*, rev. ed. (New York: Oxford University Press, 1981), pp. 194–97, 263. Popper refers to ''structure'' questions as ''what-is'' questions and to ''behavior'' questions as ''how'' questions. He rejects all ''what-is'' questions (*essential* questions, as he calls them) on the ground that they smack of animism, maintaining that scientific hypotheses about things should be in terms of universal laws of nature, which are neither inherent in the singular things nor Platonic ideas residing outside our phenomenal world in some suprasensible domain. Such theories, he continues, should describe structural or relational properties of the world. Structural properties, however, are what ''what-is'' questions are about, and it seems false to make an artificial distinction between ''individual things'' and ''the world.'' The world, after all, is composed of individual things that, in turn, are composed of those modern animae or ''spirits'' known as ''nuclear particles,'' all of which are regulated by Quantum Theory as by Einstein's Relativity Theory. The so-called structural properties of the world with which hypotheses should deal are no more than the structural properties of the things composing the world. Consequently, the universal laws of nature turn out to be ''inherent'' in the individual things that are regulated by them.

   Popper seems to have been led to his nonessentialist view by his concept of an objective and autonomous world of language, mathematical and scientific theories, arguments, problem situations, et cetera, contained in libraries—the product, but independent, of man—by use of which knowledge and particularly scientific knowledge about things increases. This domain he terms "World 3" as opposed to "World 1" (the physical world) and "World 2" (the world of subjective ideas). "World 3" is merely "World 2" brought down into, and registered in, "World 1" of human minds and books. Popper's error in regard to "World 3" consists in the fact that this so-called objectified knowledge serving as the nongenetic, exosomatic "organs" of man, interacting with man and controlling his further evolution is not, as Popper believes, objectified knowledge without a knower (it has to be known in order to be used) nor autonomous (it cannot increase or decrease independently of human agency). Even if such knowledge is contained in libraries, it takes the human mind to activate it. If it were really autonomous it would smack of that animism that Popper seems to dislike so much. See Popper, op. cit., pp. 109, 111–20, 153–61.

5. And Karl Popper as well. See note 2.

6. Theological "heresies," as we have seen (Book Two, Section B, chapter 14) could arise in this manner. They are no more than divergent meanings or nuances arising from reinterpretations and/or transvaluations of a basic myth to suit different theological needs. Since there is often no possibility of complete agreement on an objective meaning through conciliar debates, nor of sense-empirical verification of meaning, there is really no a priori question of truth or error, right or wrong, orthodoxy or heterodoxy, involved. It is simply a matter of which meaning prevails in the long run. The surviving meaning becomes "orthodox" and "right," *ex posteriori*, by the very fact of the defeat of its rivals.

7. Aristotle, however, made what seems to have been the first effort to overcome the gulf that separated meaning and essence by stressing the role of experimentation in philosophy. However, his lasting contribution was the invention of the syllogism as an abbreviated, superior method to the Socratic dialectic (two) and dialogic (two or more) method of discussion for ironing out contradictions and arriving at consistent and meaningful positions. Even Aristotle could not overcome the gulf created by the traditional distinction between *thinker* and *doer* that was the hallmark of Greek philosophy and stamped the philosophy of Plato and his school. In this tradition the concept of the philosopher was that of thinker and of the slave that of doer who was, perforce, necessary in society in order to maintain the thinking activity of the philosopher by performing all the drudgery of society.

It was not until the sixteenth century that Francis Bacon introduced a systematic method for bridging the gulf between meaning and essence. But the social effect of the separation continued for centuries after, in the pernicious custom of slavery. Such is the power of ideas both when they are wrong and when they are right—as J. M. Keynes reminds us (*The General Theory of Employment, Interest and Money* (New York: Harcourt, Brace & Co., 1956, chapter 24, section V).

8. There is, of course, a vast practical difference between the objective-empirical and the objective-conventional. The empirical is that which is supported in intuitive and sense experience, the conventional that which is accepted by common agreement, whether empirically verifiable or not, like the various conventions of mathematics as expressed in symbols or the horological and calendrical conventions in regard to the measurement and recording of the passage of time. The one can exist without, or coexist with, the other. They coexist in the physical sciences; are mutually exclusive in the various theologies, these evincing no empiricism but only convention within each particular theology; and are nonexistent among all theologies taken together—neither empirical nor conventional.

287

9. This is a game at which Plato excelled in his account of the ideal state. (See his *Republic*.)

10. They may, however, in satirical or parabolic use, have oblique reference to the world of sense experience—e.g., Sir Thomas More's *Utopia*, the parables of Jesus in the New Testament, et cetera. Many outside–space-time worlds are created and celebrated in myth. All these may be legitimate to the extent that they seek to influence behavior, but not to the extent that they pretend to be goals in themselves—e.g., the myth of heaven and hell.

Chapter 2

Protology and Cosmogenesis

1. NATURE AND SCOPE OF
PROTOLOGY AND COSMOGENESIS

Protology is the study of first things. It postulates that all things and events, the cosmos itself, had an origin and will also have an end. It seeks to discover and interpret such an origin. Why the phenomenal world—things in general—should have a beginning and an end has never been answered satisfactorily by protologists. Since it is man who makes the assumption of origination of things and invents protology, it is natural to assume that ths entire field of speculation arises from a projection of the human paradigm of manifest beginning and ending of an *individual* human life onto the cosmos. A projection of the life of the *entire* human species onto the cosmos would, of course, raise doubts about the assumption of a beginning and an end of the cosmos, since it is not so obvious that the human species—myth and fable aside—had a beginning and will also have an end. But it may also be *assumed* that the human species had a beginning and will come to an end sometime in the future—in the same way that the human individual begins and ends. Thus what is true of the individual is assumed true of the species—a palpable non sequitur.[1] Similarly, then, the entire cosmos would go the way of the human species and the human individual. This may seem satisfactory, but only to the most ardent protologist; for while it is easier, though unnecessary, to base the fact of the beginning and ending of the human individual on a parallel assumption for the cosmos, it is more difficult to build an argument for a beginning and end of the cosmos on the *fact* of a beginning and end of the human individual.

No one, of course, is obliged to postulate, or accept the postulate of, an origination of the cosmos as a onetime affair or unique event. There is enough evidence, or lack of it, to cast doubt on the origination theory, and support the opposite view that the cosmos is exactly what it seems to be and as man has found it: an ongoing process of change without beginning or end, in which mankind finds itself inserted, somehow, along with everything else. But an Indo-Persian tradition shared by the ancient Greeks and a large part of mankind, both ancient and contemporary, has fostered a prejudice of distrust of the evidence of the senses, except insofar as concerns the pattern of individual human life, regarding which there is a certain ambiguity, and the life of other animals regarding which there is a clear contradiction. Thus the evidence of the senses is regarded as untrustworthy as to the reality and nature of things. Yet, on the one hand, the physical finiteness of human beings is accepted while, on the other hand, the Indo-Persian tradition postulates a postmortem continuation of man, with Hinduism espousing a series of phenomenal existences for man ending with ultimate extinction and merging with the amorphous World Soul. Thus devotees of the orphic rites deriving from the Dionysian cult—a group that included Socrates and the Stoics—as well as Christians have rejected the physical end of man as final, replacing it with an infinitely continuing phase of soul or spiritual body. So attached is man to his corpus. Yet many of these same believers would deny this continuity after death to nonhuman animals—so anthropocentric are they in their belief. Similarly, the possibility of an infinitely continuing cosmos is ruled out.

Protological theories fall into two types: (1) secular and (2) theological. The secular theories are represented today by astrophysical theories of cosmic origination (cosmogeny)—chiefly, the big bang, continuous creation, and oscillation theories. The theological theories, of various kinds, share in common the assumption of divine origin of the cosmos. According to this assumption, a god or gods, whose characteristics and comportment are more or less those of human beings, gave a start to the cosmos. None of the existing cosmological theories is protological, in a strict sense: the secular theories do not explain the origin of matter (mass and energy); of the theological theories one only—the biblical account of the Book of Genesis—pretends to do so, as will shortly appear.

Any satisfactory theory of the origin of the cosmos must account for or interpret the origin or presence of matter in the cosmos. Current cosmological theories of the secular variety are not theories of the origin of matter, but of the evolution of the *structural pattern* or order of the cosmos. Christian theological cosmology often described as divine creation *ex nihilo* (Genesis 1 and 2) is billed as creation by the magic word or myth, by a mere fiat: "Let there be . . . and there was . . ." But this myth of so-called *creatio ex nihilo* is apparently a misunderstanding or misinterpretation of the Genesis account, which, however, makes no mention of creation out of nothing and is similar in type to the cosmology of Plato.

The basis for this view rests, prima facie, on the fact that Judaism, which recorded the myth, does not describe creation as *ex nihilo*. There is other evidence, however. In the Genesis account the fiat "Let there be . . ." is often accompanied by a subsequent act of creation ("And God made . . ."). This would seem to indicate that the fiat is less a magic formula than a declaration of intention to create, mold, or form the intended object or species out of *something* already existent. What that is, is not stated in the case of the heaven and the earth (Genesis 1:1), light in general (Genesis 1:3) and the lights in the firmament (Genesis 1:16), but it is clearly stated or implied in the case of other things: grass, herb, trees, and seed are transformed out of the earth (Genesis 1:11–12), marine life out of the seas (Genesis 1:20–21), land animals out of the earth (Genesis 1:24–25), and man among them (Genesis 1:26–27, 2:7). Even if we accept the alternative account that Eve came out of Adam's rib (Genesis 2:21–25), for the sake of indulging male chauvinist superiority, it is still established that Eve came out of *something*, not out of nothing. The fact that the matter or component of the celestial bodies is not stated is not evidence that they were made *ex nihilo*. On the contrary, it is likely that the Genesis story, which was borrowed by Judaism from Near Eastern (Mesopotamian and Egyptian)[2] sources similar to those used by Plato in the *Timaeus*, was an adaptation that cut out references to matter, form, and the demiurge, in order to suit the Jewish prejudice in favor of the primacy of Jahweh, their tribal god. This gave Jahweh, in Genesis, the look of a magician who brought things into existence by simple fiat. But only a superficial reading that overlooks that nothing materialized from the fiat without an *act* of creation would mistake the account (as did the Christians) for *creatio ex nihilo*.

Another evidence of the kinship of the Genesis story with Plato's cosmology based on the metaphysical elements of God, the forms and matter, is clearly indicated by the fact that the creationist account in Genesis deals with archetypes—original fixed and final types—that recall Plato's forms or ideas as the inspiration of the images or semblances given to the various species. Even man seems to be made, not in God's form or archetype, but in an "image" or "likeness (i.e., "copy of a copy") of God's form (Genesis 1:26–27). A defense of the creationist myth in Genesis thus turns out to be a defense, not of creation *ex nihilo* but of Plato's cosmology as set out in his dialogue, *Timaeus*—or a cosmology very similar to it.

Be all this as it may, the creationist account in Genesis is unsatisfactory from the viewpoint of a thoroughgoing cosmogenetic theory, if such a theory is supposed to account for the origin of matter—a point not touched upon by the Genesis account or by Plato's account. The point is left open, rather than implied, by the creation *ex nihilo* interpretation, if only for the very fact that "nothing" is not an empirical concept—it is not given in human experience, for if it were it would be "something." Even if we were to accept "God" unquestioningly as the creator of matter (instead of as originator of the cosmos—ordered matter—and one of Plato's metaphysical elements) in order to start somewhere and escape the slide into infinite regression[3] or, more likely, a vicious circle, there is still the difficult postulate of fixed and final species *ab initio:* a postulate that has been effectively challenged by evolutionary theory, both on the theological right by Irenaeus, Bishop of Lyons (130–202 C.E.), and on the secular left by the naturalist, Charles Darwin (1809–82). According to Irenaeus, human history is one of moral progression from immaturity to perfection, thereby implying that man's goodness at creation was physical but not moral.[4] Darwin, on the other hand, satisfactorily demonstrated—though without incontrovertible proof, since the various phyla of different species, especially man, could not be traced—that man as well as other biological species is the product of the evolutionary forces of genetic mutation and environmental adaptation. Consequently, there were, are, and will be no fixed or final species over time.[5]

For all the foregoing reasons—not the least being its involvement in infinite regression or a vicious circle—the Christian doctrine of creation *ex nihilo* is unsatisfactory and untenable. Consequently, it has been until now more satisfactory to assume that the origin of matter, hence of the cosmos (as distinct from the evolution of the ordered structural pattern of the cosmos), is unaccountable—in short, that it has no beginning and no end. This assumption is not new, but dates back to antiquity. It was the starting point of reflection on the cosmos by many ancient peoples, including the Greeks, who simply started with certain existential elements as given—matter among them—and developed their cosmology from there on. This is still the best and only possible approach today.

We must, therefore, conclude that there does not exist at the present time, and never has existed, any viable protological theory in the sense of a theory explaining or demonstrating the *origin* of things, in particular, matter (mass-energy). Consequently, the term *protology* as interpreted from this point on will not be in its strict sense of "the origin of first things" (as opposed to eschatology, "the last things") but only in the sense of the genesis or formation of the ordered structure of the universe, that is, in the conventional sense of cosmogenesis, which term will be substituted henceforth for protology.

As we shall see subsequently, secular and theological cosmogenetic theories lead inevitably to the process view and interpretation of the cosmos. The big bang and steady state astrophysical theories of the cosmos seem to fit conveniently into the more general and comprehensive oscillation theory of cosmic process. The oscillation theory is based on a metaphysical system, the general elements of which have been explored considerably by modern nuclear physics. But this seems only the beginning of a labyrinthine journey. On the other hand, starting from an anthropocentric and anthropomorphic theological cosmogenetic theory and generalizing this theory across the biological spectrum also leads us, logically and inevitably, to a process view and interpretation of the cosmos.[6] And so we progress from secular and theological cosmogenesis to a nuclear-based metaphysics that itself is in the process of evolution.

2. SECULAR COSMOGENESIS: ASTROPHYSICAL THEORIES[7]

There are three major contemporary theories of cosmogenesis advanced by astronomers and astrophysicists: Big Bang and Continuous Expansion, Continuous Creation or Steady State, and the Oscillation or Pulsation Theory of the cosmos. The third is the most comprehensive theory of structural formation of the cosmos.

A. THE BIG BANG AND CONTINUOUS EXPANSION THEORY

This theory postulates that all the matter in the cosmos was concentrated at one time in a very small volume, and that at a precise point in time—estimated at some 15 billion years ago—a violent explosion or "big bang" occurred, for "unknown and still mysterious reasons," which hurled fragments of matter in all directions. From these fragments, which have continued to travel at dizzying speeds, have been formed, and continue to be formed, the billions of galaxies, including the Milky Way, in which our own solar system is situated. Observations and calculations made in the laboratories and observatories of the world are held to have confirmed this theory.[8]

Hubble and the Bubble Expansion Theory of the Cosmos (1923)

California astronomer, Edwin Hubble, discovered in 1923 that the Andromeda Nebula was a galaxy independent of the Milky Way. Applying the Doppler-Fizeau Effect[9] to his discovery, Hubble observed that the lines of the spectrum of this and other galaxies were shifted toward the red end of the spectrum, thus indicating that they were fleeing away in every direction from our Milky Way and the earth at continuously increasing speeds but at a constant rate of acceleration. He concluded that the cosmos was expanding at more or less the same rate. This finding also implied that the matter of space is finite in quantity, though growing enormously like a balloon or bubble as it expands.

Penzias and Wilson and the Discovery
of Low Cosmic Thermal Radiation (1965)

The big bang theory states that the cosmic explosion generated, or was accompanied by, excessively high temperatures that, it predicted, would be followed by a period of cooling. This cooling, despite the lapse of 15 billion years, would leave some residue of the original heat even at the present time.

The discovery in 1965, by Arno Penzias and Robert Wilson of Bell Laboratories, of cosmic radio noise corresponding to a thermal radiation of 3° Kelvin or 5.4°F above absolute zero—the point at which there is no molecular motion and no heat—was thought to have clinched this prediction, the discovered temperature being almost exactly that predicted by the theory, and to have furnished further confirmation of the theory of an expanding cosmos.

B. CONTINUOUS CREATION OR STEADY STATE THEORY: FRED HOYLE, HERMANN BONDI, AND THOMAS GOLD (1948)

This theory assumes the opposite of the Hubble theory, namely, that the cosmos is eternal and infinite, without beginning and without end in space or time; that the cosmos is eternally homogeneous and stationary; that the galaxies expand into nothingness, being replaced by new matter, which is continuously created everywhere.

The theory has had short shrift from subsequent astrophysical discoveries, which have all tended either to confirm the big bang theory or to be not inconsistent with it.

C. OSCILLATION OR PULSATION THEORY OF THE COSMOS

This is the latest cosmological theory arising from speculation about the future velocity of the expanding cosmos in the context of the big bang theory. If this velocity should remain constant, then the cosmic order would be a phenomenon that had a beginning but no end, expanding to infinity. If, however, it should slow down then, eventually, gravitational forces would slow the expansion to a halt and reverse it. The cosmos would have reached the limit of its expansion at zero velocity and then begin to contract back to the original situation where matter would be compressed into a small volume, from which another big bang would trigger another expansion, thus repeating the process of expansion and contraction in an infinite series of big bangs and oscillations.[10]

Thus the single big bang version of an infinitely expanding and eternal cosmos is replaced with a finite and oscillating cosmos with numberless big bangs.

Black Holes

Astrophysicists had predicted that as large stars, larger than our sun, burn out and use up their hydrogen fuel, their colossal mass would compress into tiny spheres of infinite density and gravitational force—so-called back holes—which would trap light and prevent it from escaping from their gravitational field. The discovery by satellite, in 1971 and since, of areas in the cosmos from which X rays (which cannot be detected except from space) stream out continuously has been interpreted as indicating and confirming the existence of these black holes. The black holes are supposed to account for the large amount of missing cosmic mass represented by the difference between the calculated total mass and the observed mass of the cosmos. It is also thought that they may well represent the fate of all the galaxies and individual stars in the cosmos. Eventually, the cosmos would be compressed into an enormous black hole from which another big bang would ensue.[11] Thus, again, we come full circle: black hole—big bang (big burst or Heraclitean big burn)—expansion—halt—contraction—black hole. And so on, ad infinitum.

The most important conclusion deriving from the oscillation theory, assuming its validity, is that we can never know how many big bangs and oscillations had already occurred prior to the last one, which is said to have occurred some 15 billion years ago. Consequently, we can never know if and when the cosmogenetic process ever had a beginning, even if every cosmos had a commencement and terminal phase represented, respectively, by big bang and black hole. Even if the present cosmos runs down at the end of its term (as predicted by Newton's Third Law of Entropy and the oscillation theory) this would not be the end of the story.

We end, therefore, with a continuous process theory of cosmogenesis and metaphysics and an eternally self-renewing cosmos, without beginning and without end.

3. DIVINE COSMOGENESIS: THEOLOGY

Theology, as a special kind of cosmogenetic theory, postulates not only that everything has an origin but that the origin is divine—in short, a god or gods. The term *god* has been variously conceived and defined. Some of the main concepts will be examined in a subsequent section, later in this chapter. For the time being we content ourselves with the fact that all the concepts share in common the idea of an agent, a creative agent that *makes* things and *does* things, originates entities and events. A good example of the concept is the demiurge—Plato's artificer-god. All god-concepts are just that: concepts, without empirical content—with the exception of those definitions that identify the concept with specific natural forces, such as wind, fire, water, et cetera. But such naturalistic concepts of god fall in a different category, outside the realm of cosmogenesis, in that they do not claim to be the origin of anything but are themselves made by a prior and older god. They are themselves part of what cosmogenesis seeks to account for or interpret. Consequently, it was generally accepted as one of the ground rules that the postulated originator of anything must not be a part of that thing, but separate from and outside it. Nor could it be of the same type as any of the things that it originates lest it fail to be an adequate interpretation of those things. For all these reasons and more,[12] the god-concept has generally remained little more than a concept, with no empirical content. By contrast, it has always been the empirical—the phenomenal, material world—whose origin has to be accounted for. It thus came to be generally accepted that the originator of the empirical world, of the cosmos, must be nonempirical; that is, it must remain purely conceptual.

A term like *god* (or *God*) is not meaningless, simply because it may not have empirical content, provided it has enough conceptual content agreed upon by any group or groups using the term. For example, we may take the terms *phoenix* and *sphinx*, respectively legendary bird and monster, with precise description but no empirical equivalent; or, again, the concept of "nonbeing" or "nothingness," clear enough in meaning but with no empirical content since this concept is not given in or open to human experience.

Thus theology is one of those disciplines, like mathematics, that have only conceptual content (mostly supplied from characteristics or qualities drawn from the empirical world) but whose object of study, "God" or "god," cannot be identified empirically as a phenomenal entity possessing its stated qualities. Indeed, the ground rules of origination of the phenomenal world, as we have seen, require that no such empirical entity exist.

God, the originator of the cosmos, is therefore a concept replete with characteristics or qualities whose number, nature, and combination distinguish one definition of God from another and, therefore, one God from another God.

A. THE THEOLOGY OF THE PHILOSOPHERS

Plato's Imitation Theory of Creation

God, keeping an eye on its pure form, "creates" or molds the demiurge out of matter, imitating the outline of its pure form. The demiurge, in turn, keeping his eye on the various other forms, molds various objects in matter, imitating the outlines of the various forms or patterns. Plato's "creationist" theory was thus an "imitation" theory of creation. At least, this was what Plato intended it to be. In fact, however, it fell short of being a thoroughgoing imitation theory, as can be seen from what Plato actually achieved:
(a) God and the archetypal forms were on one side (suprasensible), matter on the other (sensible).
(b) The archetypal forms merely served as patterns, imitations, semblances, or poor copies of which were what was actually incorporated in the molded or "formed" objects.
(c) The separation between God and forms, on the one hand, and matter, on the other, was breached by God molding matter for the production of the demiurge. God thus constituted a link or contact point between the suprasensible world of forms and the sensible world of matter, a link continued by the demiurge in a proxy capacity.

The "creationist" act by God in molding the demiurge made nonsense of the distinction as well as the separation between the suprasensible and sensible worlds. And Plato's theory was no longer the "imitation" theory it was supposed to be since, with the direct link through God, it was a matter of an archetypal form molding matter directly; so that there was no more reason why the perfect form, instead of an imitation of it, should not be reproduced in matter. For God, being perfection itself, could not "create" or *mold* something in less than the perfection of its archetypal form. This follows from Plato's own reason for the creation of the phenomenal world by God; namely, that God was goodness itself and that it was the nature of goodness to overflow into the creation of things as good as itself.

297

Aristotle set out to repair the damage done by this contradiction to Plato's theory of the forms, the suprasensible and sensible worlds, and the imitation theory of creation. With the aim of producing a thoroughgoing imitation theory, he thought it logical that imitation should be a self-directing activity (that is, an autonomous activity) on the part of matter, not on the part of God. God did not have to *do* anything but just *be* himself: perfect form, thought or reason in love with, and contemplation of, himself (like any self-respecting Greek philosopher). Other forms should also be their own perfect selves, while matter sought to imitate God and the forms, striving to reproduce their patterns in itself—both the form of the demiurge as well as the forms of the phenomenal objects in the cosmos.

First, Aristotle, in what appears to anticipate William of Occam's rule of economy, combined God and the forms so that God thought out the forms that thereby became the pure thoughts of God. Thus God contained all the forms in himself, becoming a collective super-Form, the Form that contained all forms, the Form of forms. In effect, Aristotle reduced the basic metaphysical elements from Plato's three (God, forms, and matter) to two (form-containing God and matter).[13]

In order for matter to imitate form, it was necessary that it be endowed with the *capacity* to imitate. That is to say, it had to have some intelligence—the same intelligence by means of which God and the demiurge perceived the patterns of the forms—as well as the ability or desire to imitate the forms. In short, matter had to have some of the *mind* of God as well as the *desire* to imitate. These two qualities were incorporated in a single mechanism, the soul, which was part mind or reason (the divine element) and part appetite or desire (the material element); appetite or desire in the case of zoological entities and vegetativeness in the case of botanical entities.

Second, therefore, Aristotle endowed matter with soul, a mechanism attached to matter by means of appetite or vegetativeness and containing the divine (that is, the intelligent and perceptive) element of mind that was an immortal element. Appetite or vegetativeness, being material, decomposed along with matter at the death or dissolution of the human being, mind (a simple, noncomposite element) remaining intact and integral and liberated to join the divine mind.

Aristotle's imitation theory of creation, unlike Plato's, which was based on goodness, was now based on love: the attractive power of the condescending and sharing love (agape) of God attracting matter to become like God and the forms of his thought and the aspiring or seeking love (eros) of matter fueled by its appetite or vegetativeness to strive to become like, and incorporate, the perfection of God and the forms. This striving was called *nisus*.

In this manner, Aristotle propounded a more logical imitation theory of creation than Plato, achieving the following results:

(a) two metaphysical elements: God-incorporated archetypal forms on one side (suprasensible), matter on the other (sensible);
(b) a unidirectional attractive-seeking force (love) motivating matter to imitate and incorporate semblances of the pure forms in itself;
(c) the abolition of the separation between God and the forms, on the one hand, and matter, on the other, through the incorporation of mind in soul and the attachment of soul through its appetite or vegetativeness to matter. Mind thus became the link between matter and God.

The link constituted by mind between matter and God in Aristotle's system of imitative creation had the same effect as the action of God in creating the demiurge in Plato's system of imitative creation: both made nonsense of the distinction, as well as the separation, between the suprasensible and sensible worlds. This put Aristotle's imitative creation theory in jeopardy since, with mind (a perfect element in God) being incorporated also in matter, there is no logical reason why perfect forms (rather than poor semblances of them) should not be reproduced in matter; and especially so since mind brought matter within the ambit of God's perfection in both his self-knowledge and his love.

It may be concluded, therefore, that the Plato-Aristotle imitation theory of creation is inconsistent with their doctrine of the two separate worlds of mind and matter since, in effect, it turns out that there is only one composite world closely linked by the element of mind (or God). This is not surprising, considering that the metaphysical elements are assumed to be coetaneous and eternal. Any attempt to place them in separate worlds, as Socrates, Plato, and Aristotle did, is likely to be both artificial and arbitrary. This is, undoubtedly, a result of the fact that this philosophic trio were attempting the difficult task of incorporating the Indo-Persian religio-theological doctrine of two worlds (nirvana and maya, Light and Darkness) into their metaphysical system: a doctrine that was likely to prove indigestible. For theology and metaphysics have different perspectives; theology being concerned with the *divine origin* of being, while metaphysics is concerned with the *elements* of being and the process of *becoming*. Failure to distinguish between these two perspectives led to their being utterly confounded, the one with the other.

Indeed, *theology* and *metaphysics* were employed as equivalent terminology in Aristotle's philosophical system.

There is no way that a two-world theology can be married to a one-world metaphysics. Socrates, Plato, and Aristotle were unable to overcome the contradiction between the two disciplines, and the one-world metaphysics gained the upper hand, in spite of their theological predilections. Occidental philosophers of a later age who adopted the Platonian tradition of confusing metaphysics with theology, and regarding metaphyics as being concerned with a suprasensible world of God and the forms and utterly unconnected with events in the phenomenal or sensible world, merely continued to perpetrate the errors of their predecessors.[14] For there is no world of metaphysics separate and unconnected with the phenomenal world. There is only one metaphysical world, the phenomenal world of change.

B. THE THEOLOGY OF THE DIVINES

All attempts hitherto—that is, until the twentieth century—at inquiring into the *origin* of things have proved incapable of surmounting the hurdle of species-centrism. Consequently, the origin of things has been interpreted until now in hominoid or anthropomorphic terms, just as it would, undoubtedly, be interpreted in theriomorphic terms if the inquiry was being conducted by nonhuman animals—as Xenophanes pointed out ages ago.[15] In the case of the human species, the anthropomorphic male god (deus faber = homo faber) who originates (i.e., creates) the cosmos is conceived as either "wholly other," absolutely separate from its creation (transcendent) or incarnated in its creation (immanent), or both. Eventually, the inquiry ends, logically, in each species (the part) creating the cosmos (the whole).

Summing up—or generalizing—the individual creative effort of each species yields the altogether striking, but totally different, result that the whole generates itself through its parts. In other words, the cosmos, God, or whatever name one chooses to designate the totality of all that exists, is self-creating; in the apt words of the Creed of Saint Athanasius, it is "nor created, nor begotten but proceeding,"[16] that is, a self-generating process. Thus the question of *origin* of existence or existent things resolves itself, through a generalization of the species-centric creationist approach, into a matter of process—a self-generating process. It implies that a species-centred or zoomorphic creationist theology of the cosmos is acceptable only as a partial or first approximation to the genesis of the cosmos and must eventually yield place to a process theory of the cosmos.

300

Theology, that is to say, must yield eventually to process metaphysics. This conclusion remained hidden from the early Church Fathers, as it still does to modern advocates of the creationist theory of the cosmos.

Immersed in anthropology, the early Church Fathers could not grasp the fact that separating their man-god from the rest of the cosmos was an illusion resulting from their partial approach to the problem of cosmogenesis. Failure to generalize their approach on a zootheological basis—understandably, because of their anthropocentrism—prevented them from recognizing that the cosmos was, indeed, the self-generating or "proceeding" God that they sought. Because of this methodological defect they unknowingly attacked the very result they sought as atheism or pantheism when it was presented to them through other routes of inquiry. By these various other routes, pursued since antiquity—by hylozoists or animists of all time (a living cosmos), by Thales ("the world is full of gods"), by the atomist philosophers, Democritus, Leucippus, and Lucretius (the atom is the basic ingredient of the cosmos) and their modern offspring, by Feuerbach (humanism, i.e., "man is the god of man"), and by Karl Marx (materialism)—had been foreshadowed the very result (process metaphysics) that the Church Fathers intuited, but failed to fully recognize, in their credal formulations under the leadership of Athanasius around 400 C.E.

The Creed of Saint Athanasius foreshadowed the demise of classical zoomorphic (but especially anthropomorphic) theology as an inquiry into the *origin* of things through its absorption and replacement by process metaphysics as the science of becoming: indeed, Aristotle had used the term *theology* as equivalent to, and interchangeable with, *metaphysics* without being fully aware of the difference between the two or the process by which the one became absorbed into the other. In the light of the discussion in the preceding paragraphs, it would seem a waste of time to continue henceforth the pursuit of theology as traditionally and currently conceived and executed.

Not without good reason, therefore, given a tradition of brilliant thinkers such as Xenophanes, did the Greek philosophers from Plato on eschew the ancient theriomorphic and anthropomorphic approach to theology—an approach that had marked both Greek and other religions before their time. They, wisely, decided to start their investigations into the world of existent things by taking as data preexistent matter (space), forms, and God (a super-Form containing all forms, according to Aristotle), without inquiring into the unprofitable question of origin of their preexistent elements.[17] They had, no doubt, discovered that such an inquiry would start a train of infinite regression—a sure sign that the question of origin was a wrong or inappropriate one. Rather did they emphasize change and becoming as an ongoing and unending process, using the god-concept as a device for preventing the investigation from degenerating or backsliding into the profitless path of infinite regression.[18]

The myth of big bang and oscillation with which modern physicists and astrophysicists start their investigation into the existential process serves them in exactly the same way as the myth of God and the demiurge served Plato in his similar inquiry: these myths enable their proponents to skirt the path of infinite regression. Unless, therefore, one is prepared, like the Greek philosophers from Plato on, to talk about a preexistent cosmos-god as merely another name for the dynamic principle of continuing change and becoming that is metaphysics, all preoccupation with theology in its traditional form is unproductive. But regarded in its proper empirical status as metaphysics (in the Aristotelian sense of what follows after, and is based on, physics), there is nothing that theology can disclose to us that metaphysics cannot reveal as a study of the various modes and relationships of being and becoming within the cosmos.

C. THE GOD OF THE PHILOSOPHERS AND THE GOD OF ABRAHAM, ISAAC, AND JACOB

The philosophers' God, as interpreted by Plato and Aristotle, knows and loves no one but himself; as he is all-perfect and self-subsisting, there is nothing outside of himself that he lacks and to which he would aspire. He fashions or molds preexistent matter because his overflowing goodness leads him to fashion things that would be as good as himself. He does this, according to Plato, not directly but by proxy through a demiurge, an artificer-god that he creates (i.e., fashions) specifically for that purpose. The process is then continued on a self-sustaining basis by biological reproduction on the part of living organisms.

According to Aristotle, the philosophers' God is pure thought thinking itself, pure reason or intelligence. His relationship with man is indirect, through man's sharing or participation in the divine intelligence (Greek = *nous*). Through this participation, man comes within the circle of God's self-knowledge and self-love. Man, being imperfect, aspires to become like God, who is perfection itself. His love of God is thus an aspiring and seeking love (eros) whereas, insofar as man comes within its ambit, God's love is a condescending love (agape) of something that is good and proper for its allotted function and in its proper place.

The philosophers' God, moreover, was originally a tribal God of the Greeks but became more or less universal with the spread of Greek and, subsequently, Roman, colonial power, culture, and civilization.

302

The God of Abraham, Isaac, and Jacob—Jahweh—was originally, like the philosophers' God, a tribal God—in this case, of the Jews. His presumed acts in history were interpreted by Jews as evidence of a special relationship with the Jewish tribes of Israel: a relationship of salvation from Egyptian slavery because of his special love for this, his special people. Jahweh loved the Jews and, proxywise through them, the rest of the human race—at a price: the price of conversion to the theology and religion of Judaism (as enshrined in its Law and Prophets), and to ethnic Jewishness as required by the rites of circumcision and the observance of Jewish dietary laws.

Israel—on its own admission—was a stiff-necked people, periodically falling out of favor with Jahweh, who chastised them by handing them over to their enemies and into exile. They, nevertheless, did not forfeit the special love of Jahweh, not because they were more righteous than their enemies but, supposedly, because these were more wicked. In the end—at the last day of judgment—everything would be made right: Israel's enemies would be punished and Israel restored to its special place of honor at Jahweh's right hand—a very beguiling and self-serving myth.

The Christians, followers of the sect of Jesus of Nazareth, extended the special relationship of Jahweh with the Jews directly to the rest of the human race, the non-Jews or Gentiles—at a price: the price of faith in, and acceptance of, the super-Jew, Jesus, as the Son of God as well as the incarnation of Jahweh himself. This faith converts non-Jews into spiritual Jews through its circumcision of their hearts, not ethnic Jews through the circumcision of their foreskins. (Women, as always, were by implication taken along with their men since, according to Jewish-Christian myth, they were but ribs of man. But even they, according to Paul, needed conversion to the faith.) In the view of the non-Jerusalem Jewish apostles of Christianity (like Paul) and the Gentile Apostles, this faith did not require the supporting works of the Jewish Law (Torah). But the Jewish Christian apostles (like James) thought it did.

On a superficial view, therefore, one may conclude that the philosophers' God had transcended the naturalistic and anthropomorphic stage of early Greek religion and theology, while that of the Jews continued in that stage.

D. SOME CONCEPTS AND DOCTRINES OF GOD:
A SUMMARY VIEW

(a) Concepts of God

This is not a wide-ranging review of theological doctrines. Rather is it a brief examination of some major approaches to the concept and doctrine of God with which the author, by reason of previous exposure, is acquainted. These various approaches revolve around the single criterion of *knowledge* (or its absence, *ignorance*), that is, whether or not God can be known. Although the issue presumes some *concept* of God, the question of *knowledge* of God is not dependent thereon. This is because knowledge of God, even when defined in terms of *experience*, has never meant *direct*, but only *indirect*, experience through a third party or an analogy based on such indirect experience. Consequently, in the absence of direct experience, there has never been formulated an empirical definition of God

To take, first, the matter of concept, this resolves into the simple issue of whether or not God can be conceived. Judaism and Islam answer in the negative: God cannot be conceived. They go further to forbid any attempt to develop a concept of God, as evident in the interdiction of any graven image or other representation of God. God not only *cannot* be conceived by also *should not* be conceived. Judaism, in the beginning, went even beyond this to forbid any name of God—a logical requirement in that if God could (should) not be conceived, God could (should) not be named. This interdiction was based on the superstitious fear that anything that could be conceived could be named, and anything that could be named could be manipulated or controlled—presumably, like a pet dog. Superstition aside, however, it is a fact that naming and conception go hand in hand and that naming opens the floodgates of interpretation—something Jewish rabbis are traditionally good at—which would consequently rob any concept of a desired *unique* meaning. In the event, even Judaism had to bow to reality. There was no way an interdiction of conceptualization and naming of God could be made to stick. So Judaism, like Islam, fell back on (a) analogy as an acceptable means of circumventing direct conceptualization and (b) emphasis on the inadequacy of any analogical description of God. Consequently, depiction of such analogy in any shape or form as a representation of God was forbidden.

Christianity, an offshoot of Judaism, has, by contrast, succumbed to analogical representation of God, in the form of icons in the Roman Catholic Church and Eastern Orthodox Church. Islam, an offshoot of both Christianity and Judaism, has succumbed, similarly, as it spread eastward to India and the frontiers of China.

African theology has made an accommodation similar to that of Semitic theology. Traditional African theological doctrine holds that God is so far removed from man as to be inconceivable. Nevertheless, while in no way forbidding any attempt at direct conceptualization, it welcomes the use of analogy or indirect conceptualization, for God. Thus analogy plays an important role in Semitic and African theology: God is (like) the creator of the cosmos, (like) the sustainer of the universe, (like) the father of all mankind, et cetera. Analogy eventually becomes metaphor as theological doctrine ends up concentrating on the functions and attributes of an analogical God; God then becomes *the* creator, sustainer of the cosmos, *the* father of mankind who provides for its sustenance, et cetera.

Oriental, especially Hindu, theology is not only replete with multiple divinities but with direct conceptions and representations of such divinities as well as of their functions and attributes. In this type of theology there is free rein for the imagination, in the same tradition as ancient Greek and Roman theology.

Passing on to the criterion of knowledge, all theologies are fairly well agreed on one thing: the impossibility of *direct* knowledge of God. This tenet was the central pillar of Gnosticism, which, unlike other theologies, did not admit of even *indirect* knowledge of God. Thus Gnostic knowledge of God was knowledge of man's ignorance of God as well as of the unknowability and incomprehensibility of God. It was the unknown—and unknowable—God of the Gnostics that was the subject of the inscription on Mars's Hill at the Areopagus or supreme tribunal of Athens, whose members Paul sought to convert to Christianity.[19] The God of the Greek philosophers was, basically, a Gnostic type—intelligible but unknown to man, just as man was unknown to him. Aristotle's God was pure thought without matter, who neither knew nor loved anything—man included—but himself, and this notwithstanding that man was brought within the ambit of God's self-knowledge by sharing the divine intelligence (mind). Man and God were mutual unknowns. The God of Socrates whose voice, he claimed, spoke to him on occasion to discourage him from certain courses of action was indirectly knowable through self-knowledge, as advised by the inscription of the Delphic Oracle: Know Thyself. A God known to man through man—a position very similar to that adopted by Christianity several centuries later.

The God of the Jews, Jahweh, was directly unknown but, supposedly, indirectly known in history through Jewish experience interpreted as divine history. Thus the history of Israel since the Exodus was interpreted as the history of a people known, loved, and liberated by God—divine history. God was known in and through Israel. Other Semitic Gods are similar. The God of Christians is known to them in and through the person of the man Jesus Christ (subsequently deified by Gentile converts). Like the Hebrew God, the Christian God knows, loves, and liberates Christians through their deliverer, Jesus—a latter-day Moses. Like Moses to the Jews, Muhammad, the Messenger of the Arab God, Allah, declares him to the Arabs, Allah is known indirectly to man through the witness of Muhammad, his Prophet and Messenger.

305

The closest Hindu theology comes to experiencing God is through the experience of mysticism that foreshadows the merging of the individual human spirit (Atman) with the world spirit (Brahma). This experience is supposedly open to ascetics, holy hermits, and other mystic types. Since it is an ineffable experience, little can be known or said about it.

In none of these theologies is God directly known to, or experienced by, man. God remains a concept by analogy and nonempirical.

(b) Types of Theology[20]

Theology, in simple language, is the doctrine about god; that is, in conventional terms, the doctrine about a superior, all-powerful being. Various types of theology may be identified and classed into four main types: investive (or investitive), agnostic, synecdochic, and scientific.

Investive (or Investitive) Theology. The earliest known type of theology is the investive kind. In this brand of theology some simple or composite animal is invested with all the attributes of divinity (e.g., power, source of light and life, goodness, wisdom, et cetera) and accorded all the devotion due it in these respects. Thus the ancient Egyptians had their sun-god, Ra, which was regarded as a kind of planetary animal having the head of a hawk and wearing a solar disk as a crown; various therianthropic (or composite animal = man + other animal) divinities—a tradition also shared by the ancient Greeks—such as different types of sphinxes, satyrs, centaurs, et cetera, as well as various theriomorphic (zoomorphic)—or simple animal—divinities, also shared by the ancient Greeks.[21]

Investive theology combines concept and empirical form, even though the form may be an unnatural mix such as the therianthropic forms of human invention. A subspecies of investive theology of the simple zoomorphic type was confined to the human being, male as well as female. It developed, and was widespread, in the ancient world of Sumer, Babylon, Egypt, Greece, and the oriental reaches of the Roman Empire. According to this special brand of zootheism, known as anthropotheism, outstanding individuals—heroes, founders of tribal groups, distinguished military figures, et cetera—were deified, that is to say, they were credited with some putative divine paternity, hence invested with some or all of the conceptual attributes of divinity. The entire Greek pantheon was of this type. The genre was raised to the level of statecraft by the Romans, who deified their Caesars.[22]

Agnostic Theology. While the ancient Greeks and their city-states engaged in investive theology, combining both concept and empirical form, their philosophers did the opposite: they disinvested theology of empirical

306

form, confining it to a mere concept or idea. Their God was a mere idea without any empirical content, but determining the empirical shape and content of all phenomenal objects. It was the *master idea* that spawned and contained all the various ideas associated with empirical objects, the First Cause and Prime Mover of the world of things. In empirical terms, therefore, the God of the ancient Greek philosophers could not be known—only intuited, that is, understood intelligibly. Their type of theology may be designated *agnostic* theology. They did not know for sure, by experience, whether God existed or not; they merely postulated his existence, conceptually. Although the Hindus portrayed their various gods in human guise, even they had no empirical equivalent for their greatest god of all, the world spirit or Brahma.

The ancient Israelites, likewise, never got beyond the conceptual stage of divinity, and they feared symbolism because they thought it carried the risk of being mistaken for the empirical reality, rather than being properly regarded for what it is, namely, something pointing beyond itself to *something else*—to use Paul Tillich's apt characterization of the nature of symbols and symbolism.[23] They had not discovered that *something else*, namely, the appropriate corresponding empirical reality for their conceptual God. Thus any symbol, even the most useful, could be only a partial representation, hence, inadequate. Besides, it carried the risk of synecdochic confusion, for since the whole was unknown, there was a danger that the part might be mistaken for the unknown whole. The main part of their caution was that they had not only *not* discovered the empirical counterpart to their conceptual God, but also despaired of *ever* finding such a counterpart.[24] They therefore, wisely, decided to leave their God at the conceptual stage,[25] in which they emphasized only the (necessarily infinite) qualities of their concept. Their leader, Moses, went even further to denounce and forbid any form of symbolic representation of their God.

This brand of timid or cautionary theology also falls under the rubric of agnostic theology. The Christians as well as the Moslems followed in the footsteps of the ancient Israelites. In this respect, therefore, Semitic monotheism was no different from that of the ancient Greek philosophers. African theology, as indicated earlier, is even stricter than Semitic theology in denying both conceptual and empirical content to its God, beyond the vague assertion that God is creator and sustainer of the cosmos.
Synecdochic (or Symbolic) Theology. Modern Christian theologians, however, boldly accept and emphasize the utility—even the need—of a symbolic crutch, being careful to emphasize at the same time that it points beyond itself. They accept the risk of acknowledging their ignorance of what it points *toward*. They grasp at what they consider the unknown

part—euphemistically called the "revelation,"[26] whether burning bush, shekinah, Jesus, et cetera—for want of the unknown whole. They also rationalize the crutch or symbol—ikon, prayer beads, et cetera—as an aid to concentrating the attention or devotion of the faithful, which would otherwise tend to wander.

Modern Christian theology (now identical with Christology) has evolved into an eclectic mix of investive, agnostic, and synecdochic elements: investive from its Greek contribution, agnostic from its Judaic-Hebrew (Samaritan) origins,[27] and synecdochic, from its Roman Catholic heritage. Symbolism was ever present in ancient Judaism, to be sure, but was never emphasized. On the contrary, as already noted, it was discouraged, and condemned and this condemnation used, whenever possible, to generate fear and achieve social control of the illiterate Israeli nomads by the priestly class.

Scientific Theology. The unfinished quest of the ages has always been and continues until now to be the *total* revelation of God—what may be called the scientific god[28] or the god of scientific theology: the empirical god that appropriately confirms our conceptual image of it in its infinite scope and variety of natures and qualities. The only empirical god that conforms to this concept is *the cosmos itself*, our cosmic god, infinite in its variableness and its qualities, unchanging in its changingness: the only god that is intuited, yet neither conceptually nor empirically fashioned by man—completely independent of, yet including[29] man, and empirically confirmable by third parties.

(c) Monotheism

The discussion of concepts and doctrines of God may fittingly close with some observations on monotheism. With the exception of Gnostic dualism, which derives from Zoroastrianism, the theologies of the various groups of mankind are unqualifiedly monotheistic in the sense that they proclaim or espouse the concept of one supreme deity, whether or not minor deities are also postulated.

It is to be expected that the monotheism of each people will be shaped by its culture, so that the concept of one supreme God will in some degree vary from one people to another. In general, no group of mankind claims that its conception of a supreme deity is the only valid one, with the curious exception of the Semitic peoples whose religions (Judaism, Christianity, and Islam) claim to have the only valid theology and conception of monotheism. This theological claim exhibits two of the principal cultural characteristics of that group: intolerance in religious and theological matters and the mercantile culture of the oriental bazaar.

Both these characteristics are very closely linked.

In typical oriental-bazaar fashion, the Semitic peoples adopt a mercantile approach to theology, seeking to put a corner on the market for God as supreme being, by setting themselves up as sole seller (monopolist) of the one and only genuine God-product in all the world—monotheistic monopoly or monotheopoly. This presumptuous claim underlines the uniqueness of Semitic theology as consisting not in monotheism—contrary to the claims of Judaism, Christianity, and Islam—for the Greek philosophers as well as the rest of mankind (including so-called primitive peoples and animists) have all been and continue to be monotheists, but in its claim that its brand of monotheism is the one and only genuine product. No other group of mankind has ever dared to be so presumptuous. In the Johannine Gospel, Jesus (reportedly) went even further to make the following claim: "I am the way, the truth and the life: no man cometh unto the Father, but by me" (Saint John 14:6.) And again: ". . . he that hath seen me hath seen the Father" (Saint John 14:9).

APPENDIX

A NOTE ON CONVENTIONAL THEOLOGY, RELIGION, AND MATHEMATICS

Theological, as opposed to religious, events as traditionally conceived and discussed are *either* (a) nonrepeatable or, which is effectively the same, repeatable at infinite intervals of time (for example, eschatological events); *or* (b) outside the realm of sensible, human experience (e.g., hell). In practice, both (a) and (b) are the same thing: outside the realm of human experience hence beyond human knowledge. Thus the unknown God of Gnosticism, about whom Marcionite Gnostics claim special knowledge, namely, that it cannot be known, is a theological event par excellence: it is a nonevent, empirically speaking.

Religion, in contrast to theology, is *always*, in principle as in practice, within the realm of human experience and, therefore, of human knowledge.

Theology, therefore, pertains to the realm of human ignorance, being a special branch of protology, religion to the realm of human knowledge, being in the domain of human experience.[30] Notwithstanding that theology, in its conventional acceptation, lies in the realm of ignorant and nonempirical speculations, it can, and does, cohabit with religion and other empirical studies—but on one condition: that its untestable speculations conform to (that is, do not conflict with) the tested knowledge and results of human experience. This condition it normally satisfies by illustrating its theses by means of analogies drawn from human experience—e.g., illustrating the God-concept and related theses by means of the human paradigm, in short, by making God in the image of man. Among all theologies only Gnosticism, as we have seen, owns up honestly to its ignorance by admitting the impossibility of any human knowledge of an entity normally postulated as being completely beyond the range of human experience.

Theologians, therefore, are like mathematicians, of whom Bertrand Russell affirms: "they never know what [they] are talking about, nor whether what [they] are saying is true."[31] And the propositions of theology share similar characteristics with those of mathematics, of which Einstein remarks: "as far as the propositions of mathematics refer to reality, they are not certain; and as far as they are certain, they do not refer to reality."[32] (For "mathematics" substitute "theology.") All this follows from the fact that theology, like mathematics, is a human invention constructed out of bits and pieces borrowed from experience. These bits and pieces are then idealized, literally, in superlative terms (positive as well as negative), but put together in such a way as to be untestable by experience. There is thus no way that knowledge can be mediated out of the suprasensibilities of theology.

It therefore results that while religion, relating to human experience, can—in principle—be made scientific, theology, in its conventional forms, cannot. Scientific methods may be applied to the one but not to the other. Yet theology may be conformed to science by taking care that it does not conflict with the tested results of science either by its propositions or by their implications.

There are other areas of similarity between conventional theology and mathematics. First, both are marked by dogmatic certainty, that is, certainty under all conditions; being matters of definitions and postulates, both are a priori certain. Second, conventional theological concepts, like those of mathematics, for instance, geometry, are invented for interpretive purposes and uses: theological concepts in order to account for the origin of things, mathematical concepts as tools for describing the various elements of matter and their interrelationships, effectively used by Plato and others down to Einstein in elucidating important aspects of the cosmos. Mathematics also serves the more mundane purposes of accounting and computing.

Both religion and mathematics deal in relationships: among entities (mostly human beings) encountered in sense experience in the case of religion; among entities (concepts) without empirical content in the case of mathematics.

As regards the relationship between religion and mathematics, this

310

is the same as between religion and theology: the empirical as against the nonempirical. All three studies possess conceptual content. Only religion possesses empirical content as well.

NOTES

1. Known in the logic textbooks as the fallacy of composition.
2. See Trevor Ling, *A History of Religion East and West* (London: Macmillan Press, 1984), pp. 16–19.
3. This is not necessarily so. The answer to the question about the origin of God is more likely to lead to a vicious circle, as Ludwig Feuerbach convincingly argued in his *Essentials of Christianity*, where he showed that God is a human projection and objectification of the best qualities of the human species, so that, in effect, "man conceived (created) God in order that God, in turn, may create the cosmos and man."
4. See Trevor Ling, op. cit., pp. 170–71.
5. Charles R. Darwin, *The Origin of Species*. Incidentally, Plato's forms or ideas and Aristotle's God (as *the* Form of all forms) are equally vulnerable on this same point. They also evolve to the extent that, as intelligible entities, the way they reveal themselves to us—our intellectual apprehension of them—is subject, like us, to change and evolution over time. At least, Plato's own thought on the subject showed evidence of change over time.
6. The generalization of the anthropomorphic view of theological cosmogenesis across the entire biological spectrum is nothing new. Xenophanes, the sixth century B.C.E. Greek philosopher, had pointed out satirically that if they could talk, the various nonhuman animals would reveal their concept of God in their own likeness. But he did not seem to have taken the matter to its logical, metaphysical conclusion.
7. Various sources of information on these theories abound, including the works of Isaac Asimov. An excellent summary may be found in Stephane Groveff, "Cosmology: will it ever disclose our destiny?" in *Realités*, January 1979, pp. 68–75.
8. It is interesting to reflect that if the light from celestial bodies in expanding trajectories take millions and billions of light-years to reach us on earth, so that what we are now seeing of them is not what they currently are but what they were and at points millions and billions of light-years ago, then since these bodies were never stationary at the point and time of the cosmic big bang, we can never see either the explosion or where any celestial body is at any current time; so that we can never be sure that a big bang did, in fact, occur.

   What we ever see of any part of the cosmos outside our solar system at any time is always at some intermediate stage between its unknown, presumed origin in a cosmic explosion and its current unknown state and location. We never know its past origin (if any), its present, and, of course, its future. This same conclusion applies, with a longer time lag than that of light, to the radio signals we receive (hear) from celestial bodies. On earth, therefore, we live simultaneously in our present and the cosmic past, at any given time. We see and hear the cosmic past in our present and shall see and hear the cosmic present in our future.

   All these aspects of galactic evolution are consistent with Darwin's theory of evolution in the biological field, according to which evolution is a movement that proceeds from an unknown past to an unknown future.
9. So named after its discoverers, who established that luminous objects moving away

311

from our galaxy have the lines in their spectra displaced toward the red end of the spectrum, which indicates longer wave lengths, whereas those moving towards our galaxy have their lines shifted toward the violet end, the shorter wave lengths. The greater the speed of travel, the greater the shift.

10. The theory and its conclusion recall the similar theory by Heraclitus, the sixth–fifth century B.C.E. Greek philosopher, of continuous creation and destruction of the cosmos, preceded in each cycle by a great conflagration (Big Burn).

11. The compression of matter would trigger an implosion rather than an explosion, once a critical point is reached.

12. It has also served the purposes—legitimate as well as illegitimate—of specialists in divinity (the "divines") interested in getting their special brand of theology accepted by as large a following as possible. A conceptual God offers every divine a free field of competition in marketing his own monopolistic brand of theology.

13. It is relevant to recall that Karl Marx went Aristotle one better, reducing the metaphysical elements from Aristotle's two to one—matter, on the ground that ideas and ideology (Aristotle's forms) are the by-product ("superstructure," in Marx's terminology) of matter (in the shape of man) and the material arrangements for production in any society.

14. Notably, Descartes, Kant, Hegel—to name the principal standard-bearers—and their present-day followers.

15. Gilbert Murray, *Five Stages of Greek Religion* (Westport, Connecticut: Greenwood Press, 1976), p. 27, and Bertrand Russell, *History of Western Philosophy* (Unwin Paperbacks, 1979), pp. 58–59.

16. *The Book of Common Prayer* of 1662 (with amendments of 1964, 1965, and 1968).

17. See Plato's *Timaeus*.

18. The use of the term *God* as an "infinite regression argument stopper," as by the medieval schoolmen who variously defined it as First Cause, Necessary Being, et cetera, transforms the concept from its original meaning of "a specific mode of beingness" to one of "a technical device for signalling, and arresting, a slide into the *reductio ad absurdum* of infinite regression." The schoolmen missed this nuancing of the concept and its consequences, namely, a change in conceptual content as well as an indication that an irrelevant question of origin has entered into the discussion.

19. Acts 17:16–34.

20. This is not intended to be an exhaustive study but a brief summary of the (nonlinear) evolution of theological doctrine.

21. In a sense this tradition of zootheism has survived in the animal symbols emblazoned as mascots on the heraldry of various countries.

22. The deification of Jesus may be justly traced to this ancient practice, owing its introduction into Christianity to its Greek converts. (See Part two, Section B, chapter 10, above.)

23. Paul Tillich, *Dynamics of Faith* (New York: Harper Torchbooks, 1958), p. 41.

24. Cf. Job 11:7–8: "Canst thou by searching find out God? canst thou find out the Almighty unto perfection? It is as high as heaven; what canst thou do? deeper than hell; what canst thou know?" Yet God was a ubiquitous as well as infinite—hence empirically vague—being, as recorded in Psalm 139:7–12.

25. The danger presented by a purely conceptual god has already been noted (Book Three, chapter 1, section 4). It is, in the proper sense of the term, a "smart" god; it cannot be identified, hence empirically pinned down. And therein lies the danger. It becomes a prey to all sorts of charlatanism—it is *all* things, and *no* thing to all men. It can be invoked in support of, and as approving, all sorts of causes, conditions,

and hopes of the human race, no matter how mutually inconsistent or (on the human plane) evil these may be: Thus, outside–space-time gods, like outside–space-time worlds, are the blessed will-o'-the-wisp, the beatific vision, and the happy hunting ground of philosopher, divine, and charlatan.

26. This is the essence of the oft-quoted Pascalian reference to "the God of Abraham, Isaac and Jacob": a God revealed in history through dreams, pillar of fire, voice, burning bush, et cetera, a symbolic or synecdochic theology.

27. See the Johannine Gnostic-agnostic reference at Saint John 1:18: "No man hath seen God at any time; the only begotten Son, which is in the bosom of the Father, he hath declared him." And at 1 John 4:12: "No man hath seen God at any time."

28. No one needs take offense at the lower case denotation of *god* since this is all a matter of the point of view, and the point of view adopted here is that man is a part of the scientific god—and an infinitesimal part at that, whether as a species or as an individual—hence does not need undue inflation by capitalization, whether taken separately or inclusively. Those who capitalize *god* do so because they conceive it as a being infinitely vast and wholly other than man, who thus stands in shabby contrast; or else because they reflect man's primitive awe of the cosmos, which the ecclesiastical group seeks to use as a means of social control.

29. See the preceding note.

30. The author's conception of religion that is employed in Book Three of this work is defined and discussed in chapter 3 and at greater length in chapter 7.

31. Bertrand Russell, *A Free Man's Worship* (Unwin Paperbacks, 1976), p. 76.

32. *Ideas and Opinions by Albert Einstein* (New York: Bonanza Books, 1954), p. 233.

Chapter 3

Philosophy and Metaphysics as Systems of Interrelationships

1. THE ANCIENT GREEK IDEAL OF PHILOSOPHY AND THE PHILOSOPHER

Among the ancient Greeks philosophy began, and developed gradually, as an empirical investigation into the nature of the matter and form (structure) of things.[1] They were interested in the *what* of things—what things were made of, in what they consisted. They were not interested in the *whence* of things, that is, the origin of things—of matter and the forms or prototypical patterns of things. Nor in the *why* of things. Philosophy was thus conceived as *thought* about the *what* of things, and anyone engaged in this pursuit was, naturally, one who loved it, hence a philosopher; that is, one who loves[2] *thought*[3] *about the nature of things* (= wisdom, Greek *sophia*). "Lover of thought about the nature of things" and "lover of wisdom" thus became equivalent definitions of *philosopher*, and the pursuit itself, namely, "thought (thinking) about the nature of things" or "wisdom," became the definition of philosophy. The "nature" or "essence" of a thing was, strictly, the external,[4] suprasensible "form" or fixed pattern that the phenomenon strove to reproduce inadequately, or to share in, and that manifested its presence (parousia) in the phenomenon as a "likeness," "semblance," or "image."

Aristotle considered philosophy as being concerned with contemplation, which is the perfect activity of God, the unmoved mover of the cosmos; God being defined as pure thought or mind, no matter (or space). Whence philosophy was ideally regarded as contemplation or pure thought in an environment of physical inactivity: pure thought motionlessly contemplating—what else?—pure thought, namely itself. Thus the philosopher par excellence is a thinker; the ideal thinker, pure thought (that is, God); the activity, pure thought; the object, pure thought; the hallmark

314

of thought, lack of physical activity as a result of lack of motion. Whence God was the philosopher's ultimate philosopher: pure thought thinking itself in the static posture of the unmoved mover. The total effect: static contemplation attracting plastic matter to itself, like a magnet, and setting it in motion to produce the ordered cosmos.

At the human level, philosophy becomes the activity of a man not involved with physical work or any kind of activity other than contemplation, the physical drudgery being left to others (nonphilosophers) —ideally, slaves, i.e., noncitizens. This meant that the philosopher was an upper-class citizen or aristocrat, a privileged minority with inherited wealth and social position, living a life of contemplation at leisure, a member of the veritable upper crust. A system of slavery and caste was thus, inevitably, bound up with the ancient Greek concept of philosophy and the exercise of the philosopher's *metier*.[5]

What the Greek Academic philosophers—and the Ionian philosophers before them—wanted to account for was not the *origin* or source of form and matter, but the *activity* by which matter was led to take on form, and form to be imperfectly incorporated in matter to produce individually identifiable objects or phenomena. This activity was soul (appetite or vegetativeness), whose essential quality was to seek or strive toward the incorporation of form in matter—the quality termed *nisus*. The external, activating principle of soul—the great unknown, X—was God.

Both Plato and Aristotle thought of God metaphorically, in almost androgenous terms. But apart from this similarity, their conceptions of God differed markedly. Plato defined him as the molder of matter according to various forms, first molding a proxy—the demiurge or artificer-god—who then carried out the rest of the work of molding the remaining matter according to the various forms of things. (The demiurge was the divine slave who carried out the work of God, as was fitting for an aristocrat's aristocratic God. Since this God had to have a slave, he first had to make one from scratch—the only truck he ever had with labor.) This process may be loosely referred to as the "creation" of things (but only loosely, since *creation* has come to mean "creation ex nihilo" in occidental society). Aristotle, however, defined God not, like Plato, in the impulsive sense (i.e., as an impetus or *active* force that moves or sets in motion the "forming" process), but as a *passive*, immobile force that, by a gravity-type process, attracted matter to assume one or other of the various forms. Thus "creation" changed from being an active process of "formation" or molding of matter *from without* and according to forms, to the passive one of "in-formation" or molding of matter *from within* by the force of God's attraction (seeking or love, on the part of matter).

315

In order to convert the force that acted on matter from one of impetus to one of attraction, Aristotle was logically compelled to assimilate the forms to God, who thereby became a sort of container of forms—the Form of forms, the Idea of ideas. In this way the Aristotelian God became a being who thought out the various forms or ideas in his divine mind and attracted matter to assume one or other of the various forms issuing from his thought. It was not so much that God became a philosopher as that the philosopher was projected into God, from which position it was no great thing for the philosopher to become king. For if, unlike God, he could not rule the cosmos (which, no doubt, was a pity from Plato's point of view), he, at least, qualified to rule the city-state (as Plato very strongly believed).

The change in conception from an "activist" to a "passivist" contemplative God is significant. Aristotle's definition was more consistent with the Academy's definition of philosophy as an outwardly passive process—which, indeed, is the essence of the contemplative posture. When, therefore, following Blaise Pascal, Christian theologians make reference to the God of philosophers and scholars, they mean the passivist, contemplative Aristotelian God who thinks only his own thoughts and, being the hypostasis of perfection (pure thought), lacking nothing, can only love himself.[6]

2. PHILOSOPHY AS A SYSTEM OF INTERRELATIONSHIPS

It is evident from the discussion in the preceding section that what was under investigation by the Academic philosophers was the process by which a semblance of form became incorporated in matter and became inseparable from it so long as the "formed" and identifiable object persisted. This process was resolved into a relationship between form and matter, termed *soul*, by means of which the semblance of form and matter came together; for, given this relationship and its nature, the presence of entities among which it held was necessarily implied. This basic factor of relationship seems to have been overlooked by the Greek philosophers as constituting the essence of their investigations; hence their preoccupation, instead, with inquiries into the nature of form and of matter. Not that they were completely unaware of relationships. On the contrary, they recognized two types of relationships between semblances of form and matter: (a) inseparable association, in the case of physical objects, and (b) nonassociation, of which there were two well-known cases—in mathematics (geometrical forms) and ethics (moral forms). Mathematical forms were pure forms without known spontaneous association with mat-

316

ter.[7] Nevertheless, one of them, notably the circle, was thought to regulate the orbital motions of the heavenly bodies as well as their shapes. Moral or ethical forms also had no matter but regulated the behavior of one type of organized matter—human beings—through their being perfectly, intellectually comprehended by man. Unlike the planets, human behavior did not conform to any of the mathematical forms, although certain mathematical notions—like the asymptote—were useful in demonstrating the impossibility of perfection in human behavior in practice (as distinct from its possibility in principle) owing to the recalcitrance of matter.

As we have seen, the name *soul* was given by the Greek academic philosophers to the unitive principle that held together, in a complementary relationship, the various heterogeneous elements of organic structures, as these evolved. Yet these philosophers do not seem to have followed up the investigation of interrelationships, and so missed the fruitful avenues to which the investigation would have led them.

It is our purpose here to show that the relational approach to philosophy, namely, the investigation of interrelationships among entities, not only absorbs the traditional approach that investigates the essence (form and matter) of entities, but also leads to very fruitful results both for philosophy and for its constituent or derivative studies, such as metaphysics, theology, religion, ethics, et cetera. In short, *relational* philosophy absorbs and supersedes *essential* philosophy. Simultaneously, it will be shown that the essentialist approach not only cloaks the more important relational approach, but also leads to some erroneous results.

Philosophy is not, as the ancient Greek philosophical tradition would have it, about thought or contemplation per se or the love and search for truth or wisdom; truth being interpreted as the unchanging ideas or forms (verities) of things, which lie outside of time—hence are eternal or unchanging. Rather is it primarily about *relationships*: the investigation and interpretation of relationships among entities (things, ideas, concepts) by the application of thought. Leibniz described space as a system of relationships. Philosophy is no less like space in this respect: a system of interrelationships. Being thus concerned with interrelationships, philosophy is not interested in absolutes or individual situations but in relativities, comparative situations involving at least two entities connected in some way or other. The relational situations of interest to philosophy are such as reciprocity, mutuality, equality, inclusivity, exclusivity, opposition, cooperation, preponderance, domination, subservience, and so on.

Absolute (changeless and timeless) values and situations belong, rather, in the realm of theology as conventionally conceived and dealing with origins, or in the realm of ethics, dealing with principles. But this

317

is only the dogmatic part of ethics. (The nondogmatic, relational part of ethics deals with interests.)

It is in the relational sense that truth becomes a proper object and pursuit of philosophy, being a relationship of correspondence between two entities such that the one empirically conforms to, and confirms, the other: a relationship of empirical validity. All relational situations are, normally, provisional, not fixed and unchanging. Thus the relationships in which philosophy is interested are changing and changeable.

The proper business of philosophy, therefore, consists in the investigation and empirically verifiable interpretation of the cosmic (or less than cosmic) interrelationships among the objects of thought (concepts) as well as their phenomenal bases, where applicable. For this purpose, it is unnecessary to distinguish between concepts and phenomena, given that the proper concern is with *all* types of interrelationships, per se, regardless of the nature of the interrelationships and of the entities among which they hold. It is this absence of constraint on the nature of the interrelationships and the entities among which they hold that constitutes the distinguishing hallmark of philosophy—the characteristic that sets it apart from any of its constituents or derivatives, such as science, religion, ethics, psychology, history, et cetera. These derivatives are marked off by constraints on the interrelationships and/or entities with which they respectively deal. Thus philosophy, not theology or mathematics, is the true queen of the sciences. For example, what marks off science from philosophy is the physical nature of the phenomena involved in the relationships studied by science. Religion, on the other hand, is merely philosophy with a human face and, therefore, with a human bias; that is to say, religion deals with the interrelationships between man, on the one hand, and each of the other entities in the cosmos, on the other. Ethics is marked off as a subcategory of religion involving complete mutuality or reciprocity of interrelationships among empirical entities.

This restriction is generally—though incorrectly—regarded as valid only for human entities because of the fact that religion is biased toward human beings. However, the restriction, as given in the definition, is not intended to limit ethics to religion, nor to human beings, for it can be derived directly from philosophy and involve a wide variety of mutual relationships: among human beings; between human and other animals (e.g., domestic pets such as dogs, cats, et cetera, and tamed or domesticated wild animals such as lions[8] and chimpanzees) though to a more limited extent as compared to mutual relationships among human beings; and among other animals (e.g., in regard to the behavior of the vanquished towards the victor in a fight). Psychology is identified by its concern with

318

the mutuality of the interrelationships among mental phenomena or activity (inner) and behavioral responses (outer) of biological (strictly speaking, zoological) entities. History concerns itself with the interrelationships among human actions within and among human communities. And so on.

3. INTERRELATIONSHIPS IN GREEK ACADEMIC PHILOSOPHY AND METAPHYSICS

The philosophy and metaphysics of Plato and Aristotle (derived, in part, from Socrates) may be reviewed in the light of the relational approach in order to identify relational elements in their system. The following examples are indicative:

(a) Relationship between phenomena and ideas: This consisted in the verisimilitude of the form incorporated in the matter of the phenomenon, which resulted from the creative act of the demiurge (according to Plato); or (according to Aristotle) from the attraction exerted by God's ideas on matter, on the one hand, and the emulative propensity of soul in matter, on the other. The Aristotelian relationship is best described in mathematical terms as asymptotical, with the static, eternal (timeless), and perfect idea constituting the asymptote toward which the form incorporated in the phenomenon develops dynamically in time. Consequently,

(b) God (the collectivity of ideas) stands in
  (i) creative-impulsive-dynamic relationship to a part of matter (the demiurge) and the demiurge similarly to the rest of matter (according to Plato);
  (ii) static-attractive asymptotic relationship to matter (according to Aristotle).

(c) Knowledge stands in a *mnemonic* relationship to the dialectic (or dialogic) process and, in the conception of Socrates, in a *maieutic* relationship to the philosopher.

(d) Time stands in a dynamic relationship to eternity (timelessness).

(e) Soul stands in a dualistic relationship to God and matter: mental-intellectual to God and formal, unitive-organic to matter (Aristotle).

(f) Virtue (moderation, i.e, individual salvation or happiness) defines the relationship between the good (as existing in thought, contemplation, or idea) and right action, namely, the practical activities resulting from the emulative propensity of soul in its attempt to achieve the good. (Just as the verisimilitude of ''physical'' form

319

defines the relationship between perfect "physical" form and phenomenon, so virtue or the verisimilitude of "moral" form defines the relationship between perfect "moral" form and right conduct. Both the verisimilitude of "physical" form and of virtue are neither exact or perfect reproductions (facsimiles) of their originals, nor atrocious representations, but moderate or recognizably similar copies of their originals.)

(g) Morals (or morality) define the relationship of choice (preference) in regard to several possible courses of action.

4. IDEALISM AND THE DERAILMENT OF PHILOSOPHY INTO PHILOLOGY, SYNTAX, AND EMPIRICAL PROPOSITIONS

One adverse consequence of Plato's idealistic conception of philosophy emerged about two millennia later with the confusion of philosophy with philology, syntax, and empirical propositions. This appeared in the thought systems of Kierkegaard, Heidegger, Nietzsche, and the Logical Positivists. Since thought was held to be the essence of philosophy, it was only a short step from thought to the *expression of thoughts in words*, hence to language (philology) as the essence of philosophy.[9] The philosophers of language were led by the idealist tradition to mistake the meanings of words for philosophy. The position of the "philosophy as philology" school may be aptly expressed in the following statement:

> In the beginning was the idea or concept (Gk. = noumenon) which remained hidden until it was revealed by being expressed (incarnated) in speech. It then became a *verbalized* concept (Gk. = logos), a concept no longer hidden but open for all to see and examine. In its openness, the formerly hidden concept now became a word (Fr. = verbe, Gk. = logos) containing the original concept or idea which (according to Plato) automatically has a corresponding sense-empirical counterpart in matter, as a phenomenon, or in behavior, if it is to be at all meaningful.[10]

Martin Buber, acknowledging his debt to Ludwig Feuerbach and with a surer instinct than the philosophers of language, extended the conception of philosophy as concerned with the meanings of words to include syntax, that is, the *relationships* between and among words in propositions (in particular, among personal pronouns) in the domain of philosophy. It is true that philosophy deals with relationships, but with relationships *in general*, not with *particular kinds* of relationships. While relationships of particular kinds do fall within the general domain of

320

philosophy, they do not cover the entire realm of philosophy in its generic sense, but the narrower *philosophy of* a particular area of study: in the case we are considering, the philosophy of grammar or syntax—or ethics, in Buber's application of syntax. It is in this sense that we speak of the philosophy of metaphysics (the interrelationships among the elements of being or becoming); the philosophy of religion (the interrelationships *within* specific religions or the interrelationships *among* religions, otherwise known as comparative religion); the philosophy of mathematics (interrelationships within mathematics, that is, among mathematical concepts and operations, as well as among the various kinds of mathematics—algebra, Euclidean and non-Euclidean geometry, trigonometry, calculus, et cetera); the philosophy of science (interrelationships within a given science or among various sciences); and so on. For, obviously, the only conclusion that can emerge from such a general and wide-ranging field as philosophy is that everything is related to everything else. It is an unwieldy field to handle unless broken up into specialized areas of interrelationships—as has, in fact, happened. However, what is important in philosophy is not the entire range that it encompasses but, eventually, its method and approach through interrelationships. *Interrelationships, it cannot be overemphasized, constitute both the emphasis and the method of philosophy.*

The school of Logical Positivists (of whom Ludwig Wittgenstein was among the most famous, others being Moritz Schlick and Rudolf Carnap and, later, A. J. Ayer) moved on from syntax to language analysis as the proper domain of philosophy, according to their claim: that is, the analysis of concepts and propositions and the expression of concepts and statements in clear and empirically verifiable propositions. What may almost be regarded as the slogan of the school consisted in the two famous dicta of Wittgenstein:

(a) What can be said at all can be said clearly.
(b) Of what one cannot speak, thereof one must keep silent.

That is to say, in order for concepts and propositions to have meaning and be clearly understood they must be expressible in empirically testable propositions; otherwise, they are non-sense, hence nonsense.

The contribution made by the Logical Positivists was, in any case, a very useful one in underlining the importance and the need for clarity and precision in thought, concept, and language as a preliminary to correct thinking. This is a requirement that extends beyond the confines of philosophy, necessarily, into every other of its constituent fields of study;[11] but the requirement does not constitute philosophy in its general relational sense, as we have here defined it. For philosophy covers the entire gamut of interrelationships among concepts, words, phenomena, human and nonhuman entities, et cetera. Any and all kinds of interrelationships fall within the province of philosophy, its essence and its method.

Enough has been said to make clear that although the philosophy of language (linguistic philosophy) is a *part* of philosophy, in general, it is not the *whole* of philosophy. Even less related to philosophy is logical positivism or language analysis. The Logical Positivists were not only in error; they claimed too much.

NOTES

1. Cf. Plato's *Timaeus* and R. G. Collingwood, *The Idea of Nature* (London, New York: Oxford University Press, 1945) Part I, chapter I.
2. Greek *philos* = loving, from *philein* = to love.
3. This emphasis on thought, mind, or idea is the reason that Greek (especially Platonian and Aristotelian) philosophy is called *idealistic* philosophy or *idealism*. The tradition was continued in the Occident and culminated in Hegel. Karl Marx reversed it by putting the emphasis on the role of matter in philosophy; hence his approach to philosophy is described as *materialistic* or *materialism*.
4. Karl Popper's idea that the properties of things are not inherent but external to individual things is a reflection of this Greek thought, with the difference that these properties, in Popper's view, are found within our phenomenal world not, as with the Greeks, in a suprasensible world.
5. One corollary is that slaves are automatically excluded from the "practice" of philosophy. At the same time, the enslaved class is likely to disapprove of philosophy as an idle pursuit (idle speculation) and of philosophy-supporting societies as oppressive regimes. This has been true in the history of Jews and American Negroes, both historically oppressed groups.
6. See Hans Küng, *Does God Exist?* (New York: Vintage Books, 1981), pp. 57–59.
7. As we have already seen, Plato's *Timaeus*, which presents various solid structures (composed of isosceles and scalene triangles) as the basic constituents of the elements fire, air, water, and earth, invalidates his own tenet regarding the nonmaterial nature of mathematical forms. His doctrine of the elements was interesting, given the investigative tools then available—which were nothing but pure speculation, without the possibility of empirical verification. The planets were supposed to be spherical in shape (or form) from the evidence of eclipses of these heavenly bodies—especially of the sun and moon.
8. It is known to hold also between human beings and lions and other animals in their untamed state, both within the separate groups and in direct dealings between man and such animals. This has been observed, for example, between men and other animals in the Ngorongoro Crater in Tanzania and between a group of men digging ponds and a family of lions in the Waza Game Park of North Cameroun.
9. This was not the first time, however, that language had been misconstrued for something else. Parmenides, before Socrates and Plato, had derived metaphysics from language through logic, equating every concept automatically with a sense-empirical phenomenon corresponding to it. In this respect he was the precursor of

322

Anselm, the eleventh-century Italian Archbishop of Canterbury, who reasoned that the concept of God as the greatest possible existent implied the phenomenal existence of God. Parmenides also held the view that change was impossible, regarding the evidence of the senses as untrustworthy. His error in mistaking metaphysics for language was only partial (as we shall see, subsequently, in chapter 5), but his view about the impossibility of change was completely in error.

10. It is in this sense that, in the Fourth Gospel, Jesus was the Word/Verbe/Logos of God (the Idea of all ideas), which became automatically incarnated in the phenomenal garb of a human being, though a perfect, rather than an imperfect, empirical manifestation of God in both phenomenon and conduct. This idea of Jesus as a perfect phenomenal incarnation of God was utter "foolishness" to the educated Greeks versed in Plato's philosophy. (It turns out that the author of the Fourth Gospel, no doubt a Plotinian and a Gnostic, was, logically, a better philosopher than was Plato.)

11. For this reason, one must disagree completely with Karl Popper's extreme view that "we should altogether avoid, like the plague, discussing the meaning of words. Discussing the meaning of words is a favourite game of philosophy, past and present: philosophers seem to be addicted to the idea that words and their meaning are important, and are the special concern of philosophy" *Objective Knowledge* (New York: Oxford University Press, 1981) p. 309. Popper is right in his implied criticism of the logical positivists but wrong in dismissing the importance of the meaning of words. For his elaborate defense of Alfred Tarski's doctrine of meta-language, in connection with the "correspondence theory of truth," as a requirement for speaking about correspondence between a statement S and a fact F, not only does not avoid—as intended—Wittgenstein's objection to discussing language by language, but also leads to the awkwardness of having to learn and use a new language in which to transpose and discuss about another language or two, when one language is enough to discuss itself and any other. And all this merely to state the conditions for correspondence between S and F, while the meaning of "correspondence" itself is ignored or assumed, in the first place. It is not legitimate to replace the meaning of a word by an assumption that its meaning is self-evident. Nor is it true to hold, as did Tarski and Popper, that "logical consequence is truth transmission." What logic transmits is consistency or inconsistency, not truth, which, beyond consistency, is an empirical matter.

Chapter 4

Methodology of Understanding and Knowledge

1. THE CASE FOR METHODOLOGY

Any attempt at interpretation of any given phenomenon requires a methodology—even if only a paradigm—for all knowledge is mediated through paradigms out of ignorance: the known from the unknown through the known. In his book titled *Against Method*,[1] Paul Feyerabend argues, convincingly, against relentlessly sticking to any method, in particular the so-called scientific method. He makes the point that anarchy, rather than rationalism, has marked scientific progress and cites the case of Galileo defending the Copernican heliocentric theory by subterfuge, rhetoric, and propaganda rather than by rational argument. As he puts his case:

> . . . research always violates major methodological rules and cannot proceed otherwise. . . . In order to progress, we must step back from the evidence, reduce the degree of empirical adequacy (the empirical content) of our theories, abandon what we have already achieved, and start afresh.
> —p. 113

Or again:

> . . . Reason grants that the ideas which we introduce in order to expand and to improve our knowledge may *arise* in a very disorderly way and that the *origin* of a particular point of view may depend on class prejudice, passion, personal idiosyncracies, questions of style, and even on error, pure and simple. But it also demands that in judging such ideas we follow well-defined rules: our *evaluation* of ideas must not be invaded by irrational elements. Now, what our historical examples seem to show is this: there are situations when our most liberal judgements and our most liberal rules would have eliminated an idea or a point of view which we regard today as essential for science, and would not have permitted it to prevail—and such situations occur quite frequently . . . The ideas survived

and they can *now* be said to be in agreement with reason. They survived because prejudice, passion, conceit, errors, sheer pig-headedness, in short because all the elements that characterize the context of discovery, *opposed* the dictates of reason *and because these irrational elements were permitted to have their way.* To express it differently: *Copernicanism and other "rational" views exist today only because reason was overruled at some time in their past.* (The opposite is also true: witchcraft and other "irrational" views have *ceased* to be influential only because reason was overruled at some time in *their* past.) . . . the cosmologists of the 16th and 17th centuries did not have the knowledge we have today, they did not know that Copernicanism was capable of giving rise to a scientific system that is acceptable from the point of view of "scientific method". They did not know which of the many views that existed at their time would lead to future reason when defended in an "irrational" way. Being without such guidance they had to make a guess and in making this guess they could only follow their inclinations, as we have seen. Hence it is advisable to let one's inclinations go against reason *in any circumstances*, for science may profit from it.

—pp. 154–56, italics in original

Feyerabend makes a most convincing general case if his main aim is, as one suspects, to argue for *flexibility* in scientific methodology; for even anarchy can be said to be a method rather than an absence of method. There seem to be certain misconceptions, however, on Feyerabend's part that need to be dispelled. His persistent contrast of "rational" and "irrational" and his emphasis on the role of the latter in scientific discovery (or advance), leading on to his prescription to let inclination overrule reason frequently or even suspend it altogether, indicates a misconception on his part regarding the role of reason (hence of methodology) in scientific research. He tends to leave the reader with the impression that reason had sometimes been heuristic rather than a methodological tool. Since reason does not, of itself, lead to new knowledge, but only hypotheses (however derived) do, as they are confirmed by empirical evidence; and since reason, like methodology, becomes operative only in the testing of hypotheses, in explicating their consequences both before and after testing (if confirmed); reason and methodology, per se, are therefore not obstacles to scientific progress, unless by misuse. They are the servants of whatever hypotheses are to be tested, however these may be derived or however absurd they may be. Or, as an ancient Gnostic would have put it, reason, like methodology, is a whore to whatever scientific (or nonscientific) postulate or starting point of research is adopted.

The fact that laissez-faire anarchism (the "anything goes" method) has sometimes led, in practice, to some good and unexpected results in

325

science (e.g., Galileo's nonrational justification in support of the Copernican heliocentric theory) is no argument against *method* (even Galileo's approach, however unconventional and unsystematic, was a methodology) applied to the solution of a specific problem. And the fact that, given a specific problem, conventional methodology has sometimes failed to find a solution to it and has rather resulted, by serendipity, in discovering unintended solutions to other problems is no argument in favor of anarchism as a tool for scientific research and the expansion of knowledge.

There is a case for *systematic* method as for free style in scientific research, as well as for a combination of both (as has occasionally been the case, according to Feyerabend's account of Galileo). The case for the one does not destroy the case for the other, for it is not reason, methodology, or anarchy that *discovers*, but experience.

Given specific problems and goals, systematic and consistent method is more likely to win most of the time over anarchy (unstructured methodology) in the achievement of intended results, for even serendipity is a by-product of systematic method, not of laissez-faire or "anything goes." It was consistent and systematic method rather than free-style that placed a man on the moon.

The crucial point about scientific progress, however, has been made by Thomas Kuhn in his book *The Structure of Scientific Revolutions*[2]: it comes not by refutation but by supersession of existing enthroned theories—for whatever reasons—by new theories. Even so, one could still argue, as does Kuhn, that it would be desirable if new theories included the results of old theories as well as solutions to hitherto unsolved problems under the old theories and to new problems.

Feyerabend argues, unconvincingly, that rigid application of scientific methodology could stifle scientific progress. Since methodology is not a heuristic tool, but a useful servant only when productive hypotheses (however derived) are in play, it is not clear why application of methodology should stifle scientific progress. And even if there were such a danger one could count on the real scientists following their own inclinations (as Feyerabend assures us they do all the time) to abut in fruitful results. The verdict on method and lack of it should therefore be the same as for the wheat and the tare in the New Testament parable: "Let both grow together until the harvest."[3] That should enable us to see which method (or lack of it) leads to more fruitful results.

It may seem that a considerable amount of attention has been given to Feyerabend's arguments, but not unduly so, because it is necessary to clear the way for our own discussion and approach to method as well as to present it in a relevant context. For myth has hitherto not been regarded as a heuristic tool, nor considered as serving the same function as so-called scientific hypotheses.

326

In general, scientific method leading to a new and/or better understanding of phenomena proceeds normally by the following steps, starting with a given hypothesis, myth, model, or paradigm:

(a) conceptualization: hypothesis, myth, model, paradigm;
(b) objectification of conceptual meaning: convention;
(c) sense-empirical test within a given paradigm: empirically testable propositions;
(d) paradigm variation.

As we shall see in due course, newer and better understanding can be more easily and more frequently achieved if instead of testing one paradigm only and then waiting till events compel a change of paradigm, several paradigms or a multi-tier structured paradigm were used and tested at the same time. This would mean interchanging the last two steps in the investigation so that the preferred arrangement becomes:

(a) conceptualization: hypothesis, myth, model, paradigm;
(b) objectification of conceptual meaning: convention;
(c) paradigm variation;
(d) sense-empirical test within each paradigm: empirically testable propositions.

A multi-tiered paradigm has the advantage over several different paradigms in examining the same phenomenon or problem progressively at various and increasing levels of comprehensiveness. The biocosmic paradigm will be seen to provide this advantage and is therefore favored as a methodological choice.

2. THE ROLE OF HYPOTHESIS, MYTH, MODEL, OR PARADIGM IN SCIENTIFIC INVESTIGATIONS

Myths, models and paradigms are like any ordinary hypothesis in function: they organize and interpret information gathered from experience or any other source. Specifically, a model, paradigm, or myth fulfills the function of providing a handy framework for (a) *organizing* and (b) *interpreting* facts and phenomena under investigation. It is the equivalent of a testable hypothesis and likewise contains certain implicit questions and their corresponding answers—*both strictly relevant to the model*. But the model or hypothesis, per se, is not necessarily relevant to the matter under investigation (nor, for that matter, are its implied questions and answers) unless the necessary steps are (or have been) taken to make it so. To become relevant, the model (hypothesis) must have some *connection* with the facts and phenomena clearly established by direct testing for compatibility of the answers that it provides with the facts and phenomena, as these are known from sense experience. If the connection holds, the empirical test simultaneously provides direct confirmation of the relevance of the questions implied in the model, as well as of the model itself, to the facts and phenomena under investigation. It is then that it can be said that the model or hypothesis provides a valid interpretation of the facts and phenomena: it becomes a *scientific* interpretation; that is, one that is *provisionally* true, until a better model or theory comes along that gives a better interpretive fit to the known facts and phenomena, as well as to other additional relevant facts that were not accounted for adequately or at all by the previous model. Truth belongs in the realm of experience, knowledge and understanding to man's interpretation of that experience.

Thus every scientific hypothesis or interpretation is *always* provisional at the same time as it is empirical. No scientific interpretation is, therefore, sacrosant or fixed. This is why the question of belief, in the sense of unquestioned acceptance as well as emotional commitment to any position, can never arise as a relevant issue in matters of scientific truth, for belief is not only *unnecessary* in view of the provisional nature of scientific truth which is always, therefore, on trial; it is also *misleading* because it falsely confers the status of "fixed and immutable doctrine" on what is, by nature, always subject to change. Hence, *provisional acceptance* only is ever required and necessary for a scientific truth. In life and experience there are no fixed reference points. Whether absolute or relative, *everything* is effectively mutable—except the fact and process of mutability, of change itself.[4] If belief is both misleading and unnecessary in regard to empirical truth then it is, a fortiori, more so in regard to nonempirical propositions and conclusions, for in these cases there is nothing empirically valid that could constitute the basis of any useful, even if meaningful, discussion or of consensus. And since no man is an island, it may even happen that one man's belief obstructs or harms another person—which is also unacceptable. While we may concede the right of anyone to believe as he wishes, no one has a right to impose his beliefs on another or, through such beliefs, cause harm to another. This is also to say that anyone is fully entitled to reject another's belief, even while respecting the other's right to hold to it.

PARADIGM AND PROBLEM SOLVING

A problem is solved only when it finds its place within a proper, that is, relevant, framework or paradigm—not by being displaced or eliminated by another problem. Problem substitution is not the same as problem solving, for the displaced problem continues unresolved if it does not arise or find a place within the new paradigm or framework. It is merely forgotten, not resolved. The conventional wisdom that a problem is never resolved, only displaced by another problem is only partly true. It says more about paradigm change than about problem resolution. What it really means is that, frequently, the new paradigm is inadequate to the old problem, which continues unresolved, since it does not find a place within the new paradigm. The conventional wisdom, rather, carries an implicit plea to scientists and problem solvers to search for proper paradigms, rather than take whatever paradigm just happens to come along. In other words, the conventional wisdom should be regarded as a plea for connection and continuity, rather than discontinuity, between paradigms. This is the only guarantee of scientific progress, conceived as continuity and increasing comprehensiveness in the scope of interpretation, hence of understanding and knowledge.

Thus a standard is established for paradigm change. An appropriate paradigm—that is, one that promotes or serves the cause of scientific progress by continuity and comprehensiveness—is one in which old unresolved problems find their resolution. The new paradigm must contain the old as an element within its framework. Both the old paradigm and its problems must be, respectively, integrated and resolved within the new paradigm. It is thus possible to distinguish between new paradigms that serve the end of scientific *innovation* (that is, merely lead to new knowledge without resolving old problems) and new paradigms that serve the end of scientific *advance* (that is, *both* lead to new knowledge *and* resolve outstanding problems).

Problem solving is, therefore, seen to be an integrative affair, a matter of resolving a problem—just what it says—not a matter of displacement of old by new problems. If the problem is solved within the existing framework applied to it, then that framework is still valid; if within a new framework, then the new framework must also incorporate—integrate—the old framework within itself. Resolution of an old problem within a new framework *may* be taken as an indication that the new incorporates the old framework. But this has to be confirmed.

329

3. FAILED METHODOLOGIES

Modern scientific method has come a long way from its crude beginnings. It is the method of establishing knowledge of phenomena or events on the basis of collected data (observations, records, et cetera) interpreted with the aid of hypotheses, models, or paradigms, which are then tested against the data and, if valid, confirmed by experience. Its aim is to determine the nature of an action, phenomenon, or event on the basis of collected data. And the hypothesis or paradigm, if validated by experience, provides a basis for the prediction of future occurrences of the phenomenon or event.

Scientific knowledge starts with the collection of information or data about the phenomenon to be investigated. In the past, attempts had been made to gain knowledge about phenomena without first assembling the relevant data by which to determine their nature. This procedure was adopted because the dominant interest was not in establishing and understanding the nature of the phenomenon itself—this was assumed or taken as self-evident—but in

(a) determining the agency or cause of the phenomenon (agency and cause were regarded as equivalent, both being assumed to be human in character);
(b) predicting future events or their courses;
(c) establishing the validity of conclusions about a given phenomenon that were derived from axioms or self-evident truths.

Each of these foci of interest had a corresponding method considered to be heuristic, i.e., leading to the discovery or disclosure of the focus of interest. And each method failed because of ignorance of the basic characteristics of the phenomenon in question.

The hypotheses, models, or paradigms used in scientific investigations to interpret data are always provisional—hence, also, the knowledge based on them—because, firstly, they deal with phenomena that are subject to change in various ways: phenomena manifest themselves and undergo change through the influence of various factors; the sensual modes of experiencing the same phenomenon are different (sight, touch or feel, taste, smell, and hearing) and each mode varies according to the efficiency of its sensing mechanism at different times and under different circumstances. Secondly, hypotheses or paradigms may be formulated on the basis of single criteria, of which there are several possibilities. And the hypotheses change with changes in the criteria. Thirdly, the hypotheses or paradigms themselves are not always subject to direct empirical verification—hence they may or may not be relevant to the phenomenon to be interpreted. However, their implications may, indeed have to, be relevant if the hypotheses or paradigms are to be relevant to experience of the phenomenon under investigation. This had not always been the view about hypotheses or paradigms. In the past they were apt to be regarded as immutable laws of nature (in the case of natural phenomena) and as standards or norms from which actual occurrences deviated (in the case of social phenomena). This view, though it has turned out to be invalid, has resisted modification in the light of experience, being held in many quarters even at the present time.

Because of the provisional, hence approximative, nature of hypotheses, models, and paradigms and the interpretations based upon them, they cannot be proved or disproved—this is so from a metaphysical point of view, as will appear in due course. They merely become displaced by better and more comprehensive hypotheses, models and paradigms providing better and, it is hoped, more comprehensive interpretations than before, according as changing circumstances and experiences dictate. However, this view is of comparatively recent date.[5] The traditional, but inaccurate, view that prevailed in the past led to the conclusion that scientific hypotheses could only be shown to be true or false and, once proved false, abandoned but not otherwise. Their truth was held to be subject to proof or disproof, a single contrary case being regarded as adequate for their disproof.

We shall deal, first, with the methods that were believed to be heuristic without prior need of data regarding the nature of phenomena, then with the nature of scientific "laws" governing different types of phenomena, finally with the question of proof and disproof of hypotheses or paradigms.

A. METHODS WITHOUT DATA

The method used in the past to determine agency or cause of an action, phenomenon, or event operated on the basis of the human paradigm, making no distinction between agency and cause, since both were assumed to be of human origin. Thus in establishing *agency* the aim was to know *who* stole an article, committed a murder, et cetera. Both the *nature* and the *agency* of the action are *assumed*, not established. Thus the action committed is a theft, not misplacement of the article in question; the death is not from natural causes, but the result of a crime—a murder, not a suicide. Similarly, the agency is assumed to be human, not non-

331

human, and the task is to determine *which* human being is responsible.

In establishing the cause of an action, phenomenon, or event a *human* cause is assumed, not established, the *nature* of the action, phenomenon, or event being likewise assumed rather than established. The operative question is, Why? Why does the theft occur in this case and not another? What maleficent human agency caused the theft? Why does the murder occur in this case and not another, and what maleficent agent caused it? Or, to take another example, why is this particular family member and not another sick at this time, and which human agency is responsible for the illness?

The method used in searching out or disclosing human agency or cause is a *detection procedure*: by means of signs or trial by ordeal (fire, water, poison, et cetera). These detective means are regarded as reliable by those who employ them, but there is no way of establishing their reliability. A sign may, in fact, be misleading; a man who survives ordeal by fire, water, or poison may, in fact, be guilty of the suspected action or crime. On the other hand, the methods being often such as to leave little room for survival, in the case of trial by ordeal, are guaranteed to secure conviction of the crime, whether the accused is guilty or not. A guarantee of conviction was more important, in the interest of social stability and tranquillity, than the risk of error in detection or of non-detection. Thus the detective methods were both faulty and unsatisfactory.[6]

Future events were in the lap of the gods, being the work of divine, not human, agency. Therefore, it was necessary to devise methods for securing advance knowledge of the intentions and actions of the gods. The methods of prediction were those of *divination* (literally, searching out divine intention): augury by means of omens, portents, and auspices of the outcome of, say, a battle, illness, business venture, et cetera. Specifically, such omens and portents included lightning, a storm, a shipwreck, the flight pattern of birds, or one could take the auspices by examination of the contents of human and other animal entrails, the pattern of tea leaves at the bottom of a cup, tarot cards, et cetera.[7]

The method of augury, famous in Roman times, was even then known to be unreliable as a means of prediction. Hence it was substituted or reinforced by the vow—a purely contractual transaction between human client and divine agent regarding the future event of interest to the client: "If I win this battle, I shall build you a temple, O Mars, God of War," "If I succeed to this high office, I shall make a sacrifice to you, O Fortuna, Goddess of Chance," et cetera[8]—a purely business affair in which a quid pro quo was established.

Where the focus of interest was in establishing the validity of conclusions connected with a given phenomenon or event or derived from so-called axioms or self-evident truths, *forensic* methods or *argumentation* constituted the "heuristic" tool. These methods may be classed in two categories. The first category consisted of a set of interlocking or mutually supporting methods serving as checks and balances on one another: dialogue, rhetoric, sophistry, and determination by jury. The other category was *deductive reasoning* on the basis of the Aristotelian syllogism.

Forensic Checks and Balances

(i) Dialogue. The eliciting of desired information or response by the method of question and answer was favored by the ancient Greek philosopher, Socrates, and his pupil, Plato. Its invention is credited by Aristotle, Plato's famous pupil, to Zeno of Elea. In essence, it is the method of argument in which one starts with his opponent's basic premises and shows that they lead to unacceptable conclusions. It is the method still in use by the Oxford Debating Society. In the hands of Socrates it was a question and answer method by which, in eliciting the desired response, the questioner's position was confirmed directly by the answer, or indirectly by an implied and unacceptable contradiction (*reductio ad absurdum*). It was the method by which Socrates enunciated his famous doctrine of "knowledge as reminiscence," or the eliciting, by question and answer, of information one already possesses (from a previous existence)—just like the delivery of a baby already in its mother's womb by a midwife (the profession of Socrates' mother). This debating technique was taught in courses on rhetoric in the Greek educational system. Its aim is to arrive at a single consistent position by the elimination of contradiction. Its basic assumption is that there is only one right answer, and two sides only to every question—one true, the other false.

(ii) Rhetoric. This debating technique seeks to establish a position as valid, not by restricting the argument to the facts in dispute, but by appealing to the passion and sympathy of the listener (*argumentum ad hominem*).

(iii) Sophistry. The Sophists were a class of Greek philosophers contemporary with Socrates and adept in the art of contradiction. They strove to show that consistent arguments could be made out for both of two contradictory positions or interpretations of the same facts (in much the same way as Kant's famous antinomies in his *Critique of Pure Reason*), regardless of the ethical value of the conclusions. Carneades, who succeeded Arcesilaus as head of Plato's Academy, gave a brilliant example of sophistry during a diplomatic mission with two other philosophers

333

from Athens to Rome in 156 B.C.E., when he argued opposite conclusions on the position taken by Plato's Socrates that to inflict injustice was a greater evil to the perpetrator than to suffer it.[9] The Sophists' skill in contradiction tended to strengthen scepticism and the view that between two extreme positions truth, like virtue, lay in the middle.

(iv) Jury Determination. Given that equally good arguments could be advanced on both sides of a question—as the Sophists demonstrated—to which should be added the risk of persuasion by rhetorical appeals to the passion and sympathy of listeners, it seemed both practical and convenient to determine which argument, and therefore which conclusion, was valid by a show of hands. "Truth by majority vote" was thus invented as the basis of the jury system, used by debating societies and the courts of law.

All four forensic techniques operated as a system of mutual checks and balances but failed, nevertheless, in achieving their objectives. Dialogue, the method of pro and con, is a primitive technique of argumentation based on the erroneous assumption that there are only two sides to a question—true and false—and that the task is therefore to decide which side is true. There is no middle ground or gray area. But not every issue permits of a dialectic or adversary position, and not every apparently adversary position is indeed one, or resolvable in favor of one party or the other. An appropriate decision may favor or disadvantage *both* parties. Thus the dialectic system on which the judicial systems of the world as well as debating societies are based is both primitive and invalid, hence an outdated system. Worse, in the case of the judicial system, the jury method not only buttresses an outworn technique but also a legal system generally dedicated to the preservation of the "inalienable rights" of property.

Rhetoric plays on passions, not on intellect or reason, and sophistry is not necessarily valid reasoning or argumentation. Two contrary positions could be sustained on premises that are invalid. Neither rhetoric nor sophistry does much to establish the validity of premises on either side of a dialectic. Sophistry has the merit, at least, of revealing the true nature of logic as having no connection with truth or error—only with consistency. Thus logic has no heuristic properties. Considering these defects of rhetoric and sophistry, their use as forensic techniques in legal argumentation condemns the legal systems of our age.

As to the jury system, it hardly needs pointing out that truth is not revealed by majority vote or by consensus. Majority vote reveals merely the opinions, wishes, and prejudices of the majority without any necessary implication as to the validity or otherwise of either their opinion or the subject of their opinion. Majority vote is merely a convenient technique for resolving disagreements in favor of the majority and has no merit or wisdom in itself, nor any empirical validity for its decision. Trumped up as the bastion of so-called democracy, it therefore carries no built-in standard of validity or truth, rightness or justice, other than the brute force and weight of numbers. Thus adding the defects of the jury system to those of the other forensic techniques, it is no wonder that the courts are rightly called courts of law not of justice, and that the quality of, and respect for, legal decisions are so often called into question.

Deductive Reasoning: The Experimental Method of the Ancient World

Following its invention by the Greek philosopher, Aristotle, the syllogism became the experimental method of scholars of the ancient world. By its means deductive reasoning was applied to axioms or propositions regarded as self-evident truths. It was assumed that true conclusions would follow from self-evident truths through the application of the rules of the syllogism and that by this method one could arrive at knowledge of the external world without further ado: that is, without further examination or checking of the conclusions arrived at against the empirical facts of the external world of phenomena. As a result, deductive reasoning was misconceived as heuristic and highly overrated, in the place of sense-experience, as the ultimate test or touchstone of the discovery of truth. Nor was it recognized that the conclusion of a syllogism was really nothing new but already implied in the axiom or postulate, and that all that the process of deduction achieved was to make explicit this implied conclusion as well as its other implications.

Without verification of the conclusion as well as the axiom against the phenomenal world, the procedure was bound to be faulty. It was, moreover, unfortunately buttressed by an erroneous two-world conception of metaphyics founded on the assumption that the sensible phenomenal world was a derivative product of a supra-sensible world of intellect and intelligible concepts—hence, of deductive reasoning. It was, therefore, easy to conclude, erroneously, that at the end of the process of deductive reasoning, symbolized by the Aristotelian syllogism, lay a conclusion to which automatically corresponded some fact or entity of the phenomenal world. And, if it did not, the worse for the phenomenal world, as the lack of correspondence was further assumed to be due to the continuing change and, therefore, unreliability of the phenomenal world. Either way, in the final analysis, the facts of the phenomenal world did not really matter, and philosophers and metaphysicians could pursue their inclinations in blissful disregard of the external world around them.

The problem of verification thus arose, at the very beginning, with the basic axiom itself—the so-called self-evident truth, based on no more than the so-called intelligible concepts. If the axiom was, indeed, guaranteed to be as true to experience as it was self-evident, the result of the process of deductive reasoning—albeit already implied—would also be empirically valid. But there was no guarantee that what *seemed* self-evident was actually so in experience, in the absence of the simple precaution of cross-checking conclusions against experience or carefully assembled data.

The faulty two-world metaphysics was, in turn, hitched to, and thought to be confirmed by, mathematics—specifically, geometry—a self-evident, self-consistent, intellectual, and eminently intelligible system. It was regarded as the paragon of ideas and idea-systems applicable to the "real" world (i.e., the world of ideas) as well as to the "actual" or phenomenal world, by virtue of the conventional belief that its axioms and theorems were true of space, which was something given in experience. There was a general unawareness of the fact that mathematics, like deductive logic, was a human invention, not something discovered "out there" and that its axioms, like those of logic, were in need of verification against sensible experience as a test of their validity.[10]

All the foregoing methodologies have failed to qualify as effective instruments guaranteeing the attainment of their respective objectives, whether it be detecting the agency or cause of phenomena or events, predicting the shape of things to come, or establishing the validity of conclusions derived from so-called self-evident facts.

B. NATURAL VERSUS NORMATIVE LAW: A FALSE DISTINCTION

There is, in practice, no formal or essential difference between the laws governing the occurrence of "natural" phenomena and those governing the occurrence of "social" (including "moral," "political," and other so-called nonnatural) phenomena. On the contrary, the difference would seem to lie in our greater knowledge of the conditions governing the occurrence of "natural" phenomena and in our greater ignorance of those governing the occurrence of "social" phenomena. Certainly, also, there may be less tendency to express personal judgment on the occurrence or nonoccurrence of natural phenomena than in the case of social phenomena. But this, in itself, does not constitute a point of difference between the kinds of phenomena involved; rather, is it a reflection of the *attitude* of the observer toward phenomena, based on his likes and dislikes, on the extent of his knowledge or his ignorance.

Insofar as they occur under conditions consistent with their occurrence, social phenomena or events are no different from natural, for in both cases the laws governing their occurrence are the conditions necessary for, and consistent with, their occurrence. These laws may, therefore, be called "natural laws" in *all* cases.

Norms, by contrast, do not define occurrence conditions for phenomena. All they do is lay down supposedly nonempirical limits, asymptotes, or standards with regard to which actual conditions in which phenomena occur can be measured as *deviations*. For they would not, strictly speaking, be norms if they were ever fulfilled. The conventional definition of norms as standards of what *should be* (ideals) rather than of what *is* harks back to Greek academic philosophy, which postulated nonsensible, that is, "ideal" or "pure" forms of things from which the actually occurring (sensible) cases diverge. For Plato, the norm was the archetype or perfect version of things (the "idea"), which was only intelligible in its perfection. This idea (noumenon) could not exist in the world of things apprehensible by the senses, the world of imperfect versions of things (phenomena); the reason for this being the recalcitrance of matter that causes it to resist "perfect forming." Whence originated the contrast between what should be (the perfection that should result were it possible to reproduce it in matter) and what is (all that could ever be achieved in matter—the imperfect forms of things).

A simple and practical way of interpreting the distinction between things as they *are* and as they *should be* is in terms of the distinction between *conceptual* and *empirical* existence; conceptual existence being pure form, idea, or concept, empirical existence being sensible existence incorporating a debased version or semblance of its corresponding concept. Thus things as they are would be empirical existence, things as they should be conceptual existence. This falls squarely within the context of Greek academic philosophy. However, the Greek Academics were not consistent in their application of the distinction to physical and to social (human behavior) phenomena. First, they distinguished between "physical" and "moral" forms as relating, respectively, to material objects and nonmaterial objects, i.e., human behavior. Matter was supposed to prevent pure form from showing through in its perfection, while its absence allowed it to come through. But instead of making the obvious conclusion that since behavior contained no matter, it reflected perfectly its pure form ("moral" form), whence human behavior as it is corresponds perfectly to human behavior as it should be, Aristotle went on to complicate matters by recommending that *virtue*, the mean between two extreme or opposite moral forms, was what human behavior *should be*. This inconsistent treatment of physical and moral forms made nonsense of the attempt to distinguish between empirical and normative criteria.

One consequence was that the Greek philosophers accepted *things as they are* in the case of physical objects ("semblances of pure forms") but rejected them in the case of human behavior, where they were supposed to be identical with *things as they should be* ("pure moral forms").

On the other hand, they did not require *things as they should be* in the case of physical objects, while an artificial standard (virtue) was required instead of the pure moral forms as *what things should be* in the case of human behavior.

No reason was given for this artificial and different treatment of social as opposed to physical phenomena. It was one of many examples of how the Greek academic philosophers allowed their personal prejudices to color their philosopical positions. This is also an area in which ancient Greek wisdom has been reversed by modern wisdom (as will be seen in section 9, following).

It is clear from the foregoing discussion that Plato's "idea" or form is the equivalent of the *norm* of things and is nonempirical,[11] constituting a criterion that is never fulfilled—a criterion of *nonoccurrence* for *what is*, rather than for the *occurrence* of *what should be*: in short, a criterion of what *cannot be*.

We shall follow Plato and conventional practice—at least in the social field—and regard *nonoccurrence* of *what is* as the *primary meaning and objective of norms*. Thus norms seek, in the first place, to *eliminate* occurrences, make them *disappear*. This involves a knowledge of the conditions necessary for the *disappearance* of *what is* or, what comes to the same thing, a knowledge of the conditions necessary for the *occurrence* of *what should be*. Expressed another way, this means knowing how to bring about *what should be* in a manner consistent with the disappearance of *what is*; in short, knowing how to bring about the *corrective* of *what is*. And once the corrective was brought about it would no longer be in the realm of *what should be* but in that of *what is*.

A caveat is necessary here regarding the use of the word *corrective* to imply the substitution of one phenomenon (what should be) for another (what is). This is not the same in meaning as the term *compensation* or the term *punishment*. These carry the meaning of *balance* or *equilibrium*, not of *disappearance*, which is the essence of the term *corrective*; for the target of equilibrium—the phenomenon that *is*—remains very much in evidence. *Corrective*, on the contrary, implies *both* the disappearance from view of the phenomenon or object that is *and* its replacement by the desired substitute. And a corrective would be very much an empirical event, not a nonempirical concept like Plato's ideal form.

To illustrate: In any contemporary society, where one of the norms is a crime-free society, the absence of this norm (that is, the occurrence

338

of crime) is compensated for by punitive measures intended (so it is maintained) to discourage crime. As is well known, however, punitive measures generally fall very far short of their intended effect: they neither discourage crime nor make it disappear. They do not bring about—and are not expected to bring about—the norm, namely, the ideal of a crime-free society. A corrective, on the contrary, in such circumstances would be an action or policy that *does* make crime disappear, that *does*, at the same time, bring about a crime-free society.

This illustration confirms that the difference between "natural" and "normative" is a matter of ignorance or of knowledge, of the nonavailability or availability of *information*. Thus, if there were nonchanging states and Plato knew enough about them on the basis of experience, he would not have had to postulate a nonempirical, suprasensible world in order to define such a state. Likewise, if human society throughout the ages knew enough about the conditions responsible for the occurrence and the absence of crime, it would not be necessary to decree ineffective sanctions like imprisonment, canings, and the death penalty—merely compensatory or retributive measures—which neither discourage nor eliminate crime. Ancient and modern penal codes are a testimony to futility born of ignorance.

Thus, given enough information, the distinction between "natural" and "normative" (elimination of one natural by its correlative) disappears completely. For the normative, like the natural, will then occur as expected, that is, *naturally*, under the appropriate conditions—whether or not these conditions occur spontaneously or are contrived (as in the case of experiments successfully replicated outside the laboratory).

We are thus left, in the final analysis, with only *one* type of phenomenon—*what is*: that is, empirical phenomena occurring (appearing or disappearing) under natural or appropriate conditions. And *one* type of law—*natural* law.

Since Plato's time, the concept of a norm (pure form, idea, noumenon) has undergone an evolution in meaning. From the original meaning of a standard of perfection that is empirically impossible—that is, from the concept of things as they *should be* as contrasted with things as they *are*—the norm has descended into the realm of the possible. "Should be" has been assimilated to "is" under the influence of developments in the physical sciences, so that a norm has come to mean what *should and can be*: the way things *are, in the best possible circumstances*. This equation of norm with actual occurrence in certain circumstances is only possible by introducing the bias of value judgment, a bias that comes from regarding certain occurrences in the various fields of physical science as both natural (what is) and ideal or desirable (what should be). This dual standard was then transferred to the social field and applied in such a way that what should be came to mean what is, in the best possible circumstances (i.e., what is *desirable*); and what is, under less than the best possible circumstances (which was virtually all the time), was also what was *undesirable*. The objective in the social field was, therefore, to try to ensure that what is should approximate as closely as possible its empirical ideal of what should be.

What has happened, then, since Plato's time has been the transfer of his conceptual norm from a suprasensible, nonempirical world to the sensible, empirical one, from the plane of the transcendent to that of the immanent. The new distinction of meaning between what *is* and what *should be* is best seen in connection with the word on which discussion of natural versus normative has traditionally centered: *law*, as used in the physical sciences and as used in the social field (government, religion, et cetera). In the physical sciences, where the normative has lost its meaning—and bias—by being assimilated to the actual, empirical hypotheses are called laws (of nature, or natural laws). In the social field, where what *is* is undesirable and what is desired is what *should be*, "law" has come to mean what is normative or ideal (should be) and, presumably, can be. Thus, in government and politics, parliamentary commands and prohibitions to citizens are also called laws (of parliament or legislature); and in the field of religion ethical recommendations presented in the guise of commands and prohibitions by a superhuman agency, are similarly called laws (of God, or divine laws). In this way, it has come about that the same word, *law*, is used to denote actual or existing situations in the physical sciences, but normative or ideal situations in the social field. In order to avoid confusing the unsuspecting by using the same word, *law*, in an opposite sense in fields other than the physical sciences, and in order to save time and effort now spent in learned dissertations and other discussions distinguishing between normative and natural laws, it would seem advisable to use different words altogether for the different senses of "law."

The use of *law* exclusively to denote the empirical hypotheses stating the general conditions under which phenomena and events occur, regardless of the field of their occurrence, has much to recommend it. "Parliamentary commands" or "state edicts" requiring or prohibiting certain actions or kinds of behavior would take the place of "parliamentary laws" or "state laws," while "ethical rules" would describe very well the formulations designed to govern behavior in the religious arena. Thus *law*, *edict*, and *rules* would not need to be further distinguished from each other, as is now the case with the word *law*, used in these three different senses. There is also a net gain when the three different terms need to be applied in the same field, e.g., the formulation of ethical rules and the issuing of edicts governing the application of biological laws in genetic engineering. Or, again, when the same topic is the object of command or prohibition in two different fields—as when murder, adultery, theft, and perjury are simultaneously the objects of ethical rules and state edicts proscribing them.

It should be noted, however, that by branding what *is* as undesirable and what is desired as what *should be* (the norm) contemporary practice in the social field has not only imported bias into the concept of the norm—a bias from which the physical sciences are largely free[12]—but has also in some, though not all, cases eliminated the family resemblance that marked both the Platonian norm and its natural counterpart. Thus where the actual (undesirable) percentage of, say, 15 percent literacy is to be raised to the desirable norm of, say, 100 percent, the family resemblance exists. But where the actual (undesirable) is a crime-infested society and the normative (desirable) a crime-free society all notion of family resemblance disappears and the norm becomes that which is *inconsistent* with current conditions.

As has been shown already, there is no formal or essential difference between the hypotheses governing the occurrence of phenomena in the physical sciences and those governing the occurrence of phenomena in the social science fields—given enough information in these fields. Parallel procedures would apply for specifying the conditions under which a phenomenon under study occurred, be it mass/energy transformation, diffraction of light, crime, divorce, et cetera. A hypothesis would be formulated and its implications tested for empirical validity.

It is by this means that laws are "discovered" in the physical sciences and then experimentally put to use to produce or control specific results. Ignorance prevents this procedure from being fruitfully adopted in the social science fields, where "magical" methods still prevail. For example, in meteorology, knowledge of the conditions of precipitation has led to cloud seeding experiments to control the weather, albeit to a very limited extent. By contrast, in the social field governments depend on the magic power of a fiat to control crime (like King Canute commanding the waves to advance no further); when magic does not work they resort to wreaking vengeance on those found guilty of infractions of the edicts.

This example highlights the difference in approach between the physical sciences and the social sciences. In the former, information is first collected with a view to formulating hypotheses or statements of *consistency* (or correspondence) between conditions and occurrences of phenomena. Whether the phenomenon in question is desirable or not is a totally irrelevant matter at this stage. In the social field, however, the cart is put before the horse: a *desired* phenomenon is specified on the

341

ground that it is good for society, before the relevant information regarding the phenomenon has been collected. The phenomenon is supposed to occur spontaneously by a mere fiat and because it is judged desirable on logical grounds, without any appropriate action being taken to bring it about. Inevitably, as must be expected, the phenomenon does not occur. This procedure is the essence of magic, and magic is the essence of normative behavior and norm-setting activity.

It is thus that it comes about, as explained earlier, that unlike a hypothesis, a norm is a statement of *inconsistency* between existing conditions and those necessary (though unknown) for the occurrence of a desired phenomenon. The element of bias (desirable, undesirable) prevails to a much greater degree in the social than in the physical sciences. It seems clear, from all that has been said, that ignorance and bias, rather than alleged unusual complexity of social phenomena or the alleged inappropriateness of application in the social sciences of the methods of investigation employed in the physical sciences, are the twin barriers to progress in the social science fields. This is especially true in the areas of delinquency and crime. In other areas, however, such as education and health, where standard scientific procedures are increasingly, adopted, progress seems to be achieved in corresponding degree, backed by appropriate measures, and the norm tends to become the natural occurrence.

C. IMPOSSIBILITY OF PROOF AND DISPROOF

Disproof is one of the operational criteria in modern science. It accepts as provisionally valid what has not been disproved. Scientific truth and scientific law are, therefore, always *on trial*, provisional until disproved or, more likely, superseded by another and better truth or law. Underlying this procedure is the principle of *philosophical uncertainty*,[13] a basic pillar of philosophy.

Science is correct, from a philosophical point of view, in asserting the impossibility of *proof*—a consequence of the Parmenidean principle of the impossibility of nonexistence,[14] for to prove anything is the same as to prove its existence. But existence is all that is given in human experience and, in the absence of any experience of nonexistence, is impossible to prove. For exactly the same reason, however, science is in error, philosophically as empirically, in espousing the criterion of *disproof*. To disprove anything is to prove that it does *not* exist, which is even more difficult than proof of existence, since nonexistence is not given in human experience, whereas existence is.

Philosophically, therefore, as well as empirically, all that we can know is existence and in this connection we can only *sense-verify* the existence of anything, not *prove* it, and even when verified, knowledge of the thing remains provisional. Our knowledge remains provisional because we can never be certain of all the conditions governing the occurrence and recurrence of any phenomenon; consequently, any statement or hypothesis concerning its occurrence can, at best, be only provisional, pending further or additional information that may become subsequently available.

Given that existence is all that is known to human experience, that things do not nonexist once existing, we are left with the principle of change as the only event that can happen to, and affect, things. And change occurs through *transformation*, this being the only way in which change takes place in nature. In short, things do *not disappear* from existence; they merely *change by transforming*. It follows that the *absence* from view of a *given form* or mode of existence of a thing through transformation argues neither against its existence nor against the possibility of its recurrence in exactly the same given form or mode; for a given phenomenon may be absent at a given time and place but present at some other place simultaneously or in the future, just as it may recur where it is absent at present—not forgetting its previous occurrence in the past. Whence the criterion of disproof is metaphysically untenable.

Linked to the preceding consideration is the fact that it cannot be demonstrated with certainty—even under controlled laboratory conditions—that the conditions associated with the occurrence of a phenomenon were the only conditions involved, both when it occurred and when it did not; for there may have been a previously unknown condition that, in addition to those known to be present, was responsible for the occurrence of the phenomenon.

The invalidity—not only uncertainty—of the scientific criterion of disproof is a consequence both of the dialectics of existence (the principle of transformation of a phenomenon into what it was not—whence derives the principle of philosophic uncertainty and of the open-endedness of evolution) and of the organic unity of heterogeneous phenomena (the principle of organic unity of the cosmos).

But, basically, it follows uniquely from the Parmenidean principle of the *impossibility of nonexistence*.

We are therefore led by all the foregoing considerations to conclude that the time has certainly come for the dethronement of the "scientific" criterion of *invalidation by disproof* and its replacement by the truly scientific principle of *subsumption of a narrower in a wider hypothesis or synthesis*, itself based on the principle of organic unity of contraries or heterogeneous elements in the cosmos. The effect of the new principle is not the abandonment of the old hypothesis or "law" but a closer and more critical examination of its conditions, with a view to determining whether there may be hitherto undetected *additional* conditions associated with the occurrence of the phenomenon in question, the absence of which may be responsible for the unexpected exceptions to the reigning hypothesis. It is by this procedure that the subsumption of the previous (or reigning) hypothesis in a wider hypothesis takes place, in order to account for exceptions to the narrower hypothesis as well as to include them in the wider.

Thomas Kuhn, in his path-breaking study, *The Structure of Scientific Revolutions*, has shown how scientific knowledge is advanced not by disproof of previously reigning hypotheses but by their displacement by other and wider hypotheses. But he also argues that, correspondingly, unsolved problems under the old hypothesis may not be solved under the new but may simply be displaced by other kinds of problems. The old problems, therefore, are simply forgotten and continue to be unresolved, their place being taken perforce by the more urgent and commanding problems of the new hypothesis.[15]

Our argument is related to, but slightly different from, that of Kuhn. We are not arguing in favor of *any* kind of displacement hypothesis that may result in old problems being simply forgotten, unresolved. Rather are we arguing for what may be called family-related displacement hypotheses, that is, displacement hypotheses that not merely displace but, being related, also subsume or integrate the displaced hypothesis within their wider framework, with the result that they both resolve the old unresolved problems as well as give rise to new problems. Such type of displacement hypotheses preserves the principle of organic unity and, therefore, continuity with the old hypotheses. It is only in connection with this type of hypothesis that we can truly speak of scientific progress, that is, continuity in advancement, as opposed to scientific innovation or advancement without continuity.

The principle of subsumption of narrower in wider hypotheses by which proper scientific progress is made does not in any way affect the provisionality of scientific "law." This remains intact. All it does is eliminate from the scientific vocabulary two hitherto hallowed terms: *proof* and *disproof*. In our cosmos, "all things are possible" because existence—another name for possibility—is all that is given to us. In consequence, the terms *proof* and *disproof* do not apply in our cosmos—they have no empirical meaning.

Notwithstanding the gain in progress through continuity, the principle of subsumption of hypotheses leaves unaffected the existing limitations of modern scientific procedures—chiefly the following, on which, in the final analysis, rests the principle of provisionality of scientific knowledge:

(a) The uncertainty principle regarding the range of conditions on which every scientific law is based.
(b) The ambiguity and inadequacy of the single-criterion classification of phenomena. This criterion rests on the principle of homogeneity as the basis for inclusion/exclusion of instances examined for relevance to the phenomenon under study. The single-criterion classification (which also underlies the Aristotelian syllogism) is too narrow a basis for handling phenomena, for since the same phenomenon can belong to different groups based on different classifications, any principle of classification is not exclusive with regard to the phenomenon, but only with regard to other principles. It does not therefore eliminate ambiguity, as it is supposed to do.
(c) The irreparably disintegrative effect of the analytical method. While this method promotes a better understanding of how things (or phenomena) are constituted, it is impossible to reintegrate what has been disintegrated by analysis. The best that can be achieved is an "aggregate of differentiates" rather than the original "integrate of differentiates," or integrated whole.

There is, among other things, an urgent need to develop and use a *logic of heterogeneity* or *logic of heterogeneous consistency* to complement the traditional *logic of homogeneous consistency*. Its development and use—in accordance with cosmic realities—will not only reflect the organic unity of the cosmos itself, including all its diverse elements; it will also promote the habit of seeing things whole, each element in the context of all the other elements composing the whole organism, thus opening up a fruitful and pragmatic approach toward problem solving.

The Hegelian dialectic method of thesis, antithesis, and synthesis, which reflects the principle of organic unity, is the obvious basis for the development of a logic of heterogeneity (dialectic logic).

Even with the development and use of dialectic logic, however, the *impossibility of integrating what has been disintegrated by analysis and the experimental method* will continue unaffected, as well as the *uncertain tenure of every scientific hypothesis*, even the most reasonably well established.

4. THE HUMAN PARADIGM:
ITS EXPLOITATION AS AN INTERPRETIVE TOOL

A. THE HUMAN PARADIGM

Confronted with the task of interpreting the cosmos in which he found himself, man simultaneously confronted a Hobson's choice: to interpret everything in terms of what he knew best, himself and his community group. Thus was born, simultaneously with the Human Paradigm, the original rule that first incorporated Hobson's choice: interpreting the "unknown in terms of the known"—the rule that may be erroneously thought to originate with algebra in the form "from the known to the unknown." Both versions of the rule mean the same thing: use the known to interpret the unknown.

The human paradigm was first used by man to orient himself within the cosmos by the simple expedient of "anthropo-geo-cosmo-centrism," that is, centering the cosmos on the earth and the earth on man. Thus the earth on which man found himself was assumed to be the center of the cosmos[16] and man the master of the earth, ergo, of the cosmos. From the outset, it was implied in this view that man was the apex and raison d'être of the cosmic enterprise.

Turning next to the cosmos, man interpreted it in two possible ways: first, as a being more or less *like man himself*, with beginning (birth), development (growth), decline (aging), and end (death). This was *anthropocosmology* at its best. Second, as being an artifact created by a manlike creator who behaved very much in the manner of a man making implements (*homo fabricus*). This second interpretation comprises two component interpretations: (1) that the cosmos was a dead implement and thus *inferior to man*; (2) that the creator of the cosmos, although manlike, was more powerful than man in creating the cosmos, including man himself: he was a god, a manlike creator-god (*homo fabricus divinus*). Thus arose *anthropotheology*, the doctrine of an *anthropomorphic god*.

In interpreting the cosmos as the work of a manlike creator-god, man had automatically applied the human paradigm to the cosmos-creator and simultaneously implied that man himself could become a god just as much as the cosmos-creator. Man had conceptually created the cosmos-creator in man's image and man himself in the image of the cosmos-creator. (Which, of course, amounted to the tautological statement that man is created in man's image: an indication that an attempt to equate a cosmos-creator to man and vice versa, imagewise or otherwise, was both meaningless and irrelevant.)

B. GENDER

The application of the human paradigm at the cosmic level spawns several anthropo-basic views, as we have seen: anthropo-geo-cosmo-centrism, anthropocosmology, anthropotheology, and anthropomorph-ism. This was not the limit, however, for the human paradigm invaded the intra-cosmic domain as well more thoroughly than at the cosmic level, male and female genders being fully exploited. Thus while the cosmos-creator was unquestionably male, for the most part, or a male-female combination (androgynous), at the intra-cosmic level gender differentia-tion was essential for a satisfactory interpretation of various phenomena. Anthropomorphism had to be differentiated into *andromorphism* and *gy-nomorphism*. Thus the earth stood in a feminine relationship to the cosmic god, so that the fruitful showers of rain could be his seminal fluid that fertilized the earth, resulting in the production of its lush vegetation as well as the first men, women, and other animals who subsequently took over the task of reproduction by both sexual and asexual means.

By a kind of feedback, the gender issue had to be faced with respect to other planetary bodies. Earth and its cargo of animals and plants were easy enough—it was man's home. But other planets presented a problem because of human ignorance of their nature and what went on on them. On the analogy of human reproduction, male and female had to be rep-resented at the level of cosmic deity, separately or hermaphroditically, in order to interpret other intra-cosmic phenomena as divine offspring. In addition, human gender institutions (patriarchy and matriarchy) also had to make their contribution to the interpretive enterprise at all levels. The exploitation of the human paradigm was never complete nor entirely successful at the cosmic level, where the struggle to bisexualize the cosmos-creator has been on and off throughout the centuries, with the male sex tending to gain the upper hand. Thus in early Christianity, some Gnostic sects espoused God the Mother instead of God the Father. And, in twentieth-century America, the movement for equality of the sexes spearheaded in the 1960s by the National Organization of Women led to pressure to thoroughly bisexualize the cosmos-creator as God the Father *and* God the Mother. *Anthropotheology* is thus being genderized into *androtheology* and *gynotheology*, in preference to a *gynandromorphic* (or hermaphroditic) cosmic deity. The latter would have been more eco-nomical, but would certainly be more difficult to accept and understand, as well as to make references to in pronominal usage.

In the domain of language and communication the gender aspect of the human paradigm has also fulfilled an interpretive role, with the male gender traditionally predominating. Concepts and words were differentiated according to gender (as in the classical languages), a practice that survives until the present time. Thus *anthropolinguistics* was differentiated into *androlinguistics* and *gynolinguistics*, with dominance being accorded to the male sex in the rules governing language and syntax. One of the consequences of the storming of the male bastion of theology has been not only the feminization of the deity and the priesthood, but also of theological language and scripture.

C. PERSON

The human organism as well as its gender relationships, we have seen, constitutes a paradigm of interpretation at the cosmic and intra-cosmic levels. Thus interrelationships within the cosmos also tend to be interpreted on the basis of *human* interrelationships. In this setting, human language or speech assumes importance as an instrument for designating various elements and activities within the cosmos, as well as their status or relationship, vis-à-vis the human being in an individual or group setting. Of paramount importance in this connection are *nouns* and *pronouns*, the former for designating the particular elements and activities as manifestations of existence within the cosmos, the latter for indicating their relationships as individuals or groups on the model of human *personal* relationships.

From the viewpoint, therefore, of philosophy as an empirical investigation and interpretation of relationships within the cosmos, pronouns are important as the category of speech most appropriate to the study of these interrelationships modeled on the human paradigm. Similarly, it can be shown that, on the basis of the human paradigm, pronouns are appropriate to the study of interrelationships within the derivative and related fields of philosophy, such as metaphysics, theology, religion, and ethics. Not only have human interrelationships been applied to study in these fields, but they have also been correctly and appropriately applied in those of these fields that are essentially focused on man, namely, religion and ethics. Furthermore, the human paradigm can be correctly and meaningfully applied to relationships that are parallel to those of human beings, for example, relationships within and between various animal groups that parallel those within and between human groups.

Metaphysics

Viewed from the man-biased approach adopted by mankind in its interpretive activities, the basic existential units consist of "I" and "not-

348

I,'' the two being constitutive of the cosmos. Metaphysics thus becomes the study of existential units singly (''I,'' ''not-I'') or collectively (''I'' + ''not-I'' = cosmos) as regards their nature.

In man's investigation of the nature of the basic metaphysical units, his human bias leads to an assimilation of the ''not-I'' to the ''I.'' In other words, man makes the simple assumption that the ''not-I'' is similar to the ''I.'' The ''I'' being alive and active, it is assumed that the ''not-I'' is similarly alive and active. This assumption involves the *personification* of the nonhuman, including the nonanimal, ''not-I'' (the nonanimal ''not-I'' being the various kinds of ''It'') and constitutes the basis of hylozoism or animism—the doctrine that *all* matter in its distributive aspect is animated or alive. In this manner one could derive the doctrine of Thales, the seventh–sixth century B.C.E. Ionian philosopher, that the world is full of gods (living things).

Aside from revealing its anthropocentric bias, *personification* provides a common (human) standard for studying and dealing with all cosmic manifestations in treating them all as entities that are as much alive as human beings. This approach was not without some fruitful results: it apparently constituted the basis for the atomist metaphysics of Leucippus, Democritus, Epicurus, Lucretius, and other advocates of that brand of metaphysics. In modern science it has produced—by a different route and more empirical methods—the discipline of subnuclear physics in the directions of progressively diminishing magnitude and molecular chemistry in the opposite direction.

Animistic metaphysics has its counterpart in the religious field, notably in Buddhism, which makes no distinction between man and any other kind of manifestation within the cosmos. Modern physics confirms this by establishing that man is constituted of the same basic and active elements as the stars and the rest of the cosmos.

Theology

Given the existential facts on which the human paradigm is based—birth, growth and development, decline and death—the application of the paradigm to the interpretation of the cosmos and intra-cosmic relationships implicitly contained similar questions concerning the origin and destiny of the basic existential units: Who/what am I, whence and whither? Who/what is the not-I, whence and whither? Who/what is the cosmos (I + not-I), whence and whither?

Theology is the study that concerns itself with questions and speculations about the (divine) *origin and destiny* of the basic existential units, while metaphysics investigates the ''what'' or *essence* of these units.[17]

349

Logically, origin (theology)—if there is one—precedes essence (metaphysics), but for practical purposes essence takes precedence to origin in order that we may have a subject of discussion, about whose origin we may speculate. Thus, for convenience, theology is treated after metaphysics.

We have seen that the application of the human paradigm to the interpretation of the cosmos leads, in metaphysics, to personification, hence to hylozoism, animism, or spiritism. On the theological plane, the identification (or association) of *spirit* with *origin* of the cosmos results in viewing spirit as the god or active principle behind the "creation" of the cosmos. Thus spiritism in its distributive aspect becomes *pantheism* (as we have seen in the conclusion of Thales) and in its collective aspect becomes *monotheism-cum-pantheism*. The singular personification of collective spirit becomes *theism*, resulting in the divorce of god (theos) from cosmos and world.

In practice, theology and metaphysics have usually been discussed together since the time of the Greek Academic philosophers. This was because God was one of the three metaphysical units postulated by them (the others being form and matter) so that, for the Greek philosophers, theology was automatically a *part* of metaphysics (but not identical with it). This was Plato's schema. Aristotle combined God and the forms, thus giving birth to *ideo-theism*, which in Hegel's philosophy became Absolute Idea or Spirit. Spirit, according to Hegel, is a dynamic, because dialectic, concept that, entering and disclosing itself in history, alienates itself from itself—by virtue of its generating its opposite—but eventually collects itself again in a synthesis and moves on, relentlessly, with history.

Feuerbach identified God as a human concept whose meaning content was the ensemble of all the best qualities of the human species, so that theology was, in fact, *anthropotheism*, which becomes anthropology once man reclaims his best qualities from God for himself. Anthropology, in turn, leads to humanism, the doctrine that man is the God of man, his own savior.

Julian Huxley developed an evolutionary humanism based on an existential trinity of matter (the first person of the trinity), man (the second person), and ideas (the third person). Man thus replaced Plato's God in Huxley's scheme and is conceived as spearheading the next phase in the evolutionary process (whence evolutionary humanism) toward new possibilities for the entire terrestrial sector of the cosmos. These possibilities are described by Teilhard de Chardin as a more complex organization and further development of mind—Aristotle's soul—into an all-mind-no-matter state, called the noosphere.

Following in the footsteps of Feuerbach, Karl Marx recognized matter as the only metaphysical element, ideas (including the God-concept) being mere ideological superstructure deriving their existence from, and conditioned by, the material arrangements for the production and distribution of goods and services in any society. Marx, adopting the dual precedent of both Democritus and Feuerbach, simply had no need for God (or a God) in his metaphysical system—a one-element system—which was promptly dubbed *atheistic materialism* by the Church theologians in his day and since.

The foregoing metaphysical and theological systems—with the exception of the nontheological systems of Feuerbach and Marx—are either Platonian or variations upon Plato's metaphysics and theology, hence Platonian in inspiration. One remaining variation that has not yet been mentioned is that which identifies the cosmos with God, the cosmos being endowed with qualities of self-subsistence, indestructibility, eternalness, and infiniteness. This is the case of *theistic materialism* or *cosmotheology*. This case will be the subject of detailed examination in a subsequent discussion on *metatheology* in chapter 6 following.

Religion

The "Thou" is the "not-I" brought into personal relationship with the "I." The "not-I" is the general category comprising all the various "He," "She," and "It." When any of these elements is brought into personal relationship with the "I," the result is a *personalization* of the relationship—as distinct from personification of the element. Personification of the "not-I" merely recognizes its right to exist on the same footing as the "I," but nothing more. It does not, by itself, imply personalization of the relationship with the "I." Nor does either personification or personalization imply an equal regard for the interests of the "Not-I" on the same basis as regard for one's own self-interest. On the contrary, it is possible to personalize the relationship with the "not-I" and yet make its interests dependent on those of the "I." Equal regard for the interests of the other on the same basis as one's own interests belongs in the realm of positive ethics.

Philosophy deals indifferently with all interrelationships between and among the "I's" and "not-I's," while religion is partial. Religion *personalizes* the interrelationships among human beings and between human beings, individually and collectively, on the one hand and the rest of the cosmos (effectively, the biosphere, though not necessarily so limited) on the other. In short, religion is the personalization of interrelationships between the "I," on the one hand, and any and each "not-I," on the other. It is this personalization of his interrelationships with others by man that distinguishes religion from philosophy, that converts philosophy into religion, and that stamps religion as "philosophy with a human face"—that is, philosophy regarded from the focal point of view of man's personalized relationships with the rest of the cosmos.

Ethics

Mutuality or reciprocity of personalized interrelationships takes religion one stage further, transforming it into ethics. And since the type of interrelationships that can be both personalized and reciprocated more or less fully are usually those obtaining among human beings, ethics is usually regarded as limited to human beings. This limitation, however, is an error. Some interrelationships, for example, those between man and some other animals, domesticated and wild, are capable of being both personalized and mutualized in more or less degree. The case of man's relationship with the dog or the cat is pertinent in regard to domestic animals. Wild animals in their natural surroundings, e.g., baboons, chimpanzees, and lions, are capable of personalizing and mutualizing their relationships with man.

As in metaphysics, so in ethics a bit of personification, aided by internalization of the mutuality principle, helps in establishing ethics on an effective and meaningful basis; in short, in conferring on it some degree of automaticity in its operation, as will become evident in due course.

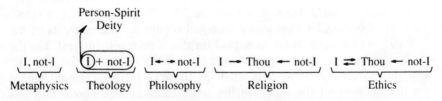

Diagram Illustrating the Human Paradigmatic Approach
in Philosophy and Related Studies

The object of this section has been to show how man has served himself by making pervasive use of the human paradigm in its various dimensions as an interpretive tool at all levels, cosmic and intra-cosmic. Inevitably, one of the principal drawbacks of this paradigm has been its indiscriminate use without regard to its aptness or relevance as an interpretive tool in specific cases. One obvious case is its use at the cosmic level, where it is clearly illegitimate to use a part of the cosmos to interpret the whole of it, which is more complex and heterogeneous: anthropocosmology and anthropotheology result from this misapplication of the paradigm. Less inappropriate is its use at intra-cosmic level, where it is easier to establish parallels as well as differences between one part of the cosmos (man) and another part of it. Naturally, the paradigm is likely to be most successful in those areas where the focus is on man himself, such as religion and ethics.

In section 7 following we shall show the importance and necessity of paradigm change in the search for wider and more efficient interpretations. Nevertheless, tribute must be paid to the Human Paradigm for the service it has rendered to man, even under impossible and irrelevant circumstances, in his search for meaningful interpretations, for contradiction serves as much as corroboration in promoting a better understanding of what is to be interpreted. Even in such a difficult area as anthropolinguistics, where it is clear that human language has obvious and serious limitations when applied to objects outside of the human orbit, there is little doubt that the Human Paradigm will survive for yet a very long time to come—at least for as long as human language remains the medium of discussion of relations and interrelationships involving mankind, and so long as man remains not only the reference point but also the principal beneficiary of the discussion. This accident of biological evolution does not necessarily make the anthropolinguistic exercise valid from a cosmic viewpoint, although it is, undoubtedly, interesting in itself. It only indicates the scope of the difficulties confronting any attempt that may be made to develop a language free of human bias and misconceptions and more suited to cosmic realities. Such a language would have to invent pronominal terms to accommodate a wide range of biological structures featuring, besides the usual human male-female sexual differentiation, androgyny (hermaphroditism), combined organic-inorganic characteristics such as exhibited by the tobacco mosaic virus; they would also have to accommodate groups containing male and female without bias to either sex,[18] as well as energy elements and concepts such as God, soul, or spirit without in these cases involving the notion of inferiority usually associated with the gender-neutral pronoun *it*.[19]

5. THE HUMAN PARADIGM:
ITS DEFECTS AND STRENGTHS

A. DEFECTS

The human paradigm has been the most exploited and generally used standard of reference in man's interpretation of the cosmos. And it is at the cosmic level that its weaknesses have been most glaring: in particular, the interpretation of the cosmos by means of anthropomorphism, anthropolinguistics, anthropobiology, anthropotheology, and anthropogenesis.

Anthropomorphism applies the behavioral characteristics of man to an assumed cosmos-creator or God. This model achieves, simultaneously, the hominization of God (God presented in human form) and the deification of man, both being the two sides of the same coin of anthropomorphism: man creates God in man's image so that the (human) God may then create man in his (God's) own image (image of man). This results in a tautology as well as a vicious circle: man creates God creates man in man's image. Furthermore, as Feuerbach pointed out, *creation* or *making* is a human idea and activity. Nature *manifests* itself through *reproduction*.[20] The attempt to establish the concept of a cosmos-creator, a fashioner of artifacts, like man, on the basis of the logic of analogy was no more successful, leading to the collapse of the human paradigm in the process. Anthropotheology collapsed simultaneously. Thus the idea of creation is inapplicable to the cosmos, as all the evidence shows only reproduction, sexual and asexual.

Furthermore, the gender aspect of anthropomorphism applied to a cosmos-creator is likewise irrelevant. It reveals itself in the andromorphic (male) behavior of deity (e.g., Zeus the philanderer, God in the biblical Garden of Eden), with gynomorphic (female) behavior brought in to complete the picture. In Greek mythology, the latter was done on a token basis, with three females among the dominant patriarchate of Olympus (Hera, Semele, and Psyche). In a later period, gynomorphism gained the upper hand in some branches of Gnosticism, but eventually lost to andromorphism. Modern-day developments have restored the female to a place in the deity, this being accompanied by the feminization of God, the priesthood, theological language, scriptures, et cetera.

Anthropolinguistics—through the attempt to interpret the cosmos in human language—led to a facile misunderstanding of the total web of interrelationships within the cosmos that we have defined as the content of philosophy. It was misconceived, as we have seen,[21] as philology or word history and word play (Martin Heidegger, Friedrich Nietzsche) or as verbal clarification of concepts and propositional statements that are empirically testable (Wittgenstein). Furthermore, Wittgenstein and other members of the school of Logical Positivism were so preoccupied with the meanings of words in sense-empirical terms as to overlook or downplay meanings of words at the conceptual level. They ruled that in order that words may have meanings and be understood, they should be capable of being used in empirically testable propositions. Any word that could not be so used (e.g., words in philosophy and metaphysics) had no meaning, they pontificated, and for all practical purposes was non-sense, hence nonsense. This view ignores the dual aspect of experience and, therefore, of existence: namely, conceptual and sense-empirical, the latter involving the former. A purely conceptual experience (e.g., the concept of a dragon or a unicorn) can be meaningful without being sense-empirical, and both types of experience (conceptual and sense) can be expressed in meaningful propositions. Thus conceptual theology and metaphysics remain meaningful, even without being sense-empirical.

The gender aspect of language results in arbitrary sexualization of concepts of cosmic dimension, for example, sexualization of God as male and, in the romance languages, of the universe as male, but of individual manifestations such as the moon as female, the sun and some of the stars as male.

Anthropobiology—through the application of the biological aspects of man to the cosmos—results in the conception of the cosmos as similar to the human organism, exhibiting birth (origin), growth, decline, and death. Modern cosmological theories, especially the most comprehensive of all—the oscillation theory—tend to reveal the cosmos as a never-ending process of oscillation, of forming and unforming of itself. This is very unlike the individual human being who is a contingent manifestation subject to a process of reproduction, rather than of oscillation.

Anthropogenesis applies (or misapplies) the evolutionary aspect of man to the cosmos, but in particular to the planet Earth. This takes two forms. First, the special theory of evolutionary humanism developed by Pierre Teilhard de Chardin, the palaeontologist and Jesuit priest, who theorized that the next stage in the evolution of the cosmos will be a noospheric phenomenon, with man evolving into "almost all mind, almost never matter." Second is Julian Huxley's evolutionary humanism, which postulates that the future transformation of man will determine the total course of evolutionary biology in the terrestrial sector, man being the spearhead and agent of the evolutionary process. Needless to say, all of this is bad evolutionary theory in that the biological theory of evolution developed by Darwin and his followers expressly rules out any known or preordained goal of the evolutionary process, for evolutionary biology

355

is not a predictive science, being a movement from an unknown past to an unknown future (Darwin) and is a blind force (Bergson). Consequently, it is impossible to know how the process will develop in the future or how each organism will evolve and which will survive, for all evolution is contingent. One thing is certain: man cannot be spearhead and agent of an evolutionary process to which he himself is subject.

Humanistic theories like those of Teilhard de Chardin and Julian Huxley merely show how pre-Copernican ideas die hard, for as we have seen,[22] the great achievement of Copernicus was to demonstrate that the cosmos has no particular center—that *any* stellar body or planet could be regarded as *a* center, and that earth (and therefore, man) has no privileged position in the cosmos. It is, indeed, remarkable that these two world-renowned scientists—one a palaeontologist, the other a biologist—were so firmly committed to an idea that, by their time, had been demonstrated for over three hundred years to be manifestly *dépassée*: man as the *raison* d'être of the cosmos.

One of the most interesting but little recognized consequences of the application of the human paradigm to the cosmos is its effect on man's attitude toward himself in relation to the cosmos—an attitude that is purely a consequence of the methodological defect of the paradigm as a cosmic interpretive tool. Using man as a paradigm for the cosmos has the effect of automatically alienating man (as it also does the anthropomorphic God) from the cosmos of which he is an integral part. Unfortunately, this built-in methodological defect of the paradigm has been exalted to the false status of theological as well as existential dogma[23]—of cosmic proportions, naturally. The doctrine of man's alienation from God and/or world that plays such an important role in the Semitic concept of sin, in the Marcionite Gnostic doctrine, and in the theological existentialism of Kierkegaard is no more than a built-in methodological defect of the human paradigm applied to the cosmos—in the same way that the frame is regarded as separate from the picture—except that, in the case of the human paradigm the paradigm frame is an integral part of the picture. But this tends to be overlooked. The reverse side of this same defect is the error of pride: the pride of man creating the cosmos through a manlike cosmos-creator[24]—the proper original sin, if ever there was one.

Given the built-in defect of alienation of man from God and cosmos which is involved in the human paradigmatic interpretation of the cosmos, the development of soteriological doctrines that reconcile or reunite man and God or man and cosmos is an inevitable consequence, the effect of which—whatever may be its purpose as conceived by theologians—is to repair the original defect of methodological alienation. Inevitably, the reconciler, atoner, or savior has to be man himself: *homo redemptor*, whatever the guise—Buddha, Jesus, Muhammad, or whoever. This mediator has to reconcile man not only to his cosmos and his God (in the context of the human paradigm) but also to his earth. In this reconciliation human sacrifice must, naturally, play a part as the price of appeasement or atonement for the error of alienation. Whether the sacrifice is that of Jesus in Christianity, of men and women in so-called heathenish cults, or the spilling of productive human blood on fields in order to fructify them, the basic idea remains the same: reunite man to his earth and his cosmos where he belongs, but from which he alienates himself in his effort at (mis)interpretation. All this is built into the human paradigm.

B. STRENGTHS

So much for the defects of the human paradigm as an interpretive tool at cosmic level. At the subcosmic (or intra-cosmic) level the results are likely to be less error-prone because comparisons at this level are likely to be more apt and relevant. Thus the part (man, the human paradigm) cannot contain the whole (cosmos)—except in mathematics and holographic representations.[25] But the part (man) can be an adequate measure of all relationships focused on man, such as existentialism, religion, and ethics.

As a microcosmic interpretive tool the human paradigm may suffice for interpreting nonhuman animal behavior, for example, and vice versa. Thus it may be used for interpreting the behavior of lions, while the lion paradigm may be used for interpreting human behavior. Either paradigm could illuminate the other. The male lion, for example, is said to be monogamous and would guard the cubs while the female goes out to hunt. She brings the kill to the male to first have his fill, then shares the remnants with the cubs. This pattern of animal behavior may illuminate human monogamy—if, indeed, it is not the source of it—as well as parallel feeding habits of families in some so-called primitive human societies. These parallel feeding patterns (if they have not been borrowed by humans from the animals) have been regarded by some as confirming male dominance as a "law of nature." This, however, is only one possible interpretation. Another is that the maternal instincts and solicitude of the female, human as well as nonhuman, are so powerful that she tends to regard all adult males as merely grown-up offspring of some female, and feeds the adult male first because of his great utility to the family as procreator and protector, and the younger (and weaker) members after. This interpretation seems to fit the human family very well.

357

This alternative interpretation is both interesting and worthy of further investigation. To the extent that it is valid for the human family it indicates maternal tolerance and, therefore, responsibility for what may well look like male dominance, but may, in fact, be evidence of male irresponsible behavior; the male interpreting as a right due to his position what is only a condescending submission to a grown-up boy on the part of the female. In that case, men would have to take a closer look at their male supremacist attitude and machismo as no more than a carryover from the "look-ma-no-hands" type of adolescent immaturity.

The discussion of the human paradigm has now arrived at the point where it should have become clear that its usefulness increases when viewed not as a unique model but as only one of many zoological models—as only one instance of a more general *animal model*. In particular, its interpretive and problem-solving functions increase as its scope is widened through its various levels of comprehensiveness: (a) individual or nuclear, (b) family, (c) social (group or community), and (d) global or international. Problems referred to this paradigm assume a different character as they are viewed in this progressively wider context, using the same basic animal paradigm. However, the interpretations cannot exceed the limits of the paradigm. Thus, as we have seen, the human paradigm cannot yield an interpretation higher than humanism, its highest religion and doctrine: man as the instrument and goal of his own development and welfare—so far, so good, but not when it goes on to add: as well as that of the cosmos. For then the doctrine (*Menschen über Alles*) becomes suspect (whether enunciated by Teilhard de Chardin, Julian Huxley, or other), being an implied assumption of the human paradigm rather a result arrived at independently and open to independent confirmation.

The stages of the general animal (i.e., zoological) paradigm are also adaptable to botanical life, so that it becomes appropriate to talk about a *biological paradigm* that would apply to all forms of life, animal and plant, and lead on, naturally, to the wider *cosmic paradigm*, which includes it as well as all inorganic entities.

C. ADDENDUM ON THE DOCTRINE OF ANALOGY AND ITS INAPPLICABILITY TO THEOLOGY[26]

The term *analogy* implies some element of "likeness." In the analogy of attribution two objects (known as analogates) are unlike physically, but possess a common abstractible characteristic (known as the analogue), which can be *formally* (that is, univocally or unequivocally) predicated of one analogate only, but only in a relative or derivative sense of the other. That is to say, while one analogate possesses a given characteristic, the other analogate can only be said to possess not the *same* but a *like* characteristic. This manner of speaking is foggy, at best, for a characteristic cannot at the same time be a *common abstractible characteristic* of two analogates (that is, belonging to both) as well as properly belonging to one but only relatively or derivatively belonging to the other in a *like* sense. It must belong to both (for a comparison of similarity) or to neither (no comparison). If it belongs properly to one but not to the other there can be no comparison, no likeness, and, therefore, no analogy. Therefore, the analogy of attribution as classically presented is invalid.

Even if one were to accept the presentation on the basis of a common abstractible characteristic, it would not work with a theology that emphasizes that God is "wholly other" to man, for the affirmation of a common abstractible characteristic would imply a denial of man's humanity and finitude vis-à-vis God as divine and infinite, or a denial of God's divinity, infinitude, and "wholly otherness" vis-à-vis man.

In the analogy of proportionality, both analogates possess the analogue (or common characteristic) literally and properly but only in proportion to the nature of each analogate. By implication, the "nature" of each analogate is different or unequal. For those who argue that God is infinite and man finite the analogy of proportionality cannot hold, for if "goodness," however defined, is a characteristic of both man and God, then

goodness in man : man as goodness in God : God

or, transposing the terms of the analogy,

goodness in man : goodness in God as man : God

While both presentations of the proportionality are equivalent and formally correct, they are really both conceptually and objectively meaningless if man is finite and God infinite, for there can be no proportion between finite and infinite, whether of man to God or (which is equivalent) of human goodness to divine goodness.

One must conclude that the classical doctrine of analogy as employed in theology is either *invalid* (for attributive analogy) or *meaningless* (for proportional analogy).

The defects of the analogical method in theology arise from the failure of its advocates to take into account the imperatives of clarity and comparability of concepts as well as their sense-empirical verification.

Any analogy is but a hypothesis that, in order for it to be both meaningful and applicable in human affairs, must be tested for both clarity and comparability of concepts and empirical validity of its consequences as well as consistency of those consequences with other known valid results. For example, the theological assumption of a creaturely relationship between man and God (so prominent in Reinhold Niebuhr's writings) and such as we know it in human terms (e.g., the creaturely relationship between his artifacts and man) is testable in regard to its consequences. If this creaturely relationship truly holds, then the following consequences, among others, should hold:

(a) Since man can use his creatures (such as atomic and nuclear weapons) to destroy himself, God must likewise be capable of using man to destroy God.
(b) Since his creatures do not know man as their creator, likewise man cannot know God as his creator.
(c) Since man's artifacts cannot war amongst themselves spontaneously, likewise man should be incapable of warring spontaneously with his fellowman.

We do not know whether (a) is true of God. All we know is that so far, God (as a recurrent theme, and whoever or whatever it may be) does not seem to have used man for God's self-destruction; for since it is assumed that God is "wholly other" than man and that man is God's creature, and since man continues to be "produced" or "created" (assumedly by God), God, apparently, continues undestroyed by man.

Some people claim to know God as their creator and so contradict their assumed creaturely relationship to God, such as exists between man's unknowing artifacts and man. If this relationship were true, man should not claim to know God (as the Gnostics maintained) or to know God as his creator. It must be concluded on this test that a creaturely relationship between man and God does not hold, as is clear from (b).

In regard to (c), one must again deny the creaturely relationship of man to God, since interhuman conflict is a clear denial of the existence of such a relationship.

With the exception of (a), for which no meaningful test can be devised, our results show up negative for the hypothesis of a creaturely man-God relationship. It is futile to attempt to escape this conclusion by arguing that the creaturely relationship is a symbolic, not a real one, for if symbols, as Paul Tillich maintains, "point beyond themselves to something else"[27]—a something that is not specified—and if God, to which the symbolic creaturely relationship refers in this case, is "wholly other"

360

and "infinite" then the symbolic relationship is meaningless, since the something referred to is a woolly, rather than a clear, concept.

Nor is it worth advancing the argument that creation by God is out of nothing, while by man it is the molding of preexisting materials, for "creation out of nothing" is pure myth, without empirical validity, while the molding of materials is an empirical one. The two kinds of creation are therefore not equivalent, hence not comparable, and God's nonempirical kind of creation cannot form the basis for any serious discussion.

The other test, that of consistency of the assumption of creatureliness with other valid (empirical) hypotheses, can now be applied. Human reproduction is an empirical fact, a biological process that occurs between male and female human beings, not a mechanical relationship between an artificer-God and a human artifact. Thus man is not God's creature. Nor is it permissible to argue that the creation process has been delegated by God to biology ("pro-creation"), for this argument cannot be verified. Other animals are, for the same fact of biological reproduction, not God's creatures.

It could be argued, however, though from a slightly different perspective, that the relationship between man and other animals, on the one hand, and God, on the other, is indeed mechanical and creaturely, on the Hellenic mythical interpretation that God made the human and other animal (and plant prototypes, but with built-in reproduction systems to carry on the reproduction process mechanically through biology. This, of course, is no serious argument, since the myth of the first creative activity of God—the creation of fixed and final prototypes—lies outside the realm of human experience, hence is not open to empirical verification.

One can conclude overall that theological assumptions cannot be established by analogy, nor is the hypothesis of man's creatureliness vis-à-vis God empirical or consistent with other empirical facts, being in the nature of pure myth. As pure myth, however, it serves the socially useful purpose of promoting peaceable relations among mankind on the basis of an assumed common creatureliness and brotherhood of man.

6. THE COSMIC PARADIGM

Where interpretations of cosmic dimensions are desired it becomes necessary to break out of the restricting mold of the human paradigm and see the cosmos—at least, figuratively—round and whole. This requires that one start one's theorizing or interpretation with the cosmic process itself and with the human being as an integral part of it. The essence of the cosmic paradigm is change and flow (or change-flow) and has been known to man for millennia. The sixth century B.C.E. Greek philosopher, Heraclitus, summarized it all in his theory of cyclical or periodic conflagration and destruction of the cosmos, followed by its renewal, phoenixlike, from its ashes. The current cosmological theory of oscillation bears a striking family resemblance to Heraclitus's theory. Just as all Western philosophy consists of footnotes to Plato, in the view of the mathematician-philosopher A. N. Whitehead, so may it be said, with equal truth, that modern cosmological theory is little more than a gloss on Heraclitus, with details about supernovae, stellar burnouts and collapsed stars in the form of black holes being substituted for Heraclitean conflagration and destruction as the final cosmic state from which the new cosmic phase emerges in a colossal bang. All cosmic phenomena have to be interpreted against, as well as inserted into, this general background of continuous cosmic oscillation or flux: theology (appropriately defined), metaphyics, evolutionary theory, ecology, religion, ethics, et cetera, in particular, the phenomenon of man and his destiny. This last involves a review of existentialist doctrines, including the meaning and relevance of doctrines of eschatology and soteriology; for, once it is granted that man can no longer be regarded as an alien existent in the cosmos but an integral part of its flora and fauna in the terrestrial sector, soteriology has to yield to evolutionary adaptation.

Originally conceived as a doctrine about the rescue of man from an alien and apparently hostile environment, soteriology became narrowed down (in the context of planet Earth and the human paradigm) to *the rescue of man from man by man*, the rescuer being the Zoroastrian Saoshyant, Buddha, Jesus, et cetera. In Kierkegaardian existentialism, human society replaced the cosmos as the hostile agent, and the individual human being aimed to be *in* but not *of* it. Salvation then consisted not only in rescue by a superhuman or man-god but in the exaltation of the human self, both as an end in itself (according to Kierkegaard, in contradiction to the Copernican revolution and the Darwinian doctrine of evolution). All this has to be changed—abandoned or revised—within the wider context of the cosmic paradigm.

The cosmic paradigm is the ultimate paradigm, and all ultimate values have to be evaluated within its framework. The God-concept is an ultimate value in this context—a value held as guaranteeing and justifying all other values. The concept of a god alien, wholly other and separate from the cosmos, must, in the context of the cosmic paradigm, yield to that of a god identified with the cosmos. And the cosmos itself is then no longer in need of "explanation" by philosophers, nor of change, Marxian-style, but of acceptance as a brute fact, a *Dasein*, in

362

Heidegger's terminology. Naturally, the age-old concept of god is unlikely to be surrendered without a struggle (intellectual, moral, and existential) or the recriminations that are bound to ensue, in sheer self-preservation, from those who espouse the age-old concept. Needless to say, god, whether in the cosmic or the human paradigm, continues to be that which does not change—being, in the new paradigm, change itself. And the struggle that the new paradigm will engender is an index, not of the distance separating man from god (man being an integral part of the cosmos, now the new god and paradigm) but of the distance that man—a changeable being like everything else in the cosmos—in his pride puts between himself and the cosmos, between himself and his god.

CONSEQUENCES FOR MAN

The displacement of the human by the cosmic paradigm as the framework for interpreting phenomena within the cosmos entails certain important consequences for man. *Firstly, change*, not man or a man-god, becomes the factor of reconciliation of man to the cosmos: man reconciles himself, through change, to the cosmos. *Secondly*, in accepting change as the principle of existence, man works out his own salvation through his reconciliation to change. This implies a *willingness* and a *readiness* to change in order to conform himself to the cosmos as circumstances dictate. *Thirdly*, there is an implied openness of attitude toward the good of the whole and a corresponding retreat from selfness, selfishness, and pride. *Fourthly*, in reconciling himself to the cosmos, man accepts his place in the cosmos as an integral part of it, not, as in the human paradigm, as a being apart from and superior to it, the darling of the gods. *Fifthly*, in accepting his integrality with the cosmos man accepts his *contingency*, like everything else; for with the next meandering of the evolutionary process all bets are off, and who knows whether man will survive it or what species, animal or plant, will rise to temporary dominance at the top of the evolutionary totem pole? *Sixthly*, with the loss of the special place he assigned himself in the cosmos under the human paradigm, man's primary concern ought to shift from himself and his fate to that of the cosmos of which he now regards himself as an integral part, and especially that of spaceship Earth, which he shares with numerous other manifestations of existence, each having its rightful place on it. The mistaken attitude of superiority and domination of biospheric resources, which naturally evolved from the human paradigm, should give place to an attitude of *adaptation to, and conservation of, the biospheric heritage*. For man happens to have survived until now not by biological mutation or any superior biological endowment, but by cultural and technological adaptation to his environment.[28]

Adaptation is the key word in the cosmic paradigm. And adaptation implies change as well as conformity to change. Culture and technology ought to adapt to the environment, not the other way round as, so far, has tended to be the case.

7. THE BIOCOSMIC PARADIGM OR HELICAL METHOD

Our discussion of the human and cosmic paradigms suggests the possibility of (a) combining both paradigms into an eclectic and integrated paradigm that combines the strengths of both paradigms in their practical application, but (b) liberating the human paradigm from its anthropocentric moorings by converting it into a general biological paradigm. The combination results in what may be appropriately termed the *biocosmic paradigm*. This paradigm provides for continuing paradigm change on an increasingly wider basis so that the same phenomenon examined within the increasingly comprehensive framework yields differing aspects and interpretations. The method of using an increasingly comprehensive framework operates like a spiral or helix, hence may be called the *helical method*.

The biocosmic paradigm is thus marked by a built-in provision for paradigm change by a spiral or progressive widening of the framework of the paradigm to yield new interpretations and new problems, while simultaneously offering the possibility of resolving old problems within the progressively comprehensive framework. The pattern of this integrated paradigm and its various levels, read from the base upward, is the following:

5. Cosmic	cosmic
4. Global (species, international)	↑
3. Social (class, group, community, nation)	bio-
2. Family (genus)	↑
1. Individual or nuclear	Paradigm

The type of thinking involved in this methodology may appropriately be called *helical thinking*: it is creative, dialectical, and dynamic. It is creative in leading to new insights and interpretations. It is dialectical in that each higher level of the paradigm and its associated interpretation takes into account the contrary cases that did not fit into the preceding lower level of the paradigm and attempts to provide a resolution of the contradictions. It is dynamic in that each successively higher level of the paradigm moves the argument along into a new and more revealing phase. It habituates the researcher to examining a given problem not in the context of a single fixed paradigm but in the context of the various levels of a multistage paradigm, thus leading to a flexible interpretation of the problem. It provides him with a method by which problems are transformed by increasingly widening the framework in which they are interpreted and assessed.

The procedure that has just been described is not new. It is the eventual path actually followed by scientific thinking *over time*, though in a haphazard manner.[29] What *is* new is that, instead of leaving the process to the laissez-faire-ism and attendant hazards of time, it consciously organizes it by a regular and systematic method of thought based on a multistage paradigm by which new and increasingly comprehensive hypotheses are devised and tested, with a view to accelerating the process and increasing the yield of scientific discovery. The intention is to ensure, by the systematic application of this method, that scientific breakthroughs are made to occur at shorter interals than the centennial and multicentennial intervals that it has taken, for example, for Newton to follow up on Copernicus, and Einstein on Newton. The method may be described, structurally, as Hegel's dialectical idealism—which he thought was revealed empirically in the dynamic process of history through thesis, antithesis, and synthesis—consciously organized and raised to the level of scientific method.

8. EMPIRICAL CONFIRMATION OF INTERPRETATION

A. TRUTH

Truth as Empirical

Truth is a relationship of correspondence with empirical fact *at any given time*.

Hence it is a *provisional* relationship, that is, one that is subject to change. It also implies consistency as well as coherence, subject to the overriding possibility of change. However, not all kinds of coherence and consistency imply a relationship of truth. Thus the kind of unchanging coherence and consistency associated with mathematics, definitions, and dogmas, which we otherwise denote by the term *certainty*, is not the kind associated with truth, for it is independent of experience and, therefore, of change. Only the consistency and coherence that are subject to change fall within the province of truth.

Accordingly, the following assertions are true:

(a) Empirical or sense-verifiable facts are true.
(b) Internally and externally consistent statements about empirical facts are also true.
(c) Consistency, correspondence, or coherence per se does not necessarily imply truth unless it concerns a sense-verifiable fact or experience. Hence,
(d) The difference between truth (an empirically consistent relationship) and logic (a conceptually consistent relationship) is the presence or absence of sense experience.
(e) Truth is a provisional relationship, hence subject to change with changing experience. (It is not necessarily a unique relationship, that is, a one-to-one correspondence between a sensation and the object of that sensation; for the same object may be experienced by the same person in several different ways, simultaneously as well as consecutively, on the same or different occasions.)

Truth may be subjectively or objectively empirical:

(a) Subjective or solipsistic truth is a relationship of correspondence of the subjective sense-empirical evidence with regard to the senses themselves (Epicurean definition of truth).
(b) Objective truth is a relationship of correspondence between *subjective expectations* and an *objective empirical event* as confirmed by others; that is, verification by third parties of the objective event corresponding to one's subjective expectations. (In this connection, things may turn out the other way when error results from misinterpretation or from disappointment of expectations. But repeatability of the event and third party verification serve to fortify experience and help guard against error.)

Veracity versus Truth. Truth may be distinguished from veracity, which is exactitude or accuracy. Veracity is a one-to-one correspondence between the content of a message or communication before *and* after its transmission; that is, correspondence between the message as dispatched and as received, or between the sequence of an event and the report or account of it. Thus veracity is a condition of correct communication and understanding of what is communicated. Truth, as we have seen, is an empirical condition, but not necessarily a unique, one-to-one relationship

366

as in the case of veracity. Veracity, like consistency, is formal rather than empirical correspondence between two entities.

Truth as a Value Created by Man and Actualized in Experience

A practitioner in any field of natural science tends to regard truth as experience of something given to man. While this is correct, the *givenness* of that which is experienced is not a criterion, nor an essential part of the definition, of truth. The criterion or essence of truth—scientific truth—is *experience*. In this respect there is no difference between the truth of the physical sciences and that of the social sciences, including disciplines such as religion and ethics. Their common criterion is experience.

Thus, in the religious field, any doctrine of Christianity is true if it attracts people to live by it in their daily activities. In so doing, they experience it by practicing it, make it come alive, make it true—regardless of whether or not there actually lived someone called Jesus the Christ to whom it may be attributed as originator. [30]

Similarly, if there was someone called Jesus the Christ who preached an acknowledged doctrine, known and practiced as a Christian doctrine, what is practiced is not necessarily the doctrine preached by Jesus but the understanding of that doctrine by its practitioners. Accordingly, it would be futile to think it possible to recreate and live the lives of the early Christians exactly as they interpreted and lived the doctrine of Jesus. While this does not, and should not, prevent one from trying to actualize one's interpretation of how the early Christians lived, the distinction between doctrine and interpretation of doctrine is important and should be kept very clear.

Insofar as man *creates* as well as *experiences* an entity, object, or value as true, truth has the same status here as in the experience of that which is *given* to man. And insofar as man creates or recreates and lives the past, what he does so re-create and live is not an absolute but a *relative* past—relative to his understanding of that past. Therefore, just as there is no absolute past, so there is no absolute truth in relation to the past. Truth is always relative to our understanding of the past as (re-)created and experienced.

The past is, therefore, nothing more than our understanding of it and truth nothing more than correspondence with empirical facts, as we understand them. This being the case, "behold, (we) make all things new." [31] The past has become the future in a different sense, and the present is the key to both in the profound sense that George Orwell expressed. [32]

Again, insofar as our experience of the truth depends upon our understanding of what is experienced, and insofar as what we understand is a product of our own creation, the possibility arises of a divergence between what was and our understanding of it. Technically speaking, if what we create, in accordance with our understanding of the past, differs from what that past actually was, our creation is a "lie"—just as living the life of Jesus would be living a "lie" if Jesus never existed. Yet in both cases the present experience would be true, though untrue in comparison with the past. It would therefore seem that occasions could arise where a "lie" becomes confounded with, and indistinguishable from, the "truth," since both the "lie" and the "truth" are *true to experience*. Is the experiential conception and definition of truth therefore amoral? Only *apparently* so; for the real test of a lie consists not in the fact of divergence or conflict between two separate experiences that are supposed to be the same, but in the fact of *experiencing two different experiences and pretending that both are the same* when they are *knowingly different*. The absence of such pretense removes the taint of lying.

Truth and Faith: Truth as Actualized Faith

"What is truth?" Pilate is reported to have asked Jesus at the latter's arraignment.[33] The answer, of course, in the context of Jesus' teaching, is: actualized faith—faith in the "kingdom of God," which is within every man.[34] The faith content of the belief in the kingdom of God, as expounded in exhortations such as those in the Sermon on the Mount[35] and various parables, becomes truth when actualized in experience through practice. Thus, once more, truth is a value—in this case, the faith content of a belief—created and actualized in experience by man.

It is thus clear that there is only one standard and definition of truth valid for the natural sciences as for the social sciences: experience, regardless of whether the object of experience is given to, or created by, man.

B. PROOF AND TRUTH

Proof is not necessary to truth in a world of relativities where only corroboration is necessary and possible. The most that could be asked for in establishing any proposition, or empirically verifiable statement, is corroboration. This is well understood in the domain of law. That the sun will rise tomorrow (to take an example) cannot be experienced in advance but can be established—corroborated, not proved—nonetheless, by the rotation of the earth on its axis.

Corroboration is thus something external to that which is to be corroborated. This, however, has been confused with the nature or essence of a thing—with the "essential question" of "what a thing is made or composed of." The latter, quite obviously, is a *property* of the thing—inherent in it. Equally obviously, the nature or property of a thing can be established directly by empirical verification (e.g., by dissection and analysis) or by corroboration by means of an external factor (e.g., the revolution of the moon around the earth being corroboration that the earth exerts a gravitational pull on the moon). Thus, while corroboration can substitute for direct determination, by experiment, of the nature or property of a thing, it is not the same thing as proof. The confusion of the two has been at the heart of the mistaken notion that essential questions smack of animism and that it is preferable and more informative to investigate the structural properties of things, which are supposed to be properties lying outside of the things themselves, and describable by universal laws of nature.[36]

As we have already seen in section 3 of this chapter, proof and disproof are metaphysical impossibilities. Empirical confirmation and corroboration are all that is possible.

C. THE OBJECTIVE NATURE OF NATURAL LAW

The view has been expressed by some scientists and philosophers that man is so constituted, anatomically and physiologically—and especially in respect of one particular organ, the eye—that he tends to see uniformities or laws in Nature, by which phenomena are governed; that Nature is an unorganized jumble of occurrences and impressions on which man seeks to impose some intellectual order; and that these so-called laws of Nature do not have an independent, objective existence but are projected onto Nature by man in pursuit of his intellectual organizing activity. Right or wrong, it is also a fact that man has been able to use these uniformities or laws to his advantage. Take, for instance, the principles of aerodynamics that he has been able to exploit in putting an airplane in the skies. This is clear evidence that these principles and other uniformities have an independent objective existence, since if they had only been imagined or "put there" by man, they would not have been operational for the activities undertaken by man. This, however, does not rule out the possibility that, *additionally*, man may, indeed, be so constituted as to be able to detect these independently existing universal principles or laws of Nature. In short, man's anatomy and physiology may be independently coordinated with the objective and independent laws of Nature.

Now, it is clear that there exists in Nature not only independent and objective uniformities but also an unceasing process of flow-change. These two principles, law and change, are basic to any serious study of Nature as well as compatible, since natural change can only occur according to natural laws.

It is a curious fact that, whether condemned to detect uniformities in Nature or not so condemned, man, *qua* man, has no particular interest in universal or fixed laws of nature for their own sakes nor, for that matter, in change for its own sake. His sole concern is with, and for, his own interests and how they may be affected by natural laws or by change. If his interests are, or are likely to be, affected adversely, then man will attempt to modify or change the laws, if he can (like seeding clouds with mercury in order to cause rain during a period of drought) or to resist change (like taking preventive or curative action to forestall or reverse an adverse change in his social situation or his health). The same holds for man-made or social laws and changes. These will be tolerated only for as long as they do not adversely affect his interests[37]; otherwise, he will take action to make them more amenable by exerting individual or group pressure on the relevant levers of influence and power. For instance, a law may provide for state housing or educational assistance only to certain income groups. An individual coming within the provision and currently benefiting from it may find himself automatically excluded by reason of an increase in his income level above the qualifying limit. In order to preserve his advantage from the law, he may seek either a change in the law in his favor by having his new income brought within the qualifying provision, or bend the law to his advantage by corruptly and illegally securing coverage. Similarly, some individuals currently excluded by the law may seek, nevertheless, to profit therefrom by irregular means. Or, again, a dominant social group may find its advantages being eroded by the accession of other groups to these same advantages, or by displacement by formerly excluded groups. It may consequently move heaven and earth to preserve its exclusive advantages either by blocking access by other groups or by preventing its displacement by the new groups. Plato even developed his entire system of philosophy around his intense dislike of change of any kind, natural as well as social, that threatened the aristocratic privileges of the ruling class to which he belonged.[38]

It is thus clear that mankind has no permanent or particular interests in natural or social laws or in natural and social changes for their own sakes. It only has its own interests to consider. Rather than accommodate his interests to the natural and social laws and changes, it would seek, if it could, to amend or conduce those laws and changes to serve its

370

interests. Despite any recognition of, or lip service to, the rule of law and of change according to law, mankind—notwithstanding all exhortations to the contrary—is not necessarily or by nature law- or change-abiding. The only difference, so far as man is concerned, between natural laws and changes, on the one hand, and social laws and changes, on the other, is not one of kind or degree but of the extent of man's knowledge of and, therefore, control or influence over them. Man has less control and influence over natural laws and changes, more over social laws and changes; more knowledge in regard to natural laws and changes, less in regard to social. But his attitude to both is uniquely the *same*—determined by his interests: he will attempt, wherever and whenever he can, to change, influence, or bend the laws and changes to his advantage.

9. THE MODERN REVERSAL OF MAINSTREAM GREEK WISDOM

ANCIENT GREEK WISDOM

The essence of ancient mainstream Greek wisdom—as we saw earlier in Book Two, Section A—is the Platonian theory of forms, the doctrine that archetypal and intelligible forms or ideas take precedence to objective entities (phenomena) and subsist in a suprasensible, nonphenomenal world. This "wisdom," however, turned out to be the "foolishness" of the ancient Greeks, for the activity of conceptualization—which is basically what the theory of forms is all about—is a subjective and mental activity based upon the objects of the phenomenal world, not an independent activity in its own right or of equal status with matter.

Plato's doctrine was an attempt to give a philosophical and ontological formulation to Socrates' doctrine that knowledge is inborn and born with man from a previous existence in a suprasensible world, and that all education does is bring out, by the method of dialogue (question and answer) what is already a natural endowment. Actually, the doctrine was a theory of conceptualization disguised as a theory of knowledge as well as an ontological theory. This so-called theory of knowledge—erroneous and nonempirical as it is—has been, nevertheless, the foundation stone of Euro-American theories of education.

The two basic ontological axioms of Greek Academic Philosophy were:

(a) the preexistence and coevality of God, form, and (unformed) matter

(b) the primacy of God and form—and (unformed) matter—over phenomena or formed matter.

It should be made clear that the Greeks never asserted the primacy of idea over matter but only over *formed* matter, i.e., phenomena.

MISUNDERSTANDING AND TRANSVALUATION OF GREEK WISDOM BY THE EARLY CHRISTIANS

The early Christians were introduced to Greek philosophy and metaphysics through the writings of Plotinus, an Egyptian-born Roman philosopher of the third century C.E. and founder of Neo-Platonism. To these Christians the Greek doctrine of organization of the cosmos (formed matter) from matter on the patterns provided by the pure forms or ideas (which contained no matter, i.e., no thing) was misinterpreted to mean the "creation" (rather than "modeling") of the cosmos out of "no thing," hence, "nothing." Thus they made no distinction between unformed matter (Greek *chaos*) and formed matter (phenomena). In their confusion they concluded that formed matter (phenomena) came from "no matter" (form) and matter itself from "no thing," hence, "nothing" (form).

Parallel to their erroneous doctrine of "creation out of nothing" the early Christians misinterpreted the Greek concept of "recalcitrance" of matter in a pejorative sense to imply that this resistance of matter to the reproduction of perfect forms was evil. From this it was but a short step to regarding all phenomena, including the human body (a corpus of matter) and all its passions—especially sexual—as evil. This transvaluation of sexual passion as evil was the special contribution of the Hellenistic Christian divine, Origen, who attributed the fall of Adam and Eve in the biblical myth to this evil passion.

Notwithstanding their pejorative view of matter and the human body, the early Christians came up with a totally un-Hellenic theological doctrine of the perfect man-God, Jesus, perfect in his human body, which reflected the perfection (or perfect form) of God.

Thus the three early Christian doctrines of "creation out of nothing," "matter as evil," and the "perfect human body" of God in the person of Jesus were totally un-Hellenic as well as being transvaluations of Greek philosophy, and would have been utter foolishness to the Greek Academic philosophers as they were to the later Hellenistic philosophers: for example, those encountered by Paul at the Areopagus who mocked his doctrine of the resurrection of the dead.[39]

372

KARL MARX'S CHALLENGE TO THE
GREEK PHILOSOPHICAL DOCTRINE OF THE COEVALITY
OF FORM (IDEA) AND MATTER

Hegel, in true Greek philosophical and ontological tradition, espoused the doctrine of the primacy of Idea over formed matter (Nature or Cosmos), implicitly accepting the concomitant doctrine of the coevality of Idea and Matter. Karl Marx broke with tradition by being the first to challenge both the doctrine of coevality of Idea and Matter and the doctrine of primacy of Idea over formed matter. Instead, he argued that Idea (or Ideology) was merely a superstructure raised on prior foundation of Matter. He applied his argument without distinction to both matter and phenomena (formed matter), thus propounding a doctrine of primacy of Matter to Idea (Ideology). Marx's argument was based on the obvious fact that concepts derive from objects (phenomena) and, contrary to the Greek philosophers, do not exist independently in their own right, outside of the human mind. They are, that is to say, abstractions and generalizations of qualities or characteristics of objects, including the produced means of production (capital).

Marx thus brought an important correction to Greek philosophy, a correction that revealed the phenomenal world as the proper basis of conceptualization (ideas or ideology) and simultaneously located the Platonian form or idea in the same world with matter and material phenomena. This completely eliminated the suprasensible world of the Greeks and showed matter to be the sole ontological element. In short, God (as Aristotelian super-Idea or Hegelian Absolute Idea or Spirit) was automatically eliminated as an ontological entity; for, as with all ideas, it was part of the ideological superstructure erected on a material base. Hegel had argued in favor of the primacy of Absolute Idea or Spirit over cosmos, of Absolute Idea as creator of cosmos, and of cosmos as the generator of the human mind and its ideas. Marx eliminated Absolute Idea, left open the process of cosmogenesis, and agreed with Hegel on the generative dependence of mind and idea on cosmos.

It was the elimination of God from the Marxian system that shocked his Victorian world, which promptly accused him of atheistic materialism. What he had really done was simplify the Aristotelian metaphysical system, basing himself on Democritus and other Greek Atomist philosophers. Aristotle had endowed matter with mind-containing soul, thus combining idea with matter. Effectively, this was no different from the "living matter" of the Greek hylozoic philosophers (the Stoics, for example). Marx merely went one step simpler, taking matter as the only existent and deriving ideas therefrom. He thus reversed the Cartesian tradition from thought as the basis of existence to material existence as the basis of thought.

MODERN WISDOM THE REVERSE
OF ANCIENT GREEK WISDOM

Subsequent to a long tradition of discussion of ancient Greek philosophy and ontology, modern wisdom has reversed ancient Greek wisdom. The doctrine espoused by Socrates, Plato, and Aristotle of the primacy of conception (noumenon) over its material object (phenomenon)—though not over matter itself—has yielded place to the view that ideas and theories, in order to be valid, must be confirmed by repeated observations of material phenomena. This view could be traced from its shadowy antecedent in Greek atomist philosophy, through Hegel's derivation of mind from Nature and Marx's blatant declaration of the primacy of Matter (Materialism) over Idea (Idealism), to the present-day view that concepts portray common qualities or characteristics of phenomena. The most important consequence of this new wisdom has been to emphasize not only the reality of matter as an ontological element, but also of phenomena as processed matter. This view is consistent with the view that mind is a potential inherent in matter and develops itself and its concepts in response to the presence of phenomena. In short, the exercise of conceptualization and the development of thought find their full scope against the background of the phenomenal world. This, in turn, becomes the sole source of empirical knowledge. Reason is thus dethroned from the divine preeminence and ontological status (as well as its presumed heuristic role) accorded it in ancient Greek philosophy, to a more modest and derivative role—that of cognition and explication—whose results are strictly relative to the environmental conditions in which it operates.

Modern scientific philosophy and methodology are the indirect and unintended offspring of ancient Greek philosophy. Sense experience based on phenomena that change and flow, one into another, has become the test of reality, of truth and knowledge—contrary to the ancient wisdom of the Greeks that survives to this day, albeit as an anachronism. There were exceptions to the ancient wisdom in Heraclitus and his school, who emphasized flux as the essence of reality; and the Epicureans, who emphasized the reality of phenomena, of the senses as the means of apprehending phenomena, and of sensations as true to themselves. But it was the Socratic-Platonian-Aristotelian wisdom that mostly survived and was handed down in the Occident.

374

Modern scientific thought is now rediscovering the wisdom of the Tao of Lao-Tzu and of Heraclitus, who lived later than Lao-Tzu and probably derived his philosophy from the Tao. According to this Eastern wisdom, nothing in the phenomenal world is certain except change and uncertainty. Knowledge is no longer, as with the Greek Academic philosophers, a pure form derived from a previous supra-sensible world but the result of sense experience of material phenomena. Sense experience has now become *episteme* (knowledge), and idea or ideology unverified by sense experience has become *doxa* (opinion). Change-flow of phenomena alone is certain, real, eternal. So is uncertainty. And, as always, philosophy bids us to be certain about nothing else but change. Contemporary wisdom is thus the antithesis of the wisdom of the ancient Greeks.

NOTES

1. Paul Feyerabend, *Against Method* (Verso, 1978).
2. Thomas S. Kuhn, *The Structure of Scientific Revolutions* 2d ed., enlarged (Chicago: University of Chicago Press, 1970) chapters VIII, IX, XII and XIII.
3. Saint Matthew 13:30.
4. This raises the question of the relevance and proper sphere of belief. Theologians, like Reinhold Niebuhr, are right in condemning belief in mutable goods as idolatry, but wrong in defining God as that which does not change, which is static—a Platonian concept—and therefore the only object worthy of belief. Belief—unquestioned acceptance and emotional commitment—is supposed to be merited only by this static God. The error, of course, lies in their conception of God as static, for there is *no* immutable *good* and, therefore, no immutable God. There is only immutable *process*, change itself, which alone does not change. And, as always, "time makes ancient good uncouth." If belief is desired, one can, therefore believe in the *process of change*—the only immutable "good," but not in things or objects, these all being mutable goods.
5. See Thomas S. Kuhn, op. cit.
6. Some would want to make exception of the so-called magical methods of detection used, for example, in African society. This author does not know enough about those methods to be competent to render opinion or judgment.
7. Again, there are those who would claim magical or scientific basis for certain types of auspices—e.g., divination by the fall pattern of cowrie shells by marabouts in Senegal and other African countries. The author must again plead ignorance about the validity of such claims. On the other hand, dowsing for water by a divining rod or witching stick is known to be scientifically based on electromagnetic poles linking the diviner and the underground water.
8. Alternatively, the vow may be interpreted as an attempt to influence or change the divined outcome.
9. Bertrand Russell, *History of Western Philosophy* (London: Unwin Paperbacks, 1979), p. 245.
10. For example, if it were possible to draw the mathematical line (unidirectional and without thickness) on the surface of the globe, one end would meet the other, thus

modifying the assumption that a line would be an indefinite and unending prolongation of a point.

11. In Plato's day, experiences—the realm of the empirical—were limited to the various kinds of sensation, intuition being regarded as intellection (the realm of the intelligible) and therefore outside the realm of sense experience. Thus intuition was in the same class as "idea" or "thing itself" (different from Kant's "thing-in-itself," which is equivalent to Plato's "semblance" of form or idea).

12. Largely, but not entirely. Thus the advent of nuclear energy is now regarded as undesirable because of its disastrous effects when accidents occur in nuclear-powered plants. Similarly, earthquakes are undesirable because of the damage and loss of life that they cause but no one makes an issue of them for lack of knowledge of how to prevent or control them. These examples clinch the point of the discussion, that there is no essential difference between "natural" and "normative" other than knowledge or the lack of it.

13. There is, no doubt, some relevance here to the Heisenberg Uncertainty Principle whereby the behavior of aggregates *or* particulars is determinable in quantum physics, but *not both* simultaneously.

14. See chapter 5, section 4, following.

15. It is only for this type of displacement hypothesis that, lacking any link to the old hypothesis, displaces old problems by new ones rather than resolving them that the conventional wisdom is true, namely, that problems are never resolved but only displaced by other problems. It is not true for displacement hypotheses that are linked to those being displaced by subsumption. The difference here is that between Copernicus's relative to Ptolemy's theory (displacement) and Einstein's relative to Newton's theory (subsumption).

16. There was nothing essentially wrong with the geocentric assumption. Confirmation lies in the fact that the Ptolemaic astronomy based upon it yielded, with its epicycles, practically the same results as the heliocentric astronomy established by Copernicus. Indeed, modern relativity theory indicates that the earth goes round the sun as much as the sun goes round the earth. The only fault with geocentrism was the one of mistaken emphasis: that the earth was *the* (only), instead of *a*, center of the cosmos. It was, however, a mistaken emphasis pregnant with most astounding consequences. Copernicus's achievement consisted in establishing that (a) the earth was one of several planets located within our solar system, (b) the sun was the center of this system, which was one of millions of such systems, thereby indicating that the cosmos has no specific center at all, or, which is the same thing (as Copernicus's editor pointed out), that any point could be regarded as its center. (See R. G. Collingwood, *The Idea of Nature*, [London, New York: Oxford University Press, 1945], pp. 96–97.) The net effect of the Copernican revolution was to dethrone man from his self-assigned position of dominance in the cosmos by showing that there were as many positions of dominance as there were celestial bodies.

17. This distinction is not often made, with the result that in ordinary discussions the *what* of the existential units is often admitted into both metaphysics and theology, resulting in an overlap as well as occasional confusion.

18. The awkward nouns like *chairperson, salesperson,* et cetera, which developed with the women's liberation movement, were designed to overcome male sexual bias involved in nouns like *chairman, salesman,* et cetera, with the gender-neutral "person" being substituted for both *man* and *woman*. They failed to achieve their objective in that they merely invented other gender words that are actually feminine without seeming so, for their corresponding personal pronouns are "her" and "hers."

376

19. It was hoped to tackle this problem in the process of writing this book, but the task had to be abandoned when it became obvious that it would prove insuperable unless dealt with as a separate exercise, for which the author does not consider himself qualified.
20. Ludwig Feuerbach, *The Essence of Christianity* (New York: Harper Torchbooks, 1957), p. 220: "Making is a genuine human idea. Nature gives birth to, brings forth; man makes." Bringing forth (Nature's way) involves a physical giving of a part of oneself. Creating or making (man's way) does not.
21. See preceding chapter.
22. See note 16 preceding.
23. See Book Two, Section A, Part II, chapter 4, section 5 and Book Three, chapter 2, section 3B.
24. See note 2 in the Introduction to this book.
25. For example, in summing up a natural number series to infinity the part contains the whole:
$$1+2+3+4+\ldots+n = X(2^0+2^1+2^3+2^4+\ldots+2^{n-1}+2^nY).$$
where $X = 1+3+5+7+\ldots+2n-1\ldots$ and $Y = 1+2+3+4+\ldots+n$ = the original infinite series. Similarly, in a holographic plate a section of the plate contains all the information found on the whole plate.
26. This addendum owes much to Frederick Ferré, *Language, Logic and God* (Westport, Connecticut: Greenwood Press), chapter 6, "The Logic of Analogy."
27. Paul Tillich, *Dynamics of Faith* (New York: Harper Torchbooks, 1958), p. 41.
28. See V. Gordon Childe, *Man Makes Himself*, 3d ed. (London: Watts and Co., 1956), chapters II, VI & VII.
29. See Thomas S. Kuhn, op. cit.
30. This fact demonstrates the irrelevance of a concern to establish the historicity of Jesus as a necessary condition for the validation of Christian doctrine. Cf. A. Schweitzer, *The Quest of the Historical Jesus* (London: S.C.M. Press, 1981).
31. Revelation 21:5.
32. George Orwell, *Nineteen Eighty-Four* (London: Penguin, 1977), p. 31: "Who controls the past controls the future. . . .Who controls the present controls the past."
33. Saint John 18:38.
34. Saint Luke 17:21.
35. Saint Matthew 5.
36. See the discussion of this issue in section 4 of chapter 1 of Book Three. One reason for the confusion is failure to make a distinction between the *understanding* of a thing—which is only possible *in relation to something else*, rather than absolutely in relation to the thing itself—and the *nature* or *properties* of a thing, which are inherent in it, absolutely.
37. Often his interests may not be in any way affected—he may just wish to profit, if he could, from the laws or changes.
38. See Karl R. Popper, *The Open Society and Its Enemies*, vol. I, *The Spell of Plato* (London: Routledge & Kegan Paul, 1945).
39. Acts 17:16–32. It should be recalled that Greek philosophy allowed for only the mental part of the human soul to join God's reason in the suprasensible world at death, the body—the material part of man—disintegrating along with its physical appetite (or soul proper).

Chapter 5

Metaphysics: Existence Theory

1. INTRODUCTION

Metaphysics is the discipline that studies the interrelationships among the elements that constitute the entire realm of being and becoming. This realm is revealed in the phenomenal world of matter, or mass energy, and in and through man's sense impressions and intuitions. The subject matter of this discipline may be subdivided among the several disciplines of physics, chemistry, and biology. These disciplines may be properly regarded as the ideological superstructure (or idea systems) erected upon the physical world as foundation or infrastructure.

In the philosophical system of Aristotle, *metaphysics* and *theology* are used as equivalent terms referring to the subject matter treated *after* "physics." In order of arrangement, it came after physics because it consisted of discussions on subjects oriented *toward* the physical. This has usually been interpreted as implying that metaphysics is related to physics and depends on the results and conclusions in that field. Hence metaphysics coexists with physics *within* our phenomenal world. While this interpretation is logically and substantially correct, the treatment of metaphysics by Plato and Aristotle has not been entirely consistent with the phenomenal world. These two philosophers postulated three coetaneous and eternal elements of being: God, ideas or forms, and matter.

However, all three elements were not assigned to the same world. Their distrust of social change, eventually *all* kinds of social change, including change within the phenomenal world, was so great as to lead to a distrust of matter and the entire phenomenal world. In consequence, they assigned "realness," authenticity, or genuineness only to "being" or "thing itself," meaning the static metaphysical elements—God and the forms—consigning them to a nonphenomenal world, while they treated "becoming" or the entire dynamic, phenomenal world composed of matter as "unreal"—not true to its appearance, hence to itself—and opposed to the static elements of "being."

378

In this arbitrary fashion, the one metaphysical world of "being and becoming" was split into two, yielding a two-world metaphysics, respectively of "being" and "becoming." This split was only partly the result of the distrust of change. It was also partly due to an eclectic borrowing and incorporation into Greek metaphysics of the Indo-Persian religio-theological dual concepts of World Soul (Hindu Brahma) or God (Persian Ahura Mazda) inhabiting the separate world of Nirvana (Hindu) or Light (Persian), and individual soul (Hindu Atma) inhabiting the deceptive phenomenal world of Maya (Hindu) or Darkness (Persian).

Plato and Aristotle went further to derive the phenomenal from the nonphenomenal world, according to a process that may be aptly described as "creation by imitation"; by this process, the pure forms, "things themselves," or real essence of phenomena were located outside of such phenomena in the nonphenomenal world, instead of within the phenomena themselves. The phenomena bore only a poor resemblance to their pure forms, which they strove to imitate. Thus a schismatic principle was introduced into the process of modeling phenomena in matter, into the very core of metaphysics.

This fiction of the "two worlds" has led to the erroneous view that metaphysics deals only with the nonphenomenal world that lies outside the world of physics, chemistry, and biology and that its conclusions do not therefore need to be validated by the results of these sciences.[1] It has also led to a resurgence in the modern garb of "objective knowledge"[2] of the Platonian-Aristotelian concept of autonomous pure forms, that is, a self-subsisting world of knowledge entities.

Given that the metaphysical world is the one and only phenomenal world of sense and intuition, several conclusions follow, among them the following:

(a) Ideas and concepts both derive from, and exist in, the phenomenal world, not in some previous existence or suprasensible world; indeed, it could hardly be otherwise, circumscribed as human existence is by the phenomenal world.
(b) Concepts and conceptual systems (mathematics, for example) are always open to the possibility of empirical validation in the phenomenal world.
(c) Reality (being and becoming) consists and occurs in the phenomenal world, a world that is both sensible and intelligible.
(d) All assumptions and conceptual systems involving a second or suprasensible world must be discarded as erroneous—along with the assumption of a two-world metaphysics—or reexamined on the basis

of a single phenomenal world of being and becoming. Examples of errors to be discarded are:

(i) the doctrine of a theological and suprasensible origin of the phenomenal world and theolatry as being the proper relationship between man and the assumed gods of a suprasensible world, entities whose characteristics and behavior cannot but be conceived in human terms;

(ii) religion and mysticism regarded as a relationship between man and a suprasensible world of states such as hell, purgatory, and paradise, these being no more than elaborations on parallel states within the phenomenal world;

(iii) metaphysics as concerned with "being-in-a-suprasensible-world," a conception held from antiquity down to the time of Descartes, Kant, Kegel, Kierkegaard, and all their contemporary followers; instead of as concerned with "being-and-becoming-in-the-phenomenal-world," as several thinkers have valiantly tried to show, beginning in antiquity with the Greek atomist philosophers, Leucippus, Democritus, Epicurus, Lucretius, and their followers, down to La Mettrie, d'Holbach, Laplace, Feuerbach, Marx, and Darwin.

Theology and religion, like metaphysics, have to come to terms with the phenomenal world, if they are to continue to have any relevance to the concerns of everyday life in future centuries. They will have to return to the tradition of animism or hylozoism established by the Ionian philosophers and their successors, the Stoics. The task of the twenty-first century—if it is not to jettison theology and religion along with the suprasensible world of ancient and modern times—will be to define these disciplines in meaningful terms consistent with a phenomenal, empirical world.

Although properly concerned with the entire phenomenal realm of being and becoming, metaphysics no longer spreads its net so widely as to take in every manifestation of being and becoming. Because of continually growing specialization within its domain, it has had to surrender certain legitimate areas. Thus it no longer concerns itself with the stellar bodies and the cosmos at large. This is now the special domain of astrophysics. Nor does it concern itself with the metaphysics of plants and nonhuman animals, an area now become the specialization of evolutionary biology. Rather does it concern itself with the metaphysics of human being and becoming, the elements involved and the interrelationships among them and among the various phases of human being and becoming.

This is, nevertheless, an area shared with evolutionary biology, as well as with chemistry and subnuclear physics.

The narrowing of the general field of metaphysics, combined with man's anthropocentric bias, has resulted in limiting contemporary metaphysics exclusively to the human animal as its goal and justification, with mixed results in such currents of thought as existentialism and evolutionary humanism. This, however, should not obscure the need for relating metaphysics to other scientific studies, and for constantly reminding ourselves that mankind is not the darling of the cosmos. Because of its dependence on the basic assumptions, first principles, and results of the natural and physical sciences, metaphysics is science-based speculation at the limits or fringes of these sciences. It is an activity of hypothesizing, subject to verification empirically by other scientists. It aims at exploring the interrelationships within its field as well as at providing new directions for exploration by the other sciences. Thus it ultimately serves to advance the general field of science. It is an activity of interest to scientists and nonscientists. Many scientists are metaphysicians. A good metaphysician, likewise, must be acquainted with the latest developments in the sciences that bear on his field—at least, in a general way—in addition to being au courant with the latest advances in his own field.

Metaphysics is thus involved with the next steps in the advancement of science. In its inquiry into the nature of being it is eminently concerned with the examination and reexamination of the existing basic assumptions, first principles, or apriorisms of contemporary science. Metaphysical speculation is no different from any other kind of intellectual speculation in that it involves abstraction of common qualities or characteristics from groups of objects or entities and their further development or processing by the human mind into reasonable empirical hypotheses.

Some of the kinds of questions of interest to the metaphysician, about which he may wish to frame hypotheses, include the following, chosen at random:

(a) What difference does the discovery of DNA make to our conception of the nature of being and becoming?
(b) How valid is the Teilhardian concept of noosphere from the viewpoint of the nuclear physicist? How does it compare with and differ from:
   (i) the intelligible, suprasensible world of the Greek academic philosophers?
   (ii) the Hindu-Buddhist concept of Nirvana?
(c) What is the difference between the Darwinian and Bergsonian views on evolution, and how does the evolutionary concept of biological

change differ from the economist's concept of development (growth with structural change) or stages of growth?

(d) Can a valid distinction be made between existence and its manifestations?

It is obvious that in attempting answers to these questions a good deal of scientific knowledge on the topics involved must be assumed as a necessary background; for metaphysical speculation is not wild or meaningless speculation, as was falsely assumed by the adherents of the school of Logical Positivism.

Because it is science-related, metaphysics requires that its concepts as well as hypotheses based on those concepts be empirically testable. This must be the case if metaphysics should be interesting and useful to scientists. Furthermore, concepts and the implications of hypotheses in metaphysics should ride well with existing facts and empirical results of other branches of science. Besides helping to advance the frontiers of science, metaphysics contributes to preparing the way for the interpretation of interrelationships within the cosmos, which is the essential task of philosophy. Thus philosophy, as always, is an essential follow-up activity from metaphysics.

2. DEFINITION AND DIMENSIONS OF EXISTENCE

Existence has been defined as a condition or state of "being there," of "thereness," as expressed by Martin Heidegger's *Dasein*.[3] Existence is not a predicate or property of things, as Kant correctly pointed out in criticism of the predicative use of the word *existence* by Anselm and Descartes. Although not a predicate, *existence* can take or have a predicate. Thus we could say, "Existence is conceptual" or "Existence is sense-empirical." These two sentences are purposely used in illustration in order to specify the two types or dimensions of existence: (a) conceptual and (b) sense-empirical.

Conceptual existence[4] is mental "thereness" as implied in "God exists," God being a concept to be defined. Sense-empirical existence is *both* conceptual *and* empirical "thereness," as in "Man exists," man being an entity that exists both in concept (mentally) and in sense experience. If the existence of an entity is conceptual it could also be sense-empirical. But not necessarily so. If, however, its existence is sense-empirical it is also, necessarily, conceptual.[5] Thus existence in any particular form or manifestation always assumes both dimensions: conceptual (or conceptual-empirical) and empirical (or sense-empirical).[6]

Existence is all we know in concept and in sense experience. Nonexistence is not given in human concept and sense-experience and, therefore, cannot be meaningfully discussed. What once exists, conceptually and/or sense-empirically, cannot nonexist. It can only be transformed into something else.[7] Existence being all there is in concept and sense-experience, the "thereness" of things, in general, is an incontestable fact, that is to say, the question of the necessity or nonnecessity of existence is completely irrelevant. So are questions relating to nonexistence. "Why do things exist in general?" "Why does anything exist at all?" are irrelevant questions because they cannot be meaningfully discussed or answered. The best that one can do is give a tautological, noninformative answer: "Because they do" or "Because it does."

One or more interesting questions may be raised at this point. For example:

(a) If everything thought or conceived exists conceptually or sense-empirically, what gives them all a coherent unity if they are not to be left hanging disjointedly?
(b) Since man is beginning to take ecology seriously, to worry about, and try to preserve endangered species, does this not imply some question about the necessity and purpose of existence? Does not the very fact of taking action to preserve endangered species testify to the relevance of questions about the necessity and purpose of existence?

The answer to both questions is essentially the same: any unifying principle and any conservation program is evidence of man's interpretive or meaning-bestowing activity. The unity of the cosmos is a principle hypothesized by man, in the first place. If, additionally, it is confirmed sense-empirically, then it becomes a scientific law independent of man's having imposed it as a unifying principle on the cosmos—a provisional law, nonetheless. The various species-conservation programs are also the result of man's interpretation of their respective roles, within the ecological context, as being one of mutual support. Again, this is an interpretation that has been confirmed empirically—provisionally. Either interpretation is a far cry from being an answer to the question, "Why does anything exist?" We may assign a purpose to the existence of various species and interpret that purpose as one of mutual support. Or we may interpret the extinction of certain species as due to climatic changes or human agency. These interpretations may seem confirmed empirically for the time being. But we still cannot give any meaningful answer to the question, "Why does anything exist or become extinct?" or "Why existence?'' without finding ourselves on the slide into infinite regression. Interpretations, whether scientific or not, are merely provisional devices, landmarks intended to give us the orientation we need in order to function at all in a cosmos essentially ungraspable, in any relevant or meaningful sense, by any answers we may give to the existential questions which we pose to ourselves.

We may therefore conclude this section by saying:

(a) Existence (being and becoming) is not a subject that can be discussed meaningfully in regard to necessity or non-necessity, logical or otherwise. This is similarly the case, and even more so, with nonexistence. Neither logically necessary nor logically unnecessary, existence is, simply, just "there." To say that there is no logically necessary or unnecessary existent (i.e., any particular manifestation of "thereness") is equivalent to the contingency argument.

(b) The medieval Schoolmen's argument for a logically necessary being or God, namely, in order to arrest the infinite regression in the answer to the question, "Why does anything exist?" (e.g., tracing the existence of an individual human being through his or her regressive chain of ancestors) is absurd as well as a non sequitur—absolutely irrelevant. An infinitely regressive answer is a sure indication that the question asked is inappropriate, irrelevant, and meaningless and, therefore, should be reformulated.

(c) The question of existence can only be discussed meaningfully if dissociated from any notion of necessity, logical or otherwise.

3. AFFIRMATIONS OF EXISTENCE OR NONEXISTENCE OF GOD

Affirmations of existence are superfluous, and of nonexistence irrelevant, both generally and with respect to God defined as Existence or as the ground of all being.

We may define God alternatively and equivalently as: (a) Reality, (b) Existence, (c) Being and Becoming, (d) The Ground of All Being and Becoming, and (e) manifestation of being and becoming. The essence of godhood, Reality, Existence, or Being and Becoming is *manifestation* in no matter what phenomenon or shape. *All* manifestations of being and becoming *taken together* may be regarded as *predictable, certain*, but *any particular* manifestation is *contingent*, in the sense that there is no reason why that particular manifestation rather than another should occur. Therefore, because of the factor of contingency of particular manifesta-

384

tions, it makes no difference to God or Existence whether or not man (or the human species) exists. Similarly, man's belief in the existence or nonexistence of God makes no difference to the being and becoming, the existence, of God. Such belief is absolutely irrelevant.

It does make a difference to man, however, that God exists, since man cannot exist otherwise than as a manifestation of God, of that whose nature and essence is to manifest itself in various forms. Thus man is a consequence, but not a *necessary* consequence, of the existence of God—or of existence—whereas the existence of God is a *necessary* and *sufficient* condition of the existence of man or other existent.

We may reiterate the preceding argument differently. The fact of manifestation of God (in the sense of any of the preceding definitions) is predictable, but individual manifestations of God (whether as man or in any other form) are not, since they obey the rule of evolution or chance. God, as the totality of manifestations involving change, is predictable because, being change itself, it does not change its character in this regard. But God evolves in its various manifestations, following the rule of chance and playing at dice—a fact Albert Einstein found very hard to accept. Each manifestation is dicey, proceeding from an unknown past to an unknown future.

The fact of existence being all that is given to, and known by, man, it follows that, once God is defined as existence, the question "Does God exist?" is tautologous. And to assert the nonexistence of God (however defined) is both irrelevant and meaningless, as well as dishonest, since nonexistence is beyond the scope of human experience. Thus atheism, defined as affirmation of the nonexistence of God, rather than as a metaphysical system without God, is not only time-wasting but also frivolous. Likewise, affirmations of theism are superfluous since there can be only one answer—the affirmative—to the question "Does God exist?" once God is defined as existence or the ground of all being. As will become clearer in the next chapter, the nature of things is such that God—however defined—*always* exists, at least conceptually.

4. ANCIENT METAPHYSICAL ARGUMENTS REVIEWED

A. PARMENIDEAN METAPHYSICS

Parmenides, the fifth century B.C.E. Greek philosopher, was a metaphysician or philosopher of existence and is generally acknowledged as the father of metaphysics. His claim to fame rests on such pithy affirmations as the following:

(a) Thou canst not know what is not—that is impossible—nor utter it; for it is the same thing that can be thought and that can be.
(b) How, then, can what *is* be going to be in the future? Or how could it come into being? If it came into being it is (was) not; nor is it if it is going to be in the future. Thus is *becoming* extinguished and *passing away* not to be heard of.

The thing that can be thought and that for the sake of which the thought exists is the same; for you cannot find thought without something that is, as to which it is uttered.[8]

Interpretation

Parmenides' thought becomes very clear once the distinction is made between conceptual (or conceptual-empirical) and empirical (or sense-empirical) existence and may be interpreted, correspondingly, as follows:

(a) Existence is all that is given to human experience and that we know. Nonexistence is nonconceptual and nonempirical, hence unknowable. Whatever is orally expressed issues from thought, and whatever is thought exists, not only conceptually but also sense-empirically. Hence it is impossible to orally express what does not exist, conceptually and sense-empirically.
(b) Whatever exists cannot come into being in the future or in the past, since whatever exists has always existed and always will. Hence becoming or coming into being, whether in the past or in the future, is impossible. Nor can what exists pass away.

The thought and the thing thought of are one and the same; that is to say, to everything thought of there corresponds automatically a conceptual existent as well as a sense-empirical (or phenomenal) equivalent.

Commentary

As interpreted, the first quote is true: conversation can only be about what exists either as an idea or concept or as both idea and sense-empirical entity. This is a truism—a tautology.

The second quote contains two thoughts:

(a) Existence has always been and always will be, without beginning and without end. This is a reasonable hypothesis that, however, should not be taken to imply that there is, or can be, no change. An existent can change without ceasing to exist, simply by ending one phase and beginning another—as happens with entities in a continuous process of change.

Parmenides was wrong to equate existence with no change.

(b) The thought and the thing thought of are the same. The simplest meaning of this is that the *meaning* of an idea as idea and as an empirical objective entity is the same, since both contain the concept. Thus one hundred dollars in cash or in figures means the same thing—one hundred units of any currency denoted in dollars. But this should not be taken to imply (as Parmenides did) that the cash and the figures are identical.

The Greek academic philosophers who succeeded Parmenides committed the error of assigning concept and sense-empirical entities to two separate metaphysical worlds and, correspondingly, affirmed two metaphysical principles based on their formal derivation of the phenomenal from the conceptual world:

(a) the "realness" of ideas, concepts, and thoughts (archetypal ideas) and

(b) the uncertainty—hence philosophical doubt—concerning the phenomenal world, owing to the unreliability associated with the evidence of the senses.

These two principles—*thought* and *doubt*—constituted, for them, the unshakable evidence (and argument) for existence.

There was, however, a third principle associated with, and implied in, these two basic principles, namely:

(c) conceptual existence was automatically presumptive evidence for a corresponding sense-empirical existent. (This third principle was a non sequitur, since the derivation of the phenomenal from the conceptual world does not necessarily imply that there is a corresponding phenomenon to every concept.)

These, then, were the three basic metaphysical principles of the ancient Greeks and may be summed up in the simple statement: idea plus doubt implies existence in both dimensions—conceptual and phenomenal. Thus, in order to establish "real" existence it was deemed sufficient to show (a) the presence of a thought (or the ability to think), an idea or concept, corroborated by (b) philosophical doubt concerning the phenomenal evidence of the senses. This was not a matter of logical argument but of demonstration by the application of accepted existential principles.

B. THE ONTOLOGICAL ARGUMENT

It is against the metaphysical background outlined in the preceding section that the existential arguments of Anselm (concerning the existence of God) and of Descartes (concerning his own existence) should be examined and evaluated, not against the background of syllogistic logic. For Plato's metaphysical system was established on the basis of Socratic dialogue without benefit of the syllogism, which was a later invention by his pupil, Aristotle.

Anselm and Descartes merely followed Plato's metaphysical system (which they both accepted without question and, apparently, without distinguishing between the two dimensions of existence). Thus Anselm "established" the existence of God by demonstrating the presence of a *concept* of God ("a being than which nothing greater can be conceived") and counting on the implied automaticity of phenomenal on conceptual existence, concluded that God must exist phenomenally as well as conceptually. Descartes supported Anselm's ontological argument for God's existence and "established" his own existence by showing the presence of *thought* (himself as a thinking being) and of *doubt* about himself as a phenomenal entity. Thus he satisfied the dual conditions for establishing his own existence within the Academic metaphysical system.

It should be noted that, notwithstanding the inescapably syllogistic nature of Descartes cogito in both form and substance, neither Anselm nor Descartes sought to establish God's or Descartes's personal existence on the basis of syllogistic argument, although neither man was ignorant of syllogistic logic. The reason for this (as we have seen) is that the ground rules for establishing existence did not need the help of logic, since existence cannot be established by deductive reasoning,[9] only by experience—conceptual and/or sensible experience; for existence is an all-pervasive empirical fact, nothing more and nothing less.

Immanuel Kant was able to refute Anselm's and Descartes's ontological argument for God's existence by showing that *existence* is not a predicate, as Descartes had argued in behalf of Anselm. However, Kant's argument, though valid, does not really touch the point at issue, which is conceptual versus sensible existence; for both Anselm and Descartes were able to establish the *conceptual* existence of God by merely thinking and defining a *concept* of God, and Descartes was able to establish his

388

own conceptual existence similarly. Neither could clearly establish the sense-empirical existence of God. Indeed, it would have been easier for Descartes to establish his own sense-empirical existence since he could sense himself in various ways by sight, smell, taste, hearing, and touch. This would have been necessary and sufficient, but not conclusive. For his sense-empirical existence cannot be conclusively established by himself alone. That would require the testimony of others. Thus, conclusive verification of his sense-empirical existence lies with others: another way of saying that an individual can exist fully (conceptually and sense-empirically) only in community.

The ontological argument is interesting in revealing the two dimensions of existence, and that existence can always be easily established conceptually ("if one thinks it, it exists as an idea") but not necessarily or automatically sense-empirically. Automatic sense-empirical existence can only be implied if such existence is already known to be the case, or an attempt is made to assure it.[10]

Finally, the ontological argument is important in establishing man in his dual (though not necessarily unique) role as (a) creator and giver of meaning and conceptual existence; (b) confirmer of sense-empirical existence of both himself and every other cosmic entity, including the entity, God. Thus man is truly *a* measure of all things, including existence, *but only from a human point of view.*[11]

5. THE PHENOMENON AND ROLE OF DEATH IN EXISTENCE

DEATH AND THE HUMAN PARADIGM

For most people, the anxiety caused by the problem of suffering, pain, good, and evil is exceeded only by the anxiety caused by the phenomenon of death. Indeed, some go so far as to say that theology and religion are mankind's reaction to the phenomenon and unresolved problem of death. Like Heidegger's man—*Dasein*—it is simply "there," a brute fact of existence, with all its consequences and accompanying human anxiety. Just as mere "thereness" of a mountain provokes in some people a challenge to climb it, so may the "thereness" of death provoke a challenge to surmount the feeling of anxiety created by it. We could never climb a mountain if we just threw up our hands at its height and the difficulty of climbing it. Similarly, we could never surmount the anxiety of death if we did no more than bow before its inevitability. But to surmount the anxiety requires an appropriate and adequate framework for its interpretation.

Much of the anxiety created by death is a consequence of the inadequacy of the human paradigm within which it is, inappropriately, handled and interpreted, for death is a cosmic phenomenon, not a uniquely human one. It can therefore be adequately interpreted only within a cosmic framework, paradigm, or model. The human paradigm, moreover, is too close to us for comfort, for us to be able to handle our own death as well as the deaths of family members and friends within it and without great anxiety. This paradigm therefore confronts us with a situation that paralyzes our thinking as our anxiety mounts and leads to neurosis and schismatic behavior. In such a state we are apt to grasp at straws—any straw—that promises to temporarily, if not permanently, allay our anxiety.

The crudest of such straws is the dogma that we can "vanquish" death—almost *the* cardinal dogma of Christianity, and second only to its doctrine of love. Even a child could see and understand that we do not "conquer" death, nor remove its "sting" by *dying* rather than by *not* dying, which latter is not within our power. Neither my death nor that of anyone else, obviously, achieves any such "conquest." It shows to what depth of paralysis of thought the anxiety over death can sink us and to what moronic state it can reduce us, for anyone to grasp at the straw that promises to "conquer death by dying" so that the "victor" can go on to live in the "mansions of the sky."

We may continue to weave such beautiful, wishful, but nonempirical mythologies and feel more comfortable that way within ourselves, in our frantic attempts to allay the anxiety of death or to escape death itself, if it were possible. We merely indulge our neurotic fantasies, for a wish or a longing is not a fulfillment, and there is no way, on earth, that we can know or determine, in advance, whether a heaven or a hell empirically exists or not after death.

DEATH WITHIN THE GLOBAL PARADIGM

The most generally known interpretation of the phenomenon of death is an adaptation of that implied in the Malthusian man-resources theory of population,[12] applied across the entire biological spectrum. It goes as follows, in a four-step argument. Given

(a) the limited earth resources and the limited ecological resources, generally,

390

(b) the reproductive function of various biological species, resulting in numerical pressure on the limited earth and ecological resources,

(c) the aggravation of the pressure on these resources by their unequal distribution, control, and use,

then:

(d) death is the inevitable regulator that by recycling a part of the existing life forms (or manifestations of existence) maintains the overall balance between the limited volume of earth and ecological resources, on the one hand, and the demand by existing and future (in gestation) life forms for those resources, on the other[13]; death puts an end to one manifestation without any inkling or promise as to the kind of manifestation to be assumed by the resources released by, and from, the extinct manifestation for recycling.

Death is thus an economic factor serving as an equilibrator, at the margin, of the global supply and demand equation for limited life-sustaining resources. It operates in various ways, through:

(a) *internal organic disequilibrium*, that is, natural wastage of life forms from old age, infirmity and sickness;

(b) *external organic disequilibrium*, that is,

    (i) accidents and catastrophes (flood, fire, drought, famine, epidemics, war, et cetera);

    (ii) intra- and inter-species cannibalism and mutual destruction.

In the light of this interpretation, death appears as the fairest possible form of equilibration of the species-resources equation on spaceship Earth, since every individual organism of every species is equally affected. This is true democracy, if ever there was one, on a global scale—and a far cry from the naïve, punitive, anthropocentric interpretation of the biblical Book of Genesis.[14] The poet and dramatist, James Shirley (1596–1666), eulogizes this global form of justice and democracy in his celebrated verse:

> The glories of our blood and state
> Are shadows, not substantial things;
> There is no armour against fate;
> Death lays his icy hand on kings;
> Sceptre and crown
> Must tumble down,
> And in the dust be equal made
> With the poor crooked scythe and spade.[15]

Thus, Existence, God, or whatever, operates a global—indeed, a cosmic—economy. In this context, species-specific interpretations of the incidence of death, such as that in the Book of Genesis, appear both deficient and ridiculous in according cosmic importance only to the death of human beings, to the neglect of death among other biological species. Ridicule passes into absurdity when human pain and suffering and death are regarded as adequate proxy for the pain, suffering, and death of nonhuman species.[16]

The Malthusian interpretation of death, however, is only a plausible one at best, since a disequilibrium between species demands and ecological resources is only a death-reinforcing, not a death-originating, factor; for we may assume that death will still occur even if ecological resources were unlimited, biological pressure on such resources absent, and the distribution and use of ecological resources equitable and optimally managed. There may then be a corresponding modification in the modus operandi of death—e.g., less intra-species cannibalism, fewer ecological disasters because of minimal ecological imbalance, and probably fewer deaths from illness. But death there still will be: death from natural wastage of biological organisms due to old age and infirmity (metabolic imbalance—katabolism exceeding anabolism) would continue inexorably and even increase.

No entirely satisfactory interpretation of death is therefore provided within the global paradigm by Malthusian theory, which in any event was formulated in order to refute William Godwin's argument about the inevitability of progress and happiness, not to account for the phenomenon of death. Malthus merely tried to show how the imbalance between the supply of life-sustaining resources and the normally excessive biological (notably human) demand for those resources was always bound to result in catastrophic consequences for human happiness—unless such measures of "moral restraint" as celibacy and postponement of marriage were adopted by the working classes in order to keep population growth, and therefore the demand for resources, in check. It is therefore necessary to change the paradigm and examine the problem within the wider framework of the cosmic (or biocosmic) paradigm.

DEATH WITHIN THE BIOCOSMIC PARADIGM

A. Death as an Existential Necessity

We have seen that the essence of existence is manifestation in an infinite variety of contingent forms with limited life-sustaining resources. This necessitates the recycling of the limited resources in order that the process of manifestation may continue in its infinite variety. The recycling process operates through death (or transformation) of existing manifestations arising from *internal disequilibrium*.

Death is therefore an existential necessity, a condition for the continued manifestation of existence in its essential mode, i.e., an infinite variety of contingent forms. It is therefore an essential part of the definition of existence. From the current state of our knowledge—at least in regard to man and probably other animals—it seems that a death-producing mechanism is built into the structure of biological organisms.[17] Biologists affirm that the cells of the human body, except the brain cells, are renewable. The brain cells are not only nonrenewable but also have a limited span of life estimated at 125 years at the maximum.[18] Consequently, human life span is limited by the life span of the brain cells, so that when these are worn out the rest of the body dies. Brain death, therefore, becomes the obvious scientific criterion of death.

This interpretation of death at the individual level is both interesting and revealing. The nonrenewable brain cells and their limited life span thus constitute the mechanism that triggers death in, and regulates as well as facilitates the mode of existential manifestation among, zoological life forms. A similar mechanism, no doubt, operates in the case of botanical life forms. Subnuclear particles, in like manner, have a built-in life span regulating their natural process of decay.

B. Death as a Bio-economic Necessity Built into the Structure of Living Organisms

Viewed from an economic perspective, the cellular components of the human organism can be classified into two groups: the first group consisting of the brain cells, which are nonrenewable and constitute the body's *fixed capital*; the second group consisting of the rest of the cells, the body cells, renewable, which constitute its *variable capital*. The combination and cooperation of these two groups of cells in the human organism are regulated by an economic relationship in which the variable applied to the fixed capital results in diminishing returns in terms of activity, energy output, and organizational efficiency of the human enterprise entity. Barring premature death from accident and disease, the using up of the body's fixed capital arrives eventually at its term, resulting in the exhaustion of the brain cells, brain death, and consequently the death of the rest of the entire organism.

C. Species Maintenance through Counteracting of Death

The function of death in the cosmos is to facilitate, not end, the

393

manifestations of existence. To ensure that death achieves this function rather than its opposite, there is a cosmic *back-up system* in built-in reproduction processes, both sexual and asexual—the corresponding equivalent of reproduction by fusion and by fission among nuclear particles—in all the various manifestations of existence. Thus sexual and asexual reproduction, nuclear fusion and fission repair the ravages of death and decay and ensure the continuation and maintenance of the various species, organic and inorganic. *Reproduction* (sexual and asexual, by fusion and by fission) is therefore the *true vanquisher* of death, not death itself; not the death of any manifestation, but its reproduction, "swallows up death in victory."

Moreover, while existence—the cosmos itself—implies, by definition, a tendency toward excess demands on limited cosmic resources by the process of manifestation in an infinite variety of forms, this tendency is accentuated by reproduction systems operating for the maintenance of existing species of manifestation. Simultaneously, death operates as a regulator or equilibrator to keep in check the tendency toward excess pressures on cosmic resources, while also serving, through the process of transformation of expired resources, to facilitate both contingence and infinite variety in cosmic manifestations.

The view, at the cosmic level, that death is directly linked to reproduction for the maintenance of the cosmic enterprise, is often transferred, by the fallacy of decomposition, to the individual or microcosmic level. There it is argued that the power of the individual human being to reproduce new beings is closely linked to the necessity of the individual's disappearance by death. This argument, otherwise true at the cosmic level, is weak at the level of the individual human being, since the individual is doomed to death, whether or not he or she engages effectively in the reproduction process, while reproduction per se does not necessarily involve the death of the human beings concerned. In other words, there is no direct link between death and reproduction at the individual level as there necessarily is at the cosmic level.[19]

D. Equilibrium of Infinite Variety of Existential Manifestations with Limited Cosmic Resources, through Death

The existential necessity of resource recycling through death constitutes a check or reinforcement against any tendency toward over-manifestation through excess cosmic demand pressures on the limited cosmic supply of life-sustaining resources. This check operates through *external disequilibrium*, that is, through accidents and catastrophes such as war, famine, et cetera, and through intra- and inter-species mutual cannibalism and destruction. Thus we have death constituting a *back-up system* against excess cosmic pressures on limited cosmic resources and excess cosmic manifestations.

E. Some Speculations about the Factor That Activates the Death-Trigger Mechanism

We have seen that death is an essential feature of the cosmic economy whereby the continuing process of cosmic manifestation in an infinite variety of contingent forms is achieved through the recycling of cosmic resources. Death is the *transformation (or change) factor*, linking together the infinite variety of cosmic manifestations, one with another. Sex and sexual reproduction as well as asexual reproduction—reproduction by fusion and by fission—constitute the other side of the same coin of resource recycling through death, and serve to maintain the balance and continuation of existing manifestations.

Little is known about the process that activates the mechanism that triggers death—other than accidental death from the impact of external factors. One may be allowed, however, to speculate on the basis of available information about the possible link of the trigger mechanism with such other factors as entropy—the running down or outflow of energy (an aspect of the dying process), the behavior of nuclear particles, and the supply of solar energy. One speculation is that the condensed energy or mass of our spaceship, Earth, is limited so that it can only receive and use a limited, marginal amount of the endless stream of solar energy reaching it. The amount of solar energy that it can so accommodate is used in photosynthesis by plants and in other ways by animal organisms. If the mass of the earth and its cargo of biological organisms and other forms is to remain constant, alive, and active, some of the energy in the earth must be given up, in marginal exchanges, for renewable energy from the sun. The process of exchange works itself out through entropy in various and complicated ways: plants convert solar energy and absorb carbon dioxide released by animals, while in turn releasing oxygen for use by animals; the continual collision of nuclear particles, both free and committed in various mass-forms, limits their longevity mutually, causing each particle to disintegrate in accordance with its life span and simultaneously reproducing similar as well as different particles by fission and by fusion. There is thus continual creation (birth) of new, and destruction (death) of old, energy particles. This translates at the molecular level into processes of reproduction and death of biological organisms. Surplus solar energy not required or used to maintain biospheric equilibrium is, presumably, released again into space to maintain the energy balance of our solar system and/or create new stars and solar systems to replace those that wear out and die. And so the process goes on and on, infinitely.

395

The entire basis of the foregoing speculation is the necessary assumption that the biophysical mass of spaceship, Earth, is maintained at a more or less constant volume. Why this should be so is beyond the scope of this book and the author's knowledge. Astrophysicists may one day tell us the facts in this connection, as they come to know them. And it may well turn out to be the case, as predicted by some astrophysicists, that the cosmos itself is an oscillating but fixed quantity. One may let the matter rest at this point.

Whether or not the foregoing speculation is valid, it is clear that death is not uniquely a human biophysical or a geophysical phenomenon but a cosmic one as well as the regulator of the cosmic economic equation connecting the exchange (supply and demand) of cosmic energy, and its transformation into an infinite variety of mass-forms or manifestations of existence. This interpretation of death within the framework of the biocosmic paradigm is not only a more reasonable and satisfactory one vis-à-vis that provided within the conventional human paradigm; it also puts the death of human and other species in a single coherent context. And while not, in any way, depriving those who would retain the human paradigmatic interpretation of whatever satisfaction and comfort they may derive from their death-related angst and its theological solace, it brings out the following conclusions:

(a) Death, like life, is an integral part of existence and the cosmic economy and is of no more significance for man than for other life forms or manifestations of existence. Furthermore, death is the very condition of man's mode and manifestation of existence as a living entity, as it is for other life forms. Death is thus a blessing for man and other biological organisms—paradoxical as this may seem—rather than a punishment, as the Semitic religions would have it.

(b) Human beings have it within the scope of their rational abilities and possibilities to minimize the death-reinforcing pressures resulting from an adverse imbalance in the species-ecological resources equation and from the lopsided distribution, control, and use of ecological resources. This may postpone, not eliminate, death.

(c) Appeals to whatever gods there be to save man from himself and the consequences of his folly in the misuse of ecological resources create a less than flattering view of the human species and its level of intelligence, while attesting to the paralyzing effects of human greed on necessary corrective action.

The preference shown in this chapter for an interpretation of the phenomenon of death within a cosmic framework is based on the obvious fact that death is a cosmic phenomenon, rather than a purely human or biological one, and therefore cannot be appropriately or satisfactorily interpreted within the framework of the human or the biological paradigm.

NOTES

1. See Claude Tresmontant, *Scienses du l'univers et problèmes métaphysiques* (Paris: Editions du Seuil, 1976), pp. 8–15, 34, where the author rightly takes to task those ancient and modern philosophers—Parmenides, Descartes, Malebranche, Leibniz, Spinoza, Heidegger, Sartre, Simone de Beauvoir—who engage in philosophy and metaphysics without regard for the results of physics. But they were only following an erroneous tradition hallowed by antiquity.
2. The reference is to Karl Popper's "objective knowledge" discussed above in note 4 of chapter 1 of Book Three.
3. This definition is only partly correct. It is erroneous or incomplete in portraying existence as a static condition—just "being there," whereas it is a dynamic state as portrayed in Jean-Paul Sartre's analysis of it as a standing before possibilities and continually orienting oneself accordingly. Hence it is both a "being (there) and becoming (something else)."
4. The Schoolmen's "essence" or "essential existence."
5. Accordingly, the earth, unicorns, et cetera, exist, once they can be conceived or thought of—clearly, one might add. They exist conceptually. In addition the earth, but not the unicorn, exists sense-empirically.
6. The act of thinking or conceptualizing is an experience involving the expenditure of some form of energy—electrical, nervous, et cetera. Therefore, conceptual existence is, properly speaking, conceptual-empirical. In ordinary language, *empirical* means experienced through the senses, hence sense-empirical.
7. Extinct animals may seem like an exception but are not: they are preserved in fossil forms or transformed by decomposition.
8. Bertrand Russell, *History of Western Philosophy* (London: Unwin Paperbacks, 1979), pp. 66–67. Emphasis supplied.
9. One only has to try to establish existence syllogistically in order to discover the impossibility of the exercise.
10. The point is made in one of the author's poems, which begins: "Whatever is conceivable within the compass of man's mind exists, or can be made to be."
11. This would seem to explain the seeming paradox in Judaism whereby the Jewish God, Jahweh, is both omnipotent and yet dependent on the Jews for his existence and recognition. "The dead praise not the Lord, neither any that go down into silence." (Psalm 115:18). Thus Israel's God is a "God in search of men" to recognize and praise him. All of which is a recognition of man's role as creator and giver of conceptual existence.
12. T. R. Malthus, *An Essay on the Theory of Population*, 1798.
13. The obvious implication of this is that the physical embodiment or incarnation of all manifestations of existence—including man—consists of borrowed elements for a finite period of time. Existence is thus the equivalent of a *term loan* to every existent, as well as an unsolicited gift. Indeed, existence is a loan transaction, every existent a debtor to existence, and death is the amount (principal + interest) paid by every existent for borrowing and using scarce cosmic resources. Payment of the amount is made by every existent by the simple act of rendering those resources at death.
14. Genesis 2:17, 3:19.
15. James Shirley, *Death the Leveller*.

397

16. The reference here is to C. S. Lewis, *The Problem of Pain* (Fontana, 1976), chapter IX on "Animal Pain." It is, indeed, presumptuous of Lewis to argue that animals have no consciousness of pain in the same way as human beings and that human beings and their pain are sufficient to account for other animals and their pain in the sight of God.

17. In this respect, compare Martin Heidegger's description of human existence as "a being unto death" in his book, *Being and Time*.

18. See D. Ikeda, *Life: An Enigma, a Precious Jewel*, trans. Charles S. Terry (New York: Kodansha International/Harper and Row, 1982), p. 172.

19. One of the strong features of Darwinian evolutionary theory is its demonstration of the close links between evolution (genetic mutation and environmental adaptation), reproduction, and death. Reproduction is the vehicle of species maintenance as well as of the manifestation of evolution. All that is needed to close the links and complete the picture—and Darwin's evolution theory—is bring into the relationship the limited volume of life-sustaining cosmic resources. We then see the inevitability of evolution/reproduction and the recycling of cosmic resources through death/transformation: reproduction as the vehicle of evolution, and death as a function of species reproduction and limited volume of life-sustaining cosmic resources.

Chapter 6

Metatheology:
The Metaphysics of Theology

Mankind has always had some difficulty concerning the empirical reality of a Supreme Being or God. The Jews and other Semites even had a genuine despair of ever finding it, notwithstanding that they had no difficulty creating a conceptual God who sought out man. The ancient Greeks, especially the Ionians and the Stoics, traveled various roads toward an empirical equivalent of divinity and a Supreme Being. Thus Thales had no difficulty about the empirical equivalents of various gods, holding that all things are full of gods—an espousal of pantheism. Nor did Parmenides, the philosopher of the One. Cicero accepted the planets as gods. All these philosophers had notions of the physical manifestations of divinity. In time, however, men learned to shy away from the search for empirical equivalents, finding it more advantageous in terms of psychological, social, and political control of the masses to have this aspect as vague as possible. For the same reason, modern theologians seem determined not to know or to search for a physical counterpart of God. A purely conceptual God, however, has both advantages and dangers.[1]

While mankind, in general, agrees that, conceptually, a Supreme Being or God exists, as regards its empirical equivalent opinions have varied from *agnosticism* (the view of those who do not know whether or not God exists empirically), to *synecdochism*, whereby a symbol of some sort (an empirical animal or a mythical composite) is held to stand in place of a greater but unknown empirical whole of which it may be a part, to *ascription*, whereby distinguished humans are deified. All these compromises fall short of a systematic attempt to correlate concept to empirical equivalent. The unfinished theological task of the ages, until now, is therefore the empirical revelation of God—a God that appropriately mirrors, conforms to, and confirms men's conceptual image of deity in its infinite scope and qualities.

As indicated in the preceding chapter, there are two dimensions of existence, the conceptual and the empirical. Similarly, there are two dimensions of God: (a) the God we create, the conceptual God, and (b) the God we do not create, the sense-empirical God that is given to us, a datum existing independently of us. The trick—and the scientific task—as always is to find or discover which empirical reality fits which concept of God. The moment the effective coupling is made, our dream, our theory, has come true and is *known*.

God *is*, and *always will be*, what we conceive and define this entity to be, existing automatically as such. It is in this sense that man creates God. Thus if we conceive and define God as a Being devoid of material properties—as did the Greek Academic philosophers—this entity will automatically exist conceptually as such a Being, capable of entering and departing our phenomenal world—and history—without detection by our sensing mechanisms, a self-fulfilling definition. Such a God will be both immanent and transcendent, without question (as an automatic consequence of our definition) and, equally without question, will be separate and "wholly other," completely different from our material world—a simple fact of *words*, their meaning and consequences.[2] Similarly, if we conceive and define God as a Being wholly perfect, good, loving, eternal, immortal, invisible, all-wise, all-knowing, omnipotent, uncreated, the ground of all being, et cetera, we have an instant conceptual product satisfying all these qualities. Conceptually, therefore, theology is clearly man's invention, the product of his imagination.

Feuerbach was, undoubtedly, right about the nature of the Christian anthropomorphic God as a human conceptual product possessing all the best attributes of the human species, alienated from it and projected as an independent conceptual entity. His one error in this respect was failing to recognize that the Christian God was not one, but several Gods in one: the anthropomorphic God was only *one* of several disguises or manifestations (or conceptual incarnations); another disguise was Spirit, and there were many others besides—such as fire, tempest, light, et cetera. But all Christians would insist that this God was, nevertheless, one. The shock created by Feuerbach's thesis was thus probably due less to the truth of what he said than to the limitation of the manifestations of the Christian God to purely human qualities, when most Christians would prefer to set no qualitative limits.

The Christian—or any other—God may be recognized in all and various possible manifestations, but not limited to any one of them, or any selection of them; for the moment one limits or stereotypes him—it was a male God, of course—he becomes dead in that manifestation (as Sartre's existentialist theory avers) but goes on to survive in all the rest of his infinite manifestations. "God is dead!" correctly declared

Nietzsche, once he had been stereotyped in his anthropomorphic disguise, but forgot to add: "Long live God"—in his other disguises henceforth.

Conceptually, therefore, God exists and always will, so long as man wills it. And man always will.[3] What man has shrunk, so far, from doing is to provide God with sensible existence. This is probably due to the feeling that this will provide a limitation to God's personality by making him easily identifiable, thereby losing that infinite flexibility that he possesses conceptually and is his guarantee of immortality, mystery, and awe.

One thing is clear, however. In a material world of mass-energy, human concepts derive directly or indirectly from this environment—exceptions made of concepts implying nonexistence or immaterial existence. Such concepts, we have seen, are metaphysically invalid and are no more than words devoid of meaningful content. It follows that the God-concept, to the extent that it has meaningful content, derives from material inspiration. From a one-world metaphysical view-point, therefore, God and man are existentially the same: material in essence and in conceptual origin. Man is inseparable though not coextensive with his God.

Man does not know everything about the cosmos and very likely never will. But modern cosmology and science provide us with enough information to guarantee that the cosmos will forever be a perpetual source of wonder, respectful (not fearful) awe, and unending curiosity. Man, as well as every other organism and inorganic entity, shares in this aura of wonder, awe, and curiosity. What better than the cosmos, the total spectrum of sensible existence, qualifies as the matching, sensible body of man's conceptual God? At once eternal, indestructible, uncreated, the same yesterday, today, and forever[4]—the *same*, because it is always in a process of perpetual change, change being the only thing that does not change within the cosmos; in perpetual change because the process of change is a perpetual oscillation without beginning or end.

The inquiry or discipline that treats theology in the context of the cosmos and regards the cosmos as the intuitive and sense-empirical counterpart to the conceptual existence of God is *metatheology* or the metaphysics of theology. It treats all existence and its manifestations, conceptual as well as sense-empirical, as the existence and manifestation of God, the "being and becoming" of God.

Metatheology comprises two parts: (a) *cosmotheology*, which conceives God as the cosmos and constitutes the ideological foundation of metatheology; and (b) *cosmotheogenesis*, which treats the cosmos as the intuitive and sense-empirical aspect of God. Cosmogenesis is then the study of the structural formation and processes occurring within the em-

401

pirical existence of God. In practice, as a result of specialization, cosmogenesis is now the special domain of astronomers and astrophysicists and should continue to remain so. But the metatheologian needs to be aware of what goes on in that field and to keep in touch, in order that both cosmotheological ideas and cosmotheogenetic studies may benefit from the data generated by the cosmogenetic studies undertaken by astronomers and astrophysicists.

The establishment and pursuit of metatheology are bound to necessitate considerable modification to contemporary theological doctrines and ideas. The nature of such modification will appear more clearly after the main ideas in cosmotheogenesis have been outlined in the following section.

1. COSMOTHEOGENESIS

Cosmotheogenesis invests the cosmos as the empirical body of God. The cosmos is "there" in its eternal, unchanging changingness. In cosmotheogenesis we start with this existential fact and proceed to other related facts, as follows.

A. NO ALPHA, NO OMEGA

The cosmos is an ongoing process in perpetual change, without beginning and without end. Plus *ça change, plus c'est la même chose:* the more things change, the more they remain the same. This French proverb gives a precise description of the cosmic dynamic process—a perpetual oscillatory cycle of structural change, according to all the currently available evidence.

B. CONTINGENCE IN SAMENESS

The cosmos reveals contingence in its microdynamic aspect. It is at this level that Darwinian evolution occurs—from uncertain past to uncertain future.[5] At the macrodynamic level there are no surprises, for it is all a sameness—the sameness of perpetual oscillation. At this level, therefore, one may legitimately talk about teleology, the macrodynamic goal of the evolution of the cosmic God: from certainty to certainty, from sameness to sameness. Evolution and uncertainty at the microdynamic level yields to *telos* at the macrodynamic level. Cosmic manifestations

402

are contingent and finite. The cosmic God is certain in its changingness and infinite in its manifestations.

C. THE RULE OF COSMIC MANIFESTATION: SHOW AND PASS ON

The essence of the cosmos is manifestation, revelation, hierophany: "show and pass on," one manifestation metamorphosing into another. *Manifestation through transformation* is the ground rule of the cosmic process. The essence of cosmic divinity is the Protean quality of continuing and changing manifestation.

D. FINITE MATTER TRANSFORMED INTO AN INFINITY OF MANIFESTATIONS

The economy of the cosmogenetic process reveals that cosmic manifestations are *infinite* (which is the basis of contingence) as well as *linked through transformation*. This is prima facie evidence that cosmic matter is limited or finite. This limitation is manifested in the phenomenon of *finitude and death* (transformation) of every manifestation, as well as in the cosmic phenomenon of recycling of renewable (e.g., climatic) resources.

It follows that transformation (or *finitude plus death*) is the very essence of the cosmos imposed by the limited matter at its disposal. The Cosmo-Theos is first and foremost an economist, whatever may be its other characteristics.

It may be concluded that death or transformation is not a punishment for some presumed sin or wrongdoing by any cosmic manifestation but a cosmic necessity, an existential feature, a characteristic of the material being[6] of the Cosmic God, a condition of existence and its continuing manifestation in infinite forms. The topics of suffering, pain and death are treated in greater detail subsequently (chapter 8).

E. IMMANENCE AND TRANSCENDENCE OF THE COSMO-THEOS

The basic nuclear elements of the cosmos are immanent in all its manifestations, but the cosmos in its entire complexity of manifestations transcends every single and contingent manifestation. In theological language this reduces to pantheism (God in each and every manifestation)[7] and pan-en-theism (each and every manifestation in God). The two are indissolubly linked, pan-en-theism being a diversity-in-unity brand of monotheism.

F. THE COSMOS AS A LIVING ORGANISM

The cosmic God is alive, its body a living organism (hylozoism or animism). This follows from the organic nature and unity of the cosmos as well as from the fact that it contains living forms. It follows also from the active nature of its constituent nuclear particles.

G. ORGANIC INTEGRITY OF THE COSMOS WITH EACH OF ITS MANIFESTATIONS: "WHOLLY SAME," NOT "WHOLLY OTHER"

The cosmos is integrally one with its manifestations, so that no essential distinction exists between it and any of its manifestations. Man, like any other cosmic manifestation, is contained in, and one with, the cosmic God. The heterogeneity of manifestations and their integrality with the cosmos indicate an organic relationship.

The distinction between manifestation and manifestation and between manifestation and cosmos is a formal not an essential one. Thus individuation is a *formal* separation and involves alienation of one manifestation from another as a purely formal characteristic. The essential oneness of all manifestations with cosmos converts individuation and alienation into what in Hinduism-Buddhism is called maya (the illusion of formal separateness appearing as essential discreteness) and in Greek Academic philosophy unreality (since the changing nature of phenomena is a superficial characteristic that does not disclose their fundamental and essential unchanging sameness).

Thus the cosmos is not "wholly other" than, but "wholly same" as, its manifestations, in the language of physics as of theology.

H. THE COSMOS AS NECESSARILY POSSESSING THE COMPONENT QUALITIES OF ITS MANIFESTATIONS

Traditionally, God has been credited with mostly human qualities: wisdom, love, mercy, forgiveness, justice, prudence, jealousy, wrath,

404

hatred, power, et cetera. While all these qualities are necessarily true of the human part of the cosmos and include qualities shared by nonhuman animals, there are also other human qualities (shared also by nonhuman animals) that are not often associated with God but also characterize the cosmos: destructiveness, mutual cannibalism, procreativeness, profligacy or (apparent) wastefulness of resources, et cetera. The cosmic God is necessarily all these and more. It is not a mere projection of only the good qualities of the human species as Feuerbach revealed of the anthropotheology of Christianity. It possesses *all* the qualities—positive, negative, neutral—found in all its individual manifestations, as seen from the human point of view. However, the human point of view needs to be corrected by being referred to the biocosmic paradigm for an accurate assessment.

I. TIME NOT RELEVANT AT (MACRO-)COSMIC LEVEL

Since the cosmos has no beginning and no end, time is not a cosmic (i.e., macrocosmic) concept. It operates only at the microcosmic level in regard to its finite manifestations—and then only as a relative concept. This indicates that attempts at dating the cosmos are misleading, if not misguided, since it cannot be dated for the simple reason that it is a perpetually oscillating process of creation (organization) and destruction (disorganization) without any known or discoverable beginning or any likelihood of ending.

At the micro- or intra-cosmic level, where concepts like *Past, Present* and *Future*, and *direction of time* are relevant, the element of relativity confers considerable flexibility on the meanings of these concepts, as well as a bit of confusion. For example, given cosmic time lags, it is difficult to know whether the light that takes billions of light-years to reach planet Earth is from the cosmic ''past'' or from the cosmic ''future.'' From the vantage point of Earth, the cosmic ''past'' and the cosmic ''future'' are light-visible in a nonlinear context in the Earth-''present,'' though not in the cosmic ''present.'' Yet, contemporary astrophysical lore holds that all Earth-visible light is from the cosmic ''past.'' (The topic of intra-cosmic time is further discussed in chapter 9, following.)

2. COSMOTHEOLOGY

We pass on to consider cosmotheology, that is, theology within the framework of the biocosmic paradigm. It has been shown in previous discussion that existence is a state of ''being and becoming,'' of ''thereness," in two dimensions, conceptual and sense-emprical, and that existence is all that human beings (at least) can conceive and experience in any meaningful sense. Consequently, to conceive anything is to bring it into existence conceptually. Hence the question "Does God exist?" receives an unequivocal answer—"Yes, at least conceptually." In any theological discussion, therefore, we must begin by assuming the conceptual existence of God. The relevant question, then, is no longer whether God exists but how God is (or can be) defined conceptually as well as sense-empirically.

Up to the present time, God has been mostly a mere conceptual existent, a vague solipsistic concept lacking objective definition, hence empirical verification.

This conceptual existence of God is all that traditional theology has to offer, an existence that is both vague in definition and incomplete in substance. The vagueness has provided maximum freedom and flexibility in interpretation and manipulation and, consequently, facilitated all sorts of pronouncements about God, without fear of contradiction from any quarter. By means of this vagueness, God becomes all things to all men. Even when pretending to precision of meaning the concept has remained amorphous. Examples of theological statements with a false claim to precision are: "God our Father in Heaven," "God the Creator of Heaven and Earth," "God the Redeemer of Mankind," "the God of Abraham, Isaac, and Jacob," et cetera. Examples of theological statements of undisguised vagueness are: "individual encounter with God," "God is Spirit," "God is Love," "God is Wholly Other," "God the same yesterday, today, and forever," et cetera.[8]

The incompleteness of God's existence stems from the illusory idea, held since time immemorial and incorporated, for example, in Platonian metaphysics, that there is a reality separate from and underlying the phenomenal world: the "two worlds" illusion. This illusion is reinforced by the fact that it is possible to conceive entities that have no phenomenal counterpart—for example, phoenix, unicorn, dragon, et cetera, from which it would seem as though there were a separate and distinct world of conceptual existents. That there are conceptual existents cannot be denied. But that they occupy a separate world of their own is an illusion into which one may fall only if one forgets that the activity of conceptualization occurs in, rather than outside, the mind of man, who is an empirical existent in the phenomenal world. Without denying the reality of conceptual existence, complete existence involves both conceptual and sense-empirical dimensions of the same reality, and these two dimensions occur only in sense-empirical entities, since such entities alone entail conceptual existence as well.

Once we accept the cosmos as the sense-empirical manifestation, the body—so to speak—of God (which is the same as defining God, sense-empirically, as the cosmos) God's existence becomes complete. All that then remains is to give precise and objective (i.e., conventional) meaning-content to the concept *God*. Only then can any kind of meaningful discussion about God in sense-empirical terms become possible. Only then can God become what man has always wanted—the living God. Defining God empirically as the cosmos implies the use of the biocosmic paradigm, from which it becomes possible to derive the main elements for an objective meaning-content for the God-concept. It then appears clearly in what respects the traditional God-concept has to be reworked or modified in order to accord with its sense-empirical counterpart, the cosmos. For instance, the basic feature of the biocosmic paradigm, that of transformation through flow-change, has to become a part of the God-concept, as well as the idea of permanence of the flow-change process, its eternal abidingness. Species-centered ideas of God (such as the anthropomorphic or theriomorphic ideas that have held exclusive sway until now) need to be abandoned and replaced by process-oriented ideas that are simultaneously valid for the individual, the family, the social and global group, regardless of biological type (microbe, man, nonhuman animals, plant life, et cetera).

The essence of cosmic existence is flow-change, of continuing and changing manifestation in accordance with the rule, "show and pass on." What is true of one manifestation may not necessarily be true of another, since each manifestation is contingent and the cosmos is the cradle of infinite possibilities. All these characteristics must be equally asserted of the God-concept—all these and more. We thus see the sense-empirical basis for the varied assertions that could be made by theologians about God. We realize that God is both X and more than X, which is the same as saying that God is X and not-X: all-inclusive as well as dialectic—thesis, antithesis, and synthesis.

In abandoning the various separate paradigms—anthropomorphic, theriomorphic, et cetera—we do so not because each is completely wrong but because each is only partially, very partially, valid and requiring subsumption in a more inclusive model: the biocosmic model, which includes all these partial models. The error in each partial paradigm is its pretension to inclusiveness when, in fact, it leaves out more, much more, than it can ever tell, whence the need for its abandonment.

Nothing said in the preceding paragraphs forbids man from deriving what selfish comfort he can from his species-paradigm view of the cosmos, of God. What is forbidden is the pretense that God is only what this myopic and blinkered view presents. Nothing forbids the theologian from continuing his traditionally vague and vaguely precise assertions

407

about God. What is forbidden is that he should continue to make those assertions henceforth without providing the sense-empirical verification necessary for their support. God is, indeed, all things to all men, but we must know the reason and show the sense-empirical evidence why this is so. Similarly, if there is a heaven and a hell we must be shown their sense-empirical location. We cannot, do not, need to take any assertion about God for granted or on trust when the evidence is all around us. Faith or belief is ruled out where the evidence exists. Faith or belief has a place, but only a temporary or provisional one until it can be verified sense-empirically. Where it cannot be so verified, it has a duty not to be in conflict with the sense-empirical evidence that we know, for there is only *one* world—the world of existence—not two. And existence does not require faith or belief: it is "there"; it is all that there is and does not need to be taken on trust. It is God.

Any particular existent assumes a different aspect to man according as it affects him favorably or unfavorably and according to which end of the quantitative scale it is viewed from. It is thus that what appear to be problems, sometimes so-called insuperable ones—such as good and evil, pain, suffering, and death—find their resolution if viewed within the biocosmic paradigm in a way that is not possible within the human paradigm. Within the biocosmic paradigm these so-called problems of human existence appear in their true aspect as consequences or aspects of divine (cosmic) manifestation, rather than as moral contradictions within the godhead or within the cosmic order.

At the nuclear particulate level, all is change and motion, combination and separation (or annihilation) of combinations or recombinations—perpetually. No one would think of associating notions of good or evil with what goes on at this level. And no event, whether volcanic eruption, earthquake, flood, nuclear fusion or fission, et cetera, makes any difference to the fundamental behavior of such particulate elements. Yet, such manifestations would be regarded as "evil" if they had adverse effects on man—except if they were to be brought about by conscious human action (e.g., experiments in nuclear fusion and fission). At the basic particulate level of existence occur all the changes and chances of existence, mostly imperceptible to man but accepted as "normal" in nonhuman phenomena—even as "beneficial" to man if they concerned, for example, climatic and other seasonal changes. Yet the moment such changes occur at molecular and quantitatively higher levels but with an adverse impact on man they become suspect, "evil," and are regarded as "problems."

So-called good and evil in nature are merely quantitative and qualitative aspects of change assuming striking proportions at the molecular

408

level and above, but having *perceived* "beneficial" and "adverse" effects on human welfare—from man's point of view, a rather narrow point of view in the cosmic context. In short, *good* qualifies any quantitative or qualitative change, event or consequence that is *form-constituting* and *form-conserving, evil* any quantitative or qualitative change, event, or consequence that is *form-threatening* or *form-dissolving*. A parallel interpretation underlies the concepts of "heaven" and "hell." This entirely human reaction rests upon the anthropocentric prejudice that the cosmos exists for the benefit of man, its be-all and end-all. In the same manner death, being *form-threatening* and *form-dissolving*, is regarded by man as evil insofar as it affects man; likewise pain and suffering, which are concomitants of change and transformation. Only outside the framework of the human paradigm does it become possible to see death as merely transformation through change and as a basic feature of existence, rather than as the "wages of Adam's sin." Only within the framework of the biocosmic paradigm do pain and suffering cease to be a paradox of human existence or a contradiction to the goodness and benevolence of the Cosmos-God; for only in this framework does man's unwarranted prejudice disappear whereby the cosmos is thought to exist for the sake and benefit of the human species.

Within the biocosmic paradigm also, inter- and intra-species parasitism—including mutual cannibalism—appears in its true light as organic symbiosis, another basic feature of existence. And change or transformation that appears as the phenomenon of mass-energy at the physical level becomes apparent as the only *permanent* feature of existence, the essence of the Cosmos-God; whereas in the human paradigm it becomes misconstrued as an exceptional event afflicting mankind, while the normal state of the Cosmos-God is held to be static:

Change and decay in all around I see:
O thou who changest not, abide with me

goes a popular Protestant hymn.[9] In fact, the Cosmos-God changes all the time. This, paradoxically, is its only unchanging feature, but this is not what these verses imply.

It becomes clear, therefore, that reference to the nuclear and subnuclear level of existence is a basic requirement in order that change and events at the molecular level and above may be seen in their true light. This can be done easily only within the biocosmic paradigm. As a result it becomes also easy to see that the so-called problems of existence are species-specific, especially man-specific and human paradigmatic, rather than cosmic or existential problems in the proper sense. It is also easy to see how these so-called problems disappear *as problems* and reveal themselves as basic features when viewed at *all levels* of the biocosmic paradigm. In general and from the human point of view, as one descends in the quantitative scale of existence, that is, down the nuclear ladder, so-called human problems become transformed or disappear into basic features of existence. We get down to the basic simplicities of existence as we jettison the anthropomorphic or any other species-specific paradigm, subsuming it in the biocosmic paradigm. Similarly, as one ascends in the quantitative scale of existence, that is, up the molecular ladder, basic features of existence assume the guise of "human problems" and become differentiated. Simplicities turn into complexities and we wonder at the "complexities of existence." In fact, however, existence is both simple and complex, depending on the direction of view—whether nuclear or molecular. Both views are necessary for a proper perspective on existence. Miniaturization seems to accompany increasing simplicity and magnification increasing complexity, within the biocosmic paradigm.

To summarize, the *cosmo-theos* is simple as well as complex in its manifestations and, within the biocosmic paradigm, there are no existential problems, properly so-called. So-called problems of existence, like suffering, pain, and death, do not arise within this paradigm as they reveal themselves only as basic existential features. These so-called problems, as well as the associated qualitative moral judgments of good and evil, are no more than human reactions to basic cosmic processes viewed against the biased background of the human paradigm and its implied assumptions.

Furthermore, the *cosmo-theos* is both immanent and transcendent within the biocosmic paradigm: transcendent with respect to each cosmic manifestation taken singly (panentheistic), immanent in each and every cosmic manifestation, singly as well as collectively (pantheistic). Being identical with the cosmos, the *cosmo-theos* cannot transcend itself. It is the one and only god.

In concluding this section it is important to stress that traditional theology (anthropotheology) can only survive if transformed and reinterpreted within the framework of the biocosmic paradigm. In this connection, general macrocosmic features need to be distinguished from the microcosmic features. At the macro-level there is neither beginning nor end to the cosmos, whatever may happen to individual manifestations, and at the micro-level the ways of the cosmo-theos remain past finding out, because of the contingence and evolutionary goallessness of each of its manifestations—including man. This means that man loses his self-assigned special place in the cosmos, on the basis of the human paradigm, when he is relocated within the biocosmic paradigm. Simultaneously and unfortunately for man, such recent anthropotheological developments as the androgynization of God; equal access of men and women to the priesthood consequent on the women's liberation or, (in the light of early Gnostic Christianity), reliberation movement; the desertion of priests and nuns from celibate to marital life following the increasing reacceptance of the sexual function as normal and compatible with devout religious life,[10] and the associated decline of postulants—all these developments, though not without a certain interest, are irrelevant within the biocosmic framework of cosmotheology. They represent a filling out or completion of anthropotheology within the long obsolete framework of the human paradigm in a more meaningful way, while this paradigm is superseded by the biocosmic paradigm as an interpretive tool and relegated as an outworn skeleton to the museum of the evolution of human intellectual and theological thought.

Out goes, as well, that branch of traditional theology known as soteriology (or human salvation theology)—at least, in its present form—to be replaced by a reinterpreted concept of soteriology. True salvation no longer consists in the assimilation of man to God or vice versa—for man is a manifestation and automatically a part of the Cosmo-Theos and always has been—but in reconciliation of man to the "divine" essence, the fact of *change*. This should ensure not only that man accept his place in the cosmos and his uncertain fate, along with other cosmic manifestations, as the contingent evolution of the manifestations of the Cosmo-Theos proceeds; but also man's acceptance and internalization of the fact that no condition, however onerous or pleasant, lasts forever—in accordance with the rule, "This also will pass."

The most important consequences for man resulting from the essential and organic integrality of the Cosmo-Theos and its manifestations and from relocating man within the biocosmic paradigm are the following:

(a) There is no need to offer prayer to the Cosmo-Theos as this would be the same as praying to its manifestations, *including* man. For this same reason of human participation in cosmic existence,
(b) There is no need for songs of praise to the Cosmo-Theos.
(c) There is no need for worship of the Cosmo-Theos.
(d) There is no need for reverence, awe, or fear of the Cosmo-Theos (Rudolf Otto's "idea of the holy," the "mysterium tremendum et fascinans"), while at the same time this does not eliminate the intrigue and sense of wonder at the miracle that is the cosmos itself.
(e) There is no need to bless or curse the Cosmo-Theos.
(f) The concepts of reward and punishment by the Cosmo-Theos, an

411

afterlife, heaven and hell, and the related concepts of resurrection and transmigration of souls, as presented in contemporary theologies, are both irrelevant and dubious.

(g) There is no two-world metaphysics, only the one world of here and now, the one world of time in eternity (timelessness).

NOTES

1. The dangers involved in a purely conceptual God have already been mentioned in the discussion on the nature and meaning of things (Book Three, chapter 1, section 4). In a sense, the conceptual God is a "smart" God: it cannot be identified, pinned down. Wherein lies the great danger. It becomes a prey to all sorts of charlatanism, all things, and no thing, to all men; appealed to in support of, and as approving, all sorts of causes and hopes of the human race—no matter how inconsistent or (on the human plane) evil. Thus, outside–space-time gods, like outside–space-time worlds, are the happy hunting ground of saint and charlatan.

2. Whether such a Being exists as an idea outside of human conception is an interesting question to which the answer is definitely negative. Firstly, ideas do not have an independent existence apart from the human mind; secondly, in an all-pervasive material environment man really has no proper conception or apprehension of a nonmaterial entity, definition aside.

3. This is not in any way affected by the position taken by the atheist (antitheist) who denies or disbelieves in the existence of God; for denial or disbelief already implies the conceptual existence of the very thing denied or disbelieved.

4. Individual manifestations of the cosmos may be finite as part of the cosmic process of transformation and change, but the cosmos entire is eternally enduring, creating and recreating itself, as man has always known from before Heraclitus formulated his theory of cyclical cosmic conflagration and reconstruction until today's theory of cosmic oscillation. Thus the vine-branches, body-members metaphor used by Jesus to illustrate man's relationship to his God is no idle metaphor.

5. The Uncertainty Principle is manifested within the cosmos and reflected in the physical and natural sciences and, not surprisingly, in philosophy.

6. In view of the apparent limitation or finite amount of cosmic matter, the static term *being* is appropriate in this context, instead of the dynamic and flexible *becoming*, which is appropriate and manifest at the micro- or intra-cosmic level.

7. In a sense, this democratic quality cheapens divinity. One can therefore understand the concern of those who may be opposed to pantheism for this reason, seeking to impose a different kind of scarcity value on divinity—market scarcity—resulting in the monotheopoly or intolerant monotheism of the Semitic religions.

8. Theologians who use such "vaguely precise" terms justify them on the basis of analogy, the weakness of which has been discussed in chapter 4 of Book Three. Alternatively, a snobbish elitism is often invoked to the effect that anthropomorphic comparisons are all that the common people can understand in conversations about God. Ironically, theologians of this stripe have never been known to use any other type of language in communication among themselves!

9. The hymn by H. F. Lyte (1793–1847) beginning "Abide with me; fast falls the eventide" in *Hymns, Ancient and Modern* (no. 27).

10. One has merely to remind oneself of the Pauline epistles, which recommended monogamy for the bishops of the Church and celibacy as an optional and voluntary, rather than an institutional, obligation incumbent on all priests of the Church. See I Timothy 3:2; Titus 1:6, and I Corinthians 1–9. Likewise, Jesus on marriage, divorce, and celibacy in Saint Matthew 19:3–12.

Chapter 7

Religion

1. DEFINITION

Religion is philosophy with a human face, the personalization of man's relationships with the rest of the cosmos. This personalization of relationships—religion—is the result of an exploring and knowing through sensing and emotional appropriation of the entities (persons, objects, or thoughts) involved.[1] One aspect as well as consequence of this sensual apprehension and emotional appropriation[2] is also the apprehension and appropriation of the rhythm (beat of life) of the experience involved in the sensing, and its transformation into corresponding physical movement and the product of such movement: various art forms—music, song, dance, visual (painting and other graphic) arts, and plastic art (sculpting, collage and other manipulative forms).[3] In other words, by its sensual exploration and emotional appropriation of entities involving a personalization of relationships, religion gives birth to art and both become thereby associated.[4] It is by this same process that sex and love become associated, explicitly or implicitly, with religion and play a very significant role in it within certain cultures both ancient (e.g., Greek and Roman) and modern (e.g., Indian tantra and Negro voodoo). In monastic Christianity as in voodooism, hierogamy (marriage with divinity) is institutionalized and even formally celebrated and legally registered as in Haitian voodoo.[5]

Now, the religious approach to experiencing and knowing,[6] like the intuitive, is integrative or macro-cognitive, not analytical or micro-cognitive. Either way of knowing does not exclude the operation of the process of reasoning; for reason is not a way of experiencing, alternative to sensing, but a mere tool for explicating the implications of propositions and assumptions. The macro-cognitive approach apprehends things in their organic wholeness, while the micro-cognitive approach, being analytical, destroys their organic unity without being able to reintegrate the disintegrated elements. The most that can be achieved after analysis of

414

the organic unit is *aggregation* (mere adding up) not integration or restoration of organic unity. For this reason the two methods, while being complementary *in principle*, can only be *effectively* so if used in a certain order: the macro-cognitive *preceding* the micro-cognitive. Taken the other way round, the complementarity is lost since only aggregation, not integration, will be possible after the use of the analytical method. This imposes a certain limitation on the analytical method if it should be attempted without completely destroying the integral structure of the organism to be analyzed: it can only be *partially* employed. Only dead organisms or inorganic entities are therefore suitable for complete analysis. We are thus led to the conclusion that while the *results* of the religious experience, hence of religious knowledge, are not in conflict with those obtained by the analytical (scientific) method, *methodologically* the two—science and religion—may conflict.

2. ART AS PRODUCT AND OBJECT OF RELIGIOUS COMMUNION

We have defined religion, or religious experience, as knowing an entity through sensual exploration and emotional appropriation and transforming its essence or rhythm into corresponding physical movement, which then reveals itself in various art forms—music, song, dance, and the visual and plastic arts.[7] Now this is true of all objects of religious cognition, and particularly so of that class of entities that, by reason of their remoteness (e.g., objects such as the sun, moon, and stars) or abstractness (e.g., thought) are less accessible than proximate objects to the grasp of the complete battery of senses—visual, tactile, auditory, olfactory, and gustatory. As is the case for all entities that are targets of religious experiencing, the rhythm of these remote, almost inaccessible, and abstract entities is also transformable into concrete artistic forms that serve as suitable proxies, available for a full and effective exploration by all, instead of only some, of the senses and for full appropriation by the emotions. The religious cognition of various art substitutes for inaccessible and abstract entities is appropriately termed *communion* in religious language—that is, the sharing or the bestowing of the sensations and emotions with or on the art objects; and the art substitutes constitute the means of communion.[8]

The process just described throws a searchlight on what, by ignorant Christian or Islamic missionaries, has been dubbed fetishism and the hallmark of idolaters and pagans: the objects of "wood and stone," trees or animals "worshiped" by "the heathen in his blindness." (The an-

415

thropologists merely followed unthinkingly in the footsteps of the missionaries.) So ignorant—more so than the "heathen"—have been the missionaries about the nature and actual process of religious experiencing, of religious knowing.[9] Thus one of the many functions of art, including ready-made objects of "wood and stone," is to serve as proxies or symbolic instruments of communion—*communion*, not communication, since what is involved is a voluntary, *unilateral* act of intimate rapport, of assimilation of one entity by another through the senses and the emotions, rather than a voluntary, bilateral exchange of information, thought, or feeling engaged in by both parties, which we call communication.[10] Sometimes, the object to be assimilated is at hand, an organic or inorganic entity. Often, as has been mentioned, the object is either too distant to be physically accessible to all the senses, or too abstract, existing only in thought or mental symbolism and, consequently, completely inaccessible to any of the senses. As thought, it may be either distinct or unclear. Or, again, it may be an unknown object that is merely felt to exist somewhere, somehow, or in some form, endowed conceptually with certain attributes or qualities by the communing subject. It is in such circumstances of inaccessibility, abstractness, ignorance, and uncertainty that it is deemed necessary to substitute, in accessible form, either a symbol or semblance (image) as a stand-in for the object of religious experience, in order that it may be sensed and contemplated at close range and at leisure. Art objects, such as ritual or funerary masks in Africa, and other kinds of religious art, including "fetishistic" objects, paintings, and sculptures, et cetera, fulfill this function of mediation as tangible substitutes in accessible form for the inaccessible objects of communion.

It is necessary to mention, in this connection, another activity connected with art—critical examination and analysis of the art object, which is known also as art appreciation.[11] Here the art object serves the function of providing for its author a substitute and means of communion—that is, bestowing on or sharing of feelings and sentiments with the inaccessible object. But for the viewing public it serves, not as a substitute for the artist's original source of inspiration, but as their own original source and is completely available for criticism or appreciation. The artist's vision remains very much his private possession, inaccessible to the viewing public. What the viewer criticizes, evaluates, or reacts to is *not* the artist's source of inspiration (which remains inaccessible) but the *product* of that inspiration, as the latter is represented, transformed, or both, as the case may be.

This leads to a consideration of the basic function of art, which is to portray an experience seen, felt, heard, touched, or smelled—a sense experience; or a thought independent of, or provoked by, a sense experience, whether for religious purposes or not. The artist, however, is limited to visual and tactile media in expressing this wide range of experiences. Consequently, only visual, auditory, olfactory, and tactile experiences can be represented in visual and tactile media.[12] Thought and emotional experiences that cannot be directly rendered in visual or tactile form must necessarily be *transformed* into one or other of the available media. Thus may be distinguished two kinds of art—representational and transformational, or a mixture of both as a third category.

Representational art covers the school of artists who regard the function of art to be the imitation of nature or the reproduction of semblances of original objects: "expressionists," that is, painters and carvers of imitations or semblances of original objects. All other types of artists ("impressionists," "surrealists," et cetera) are transformists; that is to say, they seek to convey moods, feelings, and thoughts, or these in addition to the original objects of their experience.[13] The transformists necessarily have a difficult task, both for themselves and for their viewing public, who may wish to appreciate their creations.

The difficulty of transforming thought and emotional experiences into mostly visual and tactile media is reflected, correspondingly, in the difficulty experienced by the viewing public in appreciating so-called modern art. Since in nonrepresentational art, especially, the artist's vision or other type of experience is unavailable to the viewing public, the latter is left with two choices, other than outright rejection: to make a cult of the artist and/or to make what it can of the artist's work. In no circumstances can the public *appreciate* the artist's original experience, which is unavailable. Consequently, only in conventional, ritual art, whether representational or not (e.g., African funerary masks) can the artist and public come close to participating in, or communing with, the experiences mediated by the art object, by reason of their shared knowledge and common cultural background.

Let us now summarize the foregoing discussion. Art is, in a general way, an expression of the religious mode of experiencing and knowing an object or idea. And both the artist and at least some of the viewing public are in their respective ways—indirectly by the artist, directly by the viewing public—enacting a religious experience or something very close to it. Richard Wagner leaps to mind, in this connection, as a famous example of the relation of art to religion. Unlike that of the musicians whose religious experience is expressed uniquely in the medium of music and song—such as Bach, Chopin, Handel, Mendelssohn, Mozart, et cetera—Wagner's religious experience seems to have been of a far greater range and intensity, at least dimensionally, which led him to seek its expression in the triple combination of music, drama, and poetry, of which the *Niebeligung* is generally recognized as his best example. On its side, the viewing public may commune directly and religiously with a piece of music or with a sculpture on which much visual, tactile, and emotional (and sometimes financial) capital has been invested.

It would seem, therefore, that the end of art is *communion* with the art object, as representation or as symbol, of something for which it substitutes. As symbol, art, like any other symbol, is a transformation of something beyond or outside it into sensible medium. That something, however, remains vague—a feeling, a mood, a thought—to the viewing public, unknown. As representation, it is a recognizable object of sense experience or an experience that can be objectivized or stylized in a form whose meaning is common knowledge to artist and viewing public, being based on shared customs or rites. It is in this sense that mathematics and any other kind of language may be regarded as nonreligious art.

3. RELIGION AND MAGIC

We have seen that the function of art in religion is to mediate as an accessible object of communion in place of an inaccessible object or abstract entity. Magic enters into religious experience by this very act of communing with the inaccessible entity through a surrogate object. It consists precisely in the *investing* of the surrogate object, by the communicant, with all the powers and attributes held to pertain to the inaccessible entity (in this case, a force or energy source) and *actively willing and expecting* the exercise by the entity, through its surrogate, of such powers and attributes in favor of the communicant.

This interpretation of the origin of magic in, and its close association with, religion differs from that of anthropologists,[14] who interpret magic as resulting from a failure of technique to catch up with expectations, so that magic fills the gap between technique and expectations. This latter is a rational rather than empirical interpretation, to which African practice and experience do not seem to conform. The common cases of magic reported by those who have experience of the phenomenon have to do with *action* performed by some object (juju) such as a bundle of twigs, a pestle, or another object serving as surrogate or instrument of an otherwise inaccessible entity or force, at the will (or demand) of the communicant. By such action a thief may be uncovered and punished and other contraventions of the social order traced to their culprits and sanctioned. On the other hand, by such action, benefits may also be conferred on individuals—except, of course, the practitioner, who is universally precluded from any personal enrichment from his trade.

The discussion here is limited to the origin of magic in religion. It is no part of its purpose to analyze or interpret empirical acts of a magical nature. It may be said, however, that there is a parallel between so-called acts of magic (as defined above) and the transformation of religious experience into artistic, that is, sensible, media. What is unknown is the relationship between the process of transformation of religious experience into sensible form and that of inaccessible powers into concrete acts of intervention in personal affairs.

Another interesting aspect of magic is its relation to belief and the implementation of belief. This is also a religious phenomenon inasmuch as many religions are based on, or associated with, belief systems. It was shown in the discussion on the cult of Dionysus as archetype of Christianity and paradigm of faith[15] that a belief system consists of three elements: (a) renunciation of a current reality, (b) a belief-content or desired alternative to the rejected reality, (c) appropriate action to actualize the desired alternative. Now, appropriate action to bridge the gap between the desired alternative and its empirical actualization may take one of two possible forms: technology or magic. Thus magic fulfills the same implementation role as technology in achieving the desired alternative situation, serving as a substitute for, not a supplement to, technology in the implementation of belief. It is not here intended to imply that magical action is or is not always, or necessarily, as effective as technology, for not enough is known on the subject. All that is intended is to say that some view magic in action as an alternative to technology and that in practice it does appear as such.

NOTES

1. It is this process that the Senegalese poet, Leopold Sedar Senghor, describes in his "Nation et voie africaine du socialisme" (*Presence Africaine* [Paris,1961] and his other writings and considers as the distinguishing characteristic of Negro peoples everywhere—which he terms their *negritude*.

2. The process conforms well to the meaning of the Latin word for *religion* (*religio*). It has the same derivation as the verb *religare*, meaning, "to bind back (to), to latch (onto)."

3. What Leopold S. Senghor terms *negritude* is thus a shorthand for this way of relating to entities by the process of knowing them—as well as their rhythm—through sensual exploration and emotional appropriation, and the conversion of this kind of knowing experience into an appropriate physical medium—music, song, dance, the visual and plastic arts. It is, in short, a way of denoting the religious experience. Spelled out, it says no more than what already is a well-known phenomenon, namely, that the approach of black people to experience and life is predominantly religious. It does not, of course, mean that "black folk are the only religious folk." Nor does it quite mean a "philosophy of blackness," although tending to a kind of racism that even

419

a superficial reading of Senghor cannot fail to detect. Indeed, the term *negritude* is an unfortunate expression borrowed by Senghor from its coiner, Aimé Césaire, the Martiniquan poet. Cæsaire intended the term to mean the recapture of initiative by black peoples in order to assert their cultural values in all freedom and independence from colonial rule, while borrowing enriching elements from other cultures without losing their own cultural identity.

Senghor transvalued the term to connote entirely different meanings, including what in the view of his critics, may be his personal prejudices and complexes, but primarily to mean what is best called "black peoples' religious approach to experience." Similarly, the so-called "philosophy of negritude" and the "black is beautiful" movement amount to no more than the trite and uncontroversial statement that "black peoples' approach to life and experience is essentially a religious one, and this is a beautiful way of experiencing."

For all its seeming philosophic trappings, Senghor's so-called philosophy of negritude is nothing new, although his interpretation as the religious mode of experiencing and knowing is certainly new. It has illustrious antecedents in the speeches and writings of his famous African precedessors, E. W. Blyden of Liberia and Sierra Leone and J. E. K. Aggrey of Ghana and the United States. For Senghor, like Blyden, bases himself on *race* and *religion*, emotion and mysticism. And, like Aggrey, he stresses the complementarity of black and white cultural values, that is, the cultural values of Africa and Euramerica; whence Senghor's pet dream of a Eurafrican cultural symbiosis, which he baptizes in picturesque Gallicism as *"la civilization de l'universel."* (See E. W. Blyden, *Christianity, Islam and the Negro Race*, 1887 (reedited by Edinburgh University Press, 1967); R. W. July, "Edward Wilmot Blyden, Nineteenth Century Negritude," *The Journal of African History*, V (1964), no. 1, pp. 73–86; and Edwin W. Smith, *Aggrey of Africa: A Study in Black and White* (London: S.C.M. Press, 1929).

4. Details of the process whereby the activity termed *religious knowing* gives birth to art are discussed later in this chapter.

5. Jean Manolesco, *Vaudou et magie noire* (Montreal: Editions du jour, 1972), p. 96.

6. To know is to experience, and vice versa.

7. In the absence of artistic skills in the religious devotee, any ready-made object—stone, feather, tree, animal, et cetera that is to hand and answers to his artistic temperament will do.

8. The Christian rite known as the Eucharist exemplifies the religious experience and knowledge. The desired but inaccessible and absent object of religious experience (Jesus) is emotionally transformed (transubstantiated) into bread and wine, which *stand in* for (consubstantiate) Jesus and become the object of gustatory sensing and emotional appropriation, thus personalizing vicariously the devotee's relationship with Jesus.

9. This ignorant prejudice has, of course, been inherited from the traditions of Judaism. The Jews, for various reasons—inability, unwillingness, superiority complex, or whatever—refused to give concrete proxy representation to their tribal God, Jahweh, whom they had brought into conceptual existence. Thus they lacked the full measure of religious experiencing enjoyed by the "idolaters" in whose midst they put themselves. In a sense, they were in a predicament into which they unwittingly put themselves by their claim that their tribal God was more powerful than those of other tribes, being supreme over all the earth, the seas, and the heavens. Naturally, he could not be represented in the same way as other tribal gods (according to their manner of thinking), and they were at a loss as to how to represent, even by proxy, a being that was greater than heaven, earth, the sun, the moon, and stars—admittedly

not an easy task. So they decided to do nothing by way of proxy representation of Jahweh, making a virtue of their necessity by condemning the symbolic gods of other tribes. The error of the Jews and their followers in Christianity and Islam was to misunderstand symbolic representation for facsimile reproduction of the original on a smaller scale. Thus they confounded symbol with image. The fetishes of all peoples who have had them (including the Jews during periods that they regarded as lapses from the cult of Jahweh) have been nothing but symbols—not images, although likenesses or images may be used, as in the case of the sun—for no "pagan" would testify that his one, true God, Spirit, or whatever was exactly the same as his fetish or his totem. Furthermore, while fetishes may symbolize a supreme God, they do not always necessarily do so. They may symbolize what are regarded as lesser deities or spirits. Thus the essence of religion is to know by sense and emotional experience an entity—any entity—whether a God or other entity.

10. The author became aware after this was first written that there could be *involuntary* physical communication between persons and persons, persons and impersonal objects, and between objects and objects—good or bad "vibes," as the hippies first taught us—such as has been discovered by nuclear physicists to be the essence of gravitational pull. Hence the addition of the qualification *voluntary* to the terms *communion* and *communication*.

11. The thoughts expressed in this and following paragraphs owe their inspiration to my present wife.

12. Perfume makers and perfume chemists are artists in that they seek to concoct, in tactile and visual medium, their smelling experiences and experiments.

13. Caricaturists, other than cubists, seem to occupy a middle ground between representational and transformational art. Impressionists and cubists may be regarded as combining both representation and transformation rather than as being mostly transformational artists.

14. See, for example, E. E. Evans-Pritchard, *Theories of Primitive Religion* (New York: Oxford University Press, 1965, reprinted 1980), p. 40.

15. Book Two, Section B, chapter 8.

Chapter 8

Ethics

1. THE NATURE OF ETHICAL SYSTEMS

Ethics or morality is that aspect of religion that deals with mutuality or reciprocity of religious experiencing and knowing and with the resulting consequences in terms of harmony and disharmony in the prevailing interrelationships. Ethics is a goal-oriented discipline in that it seeks harmony, rather than disharmony, in interrelationships among persons and things. It is consequently not indifferent to the *quality* of such interrelationships. The goal of harmony is empirical and achievable as well as mutual among the parties concerned. When the goal of mutuality is assumed and internalized and becomes the governing rule of human action, each individual action then becomes automatically reciprocalized (or dualized) with regard to every object or entity touched by that action. In short, mutuality of benefit (benevolence, in other words) becomes built-in into every individual action. And the action, though unilateral, becomes transformed into an action in which one's personal interests include the independent interests of "the other" (person or persons, friend or foe, taking human beings as our example).[1]

Mutuality of relationships is normally regarded as holding only among human beings. But it also holds among nonhuman animals and can exist between these, on the one hand, and humans, on the other. Furthermore, considering (a) the philosophical fact of interdependent relationships among all elements in the biosphere and in the cosmos, generally, and (b) that human welfare therefore depends on a proper relationship to every element in the biosphere, including proper conservation and use of biospheric resources, the survival and welfare of mankind dictates an ethical, that is, benevolent, attitude toward every constituent of the biosphere. This implies that whether a biospheric element has the status of a person or not, it should be treated *as if* it were a person. Hence, a general rule of personification of every "other" is indicated. Thus ethics becomes a system of mutual and interdependent relationships among persons and personified entities.

422

Ethical relationships between man and various nonhuman animals are probably best exemplified by those existing between man and dog, but hold between man and other animal species, wild or tame. Reference was made earlier[2] to ethical behavior between a team of pond diggers in an animal park and some of the animals that stood to benefit from the team's activities. The diggers were amazed at the unusual behavior of the lions in their vicinity. Appreciative of the water that welled up from underground to fill the ponds being provided for the animals, the lions would fetch their kill (deer) to the workers, who would excise their choice bits. The lions took the rest away for their meal. The cubs preferred to drink the water flowing from the cisterns by which the men served themselves, and would play among themselves with the plastic jerrycans, returning them in the evening to the camp. Similarly, elephant herds coming upon the sleeping men at night would backtrack noiselessly from the camp.

All these animals—lions, elephants, and others—were aware of the great benefit they derived from the provision of water by the team in an area subject to periodic drought, and showed their appreciation in various ways, the lions in particular reciprocating in a mutually beneficial manner.[3]

An ethical system is based on the presupposition of harmony of the interests of all concerned, as well as on concrete action undertaken to ensure that such harmony exists and that disharmony is eliminated, avoided, or minimized.[4]

In summary, the salient features of an ethical system of conduct are the following:

(a) Reciprocity or mutuality of interrelationships: this implies relationships among persons and between persons and personified entities.
(b) Independent benevolence, or including in one's interests the independent interests of others—those which serve their own purposes rather than one's own.
(c) Internalization of independent benevolence by every individual in their relationships with other persons and personified entities in order to assure automatic, or near automatic, operation of mutuality or reciprocity of action and of mutual benevolence.
(d) Effective mutual benevolence on a unilateral basis, once every party in an interrelationship internalizes the ethic of "independent benevolence toward the other."

This summary reveals the dual foundation of an effective ethical system: (a) personification of "the other" and (b) internalization of independent benevolence toward "the other." It follows from this that any ethical system is likely to fail that ignores the dual foundation required for its effectiveness. It is, indeed, because Christian and Communist ethics tend to actually ignore this dual basis—especially the requirement of internalization of the ethic of independent benevolence—that these systems have proved ineffective in practice. Indeed, this is the point stressed by Jesus' statement that "the kingdom of God is within you" (Saint Luke 17:21). Without internalization of any standard, action designed to reflect that standard is unlikely to be effective. The story of Ananias and Sapphira in Acts of the Apostles 5 is a case in point. Their failure consisted in noninternalization of the early Christian communist ethic by which "all that believed . . . had all things common; and sold their possessions and goods, and parted them to all men, as every man had need" (Acts 2:44–45). Whence their practice of the ethic was defective. The same criticism applies to modern-day attempts to establish communist societies, starting with the USSR, and accounts to a large degree for their failures.

The dual foundation of an ethical system provides a touchstone for assessing the adequacy of every ethical system. Thus the ethical system of the Greek philosophers, Plato and Aristotle, is seen to be defective on both counts. First, it did not give full personal status to every human being nor treat nonhumans as if they were human with a right to independent benevolence. In Greek society there were free citizens with all civic rights and slaves (as well as women) who had none. Second, and following from the first, it did not accord to the independent interests of others the right to equal status with one's own interests. Thus the Greek system was not based on independent benevolence. As a result—as Thrasymachus argued validly and convincingly in Plato's *Republic*—the moral or ethical system of Greek society served the interests of the dominant class (the aristocrats) and took into account the interests of other classes only insofar as they served the dominant class in a dependent relationship. It is no surprise, therefore, that the apologists for this biased ethical system—Plato among them—sought both to protect the interests of the dominant class and to put them beyond challenge by providing for them what they considered an adequate authoritative basis. Both objectives were achieved by a definition of moral standards that were inconsistent and not only put them formally in a metaphysical world beyond our space-time world, but further buttressed them by a kind of mathematical concept (that of an asymptote) that made them doubly unachievable. Thus the Platonian moral standards (or forms) that governed human conduct were only very approximately achieved in human action and never completely in the space-time world of phenomena.

By contrast, the ethical system discussed in this chapter is a space-time system falling within the realm of achievement. The standards of the Greek Academic philosophers were *externalized* beyond our space-time world, so that impossibility of achieving them was an essential part of their definition, the aim being to inculcate the lesson of "perpetual striving toward" their achievement. This type of externalized ethic is the heritage of occidental society and organized (institutionalized) Christianity, though different from the ethic of Jesus himself, as already indicated. The ethical standards of the present discussion, like those of Jesus, are standards that can be *internalized* within our space-time world and within individuals and are completely achievable. They are based on a mutuality of conduct that was impossible in the Greek city-state, a society that was undemocratic as between the different segments of its population. Duties were all one way, responsibilities the other way. But in an ethics of mutuality duties and responsibilities are the same for all, without exception.

This is the place to consider the issue of "means" and "ends." Since the "end" of ethics is harmonious relationships through mutual benevolence, it follows that the "means" can only be such as promote this "end" and are qualitatively in keeping with the principle of harmony. Thus it must always and automatically be true that "the end justifies the means," given an adequate definition or description of the *end*. If, by contrast, the end sought is the selfish one of self-aggrandizement at the expense of others, it is clear that only such means as promote this end will be justified. Such is the case with Machiavellian ends. Hence the principle incarnated in the statement that "the end justifies the means" is unexceptionable. It is in its application that differences arise. Contrary to popular belief, the principle, per se, is *not* Machiavellian; its application may be Machiavellian (unqualifiedly selfish) or not. Nor is it the case—again, contrary to popular belief—that the principle implies that *any* means is justified by a given end. This is a popular misperception and misinterpretation that identifies it uniquely with Machiavellism, for the principle merely states that the nature of the "end" determines the character of the "means." And Machiavellian selfishness is no exception to this general rule. Nor, for that matter, is mutually beneficial action based on independent benevolence. Means and ends bear a close and direct correlation.

If the more energy I devote to others the less I have for myself, then the means of reconciling and harmonizing love of self with love of others, and energy for self with energy for others, is to avoid one-sided activities and engage only in such activities as are mutually beneficial to self and others at the same time. Just as the economics of supply and demand excludes activities that seek 100 percent of profits for oneself or for others, so in the same sense can it be said that mutually beneficial activities are *moral* (harmonizing) and *economic* (optimum use of energy and re-

425

sources) *although the proportion of allocation of benefits still remains open.* In this context the means is equally as important as, if not more so than, the end, for it is not so much what advantage one secures for oneself as *how* one secures it that matters. Here, as always, the end (as defined) must justify the means, and the means must be in conformity with the end.

Another source of traditional misunderstanding in ethics—deriving from the Greek habit of externalizing attributes, including moral standards, and thereby making them unattainable in practice—is the related erroneous distinction between the "ideal" and the "actual." In the Greek ethical system the *ideal* is defined as a standard of aspiration, while the *actual* (or *virtual*) is the attainable level to which practice descends—thus falling short of the "ideal," the so-called standard or norm. Thus *duty* was defined as ideal action, what *should* be done because it was *right* action. Much of the fuzziness can be taken out of this concept of "ideal," "duty," or "right action" by relating it to the concept of mutually beneficial relationships and thus seeing it in its true color as an immanent and attainable, rather than as a transcendent, asymptotic, and unattainable course of action. (That this was not done by the Greek ethicists is a reflection of the imperfect structure of Greek society wherein mutual obligations held only within the narrowly defined group of "citizens," while "duties"—toward superiors, that is, citizens—and "responsibilities"—towards inferiors, that is, women and slaves—defined the relationships between these citizens and the rest of the society.)

Accordingly, actions that promote mutually beneficial results are what properly may be called duties: they reconcile and harmonize the self-interest of all the parties concerned. Hence what "should," "ought" to be done turns out to be not, as is usually supposed, a self-sacrificing act but the contrary—a mutually beneficial one, beneficial to self as well as to other(s). A "duty" is, therefore, not an action that someone else wants to impose upon me, wishes me to take or to desire, but action that I would want to take myself because it benefits me but, beyond this, others as well. It is not Kant's conception of duty, which he defines as (unconditional) action, that I would wish to become a law of nature for myself and others—the Platonian type of externalized moral standard beyond reach and hope of fulfillment. Rather is it something more utilitarian and conditional, in the sense of benefiting the greatest number of people, including myself; nothing of self-sacrificing nature. There is, indeed, a substitution of others' independent interests for some of mine that I might otherwise wish to realize, but what this substitution implies should be made clear. First, because of the fact of interdependence with others there is no possibility of realizing one's interests to the *total* exclusion of the interests of others. Interdependence sets a limit to the volume of one's interests that could be actualized, and this is less than 100 percent. Second, since one does not give up all of one's interests in any action, there is no self-sacrifice in the sense of complete surrender of one's welfare. It is always a case of more or less benefit for oneself—but this goes as well for others in a mutually beneficial relationship. A complete surrender of one's interests in any given action would violate the bond of interdependence as equally as an attempt to realize 100 percent of one's interests. Neither type of action is to be recommended, worse, commended. Either type of action would be antisocial, unethical action.[5]

Ethical acts should thus be recognized for what they are: acts conferring mutually beneficial results, rather than acts of punishment or reward according to the conventional view. Violation of the principle of mutuality does entail inconvenience, even suffering, not only for individuals but for society as a whole. Ethical behavior is not behavior that family or society imposes on individual members but on itself as an interacting whole, if it should derive the greatest benefit for all its members.

2. MODES AND PRINCIPLES OF ACTION

Within the context of the syndrome—self → interests → other → action—various modes of human behavior are possible, as indicated diagrammatically and otherwise in what follows.

A. MODES OF PERSONAL ACTION

Some comments are in order regarding the various situations. To take first the case of symbiosis, which is normally defined as "a close association of two animal or plant species that are dependent on one another"(Collins English Dictionary [1984]). Thus would it seem that Situation 5 portrays a symbiotic relationship—a relationship of interdependence. However, in a truly symbiotic relationship the selfish act of the one party benefits the other party as well. For example, certain birds that accompany cattle, picking off their lice and nutrients from their excreta, have a symbiotic relationship in this sense since their self-serving act of feeding on lice brings relief to the cattle. Alternatively, it may be said that the cattle use the birds to get rid of their lice while thus providing food for the birds as well as transportation. Thus true symbiosis involves

427

mutual benefits in a dual sense—that is, both unilaterally and bilaterally. Consequently, Situation 8 (with or without the element of consultation) represents more accurately the truly symbiotic situation, thereby superseding Situation 5.

Situation 1:

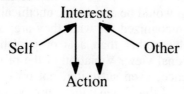

Interests

Self   Other

Action

Selfish Interests (Nonconflicting)

The self consults only its own interests and takes appropriate action without regard to the other or its interests. And vice versa. This type of behavior is successful in achieving its object only so long as there are enough resources to satisfy each person without conflict or competition for those resources. But this is not the usual situation. In general, resources are limited relative to the demands made upon them. This leads to conflict, hence to Situation 2 and its mode of behavior.

It is important to distinguish between nonconflicting interests and mutuality of interests. Nonconflicting interests are those that, formally, do not conflict with the interests of the self or those of the other, but achieve some of the interests of both. Thus Situation 8 (generalized by mutuality in Situation 9) is the only case of nonconflicting interests in this sense. Situation 1 is nonconflicting as regards the interests of the self and the other only in the narrow sense through absence of contact between the parties. This is due to the fact that resources are more than adequate

428

Situation 2:

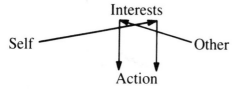

Selfish Interests (Conflicting)

The self consults only its own interests and takes appropriate action without regard to the other or its interests. And vice versa. But in view of limited resources and resulting competition for those resources, conflict arises: an unstable situation that may or may not continue indefinitely. If enough conflict and dissatisfaction result, this may lead to open hostility and an attempt by one side to exclude the other from shared enjoyment of those resources. In the absence of open conflict, however, a third and better mode of behavior results (Situation 3).

Situation 3:

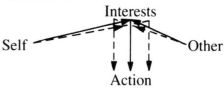

Resolution of Conflicting Self-Interests: Conflict Minimization through Compromise, Negotiation, or Bargaining

In view of their conflicting interests, the self and the other resolve to eliminate, peacefully, the conflict resulting from their competition for limited resources to satisfy their respective interests. They compromise, negotiate, or bargain for the use of the resources and arrive, thereby, at an agreement or treaty. They compose their differences by coordinating their interests and their actions.

429

Situation 4:

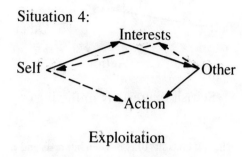

Exploitation

Here superior power or force enters into the picture. By this power the self consults only its own interests and uses the other to achieve them, or vice versa. Where this action becomes bilateral, a fifth situation and mode of behavior ensues.

Situation 5:

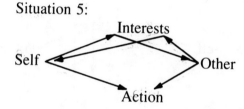

Resolution of Exploitative Relationship: Cease and Desist or Symbiosis (Mutual Exploitation)

This is a case of mutual exploitation by the self and the other, implying a stable situation of symbiosis—survival by mutual exploitation—whereby both parties derive benefit from the relationship. (Where mutual exploitation is not satisfactory, the parties will cease and desist from such action.)

430

Situation 6:

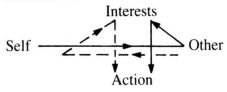

Independent Benevolence (Based on Consultation of the Other)

The self seeks only the other's interests—as the other sees them—and takes appropriate action to achieve them, or vice versa. This is the mode of behavior known as independent benevolence: one acts to preserve the other's interests as the other sees them. This implies consulting the other in order to determine what those interests may be.

Situation 7:

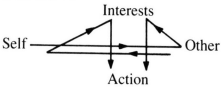

True Reciprocity (or Mutuality): Mutual Independent Benevolence (Based on Mutual Consultation)

This is the situation that results when Situation 6 is practiced on a bilateral basis, that is, achieving independent benevolence after due consultation bilaterally. The action taken on both sides is not necessarily identical, but where this is the case it tantamounts to the Golden Rule—doing unto others what one would have others do to oneself.

431

Situation 8:

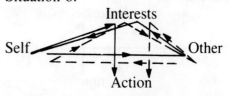

Unilateral Internalization of the Other's Independent Interests

The self consults the other's independent interests, adopts them along with its own interests, and takes action to implement the combined package of interests, or vice versa. Practiced on a bilateral basis, Situation 8 evolves into Situation 9 (loving one's neighbor as oneself, in both cases).

Situation 9:

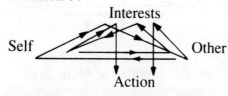

Reciprocal/Mutual Internalization of Each Other's Independent Interests

Mutual internalization of each other's independent interests, by the self and the other, results in, and generalizes, the mode of behavior and action commonly referred to as "Christian love"—loving one's neighbor as oneself.

432

for both. It is thus the *situation*, rather than the interests, that is non-conflicting. The interests are conflicting in the wider sense that neither the self nor the other promotes each other's interests by their separate action.

At this point it is necessary to observe that it is possible to have nonconflicting and mutually beneficial interests by *unilateral* action, that is, without reciprocal action by the other party. This is the case of Situation 8. Mutuality of interests, therefore, does not necessarily imply reciprocal *action* (as Situation 8 clearly shows), nor does reciprocal action imply an absence of conflict of interests but only a balancing or reciprocation of interests. These may yet be in conflict as regards the interest of the self or of the other (cf. Situations 5 and 7). On the other hand, it is possible (as in Situation 3) to have both conflicting and nonmutual interests in a nonconflict (or minimal conflict) situation. Here the respective interests of the self and the other are separately but simultaneously achieved.

Situation 8 is thus the only case of *unilateral* action with *bilateral* benefits, benefiting *both* the self *and* the other. For the rest, the benefit of unilateral action is unilateral. Only in Situation 8, therefore, do we have a truly positive and ethical *unilateral* action, one that takes the interest of the other into one's self-interest, hence fulfills the ethical rule of conduct: "Whenever—and as much as—possible, take only such unilateral action as benefits both oneself and another, simultaneously." By contrast, a simple act of economic exchange—buying or selling—is a *bilateral* act that benefits both oneself and another simultaneously. It is not a divisible act and cannot be split into two unilateral actions of a nonreciprocal nature. It is not an individual unilateral and ethical action in this regard, even though it is a mutually beneficial action to the parties involved. Although, like Judeo-Christian (self-other) love, it takes the interests of the other into account in determining and implementing one's proper interests, yet there are a few crucial differences. First, unlike an act of exchange, Judeo-Christian love is unilateral; second, although mutually beneficial, an act of Judeo-Christian love expects no *direct* benefit or favor from the other in return, no quid pro quo as in the case of an act of exchange; third, and most important of all, unlike an exchange transaction, an act of Judeo-Christian love is *not a marketable commodity*—it has no price at which it can be bought or sold; it is a non-negotiable value. Thus an act of Judeo-Christian love can never be or become in itself an exchange transaction. In the marketplace, by contrast, *all* values are regarded as commodities and thus become negotiable—including (unfortunately) Judeo-Christian love, when individuals so decide to debase it.

The greatest and most difficult task of any society, therefore, is to be able to preserve its values and prevent them from being debased into negotiable and marketable commodities by the cynical elements among its population. Unfortunately, this is exactly what is likely to happen in the corridors of power, for power is amoral, unethical. Power has no respect for values except to the extent that such values can be made to serve the ends of power. Power then clothes itself in morality, making a travesty of it, in order to achieve its amoral ends, for, in the halls of power and Machiavellian pursuits *any* means will do to achieve any given end. Power is based on pragmatism—"what works." The moral dangers of power lurk in any society that fails to inculcate in its citizens the need to internalize the independent interests of the other as a prerequisite to any individual action or that, confusing religion with theology (the bedrock and differentiated product of institutionalized "religion"), fails in its public duty to inculcate religion and ethical values in its youthful population.

B. GENERAL PRINCIPLES OF ETHICS

The foregoing modes of personal behavior—which, incidentally, are applicable between groups and societies by their representatives—can be incorporated as particular instances in more general principles of action in the field of ethics (mutual effects of human behavior). These general principles relate to nonreciprocity (or nonmutuality) and reciprocity (or mutuality) of the actions and intended effects (benefits or disadvantages) of one's actions with respect to another party or parties.

In general, as we shall see, ethical actions fall into two categories defined by (a) the mutually beneficial (or disadvantageous) bilaterality of the Golden Rule, which ultimately is based on self-interest plus fear (of revenge) of the other ("Do [do not] unto others what, in similar circumstances, one would [would not] wish others to do unto oneself"); and by (b) the mutually beneficial unilaterality of Judeo-Christian love, which is based on self-interest plus religion or religious self-interest ("Love thy neighbor as thyself").

It is appropriate at this point to mention, in passing, the crucial difference between religion and ethics. In religion, the empirical act of knowing by sensing and emotional appropriation is a unilateral act that benefits the self (or devotee) alone; in ethics, the truly ethical act is a unilateral act that benefits the self and other(s) and demands no quid pro quo, or else a bilateral act of mutual advantage (or disadvantage). Put another way, and perhaps somewhat bluntly, in religion one loves a person or thing for *their own sake*, in ethics for *one's own sake as well*.

434

On this showing, the scope of ethics—it would seem—is more inclusive than that of religion and is exemplified at its best in the domain of ecology. The benefit is self-serving in religion, mutual in ethics and ecology.

We may now show how the various modes of action are classifiable under the two general principles of ethics.

Nonreciprocity/Nonmutuality of Action

This category covers all unilateral, uncompensated actions.

1. Self-regarding, and Self-serving Actions with Unilateral Personal Benefits. All save personal interests are neglected in these cases, of which there are three:

(a) *Selfish, nonconflicting actions* where resources are more than adequate to satisfy the personal needs of every individual in a community (Situation 1).
(b) *Selfish, conflicting actions* where individual interests overlap in terms of the resources available to satisfy those interests. This implies limited ecological resources and continual conflict (Situation 2).
(c) *Resolution of selfish, conflicting actions* by agreement or treaty resulting from compromise, bargaining, negotiation (Situation 3).

2. Other-related Transactions with Unilateral Benefits. The following are the relevant cases and situations under this class of transactions:

(a) Combining one's interests with the other's disadvantages (negative interests) or, which is the same thing, pursuing one's interests to the other's disadvantage. This may be described as self-serving malevolence toward the other and includes the case of exploitation in unilateral and bilateral terms (Situations 4 and 5).
   The Gandhian response to evil—passive resistance, nonviolent noncooperation with evil ("resist evil")—is the "cease and desist" response to exploitation, neither symbiotic in the loose sense (Situation 5) nor Christian ("resist not evil").
(b) Combining one's disadvantage (negative interests) with the other's independent interests or, which is the same thing, pursuing the other's interests at one's expense. This is self-denying independent benevolence. Under this heading may be considered the various Christian responses to evil, as well as the case of ingratitude of a special kind (Situation 6).

435

(i) *Christian nonresistance actions* ("Resist not evil"—Saint Matthew 5:39)

   (a) Forbearance or nonretaliation, implying forgiveness (but not necessarily, in a non-Christian context)
- seventy times seven cases of forgiveness (Saint Matthew 18:21–22)

   (b) Appeasement or cooperation with evil
- turning the other cheek (Saint Matthew 5:39, Saint Luke 6:29)
- giving up coat plus cloak (Saint Matthew 5:40; Saint Luke 6:29)
- going the extra mile (Saint Matthew 5:41)

   (c) Compensation or rewarding evil with good (Romans 12:17, 21) (Although Jesus preached forbearance—even up to the limit of seventy times seven—he seems to have set a limit at far less than seventy times seven in certain cases; such is the case in the parable of the lord of the vineyard, where the traditional Jewish response of retaliation is approved (Saint Luke 20:9–19). This apparent contradiction merely confirms that Jesus taught and acted within his Jewish tradition, in spite of his occasional innovative interpretations of that tradition and its doctrines.)

(ii) *Ingratitude*: It is assumed that the other's independent interests are served. Where this is not so, as in the case of public almsgiving (Saint Matthew 6:12) gratitude would not seem to be called for, since the objective of the apparently charitable act was public recognition of the same rather than charity to the beneficiary. In this case, ingratitude would merit no adverse reaction.

3. Other-related Transactions with Bilateral Benefits. Cases of this kind combine one's interests with the independent interests of the other: self-serving independent benevolence. There is implied an internalization of independent benevolence (the other's independent interests) in accordance with the rule "Whenever—and as much as—possible, take only such unilateral action as benefits oneself and others at the same time." ("Love thy neighbor as thyself.")

The contrary of other-related unilateral transactions with bilateral benefits is *other-related unilateral transactions with bilateral disadvantages* (negative interests). Here one combines one's disadvantages with those of the other: "hate thy neighbor as thyself." In formal terms, self-other love and self-other hate are equivalent. This is outwardly similar to, but substantially different from, the lex talionis.

436

Reciprocal action with mutual benefits may be achieved in the following ways:

(a) Mutualization of other-related, uncompensated transactions with unilateral benefits (Situations 5 and 7).
(b) Mutualization of other-related, uncompensated transactions with bilateral benefits (Situation 9).
(c) Bilateral transactions with bilateral benefits or effects: these transactions fall into two classes—positive for benefits, negative for adverse effects—all involving a quid pro quo.

On the positive side are

(a) Gift exchange ("gift for gift")
(b) Commercial exchanges— (i) Barter
                               (ii) Export for import

On the negative side fall retaliatory or vengeful acts covered by the famous lex talionis endorsed by Judaic morality ("Eye for eye, tooth for tooth," et cetera).

To sum up, for the individual, ethical behavior, at a minimum, is governed by reciprocity—the mutual discharge of obligations enshrined in the Golden Rule and the principles of exchange. At a maximum, ethical behavior is internalization of Judeo-Christian self-other love—that is, unilateral, other-related transactions involving bilateral benefits. Thus man lives the "good life" between trade-off and self-other love, these principles being by no means confined to the human species, but applicable also to the entire range of the ecological environment on which all terrestrial life depends.

3. CONSCIENCE

The subject of conscience belongs in the domain of ethics, because it concerns human behavior. Conscience may be defined as the internalization of external rules of human behavior vis-à-vis man and his environment, but principally the biosphere. This internalization takes place on the basis of consciousness or awareness, a characteristic associated with the mind, itself associated with individuation and increasing complexity of phenomena. This conscience, this result of internalization of ethical rules, then serves as an automatic guide or check to human behavior at individual and group level—the voice of Socrates' God, the Christian's "still small voice."

To take, for example, the principle of independent benevolence—action that serves one's interests as well as the independent interests of another—the more one acts in an independent benevolent manner, the greater the reinforcement of this internalized rule—in short, the reinforcement of one's conscience in this regard. In general, all actions that conform to the internalized canons of behavior reinforce those canons and strengthen one's conscience. The more frequent the violation of those canons in action, the weaker the canons as guides to behavior, the weaker the conscience. Thus is conscience the totality of ethical rules internalized by the individual.

The question arises whether there is a basic minimum of ethical rules necessary to the formation and development of conscience through internalization. In considering the question, one must start with the very fact of one's existence—an unsolicited gift for man and other existents, a Hobson's choice. This "thereness" of one's existence itself implies an ethical rule, namely, the obligation to make the best of one's existence. And in making the best of one's existence another rule emerges, namely, to conform oneself to the organic unity, interdependence, and equilibrium of the cosmos. In regard to other existents the truly ethical and positive rule of action is what has been termed independent benevolence, a rule that recognizes the equal rights of other existents to equal consideration as interdependent and mutually supporting elements guaranteeing, as a whole, the existence of each existent in the system. All three rules (namely, about (a) making the best of one's existence, (b) conforming oneself to the organic unity, interdependence, and equilibrium of the cosmos with the least disturbance thereto, and (c) taking only mutually beneficial actions that are conducive to independent benevolence), are interrelated, and valid within the biocosmic paradigm.

Conformity to the organic unity of the cosmos is the same as adaptation to the cosmos—a view and practice common to African and other similar (so-called primitive) societies. It is in keeping with the ecological demands of any given system or community, although it is only in the second half of the twentieth century that occidental society has begun to discover it, after centuries of the delusion—nourished on the Book of Genesis—that man can dominate the biosphere with the aid of technology. Indeed, the necessity to conform and adapt to the cosmos is a Hobson's choice for mankind. This follows from the fact that existence is itself a Hobson's choice—a contingent fact, a fait accompli—with

438

which man is confronted. It may seem as though man does have a choice—to adapt or not, to conform or dominate. But one should take note of the fact that the existence of the cosmos is a given, and that whether one conforms to it or not, the biospheric and cosmic systems are such that they make automatic adjustments to disturbances of their equilibrium. And in such a fashion that the disturber of the equilibrium not only will be adjusted, *mal gre bon gre*, but in the end will pay the price of the adjustment required by the disturbance. Consequently, since through lack of complete knowledge of the nature and balance of cosmic and biospheric interrelationships, man cannot avoid disturbing their equilibria man's best guide and goal is to cause the least disturbance possible if one must consciously disturb. In economic parlance, if man must consciously disturb his biospheric equilibria, then only marginal disturbances to the system are called for.

The world in which we live exists neither to please us nor to punish us, as Bertrand Russell was fond of saying, but for our benefit as well as that of other co-denizens if we and they use it wisely; for it is what it is because of us and its other components. We are a part of it, willy nilly, and must adapt to it. We must, that is, make marginal not fundamental changes, bearing in mind that we are not its only inhabitants and that fundamental changes will hurt not only our co-denizens but ourselves, above all.

Reference was made previously, in the discussion of Marx as philosopher, to the failure of Christianity and Marxism-Communism, as ethico-religious systems, to effectively internalize their own ethic (Book Two, Section A, Part II, chapter 3). In other words, they failed to develop an adequate and effective conscience in the individual adherent. There are, of course, other possible causes of ethical failure, but the failure to develop an effective Christian or Communist conscience is paramount.

Marx's real quarrel was with theology not, as he supposed, with religion, for Marxism-Communism is nothing if not a religion, dealing as it does with interrelationships from the human focus. It was theology that was—and still is—misused to promise ''pie in the sky when you die'' to exploited workers, in compensation for the miserable life they lead in this empirical existence. It was—and still is—theology, not religion, that is the ''opium of the people.'' In misdirecting his fire at religion Marxism-Communism not only cut the ground from under itself but overlooked the function of ethics in religion, namely, to internalize canons of human behavior—build conscience into the individual—without which no religious system can be successful or effective. As it turned out, Marxism-Communism made no provision for a mechanism for internalizing the socialist-communist ethic in its adherents.

4. INTERESTS AND PRINCIPLES IN MORALITY

Interests are advantages or beneficial objectives that are pursued in action at any given time. They are provisional, changing with time and circumstance. Among themselves they may be complementary but may also be competitive and substitutable one with another, thereby indicating that they are concerned with the acquisition, distribution, and use of limited resources in manpower as well as materials. They are consequently economic in nature and scope. They confer a mutual benefit on any two parties involved only through an act of barter or exchange. For example, one gives up an interest in a company in order, with the proceeds, to acquire an interest in another (competitive interests). Or one gives up, sells, one's country home in order to acquire a car and a pleasure boat. The country home is competitive with the car and boat, and the two latter are complementary interests.

Principles are canons or rules of behavior—ethical rules, for example. Like dogmas and definitions they are held to be valid under all circumstances, whether they conflict with our interests or not and, except where they conflict among themselves, make an absolute and unconditional claim upon our loyalties and our actions. In comparison with principles, all other goals and advantages are subordinate, relative, noncompetitive, and nonsubstitutable with principles. This indicates that principles do not relate to limited resources. They are not rules for the acquisition, distribution, and use of limited resources. They are not, that is to say, economic in nature and scope. In subscribing to principles one does not seek to deprive another of any advantage or benefit to which that other is entitled. Rather, one aims to ensure that one's actions do not conflict with those principles. Any inconvenience to others, while regrettable, is merely incidental. Thus principles may, but need not, serve the specific interests of others or oneself. This is because principles are superior to interests.

There are, however, no specific or particular kinds of things called *principles*, just as there are no specific or particular kinds of things called *interests*. A principle or an interest is an attitude, a state of mind toward any given type of conduct (principle) or toward any given object or objective (interest). Both are the same insofar as they relate to an *attitude* or state of mind, but vastly different insofar as principles are purely concepts regulating human behavior while interests are, *additionally*, specifically concerned with material resources. Thus honesty and truth in one's dealings with others relate to principle, while one's livelihood relates to interest.

Moreover, principles being superior to interests, the latter cannot be

440

substituted for the former, but the former may be substituted for the latter in that interests may be *surrendered* in favor of principles without any quid pro quo in return (nonsubstitutability of interests for principles). However, interests are inter-substitutable, intra- as well as inter-personally. The latter type of substitution constitutes the subject matter of benevolence as a feature of morality.

We thus arrive at a second important difference between principles and interests. Principles take precedence to interests and are served by interests. That is to say, *interests are the price one pays—the things one surrenders without compensation in kind—for defending and maintaining one's principles.*

A third important difference between principles and interests is that one cannot be deprived of one's principles so long as one regards them as worth holding onto as principles—even if one is deprived of any and all material interests or means of defending them; for when one has lost all of one's interests or material possessions one could still defend one's principles with one's life (or death).[6] This is why no interest or material advantage can become a principle since, in theory as well as practice, one can be deprived of it against one's will.

Aside from their attitudinal characteristic, principles and interests also share another characteristic: they are likely to conflict among themselves. This means that, occasionally, two principles may not be held on to simultaneously, in regard to a given course of action. For example, truthfulness and avoiding the causing of injury knowingly to another may come into conflict insofar as telling the truth may knowingly result in detrimental action to another. One may, in such circumstances, decide against telling the truth in order to preserve the principle of avoiding hurt to another,[7] or vice versa.

We thus arrive at another, and third, similarity between principles and interests: in cases of conflict one principle may be sacrificed to another, just as one interest may be sacrificed to another. This is but the other side of the same coin of conflict between principles and between interests. (In addition, interests may be sacrificed to principles, as we have seen, where there is a clash between interests and principles.)

Principles are absolute only with regard to interests, since they take precedence to interests (nonsubstitutable by interests) but relative with respect to themselves (substitutable). We have indicated that principles are purely behavior-regulating concepts based on one's attitude and in this respect are no different from interests. This means that they remain principles only for so long as one is willing to so regard them. The moment they are no longer so regarded, they degenerate to the status of interests; hence *principles are potential interests, and interests may be degenerated or dethroned principles.*

441

There are, accordingly, three possible choices in the clash between principles and interests:

(a) We may *use* them—put them to the test and defend them in action with our interests and, if necessary, with our lives (or deaths). In this context, one goes into the world to *negotiate* one's interests, but to *defend* one's principles. Principles, so long as they remain principles, are nonnegotiable vis-à-vis interests. It is thus, by defending them, that principles have a chance to mold one's character and influence one's actions—because they are constantly being put to the test.

(b) We may *withdraw* them from the test and contemplate or enjoy them in thought only—admire them, so to speak, if we are so inclined. In withdrawing one's principles from the test, that is, from the world of action, one in effect pleads "no contest," giving up all effort to defend them. And undefended principles quickly become undefendable because no longer being put to the test and lose their vitality and ability to mold character and influence action.

(c) We may *convert* them into interests, that is, make them negotiable—in effect, surrender and forget them *qua* principles. They become downgraded to the status of negotiable interests: from being non-negotiable and priceless (principles) they become negotiable and carry a price (interests).

Since principles constitute a type of nonmaterial asset of which one cannot be deprived against one's will, they stand a better chance of influencing and molding one's character and guiding one's actions continually when internalized. Indeed, any ethical principle stands to succeed or fail increasingly with the degree of internalization or noninternalization by its adherents.

The hallmark of an integrated personality consists in the integration of its principles and of its interests among themselves, respectively, and the defense of its principles in action at the expense of its interests, if need be. The hallmark of an ethical or moral personality consists in the integration of its principles with those of others, to the extent possible, and of its interests with the independent interests of others.

A NOTE ON INTERESTS AND PRINCIPLES
IN INTERNATIONAL RELATIONS

Lord Palmerston is credited with the adage that a nation has no permanent friends and no permanent enemies, but only permanent interests. This is only partially true, since interests change and are therefore

442

never permanent. Nothing is said, be it noted, about principles. The question may, therefore, be raised: "What about human rights—the rights of the individual? What about the rule of law and justice among men?" to take the obvious kinds of questions of principle in the international arena. The plain fact, as any serious observer of the international scene can testify, is that in international relations, principles, as such, do not really exist since so-called principles are too often interchangeable with interests. The life span of principles, *qua* principles, is very short in international relations—often for only as long as it takes to declare them.

Thus Great Britain would not stand up for its often-declared principle of one-man, one-vote democracy, nor against injustice to black Africans or against unilateral declaration of independence in Southern Rhodesia (now Zimbabwe) because the principles involved were negotiable in favor of its racial and other economic interests in white Rhodesians. Similarly, despite countless United Nations resolutions and declarations, the so-called Western democracies are content to negotiate liberty and justice for black South Africans in favor of racial and other economic interests in white South Africans.

Human rights are, similarly, not principles but interests negotiable in favor of friendly military and other dictatorships in Latin America and around the world on the part of the U.S.A. and friendly military and other dictators in Eastern Europe and around the world on the part of the USSR—in both cases, against the local populations.

The international arena thus provides a good laboratory in which to observe the operation or nonoperation of the distinction between interests and principles and of the downgrading of principles to the level of interests, judging from the practice of the leading powers and loudest advocates of principles in international relations.

5. GOOD AND EVIL

A. GOOD AND EVIL AS STATES OF EXISTENCE

Manifestation in an infinite variety of phenomena has been noted as the essence of existence, so that differences and distinctions—variety, in short—constitute the spice of life, as the popular maxim goes. Without differences and distinctions there is no existence. Interest therefore centers on the quality of the prevailing differences and distinctions, and on the nature of the interrelationships holding among them.

In general, we may describe as evil a state of conflict among the different manifestations, and as good a state of harmony, minimal or no conflict, among them. Accordingly, the exploitation of differences and distinctions for the purpose of creating conflict is evil, while their exploitation for the purpose of creating harmony and integration among them is good. The mere existence of distinctions and differences is not evil, nor their elimination good. Variety is the stuff and spice of existence, the essence of organic unity or what the ancient Greeks called *justice*, and the modern economist *division of labor* or *specialization*.

If one defines God, the Cosmo-Theos, as that which manifests itself in manifold and different forms, then one recognizes that God (or the manifold of existence) is, by definition, variety (difference and distinction) and, according to this point of view, exhibits both evil (conflict of differences) and good (harmony and integration of differences). Good and evil are thus states or conditions of existence. According to this view, good and evil do not inhere in the manifestations of being and becoming, but merely describe the conditions or state of their external relationships, in short, their environment. As African philosophy expresses it, good and evil proceed from without, not from within. Specifically, it holds that all things are inherently good and that evil comes from without.

The view that the mere existence of differences and distinctions is not evil, nor their abolition necessarily good, is in accord with the nature of existence itself. It contrasts sharply, however, with the Hindu-Buddhist view, which holds that evil consists in the mere existence of distinctions and differences, and good, in their abolition. Thus Hinduism-Buddhism rejects the ontological status of distinctions and differences. This may have been due to the inadequate cosmology of the religion, which did not have the advantage of the modern view of the nature of mass-energy and its permeation by distinctions and differences among its elemental particles.[8]

The essence of the foregoing discussion may be presented in another way in summary form. If good and evil are the potential, respectively, for harmony and for conflict presented by the existence of distinctions and differences, then what we have here is either a trigger theory of good and evil, a reinforcement theory of good and evil, or both. In the first case, it is assumed that we start with a neutral situation of no harmony, no conflict and no good, no evil, so that all that is needed is a trigger to set off or actualize the potential for good or for evil. In the human or zoological paradigm, the trigger may be found in the thought and motivation (will) of animals—human as well as nonhuman—which generates the appropriate action that results in good (harmony, integration) or evil (conflict, disharmony). It would thus be true that "there is nothing either good or bad but thinking (through motivation and action) makes it so."

In the second case, good and evil are assumed to be already actualized and encountered by man and other animals whose only choice is to reinforce (or alleviate), by will and appropriate action, the preexisting situation. The third case combines the two preceding cases, where man and other animals may influence an ongoing situation of harmony and disharmony or initiate new such situations. In all three cases human (or other animal) agency is necessary to the generation and/or perpetuation of good and evil, in the context of the zoological paradigm. This has been the traditional and time-honored approach to the problem of good and evil in all religio-ethical systems—"where every prospect pleases and only man is vile."

B. RESOLUTION OF THE "PROBLEM" OF GOOD AND EVIL IN THE BIO-COSMIC PARADIGM

Once we get outside the narrow framework of the human paradigm or the general zoological paradigm into the wider framework of the bio-cosmic paradigm, things look different and what appeared at first as an entirely human (or animal) problem becomes resolved into a general condition, or sine qua non, of existence owing nothing directly or indirectly to man.

It is only natural that man should be concerned with his own pain and pleasure, with his own good (whatever conduces to his happiness) and evil (whatever conduces to his discomfort and misery). In the context of the interpretive framework of the human paradigm set against the cosmos, these problems are given cosmic dimensions out of all proportion to man's place and role as an infinitesimal speck on the cosmic panorama. When, however, the human is replaced by the biocosmic paradigm of evolutionary flow change, the problem of good and evil becomes instantly transformed, losing the urgency and importance it assumed under the human paradigm. To be sure, it does not disappear but assumes a different aspect—that of the perennial and continual phenomenon of flow change vis-à-vis limited cosmic resources, of which action reaction (the principle of compensation) and mutual destruction and cannibalism among living manifestations are essential to substaining biocosmic equilibrium. These aspects, in which man's "good and evil" are now subsumed, are the very stuff of existence, including that of man. Consequently, "good and evil" no longer appear as a uniquely human "problem" but a part of the definition of the cosmos, of existence itself. An urgent human "problem" is thus automatically subsumed and transformed within a wider framework of interpretation.[9]

This translation of the human preoccupation with good-evil or even good-bad, to a wider framework is not intended to deny its importance for man. It merely elucidates the problem as an existential characteristic as much as a moral problem to the extent that man, through his own volition, aggravates the characteristic.

Buddhist analysis attributes the root of good and evil—especially the latter—as a moral problem to man's selfness and greed at the expense of others (both human and nonhuman entities)—a type of behavior likely to provoke immediate reaction in kind under the cosmic principle of compensation, leading to pain and suffering. The ecological consequences of human greed are well known in terms of wanton human pollution and destruction of environmental resources beyond what is immediately necessary or required and without regard for principles of conservation of renewable resources. This can, in turn, provoke, via the compensation principle, not only inconvenience to man to the extent of threatening his physical survival, but also some of the apparently inexplicable natural calamities of drought, famine, and flood. Man is thus recalled to his responsibility to use environmental resources wisely on pain of forfeiting his own survival, a survival on which he carries no guarantee or perpetual lease.

C. INDIVIDUATION AND THE PROBLEM OF PAIN AND SUFFERING

One may attempt to find consolations in pain and suffering or to rationalize their presumed benefits.[10] This is the natural and easy way out, the first and common human response to a phenomenon that defies satisfactory interpretation within the human framework in which it is placed. When this occurs it is advisable to change the framework. We may thus take a closer look at pain and suffering in relation to biological individuation within the cosmic paradigm.

Biological individuation and its built-in mechanism of metabolism and limited physical survival of the organism involved has two classes of consequences, external and internal. The external consequences are:

(a) competition among organisms for limited life-sustaining resources;
(b) death by mutual destruction and consumption by and among organisms;
(c) recycling of resources invested in expired organisms.

These external consequences, as we have seen, are the means of continued cosmic equilibrium and maintenance. The pain and suffering they entail do not carry a moral stigma in the biocosmic context.

The internal consequence consists in the emergence of mental consciousness or awareness.[11] This constitutes the subject matter of psychology, defined by Karl Popper as the science of the self and its experiences.[12] The definition may be extended to include the offshoots of this science—psychoanalysis and psychiatry—and their numerous and extensive applications. The reaction at the mental level varies from that of Buddhism, which regards pain and suffering as unmitigated disaster, through that of the Greek Stoics, who held that pain and suffering should be endured with fortitude and without any sense of human guilt or blame, to the complex hermeneutic of pain and suffering developed by the Judeo-Christian-Islamic religions (as well as African religion), which discerns a human agency in pain and suffering. However, while regarding pain and suffering as a limitation on divine goodness, the Semitic religions counterbalance this with a positive view that regards pain and suffering as a mark of divine favor and love: "Whom the Father loveth he chastiseth."

Reviewing the three types of mental reaction, we see that the mental attitude of the Stoics best accords with the interpretation furnished by the bio-cosmic paradigm. This indicates that while human behavior may be an aggravating factor with moral consequences, pain and suffering are part of the definition and meaning of existence, being neither a mark of divine displeasure nor of divine favor toward man.

NOTES

1. This is the same relationship described as independent benevolence (or Type 3 Love) in Book Two, Section B, chapter 12. There it is fully described as "nonreciprocal beneficial relationships with one's 'neighbor.' " It is nonreciprocal in the strictly formal sense that the action is unilateral. But in terms of content or substance, two such unilateral actions toward each other by two different persons become effectively reciprocal. In short, when every person acts unilaterally in a manner consistent with independent benevolence, all such actions become effectively reciprocal. Consequently, *nonreciprocal* as used in the earlier chapter has the sense of *unilateral* in the current chapter.
2. Book Three, chapter 3, note 8.
3. The case referred to occurred during the pond-digging project undertaken by a joint FAO–Lake Chad Basin Commission team in the Waza National Park of Northern Cameroon during the period 1982–84. This was not a singular but a repeated occurrence.
4. The killing and serving of deer, whether by man or lion, is certainly not ethical in this sense or from the deer's point of view. It falls, however, under the rubric of minimization of disharmony in the face of the prevalence of mutual cannibalism

among animal species. The lion, it should be noted, does not, as a rule, kill deer that live in the vicinity of its lair.

5. As mentioned in Book Two, Section B, chapter 12, this raises serious doubts about "sacrifical love" and whether there ever has been, or is, such a kind of love. If ever there was, it would be antisocial, violating the ethical code of mutuality and interdependence. It was pointed out in that chapter, however, that even were there such a kind of love, it would still involve a measure of self-satisfaction at surrendering one's life for the presumed benefit of others.

6. They become, in this respect, the equivalent of what Tillich calls "ultimate concerns"—things that one is prepared to defend with one's life (or death). See Paul Tillich, *Dynamics of Faith* (New York: Harper Torchbooks, 1958), p. 1.

7. There is an obvious difference between this type of action and the silence of "omerta," the criminal oath of the Mafia. Here silence is used not to defend principles but interests. It is also immoral in that the aim is to sacrifice the interests or welfare of society to one's personal advantage or the advantage of one's criminal clique or both.

8. The basis of selfhood is individuation, which is equally the basis of self-preservation and the competition for life-sustaining resources. The Buddhist demand for the abolition of individuation, of the very basis of human and other manifestations of existence, would seem like a demand for the abolition of existence itself. This makes of Buddhism a negative, anti–life-and-existence, and impractical religio-ethical system. There is, however, another possible interpretation of the Buddhist demand for the abolition of self, which exonerates it from the charge of being anti–life-and-existence. This is that, bearing in mind that a fully reciprocal relationship is possible only among animals (including man), Buddhism merely asks for a transcendence of the zoological paradigm and its replacement by the biocosmic paradigm in which every manifestation of existence, organic as well as inorganic, counts equally. Thus the human self has no claim to preeminence among the other existents. This interpretation, reasonable on the face of it, seems, nevertheless, somewhat far-fetched.

9. In this context, what would seem at first, a matter of great profundity in Nietzsche's work titled *Beyond Good and Evil*, in which "good and evil" is replaced by "good and bad" seems utterly shallow. And for the good reason that Nietzsche's view of the problem and his alternative argument are presented within the framework of the human paradigm, which exaggerates the nature of the issue to the status of a *problem* and further distorts it to the status of a *unique human problem*.

10. As did C. S. Lewis in his book *The Problem of Pain* (Fontana, 1976).

11. This is reminiscent of Hegel's doctrine that God (Absolute Idea or Spirit) preexists Nature, which it creates and, through Nature, human mind as the crowning phase in the becoming (development) of Spirit. More complexity, more mind.

12. Karl Popper, *Unended Quest* (Fontana/Collins, 1982), p. 187.

Chapter 9

Time

1. TIME AS EVENT AND AS ACTIVITY

As an aid to the discussion two basic concepts need to be introduced and defined: (a) an event and (b) an activity. An *event* is that which occurs *without* the intervention or participation of man. An *activity* is that which happens *with* the intervention or participation of man. These concepts are useful tools in the interpretation of time.

Time is not a physical entity but a concept. It may be defined as merely a dimension of events and activities—the *flow* aspect of events and activities. This dimension is conceptually divisible into a succession of moments or instants that may be occupied by one event or activity or by several parallel (that is, overlapping) events or activities, separate and distinct and outside each other.

When the evolution of a single event is observed, relative to other passing events, we are apt to think of time in terms of motion and duration or a succession of instants and call it *chronological time*. Thus chronological time is single-eventful time or a succession of single-eventful instants of time (for example, the daily progression of the sun relative to the earth).

In observing the evolution of several activities in parallel (or overlap) we are apt to think of time in terms of *depth*, that is, *a dimension reckoned in terms of the number of such activities that take place*, and call it *activity time*.

Thus time is a dimension of events and activities and this dimension is also its depth measured in terms of the number of events or activities occurring simultaneously. Accordingly, *single-dimension time* is time occupied by *one* activity (or event) only or by a succession of different but contiguous activities (or events). It follows that *multidimension time* is time occupied by several parallel or overlapping activities (or events), each of continuing duration or succeeded by a different contiguous activity (or event). In short,

$$\text{single-dimension time} = \text{single-activity time}$$
$$\text{multidimension time} = \text{multi-activity time}$$

In all its various aspects time or the succession of instants of time, considered as a flow, is one and indivisible.

Past, present, and future are not divisions pertaining to time, but divisions of human perspective on time—descriptions of man's relationship to time in its chronological or activity aspect. The standpoint from which the division (or distinction) is made is that of man's ability to influence or affect activities over time. Thus the *present* is any duration, lapse, or period of time occupied by ongoing activities. The *past* is that duration of time occupied by activities that cannot be influenced or affected by the present, that is, by ongoing activities. The *future* is any duration of time in which activities being completed can have an impact, that is, generate or lead to new activities.

The importance of these definitions of man's relationship to time is twofold: (a) to show the *unidirectional* nature of *chronological time*, from past through present to future and (b) to show the parallel relationship of past to present and of present to future.

According to the activity definition and content of time, the past moves into, and influences, the present; the present, in turn, moves into and influences the future while, similarly, the past through its effect on the present also moves into, and influences, the future. By the same token, chronologically, the future becomes the present becomes the past. Chronologically, also, one man's past time is another's future time, and one man's present time becomes another's potential future time—all this as the world turns.

While it is true that the past consists of those activities that cannot be affected by present or ongoing activities, it is otherwise as regards one's *understanding* or *interpretation* of the activities that constitute the past. In this respect there is more flexibility and the present can reach back to alter the past. It is in both these senses that George Orwell's famous Oceania dictum is true: "who controls the past controls the future"—activitywise—and interpretationwise, "who controls the present controls the past," that is, the *recorded*, as distinct from the actual, activity-content of the past.[1] The past, in the sense of the events and activities with which it is filled, is *unalterable*; only our *idea* of its events and activities is alterable.

450

2. TIME AS RELATIVE MOTION OR CHANGE

The concept of change or motion is also relevant to an interpretation of time. We may distinguish between two types of change or motion of an entity:

(a) displacement motion under the force of attraction or an impact,
(b) inherent motion (or *mouvement sur place*) *within* an entity, at nuclear and subnuclear levels and in metabolic transportation systems.

Both types of motion constitute what is otherwise known as *change*. In discussions of *space, motion,* and *time*, however, it is displacement motion that is primarily concerned.

Occidental and African Activity Concepts of
Time, Destiny, and Development

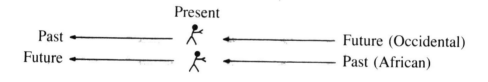

For the African—and, to a large extent, for the Occidental as well—space-in-motion, the nearest and simplest example of which is land (terra firma), is the *potential* embodiment of time, and worked land the *concrete* embodiment or expression of invested activity, that is, time-constituting activity. Worked land is thus embodied activity (embodied labor) or Marxian primitive capital. But land is only the simplest and universal example for the illustration of both potential time and time-constituting activities. There are other non–land-involving (though land-related) activities such as certain kinds of arts and crafts, the products of hunting and fishing, community rites and observances that provide an investment in time. The results or products of such activities are also as much capital as worked land.

1. For both Occidental and African, time and space are closely linked, time being space-in-motion. For both, also, there is a distinction between

"idle time"—same as chronological or passivity time (i.e., time drifting by in the face of human inactivity)—and "activity time" (i.e., time filled with human activity). Time being space-in-motion, "idle time" is space-in-motion without any modification by human activity, while "activity time" is space-in-motion modified by human activity. The relevant and significant time for both Occidental and African is "activity time," whose importance, for the Occidental, is enshrined in the dictum "(activity) time is money."[2] Idle or passivity time is less significant (although essential for recuperation and regeneration of certain life-supporting functions), being the time in which things happen, or are made to happen, to and by nonhuman entities: plants grow; cows graze, chew the cud, or give birth to calves; et cetera. Hence it is that, for the African, idle or passivity time is "time that does not pass," time in which there is no human activity.

2. In the conception of both Occidental and African the *direction of time*, that is, the direction of movement of space-in-motion, is *unique*; in short, unidirectional, the direction being that of the motion of planet Earth *relative to the sun and the stars*. (For human beings, space-in-motion is, effectively, planet Earth in its unidirectional daily rotation and annual revolution around the sun, the latter being the dominant space fragment and centre of our planetary system.)

Time is thus the relativity measure of space-in-motion; that is, of one space-fragment (Earth) with regard to another space-fragment (sun) or with regard to the rest of space-in-motion.

Man can, however, and sometimes does change his *relationship* to the direction of time, though not the direction of time itself.

3. Although man cannot change the unique direction of time (being a prisoner on the spaceship, Earth) he can alter his relationship to that direction, since he has a choice of self-orientation to time. He can face in the same direction as time or face away from it, or he can orient himself perpendicularly to the direction of time. Time flows *eastward* with the earth. One therefore has a choice of facing eastward, westward, northward, or southward. These directional orientations can, however, be interpreted metaphorically.

One who always faces the east (dawn) always sees the sun rise, tends toward expectancy, toward hope, toward optimism (the view that things are always for the best or will improve). The one who always faces west (eve) always sees the sun set, tends toward nostalgia, regret, despair—toward pessimism (the view that things are always for the worse or can only get worse). Who faces north or south, seeing neither sunrise nor sunset, may tend toward depression, melancholy, indifference (the view that nothing matters). But all this is only by way of metaphor.

452

More interesting, perhaps, is the case where relative time is reversed. Chronological (that is, day-night, seasonal, and planetary) time like biological time (biorhythm, birth-growth-decline) is unidirectional and irreversible. But relative time is reversible. In this respect, for example, we can reverse the order of the four seasons if we are prepared to move and live every other season in the northern hemisphere, the remaining seasons in the southern hemisphere. This hemisphere hopping on an alternating seasonal basis would reverse the normal rotation of the seasons to the following:

Northern Hemisphere: Winter (Spr) Summer (Aut) Winter (Spr) Summer (Aut)

Southern Hemisphere: (Sum) Autumn (Win) Spring (Sum) Autumn (Win) Spring

This is the reverse of the normal order of rotation in either hemisphere, which is: winter—spring—summer—autumn—winter. Whether, if at all and to what extent, this type of behavior is likely to affect or interfere with one's biorhythms and aging processes can be determined empirically.

4. The Occidental and the African both bestride the Present, the Now, but their conceptions of the Past and the Future differ. For the Occidental, the future is that which is to come, activitywise, into the present and is unknown until it becomes the present. For the African, however, that which is to come into the present, activitywise, is the past—that which has already happened and is known (or known about) even before it becomes the present. It is the activity in the time of the fathers, of the ancestors, about which a lot abounds in myth.

Once come into the present, the future traverses it and becomes the past, for the Occidental. It is that which is known now receding from him into the dimness and the mist of unremembered things. The past is behind him, gone forever. For the African, it is all otherwise. That which came into the present was the past, traversed it, and became the future, rapidly receding from him but destined to return. Thus while the past (that which has happened) may be the same for both the Occidental and the African, the African's concept of the future is no different from that of his—and the Occidental's—past.

5. For the Occidental, what is past is past, beyond recall and of no account to the present. "Bygones are forever bygones," the renowned economist, Lord Lionel Robbins, used to intone gravely. In the same

tradition, occidental economic wisdom dictates—contrary to the practice of the great investment monopolies at home and in the colonies—that "past (sunk) costs cannot, do not, influence future investment decisions." Only present investment decisions—apparently uninfluenced by past investment decisions, otherwise the argument fails—can influence future investment decisions. True or false, this is the economic myth.

For the African, likewise, what is past is past but not beyond recall and of every account in the present; for the past influences the future through the present by way of present actions that conform to the past. In this way, it is hoped, the future will always resemble the past. This is the African myth, except that the African is fully aware that there is no automaticity in the matter: the future cannot automatically resemble the past without human effort toward that end. The expectation is not a law of nature, so far as the African is concerned, unlike in the domain of natural and experimental science, where the Occidental expects the future to forever resemble the past, unaided by human effort and automatically.

6. Destiny, for the Occidental, is that which is to come—that which lies unknown in the future but which he may be able to influence in some way by his present actions. For the African, destiny is the past, which has already come and gone and is to come again in the future, thanks to present efforts to recreate it. While the Occidental is likely to expect his future to be "anything but the past," the African traditionalist expects his future to be "just like the past."

7. Development—an improving change—for the Occidental, lies effectively in the future, provided he acts decisively in the present. For the African, development has already happened—in the past—and is that to which he seeks to conform the present and the future. Thus development is future-oriented for the Occidental, past-oriented for the African. Through development, the Occidental expects his future to be better than his present and his past. The traditional African, by contrast, never expects his present or his future to be better than the exemplary past of his ancestors; for, by definition, all the best things happened in the past and can never be surpassed in the present or the future. The most that can be expected is to equal the exemplary past: circular time, the "eternal return."

Herein lies the difference between the Occidental and the African. The former has a model, for and in the future, which is "wide open"; the African, by contrast, has a model in the past, for the present and the future which are "closed" by the past.

8. Again, however, both Occidental and African are agreed on one thing: one cannot influence the actual content of the past, only that of the present

and the future. Correct, but the past is subject to interpretation of what was its actual content, what actually took place; and to this extent the past is myth, elastic, "wide open." Since one's interpretation of the past is thus malleable so, derivatively, is one's understanding of the present and the future. Because of the hazards of interpretation nothing is stable, everything is unpredictable—open to chance and change.

9. *Conclusion*. For the African, the interminable past stretching out before him (Zamani) comes ready-made into the present (Sasa) as a source of uninfluenceable, exemplary models by which to mold the present, so that the future will become like the past.[3] There *is* a future,[4] except that it will be like (or is expected to be like), and indistinguishable from, the past, since one is expected to *make* it be like the past. Thus to the past belongs, and from the past comes, the myth (exemplary model) and the future; to the present belongs myth-enhancing activity; and to the future (the product of past and present) belongs the task of prolonging the past and thus ensuring the eternal return of the past.

The vicious circle of the "eternal return" can only be broken, if need be, *in the present* by the adoption of other models, other myths, than those traditionally furnished by the past; or by reinterpretation of the traditional myths so that they become, effectively, new myths.[5] But the new myths fabricated must be *known widely*. Hence the role of new knowledge—education and technique—to furnish new myths. But this will not be enough. The inheritors and bearers of the new myths must be accorded a leadership role so that they can influence the future with the new myths that will return, via the past, to mold new futures—at least, for a while.

The crucial question for Africa, therefore, is this: will the new knowledge and technique be given a leadership role, a chance? But even *more* crucial and important is the question: will the new knowledge and technique be mastered sufficiently by its bearers to be applied in an ecologically beneficial manner? Or, failing that, would it not be better to continue to adapt in the traditional way, in order to save the ecological patrimony for countless futures yet? And *most* crucial and important of all: will others—more powerful, more charismatic, profiting from the openness of the African to the new, provided it comes from the outside—be disposed to let the African decide to continue to adapt or to change?

And what if the answer to each of these three questions, in ascending order of importance, is the same—No? What then? This is the ever-present challenge confronting Africa. What will be the response?

Eventually, there may be no need for any particular response, for what will be, will be. And—fortunately—no one knows for certain, in advance, what will be. In a world in which the only certain thing is change—regardless of whether we initiate it or not, and whether we adapt to change or not, a change that is independent of our volition—this is the ultimate salvation: change.

3. GEOLOGICAL AND BOTANICAL TIME: TIME AS ACCRETION OR DEPTH

As we have seen, time is a way of looking at *things-in-motion* (chronology) as well as of *things-in-action* (activity). But time is also a way of looking, literally, at *things-in-depth*. Depth can be conceived as the number of activities or events taking place independently of one another within a given time slot, as we have seen in section 1 preceding. But depth can also be looked at as the consequence of *accretion or layering of matter* (stratification) or as the consequence of weathering down or stripping off of layers of matter (denudation or erosion), e.g., by glaciation or by the action of wind, water, and temperature change.

Time regarded as a dimension of things-in-depth is *geological* time, the tool of paleontologists and archaeologists.

Geological time, however, introduces nothing fundamentally new, being pure chronology written into matter and measured not by relative motion but by relative position along a vertical.

There is, however, a similarity between geological and *botanical* time: both measure accretions, geological time in rocks and other deposits, botanical time in plants—trees, in particular. The rings in a cross-section of a tree—the giant redwood, for example—measure the passage of time as well as the age of the tree in years.

This leads to a fundamental truth: everything carries within itself the evidence, trace, or record of the passage of time, as well as of how much time has elapsed, as measured by the number of basic time units of the record—tree rings, geological layers or accretions, rotations, revolutions, et cetera. This can be discovered and known, provided we know how to read the record.

4. PHILOSOPHIC TIME

Plato defined time as "the moving image of eternity," meaning thereby that time is a unit or phase in the evolution toward complete self-realization of objects in our phenomenal world. Like the slow-motion picture of each successive stage ("time") in the opening of a bud into

456

what, eventually, becomes a full and complete flower ("eternity"), time is the *successive* or *stage-by-stage* realization of an object in all its parts and proportions. Eternity, in Plato's philosophy, is the *instantaneous and complete* self-realization of an object in all its parts and proportions.

It should be mentioned that instantaneous and complete self-realization occurs only in the ideal—that is, purely conceptual and nonempirical—Platonian world of non-change.

Time is thus the mode of self-realization that is possible in our phenomenal world of change, eternity or complete and instantaneous self-realization being impossible in such a world. Plato, however, conceives of both time and eternity as modes of existence, the former being empirical and known as *becoming* ("forming" and "unforming"), the latter nonempirical. Time is the process, eternity the goal—frozen, once achieved.

5. ANTHROPOLOGICAL TIME

In conventional usage we are accustomed to speaking of past, present, and future as phases in a dynamic continuum. The present is the dynamic rendezvous or point of intersection of past and future, ourselves (man) being always at that intersection. The past is continually behind us—what we cannot see when we face the future. But it comes around again to meet us in the future—according to the African conception of time. On this view, the past is like a complete revolution in the time continuum, the future an incomplete or perpetually incomplete revolution, and the present is wherever we happen to be on the revolving circumference or wheel of time.

Thus, in the African conception, time is a cycloid, a continually lengthening (receding or preceding) past. The sun is the guarantee that there will always be a present, the earth the guarantee of our perpetual illusion of a future (when we face the sun) and a past (when the sun lies behind us).

In a strictly anthropological sense, however, there is only *one* time facet, the present—the eteral NOW, as measured by the average life span of the human being. Anthropological time, the human life span, is, for all intents and purposes, man's effective operational time unit. Its average duration was thought by the ancient Hebrews to be "three score years and ten," with some people attaining "fourscore years" occasionally. Since one's life span is bounded by birth and death, there is no past and no future—the past being all that went on before one's birth, the future all that follows after one's death. Neither has any operational meaning or content for the individual.

Corresponding to the objective unit of anthropological time (life span) is an internal dimension given by mind, the subjective factor that duplicates the illusive duality of past and future time in terms of *experience-cum-memory* or *reminiscence* (past) and *expectations* (future). The geo-solar routine that creates the external illusion of past and future also dictates and regulates the physiological phenomenon generally referred to as man's built-in biological (twenty-four–hour) clock.

The dimensions of anthropological time may be diagrammed as follows:

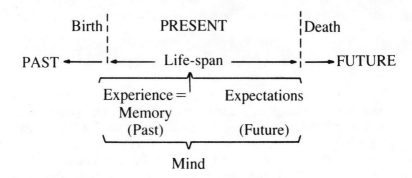

Mind is ever active during one's life span. When the body takes a rest, mind enters the domain of dreams; when mind is on holiday, it enters the domain of neurosis and mental illness, and when it abdicates its activities, the brain is dead, the body dying at the same time or subsequently.

6. INTRA-COSMIC TIME

The concepts of *motion* and *duration* are fundamental constituents in the concept of time. This is also true of intra-cosmic time. Here, the phenomenon of light, not just sunlight but light from any source within the cosmos, plays an important role. In this connection, the basic operational unit of cosmic time is the distance traveled (motion) by light per second or per year (duration).

From the focal point of man's location on planet Earth, any light apprehended has had a duration, implying that only light from the distant past (preanthropological time) reaches the earth at any present time. Thus we see only the *cosmic past* in our present (life span). The *cosmic present*—still less the *cosmic future*—is not given to man to know.

Timewise, therefore, and in a physical sense, man lives simultaneously in a dual dimension: the *cosmic past* and the *terrestrial present*, in such a manner that the equation,

$$\text{cosmic past} = \text{terrestrial present}^6$$

is always true. Literally, "a thousand years in thy sight are but as yesterday when it is past," according to the Hebrew psalmist.[7] It is the same for man, as for God, whether it is a thousand, billion, trillion, or whatever the number of years. Human history, as well as the history of the human individual, is simultaneously cosmic history compressed into a short life span.

7. TIME AND THE CONVENTIONAL NOTION OF GOD

Time may be regarded as an element as well as a function of sequential analysis or activity. Accordingly, it disappears where several stages of an event or activity occur simultaneously, or an event occurs in different places instantaneously, or if all events are known as they occur or in advance of their occurrence. These attributes of *instantaneity* and *ubiquity* may be summarized in one word, *omnipresence*, implying *timelessness*[8] (absence of time).

The philosophic notion of time is linked, through its opposite, timelessness or eternity, with the conventional notion of God, since perfection and timelessness are universally accepted attributes of the concept.[9] Time being associated with the concept of motion and sequence, the absence of motion is associated with timelessness as well as with God. Aristotle regarded God as the *unmoved* mover, perfect static equilibrium.

Time may also be looked at in two other ways: as a resource (or tool) to work with or as a barrier to be breached. In the former case, time or sequence is a given and the problem in hand has to be tackled sequentially. In the latter case, the element of time in a given problem has to be annihilated or reduced to instantness. This does not mean the freezing of all motion but merely the telescoping of all motion into an instant—the ideal example being the spinning electron within the nucleus of an atom. Ability to telescope time into an instant will depend on possession of unlimited volume of knowledge and the ability to deploy unlimited amounts of physical energy (power).

459

His biology and especially his diurnal clock prevent man from dealing permanently on the basis of simultaneity or annihilation of time, the growing use of computer technology and shared activity-time notwithstanding. He will, therefore have need of time for sequential activities for the most part of his life.

8. CONCLUSION

From this rather brief review of the myth of time two aspects stand out prominently: the purely mythical (nonempirical) and the empirical. The purely mythical aspect is the philosophical concept of time and its related extension into the concept of God. The empirical aspect of time covers any and all of the remaining aspects that have been passed in review.

Empirical time is any unit of duration of an activity or function, live or recorded, in various dimensions. It is unidirectional, that is, cumulative, and, because it is relative to motion and location within the cosmos, permits of variable (including reversible) arrangements of activity within it. Given a location and motion within the cosmos, at any specific location there is only the *present*—the NOW—which is the same as the *past* vis-à-vis any other location within the cosmos. Moreover, within the cosmos, the future, if it exists, is not for or with the living—and certainly not with the dead, nor with the unborn. As an operational and empirical fact it simply does not exist within the cosmos—if the astrophysicists are right.

NOTES

1. George Orwell, *Nineteen Eighty Four* (London, New York: Penguin Books, 1977), p. 31.
2. Money-making, however, is not the only activity that one could fill time with: carving of ceremonial masks (African) or self-improvement (Occidental) are other alternatives among many.
3. See John S. Mbiti, *African Religions and Philosophy* (London, Nairobi: Heinemann, 1969, reprinted 1977), chapter 3.
4. Idem. This author differs with Mbiti's view that the traditional African has virtually no concept of future time (p. 17) and has discovered it through missionary teaching, western-type education, and modern technology (p. 27). This is an oversimplification reminiscent of similar views propounded by those who know Africans even less. The fact is that the traditional African's concept of future time differs from the occidental. What he is supposed to have discovered through the foreign influences mentioned is not the concept of the future, but the *occidental* concept of the future: quite a big difference.

5. Obviously, the new myth or interpretation of the old myth must come from the outside—exogenous rather than endogenous—in order to have a chance of success.
6. It is interesting to speculate on the relationship between this equation and the African conception of time in which only past and present are different.
7. Psalm 90:4.
8. To the ancient Greeks, the philosophical concept of timelessness implied perfection, in the sense of the absence of blemish of any kind, but also in the sense that no improvement by way of further development or change is possible. *Eternity* was the alternative term used to express timelessness.
9. Other generally accepted attributes are omnipresence, omniscience, and omnipotence.

Chapter 10

The Myth of History

1. HISTORY DEFINED

History may be defined in two ways: first, as the flow of human events and activities; second, as written or oral interpretations of human events or activities. And human events or activities may be defined as events or activities centered around persons or groups of persons and in which such persons or groups play a dominant role.

These meanings of history are rather general and not confined to history. They are shared by other human studies—anthropology, human geography, et cetera—that examine human activities in various specific ways. For practical purposes, however, it is the *interpretation* of human activities that constitutes the focus of history, as of other human studies.

2. MAGIC, SCIENCE, AND HISTORY

Magic is the desire and the will to control and influence events according to one's liking, purpose. hypothesis, or theory.[1] A hypothesis or theory, in natural science as in history, is—as it were—a magic formula based on the desire to discover the secret pattern of connection and interaction among events through time (in the conventional sense of past, present, and future) and thus be able to control events through time. But whereas in science the objective is to control the *occurrence* of events, in history the objective is to control the *interpretation* of events as they occur. This occasionally involves *reinterpreting* past events in order, thereby, to influence the interpretation of present and future events.

Because in science it is possible to experiment repeatedly in a restricted sphere with actual events, science is magic par excellence; it serves one's purpose *consistently* with the events themselves. For all its power, natural science, however, is only a part not the whole of life. It creates events analytically and aggregatively, not organically or inte-

462

grally. It is based on the logic of consistency and disintegration (analysis), not on the logic of contradiction and integration (organicism) on which real life is based. Natural science is to life as consistency is to dialectical contradiction.

In history, unlike natural science, it is not possible to experiment, even once, with human events, because of inability to restrict the area of experimentation. Therefore, history is pseudo-science in that one is free to experiment only with the interpretation (or look) of events rather than with the events themselves. In other words, history is pure myth; it has no empirical dimension.

In sum, magic is control of events—the same as science, a purely technical matter—pseudo-magic (legerdemain) the control of the look or interpretation of events—the same as history. The natural scientist (i.e., experimental scientist) is the real magician, the historian a common magician or juggler.

History, however, could be scientific and real magic only if the historian desists from imposing on events an interpretation inconsistent with the actual nature of events—if he ceases to manipulate the look of events. But he would, in that case, see reflected in human events the biological processes of change-flow through the cycle of emergence, growth, and decline. He would become the only type of scientific historian possible: the bio-historian. This type of history is not exciting because of the spiral cyclicity of its basic pattern—its boringly predictable cyclicity, its déjà vu nature, its nothing-new-under-the-sun philosophy. This cyclo-spiral nature of history is a recurrence that, however, is not quite the same as the previous cycle. Each cycle is usually generally like yet, in detail, new and different from, the preceding cycle. Technological change alone is enough to bring about differences in detail.

3. TYPES OF HISTORIAN

We therefore have two categories of historian: the *bio-historian* and the *mytho-historian* (i.e., the meaning or cosmetic historian). To the first category belong Gibbons, Spengler, and their type, who argue that civilizations decline because they are part of the order of Nature, the order of living organisms. In other words, civilizations are a human product and decline with the human groups that produce and maintain them, in accordance with the bio-rhythm of Nature.

The second category comprises all other historians, including such as Toynbee, who impose a variety of mythical patterns on events, each pattern effectively a dogmatic interpretation because without benefit of empirical confirmation. Toynbee, for example, argues that civilizations declined because they were not Christian or inspired by Christianity. Those preceding Christianity declined because they were not Christian, and those that were Christian declined because they departed from Christianity as their central inspiration.[2] (Ergo: civilizations will not decline and disappear if they continually draw on Christianity as their central inspiration.) There is no way of putting this gratuitous view to the test.

In general, mytho-historians fall into two groups: (a) Radicals and Reformers (R and R), whose interpretation of history favors the present, and (b) Conservatives (C), whose interpretation of history favors the past. Radicals and Reformers reject the past and use the present to alter the meaning of the past in order to control the future, in the interest of the present. For them the past is malleable, and they live in the future. Communist historians and Party Theoreticians belong to this group.

Conservatives reject the present and use the past to alter the meaning of the present in order to control the future, in the interest of the past. For them the present is malleable[3] and they live in the past. Roman Catholic historians and the Pope belong to this group.

Regardless of their respective interpretive slant, however, Radicals, Reformers, and Conservatives are all agreed on one thing: control of the (meaning of the) future, the first group through manipulation of the past, the second through manipulation of the present.

Historicists—historians who believe that each period in history has its own values, inapplicable to other periods—emphasize the use of imagination to reenact and reconstruct the past in the living thought of the present. R. G. Collingwood was an advocate of this view.[4] But this, again, is a matter of interpretation and leaves open the bias (radical, reform, or conservative) in which the interpretation is done. Thus historicists will fall into one or the other group of mytho-historians.

What all this implies is that the two groups—Radicals and Reformers ("control the past in the interest of the present") on the one hand and Conservatives ("control the present in the interest of the past") on the other—constitute a dialectical tandem for which no clear or satisfactory method of conflict resolution can be found. An evolutionary situation (that is, an unpredictable future) is the most likely solution that will emerge, but neither group wants this solution nor is prepared to admit or confess to any external limitations on its power to influence the look of the future.

4. ROLE OF HISTORICAL TIME IN THE STRATEGY OF AUTHORITARIAN ORGANIZATIONS

Authoritarian organizations of all types are similar in at least one respect: they accord a dominant role to historical time (chronology) in their operational and survival strategy. They differ only in regard to which aspect of historical time—past or future[5]—they emphasize in their strategy. Authoritarian organizations and dictatorships of the left (e.g., the Socialist and Communist parties) emphasize the future; those of the right (e.g., the Roman Catholic Church) emphasize the past.

Given their historical time bias, all authoritarian organizations conform to a common organizational structure resting on three major elements: an *apparatus* (Church or Party), a *doctrine* (Communism or Christianity), and a *strategy* (resources and a membership drive). In the apparatus of the Church and the Party, the Pope and the Party Theoretician, respectively, serve the same function of defining and interpreting the doctrine of the organization.

The time plank of the Communist Party (which will here be taken as representative of all leftist authoritarian organizations) favors the future in preference to the present and views the past as malleable or mutable. George Orwell aptly summarizes the doctrine of all such authoritarian groups in his book *Nineteen Eighty-Four*:

"Who controls the past controls the future: who controls the present controls the past."[6]

The trick for achieving this control consists in *alteration of records* and in *mind control* (propaganda or brainwashing). And the resources for implementing the doctrine constitute the strategy, the success of which depends on the degree of population and environmental control. The historical time plank is a cycle that becomes closed by the third member of the triad:

"Who controls the future controls the present."

The future is the governor in this system, whose tenet may be summarized as the doctrine of the millennium or enchanted future, as follows:

"The future controls the present controls the past."

The Roman Catholic Church is the paradigm of authoritarian organizations of the right. Its time plank favors the past in preference to

465

the present the latter being considered malleable. Its corresponding maxim to that of the left goes as follows:

"Who controls the past controls the present; who controls the future controls the past."

And the circle is closed by:

"Who controls the present controls the future."[7]

Like the Communists, the Roman Catholic Church adopts the practice of altering records (including destruction and banning)—attested to by events in the course of its historical development—as well as mind control in order to achieve its purpose; and the past is the governor of its system. Its thesis may be summed up as the doctrine of the golden age or enchanted past, as follows:

"The past controls the present controls the future."

Thus the two competitive systems, Roman Catholicism and Communism, are locked in a membership contest from opposite ends of the conventional time spectrum. The Church strives to retain control over the present in order to mold it into conformity with the past, and thereby make the future in the image of the past. The Party, likewise, strives for control of the present, but in order to shape it in conformity with its future goal, altering the record of the past, if necessary, in order to achieve that goal. The competition between the two organizations is intense and pursued in deadly earnest. The following diagrams illustrate their respective positions:

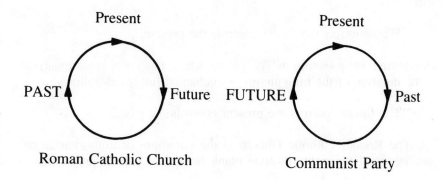

Roman Catholic Church   Communist Party

5. DOES HISTORY REPEAT ITSELF?

This perennial question is seldom satisfactorily answered because the objective is often not to establish the fact but to advance a pet theory. On the one hand are those who argue that history repeats itself, because they wish to advance the thesis that history is a thesaurus of exemplary models successfully copied by successive generations, but without avoiding or learning how to avoid the mistakes of the past. On the other hand are those who argue that history does not repeat itself, so that they may advance the thesis that history does not contain exemplary repeatable models and that while mankind learns to avoid the mistakes of the past it commits new ones.

What are the facts? Obviously, to the extent that human activities are based on natural cycles, e.g., the four seasons, some human activities tend to be cyclical and repetitive: agricultural activities, harvest celebrations and other feasts, et cetera. However, even here, every cyclical event is not quite the same as, but differs in some detail or other from, its precedessor and its successor. Even human follies, like war, "repeat" themselves as a genus, but differently as individual occurrences. Thus there is only one Battle of Hastings and one American War of Independence.

The combination of cyclical movement with difference of detail in history is best described by, and as, a spiral movement. It demonstrates, on the one hand, the influence of natural events in human affairs and, on the other, man's freedom to do things differently by adaptation and change. This conclusion applies to history both as a flow of human activities and events and as oral or written interpretations of human activities and events. The historian may see a similarity between events within the framework of his interpretation, but the details and evaluation are unlikely to be the same for any two similar events or for any two historians interpreting the events, for that matter.

6. USES (OR MISUSES) OF HISTORY

Specific interpretations of history serve various convenient purposes. Treated as a parameter or constant, a particular interpretation of historical events may be used to *interdict* change. This is the case with authoritarian regimes of the right, of which the Roman Catholic Church has been shown as a paradigm. Its doctrines and interpretations of past events are propounded as immutable and immune to any change, whence the present is to be conformed to the past.

Those, like the Communists, who regard history as a variable use varying interpretations of a given doctrine or dogma to *promote* change whenever this is deemed desirable, whence the past is malleable in the interest of current and future advantage.

There is, however, a third use of historical interpretation. This is its use as a tool for rationalizing questionable activities. A large part of national history is of this kind—a rationalization of an ethnic or group position. In short, myth is presented as history. Thus the slavery experiences of the ancient Jews had a profound impact on their self-image vis-à-vis other ethnic groups. Like every ethnic group, they had their tribal God, Jahweh, whose position, when the Jews were in slavery in Egypt, was in parallel fashion inferior to that of the Egyptian gods Osiris and Isis. Once freed from their yoke, a general transvaluation of their self-image occurred: Jahweh had become more powerful than the Egyptian gods in engineering the escape of the Jews from slavery, thus freeing them to impose slavery on the peoples whose territory they invaded and appropriated in Palestine. Their plunder of the land of other tribes was rationalized as the command of their superior god and, as is well known, superior gods and their commands are beyond question. The excuse for this aggressive act was that it was commanded by Jahweh; and not because Israel was righteous but because the other nations were more wicked. A distinction without a difference, in the final analysis: more righteous would serve just as well as less wicked, in relative terms applied to the Jews. This ancient rationalization of Jewish history has not changed and is currently being used by the modern state of Israel for similar purposes in the claims being made on behalf of "Eretz Yisrael."[8]

One should not, however, lose sight of the fundamental nature and objective of dogma of all sorts—historical, theological, et cetera—and the price at which this objective is achieved. The purpose of dogma is to save the intellectually lazy and incompetent the trouble of intellectual curiosity, along with its perplexing and uncomfortable questions and its unending odyssey, by providing "sure and unchanging answers" to their every question within a "sure and unchanging framework." It serves as a metaphysical, philosophical, and intellectual slide rule or multiplication table to be applied to every problem, every question. And they are always grateful for this service offered, and willingly accepted, at the price of the surrender of their reason. They judge the avoidance of intellectual adventure, with its exposure to dangers and pitfalls, as worth the price of blissful capitulation; and, indeed, they literally surrender their heads—blissfully.

NOTES

1. According to one psychological theory, magic is the consequence of a dispartiy between desire and technique, that is, a result of the inadequacy of technique to bring about the desired end. The efficacy gap is filled by magic to bring about the wish fulfillment. So that, technique + magic = wish fulfillment, or wish fulfillment − technique = magic, or technique = wish fulfillment − magic. (See E. E. Evans-Pritchard, *Theories of Primitive Religion* [London, New York: Oxford University Press, 1963], pp. 40–41.)
2. Arnold Toynbee, *A Study of History* (in ten volumes). Not markedly different from Toynbee's schema is that of the Lutheran Protestant theologian, Reinhold Niebuhr, who defines history as consisting only of all that transpired between the first and (expected) second coming of Jesus Christ and as necessarily doomed to failure. See Reinhold Niebuhr, "The Diversity and Unity of History," in H. Meyerhoff (ed.), *The Philosophy of History in our Time* (Garden City, N.Y.: Doubleday, 1959); *The Nature and Destiny of Man*, Gifford Lectures (New York: Charles Scribner and Sons, 1953); also, Pieter Geyl, *Debates with Historians* (Fontana, 1962, fourth impression, 1974) chapters V–VIII.
3. This is the ideological basis of the Order of Jesuits as a teaching order: control and molding of the formative years guarantees a future outcome in happy harmony with the past.
4. R. G. Collingwood, *The Idea of History*, ed. T. M. Knox (London, New York: Oxford University Press, 1980). See also H. Meyerhoff, op. cit., Introduction.
5. It is worthy of note that organizations or movements that accent the present, denying the validity of the past and emphasizing the meaninglessness of the future, are generally antiauthoritarian at first—the secular (Sartrean) existentialist movement and its offspring, the hippies and flower children—but end by seeking to reestablish some form of community and authority pattern.
6. George Orwell, *Nineteen Eighty-Four* (London, New York: Penguin Books, 1977), p. 31.
7. This is the maxim underlying the oft-quoted dictum of Saint Ignatius Loyola, founder of the Order of Jesuits: "Give me a child until the age of seven and I don't care who has him after that."
8. Jews are not the only case of ethnocentric history, of course. A similar situation is found among other emancipated groups, such as the Americo-Liberians, or the Creoles of Sierra Leone, vis-à-vis the indigenous population. "Divine right," like "civilizing mission" or "manifest destiny," is the last and ancient resort of tyrants. All colonizing groups have used it—the British, French, Spanish, and Portuguese, not forgetting the last of this genre, the Afrikaners.

Afterword

The writing of this book has been an exciting adventure full of unexpected surprises, pleasant and unpleasant. It is an intellectual biography with no holds barred. Among the pleasant surprises have been a new perspective on myth and philosophy; a new conception of religion which has thereby gained strength, in the author's estimation; of faith, which remains as unshaken as ever in its lofty and nonempirical perch; of metaphysics, whose role has become increasingly important as never before; and of theology, whose role has been absorbed in metaphysics and confined to the only God we can ever know in our human experience: Existence as manifested in the Cosmos.

Unpleasant surprises have been many, but chiefly the unsuspected widespread and age-old practice of philosophers in elevating their personal and social prejudices to the status of philosophical and metaphysical principles endowed, dishonestly or unconsciously, with divine attributes and sanctions; and the almost unshakeable hold which their spurious concepts and doctrines have had on the imagination of generations of docile and unquestioning scholars for several millennia.

To those who, shocked by some of the revelations and positions taken in this book, may be tempted to rush to conclusions about its nature and aims—despite the background given in the Foreword—or who through hasty or superficial reading or their own theological and religious doubts may feel threatened in their beliefs and persuasions, it may, perhaps, be necessary to reiterate that this exercise has been primarily for the author's own benefit: to clear away the cobwebbed thinking of centuries of misunderstanding of the nature and powerful role of myth in human life; and only secondarily to share his adventure with others who may be, or may have been, interested in making a similar pilgrimage to the strange and fascinating "kingdom of heaven" within themselves.

While its aim is both serious and diversionary—as any adventure of this nature is bound to be in the interest of perspective and sanity—it is not a part of the purpose of this book to convert or to sell anyone a bill of goods, especially so as, in true African fashion, matters of religion and theology are strictly for personal enjoyment, not for export. For all is myth, and one man's myth is just as good as another's, provided it

471

does not conflict with everyday experience and the rational functioning of the individual.

The Primal Couple, the true Adam and Eve, are Myth (Mythos, m.) and Reason (Sophia, f.)—in particular the "lower" Sophia, Sophia-Prunikos or Wisdom the Whore.[1] Myth is open to all possible propositions and interpretations, and Reason examines each of them impartially. Myth is a philanderer and Reason a whore. Both are the saviors of mankind in guarding against bias or, at least, in minimizing it. Human salvation therefore lies in intellectual whoring—examining all possible positions and interpretations—and intellectual progress depends on fruitful intercourse between Myth and Reason. Very little in the intellectual domain is essentially new, progress consisting for the most part in shedding new light on old issues by rearranging and reinterpreting the elements of old myths in new and expanding frameworks. The scientific payoff comes from applying the touchstone of Experience to the numerous offspring of Myth and Reason.

The author has examined others' myths and presented for examination his own—a fair enough deal. Criticisms and other intellectual flak will be most welcome—but, above all, new myths or reexamination of old myths, more interesting metaphysical, theological, philosophical, and religious myths. For it is the author's firm conviction that the mythopoetical resources of mankind are too rich and varied and productive of potential beneficial consequences for mankind to be stuck, uncritically, for millennia with a few well-worn myths that, no matter how great their antiquity, stifle intellectual curiosity, and initiative, generating no more than copious footnotes and commentaries, in addition to untold miseries perpetrated by one section of humanity on another.

Much of this ancient wisdom has been shown to be dubious and has long outlived its usefulness. If mankind is to progress in its accommodation to its environment, it owes itself, at the very least, new combinations and interpretations of the basic metaphysical elements that compose the existential myth, if not the invention of completely new elements to insert into the existential equation. For progress is change; not change for the sake of change, but change for the satisfaction of new needs and the better satisfaction of existing ones.

NOTE

1. See Hans Jonas, *The Gnostic Religion*, 2d ed., rev. (Boston: Beacon Press, 1963), p. 109.